CORE CONCEPTS OF
Accounting Information Systems

Fourteenth Edition

Mark G. Simkin, Ph.D.

Professor
Department of Information Systems
University of Nevada

James L. Worrell, Ph.D., CPA, CISA, CIA

Associate Professor
Department of Accounting and Finance
University of Alabama at Birmingham

Arline A. Savage, Ph.D., CA(SA)

Professor and Chair
Department of Accounting and Finance
University of Alabama at Birmingham

WILEY

EDITORIAL DIRECTOR	Michael McDonald
ACQUISITIONS EDITOR	Emily Marcoux
EDITORIAL MANAGER	Judy Howarth
CONTENT MANAGEMENT DIRECTOR	Lisa Wojcik
CONTENT MANAGER	Nichole Urban
SENIOR CONTENT SPECIALIST	Nicole Repasky
PRODUCTION EDITOR	Annie Sophia Thapasumony
PHOTO RESEARCHER	Billy Ray
COVER PHOTO CREDIT	© simon2579/iStockphoto

This book was set in ITC Garamond Std Book 10/12pt by SPi Global and printed and bound by Lightning Source Inc.

Founded in 1807, John Wiley & Sons, Inc. has been a valued source of knowledge and understanding for more than 200 years, helping people around the world meet their needs and fulfill their aspirations. Our company is built on a foundation of principles that include responsibility to the communities we serve and where we live and work. In 2008, we launched a Corporate Citizenship Initiative, a global effort to address the environmental, social, economic, and ethical challenges we face in our business. Among the issues we are addressing are carbon impact, paper specifications and procurement, ethical conduct within our business and among our vendors, and community and charitable support. For more information, please visit our website: www.wiley.com/go/citizenship.

ISBN: 978-1-119-37366-7 (PBK)
ISBN: 978-1-119-37367-4 (EVALC)

Library of Congress Cataloging in Publication Data:

LCCN: 2017054100

The inside back cover will contain printing identification and country of origin if omitted from this page. In addition, if the ISBN on the back cover differs from the ISBN on this page, the one on the back cover is correct.

In memory of my mother, Selma Simkin (Mark G. Simkin)

Thank you to my parents, Barney and Betty, for your sacrifices, to my wife, Lynn, for your support, and to my son, AJ, for the joys of being a father (James L. Worrell)

For my grandchildren: Archer, Mirabel and Lillianna (Arline A. Savage)

ABOUT THE AUTHORS

Mark G. Simkin received his A.B. degree from Brandeis University and his M.B.A. and Ph.D. degrees from the University of California, Berkeley. Before assuming his present position of professor in the Department of Information Systems, University of Nevada, Professor Simkin taught in the Department of Decision Sciences at the University of Hawaii. He has also taught at California State University, Hayward, and the Japan America Institute of Decision Sciences, Honolulu; worked as a research analyst at the Institute of Business and Economic Research at the University of California, Berkeley; programmed computers at IBM's Industrial Development—Finance Headquarters in White Plains, New York; and acted as a computer consultant to business companies in California, Hawaii, and Nevada. Dr. Simkin is the author of more than 100 articles that have been published in journals such as *Decision Sciences, JASA, The Journal of Accountancy, Communications of the ACM, Interfaces, The Review of Business and Economic Research, Decision Sciences Journal of Innovative Education, Information Systems Control Journal,* and the *ISACA Journal.*

James L. "Jamey" Worrell received his B.S. (Accounting), M.Acc. (Information Systems), and Ph.D. (Management Information Systems) from Florida State University. He is a Certified Public Accountant (Florida), Certified Information Systems Auditor and Certified Internal Auditor. Before assuming his present position as Associate Professor in the Department of Accounting and Finance at the University of Alabama at Birmingham, Dr. Worrell spent over a decade in industry, serving as an auditor for the State of Florida, an IT auditor and information security consultant for Pricewater-houseCoopers, and Lead IT Internal Auditor for Raymond James Financial. A recipient of UAB's President's Award for Excellence in Teaching, Dr. Worrell has developed courses at the undergraduate and graduate levels in accounting information systems, internal auditing, IT governance, IT audit, and IT strategy/management. His research has been published in journals such as *International Journal of Accounting Information Systems, Issues in Accounting Education, Information Technology and People,* and *Information Technology and Management.*

Arline A. Savage received her B.Com., M.Com. (Accounting) and Ph.D. (Accounting) from the University of Port Elizabeth, South Africa. Before assuming her present position as Professor and Chair of the Department of Accounting and Finance at the University of Alabama at Birmingham, Dr. Savage was the Deloitte Faculty Fellow at the Orfalea College of Busines, California Polytechnic State University in San Lius Obispo. While on faculty at the Orfalea College of Business, Dr. Savage was awarded the Ernst & Young Leader in Ethics Award, the Fluor Corporation Excellence in Teaching Award, and the Ernst & Young Outstanding Educator Award. A Chartered Accountant in South Africa, Dr. Savage is a past-president of the Accounting Information Systems Educator Association, and served as the founding editor of *AIS Educator Journal.* Dr. Savage is the author of more than 40 articles published in journals such as *Journal of Information Systems, Issues in Accounting Education, Journal of Accounting Education,* and *AIS Educator Journal.*

PREFACE

Accounting is, at its core, an information discipline. In essence, accounting is a set of inter-related components (*system*) that capture, aggregate and transform data about economic events into a meaningful context (information), which is presented to decision makers for consideration and action. Now more than ever, information technologies affect every aspect of accounting, from what data are captured (social media, blogs, sensor data), how data are captured (RFID tagging), where data are stored (cloud based databases), and how data and information are analyzed and presented (data visualization). As technologies advance, so does the accounting profession.

Because most business processes rely heavily on information technology, accounting professionals must understand how people, processes and technologies interact to transform data into decision-useful information, and also how to develop and evaluate internal controls. Business and auditing failures continue to force the profession to emphasize internal controls and to rethink the state of assurance services. As a result, the subject of accounting information systems (AIS) continues to be a vital component of the accounting profession.

The purpose of this book is to help students understand basic AIS concepts. Exactly what comprises these AIS concepts is subject to some interpretation, and it is certainly changing over time, but most accounting professionals believe that basic AIS concepts consist of the knowledge that accountants need for understanding and using information technologies and for knowing how an accounting information system gathers and transforms data into useful decision-making information. In this edition of our textbook, we include the core concepts of Accounting Information Systems. The book is flexible enough that instructors may choose to cover the chapters in any order.

ACCOUNTING INFORMATION SYSTEMS
COURSE CONTENT AREA COVERAGE

AIS Applications	5, 8, 9
IT Auditing	4, 10, 11
Database Concepts	14, 15, 16
Internal Control	6, 7
Management of Information Systems	3, 12, 13
Management Use of Information	1, 2, 4, 8, 9, 12, 15
Systems Development Work	12, 13
Technology of Information Systems	All chapters

About This Book

The content of AIS courses varies widely from school to school. Some schools use their AIS courses to teach accounting students how to use computers. In other colleges and universities, the course focuses on business processes and data modeling. Yet other courses emphasize transaction processing and accounting as a communication system that has little to do with the technical aspects of how systems gather, process, or store underlying accounting data.

Given the variety of objectives for an AIS course and the different ways that instructors teach it, we developed a textbook that attempts to cover the core concepts of AIS. In writing the text, we assumed that students have completed basic courses in financial and managerial accounting and have a basic knowledge of computer hardware and software concepts. The text is designed for a one-semester course in AIS and may be used at the community college, baccalaureate, or graduate level.

Our hope is that individual instructors will use this book as a foundation for an AIS course, building upon it to meet their individual course objectives. Thus, we expect that many instructors will supplement this textbook with other books, cases, software, or readings. The arrangement and content of the chapters permits flexibility in covering subject materials and allows instructors to omit chapters that students have covered in prior courses.

Special Features

This edition of our book uses a large number of special features to enhance the coverage of chapter material as well as to help students understand chapter concepts. Thus, each chapter begins with a list of learning objectives that emphasize the important subject matter of the chapter. This edition of the book also includes many new real world Cases-in-Point, which we include to illustrate a particular concept or procedure. Each chapter also includes a more-detailed real-world case as an end-of-chapter *AIS-at-Work* feature.

Each chapter ends with a summary and a list of key terms. To help students understand the material, each chapter includes multiple-choice questions for self-review with answers. There are also three types of end-of-chapter exercises: (1) discussion questions, (2) problems, and (3) case analyses. This wide variety of review material enables students to examine many different aspects of each chapter's subject matter and also enables instructors to vary the exercises they use each semester.

The end-of-chapter materials include references and other resources that allow interested students to explore the chapter material in greater depth. In addition, instructors may wish to assign one or a number of articles listed in each chapter reference section to supplement chapter discussions. These articles are also an important resource for instructors to encourage students to begin reading such professional journals as *Strategic Finance*, *The Journal of Accountancy*, and *The Internal Auditor*.

Supplements

There are a number of supplements that accompany this textbook. One is an instructor's manual containing suggested answers to the end-of-chapter discussion questions, problems, and case analyses. There is also a test bank consisting of true-false, multiple choice, and matching-type questions, as well as short answer problems and fill-in-the-blank questions, so that instructors have a wide variety of choices. In addition, PowerPoint lecture slides accompany the text, and all of these materials can be accessed from the book's companion website at www.wiley.com/college/simkin.

What's New in the Fourteenth Edition?

This edition of our book includes a number of changes from prior editions.

- The book is now organized into three units:
  - *Technology and Accounting in the 21st Century*: chapters discuss the transformative changes that AISs have facilitated to the practice of accounting, such as changes to the profession, the systems that capture financial and non-financial data for decision-making purposes, and the direction of AISs in general;
  - *Managing and Controlling Business Processes with AISs*: chapters cover the various control frameworks, risks and means of implementing internal controls in AISs, as well as the business processes that give rise to financial and non-financial data; and
  - *Designing and Implementing AISs*: chapters cover the development of AISs and databases that support modern AISs.
- A new chapter (*Accounting, Big Data and Data Analytics*) discusses the nature of Big Data, the data analysis process, and data analytics trends in managerial accounting, tax accounting, and assurance and compliance services.
- The book offers expanded and revised coverage of important topics, such as cloud computing, cyber-security, and COSO's pending update to the Enterprise Risk Management-Integrated Framework, as well as updated information on AIS selection, accounting and fraud, e-commerce, ransomware and other threats.
- Database examples and references have been updated to Microsoft Access 2016.
- Updated *Case-in-Points* illustrate the concepts discussed in the textbook and give students a better grasp of the material, while revised end-of-chapter *AIS at Work* features help students better understand the impact of systems in a wide variety of contexts.
- Revised discussion questions, problems, and cases at the end of chapters give instructors more choices of comprehensive assignments for students.
- Revised Test Yourself multiple choice questions help students assess their understanding of the chapter material.
- The end of the book contains an updated glossary of AIS terms.

Acknowledgements

We wish to thank the many people who helped us during the writing, editing, and production of our textbook. Our families and friends are first on our list of acknowledgments. We are grateful to them for their patience and understanding as we were revising this textbook. Next, we thank those instructors who read earlier drafts of this edition of our textbook and provided enormously valuable ideas and suggestions to improve the final version. Chief among these is Timothy L. Baker, University of South Carolina Aiken, who was invaluable in improving the quality and content for chapters 4, 6, 7, 10, and 11, as well as providing timely feedback on many others.

We would also like to acknowledge the timely assistance of Paul M. Di Gangi, University of Alabama at Birmingham, who stepped in on short notice to provide technical assistance and review on chapters 14 through 16.

In addition, we are indebted to the many adopters of our book who frequently provide us with feedback. We'd also like to thank the following people who provided feedback for the Fourteenth Edition:

Timothy L. Baker, University of South Carolina, Aiken
Michael Campbell, Montana State University Billings
Deborah L, Habel, Wayne State University
Steven Johnson, Minnesota State University, Mankato
Lois Mahoney, Eastern Michigan University
Christine Schalow, University of Wisconsin-Stevens Point

We sincerely appreciate the efforts of three additional individuals who helped us in various stages of this book: Ms. Emily Marcoux, Ms. Annie Sophia Thapasumony, and Ms. Paula Funkhouser. Emily was our primary contact with our production contractor. Annie was our Production Editor and worked to keep us on schedule and shepherd us through the production process. Finally, Paula helped us with our supplementary materials on this and several previous editions.

Lastly we thank our many students for the insightful feedback and useful suggestions. Your input has greatly improved the quality of this edition!

Mark G. Simkin
James L. Worrell
Arline A. Savage

CONTENTS

Chapter 1

Accounting Information Systems and the Accountant

After studying this chapter, you will be able to:

1. *Describe* the significant impact of information technology (IT) on the accounting profession and *explain* why you need to study accounting information systems.

2. *Identify* career opportunities that combine accounting and IT knowledge and skills.

3. *Explain* how IT influences accounting systems.

4. *Give examples of* how financial reporting is changing with advances in IT.

5. *Give examples of* how accountants use business intelligence for decision-making.

6. *Identify* what is new in the area of accounting information systems.

7. *Distinguish* between terms such as "systems," "information systems," "information technology," and "accounting information systems."

"In the accounting profession, for example, firms working with clients that own large mineral deposits or mining operations can now use drones to fly over the area, taking thousands of pictures and measurements. CPAs can then use that data to provide exact estimates of holdings. "Their balance sheets and their assets are literally sitting on the ground," and drones can quickly calculate inventory estimates by flying over the area ..."

Ovaska-Few, S. 2017. Drones set to invade accounting profession. CPA Insider, *Journal of Accountancy* (January 23): Available online.

1.1 INTRODUCTION: WHY STUDY ACCOUNTING INFORMATION SYSTEMS?

This chapter begins by answering the question "why should you study accounting information systems?" There are so many reasons, but one of the most important is because of the special career opportunities that will enable you to combine your study of accounting with your interest in computer systems. In today's job market, accounting employers expect new hires to be computer savvy. A large number of specialized and highly compensated employment opportunities are only available to those students who possess an integrated understanding of accounting and information systems and can bring that understanding to bear on complicated business decisions.

Think about it. When is the last time you went into a bank, filled out a piece of paper to withdraw cash from your bank account, and then stood in line waiting for a teller to help you? When is the last time you went to a travel agency to ask someone to find you an airline ticket for your spring break vacation to Florida or the Virgin Islands?

Or when is the last time you stood in line to fill out paperwork for the courses you wanted to take for next semester? Most likely, the answer to each of these questions is "never." And that is because of information technology (IT). Information technology is so pervasive today that it is nearly impossible to do anything that does not in some way involve technology. So ask yourself the question "how can you possibly be a successful accountant if you do not have a basic understanding of how technology influences the profession?"

1.2 CAREERS IN ACCOUNTING INFORMATION SYSTEMS

Our introductory remarks to this chapter suggest a variety of reasons why you should study **accounting information systems (AISs)**. Of them, perhaps the most interesting to students is the employment opportunities available to those who understand accounting, information systems, and the applicable technologies.

Traditional Accounting Career Opportunities

Certainly, a number of traditional accounting jobs in corporate and public accounting are available to those who choose to study accounting and information systems. Technology plays a very strong role in public accounting and auditing, internal auditing, managerial accounting, fraud examination, and taxation. Recognizing the importance to accountants of knowledge about IT and information systems, the American Institute of Certified Public Accountants (AICPA) developed a new designation, the **Certified Information Technology Professional (CITP)**, that accountants can earn with business experience and if they pass an examination. This certification signifies superior knowledge in IT, information systems, and specialized information management systems.

> **Case-in-Point 1.1** The AICPA has an Information Management and Technology Assurance (IMTA) Section that supports CPAs who offer assurance services and information management support for their clients. This section provides access to resources to help CPAs understand how the use of data and reports from information systems can lead to better business decisions. Members also gain an understanding of how they can use IT and information systems skills combined with financial insight to evaluate technology risks.[1]

Employer demand is high for employees with a combination of accounting and IT/systems skills. For example, in 2017 in the corporate world, financial systems administrators generally earned between $61,250 and $84,000, while project managers ranged from $80,250 to $110,250, and managers from $98,000 to $130,750.[2]

Systems Consulting

A consultant is an outside expert who helps an organization solve problems or provides technical expertise on an issue. **Systems consultants** provide help with issues

---

[1] American Institute of Certified Public Accountants, accessed from www.aicpa.org, March 2017.
[2] Robert, H. 2017. "Salary guide for accounting and finance," accessed from www.roberthalf.com, March 2017.

concerning information systems—for example, by helping an organization design a new information system, select computer hardware or software, or reengineer business processes so that they operate more effectively.

One of the most important assets a consultant brings to the job is an objective view of a client's organization and its processes and goals. Students who are skilled in both accounting and information systems are particularly competent systems consultants because they understand how data flow through accounting systems as well as how business processes function. Systems consultants can help a variety of organizations, including professional service organizations, public and private corporations, and government agencies. This broad work experience, combined with technical knowledge about hardware and software, can be a valuable asset to CPA clients. Because it is likely that a newly designed system will include accounting-related information, a consultant who understands accounting is particularly helpful. Many systems consultants work for large professional service organizations, such as Accenture, Protiviti, or Capgemini, as well as for the consulting divisions of CPA firms. Others may work for specialized organizations that focus on the custom design of AISs.

Consulting careers for students knowledgeable in AISs also include jobs as **value-added resellers (VARs)**. Software vendors license VARs to sell a particular software package and provide consulting services to companies, such as help with their software installation, training, and customization. That is, VARs are individuals who take a product and add value to the product for their customers, which might include services such as strategic planning, system design and implementation, technical support, database development, and other similar services. A VAR may also set up a small one-person consulting business or may work with other VARs and consultants to provide alternative software solutions to clients.

Fraud Examiner or Forensic Accountant

Due to increased concerns about terrorism and corporate fraud, forensic accounting and fraud examination are important area for accountants to study and develop their skills. An accountant can acquire the **Certified Fraud Examiner (CFE)** certification by meeting the qualifications of the Association of Certified Fraud Examiners (ACFE). To become a CFE, an individual must first meet the following qualifications: have a bachelor's degree, at least 2 years of professional experience in a field either directly or indirectly related to the detection or deterrence of fraud, be of high moral character, and agree to abide by the bylaws and code of professional ethics of the ACFE. If a person meets these requirements, then she or he may apply to sit for the CFE examination.

You might be asking yourself what sort of professional experience might be useful if you wish to satisfy the 2-year requirement for certification. Not surprisingly, these jobs may be located within CPA firms across the United States, as well as within international public accounting firms. Other such positions might include working for at business organization as an internal auditor, with a valuation expert in a law firm, with an FBI or CIA agent, or as an auditor for Medicaid, Medicare, or many other government organizations.

The AICPA also offers the Certified in Financial Forensics (CFF) designation for CPAs who want to specialize in the area of Forensic Accounting. The knowledge base for this certification includes computer forensic analysis. A forensic accountant with an IT background is very helpful in the investigation of cyber crime and breaches in cyber security.

Fraud examiners and forensic accountants use software data analytical tools like ACL Analytics and IDEA Data Analysis to analyze large quantities of data and to

Job Title	Salary Range
Fraud Investigator	$39,551–91,715
Senior Internal Auditor	$53,424–90,613
Internal Auditing Manager	$74,441–111,778
Internal Auditor	$42,971–76,480
Senior Auditor	$50,848–95,600

FIGURE 1-1 Examples of job titles and pay range for Fraud Examiners and Forensic Accountants. Source: 2017 Salary guide for accounting and finance, www.roberthalf.com, accessed March 2017.

perform advanced digital forensics. The objective is to reduce fraud risk and to detect fraud.

The salary ranges and possible job locations are varied. Most positions will likely be located in larger metropolitan areas, but may also be found in mid-sized cities. From the chart for 2017 (Figure 1-1), you can see the salary ranges for several types of positions.

Essentially, fraud occurs where there are weak internal controls or when a manager or employee circumvents the internal controls that are in place. A more detailed explanation of internal controls is contained in Chapters 6 and 7.

Information Technology Auditing and Security

Information technology (IT) auditors focus on the risks associated with computerized information systems. These individuals often work closely with financial auditors to assess the risks associated with automated AISs—a position in high demand because almost all systems are now computerized. Information systems auditors also help financial auditors decide how much time to devote to auditing each segment of a company's business. This assessment may lead to the conclusion that the controls within some portions of a client's information systems are reliable and that less time needs to be spent on them—or the opposite. Due to the growing need for this type of auditor, we devote an entire chapter to IT auditing—Chapter 11.

IT auditors are involved in a number of activities apart from assessing risk for financial audit purposes. Many of these auditors work for large CPA firms, such as Ernst & Young, PwC, Deloitte, or KPMG. Figure 1-2 identifies a partial listing of the types of services offered by Ernst & Young.

Assurance Services
- Financial statement attestation
- Internal control reporting
- Assess procedures and controls concerning privacy and confidentiality, performance measurement, systems reliability, outsourced process controls, information security

Business Risk Services
Fraud Investigation and Dispute Services
Technology and Security Risk Services
Specialty Advisory Services

FIGURE 1-2 A sample of the many types of services offered by Ernst & Young LLP, one of the largest international professional service organizations.

IT auditors might be CPAs, or they might be licensed as **Certified Information Systems Auditors (CISAs)**—a certification given to professional information systems auditors by the **Information Systems Audit and Control Association (ISACA)**. To become a CISA, you must take an examination and obtain specialized work experience. Many CISAs have accounting and information systems backgrounds, although formal accounting education is not required for certification. IT auditors help in documenting and evaluating IT controls.

According to the ISACA website, there is a growing demand for employees who have IS audit, control, and security skills. The CISA certification is therefore in high demand because CISA employees are highly qualified, experienced professionals who provide the enterprise with certification for IT assurance that has global recognition. These employees have proficiency in technology controls. They demonstrate competency in standards and practices, organization and management, processes, integrity, confidentiality, availability, and software development, acquisition, and maintenance. They also demonstrate a commitment to providing the enterprise with trust in and value from its information systems.[3]

Case-in-Point 1.2   According to Cindy Wyatt, Managing Member at Insyte CPAs, LLC in Birmingham, Alabama, who herself has passed the CISA certification examinations, "Technology is paramount in today's business environment. Accountants who understand information technology controls are far more effective in their careers, and thus, far more valuable to the organizations they serve."

Sometimes the best way to assess the risks associated with a computerized system is to try to penetrate the system, which is referred to as **penetration testing**. These tests are usually conducted within a systems security audit from which the organization attempts to determine the level of vulnerability of their information systems and the impact such weaknesses might have on the viability of the organization. If any security issues are discovered, the organization will typically work swiftly to correct the problems or at least mitigate the impact they might have on the company. But what if someone else penetrates an organization's systems? That is commonly called "hacking" and is usually a very serious problem for any company. We cover hacking in more detail in Chapter 10.

Case-in-Point 1.3   In 2013 and 2014, Yahoo Inc. had its systems hacked, affecting over a billion user accounts. The hacker(s) penetrated Yahoo's network and were able to steal user names, email addresses, dates of birth, telephone numbers, and encrypted passwords. Yahoo disclosed that it had spent $11 million in legal fees and $5 million to investigate the breach and patch the security holes. The CEO, Marissa Mayer had to also forego her 2016 cash bonus of around $2 million and her 2017 equity award of no less than $12 million.[4]

Predictive Analytics

What you will soon learn from studying this book, and hopefully through reading professional accounting journals, is that the accounting profession is constantly changing. To be successful as an accounting professional, you will need to stay abreast of these

[3] The Benefits of CISA, accessed from ISACA (www.isaca.org), March 2014.
[4] Seetharaman, D. and R. McMillan. Yahoo CEO Marissa Mayer takes pay cut over security breach. March 1, 2017, *Wall Street Journal*, accessed March 2017.

changes, or better yet get out in front of some of the expected trends in the profession. One of those trends that we want to alert you to is the rapidly growing opportunities in the field of predictive analytics, which is the result of the tremendous amount of data that is now available within organizations (e.g., data warehouses, which offer opportunities for data mining). In the future, this is the most likely area where you can add value—by being able to analyze that data and make useful business predictions for your clients.

You might be surprised to learn that a number of accounting jobs already require this type of skill set—for example, jobs such as client service analyst, quantitative analyst, risk analyst, and financial planner and analyst (responsible for preparing the annual plan and long-range or 5-year plan for a company and usually reports to the CFO).[5] So what exactly is predictive analytics, and what does this type of professional do? The predictive analytics professional uses a variety of skills and abilities, ranging from statistical analysis, data modeling, and data mining used by management to make predictions about the future.

This might require a mind shift for some accounting majors. Rather than seeking an MBA degree or an MS in accounting, consider an MS degree in analytics or business analytics. There are now over 100 such degree programs in the United States, offering full-time, part-time, and online delivery. So that you can appreciate the strong demand for this new type of credential, the first MS in Analytics program was available in 2007, and around 25% of these programs just started since 2016.[6] If you go to the website at footnote 6, you can find the universities that offer these programs, the length of each program, the cost, and the curriculum. You might also be interested in the 2016 median starting salary of $87,700 *with no experience* (see Institute for Advanced Analytics, MSA Infographic, analytics.ncsu.edu, accessed March 2017).

1.3 ACCOUNTING AND IT

IT is pervasive and impacts every area of accounting. Instantaneous online access is available via mobile communication devices such as cell phones, iPads, smartphones, and so on, which enable activities to take place anytime, anywhere. For example, managerial accountants can complete important work tasks while traveling in the field, auditors can communicate with each other from remote job sites (while auditing the same client), staff accountants can text message one another from various locations, and tax experts can download current information on tax rulings.

Figure 1-3 provides an overview of the major areas within the field of accounting impacted by information technology. This section of the chapter considers the influence of IT on each of them.

Financial Accounting

The major objective of the **financial accounting information system** is to provide relevant information to individuals and groups *outside* an organization's boundaries, for example, investors, federal and state tax agencies, and creditors.

---

[5] icrunchdata.com, accessed March 2014.
[6] "Survey of graduate degree programs in analytics," Institute for Advanced Analytics, analytics.ncsu.edu, accessed March 2017.

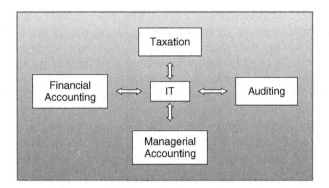

FIGURE 1-3 Overview of the major areas of accounting impacted by information technology.

Accountants achieve these informational objectives by preparing financial statements such as income statements, balance sheets, statements of stockholders' equity, and cash flow statements. Of course, managers *within* a company might also use these financial reports for planning, decision-making, and control activities. However, for most decisions within the firm, managers likely use managerial accounting reports.

Recall from your introductory financial accounting course that an organization's financial accounting cycle begins with analyzing and journalizing transactions (e.g., this data is captured when a business event occurs that has a monetary impact on the financial statements) and ends with its periodic financial statements. Accounting clerks, store cashiers, or even the customers themselves input relevant data into the system that stores these data for later use. In financial AISs, the processing function also includes posting these entries to general and subsidiary ledger accounts, preparing a trial balance from the general ledger account balances, and preparing financial statements.

Nonfinancial Data. The basic inputs to, and outputs from, traditional financial accounting systems are usually expressed in monetary units. This can be a problem if the AIS ignores nonmonetary information that is also important to users. For example, an investor might like to know what the prospects are for the future sales of a company, but many financial AISs do not record information such as unfulfilled customer sales because such sales are not recognizable financial events for accounting purposes, even though they represent important business events. The AIS is a subset of the management information system of an organization, which also stores important nonfinancial information about organizational resources, business events, and agents (customers, vendors, banks, etc.) in databases precisely because they are relevant to the decision-making processes of their users.

Inadequacies in financial performance measures have encouraged companies to consider nonfinancial measures when evaluating performance. Some of the advantages include the following: (1) nonfinancial measures can provide a closer link to long-term organizational strategies; (2) drivers of success in many industries are "intangible assets" such as intellectual capital and customer loyalty, rather than the "hard assets" that are recorded on balance sheets; (3) such measures can be better indicators of future financial performance; and (4) investments in customer satisfaction can improve subsequent economic performance by increasing revenues and loyalty of existing customers, attracting new customers, and reducing transaction costs.[7]

---

[7] Ittner, C. and D. Larcker. "Non-financial performance measures: What works and what doesn't," December 6, 2000, Knowledge@Wharton (knowledge.wharton.upenn.edu), accessed March 2017.

Several professional associations now formally recognize that nonfinancial performance measures enhance the value of purely financial information. For example, in 1994 a special committee of the AICPA recommended several ways that businesses could improve the information they were providing to external parties by including management analysis data, forward-looking information such as opportunities and risks, information about management and shareholders, and background information about the reporting entity. Similarly, in 2002, the American Accounting Association (AAA) Financial Accounting Standards Committee recommended that the *Securities and Exchange Commission (SEC)* and the *Financial Accounting Standards Board (FASB)* encourage companies to voluntarily disclose more nonfinancial performance measures.

There are several suggestions that are important to keep in mind if a company chooses to collect metrics around nonfinancial performance measures. For example, keeping track of the information, such as using a dashboard, is very helpful. (We discuss dashboards in more depth in the next section of this chapter and in Chapter 5.) Also, limiting the number of measures is important so that a company remains focused on those that are truly critical to the performance of the company. And finally, management should closely monitor the nonfinancial performance measures to make sure that they are relevant to the company's success.

Case-in-Point 1.4 The ThyssenKrupp company uses nonfinancial performance indicators to monitor sustainability, innovations, employees, environment and climate, and corporate citizenship. The company summarizes their goal in the following statement. "Our performance is reflected not only in our financial results, but also in the sustainability of our actions. We develop efficient solutions that conserve resources and protect the climate and the environment. For this we need capable employees—so we place strong emphasis on training and development and health and safety."[8]

Real-Time Reporting. Another impact of IT on financial accounting is the timing of inputs, processing, and outputs. Financial statements are periodic, and most large companies traditionally issue them quarterly, with a comprehensive report produced annually. With advances in IT that allow transactions to be captured immediately when the business activity occurs, the AIS can produce financial statements almost in real time. Of course, some of the adjustments that accountants must make to the records are not done minute-by-minute, but a business can certainly track sales and many of its expenses continuously. This is especially useful to retailing executives, many of whom now use dashboards.

Interactive Data and XBRL. A problem that accountants, investors, auditors, and other financial managers have often faced is that data used in one application are not easily transferable to another. This means that accountants may spend hours preparing spreadsheets and reports that require them to enter the same data in different formats over and over. **Interactive data** are data that can be reused and carried seamlessly among a variety of applications or reports. Consider, for example, a data item such as total assets. This number might need to be formatted and even calculated several different ways (e.g., at cost, net realizable value, book value, replacement value) for reports

---

[8] ThyssenKrupp, A.G., "Non-financial Performance Indicators," Online Annual Report 2010/2011, accessed March 2017.

such as filings with the SEC, banks, and performance reports. With interactive data, the data are captured in the database only once and can be used wherever needed.

Interactive data require a language for standardization that "tags" the data at its most basic level. As an example, for total assets, this would be at the detail level for each asset. **Extensible business reporting language (XBRL)** is the language of choice for this purpose. As of 2010, the SEC requires public companies to file their financial reports in XBRL format. In addition, many companies, software programs, and industries are beginning to incorporate XBRL for creating, transforming, and communicating financial information.

We will discuss cloud computing later in this chapter, but at this point, we want to make you aware of this technology with respect to XBRL. XBRL Cloud made a viewer available that allows anyone to examine SEC XBRL financial filings, and it is called the XBRL Cloud EDGAR Dashboard.[9] When a filing is posted on the SEC website, XBRL Cloud takes the information and adds a new line to the Dashboard that indicates the name of the filing company, the form type and date filed, the percentage of extended elements, the creation software that was used to prepare the filing, and free validation checking. A description of some of the Dashboard's features can be found at xbrl.squarespace.com. We discuss XBRL in more detail in Chapter 2, and you can learn about the current status of XBRL at www.XBRL.org.

Case-in-Point 1.5 The Federal Deposit Insurance Corporation (FDIC) insures bank deposits over a specific amount. FDIC wanted to create an Internet-based Central Data Repository that stored all the quarterly data they received from more than 7,000 banks. They convinced their software vendors to incorporate XBRL to standardize the data. The tagged data that the FDIC receives from banks now has improved accuracy and can be published and made available to users much more quickly than before.[10]

Managerial Accounting

The principal objective of managerial accounting is to provide relevant information to organizational managers, that is, users who are internal to a company or government agency. Cost accounting and budgeting are two typical parts of a company's managerial accounting system. Let us examine each of them in turn.

Cost Accounting. Due to globalization, decentralization, deregulation, and other factors, companies continue to face stiff competition. The result is that companies must be more efficient and be more adept at controlling costs. The **cost accounting** part of managerial accounting specifically assists management in measuring and controlling the costs associated with an organization's various acquisition, manufacturing, distribution, and selling activities. In the broadest sense, these tasks focus on the *value added* by an organization to its goods or services, and this concept remains constant whether the organization is a manufacturer, a bank, a hospital, or a police department.

Take health care for an example. Although much controversy still surrounds the health-care legislation that was signed into law in 2010, there is one fact that most currently agree upon—the health care industry is a very large portion of the US economy and it is growing rapidly as the "baby boomer generation" reaches retirement age.

---

[9] See https://edgardashboard.xbrlcloud.com/edgar-dashboard. Accessed March 2017.
[10] Improved business process through XBRL: A use case for business reporting, Federal Financial Institutions Examination Council, White Paper, January 31, 2006. Accessed from XBRL.org in March 2017.

These facts, coupled with increased regulatory demands on health-care providers and hospitals, suggest the need for sophisticated accounting systems to maintain critical data, as well as the need for up-to-date reports for decision-making.

Case-in-Point 1.6 Survey data from more than 100 hospital CFOs suggests five major themes regarding the evolution of financial practices in health care. Two of those themes are (1) a greater focus on internal controls (supported by information and management systems) and (2) an increased reliance on business analysis (requirement to develop and measure business performance).[11]

Activity-Based Costing. One example of an AIS in the area of cost accounting is an **activity-based costing (ABC) system**. Traditionally, cost accountants assigned overhead (i.e., indirect production costs) on the basis of direct labor hours because the number of labor hours was usually directly related to the volume of production. The problem with this traditional system is that, over time, increased reliance on automation has caused manufacturers to use less and less direct labor. Thus, managers became frustrated using this one method of assigning overhead costs when a clear relationship between labor and these overhead expenses no longer seemed to exist. Instead, managers in a variety of manufacturing and service industries now identify specific activities involved in a manufacturing or service task and then assign overhead costs based on the resources directly consumed by each activity.

Although ABC techniques have been available for several decades, they are more common now that computerized systems can track costs. These systems can move an organization in new strategic directions, allowing corporate executives to examine fundamental business processes and enabling them to reengineer the way they do business. ABC systems can also play an essential strategic role in building and maintaining a successful e-commerce business because they can answer questions about production costs and help managers allocate resources more efficiently and effectively.

Case-in-Point 1.7 Dr. Robert Kaplan, Harvard Business School, discusses how surgery centers can use ABC to improve efficiency. He explains how to look at each surgical activity and to identify the cost of that activity, how costs can be eliminated or reduced, and how ABC data can be used to make operational changes for more cost efficiency.[12]

Corporate Performance Measurement and Business Intelligence. Another example of an AIS used in the area of cost accounting is in corporate performance measurement. In a **responsibility accounting system**, for example, managers trace unfavorable performance to the department or individuals that caused the inefficiencies. Under a responsibility accounting system, each subsystem within an organization is only accountable for those items over which it has control. Thus, when a particular cost expenditure exceeds its standard cost, managers can take immediate corrective action.

In addition to the traditional financial measures, cost accountants also collect a variety of nonfinancial performance measures to evaluate things such as customer satisfaction, product quality, business innovation, and branding effectiveness. The **balanced scorecard** measures business performance in four categories: (1) financial

[11] Langabeer, J., J. DellliFraine, and J. Helton. 2010. Mixing finance and medicine. *Strategic Finance* 92(6): 27–34.
[12] AHC Media. "Activity-based costing can save money for surgery centers," January 1, 2017, accessed from ahcmedia.com, March 2017.

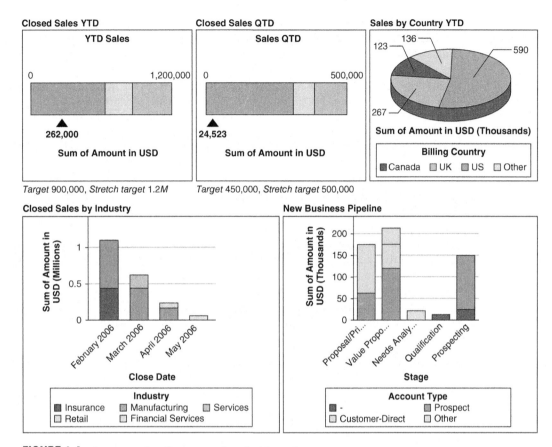

FIGURE 1-4   An example of an executive dashboard.

performance, (2) customer knowledge, (3) internal business processes, and (4) learning and growth. A company may choose to rank these categories to align with their strategic values. For example, a company may stress "customer knowledge" because customer satisfaction is important to its market position and planned sales growth.

Balanced scorecards and corporate performance measurement are not new ideas. But with the Internet, integrated systems, and other advanced technologies, balanced scorecards and other approaches to Cost Performance Management are becoming increasingly valuable **business intelligence** tools. Businesses use **key performance indicators (KPIs)** to measure and evaluate activities in each quadrant of the balanced scorecard. For example, a financial KPI might be return on investment. In the customer area, a company might track the number of new customers per month.

Dashboards (Figure 1-4) are commonly used to monitor key performance metrics. Dashboards usually appear in color, so that red, for example, might indicate a failure to meet the goal. Another indicator might be up and down arrows to show how a key activity performs over a certain time period. Dashboards are especially useful to managers who appreciate the presentation of important performance data in easy-to-understand graphic formats.

Case-in-Point 1.8   Accounting and advisory firms often work with organizations to select appropriate software to serve their information and IT needs. Most dashboards can be adapted for use at the highest level of the firm—even at the board of directors' level—or at any level below. Four of the industry leaders that offer software that can design a dashboard are IBM (Cognos), Actuate (PerformanceSoft), SAP (Business Objects/Pilot Software), and iDashboard.[13]

Budgeting. A budget is a financial projection for the future and is thus a valuable managerial planning aid. Companies develop both short- and long-range budget projections. Short-range budget projections disclose detailed financial plans for a 12-month period, whereas long-range budgets are less-detailed financial projections for 5 or more years into the future. Management accountants are normally responsible for an organization's budget.

A good budgetary system is also a useful *managerial control* mechanism. Because managers use budgets to predict future financial expectations, they can compare the causes of significant variations between *actual* and *budgeted* results during any budget period. Through timely performance reports that compare actual operating results with prescribed norms, managers are able to identify and investigate significant variations. While negative variations are normally cause for concern, favorable budget variations are not always good news either. For example, managers might find cheaper inputs and have a positive variation from the standard cost, but such a savings might cause quality problems with the finished product. Regardless of whether variations are positive or negative, managers can use the information for better decision-making.

Auditing

The two most popular career paths in auditing are external auditing and internal auditing. We briefly examine each path and the related impact of IT in the following sections.

External Auditing. The traditional role of external auditing has been to evaluate the accuracy and completeness of a corporation's financial statements. In recent years, however, the individuals working in CPA firms would probably argue that they are actually in the assurance business—that is, the business of providing third-party testimony that a client complies with a given statute, law, or similar requirement. Historically, the growth of such assurance services can be traced to a conference of the AICPA in 1993, which created a Special Committee on Assurance Services to identify and formalize some other areas (besides financial audits) in which accountants could provide assurance services. Figure 1-5 describes the first six areas identified by the committee.

Today, there are several additional areas in which auditors can perform assurance work, many involving AISs. One example is to vouch for a client's compliance with HIPAA laws, the privacy requirements of the Health Insurance Portability and Accountability Act. Another example is **CPA Trust Services**, a set of professional service areas built around a set of common principles and criteria related to the risks and opportunities presented by IT environments. Trust services include online privacy evaluations, security audits, tests of the integrity of information processing systems, verification of the availability of IT services, and tests of systems confidentiality.

Despite the rise in ancillary assurance services, auditors mainly focus on traditional financial auditing tasks. As noted earlier, computerized AISs have made these tasks more challenging. For example, automated data processing also creates a need for

---

[13] Ballou, B., D. Heitger, and L. Donnell. 2010. Creating effective dashboards. *Strategic Finance* 91(9): 27–32.

Risk Assessment
Provide assurance that an organization's set of business risks is comprehensive and manageable.
Business Performance Measurement
Provide assurance that an organization's performance measures beyond the traditional measures in financial statements are relevant and reasonable for helping the organization to achieve its goals and objectives.
Information Systems Reliability
Provide assurance that an organization's information system has been designed to provide reliable information for decision-making.
Electronic Commerce
Provide assurance that organizations doing business on the Internet can be trusted to provide the goods and services they promise and that there is a measure of security provided to customers.
Health-Care Performance Measurement
Provide assurance to health-care recipients about the effectiveness of health care offered by a variety of health-care providers.
Eldercare Plus
Provide assurance that various caregivers offering services to the elderly are offering appropriate and high-quality services.

FIGURE 1-5 Assurance services identified by the AICPA Special Committee on Assurance Services.

auditors to evaluate the risks associated with such automation. Chapter 11 discusses the audit of computerized AISs and the ways in which auditors use IT to perform their jobs.

In addition to the auditing and assurance businesses mentioned above, many CPA firms also perform management consulting tasks—for example, helping clients acquire, install, and use new information systems. The AIS at Work feature at the end of this chapter describes one such consulting area. However, the corporate accounting scandals in the early 2000s led members of the SEC and the US Congress to question whether a CPA firm can conduct an independent audit of the same systems it recently assisted a client in installing and using—a concern intensified when audit staff at Arthur Andersen LLP apparently deliberately destroyed auditing papers for the Enron corporation. Thus, the Sarbanes–Oxley Act of 2002 (SOX) expressly forbids such potential conflicts of interest by not allowing CPA firms to simultaneously act as a "management consultant" and the "independent auditor" for the same firm.

Despite this requirement, there are still many areas in which CPA firms provide consulting services to clients. Examples include business valuations, litigation support, systems implementation, personal financial planning, estate planning, strategic planning, health-care planning, making financing arrangements, and performing forensic (fraud) investigations.

Internal Auditing. According to the Institute of Internal Auditors (IIA), the definition of internal auditing is "an independent, objective assurance and consulting activity designed to add value and improve an organization's operations. It helps an organization accomplish its objectives by bringing a systematic, disciplined approach to evaluate and improve the effectiveness of risk management, control, and governance processes." Large companies have Internal Audit Departments to carry out these duties. Internal auditors in public companies report to the Audit Committee of the Board of

Directors, as it is important for them to be independent and to have wide access to all areas of the organization.[14]

Internal auditors make extensive use of technology. For example, they use electronic audit workpapers, computer-assisted audit techniques (CAATs), and software tools for data mining, data analysis, documenting business processes and systems, monitoring audit exceptions and remediation.

Taxation

Although some individuals still complete their income tax returns manually, many now use computer programs such as *TurboTax* for this task. Such tax preparation software is an example of an AIS that enables its users to create and store copies of trial tax returns, examine the consequences of alternative tax strategies, print specific portions of a return, and electronically transmit complete copies of a state or federal tax return to the appropriate government agency.

Similarly, IT also helps tax professionals research challenging tax questions—for example, by providing access to online tax libraries. Tax professionals typically subscribe to online tax services by paying a fee for the right to access databases of tax information. Online services can provide tax researchers with databases of federal and state tax laws, tax court rulings, court decisions, and technical advice.

1.4   WHAT ARE ACCOUNTING INFORMATION SYSTEMS?

Now that you know the exciting career opportunities that are available to accountants who also have technology skills and understand the impact of technology on the profession, let us now focus on the terminology surrounding AISs. What exactly do we mean by information systems, and why do we care about the difference between information and data?

Accounting Information Systems

Accounting information systems stand at the crossroads of two disciplines: "accounting" and "information systems." As a result, the study of AISs is often viewed as the study of computerized accounting systems. Thus, we define an accounting information system as a collection of data and processing procedures that creates needed information for its users. Let us examine in greater detail what this definition really means. For our discussion, we'll examine each of the words in the term "accounting information systems" separately.

Accounting.   You probably have a pretty good understanding of accounting because you have already taken one or more courses in the area. You know that the accounting field includes financial accounting, managerial accounting, auditing, taxation, and so forth. AISs are used in all these areas—for example, to perform tasks in areas such as payroll, accounts receivable, accounts payable, inventory, and budgeting. In addition,

---

[14] The Institute of Internal Auditors. "All in a day's work: A look at the varied responsibilities of internal auditors (theiit.org)," accessed March 2017.

Applications	Examples of AIS information
Finance	Cash and asset management, multicompany and multicurrency management
Human resources	Payroll and benefits summaries and management
Marketing and sales	Customer management, sales management, sales forecasts, and annual summaries
Production	Inventory management and summaries, product cost analysis
Supply chain management	Supplier management, inventory management

FIGURE 1-6 Examples of information an AIS can generate for various business functions.

AISs help accountants maintain general ledger information, create spreadsheets for strategic planning, and distribute financial reports.

It is difficult to think of a business task that is not integrated, in some way, with an AIS. As a result, accountants must determine how best to provide the information contained in an AIS to support business decisions. AISs also create information that is useful to nonaccountants, such as individuals working in marketing and sales, production, or human resources. Figure 1-6 provides some examples. For this information to be effective, the individuals working in these subsystems must help the developers of an AIS identify what information they need for their planning, decision-making, and control functions. These examples illustrate why an AIS course is useful not only for accounting majors but for all business majors.

Information (vs. Data). Although the terms **data** and **information** are often used interchangeably, they do not have the same meaning. *Data* (the plural of *datum*) are raw facts about events that have little organization or meaning—for example, a set of raw scores on a class examination. To be useful or meaningful, most data must be processed into useful *information*. An example might be to take the raw scores of a class exam and compute the class average.

Do raw data *have* to be processed in order to be meaningful? The answer is no. Imagine, for example, that *you* take a test in a class. Which is more important to you—the average score for the class as a whole (a processed value) or *your* score (a raw data value)? Similarly, suppose you own shares of stock in a particular company. Which of these values would be *least* important to you: (1) the *average* price of a stock that was traded during a given day (a processed value), (2) the price *you* paid for the shares of stock (an unprocessed value), or (3) the *last* price trade of the day (another unprocessed value)?

Raw data are also important because they mark the starting point of an **audit trail**—the path that data follow as they flow through an AIS. In a payroll system, for example, an input clerk enters the data for a new employee, and the AIS keeps track of the wages earned by that employee each pay period. An auditor can verify the existence of employees and whether each employee received the correct amount of money.

Case-in-Point 1.9 A former payroll manager at the Brooklyn Museum pleaded guilty to embezzling $620,000 by writing paychecks to "ghost employees." Dwight Newton, 40, admitted committing wire fraud by adding workers to the payroll who did not exist and then wiring their wages directly into a joint bank account that he shared with his wife. Under a plea agreement, Newton must repay the museum the stolen funds. He was ordered to forfeit $77,000 immediately, sell his Barbados timeshare, and liquidate his pension with the museum.[15]

---

[15] Brooklyn Museum Embezzlement in *New York Magazine* (nymag.com), accessed March 2014.

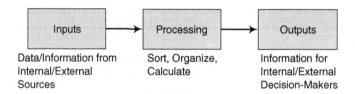

FIGURE 1-7 An information system's components. Data or information is input, processed, and output as information for planning, decision-making, and control purposes.

Despite the potential usefulness of some unprocessed data, most end users need financial totals, summary statistics, or exception values—that is, processed data—for decision-making purposes. Figure 1-7 illustrates a model for this—a three-stage process in which (1) raw and/or stored data serve as the primary inputs, (2) processing tasks process the data, and (3) meaningful information is the primary output. An AIS typically performs the necessary tasks in each step of the process. For example, a catalog retailer might use Web pages on the Internet to gather customer purchase data, then use central file servers and data storage to process and store the purchase transactions, and finally employ other Web pages and printed outputs to confirm and distribute information *about* the order to appropriate parties.

While computers are efficient and useful tools, they can also create problems. One is that computers may not automatically catch the simple input errors that humans do. For example, if you were performing payroll processing, you would know that a value of "−40" hours for the number of hours worked was a mistake—the value should be "40." A computer can be programmed to look for (and reject) bad input, but it is difficult to anticipate all possible errors.

Another problem created by computers is that they make audit trails more difficult to follow. This is because the path that data follow through computerized systems is electronic. However, a well-designed AIS can still document its audit trail with listings of transactions and account balances both before and after the transactions are processed and the accounts are updated. A major focus of this book is on developing effective internal control systems for companies, and audit trails are important elements. Chapters 6, 7, and 11 discuss these topics in detail.

In addition to collecting and distributing large amounts of data and information, AISs must also organize and store data for future uses. In a payroll application, for example, the system must maintain running totals for the earnings, tax withholdings, and retirement contributions of each employee in order to prepare end-of-year tax forms. These data-organization and storage tasks are major challenges and is one of the reasons why this book contains three chapters on the subject (see Chapters 6, 7, and 11).

Besides deciding *what* data to store, businesses must also worry about how best to *integrate* the stored data for end users. An older approach to this problem was to maintain independently the data for each of its traditional organization functions—for example, finance, marketing and sales, human resources, and production. A problem with this approach is that, even if all the applications are maintained internally by the same IT department, there will be separate data gathering and reporting responsibilities within each subsystem, and each application may store its data independently of the others. This often leads to a duplication of data collecting and processing efforts, as well as conflicting data values when specific information (e.g., a customer's address) is changed in one application but not another.

Organizations recognize the need to integrate the data associated with their functions into large, seamless data warehouses. This integration allows internal managers and possibly external parties to obtain the information needed for planning, decision-making, and control, whether or not that information is for marketing, accounting, or some other functional area in the organization. To accomplish this task, many companies are now using large, expensive **enterprise resource planning (ERP) systems** to integrate their information subsystems into one application. An example of such a software product is *SAP R/3*, which combines accounting, manufacturing, human resource, and other subsystems into an enterprise-wide information system, that is, a system that focuses on the *business processes* of the organization as a whole. We discuss these systems in more depth in Chapter 5.

SAP, SAS Institute, IBM, and Oracle have recognized the need for integrated information and therefore developed business intelligence software to meet this need. As a result, software developers are including **predictive analytics** features into their main software suites. These analytics tools include a variety of methodologies that managers might use to analyze current and past data to help predict future events or trends. In March 2010, IBM opened a predictive analytics lab in China, which is part of estimated $12 billion commitment to build out IBM's analytics portfolio.[16]

Case-in-Point 1.10 Accountants and other managers are using predictive and real-time analytics, which take advantage of data stored in data warehouses to create systems that allow them to use their data to improve performance. For example, for 2 weeks every August and September, the United States Tennis Association welcomes hundreds of thousands of spectators to the US Open tennis tournament. Predictive and real-time analytics drive IBM's SlamTracker, which identifies key actions players must take to enhance their odds of winning. These same technologies are being used by police departments to prevent crime, retailers to drive sales, and financial firms to reduce fraud.[17]

It is no secret that the amount of data in data warehouses around the globe has been exploding. As a result, managers are grappling with how best to analyze these large data sets (called "**big data**") for competitive advantage, to identify consumer trends, and for other critical decisions. In a 2012 white paper from Intel, the authors claim that "the ability to mine and analyze big data gives organizations deeper and richer insights into business patterns and trends, helping drive operational efficiencies and competitive advantage in manufacturing, security, marketing, and IT."[18]

Systems. Within the accounting profession, the term "systems" usually refers to "computer systems." As you know, IT advances are changing the way we do just about everything. Less than a decade ago, the authors never imagined that people could someday purchase a book from a "virtual bookstore" on the Internet using a wireless device, while enjoying a latte in a Starbucks! The explosion in electronic connectivity and commerce are just some of the many ways that IT influences how people now access information or how firms conduct business. Today, IT is a vital part of what accountants must know to be employable.

---

[16] Vance, J. "Business intelligence software and predictive analytics," Datamation (www.datamation.com), accessed March 2017.

[17] "Data is a game changer," IBM Smarter Enterprise, U.S. Open Case Study (www.ibm.com), accessed March 2017.

[18] Fania, M. and J. D. Miller. July 2012. IT@Intel White Paper, IT Best Practices. "Mining big data in the enterprise for better business intelligence," accessed from www.intel.com, March 2017.

Returning to our definition, you probably noticed that we did *not* use the term "computer," although we did use the term "processing procedures." You already know the reason for this—not all AISs are computerized or even need to be. But most of the ones in businesses today are automated and thus the term "processing procedures" could be replaced by the term "computerized processing" for almost all AISs.

In summary, it is convenient to conceptualize an AIS as a set of components that collect accounting data, store it for future uses, and process it for end users. This abstract model of data inputs, storage, processing, and outputs applies to almost all the traditional accounting cycles with which you are familiar—for example, the payroll, revenue, and expenditure cycles—and is thus a useful way of conceptualizing an AIS. Again, we stress that many of the "end users" of the information of an AIS are not accountants, but include customers, investors, suppliers, financial analysts, and government agencies.

The Role of Accounting Information Systems in Organizations

IT refers to the hardware, software, and related system components that organizations use to create computerized information systems. IT has been a major force in our current society and now influences our lives in many personal ways—when we use digital cameras to take pictures, access the Internet to make a purchase or learn about something, or email friends and family. It is perhaps less clear that computer technology has also had profound influences on commerce. In our current **information age**, fewer workers actually make products while more of them produce, analyze, manipulate, and distribute information *about* business activities. These individuals are often called **knowledge workers**. Companies find that their success or failure often depends upon the uses or misuses of the information that knowledge workers manage.

Case-in-Point 1.11   The Wall Street Journal reports that the rise of knowledge workers is accelerating, while routine jobs have been replaced by automation and technology. The number of knowledge workers has more than doubled over the past three decades and shows no signs of slowing down.[19]

The information age has important implications for accounting because that is what accountants are—knowledge workers. In fact, accountants have always been in the "information business" because their role has been, in part, to communicate accurate and relevant financial information to parties interested in how their organizations are performing. And this includes the increasing importance and growth of **e-business**, conducting business over the Internet or dedicated proprietary networks and **e-commerce**, a subset of e-business, which refers mostly to buying and selling on the Internet.

In many ways, accounting is itself an information system—that is, a communicative process that collects, stores, processes, and distributes information to those who need it. For instance, corporate accountants develop financial statements for external parties. But users of accounting information sometimes criticize AISs for only capturing and reporting *financial* transactions. They claim that financial statements often ignore some of the most important activities that influence business entities. For example,

[19] Zumbrun, J. "The rise of knowledge workers is accelerating despite the threat of automation," (wsj.com) May 4, 2016, accessed March 2017.

the financial reports of a professional basketball team would not include information about hiring a new star because this would not result in journal entries in the franchise's double-entry accounting system.

Today, however, AISs are concerned with nonfinancial as well as financial data and information. Thus, our definition of an AIS as an enterprise-wide system (described further in Chapter 5) views accounting as an organization's primary producer and distributor of many different types of information. This matches the contemporary perspective that accounting systems are not only financial systems.

1.5   WHAT'S NEW IN ACCOUNTING INFORMATION SYSTEMS?

The last few years have witnessed some of the most startling changes in the uses and applications of AISs, causing us to reassess our understanding and uses of accounting data. Below are a few examples.

Cloud Computing—Impact for Accountants

Cloud computing is in its second decade and impacts many aspects of IT. In Chapter 2 we identify the basics of cloud computing, but in this section we want to discuss why this technology is important to accountants and then describe some of the current issues surrounding cloud computing as it relates to accounting professionals. According to Ron Gill, **cloud computing** is a way of using business applications over the Internet—like you use the Internet for your bank transactions. Think of cloud computing as a way to increase IT capacity or add capabilities without investing in new infrastructure, training new people, or licensing new software. Mostly, we're talking about a subscription-based or pay-per-use service that makes IT's existing capabilities scalable whenever the need exists, using the Internet. Gartner predicts that for 2017, $247 billion will be spent on cloud services worldwide, with a 5-year compound annual growth rate (CAGR) of 16.5%.[20]

Cloud computing resources may be categorized as data storage, infrastructure and platform, and application software (i.e., business applications such as purchases, human resources, sales). If a firm would like to take advantage of cloud computing, it would most likely need to subscribe to all three of these categories from the service provider. For example, business applications depend on company data that is stored in the database, and data storage depends on the appropriate infrastructure.[21]

Experts identify a number of important benefits of using the cloud. One is the ability to only pay for the applications that you use, and those applications are offered over the Internet. Of course, this sort of flexibility also suggests that a firm has the ability to quickly modify the scale of its IT capability. Another benefit is that an organization may not have to purchase or operate expensive hardware and software—providers own and operate the equipment and software, much as a taxi company owns and operates its own fleet of vehicles. Also, cloud computing providers offer only one (current) version of an application, so individual firms no longer have to deal with expensive, time-consuming upgrades for software. See Figure 1-8.

---

[20] Gartner (www.gartner.com). "Forecast: Public cloud services, worldwide, 2014–2020, 4Q16. Update." Stamford, CT. January 5, 2017, accessed March 2017.

[21] Du, H. and Y. Cong. 2010. Cloud computing, accounting, auditing, and beyond. *The CPA Journal* 80(10): 66–70.

Why Is Everyone Choosing Cloud Computing?	
• Support 24/7	• Only Pay for What You Use
• Lower Total Cost of Owning	• Reliable, Sustainable, Scalable
• Secure Storage Management	• Lowers Capital Expenditures
• Freed-Up Internal Resources	• Highly Automated
• Utility Based	• Easy Deployment
• Independent of Location	• Independent of Devices

FIGURE 1-8   Some of the reasons why cloud computing is becoming so pervasive.

Case-in-Point 1.12   Food for thought: if you have used Facebook, Twitter, or LinkedIn in the recent past, you have made use of cloud computing. The same goes for your Gmail or Yahoo email account.

Accountants always talk about cost–benefit trade-offs. We just identified several possible benefits surrounding this new technology, so it is appropriate to mention that there are also costs and/or concerns. The first potential concern is reliability of the Internet since this is the medium for delivering all cloud services. Other issues include (1) data security measures that the provider offers (i.e., appropriate internal controls), (2) the quality of service that the provider gives the firm (i.e., careful crafting of the service contract is similar to that of any outsourcing contract, which includes vigilant monitoring of services for quality purposes), and (3) the reliability of the service provider (i.e., going concern issues). Accordingly, management accountants, internal auditors, and external auditors will need to evaluate the different risks that a firm may face if it decides to "use the cloud."

Corporate Responsibility Reporting

Corporate Responsibility Reporting (also called Sustainability Reporting) is voluntary and focuses on nonfinancial environmental and social measures that might impact an organization's income, value, or future performance. A 2015 KPMG survey of 4,500 companies in 45 countries produced interesting results. The current rate of corporate responsibility reporting among the world's largest 250 companies (in terms of revenue) exceeds 90%. Surprisingly, four emerging economies (India, Indonesia, Malaysia, and South Africa) have the highest reporting rates in the world. Also, including corporate responsibility data in annual reports has become a global trend, with almost three in five companies doing so.[22]

Case-in-Point 1.13   In IKEA Group's 2015 corporate responsibility report, an innovative feature is the inclusion of external stakeholder perspectives presented as challenges to senior management and management's responses. Topics include corporate growth and environmental impact, fueling a throwaway culture, and combating child labor deep in the supply chain.

You might be asking yourself how this is an AIS issue if the information is "non-financial" in nature. As you will discover in Chapter 5, enterprise-wide systems are

---

[22] KPMG. 2015. "*Current of Change: The KPMG Survey of Corporate Responsibility Reporting 2015.*" (www.kpmg.com/crreporting). Accessed March 10, 2017.

Employee Health Indicators	Employee Safety Factors	Environment
Tobacco use	Fleet car accidents	Carbon emissions
High cholesterol	Lost workdays	Waste recycled
Absenteeism	Employee accidents	Biodiversity impact

FIGURE 1-9   Examples of corporate responsibility items of interest to a firm and data that would be collected to report on each item of interest.

widely used to collect qualitative as well as quantitative information for decision-making within organizations. In fact, management control systems are the backbone of corporate responsibility reports. That is, organizations need to establish well-defined corporate responsibility strategies that identify achievable and measurable goals.[23] Figure 1-9 identifies examples of corporate responsibility items of interest to firms and their stakeholders, as well as some of the data that would be collected to report on each item of interest.

Suspicious Activity Reporting

A number of **suspicious activity reporting (SAR)** laws now require accountants to report questionable financial transactions to the US Treasury Department. Examples of such transactions are ones suggestive of money laundering, bribes, or wire transfers to terrorist organizations. Federal statutes that mandate SARs include sections of the Annunzio-Wylie Anti-Money Laundering Act (1992), amendments to the Bank Secrecy Act of 1996, and several sections of the Patriot Act (2001). Institutions affected by these laws include (1) banks, (2) money service businesses such as currency traders, (3) broker dealers, (4) casinos and card clubs, (5) commodity traders, (6) insurance companies, and (7) mutual funds. Over the years, such filings have enabled the federal government to investigate a wide number of criminal activities, gather evidence, and, in some cases, repatriate funds sent overseas. Testimony to the importance of SAR is the growth of SAR filings—from about 62,000 reports in 1996 to almost 2.0 million reports in 2016.

Case-in-Point 1.14   A cooperating witness indicated that a pharmaceutical network was selling controlled drugs through affiliated websites to customers without authorized prescriptions. To evade US laws, the owners located their headquarters in Central America and their Web servers in the Middle East. A federal investigation and a SAR filed by a financial institution involved in the matter documented almost $5 million in suspicious wire transfers. The result: indictments against 18 individuals and the repatriation of over $9 million from overseas accounts as part of the forfeiture proceedings.[24]

SAR impacts AISs in several ways. Because so much of the information within AISs is financial, these systems are often used to launder money or fund criminal activities. As a result, AISs become important sources of SAR evidence and subsequent legal action. Finally, SAR can act as a deterrent to criminal or terrorist activities—and is therefore an important control for AISs.

---

[23] Busco, C., M. Frigo, E. Leone, and A. Riccaboni. 2010. Cleaning up. *Strategic Finance* 92(1): 29–37.
[24] "BSA documents lead to repatriation & seizure of over $9 million generated by illegal internet pharmacy," published in *The SAR Activity Review—Trends, Tips & Issues*, Issue 14, October 2008.

Forensic Accounting, Governmental Accountants, and Terrorism

As we discussed in the beginning section of this chapter, **forensic accounting** is a career field that is important and growing. This area of accounting has become a popular course at many universities and some universities now have a number of specialized courses that are included in a fraud examination or forensic accounting path so that students may specialize in this area of accounting.[25] In general, a forensic accountant combines the skills of investigation, accounting, and auditing to find and collect pieces of information that collectively provide evidence of criminal activity in progress or that has happened.

Terrorists need money to carry out their criminal activities, and, as a result, forensic accountants have become increasingly important in the fight against such activities because these accountants use technology for data mining. For example, Audit Command Language (ACL) and Interactive Data Extraction and Analysis (IDEA) are popular data extraction software tools that auditors can use to spot anomalies and trends in data.

One example of the use of AISs for this purpose is using banking systems to trace the flow of funds across international borders. Other examples include (1) identifying and denying financial aid to terrorist groups and their sympathizers, (2) tracing arms and chemical orders to their final destinations, thereby identifying the ultimate—perhaps unauthorized—purchasers, (3) using spreadsheets to help plan for catastrophic events, (4) using security measures to control cyber terrorism, and (5) installing new internal controls to help detect money laundering and illegal fund transfers.

But where do terrorists get the money to finance their activities? Generally speaking, they rely on the following sources for funding: state sponsors, individual contributions, corporate contributions, not-for-profit organizations, government programs, and illegal sources—and here is where government accountants can play an important part in the fight against terrorism. Apparently, terrorists choose to live unpretentiously, they exploit weaknesses in government assistance programs, and they are skillful at concealing their activities.[26] Similar to forensic accountants, government accountants should use data extraction software to spot anomalies, suspicious activity, or red flags that might suggest illegal transactions.

Corporate Scandals and Accounting

Although corporate frauds and scandals are hardly new, more recent ones have set records for their magnitude and scope. Of particular note are the Enron scandal and the case against Bernard Madoff. The Enron scandal is important because of the amount of money and jobs that were lost, and also because so much of it appears to be directly related to the adroit manipulation of accounting records. Although the details of these manipulations are complex, the results were to understate the liabilities of the business entities and to inflate earnings and net worth. The opinion of most experts today is that the mechanics of these adjustments might not have been illegal, but the intent to defraud was clear and therefore criminal.

---

[25] Examples include University of Alabama at Birmingham and West Virginia University.

[26] Brooks, R., R. Riley, and J. Thomas. 2005. Detecting and preventing the financing of terrorist activities. *Journal of Government Financial Management* 54(1): 12–18.

Accounting rules allow for some flexibility in financial reporting. Unfortunately, some financial officers have exploited this flexibility to enhance earnings reports or present rosier forecasts than reality might dictate—that is, they "cooked the books." Examples are Scott Sullivan, former Chief Financial Officer at WorldCom, Inc., Mark H. Swartz, former Chief Financial Officer at Tyco International, Inc., and Andrew Fastow, Enron's former Chief Financial Officer. While some accountants have been guilty of criminal and unethical behavior, others have emerged from the scandals as heroes. These include Sherron Watkins, who tried to tell Ken Lay that the numbers at Enron just didn't add up, and Cynthia Cooper, an internal auditor at WorldCom, who blew the whistle on the falsified accounting transactions ordered by her boss, Scott Sullivan.

As the credit crunch worked its way through the economy in 2008, a number of financial institutions either collapsed or narrowly avoided doing so and accounting was in the news once again. In March 2009, Bernard Madoff pleaded guilty to 11 federal felonies and admitted that he turned his wealth management business into a **Ponzi scheme** that defrauded investors of billions of dollars. Named for Charles Ponzi, this is a pyramid fraud in which new investment funds are used to pay returns to current investors. The fraud relies on new money continuously entering the system so that investors believe their money is actually earning returns. The problem is that when new money stops flowing, the pyramid collapses.

AIS AT WORK
The Cost of Not Filing a SAR[27]

The name Madoff has become a household name in the United States. Bernard Lawrence "Bernie" Madoff, discussed in the previous section, was a stockbroker, investment advisor, and financier. Even before Madoff pleaded guilty to the largest Ponzi scheme in history, countless informed individuals wondered how in the world he could deceive so many people for decades—and many of these people were financial experts, including the staff at JPMorgan, where Madoff banked. In fact, as early as 1999 a man by the name of Harry Markopolos repeatedly tried to warn the authorities over a 10-year period.

As it turns out, the bank's London desk did circulate a memo describing JPMorgan's inability to validate his trading activity or custody of any assets. The memo also noted Madoff's odd choice of a one-man accounting firm. Think about that—a wealth management firm with assets estimated to be $65 billion—and Madoff employed a sole proprietor (with two nonaccounting employees) to audit his firm. That's more assets than that of Etrade ($45.5B), JPMorgan Asset Management ($63.4B), Principal Financial Group ($44.8B), or Charles Schwab ($34.2B)! Each of these firms uses the following independent audit firms, respectively: Deloitte & Touche, PricewaterhouseCoopers LLP, Ernst & Young LLP, and Deloitte & Touche.

But to the point—SARs are not optional. There are a number of laws that require a SAR filing if individuals are concerned about any suspicious financial activities.

---

[27] The Associated Press. 2014. JPMorgan to pay $2.5B for ignoring "alarm bells" on fraud. *Richmond Times-Dispatch*. January 8: D3. Also: Fitzpatrick, D. 2013. JPMorgan is in talks with US over Madoff warnings. *Wall Street Journal (online)*, December 6, 2013.

JPMorgan filed a SAR with UK regulators about 1 month prior to Madoff's arrest—but did not file a SAR with US regulators. This is especially curious since JPMorgan typically files 150,000 to 200,000 such reports every year. How can it be the case that Madoff's activities did not alert bank employees? The bank had been doing business with Madoff for more than two decades prior to his arrest in December 2008.

As you might imagine, the Justice Department was not amused! The result of JPMorgan's silence to the American authorities will cost them dearly—$2.5 billion to be exact. This is the largest forfeiture by a US bank and largest Department of Justice penalty for a Bank Secrecy Act violation. Although JPMorgan is negotiating a settlement to avoid criminal charges, that's a huge price for not filing a SAR with US regulators!

 ## SUMMARY

- ✓ There are many reasons to study AISs, and one of the most important is the availability of many exciting career opportunities.
- ✓ Information technology affects virtually every aspect of accounting, including financial and managerial accounting, auditing, and taxation.
- ✓ Financial accounting information is becoming increasingly relevant and important as advances in IT allow for creation of new reporting systems.
- ✓ Managerial accounting is impacted by IT in the following areas: balanced scorecards, business intelligence, dashboards, and other KPIs.
- ✓ External auditors perform many types of assurance services, in addition to financial statement attestation.
- ✓ Internal auditors provide assurance that corporate governance, internal control, and risk management processes are operating effectively.
- ✓ The availability of tax software and extensive tax databases influences both tax preparation and tax planning.
- ✓ IT refers to the hardware, software, and related system components that organizations use to create computerized information systems.
- ✓ Computerized information systems collect, process, store, transform, and distribute financial and nonfinancial information for planning, decision-making, and control purposes.
- ✓ Data are raw facts; information refers to data that are meaningful and useful.
- ✓ Accountants and other managers are using predictive analytics, a technique that takes advantage of data stored in data warehouses to improve performance.
- ✓ Cloud computing is a way of using business applications over the Internet.
- ✓ The basic concept of corporate responsibility reporting is that a company focuses on nonfinancial performance measures that might impact its income, value, or future performance.
- ✓ By law, the accountants in many specific financial institutions must now file SARs that document potential instances of fraud, money laundering, or money transfers to terrorist organizations.
- ✓ A forensic accountant combines the skills of investigation, accounting, and auditing to find and collect pieces of information that collectively provide evidence of criminal activity in progress or that has happened.
- ✓ Some of the recent corporate scandals involved manipulation of accounting data, which led to the passage of legislation to protect investors.

KEY TERMS YOU SHOULD KNOW

accounting information systems
  (AISs)

activity-based costing (ABC)
  systems

audit trail

balanced scorecard

big data

business intelligence

Certified Fraud Examiner (CFE)

Certified Information Systems
  Auditors (CISAs)

Certified Information Technology
  Professional (CITP)

cloud computing

Corporate Responsibility
  Reporting

cost accounting

CPA Trust Services

dashboards

data

e-business

e-commerce

enterprise resource planning
  (ERP) system

Extensible business reporting
  language (XBRL)

financial accounting information
  systems

forensic accounting

information

information age

Information Systems Audit and
  Control Association (ISACA)

information technology (IT)
  auditors

interactive data

key performance indicators
  (KPIs)

knowledge workers

penetration testing

Ponzi scheme

predictive analytics

responsibility accounting system

suspicious activity reporting
  (SAR)

systems consultants

value-added resellers (VARs)

TEST YOURSELF

Q1-1. Which of the following is NOT true about AISs?

  a. All AISs are computerized.

  b. AISs may report both financial and nonfinancial information.

  c. AISs, in addition to collecting and distributing large amounts of data and information, also organize and store data for future uses.

  d. A student who has an interest in both accounting and IT will find many job opportunities that combine these knowledge and skills areas.

Q1-2. Which of the following is likely to be information rather than data?

  a. sales price

  b. customer number

  c. net profit

  d. employee name

Q1-3. With respect to computerized AISs, computers:

  a. turn data into information

  b. always make audit trails easier to follow

  c. always catch input errors

  d. do not generally process information more quickly than humans

Q1-4. A dashboard in an information system is:

  a. a computer screen used by data entry clerks for input tasks

  b. a physical device dedicated to AIS processing tasks

  c. a summary screen of key performance metrics typically used by managers

  d. a cloud storage summary

Q1-5. The Sarbanes–Oxley Act of 2002:

  a. enables US officers to wiretap corporate phones if required

  b. was enacted as a reaction to major corporate accounting scandals

  c. allows CPA firms to simultaneously act as management consultants and external auditors for the same organization

  d. does not require that senior executives of public companies take individual responsibility for financial reporting.

Q1-6. The acronym SAR stands for:

  a. simple accounting receipts

  b. suspicious accounting revenue

  c. suspicious activity reporting

  d. standard accounts receivable

Q1-7. Which of the following is FALSE regarding assurance services provided by CPA firms?

a. Auditors of public companies are no longer allowed to provide assurance services to any public company as a result of the Sarbanes–Oxley Act of 2002

b. Assurance services may include information systems reliability

c. ABC is not a type of assurance service

d. Only CPAs can provide external audit assurance services to clients

Q1-8. Assigning overhead costs based on the resources, rather than only direct labor, used in manufacturing is an example of:

a. ABC

b. budgeting

c. cost-plus accounting

d. financial, rather than managerial, accounting

Q1-9. Which of these acronyms represents a law involving health assurance and privacy?

a. ABC   d. SOX

b. HIPAA   e. XBRL

c. CPA

Q1-10. Which of these acronyms stands for a computer language used for reporting business activities?

a. ABC   d. SOX

b. HIPAA   e. XBRL

c. CPA

Q1-11. Which of these acronyms is a certification for information professionals?

a. ABC   d. CITP

b. HIPAA   e. XBRL

c. CBA

Q1-12. Which of the following describes "cloud computing"?

a. business applications over the Internet

b. it is a subset of e-business

c. the ability of a company to exchange data with its subsidiaries

d. none of the above

Q1-13. How would you describe "big data"?

a. Cloud computing can be used to support data analytics projects

b. A combination of large, complex data sets

c. The definition depends on the capabilities of the organization that manages the data

d. All of the above

Q1-14. A forensic accountant is one who:

a. has a variety of skills, such as investigation, accounting, and auditing

b. can find and collect pieces of information that provide evidence of criminal activity

c. might be certified big data

d. all of the above

DISCUSSION QUESTIONS

1-1. Take a survey of the students in your class to find out what jobs their parents hold. How many are employed in manufacturing? How many are employed in service industries? How many could be classified as knowledge workers?

1-2. Hiring an employee and taking a sales order are important business activities, but are not accounting transactions requiring journal entries. Make a list of some other business activities that would not be captured as journal entries in traditional AISs. Do you think managers or investors would be interested in knowing about these activities? Why or why not?

1-3. Advances in IT are likely to have a continuing impact on financial accounting. What are some changes that are occurring in the way financial information is gathered, processed, and communicated as a result of increasingly sophisticated information technology?

1-4. XBRL is becoming established as the language to create interactive data that financial managers can use in communication. How do you think the use of interactive data might enhance the value of a company's financial statements?

1-5. Discuss suspicious activity reporting. For example, should such reporting be a legal requirement, or should it be just an ethical matter? Is the majority of SAR activity illegal, or are these just mostly false alarms?

1-6. Managerial accounting is impacted by IT in many ways, including enhancing corporate performance measurement. How might a university use a scorecard or dashboard approach to operate more effectively?

1-7. Look again at the list of assurance services shown in Figure 1-5. What other assurance services can CPAs offer which would take advantage of their AIS expertise?

1-8. Interview a sample of auditors from professional service firms in your area. Ask them whether or not they plan to offer any of the assurance services suggested by the AICPA. Also, find out if they offer services other than financial auditing and taxation. Discuss your findings in class.

1-9. This chapter described several career opportunities available to students who combine a study of accounting with course work in information systems, and/or computer science. Can you think of other jobs where these skill sets would be desirable?

1-10. This chapter stressed the importance of IT for understanding how AISs operate. But is this the only skill valued by employers? How important do you think "analytical thinking skills" or "writing skills" are? Discuss.

1-11. In this chapter we talked about predictive analytics and big data. Using the Internet and your research skills, identify the skills and abilities accounting majors might need (i.e., what type of courses should you take while at your university) to leverage these skills in entry-level accounting positions such as (1) public accountants, (2) internal auditors, and (3) management accountants. Discuss specifically how you would use these skills to impress your supervisor.

PROBLEMS

1-12. What words were used to form each of the following acronyms?

a. ABC	**h.** CPM	**n.** KPI
b. AICPA	**i.** ERP	**o.** SAR
c. AIS	**j.** FASB	**p.** SEC
d. CFO	**k.** HIPAA	**q.** SOX
e. CISA	**l.** ISACA	**r.** VAR
f. CITP	**m.** IT	**s.** XBRL
g. CPA		

1-13. Choose three or four issues of one of these journals: *Journal of Accountancy, Internal Auditor, Strategic Finance,* and *Management Accounting.* Next, count the number of articles that are related to IT. In addition, make a list of the specific technology discussed in each article (where possible). When you are finished, discuss the impact you think IT is having on the accounting profession.

1-14. Shervonne Thomas is the controller at a large manufacturing company located in Chesterfield, Virginia. The company has several divisions that evaluate their performance using a return on assets (ROA) formula (calculated by dividing net profit by the book value of total assets). In a meeting with the company president, Shervonne warned that ROI might not accurately reflect each division's performance.

Shervonne is concerned that managers might be too focused on short-term results.

The president asked Shervonne to identify a better way to evaluate each division's performance. Shervonne told the president that the company allocates a lot of overhead costs to the divisions on what some managers consider an arbitrary basis. She agreed to discuss this problem with the managers and to get back to the president very soon.

Requirements

a. Explain what managers can do in the short run to maximize return on assets. What other accounting measures could the company use to evaluate the performance of its divisional managers?

b. Describe other instances in which accounting numbers might lead to dysfunctional behavior in an organization.

c. Search the Internet and find at least one company that offers an information system (or software) that might help Shervonne and the managers do a better job of evaluating performance.

1-15. Select one new trend in the field of accounting information systems today that is not mentioned in the chapter, but that you feel is important. Write a short report describing your findings. Be sure to provide reasons why you feel that your choice of topics is important and therefore of interest to others in your class.

1-16. The participants of such recreational activities as hang gliding, soaring, hiking, rock collecting, or skydiving often create local "birds-of-a-feather" (affinity) organizations. Two examples are the Chicago sky divers (www.chicagoskydivers.com) or the soaring club of western Canada (www.canadianrockiessoaring.com). Many of these clubs collect dues from members to pay for the printing and mailing costs of monthly newsletters. Some of them maintain only minimal accounting information on manual pages or, at best, in spreadsheets.

   a. What financial information are such clubs likely to collect and maintain?

   b. Assuming that the club keeps manual accounting records, would you consider such systems "accounting information systems?" Why or why not?

   c. Assume that the club treasurer of one such organization is in charge of all financial matters, including collecting and depositing member dues, paying vendor invoices, and preparing yearly reports. Do you think that assigning only one person to this job is a good idea? Why or why not?

   d. What benefits would you guess might come from computerizing some or all of the club's financial information, even if there are less than 100 members? For example, do you think that such computerization is likely to be cost-effective?

1-17. Many companies now provide a wealth of information about themselves on their websites. But how much of this information is useful for investment purposes? To help you answer this question, imagine that you have $10,000, which you *must* invest in the common stock of a publicly held company.

   a. Select a company as specified by your instructor and access its online financial reports. Is the information contained in the reports complete? If not, why not? Is the information contained in these reports sufficient for you to decide whether or not to invest in the company? If not, why not? What additional information would you like?

   b. Now select an online brokerage website such as E*TRADE and look up the information of that same company. Does the information provided by the brokerage firm differ from that of the company itself? If so, how? Again, answer the question: Is the information contained in these reports sufficiently detailed and complete for you to decide whether to invest in it? If not, why not?

   c. Access the website of an investment rating service such as Value Line. How does the information on this third site differ from that of the other two? Again, answer the question: "Is the information contained on the site sufficiently detailed and complete for you to decide whether to invest in the stock? If not, why not?"

   d. What do these comparisons tell you about the difference between "data" and "information?"

1-18. The website of FinCen—the Financial Center Crimes Enforcement Center Network (a department of the US Treasury)—maintains a website at www.fincen.gov. Under "RESOURCES", you will find links to information for various types of financial institutions including banks, casinos, money service businesses, insurance companies, security and futures traders, and dealers in precious metals and jewelry, that is, the companies mandated by various federal laws to file SARs. Select three of these types of companies, and for each type, use the information provided on these secondary pages to list at least two types of financial transactions or activities that should be considered "suspicious."

1-19. In this chapter's "AIS at Work" feature, we discuss the events and SAR surrounding the case of Bernard Madoff. A financial analyst by the name of Harry Markopolos believed it was legally and mathematically impossible for Madoff to be posting such outrageous returns on investments. Mr. Markopolos notified the Boston SEC in 2000.

   a. What happened when Mr. Markopolos notified the SEC in 2000?

   b. How many more times did Mr. Markopolos notify the SEC of his concerns?

   c. What was the result of Mr. Markopolos' efforts to notify the authorities about his suspicions regarding Madoff?

CASE ANALYSES

1-20. Berry & Associates, LLP

Robert Berry is the managing partner for Berry & Associates (B&A), LLP. He was recently reviewing the firm's income statement for the previous quarter, which showed that auditing revenues were about 5% below last year's totals while tax revenues were about the same. Robert also noted that the income from auditing was 10% less than for the previous year. During the past few years, competition for new audit clients has been intense, so B&A partners decided that it would be wise for the firm to lower its hourly billing rates for all levels in the firm.

The firm's client base is closely held firms that are mostly very successful sole proprietors, as well as a number of small- and medium-sized companies. Robert and the other partners have been brainstorming ways to expand the revenue base of the organization. The partners know that information technology is a tool that the firm can use to develop new lines of business. Accordingly, the firm hired several college graduates over the past few years with dual majors in accounting and information systems or computer science. Given the recent financial results, Robert wants to encourage the other partners to consider the potential to the firm of offering additional professional services.

Requirements

1. Would it make the most sense for Robert to consider developing new types of clients or to consider offering different types of services to the types of clients typically served by B&A?
2. Robert remembers that the AICPA developed a list of various types of assurance services that auditing firms might consider offering. Describe three of these assurance services that might be a good fit for this CPA firm. (Hint: Visit the AICPA's Web page or a website of a large accounting firm for a listing of assurance services.)
3. What might B&A do to fully use the combined strengths in accounting and information systems/computer science of its new staff auditors?

1-21. Organizational Reports to Stakeholders

The annual report is considered by some to be the single most important printed document that companies produce. In recent years, annual reports have become large documents. They now include sections such as letters to the stockholders, descriptions of the business, operating highlights, financial review, management discussion and analysis, segment reporting, and inflation data as well as the basic financial statements. The expansion has been due in part to a general increase in the degree of sophistication and complexity in accounting standards and disclosure requirements for financial reporting.

The expansion also reflects the change in the composition and level of sophistication of users. Current users include not only stockholders but also financial and securities analysts, potential investors, lending institutions, stockbrokers, customers, employees, and (whether the reporting company likes it or not) competitors. Thus, a report that was originally designed as a device for communicating basic financial information now attempts to meet the diverse needs of an expanding audience.

Users hold conflicting views on the value of annual reports. Some argue that annual reports fail to provide enough information, whereas others believe that disclosures in annual reports have expanded to the point where they create information overload. The future of most companies depends on acceptance by the investing public and by their customers; therefore, companies should take this opportunity to communicate well-defined corporate strategies.

Requirements

1. The mission of the US SEC is to protect investors, maintain fair, orderly, and efficient markets, and facilitate capital formation. Identify several ways that the SEC accomplishes its mission.

2. The goal of preparing an annual report is to communicate information from a company to its targeted users. (a) Identify and discuss the basic factors of communication that must be considered in the presentation of this information. (b) Discuss the communication problems a company faces in preparing the annual report due to the diversity of the users being addressed.

3. Select two types of information found in an annual report, other than the financial statements and accompanying footnotes, and describe how they are useful to the users of annual reports.

4. Discuss at least two advantages and two disadvantages of stating well-defined corporate strategies in the annual report.

5. Evaluate the effectiveness of annual reports in fulfilling the information needs of the following current and potential users: (a) shareholders, (b) creditors, (c) employees, (d) customers, and (e) financial analysts.

6. Annual reports are public and accessible to anyone, including competitors. Discuss how this affects decisions about what information should be provided in annual reports.

1-22. North Gate Manufacturing

Neil Rogers is the controller for North Gate Manufacturing (NGM), a company with headquarters in College Station, Texas. NGM has seven concrete product plants located throughout the Southwest region of the United States. The company recently switched to a decentralized organizational structure. In the past, all revenues and expenses were consolidated to produce just one income statement.

Under the new organizational structure, each plant is headed by a general manager, who has responsibility for operating the plant like a separate company. Neil asked one of his accountants, Scott McDermott, to organize a small group to be in charge of performance analysis. This group is to prepare monthly reports on performance for each of the seven plants. These reports consist of budgeted and actual income statements. Written explanations and appraisals are to accompany variances. Each member of Scott's group has been assigned to a plant and is encouraged to interact with management and staff in that plant to become familiar with operations.

After a few months, Neil began receiving complaints from the general managers at several of the plants, claiming that the reports were slowing down operations and they felt like someone was constantly "looking over their shoulders" to see if they are operating in line with budget. They pointed out that the performance analysis staff is trying to do its job (i.e., explanation of variances). The most vocal plant manager claimed that "those accountants can't explain the variances—they don't know anything about the industry!"

The president of NGM, Ross Stewart, also complained about the new system for performance evaluation reporting. He claims that he is unable to wade through the seven detailed income statements, variances, and narrative explanations of all variances each month. As he put it, "I don't have time for this, and I think much of the information I am receiving is useless!"

Requirements

1. Is it a good idea to have a special staff in charge of performance evaluation and analysis? Explain.
2. In a decentralized organization such as this one, what would seem to be the best approach to performance evaluation?
3. What information would you include in a performance evaluation report for Mr. Stewart?

READINGS AND OTHER RESOURCES

Camgeni, M.P. 2015. Staying a step ahead: Internal audit's use of technology. The IIA Research Foundation. Download from theiia.org.

Collins, J.C. 2017, January. Data mining your general ledger with Excel: Learn how to use Microsoft's ubiquitous spreadsheet application to unlock the wealth of information stored in your company's financials. *Journal of Accountancy* 223(1): 27.

Drew, J. 2015, October. CPAs: Criminal-pursuing agents. *Journal of Accountancy* 220(4): 54.

Drew, J. 2016, June. Should CPAs switch to Windows 10 or Office 2016? The JofA's annual gathering of accounting technology experts examines the newest major Microsoft releases and identifies the most exciting technologies on the horizon. *Journal of Accountancy* 221(6): 48.

Tysiac, K. 2016, November. New path for CPAs in cyber risk management: AICPA proposals would guide companies in designing and describing cybersecurity risk management programs and create a 'cybersecurity examination' engagement. *Journal of Accountancy* 222(5): 16.

Go to www.wiley.com/go/simkin/videos to access videos on the following topics:

Accounting Songs
Cyber Net Fraud
Identity Theft
Sustainability
Accounting for Sustainability

ANSWERS TO TEST YOURSELF

1. a **2.** c **3.** a **4.** c **5.** b **6.** c **7.** a **8.** a **9.** b **10.** e **11.** d **12.** a **13.** d **14.** d

Chapter 2

Accounting on the Internet

After reading this chapter, you will be able to:

1. *Explain* some of the basic concepts of the Internet, such as Transmission Control Protocol/Internet Protocol (TCP/IP), uniform resource locators (URLs), and Web page addresses.

2. *Show how* electronic communication and social media are important to accountants.

3. *Explain* why Extensible Business Reporting Language (XBRL) is important to financial reporting.

4. *Define* electronic data interchange (EDI) and why it is important to AISs.

5. *Provide* some examples of cloud computing.

6. *Explain* the differences between B2B, B2C, and C2C e-commerce.

7. *Outline* the privacy and security issues associated with e-commerce.

8. *Explain* why businesses use firewalls, proxy servers, and encryption techniques.

9. *Define* digital signatures and digital time-stamping techniques.

" … accounting has its new address and it is known as the cloud."

Kadia, Nishat. 2016. Five tech innovations set to influence cloud accounting in 2017. *Finances Online.* Accessed from https://financesonline.com/5-tech-innovations-set-influence-cloud-accounting-2017.

2.1 INTRODUCTION

Most accountants use the Internet for research, education, and email on a daily basis. Auditors regularly evaluate their client's internal controls to ensure complete, accurate, and authentic transmissions of transactions over the Internet. It is nearly impossible to imagine how accounting professionals could accomplish their various job responsibilities without the many Internet technologies that support today's businesses.

This chapter describes some accounting applications of the Internet in detail. The first section describes Internet components such as Internet addresses and software. This section also discusses some Internet concepts of special importance to accountants (i.e., intranets and extranets). We also discuss XBRL, a financial reporting language, in this section.

One of the most important uses of the Internet is for electronic commerce (e-commerce or EC)—the topic of the second section of this chapter. While the terms *e-commerce* and *e-business* are often used interchangeably, some experts prefer to view them as different concepts. E-commerce involves buying or selling goods and services electronically. This activity can be between two businesses, between a profit-seeking company and a governmental entity, or between a business and a customer. In contrast, e-business goes beyond e-commerce and deep into the processes and cultures of an enterprise. This could include, for example, email, soliciting vendor bids electronically, making e-payments, exchanging data electronically (EDI), and using a host of specialized cloud-computing services. Thus, it is the powerful business environment that organizations create when they connect their critical business systems directly to customers, employees, vendors, and business partners using intranets, extranets, e-commerce technologies, collaborative applications, and the Web.[1] We discuss some of these topics in the third section of this chapter.

As more organizations conduct business on the Internet, managers increasingly recognize the importance of Internet privacy and security. This includes protecting consumers' privacy, defending proprietary data from hackers, and safeguarding information that businesses send to one another over the Internet. The final section of this chapter discusses these topics in detail.

2.2 THE INTERNET AND WORLD WIDE WEB

The **Internet** is a collection of local and wide area networks that are connected together via the Internet backbone, that is, the main electronic connections of the system. Describing the Internet as an "information superhighway" makes sense because over 3.9 billion people from around the world now use it, just as a set of state, interstate, and international highways connect people physically.[2] Most universities are connected to the Internet, as are most businesses, government agencies, and not-for-profit organizations. This section of the chapter discusses Internet basics, including Internet addresses and software, intranets and extranets, the World Wide Web, IDEA, groupware, electronic conferencing, and Web logs.

Internet Addresses and Software

To transmit data over the Internet, computers use an Internet address and a forwarding system that works much the same way as a post office system. On the Internet, the initial computer transmits a message to other computers along the Internet's backbone, which in turn relay the message from site to site until it reaches its final destination. If the message is large, Internet computers can divide it into smaller pieces called *data packets* and send each of them along different routes. The receiving computer then reassembles the packets into a complete message at the final destination.

An Internet address begins as a **domain address**, which is also called a **uniform resource locator (URL)**. This is a text address such as "www.name.com.uk." As suggested by this generic example, the lead item indicates the World Wide Web. The second entry designates the site name, and the third entry ("com" for commercial user) is the organization code. Other organization codes are "edu" (education), "gov" (government), "mil" (military), "net" (network service organization), "org" (miscellaneous organization), and "int" (international treaty organization). Finally, a domain address

---

[1] "Difference between e-commerce and e-business," accessed from eBusinessProgrammers.com.
[2] Internet World Stats (www.internetworldstats.com), Miniwatts Marketing Group, accessed November 3, 2017.

can include a country code as well, for example, "ca" for Canada, "uk" for the United Kingdom, or "nz" for New Zealand.

For transmission purposes, Internet computers use tables of domain names that translate a text-based domain address such as www.wiley.com into a numeric **Internet Protocol (IP)** address. IPv4 is version 4 of this standard and uses 32 bits for this. An example might be 207.142.131.248. The elements in this address contain a geographic region ("207"), an organization number ("142"), a computer group ("131"), and a specific computer or Web server ("248"). The **Internet Corporation for Assigned Names and Numbers (ICANN)** maintains the official registry of domain names, manages the **domain name system (DNS)** to ensure that all IP addresses are unique and so that each domain name maps to its correct IP address. In February of 2011, the Internet officially ran out of numbers, and administrators had to use workarounds and shared IP addresses to compensate. The new standard is IPv6, which uses 128 bits instead of 32 bits—a version that developers hope will suffice for many years to come.

IP addresses enable Internet computers to deliver a specific message to a specific computer at a specific computer site—for example, when you send an email message to a friend at another university using the standard **Transmission Control Protocol/Internet Protocol (TCP/IP)**. IP addresses are useful to auditors because they identify the sender—an important control in e-commerce applications.

Intranets and Extranets

Because Internet software is so convenient to use, many companies also create their own **intranets** for internal communications purposes. These computer networks use the same Web browsers (such as Google Chrome) and software as the Internet but are internal to the organization that created them. Thus, outsiders cannot access the information on intranet networks—a convenient security feature.

One common use of intranets is to allow users to access internal databases. Advanced search engine technology coupled with an intranet can deliver user-defined information when needed. For example, a purchasing agent can access a centralized listing of approved vendors using a Web browser and a local area network. Another valuable use of an intranet is for gathering and disseminating information to internal users. For example, employees can collaborate with each other by posting messages and data on the internal network, update records, check out job postings, complete forms to request office supplies, and enter travel expenses through their organization's intranet. Universities offer many of the same services to their employees, as well as a similar variety of services and educational opportunities to students.

Extranets enable selected outside users to access corporate intranets. Users connect to internal Web servers via the Internet itself using their assigned passwords. The user can be around the corner or around the world.

Case-in-Point 2.1 Do you access information about your university from a computer at home? If so, there is a good chance you're using an extranet that allows you to learn about your university's degree programs, find and register for future classes, pay registration fees remotely, access library resources, identify available scholarships, and even determine your final grades. Pretty convenient, huh?[3]

---

[3] From the authors.

The World Wide Web, HTML, and IDEA

The multimedia portion of the Internet is commonly called the World Wide Web, or just "the Web." As you probably already know, you view these graphics using a Web browser. A typical entity on the Web is a Web page—a collection of text, graphics, and links to other Web pages stored on Internet-connected computers.

HTML. Developers typically create Web pages in an editing language such as **hypertext markup language (HTML)** (see Figure 2-1a). Web designers store these instructions in one or more files and use the Internet to transfer these pages from a source computer to a recipient computer using a communications protocol such as **hypertext transfer protocol (HTTP)**. Your Web browser then deciphers the editing language and displays the text, graphics, and other items of the Web page on your screen (Figure 2-1b).

Because HTML is an editing language, many of its instructions are simply pairs of tags that instruct a Web browser how to display the information bracketed within them. Thus, in Figure 2-1a, note that the entire file begins with an <html> tag and ends with a closing </html> tag. Similarly, the <b> and </b> tags bold and unbold text, and the <i> and </i> tags begin and end italicized text. Using Figure 2-1b, you can probably guess the purpose of anchor tags (beginning with <a>), ordered list tags (beginning with <ol>), and list item tags (beginning with <li>). Problem 2-20 is an exercise to help you understand HTML tags.

Groupware, Electronic Conferencing, and Blogs

Groupware allows users to send and receive email and perform a wide range of other document-editing tasks. For example, these network packages allow users to collaborate on work tasks, make revisions to the same document, schedule appointments

```
<html>
<title>Some examples of HTML tags</title>
<body lang=EN-US style='tab-interval:.5in'>
<h1>Some Examples of HTML Tags</h1>
<p><b>This sentence is bold.</b></p>
<p><i>This sentence is in italics.</i></p>
<p><span style=font-size:14.0pt>
This sentence uses 14-point type
</span>
</p>
<p><a href="http://www.wiley.com">John
   Wiley web site</a></p>
<p>This is an ordered list.</p>
<ol><li>This is item #1.</li>
<li>This is item #2.</li>
</body>
</html>
```

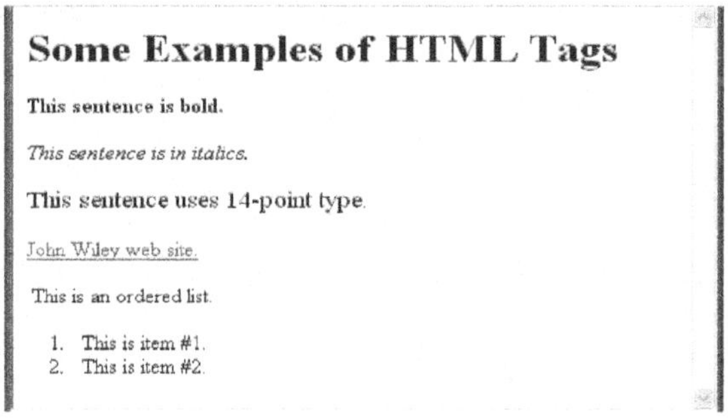

Some Examples of HTML Tags

This sentence is bold.

This sentence is in italics.

This sentence uses 14-point type.

John Wiley web site.

This is an ordered list.

1. This is item #1.
2. This is item #2.

(a) HTML code   (b) What the code in part (a) displays

FIGURE 2-1 An example of HTML code and what that code displays in a Web browser. Note the anchor tag <a>, which allows you to create a link to another Web page—in this case, the Wiley website.

on each other's calendars, share files and databases, conduct electronic meetings, and develop custom applications. Examples of such software include *Exchange* (Microsoft), *Groupwise* (Novell), *Lotus Notes* (Lotus Development Corporation), and *Outlook* (Microsoft).

Instant messaging software enables remote users to communicate with each other in real time via the Internet. You are probably already familiar with such software if you use MSN Messenger, Yahoo Messenger, or Skype to chat with distant friends. Many of these packages also support audio, video, and **electronic conferencing** (enabling several users to join a discussion instead of just two). Accounting applications include the ability to interview job applicants remotely, consult with clients about tax or audit problems, discuss projects from several remote sites, or plan corporate budgets.

Large consulting and accounting firms have access to a wealth of information within their organizations. Groupware is one of the technologies behind **knowledge management** that many professional service firms (such as accounting and consulting firms) use to distribute expertise within the organization (frequently on its intranet). This information includes descriptions of clients' best practices, research findings, links to business websites, and customized news. An employee with a client issue can access the knowledge database to learn how others handled similar issues.

Web *logs*, or **blogs**, are collaboration tools that allow users with Web browsers and easy-to-use software to publish personalized diaries or similar information online. Accountants publish a number of them. For example, some of these blogs explain general accounting concepts, comment on recent pronouncements in the profession, describe recent accounting frauds, or recount interesting CPA experiences. Case 2-31 invites you to view several of them.

Social Media and Its Value to Accountants

You now probably post comments, pictures, or videos using some form of social media—for example, on Facebook, Instagram, Pinterest, Twitter, or Baidu. At present and around the world, more than 2 billion people have some type of social media account. In aggregate, the postings logged on such sites create massive amounts of commentary that businesses can also mine for commercial purposes. Two important advantages of social media to accountants are that (1) accounts on social media are usually free and (2) they operate around the clock (24/7).[4]

One use of social media is to increase organization recognition—for example, when a company seeks to attract followers on Facebook and increase its customer base. This is also useful to accounting firms seeking new clients. A second use is for accounting teams to use social media to communicate with one another on projects at remote sites. Yet a third use is to identify and perhaps manage problems caused by corporate actions that anger consumers—before they go viral.

Case-in-Point 2.2 What company operates 6,000 fast-food stores in China? Did you guess Yum Brands, the owners of KFC and Pizza Hut? China accounts for half of Yum Brand's revenues—a problem because sales in the last few years have been flat. To boost business,

[4] See, for example, Alter, M. 2013. How accountants use social media for business. *Accounting Web*. Accessed online from http://www.accountingweb.com/practice/growth/how-accountants-use-social-media-for-business.

the company plans a social media campaign to assure customers its food is safe, improve its image, and distribute coupons for store discounts.[5]

Businesses can also use social media for recruiting employees, for example, to attract applicants for new jobs or to screen current applicants for undesirable traits. Looking for a new job? Employment counselors say that an online identity is a "must-have."

Finally, a company can use social media for monitoring purposes—for example, to gauge the effectiveness of a new ad campaign or to assess customer feelings about the company itself. For example, when accounting firms offer new services, they can now scan social media sites in search of honest reactions to the new offerings. Organizations can also hire outside firms to perform such monitoring for them. In total, experts suggest that businesses are just beginning to tap the value stored in social media commentary.

Case-in-Point 2.3 A survey of 4,200 business executives from around the world by the McKinsey Global Institute found that over 70% of them were using social media in some way. This same company estimates that social media contains around $1 trillion in untapped value to businesses.[6]

2.3 XBRL—FINANCIAL REPORTING ON THE INTERNET

While the Internet supports general financial reporting, exchanging financial information between trading partners often requires more detailed specifications. **eXtensible Markup Language (XML)** is similar to HTML in that it also uses tags such as <b> and </b> to format data (b stands for "bold"). But there are two important differences between HTML and XML. One is that XML tags are "extensible," allowing users to define their own tags such as <SalesRevenue>. The other difference is that XML tags actually *describe* the data rather than simply indicate how to display it. For example, if a business wants to report sales revenue of $1 million, it could use the XML tags: <SalesRevenue>$1,000,000</SalesRevenue>. Now, this data item has meaning.

A problem with XML tags is a potential lack of consistency among users. For example, one company might use the XML tag <SalesRevenue>, while another company might choose <Revenues>. Without standardized markers (tags), financial information may not be clear and users may not be able to extract data from XML files for comparison purposes. **Extensible Business Reporting Language (XBRL)** solves this problem by standardizing the tags that describe financial information in documents for both profit and not-for-profit organizations. In short, XBRL is a specialized subset of XML for reporting financial information. Figure 2-2 provides an example of XBRL code and what that code creates.

The **XBRL International Consortium** creates XBRL standards that anyone can use, license-free. In addition, many accounting software packages are now *XBRL-enabled*, meaning that they can insert appropriate XBRL tags automatically in user financial files. Because of its growing importance, some authorities now suggest that XBRL should become an integral part of the general accounting curriculum.

[5] Jargon, J. 2013. KFC to reboot in China. *The Wall Street Journal* (December 5): B3.
[6] McKinsey Global Institute. July 2012. The social economy: Unlocking value and productivity through social technologies. McKinsey & Company.

XBRL code:

```
<ifrs-gp:CashCashEquivalents contextRef="Current_AsOf" unitRef="U-Euros"
    decimals="0">1000000</ifrs-gp: CashCashEquivalents>
<ifrs-gp:OtherAssetsCurrent contextRef="Current_AsOf" unitRef="U-Euros"
    decimals="0">200000</ifrs-gp: OtherAssetsCurrent>
<ifrs-gp:AssetsCurrentTotal contextRef="Current_AsOf" unitRef="U-Euros"
    decimals="0">1200000</ifrs-gp:AssetsCurrentTotal>
```

What the XBRL code displays in a Web browser:

Current Assets:	
Cash and Cash Equivalents	1,000,000
Other Assets, Current	200,000
Current Assets, Total:	1,200,000

FIGURE 2-2 An example of XBRL code and what that code creates.

XBRL Instance Documents and Taxonomies

XBRL documents are called **XBRL instance documents** because they are examples ("instances") of a class of documents defined by a standard or specification. Figure 2-2 shows an example—a portion of a balance sheet in XBRL. In this example, note that XBRL tags follow conventional HTML and XML coding rules that use a beginning tag such as <ifrsgp:OtherAssetsCurrent> and an ending tag such as </ifrsgp:OtherAssetsCurrent> to define a value. The number itself sits between these two tags. XBRL tags identify financial values uniquely. For example, the term "Cash-CashEquivalents" within a tag unambiguously defines "cash and cash equivalents." The initials "ifrs" stand for "international financial reporting standard." Finally, you can use optional entries in each tag to identify currency units (e.g., "Euros") and the number of decimal places to display (e.g., "0").

To create an XBRL instance document, you need to know (1) the standard tags that define familiar items such as net revenues and operating expenses and (2) the rules that govern how to use these tags. XBRL Specification 2.1 currently defines the rules and syntax for XBRL taxonomies and XBRL documents. XBRL taxonomies define the tags that represent accounting and financial terms used in XBRL instance documents. With standard tags for each piece of common financial data, accounting software can create instance documents for income statements, balance sheets, and similar financial statements in a straightforward manner. Figure 2-3 lists a number of ways that XBRL affects accountants.

The Benefits and Drawbacks of XBRL

Perhaps the most obvious benefit of XBRL is the ability to transmit financial information in a standard format. This facilitates communications between suppliers and their buyers, companies and their shippers, and even retailers and their customers. The same standardization applies to financial filings. For example, the Securities and Exchange Commission (SEC) now requires XBRL-formatted financial statement reports such as 10-Q and 10-K reports of all US publicly traded companies. This standardization also benefits companies making loan applications, filing tax returns, or reporting to other financial agencies.

- Due to corporate scandals, shareholders, analysts, and reporters are demanding more transparent reporting. XBRL allows readers to quickly access the information they need electronically.
- XBRL permits the automatic and reliable exchange of financial information across all software formats and technologies, including the Internet.
- XBRL does not require a change to existing accounting standards of corporate disclosure policies.
- XBRL improves access to financial information because data is in a digital, reusable form.
- XBRL eliminates the need to reenter financial data for different users, which reduces the risks associated with data entry and lowers the cost to prepare and distribute financial statements.
- XBRL improves investor and analyst access to information.
- XBRL allows accountants to more quickly and easily consolidate and scrutinize internal data for use in financial reports.
- XBRL allows CEOs and CFOs to deliver more transparent information to investors and analysts, and allows a vehicle for control within the firm.

FIGURE 2-3 How does XBRL affect accounts? Source: Charles Hoffman and Carolyn Strand, *XBRL Essentials* (New York: AICPA), 2001; and www.xbrl.org.

Another important advantage of XBRL is that it defines data items uniquely. Consider, for example, how a spreadsheet stores financial information. The only way we know that a particular number *in* a spreadsheet is, say, "net revenue" is because we also see a label that identifies it as such. Move the number somewhere else in the spreadsheet and you also lose its meaning. In contrast, a "net revenue" figure remains "net revenue" no matter where it appears in XBRL instance documents as long as it remains within its tags. It is for this reason that some experts predict that some accounting systems will begin *collecting and storing* their data in XBRL formats, redefining XBRL as a *formatting* language as much as a *reporting* language.

XBRL's standardized tags also make searching for items in XBRL financial documents relatively easy. If you know the standard tag for an item of interest, you can unambiguously find and extract the information from those documents. One repository of such financial information is the Security and Exchange Commission's **interactive data and electronic applications (IDEA)**, which now contains XBRL data for over 10,000 companies—a valuable source of financial information and an important reason why standardized reporting is useful.

In business environments, the term *semantic meaning* refers to the fact that the financial data are related to one another through formulas such as "Assets = Liabilities + Equity." An additional advantage of XBRL is its ability to express such relationships in formulas, thereby making the data self-checking. This is important because organizations often need to transmit financial data to others, and XBRL provides a means of internal control.

Case-in-Point 2.4 The Federal Deposit Insurance Corporation (FDIC) insures banks and similar financial institutions throughout the United States. The FDIC exchanges financial information with member institutions all the time, and uses a set of 1,800 rules to validate such data. The FDIC was an early adopter of XBRL in part because this language has the ability to perform data-validation tasks automatically.[7]

---

[7] BLOG: Digital Financial Reporting. "Benefits of financial integrity," accessed from xbrl.squarespace.com, March 2014.

Companies using XBRL-enabled software can save their financial information in standard XBRL format, thus avoiding the errors that may come from reentering data multiple times from multiple sources. Companies can then directly upload their business information in this format onto their websites, avoiding costly rekeying costs. Another advantage is that XBRL permits the automatic and reliable exchange of financial information across all software platforms and technologies, including the Internet. Thus, anyone interested in comparing the cash and cash equivalents of several companies can search for the data and export it to a spreadsheet for analysis purposes.

Finally, it is important to note that XBRL does not constrain companies to a particular *format* for their financial reports. To the contrary, the language is flexible and therefore intentionally constructed to support financial reporting by companies in different industries or from different countries. The hope is that both the extensible capabilities of the language and this flexibility are great enough to meet business and governmental needs at all levels. Problem 2-22 invites you to explore the benefits of XBRL in further detail.

XBRL also has several disadvantages. One problem is the fact that a common reporting language requires its users to learn, and conform to, the standards of that language. Usually, accountants achieve this task by acquiring software that can output data in XBRL formats. Another problem is that evolving XBRL standards require users to conform to changing specifications—a drawback, for example, that may require organizations to update their accounting software more often. A third concern is that, at present, there is no requirement for auditors to provide assurance on XBRL filings. Finally, the transition to XBRL reporting is not without costs.

Case-in-Point 2.5   A survey by the SEC of XBRL filers revealed that the additional costs of the requirement averaged between $30,000 and $40,000, but in some cases ran as high as $82,000. However, these costs tended to diminish over time as organizations gained experience with the language and were able to reuse their software. A more recent study by the AICPA found that almost 70% of companies paid less than $10,000 to adopt XBRL standards.[8]

The Current Status of XBRL

The XBRL International Consortium has about 600 members and is in charge of developing XBRL standards. Many US accounting firms are members of this consortium, as is the American Institute of Certified Public Accountants and parallel accounting organizations around the world. The current specifications for version 2.1 of XBRL were issued in July of 2008. The website at www.xbrl.org provides additional information on both current and proposed standards, as well as recent articles about XBRL and best practices.

As you might imagine, developing global standards for financial reporting is a massive undertaking. The language specifications require classification systems for different countries, different reporting segments (e.g., different industries), and even different organizational standards such as US generally accepted accounting standards (GAAP). For example, oil and gas companies require specialized tags to identify reserve

---

[8] SEC study: Gray, G. and D. Miller. 2009. XBRL: Solving real-world problems. *International Journal of Disclosure & Governance* 6(3): 207–223. AICPA study: AICPA (2015). Research shows XBRL filing costs lower than expected. Accessed online from https://www.aicpa.org/InterestAreas/FRC/AccountingFinancialReporting/XBRL/DownloadableDocuments/XBRL%20Costs%20for%20Small%20Companies.pdf.

balances, casinos require specialized tags to identify allowances for unclaimed gambling chips, and so forth. Then too, the language requires standard tags for formulas (e.g., a price/earnings ratio) and different functions. For this reason, XBRL is best viewed as a dynamic language still in continuous development.

Most accounting software now supports XBRL, and the worldwide adoption of XBRL is moving along quickly. For example, in Germany, XBRL is already built into a software package used by 80% of the accountants in that country. The XBRL International consortium publishes a progress report several times a year, available on its website (www.XBRL.org), that contains current information about XBRL.

2.4 ELECTRONIC BUSINESS

The term **electronic business**, or **e-business**, refers to conducting business with computers and data communications. Most companies perform e-business over the Internet, but businesses can also use virtual private networks (VPNs) or proprietary data transmission lines. Recent surveys estimate the total annual revenues for e-commerce in the United States exceeds $1 trillion, and the FBI estimates that the banking industry transfers over $1 trillion *each week* by electronic means. Some general categories of electronic business are (1) e-accounting, (2) retail sales, (3) e-payments and e-wallets, (4) electronic data interchange, and (5) a variety of cloud-computing services, each of which we examine briefly in the following sections.

e-Accounting

The term **e-accounting** means performing accounting functions on the Internet. This includes normal accounting tasks such as processing payroll or accounts receivable data, as well as preparing financial reports or completing income tax returns using online software. Often the Web server is not even in the same country as the user but in Ireland or India instead of the United States or Canada.

At the personal level, e-accounting allows users to perform familiar accounting tasks such as preparing budgets or writing reports that others can see and modify as desired. The application moves online, allowing users to share files that formerly had to be emailed. Hybrid versions of such processes are also possible, in which users retain complete control of sensitive data, but who use the newest and most robust versions of online software for processing tasks.

An additional accounting use of the Internet is as a medium for publishing accounting documents such as financial statements. Posting financial information on the Web is relatively fast and inexpensive compared to printing and mailing them. Such information can also be revised, replaced, or deleted easily and quickly.

Case-in-Point 2.6 When IBM first began posting its financial reports on its website, its online version was an exact copy of its printed version, no more and no less. This quickly changed as the company realized it could post adjusted or unaudited reports online as well, expand product or services information from what it had previously published in hard copy reports, or create more extensive footnotes or addendums that provided previously unavailable or more current information to interested viewers.[9]

---

[9] Kogan, A., F. Sudit, and M. Vasarhelyi. 2009. The future of accounting and electronic commerce on the Internet. *Texas CPA*: 1–6. Accessed from raw.rutgers.edu.

Many e-accounting applications use software as a service (described below)—for example, when an accountant prepares a tax return using online software tools. Other Internet possibilities include online search tools for performing accounting research or video clips for training personnel. Such services enable businesses to avoid the costs of acquiring, installing, upgrading, or reformatting the data files required by traditional accounting software. Backup and disaster recovery also become the responsibility of the vendor organization instead of the user organization.

Retail Sales

The World Wide Web offers businesses the opportunity to create virtual stores ("shopping cart applications") for selling merchandise directly to customers. At the retail level, it is clear that such websites are really automated AISs that allow customers to create their own order forms, shipping forms, and payment documents. Testimony to the success of such retail e-commerce abounds. The number of online shoppers has increased steadily over the past decade. More than 98% of the US population is now connected to the Internet, and many now purchase items online on a regular basis. For example, consumers now reserve most of their domestic airline tickets, rental cars, and hotel rooms over the Internet. Figure 2-4 lists some of the advantages of virtual stores. Note how many of these advantages relate directly to AISs.

Internet retail sales also introduce special issues. One problem is that customers usually cannot determine whether a retail website is legitimate. Similarly, consumers must usually rely on emails to express their complaints (rather than speaking to someone in person), and returns are sometimes problematic. A third problem is that online stores frequently rely on suppliers rather than their own shelves for merchandise to satisfy orders, creating the potential for stock-out and backorder problems.

Finally, a growing e-commerce problem is **click fraud**. Many businesses are willing to sign pay-per-click contracts in which they pay a fee every time a customer clicks on

---

1. Web pages are much cheaper to create than producing and mailing catalogs.
2. Distribution is global.
3. Sales can occur around the clock.
4. Customers can search for specific products or services electronically, either within a particular website or as a hit from another site.
5. A business can easily outsource its Web business to others, enabling it to focus on core processes.
6. The websites themselves can use automated tools to verify customer credit cards.
7. Businesses can send emails to confirm orders or advise customers about shipping dates.
8. Businesses can update product descriptions, sales prices, and information on merchandise availability immediately.
9. Customers create their own sales orders online.
10. Customers can track their own orders, freeing business personnel for other tasks.
11. The sales and customer-relations personnel required for virtual stores is minimal, thus reducing labor costs per dollar of sales.
12. Users can often customize their purchases online—for example, configure laptop systems to preferred specifications or create personalized gift cards with their orders.

FIGURE 2-4   Some advantages of virtual stores on the Internet.

a link to its own website from another site (such as a search engine site). Click fraud occurs when dishonest managers or even a company's own competitors inflate the number of clicks on an advertising link, and therefore bill (or cost) the company for more referrals than actually occurred.

Internet sales also provide retailers with a wealth of data *about* their customers, raising issues about privacy. For example, you might be concerned about the fact that your Web purchase also means that a retailer now has (1) your email address, which it can use to send additional, annoying emails or sell to others, (2) your credit card information, which it may or may not protect as well as you would like, and (3) sensitive information about your purchase patterns—for example, prescription drug purchases. A later section of this chapter addresses these privacy and security issues in greater detail.

E-Payments, E-Wallets, and Virtual Currencies

Most customers pay for the merchandise they order over the Internet with a credit card, requiring vendors to use third-party affiliates to authenticate user credit card numbers. This is a problem because such credit card verification systems only indicate that a card is valid, not that the online customer is authorized to use it. A related problem with online payments is that, while online customers might not mind giving their credit card numbers to trusted merchants, they may not wish to share this information with unfamiliar businesses or unknown sellers.

E-Payments. Some merchants and auction sites solve these payment problems with **electronic payments (e-payments)**, which proponents claim is a faster, easier, and safer way for both customers and sellers to handle online transactions. The e-payment service acts as a trusted intermediary because it collects payment from a buyer and pays that amount to the seller.

> *Case-in-Point 2.7* If you start your own Web-based retailing company, one problem will be "how to handle customer payments." This is what Stripe, Braintree, and Square do—process the credit- and debit-card transactions of Web and mobile-phone customers. Processing fees charged by these companies are as low as 2.75%, and setup time can be "minutes," giving you more time to focus on your core business needs. When Stripe was 3 years old, it had already processed billions of dollars' worth of business.[10]

Businesses are not the only entities that can enjoy the convenience of e-payments—many state and local governments also have websites for e-payments. For example, the US government enables contractors to conduct financial transactions online at Pay.gov (Figure 2-5)—a site allowing both businesses and individuals to make payments to the US government electronically. Developed by the US Treasury Department's Financial Management Services (FMS), Pay.gov is a central portal through which businesses and individuals can make payments, submit forms, and send bills to federal agencies. This portal provides authentication services for secure transactions.

> *Case-in-Point 2.8* Pay.gov processes payments for several hundred government agencies, including the Department of Veteran Affairs, the Small Business Administration, the

---

[10] Helft, M. 2014. The new power player in online payments. *Fortune Magazine* 168(9): 42–48.

FIGURE 2-5 The home page for Pay.gov—an e-payment system supported by the US government.

Department of Defense, most US courts, the US Coast Guard, and the Internal Revenue Service. FMS expects Pay.gov to handle approximately 80 million transactions worth over $125 billion a year, reduce paperwork, and save agencies over 5% in processing costs.[11]

E-Wallets. Another Internet payment option is an **e-wallet**. E-wallets are software applications that store a consumer's personal information, including credit card numbers, email addresses, and shipping addresses. Shoppers pay for online purchases by providing their e-wallet account numbers to online vendors that also subscribe to the system.

One advantage of an e-wallet is that you can use it whenever you visit subscriber websites. These systems spare you the trouble of entering your personal information each time you make an online purchase. Also, because your e-wallet information is usually stored on your own hard drive, you control it. This maintains your email privacy as well. E-wallets may be as important for retailers as they are for consumers because many consumers cancel e-commerce transactions before they complete them, often because of frustration with online forms.

---

[11] To learn more about this program, log onto its website at www.fiscal.treasury.gov.

Case-in-Point 2.9   Consumers who buy products on E-bay or other online auction sites may be familiar with PayPal (www.paypal.com), an e-payment system that operates via the Internet. Customers who want to bid for items in online auctions, but who don't wish to share their credit card number with unknown sellers, may open an account with PayPal. Account holders can deposit funds in their PayPal account using credit cards, debit cards, or bank checks. When consumers purchase items, PayPal acts as an intermediary bank, withdrawing money from the purchaser's account and depositing similar funds into the seller's account (or sending a check).[12]

Virtual Currency. Imagine an international currency that eliminates the need to exchange one type of money for another, involves no extra transaction fees, escapes government scrutiny, and is widely accepted on the Internet. This is the idea behind a **virtual currency**—a medium of exchange that operates beyond the restrictions of a particular country or its monetary policies. An example at the time this book was published is bitcoin, which allows you set up an e-wallet at www.bitcoin.com.

Retailers have several reasons why they might accept a virtual currency when selling merchandise online, including (1) the ability to do more business, (2) the ease with which transactions can take place electronically, (3) no need for credit-card middlemen or check-clearing houses, (4) near-instantaneous credit of transactions to corporate accounts (like debit cards), (5) consumer wallets cannot be frozen, and (6) no transaction fees charged the retailer.

But virtual currencies also operate beyond the realm of any central bank. This exposes businesses to risks, including (1) the potential devaluation of the currency in response to market forces, (2) the fact that transactions are not independently auditable, as they would be at a bank, (3) the observation that all seven earlier virtual currencies have failed, and (4) the unwillingness of others to accept it—the ultimate test of any currency.

Case-in-Point 2.10   Virtual currencies are speculative and can therefore vary widely relative to other monies. In 4 years, the trading value of one bitcoin had appreciated to $1,250. But in November 2013, Baidu.com, the Chinese Web services company, and the Chinese central bank both announced that they would not accept bitcoins for transactions. As a result of this and other market forces, the exchange rate dropped to below $400 in 2015. By July of 2017, however, the exchange rate had recovered and climbed to over $2,500.[13]

Virtual currencies also present challenges to accountants. Assets purchased with such currencies have floating cost bases, for example, and (in the case of bitcoins) no central institution keeps records. At this time, it is also unclear whether funds held in a virtual currency are reportable to the IRS as "offshore funds." Finally, there is the question of whether the appreciation in the value of a virtual currency qualifies as a long-term asset that is subject to capital gains taxes or a short-term currency swing and therefore subject to ordinary income taxes.[14]

---

[12] To learn more about PayPal, log onto its website at www.paypal.com.

[13] Wesbury, B. How much does that burger cost in bitcoins? *Wall Street Journal* (December 16, 2013), A13. You can find current exchange rates for bitcoins and other virtual currencies at: https://www.coinbase.com/charts?locale=en-US.

[14] See, for example, Sanders, L. Another bitcoin mystery: How will the RS tax it? *Wall Street Journal*, (December 21–22, 2013), B1. For suggested answers to many of these tax questions, also see https://en.bitcoin.it/wiki/Tax_compliance.

Company	Headquarters	Year Founded	Type of Business	Description
Airbnb	San Francisco	2008	C2C	House- and apartment-sharing platform
Instagram	Menlo Park, CA	2010	C2C	Photo-sharing platform
Slack	San Francisco	2009	C2C	Workplace chat service
Snapchat	Venice, CA	2011	C2C	Photo- and video-sharing service; messages disappear after a few seconds
Spotify	Stockholm, Sweden	2006	B2C	Music and video streaming service
Square	San Francisco	2009	B2C	Supports credit card readers for smart phones
Tesla	Palo Alto, CA	2003	B2C	Manufactures electric cars
Uber	San Francisco	2009	C2C	Mobile platform for ride-sharing activities
Venmo	New York City	2009	C2C	Payment enabling platform using linked credit or debit cards, or checking accounts
Waze	Mountain View, CA	2008	C2C	platform for sharing traffic and navigation information

Source: Multiple authors (2017). Breakthrough brands of 2017. *Fortune Magazine* 175(1); 64–69.

FIGURE 2-6   Ten breakthrough Internet companies.

B2C, B2B, and C2C E-Commerce

The Internet supports several types of business models (Figure 2-6). The oldest of these is the traditional **business-to-consumer (B2C)** model—the retail sales model discussed above. Examples include the websites of Walmart, Home Depot, and Southwest Airlines. These sites typically offer goods or services from brick-and-mortar (i.e., traditional) companies. For merchandise, customers can often order online but pick up their orders at physical retail stores with no shipping charges—or can ship goods to their residences.

Another type of e-commerce is **B2B**, that is, businesses that buy or sell goods and services to each other. Buying materials online shortens the time from purchase to delivery and also allows businesses to shop from vendors all over the world. Like retail consumers, corporate purchasing agents using **B2B e-commerce** tools can select items from online catalogs, confirm purchases, track shipments, and pay bills electronically. E-commerce software can also expedite internal paperwork by first sending purchase orders to the appropriate managers for approvals and then forwarding them to the vendor, thus reducing the costs of processing purchase requisitions.

Case-in-Point 2.11   BASF is one of the world's largest chemical, plastics, and energy companies, with sales of €70.4 billion in 2015 and 112,000 employees on five continents. Company managers credit much of its recent growth in revenues to its e-commerce initiatives. According to Herbert Fisch, head of global e-commerce, "In addition to order management, e-commerce provides our customers with information and service tools. Customers benefit from greater transparency and we gain valuable time to better serve them."[15]

[15] Burridge, E. 2005. E-commerce revenues boost achieved by BASF. *European Chemical News* 83(2174): 2.

Further back in the supply chain, the Internet affects accounting activities just as strongly. Another feature of B2B e-commerce is the wider availability of real-time data that allows managers to view up-to-the-minute information. Take, for instance, a supplier whose business customers in turn sell products to end users. With current data about its customers' retail sales, the supplier can quickly increase or decrease its operations as required. Similar online information can determine the location of specific trucks (using GPS), check the estimated arrival date of incoming cargo ships, or determine the current status of finished products, parts inventories, or even working assembly lines. The term **churn** describes the number or percentage of customer subscribers lost in a given period of time—a metric of particular importance to B2B organizations. For example, a customer renewal rate of 60% means a **churn rate** of 40%.

Even vendors of inexpensive accounting software now include an e-commerce interface with their products. An example is *Peachlink (Sage)*, whose software enables users to create a shopping-cart website and accept Internet orders. Similarly, software from companies such as Time Capital allows vendors and customers to view purchase and shipping documents so that they can resolve discrepancies quickly and cut checks or make electronic payments as needed.

Perhaps the most interesting type of e-commerce is the **consumer-to-consumer (C2C)** model. In such applications, the software creates a platform or virtual market that connects consumers wishing to buy something with those wanting to sell it. One of the oldest of these is ebay, which enables individuals to sell unwanted merchandise online. Newer examples include Airbnb (which enables home owners to rent rooms to others), Uber (which provides private-car taxi services), or Venmo (which facilitates money transfers between private parties). With Uber, for example, the passenger pays the company directly, freeing the driver from handling money or making change. Uber in turn extracts a percentage of the total fare as a fee, and then transfers the remainder of the customer's payment to the driver's bank or PayPal account. Because much of the business is automated and drivers own their own cars. Uber can often offer transportation services at lower costs than those of taxi or limousine services.

Case-in-Point 2.12 Jonathan Lay, a computer technician who now works for his alma mater, especially likes to use Venmo when he and his buddies go on weekend vacations together. If someone pays for an entire meal, that person can immediately ask Venmo to transfer monies from the bank accounts of the others to his own account. This results in a pay-as-you-go system with no one needing exact change—or even cash.[16]

Electronic Data Interchange

A high percentage of companies continue to use at least some manual documents—for example, purchase orders, invoices, payment remittance forms, credit memos, bills of lading, or shipping notices. **Electronic data interchange (EDI)** enables organizations to save money by creating and transmitting the information contained in such documents electronically. Thus, EDI permits organizations to conduct many forms of commerce electronically. Government agencies also depend heavily on EDI. One example is the US Customs Service, which uses it to identify and streamline the processing of import merchandise and customs declarations.

---

[16] From the authors.

Case-in-Point 2.13 Pratt and Whitney is a large-engine manufacturer that buys over 26,000 parts from more than 700 suppliers. This company now transmits over 50,000 EDI documents per month, including purchase orders, procurement schedules, and sales invoices. The company estimates savings between $10 and $20 on every purchase order—over $6 million per year.

According to research from the Forrester Corporation, EDI usage now exceeds 20 billion documents per year—and growing. One of the most important users of EDI is those in the health industry—doctors, hospitals, and insurance companies. EDI allows such participants to gather, store, and transmit both text and imaging graphics electronically, speeding the exchange of such information and saving money in the process.

Case-in-Point 2.14 A friend of one of the authors is a cardiologist who reads EKG test results for a living. But he doesn't work at an office—he works at home, performing all the required tasks from the comfort of his house. It's a win–win situation because his company does not pay for expensive office space in town for him, and he does not waste time commuting to and from it.[17]

One potential advantage of EDI is that it enables users to take advantage of early-payment discounts. Another advantage is that EDI documents can include hand-written signatures that help ensure their authenticity. A third advantage is that EDI includes the exchange of both graphic and photographic documents—media that *can* be scanned and captured electronically. Finally, scanned documents enable business systems to automate the testing for missing information, and sometimes even to provide it.

Cloud Computing

As explained in Chapter 1, cloud computing refers to purchasing services from vendors over the Internet. The term derives its name from the cloudlike symbol often used to depict the Internet in networking diagrams. A host of activities falls into this category, including Web hosting, payroll processing, backup provisioning, emailing, and even outsourcing business phone systems. Here, we briefly discuss some examples of these services.

Processing Services. Companies that access specialized software (e.g., tax-preparation applications) on the Internet purchase **software as a service (SaaS)**. In contrast, Web hosting is an example of **platform as a service (PaaS)**. Examples of cloud vendors that provide such services include Amazon.com (data storage), Oracle (database software), and Intuit (both tax and payroll processing).

Cloud computing closely resembles other forms of outsourcing and therefore enjoys the same advantages. For example, when a hospital contracts with a second company to do its payroll, it can then focus on its core health-care mission and shift the burdensome details of payroll processing (e.g., how much taxes to withhold for out-of-state employees) to the contractor. But cloud computing also differs from traditional forms of outsourcing. For example, the data communications in cloud computing take place over the Internet and are therefore instantaneous. Another

[17] From the authors.

important difference is that transaction volumes are usually charged by the day, hour, or even minute and are billed accordingly.

Case-in-Point 2.15 Doug Askam is a partner at DKS&H—an accounting firm in Denver, Colorado, with 675 employees. The firm currently spends $25,000 per year plus $1,000 per month for each of 40 to 50 users for cloud services—an expenditure Doug thinks is worth it. He notes, for example, that employee turnover has been "drastically reduced" because employees do not have to leave the company when they move from Denver. Similarly, both clients and employees like the fact that they often no longer have to visit each other's offices—needed accounting data is readily available through Cloudnine Real Time—the firm's cloud provider. These advantages have led to one more benefit—the firm's ability to expand its client base without expanding its employee base.[18]

Figure 2-7 outlines some of the advantages cloud computing offers to companies. Cloud computing also has several disadvantages. Perhaps the most important is the loss of control that client firms experience when another company assumes responsibility for their data and data processing—a security concern. Language barriers, quality control, and time-zone differentials are additional potential concerns when contracting with overseas vendors. A third concern is that backup service providers typically involve high transmission volumes, and the timing of automatic backups is not always convenient to individual subscribers. Finally, cloud computing often promises cost savings but does not guarantee them. Performing the same work within the organization and dealing with all of its attendant problems may be the cheaper option.

The Internet of Things. Many smart devices now use sensors that connect directly to the Internet, including home door locks, automobiles, fitness monitors, and kitchen appliances. This is the **Internet of Things (IoT)**—devices that use the Internet to

Advantage	Example
Access to specialized expertise	In a payroll application, the vendor keeps up to date with the most recent tax-withholding requirements.
Cost savings	The contracting company avoids the hardware, software, and training costs involved in performing the service in house, and pays only for the services actually consumed.
Speed	In a tax-preparation application, all communications take place electronically and therefore nearly instantaneously, thereby avoiding the data-transfer delays in, say, post-office options.
Access to distant vendors	In an email application, the least costly vendor might be thousands of miles away—a factor of no consequence to the contracting company.
Avoiding peak loading problems	Sales often spike during the Christmas season. The retailer offloads these volume problems to the vendor.
Virtual remote backup	A company makes a copy of its critical data at the same time it updates the initial database. This increases security because the backup copy is by definition off-premises.
Pay as you go	The outsourcing company avoids the initial investments in hardware, software, or personnel. This can be similar to the difference between owning a car and renting a taxi.

FIGURE 2-7 Some advantages of cloud computing.

---

[18] Arrowsmith, R. 2016. Case studies: Cloud hosting: Finding time savings, risk reduction and efficiency online. *Accounting Today*. 30(10): 22.

communicate with their owners, even if these users are not in the same room, state, or country. This connectivity also helps manufacturers—for example, to learn how often customers use their appliances, how long their products last before failing, or how often customers open their refrigerator doors. Similarly, users can check whether they locked the car doors, how the baby is doing in another room, or how fast a teenage son is driving on his Saturday night date.

Case-in-Point 2.16 Domino's is one of many national pizza makers whose websites allow customers to order pizza online—a trend that will soon make "online ordering" more popular than "phone ordering." In Australia and the United States, the company now also provides a phone app and a GPS tracking system that allows impatient customers to monitor the pizza delivery vehicle's progress from store to door. This same system also allows company managers to monitor erratic driving behavior such as speeding or frequent stopping—a system credited with helping reduce accidents by 50%.[19]

The IoT is also likely to have profound effects on accountants, CPAs, and auditors. For example, some accounting data will flow directly to businesses from IoT devices, potentially changing billing practices, auditing procedures, and client–auditor relationships. Because most data will flow in real time, informational flows are likely to be more current, but also perhaps at greater risk. Finally, IoT is likely to require accountants to become more tech savvy in order to understand these new data sources and the new environment in which data flow.

Storage and Backup Services. One of the most important types of cloud computing is creating and maintaining copies of critical data and files for both individuals and organizations. Cloud vendors include Amazon, Backblaze, Carbonite, Drop Box, SkyDrive, JungleDisk, and Mozy. Most of these vendors provide low-cost, and even free, backup services for individual customers. In commercial, fee-for-service settings, most backups are synchronized and therefore occur at the same time a computerized system gathers and stores the original data, thereby creating mirror, off-site copies of vital accounting data. Additional, and usually optional, services for home computing applications include encryption, fixed-time backup schedules, expandable storage options, and Mac computer support.

Case-in-Point 2.17 The last edition of this book was the first time the authors used Dropbox to share, store, and secure the word-processing files for this textbook online. The advantages became obvious to us as we were able to see, modify, and reference each other's work. No one had to worry about maintaining backup copies either … Dropbox did that for us!

Educational Services. You probably already use Web search engines such as Google or Bing to answer personal questions of interest. Professional accountants do the same thing, using these same engines to answer asset classification, depreciation, or tax questions. In addition, the Internet provides a host of specialized educational services. One category is "software tutorials." For example, you can find explanations and videos explaining how to perform a wide variety of spreadsheet tasks by searching on the term "Excel Tutorials." Similar tutorials also explain how to use Microsoft Access, complete specific tax forms, or create PowerPoint presentations.

---

[19] McCord, N. 2015. GPS tracking your pizza delivery. Accessed online from http://gpstrackit.com/gps-tracking-your-pizza-delivery.

Another category of online education is the large number of online courses offered by prestigious schools such as Duke University, Stanford University, and the University of Washington. Many of these courses are free to individuals not seeking university credit. You can find a partial list of such courses at Coursera.org.

Yet a third category of online educational services is complete degree programs—for example, schools that offer complete online programs that lead to accounting degrees. You can earn an associate's degree, bachelor's degree, and even a master's degree of science in accounting through such "distance-learning" offerings—see for example, eLearners.com.

2.5 PRIVACY AND SECURITY ON THE INTERNET

The most important advantage of the Internet and World Wide Web—*accessibility*—is also its greatest weakness—*vulnerability*. This means that someone who *poses* as an authorized user may be able to access any email, Web page, or computer file that an authorized user can access on the Internet. This section of the chapter discusses Internet privacy and security in detail.

Identity Theft and Privacy

Identity theft refers to crimes in which someone uses another person's personal identification (credit card, social security card, or similar identifier) in some way that involves fraud or deception (usually for economic benefit).[20] A 2016 study by Javelin Strategy & Research reported that 13.1 million people were victims of identity theft in the United States—a rate of one victim every 2.4 seconds—and an estimated total of $15 billion in personal losses.[21] In 2016, new-account fraud, in which thieves open new accounts in the names of others, was among the most common type of crime.

The most common complaint related to identity theft is credit card fraud. The Department of Justice prosecutes ID theft violations under the **Identity Theft and Assumption Deterrence Act (ITADA)** of 1998. The punishment can be a prison term of 15 years, a fine, and forfeiture of any personal property used to commit the crime.

A related issue is personal privacy. Businesses need to protect the payroll data they send to service providers electronically. Online shoppers want to know that vendors protect their privacy. None of us wants our emails read by hackers. But all of these needs often conflict with other objectives. For example, managers feel they have the right to view all the email messages of employees who use company computers during working hours, and companies doing business on the Web are sometimes hard pressed not to use the wealth of data that online shoppers provide them.

Most websites accessed by online users collect personal information. What they collect and how they use it are dictated by their privacy policies. Because businesses vary widely in the amount of privacy protection for customers, it is important to read a company's policy statements carefully. State governments, prompted by concerns over consumer privacy rights, particularly in the financial and health-care industries, are introducing a variety of privacy legislation. Groups such as the Electronic Frontier

---

[20] Identify Theft and Identify Fraud, accessed from the US Department of Justice website (justice.gov).
[21] Pascual, A., K. Marchini, and S. Miller. 2016. 2016 Identity fraud: Fraud hits an inflection point. Accessed online from **https://www.javelinstrategy.com/coverage-area/2016-identity-fraud-fraud-hits-inflection-point**.

Foundation and the Online Privacy Alliance are also working to protect the privacy of data transmitted over the Internet.

While companies need strong preventive controls to help protect customer information, individuals should also use caution. For example, if you are uncertain about the authenticity of a request for personal information, ask the person to send the request in writing on company letterhead. If you question the authenticity of a particular offer on a website, do more research on the company before purchasing goods or service from it—especially if you must give your credit card number. Figure 2-8 outlines some additional steps that you can take to protect your personal information—almost all of them accounting related.

Social media also pose interesting privacy concerns because what you post online is neither private nor retractable. Moreover, employers often check postings on social networking sites in search of "red flags"—for example, substance abuse, large amounts of debt, criminal activity, or membership in extremist groups. Organizations use all this information to help them evaluate employees or disqualify job applicants.

Like it or not, managers regularly screen the postings of their subordinates, and more than one person has lost his or her job by accidentally posting candid and offensive materials that the boss could see. This is more common than you might think—a Google search by one of the authors on the terms "social networking" and "lost jobs" yielded 20 million hits! Even if you allow for duplications, that's a big incentive to be cautious about what you post!

Case-in-Point 2.18 One new employee forgot that she had accepted her boss's invitation to add him as a friend on Facebook. She later posted a note saying that she hated her job and added several additional, unflattering comments about him. He fired her on the spot.[22]

1. Only give personal information such as Social Security numbers and dates of birth to those absolutely needing it.
2. Mail checks, credit applications, and similar materials directly in locked outgoing mail boxes, not in front-yard mail boxes with red, "steal me" flags on their sides.
3. Do not leave purses, wallets, or similar carrying cases unattended—for example, in unlocked gym lockers.
4. When asked by a legitimate business person such as a bank teller for your personal information, write it down for them—do not recite it verbally.
5. Be wary of unsolicited calls from individuals claiming to be bank representatives, credit card issuers, or others, especially if they ask for personal information. A similar rule applies to emails from unknown agents.
6. Do not "lend" personal information to others, for example, a password.
7. Do not simply toss sensitive information in trash cans where others can retrieve it. Shred or burn it first.
8. Be wary of relatives in financial difficulties. Sadly, the family members of identity thieves account for a high percentage of identity-theft victims.
9. Phishing describes a website or email that appears to be from a known source but that gathers personal data for illegal purposes. Don't fall for this! For example, use your Web browser to reveal the true URL of a generic link that says "Click here."
10. Key-logging software is software that captures your keystrokes—usually for illicit purposes. Use security software to guard against it.

FIGURE 2-8 Steps that you can take to safeguard your personal data from identity theft.

[22] Poppic, S. 2014. Ten social media blunders that cost a millennial a job—or worse. *Money Magazine*; careers. Accessed online from http://time.com/money/3019899/10-facebook-twitter-mistakes-lost-job-millennials-viral.

Security

Security policies and procedures safeguard an organization's electronic resources and limit access to authorized users. For this reason, **information security** has been a high-ranking entry in each of the last 5 years in the AICPA's survey of the "Top 10 Technologies" expected to have a powerful influence over business.

Of special importance to AIS is **access security**—for example, limiting access of proprietary budget data to bona fide users. *Access authentication* requires individuals to prove they are who they say they are. The three types of authentication are based on (1) what you *have,* (2) what you *know,* and (3) who you *are.* What you *have* may be a plastic card that provides you physical access to information or a restricted area. Examples are your ATM card, debit card, or employee card that gives you access to certain premises. What you *know* refers to unique information you possess, such as a password or your mother's maiden name. You can authenticate who you are with a unique physical characteristic such as your fingerprint or the pattern of the retina in your eye. As you might guess, using security that forces a user to prove who they are is the highest level of authentication. **Two-factor authentication (TFA) systems** require a combination of authentication techniques—for example, requiring both your debit card number and your password to withdraw cash from an ATM.

Spam, Phishing, Spoofing, and Ransomware

A current Internet problem is the increasing amount of **spam**—those annoying, unsolicited email messages that clog your email inbox. However, spam is more than a simple bother—it is distracting, often illegal, and increasingly costly to organizations. AOL and Microsoft, two of the biggest Internet service providers, estimate that they each block over 2 billion spam emails per day.

> ***Case-in-Point 2.19*** Do you receive a lot of spam messages in your email inbox? You're not alone. According to a recent report by Talos, worldwide spam now exceeds 400 billion emails per day. A similar report by Appriver suggests that 4.2 billion of these emails also contain malware.[23]

Although about 35% of spam messages are harmless advertising, a greater percentage are bogus—for example, attempt to sell fictitious merchandise, steal identities, or ask for donations based on untrue stories. Clicking on the "unsubscribe button" in such messages often accomplishes the exact opposite effect because it tells the sender that you actively read such emails. Spammers sell lists of such prized, active email readers to others, furthering the problem.

Phishing means tricking users into providing valuable information such as Social Security numbers, debit card PINs, passwords, or similar personal information—for example, by requesting this information on bogus websites. Other examples are emails that request personal information for "routine security purposes" or "because we believe your account has been compromised." Phishing activity is growing. According to a survey by Kaspersky Labs, such attacks increased from nearly 20 million in 2012 to over 37 million in 2013.[24]

---

[23] See, for example: https://www.appriver.com/about-us/news-releases/2016-malware-levels-now-stand-at-nearly-four-times-2015-totals/.

[24] Kaspersky Lab Report. 37.3 Million users experienced phishing attacks in the last year. Accessed from Kaspersky Lab website (usa.kaspersky.com), June 20, 2013.

A growing type of phishing is **spear phishing**, which means attempting to collect sensitive information from a particular person or organization. These efforts are not random attacks, but focus on more specific individuals or groups—hence the name. Like other forms of phishing, the attack typically begins with an email from a trusted source and appears legitimate. "Financial gain" is only one motive for such efforts. Passwords, military secrets, or trade secrets are other targets.

Closely associated with the concept of phishing is spoofing. Within the context of the Internet, spoofing means altering the IP identity of an email sender or website link in order to hide the true source of the sender or website. Phishing becomes more effective if hackers can hide their true identities.

Finally, have you ever clicked on an email attachment, only to see your computer freeze and display a note from a "security company" offering to sell you software that can fix it? If so, you've probably been the victim of **ransomware**, that is, malicious software that denies access to computer-system resources until you pay a given amount of money.

Individuals, businesses, and even government agencies are common targets of ransomware, and the problem is growing. In 2015, for example, the Internet Crime Complaint Center of the US Department of Justice reported that over 2,500 victims paid over $24 million to cyber criminals in ransomware attacks.[25]

Firewalls, Intrusion Detection Systems, Value-Added Networks, and Proxy Servers

To gain access to a company's files, a computer hacker must first obtain access to that company's computers. The firewalls, intrusion detection systems, and proxy servers discussed here protect against unwarranted intrusions from external parties.

Firewalls. A **firewall** (Figure 2-9) guards against unauthorized access to sensitive file information from external Internet users. On networked systems, firewalls are often

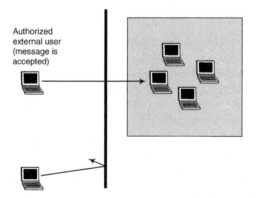

Authorized
external user
(message is
accepted)

FIGURE 2-9 A firewall acts as a barrier between unauthorized external users and organizational (internal) computers and files. Firewalls accept messages from bona fide users but reject messages from unauthorized users.

---

[25] Turkel, D. 2016. Victims paid more than $24 million to ransomware criminals in 2015—and that's just the beginning. *Business Insider*. Accessed online from http://www.businessinsider.com/doj-and-dhs-ransomware-attacks-government-2016-4.

stand-alone devices with built-in, protective software. On mainframe or host systems, firewalls are usually software.

The two primary methods of firewall protection are *by inclusion* or *by exclusion*. When firewalls protect internal systems by inclusion, the software examines packets of incoming messages and limits entry to authorized ("included") users. To do this, the software maintains an **access control list (ACL)** of bona fide IP addresses that network administrators create for this purpose. If the software does not recognize the IP address of an external user, it refuses that user access to the files he or she requested. When firewalls protect internal systems by exclusion, the software compares the incoming packet IP address to a list of known threat addresses, rejecting messages from these sources but accepting all others.

Case-in-Point 2.20   Theresa Gravenstine is a CPA and an inspector general who works for Congress in Washington, DC. Her job includes performing firewall audits. For example, she examines new computer systems at the House of Representatives, confirms their security, and ensures that outsiders cannot defraud House members. In the US government, she says, "cyber security is the 800-pound gorilla in the room."[26]

Firewalls are useful Internet security controls, but (like most security features) are not perfect. One problem is that they cannot protect against **denial-of-service attacks**, which overwhelm system resources with a volume of service requests. Another problem is **spoofing** (i.e., when a hacker masquerades as an authorized user with a recognizable IP address). A similar, but less obvious, problem is the ability of a determined intruder to alter the contents of the access control list itself—a security breach that is especially difficult to overcome. A final problem is that most firewalls can only protect against external attacks, not internal (authorized) users bent on mischief.

Intrusion Detection Systems.   Whereas firewalls simply reject unauthorized users from access, **intrusion detection systems (IDSs)** create records of such events. *Passive IDSs* create logs of potential intrusions and alert network administrators to them via console messages, alarms, or beepers. *Reactive IDSs* have the ability to detect potential intrusions dynamically (e.g., by examining traffic flows), log off potentially malicious users, and even reprogram a firewall to block further messages from the suspected source.

Perhaps the most important advantage of an IDS is its ability to both prevent unauthorized accesses to sensitive information and to alert system administrators to potential violations. This may also increase the perceived risk of discovery, dissuading would-be hackers. IDSs may also be able to detect preambles to attacks, forestalling their effectiveness. Finally, an IDS is an important tool for *documenting* an attack, thereby generating invaluable information to both network administrators and investigators.

Value-Added Networks.   Message routing is important to accountants because the security of a data transmission partially rests on the security of all the intermediate computers along a given communications pathway. Thus, the greater the distance between the sending station and the destination computer, the more intermediary routing computers there are and the more vulnerable a message becomes to interception and abuse. This is one reason why businesses sometimes prefer to create their own (proprietary) networks to transmit data electronically.

---

[26] Gravenstine, T. as told to S. Wilson. 2014. "The last word." *Journal of Accountancy* 218(3): 120.

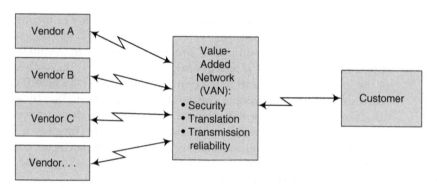

FIGURE 2-10 A VAN-based EDI system.

Value-added networks (VANs) are private, point-to-point communication channels that large organizations create for themselves—usually for security reasons (Figure 2-10). When it first implements a VAN, the business assigns each user a unique account code that simultaneously identifies the external entity and authenticates the organization's subsequent electronic transactions.

There are at least three ways to create secure networks. One way is to start with a blank slate and create everything from scratch—an approach first used by the military and later by Walmart. A second way is to lease secure, dedicated transmission lines from conventional long-distance carriers such as AT&T.

A third alternative is to create a **virtual private network (VPN)** on the Internet. As the name suggests, a VPN mimics a VAN in many of its security features, but enjoys the benefit of transmitting messages cheaply over existing Internet connections. A VPN creates secure data transmissions by (1) using "tunneling" security protocols embedded in the message frames sent to, and received by, the organization, (2) encrypting all transmitted data, and (3) authenticating the remote computer (and perhaps also the individual sender), before permitting further data transmissions. Most AIS VANs use this approach.

Proxy Servers. Given the large amount of information now available on the Web, some organizations seek to limit the number of sites that employees can access—for example, to ensure that employees do not use Web-access privileges for personal, frivolous, or counterproductive purposes. A **proxy server** is a network server and related software that creates a transparent gateway to and from the Internet and controls Web access. In a typical application, users log onto their familiar file server as before. But when they attempt to access a Web page, the initial network server contacts the proxy server to perform the requested task.

One advantage of using a proxy server is the ability to funnel all incoming and outgoing Internet requests through a single server. This can make Web access more efficient because the proxy server is specifically designed to handle requests for Internet information. A second advantage is the proxy server's ability to examine all incoming requests for information and test them for authenticity (i.e., the ability to act as a firewall). A third advantage is that a proxy server can limit employee Internet access to approved websites (i.e., to only those IP addresses contained in an ACL). This enables an organization to deny employees access to gambling, pornographic, or game-playing websites that are unlikely to have any productive benefits.

A fourth advantage is the ability to limit the information that is stored on the proxy server to information that the company can afford to lose. If this server fails or is compromised by hackers, the organization is only marginally inconvenienced because its main servers remain functional. To recover, the company can simply restart the system and reinitialize the server with backup data.

Netscape Communications estimates that between 30% and 60% of employee Internet requests are redundant. A final advantage of proxy servers is the ability to store ("cache") frequently accessed Web pages on its hard drive—for example, the Web pages of preferred vendors. This enables the server to respond quickly to user requests for information because the Web page information is available locally. This feature also enables managers to obtain some idea of what information employees need most and perhaps take steps to provide it internally (rather than through Web sources).

Data Encryption

To safeguard transmitted data, businesses often use **data encryption** techniques that transform plaintext messages into unintelligible ciphertext messages. The receiving station then decodes the encrypted messages back into plaintext for use. There are many encryption techniques and standards. The simple method shown in Figure 2-11 uses a *cyclic substitution* of the alphabet with a constant displacement value of "5" to transform the letters of a plaintext message into alternate letters of the alphabet. To decode the message, the recipient's computer performs the encryption process in reverse, decrypting the coded message back into readable text. To make things more secure, the sender can use a different displacement value for each coded message, each *portion* of a coded message, or even each word of the coded message.

In Figure 2-11, the encryption system encodes each *letter* of the message separately. With **block chaining**, the encryption system encodes an entire set or block of characters, treated as a set. A key aspect of block chaining is that the decryption of a block depends upon the prior blocks. This causes the entire decryption process to depend upon an initialization vector.

The method that computers use to transform plaintext into ciphertext is called the **encryption key**. This is typically a mathematical function that depends on a large prime number. The **data encryption standard (DES)** system used by the US government to encode documents employs such a system. DES uses a number with 56 binary digits to encode information, a value equal to approximately 72 quadrillion. Thus, to crack a code, a hacker must guess which of 72 quadrillion values was used to encrypt the message.

The data encryption method illustrated in Figure 2-11 uses a single cryptographic key that is shared by two communicating parties and is called **secret key encryption**.

Encryption Scheme

Letters of the alphabet:	A	B	C	D	E	F	G	H	I	J	...
Numerical equivalent:	1	2	3	4	5	6	7	8	9	10	...
Plus displacement key:	5	5	5	5	5	5	5	5	5	5	
New values:	6	7	8	9	10	11	12	13	14	15	
Letters to use in code:	F	G	H	I	J	K	L	M	N	O	...

Example
Plaintext message: HI, ABE!
Ciphertext message: MN, FGJ!

FIGURE 2-11   A simple substitution encryption method.

This system derives its name from the fact that its users must keep the key secret and not share the key with other parties. The most common encryption methods today use **public key encryption**, a technique that requires each party to use a pair of public/private encryption keys. Two examples are Secure Socket Layer (SSL) and Secure Hypertext Transfer Protocol (HTTPs).

To employ public key encryption, the sending party uses a public key to encode the message and the receiving party uses a second, private key to decode it. A major advantage of public key encryption is that the same public key cannot both encode and decode a message. Data transmissions using public key encryption are likely to be secure because the transmitted message itself is scrambled and because neither party knows the other's key. This is the main reason why most Web applications use public key encryption systems.

Digital Signatures and Digital Time Stamping

Many businesses want proof that the accounting documents they transmit or receive over the Internet are authentic. Examples include purchase orders, bids for contracts, and acceptance letters. To authenticate such documents, a company can transmit a complete document in plaintext and then also include a portion of that same message or some other standard text in an encrypted format—a **digital signature**.

In 1994, the National Institute of Standards and Technology adopted Federal Information Processing Standard 186—the **digital signature standard (DSS)**. The presence of the digital signature authenticates a document. The reasoning is straightforward: if a company's private key decodes a message, then an authentic sender must have created the message. For this reason, some experts consider digital signatures even more secure than written signatures (which can be forged). Further, if the sender includes a complete message in both plaintext and ciphertext, the encrypted message provides assurance that no one has altered the readable copy. If someone has altered the plaintext, the two copies will not match.

Another authentication technique is a **digital certificate**—an authenticating document issued by an independent third party called a **certificate authority** (e.g., Thawte or Verisign). The certificates themselves are signed documents with sender names and public key information. Certificates are generally encoded, possibly in a certificate standard such as the X.509 certificate format. Customers can also use digital certificates to assure themselves that a website is real.

Many important business documents are time sensitive. Examples include bidding documents that must be submitted by a deadline, deposit slips that must be presented to banks before the close of business, purchase orders for common stocks that depend on the date and time of acquisition, and legal documents that must be filed in a timely fashion. Then, too, most businesses also want to know when customers made particular purchases, when they paid particular bills, or when specific employees entered or modified data items in important databases. Finally, a good way to protect intellectual property such as computer software is to establish clearly the date and time it was first created or distributed.

What these items have in common is the need for a **time stamp** that unambiguously indicates the date and time of submission, filing, or data entry. PGP Digital Time Stamping Service and Verisign are two of several **digital time stamping services (DTSSs)** that attach digital time stamps to documents either for a small fee or for free. In a typical application, the user sends the document to the service's email address along with the Internet address of the final recipient. When the service receives the document, it performs its time-stamping task and then forwards the document as required.

Case-in-Point 2.21   The DigiStamp time-stamping company was founded in 1988 and has now performed over 1 million time stamps. While some customers use its services to establish regulatory compliance, others use it to document ownership of important intellectual property. The company first charged $5 for a time stamp—a figure now as low as 40 cents.[27]

Digital time stamping performs the same task electronically that official seals and other time stamps perform manually—it authenticates the date, time, and perhaps place of a business transaction. This can be important over the Internet. Although most documents are transmitted instantaneously, time delays can occur when file servers temporarily falter or power failures disrupt wide area networks. DTSSs enable businesses to overcome these problems.

AIS AT WORK
The Benefits of Online Accounting Outsourcing[28]

The advantages of outsourcing accounting functions such as payroll or tax preparation are well known, but outsourcing additional accounting tasks to online providers is a different matter. Can a cloud provider, perhaps located offshore, perform general ledger or deprecation computations as well? A growing number of businesses say "yes!"

The most common reason why organizations outsource a given business process is to reduce costs, and this applies to accounting applications as well. Additional benefits include faster turnaround, improved quality, enhanced access to expertise, improved ability to handle both high and low processing volumes, and reduced capital expenditures (e.g., realized savings in computer hardware and software). Experts note that outsourcing also enables clients to reduce in-house labor costs, pay only for the services they need, and focus on only their core businesses.

Perhaps the most commonly cited objection to outsourcing is a loss of control. In a recent survey of over 800 businesses by Accenture, however, over 85% of the respondents said that outsourcing actually gave them more control—especially in the ability to plan. In addition, over 55% thought that accounting outsourcing enabled them to implement strategic changes faster and at more controlled rates. But the biggest benefit of outsourcing may be the increased business for those accounting companies providing these services—yet one more opportunity made possible by the Internet.

SUMMARY

✓ The Internet is a collection of local, wide area, and international networks that accountants can use for communication, research, and business purposes. Most accountants also use the World Wide Web—the multimedia portion of the Internet—for similar purposes.

---

[27] From the company website at: https://www.digistamp.com/about-us/aboutus.
[28] May, A. R. 2016. Are you ready to take some work off your plate? *Collector* 81(8): 32–39; and Ferber, K. 2008. Why outsourcing accounting is a good idea for you! Accessed from www.articlesbase.com.

✓ Intranets are private networks that businesses create for internal purposes such as distributing email. Extranets are similar to intranets, except that they also allow approved external parties to access internal network files and databases.

✓ Groupware is software that supports email on business networks, plus allows users to share computer files, schedule appointments, video-conference, and develop custom applications.

✓ Social media contains information of value to accountants. For example, it can help them recruit new employees, screen applicants for red flags, and help them communicate with one another.

✓ To exchange financial information on the Internet, businesses can use XBRL—a standardized form of XML that provides a common format for financial data and allows searches of the data and extraction for comparison purposes. The XBRL International Consortium develops XBRL standards.

✓ The term e-accounting means the ability to perform accounting tasks on the Internet—for example, preparing budgets, posting financial statements, or training employees.

✓ E-payment systems, e-wallets, and virtual currencies allow Internet users to pay for Internet purchases without using their credit cards. For various reasons, such alternatives can benefit both the Internet seller and the online buyer.

✓ Electronic business includes retail sales on the Internet and EDI. Three examples of Internet-based accounting activities are B2C (business to consumer), B2B (business to business), and C2C (consumer to consumer—typically using a platform supported by a business).

✓ Accountants can use cloud computing services to outsource selected data processing, to store copies of important files for both backup and file-sharing, and to access vital educational services.

✓ The Internet of Things (IoT) refers to the ability of smart appliances and machinery to communicate over the Internet—an ability of importance to accountants if the communication involves accounting transactions.

✓ For security reasons, some businesses prefer to use private, value-added networks (VANs) rather than the Internet to support e-commerce applications.

✓ Internet privacy and security concerns include hacking, identity theft, spam, and phishing, all of which impact AISs. These concerns prompt many businesses to use firewalls, IDSs, proxy servers, data encryption techniques, digital signatures, and digital time stamping to achieve control objectives.

✓ Authentication requires users to prove they are who they say they are. Digital time stamps and signatures help in this process.

✓ Privacy concerns also include the need to protect users' private information and the growing threat of identity theft.

KEY TERMS YOU SHOULD KNOW

access control list (ACL)
access security
block chaining
blogs
business-to-business (B2B)
  e-commerce
business-to-consumer (B2C)
  e-commerce
certificate authority

churn rate
click fraud
consumer-to-consumer (C2C)
  e-commerce
data encryption
data encryption standard (DES)
denial-of-service attacks
digital certificate
digital signature

digital signature standard (DSS)
digital time stamping service
  (DTSS)
domain address
domain name system (DNS)
e-accounting
e-business
e-wallet
electronic conferencing

Electronic data interchange (EDI)
electronic payments (e-payments)
encryption key
Extensible Business Reporting
  Language (XBRL)
eXtensible Markup Language
  (XML)
extranets
firewall
groupware
hypertext markup language
  (HTML)
hypertext transfer protocol
  (HTTP)
IDEA
identity theft

Identity Theft and Assumption
  Deterrence Act (ITADA)
information security
instant messaging
Internet Corporation for Assigned
  Names and Numbers (ICANN)
Internet of Things (IoT)
Internet Protocol (IP)
intranets
intrusion detection systems
  (IDSs)
phishing
platform as a service (PaaS)
proxy server
public key encryption
ransomware

secret key encryption
software as a service (SaaS)
spam
spear phishing
spoofing
TCP/IP
time stamp
two-factor authentication (TFA)
uniform resource locator (URL)
value-added networks (VANs)
virtual currency
virtual private network (VPN)
XBRL instance documents
XBRL International Consortium

TEST YOURSELF

Q2-1. Which of the following is most likely to contain only numbers?

  a. domain address

  b. URL address

  c. IP address

  d. postal address

Q2-2. Which of the following enables users to view data with a Web browser?

  a. intranet

  b. extranet

  c. Internet

  d. all of these

Q2-3. All of the following are protocols for transmitting data over the Internet except:

  a. IP

  b. HTTP

  c. XML

  d. all of these are protocols

Q2-4. All of the following are markup languages (that use edit tags) except:

  a. HTML   **c.** XML

  b. IP   **d.** XBRL

Q2-5. Which of these is *not* an acronym?

  a. HTML   **c.** IDS

  b. blog   **d.** Internet

Q2-6. Which of the following is true?

  a. XBRL is a subset of XML.

  b. XML is a subset of TCP.

  c. PBX is a subset of HTML.

  d. None of these is true.

Q2-7. A document file containing XBRL tags is a(n):

  a. extranet document

  b. intranet document

  c. instance document

  d. URL

Q2-8. Which of these identifies a private, point-to-point network?

  a. EDI   **c.** IP

  b. DES   **d.** VAN

Q2-9. Which of these statements is correct?

  a. A VPN is a type of private network.

  b. DES stands for "data entry system."

  c. An IDS is the same as a firewall.

  d. All of these statements are correct.

Q2-10. Spoofing means:

  a. kidding someone about their computer

  b. simulating a disaster to test the effectiveness of a disaster recovery system

  c. posing as an authentic user to gain access to a computer system

  d. encrypting data for security purposes

DISCUSSION QUESTIONS

2-1. What are intranets? What are extranets? Why are intranets and extranets important to accountants?

2-2. What are blogs? How are they used? Who is using them?

2-3. Is bitcoin still a viable currency? Use an Internet search engine to find out. If so, what is the exchange rate for one bitcoin in the currency of your country? Would you buy a bitcoin? If so, why? If not, why not?

2-4. How are the comments on social media sites useful to businesses? How are these sites useful to accountants?

2-5. What is HTML? How does it differ from XML and XBRL? (Note: For a more comprehensive description of the differences, you may want to search the Internet.)

2-6. How does XBRL compare to the IDEA database?

2-7. Describe some important uses of electronic commerce and explain why electronic commerce is important to accountants.

2-8. What are electronic payments? How are they different from credit card payments?

2-9. What is EDI? Why do companies use EDI?

2-10. Most retail sales websites require customers to use their credit cards to make purchases online. How comfortable are you in providing your credit card number in such applications? Why do you feel this way?

2-11. What is click fraud? Who benefits and who loses when click fraud occurs?

2-12. What is spamming? How is spam related to accounting information systems? Should all spamming be illegal? Why or why not?

2-13. What are Internet firewalls and proxy servers? How are they created? How do businesses use them for Internet security?

2-14. What is data encryption? What techniques are used for data encryption?

2-15. Describe and contrast the three types of authentication. Can you think of a business situation where someone would need to use a combination of all three levels to gain access to information?

2-16. What are digital signatures? Why do businesses use them? How can businesses use a digital certificate for Internet security?

2-17. Analysts claim that businesses can increase sales on the Internet, but not profits. What evidence does this chapter provide to support or refute this claim? Discuss.

PROBLEMS

2-18. The Internet uses many acronyms. Within the context of the present chapter, what words were used to form each of the following?

a. B2B	**h.** HTTP	**o.** ISP
b. B2C	**i.** ICANN	**p.** SaaS
c. C2C	**j.** IDEA	**q.** URL
d. DNS	**k.** IDS	**r.** VAN
e. EC	**l.** IETF	**s.** VPN
f. EDI	**m.** IoT	**t.** XBRL
g. Email	**n.** IP address	**u.** XML

2-19. In Discussion Question 2-1, you discussed intranets and extranets, and identified the importance of each to accountants. Now, assume that you are a partner in a medium-sized, local CPA firm. Your firm has 4 partners, 10 staff accountants, 1 research assistant, and 1 administrative assistant. Your firm is considered a technology leader in the local area, and this is considered a competitive advantage for your firm. At the weekly staff meeting next Friday you want to discuss the topic of developing an intranet for the firm. To be sure everyone is prepared to discuss this topic, you want to develop a "talking paper," which is a one-page summary of salient points that you want to be sure you cover in your presentation to everyone. What would you include in this one-page discussion aid?

2-20. Create an HTML document of your own, using the example in Figure 2-1 to guide you. Put the name of this assignment in the tag for the heading. Put your name in bold. Include at least one hyperlink to a favorite Web page using the anchor <a> tag. Finally, include an ordered list in your Web page with at least three items—for example, a list of your favorite books, favorite restaurants, or the courses you're taking this semester. You will find it easiest to work in Notepad for this problem, but you can also use a word processor—as long as you save your document as "text." Also, be sure to add the extension "html" to the end of your file name. View your completed document in your Web browser—for example, by selecting File/Open in Microsoft Internet Explorer—and screen capture your work.

2-21. At the time this book was written, the US Securities and Exchange Commission still supported Edgar—a depository of corporate accounting filings. Log onto Edgar at www.sec.gov/edgar.shtml, click on "Search for Company Filings." Finally, find and select two companies in the same industry (either your instructor's choice or your choice) so that you can compare various financial data. Note that you can select either "text" or "html" formats. Compare these formats to Figure 2-1. Are they similar? Looking at either image, can you download the financial information into a spreadsheet? Can you easily do financial comparisons such as ratio analysis? What do you have to do if you want to make financial comparisons?

2-22. Visit the XBRL home page at www.XBRL.org, and read the section entitled "What is XBRL." Then, do each of the following:

a. Select an article from the "What" list of on the home page and write a one-page summary of your findings.

b. Search the Internet for articles on the topic "benefits of XBR."

When you have found at least three good articles, write a one-page summary of this topic.

2-23. Write a one-page paper on each of the following topics as they relate to XBRL:

a. What is the history of XBRL? What professional accounting organization helped in the early stages of this concept?

b. What is an XBRL specification, and what is the latest version? When was it released? By whom?

c. How could XBRL help a company engage in "continuous reporting?" Find a website or an e-journal article that discusses XBRL

and continuous reporting. What are the main points of the article?

d. Find at least two other companies (other than Microsoft) that are publishing their financial statements on the Internet using XBRL. What business are they in (what industry)?

2-24. Select three Internet websites whose owners sell goods or services and create a table similar to Figure 2-6. Classify each of your websites as B2B, B2C, or C2C. If you are not sure, feel free to use more than one classification. How does this company make money?

(Hint: It may primarily be through advertising.)

2-25. The business models of the breakthrough Internet companies in Figure 2-6 have often been controversial. For example, homeowners often violate local rules governing the rental of their private dwellings, Tesla's plans to sell cars through company-owned dealerships ran afoul of those state rules requiring independent dealerships, the singer Taylor Swift withdrew her music offerings from Spotify to protest its reimbursement policies, and Uber's ride-sharing system often breaks local ordinances limiting public conveyances to licensed taxis. Select a company from those listed in Figure 2-6 (or from a list provided by your instructor) and write no more than a one-page description of such a controversy that is of interest to you or your local community. What do you feel is a fair resolution of the problem you describe?

2-26. Examine the data encryption technique illustrated in Figure 2-11. Use a displacement value of "8" to encrypt the following message. Hint: This task becomes easy if you use an Excel spreadsheet and VLookUp formulas that reference a table of letters and their numeric equivalencies.

"Those who ignore history are forced to repeat it."

2-27. The messages below were encrypted using the technique illustrated in Figure 2-11 (using displacement keys other than 5). Using trial and error, decode them. Hint: This task becomes easy if you use an Excel spreadsheet and VLookUp formulas that reference a table of letters and their numeric equivalencies.

Message 1 OZ OY TUZ CNGZ CK JUTZ QTUC ZNGZ NAXZY AY OZ OY CNGZ CK JU QTUC ZNGZ PAYZ GOTZ YU

Message 2 QBZAPJL KLSHFLK PZ QBZA-PJL KLUPLK

Message 3   FAA YMZK OAAWE EBAUX FTQ
NDAFT

2-28. A number of accounting journals now post back issues or even publish their entire journals online. Access the *Journal of Accountancy* website at www.aicpa.org (or another website selected by your instructor). Select an article that pertains to a topic in this chapter and write a one-page report on it. Be careful to cite correctly any information that you use from this article!

2-29. Visit the home page of a DTSS. How much does your service charge? Do you think these fees are reasonable? Why or why not?

CASE ANALYSES

2-30. Small Computers, Inc. (Evaluating privacy policies on the Internet)

The following stated policies pertain to the e-commerce website for Small Computers, Inc., a personal and handheld computer manufacturer and seller.

Privacy Statement

We will only use information collected on this website for legitimate business purposes. We do not give away or rent any information to third parties.

We will only contact you for legitimate business purposes, possibly from time to time, as needed. Please be 100% assured that we hold all transactions between you and our company in the strictest confidence.

Disclosure of Business Practices, Shipping, and Billing

- We will ship all items at the earliest possible date.
- We will not require you to accept items that you did not order.
- We will accept any returns from you of damaged or defective merchandise.
- In the event that we should accidentally bill you more than once for the same item, we will immediately issue you a refund.

Requirement

Evaluate these stated policies in terms of how well they promote customer trust and confidence in Small Computers, Inc.'s electronic business operations.

2-31. Accounting Is Mind Blogging (Accounting Blogs on the Internet)

There are many accounting blogs on the Internet. Here are some examples.

Education

Accounting Coach (www.accountingcoach.com/blog)
The Accounting Onion (www.accountingonion.com)
Sleep on CPA (http://sleeponcpa.blogspot.com/)

Fraud

The Forensic Accounting File (www.bbforensic.com/blog)
The Fraud Files Blog (www.sequenceinc.com/fraudfiles/)

Motivational

CPA Success (www.macpa.org/blog)
The Lighter Side of Accountancy and Tax (marksaccjokes.blogspot.com)

Industry Specific

Not-for-Profit (nonprofit.belfint.com)
Farm CPA Today (www.farmcpatoday.com)
Home School CPA (homeschoolcpa.com/blog)
Dental CPAs (dentalcpas.blogspot.com)

Requirement

1. Pick one of these blogs, a site recommended by your instructor, or one of your own, and write a one-page report on it. Your report should describe what the site contains, provide some examples of the articles it contains, and include your reactions to it—that is, an explanation of why you did or did not like the site.

2-32. Me, Inc. (The Dos, Don'ts, and Ethics of Social Networking Sites)

Even if you are now only a student with limited or no work experience, it is not too early to begin building a professional identity and your own company—Me, Inc. This is an identity that you'll want to post and carefully cultivate on some of the popular social networking sites and that will establish you as a serious, desirable employee.

Obviously, Me, Inc., has only one, part-time employee (you) and probably hasn't been in business very long. But, given the discussions about social networking in this chapter, there is much you can do to enhance your identity as time goes on—and also some things you can also do to avoid mistakes.

Requirements

1. Identify at least four strengths that you think would make you a desirable employee. Is "education" one of them?
2. Identify at least four mistakes that individuals make to hurt their employment chances. Do you think you would ever make such mistakes?
3. Which social networks or other websites would you use to market Me, Inc.? Name at least three of them.
4. Suppose that you ultimately land an entry-level job at a large company with several levels of management. After working 4 months on the job, a senior manager several levels above you notices your account on Facebook and requests to be added as a friend. Would you approve him or her? Do you think such a request is appropriate? Why or why not?

5. Continuing Question 4, suppose the probationary period for your job is 6 months. Until now, you've received monthly job evaluations of "satisfactory" or "exceeds work requirements." However, you post a comment on a social networking site indicating that you don't like the job and hate your boss. At your next job evaluation, your boss mentions that posting and terminates you "for cause." Do you think this is ethical? Why or why not?

2-33. Anderson Manufacturing (XBRL-Enabled Software)

The Anderson Manufacturing Company (AMC) is located in Las Vegas, Nevada, and manufactures specialty parts for high-end sports cars. The company currently has an accounting information system, but over time, has found that it would like its system to do more. For example, the finance department finds an increasing need for reporting financial data about the company in alternate report formats that the current system cannot perform. Rather than revise its existing accounting system piecewise, the company's managers have begun to think about acquiring a new one. But which one? There are many packages available with various degrees of capability.

To help it make a decision, AMC hires Kuechler Associates, a consulting firm that specializes in software acquisitions and implementation. One of KA's areas of expertise is implementing enterprise resource planning systems (ERPs). One of its suggestions is that AMC consider selecting XBRL-enabled software to help it with its financial reporting needs.

Requirements

1. What does it mean when software is "XBRL-enabled?"
2. Identify at least five advantages that KA might discuss with the company regarding an XBRL-enabled software solution. Identify any disadvantages that might also be relevant for AMC.
3. Assume that you are KA's research assistant. Draft a memo to AMC that explains how XBRL works. Remember to keep in mind your audience. This should be an executive-level piece of correspondence.
4. As the research assistant, develop a PowerPoint presentation for AMC explaining exactly what benefits it could realize with an XBRL-enabled software solution. Be creative, and use diagrams and examples where appropriate.

2-34. Barra Concrete (XOR Encryption)

Barra Concrete specializes in creating driveways and curbs for the residential market. Its accounting software uses exclusive OR (XOR) operations to convert the individual bits of a plaintext message into ciphertext. The rules are as follows:

	Exclusive OR rules			
	Rule 1	Rule 2	Rule 3	Rule 4
Plaintext bit	0	0	1	1
Bit in key	0	1	0	1
Ciphertext result	0	1	1	0

In other words, exactly one of the bits must be a "1" and the other a "0" for the result of an exclusive OR operation to be a "1." To illustrate, suppose that the bits representing a single plaintext character were 1010 0101 and the secret key used just the four bits 1110. Here are the results of the XOR operation, using this key:

Plaintext bits	1010	0101
Key (repeated)	1110	1110
Ciphertext result	0100	1011

The encrypted bits are the ciphertext, or 0100 1011 as shown. These (encrypted) bits are what the software would transmit to the final recipient.

Requirements

1. Decrypting the ciphertext created by an XOR operation is easy—just use the same XOR operation on the encrypted bits! Demonstrate this for the example above.
2. Suppose the secret key were longer—the eight bits 1100 0011. Using this key and an exclusive OR, what is the ciphertext for the plaintext message "Go, team" if the bit configuration for these letters is as shown below.
   (Hint: The final answer consists of seven sets of data, each containing 8 bits.)

	G	O	,	T	E	A	M
Message:							
Binary:	0100 0111	0100 1111	0010 1100	0101 0100	0100 0101	0100 0001	0100 1101

READINGS AND OTHER RESOURCES

Arrowsmith, R. 2016. Case studies: Cloud hosting: Finding time savings, risk reduction and efficiency online. *Accounting Today* 30(10): 22.

Kaya, D. and P. Pronobis. 2016. The benefits of structured data across the information supply chain: Initial evidence on XBRL adoption and loan contracting of private firms. *Journal of Accounting and Public Policy* 34(4): 379–403.

Needleman, T. 2016. Accounting software in the cloud today—and tomorrow. *Accountingtoday.com* (12/28): 1.

Page, E. and C. Wright. 2016. Putting the cloud at the heart of your accounting practice. *CPA Practice Advisor.* 26(9): 24.

Segal, S. 2016. Accounting frauds—review of advanced technologies to detect and prevent frauds. *Economics and Business Review* 2(4): 45–64.

Whitehouse, T. 2016. FASB, SEC offer some new insights on XBRL. *Compliance Week* 13(146): 7–8.

Go to www.wiley.com/go/simkin/videos to access videos on the following topics:
   How XBRL Works
   Intro to Identity Theft
   E-Wallet Demo Video (click on the High Res choice)

What Is a Bitcoin
Social Media Tips for Professional Service Firms
Why Use Cloud Accounting Software
Digital Signature Video Demos

ANSWERS TO TEST YOURSELF

1. c **2.** d **3.** c **4.** b **5.** d **6.** a **7.** c **8.** d **9.** a **10.** c

Chapter 3

Information Technology and AISs

After studying this chapter, you should be able to:

1. *Describe* why information technology is important to accounting information systems (AISs) and why accountants should know about this technology.

2. *Explain* why computer processor speeds are not particularly important to most accounting information systems.

3. *Identify* source documents and *explain* why they are important to AISs.

4. *List* some common AIS uses for point-of-sale (POS) input, magnetic ink character recognition (MICR) media, and optical character recognition (OCR).

5. *Explain* in general terms the value of secondary storage devices to AISs.

6. *Summarize* why data communications are important to AISs.

7. *Describe* some advantages of client/server computing.

8. *Explain* the advantages and disadvantages of cloud computing.

The pervasive use of IT in accounting information systems have produced unique control risks that auditors need to understand. For example, Goodyear Tire & Rubber Company announced a $100 million restatement of its profits from 1998 to the first half of 2003, resulting from errors during the integration of a new ERP system with its accounting system. The firm's external auditor had failed to identify the problem.

Han, S., Z. Rezaee, L. Zue, and J. H. Zhang. 2016.
The association between information technology investments and audit risk.
Journal of Information Systems 30(1): 93–116.

3.1 INTRODUCTION

In automated accounting systems, information technology (IT) serves as a platform upon which other system components rely. The purpose of this chapter is to discuss IT subjects in detail—especially as they relate to accounting information systems (AISs). Since most students in AIS courses have already taken a survey computer class, the discussions here are brief. This chapter may nonetheless be useful as a review of computer hardware and software concepts or as a study of how IT helps organizations accomplish strategic accounting goals.

It is helpful to view an AIS as a set of five interacting components: (1) hardware, (2) software, (3) data, (4) people, and (5) processes. Computer hardware is probably the most tangible element in this set, but "hardware" is only one piece of the pie—and not necessarily the most important piece. For example, most organizations spend more money on people (in wages and salaries) than they do on computer hardware and software combined. Similarly, computer hardware must work together with the other system components to accomplish data processing tasks. Without computer software, the hardware would stand idle. Without data to process, both the hardware and the software would be useless. Without processes, accounting data could not be gathered accurately or distributed properly. And finally, without people, it is doubtful that the rest of the system could operate for long or be of much use.

What all this means is that "information technology" is a fuzzy term that includes more than computer hardware. In this chapter, we concentrate on computer hardware (in the next three sections of the chapter) and software (in the final section). But you should remember that these items must interact with all the other system components to create successful AISs.

3.2 THE IMPORTANCE OF INFORMATION TECHNOLOGY TO ACCOUNTANTS

Although it may be tempting to dismiss "information technology" as more important to computer people than accountants, this would be a mistake. In fact, most of the references at the end of this chapter make it very clear that "IT" and "accounting systems" are intimately related. Here are six reasons why IT is important to accountants.

Six Reasons

One reason for IT's importance is because information technology must be compatible with and support the other components of an AIS. For example, to automate the accounting system of a dry-cleaning business, the owners will have to consider what tasks they'll want their system to accomplish, identify what software package or packages can perform these tasks, and perhaps evaluate several different computer hardware configurations that might support these packages. These concerns are the subject of "systems analysis"—the topic covered in Chapters 12 and 13.

A second reason why information technology is important is because accounting professionals often help clients make hardware and software purchases. For example, large expenditures on computer systems must be cost justified (i.e., the benefit must exceed the cost)—a task usually performed with accounting expertise and assistance. For this reason, many consulting firms now specialize in, or have departments for, management advisory services to perform these consulting tasks. Understanding IT is critical to these efforts.

A third reason why information technology is important to accountants is because auditors must evaluate computerized systems. Today, it is no longer possible for auditors to treat a computer as a "black box" and audit around it. Rather, auditors must audit through or with a computer. This means that auditors must understand automation and automated controls and also be able to identify a computerized system's strengths and weaknesses. We cover these matters in Chapters 6–11.

A fourth reason why IT is important to accountants is because they are often asked to evaluate the efficiency (e.g., costliness and timeliness) and effectiveness (usually strategic value) of an existing system. This is a daunting task, requiring a familiarity with the strengths and weaknesses of the current system as well as an understanding of what alternate technologies might work better.

A fifth reason why information technology is important to accountants is that IT profoundly affects the way they work today and will work in the future. This includes new ways of gathering and recording information, new types of systems that accountants will use (both to perform personal tasks and to communicate their work to others), new types of hardware, software, and computer networks upon which these systems will run, and new ways to audit these systems.

A final reason why information technology is important to accountants is because understanding how IT affects accounting systems is vital to passing most accounting certification examinations. For example, sections of both the CPA and CMA examinations contain questions about information technology.

The Top 10 Information Technologies

Annually, the American Institute of Certified Public Accountants (AICPA) conducts a voluntary annual survey of its members to identify the "top 10 information system technologies" affecting the study and practice of accounting. Figure 3-1 provides this list for the United States and Canada for 2014, the most recent survey. The results for the two countries are identical for this survey. The top technology in both countries is "securing the IT environment." Due to technological advances, firms capture, analyze, and generate information from large volumes of data. CPAs are obligated to deal with this risk by managing and protecting data for themselves and their clients. Coming in second in both countries is "managing and retaining data," recognizing the fact that many companies collect huge amounts of raw data in the natural course of doing business. This is the concept of "big data" discussed in Chapter 1. Managing and retaining data means storing this data intelligently, analyzing it appropriately, and protecting it from would-be hackers.

Case-in-Point 3.1   In December of 2013, hackers broke into Target Corporation's vast online credit card system, compromising at least 40 million credit and debit cards, including the personal identification numbers (PINs) of its customers. The hackers gained access to Target's system by using the stolen login credentials of a Target vendor—a heating-and-air-conditioning contractor. In 2017, this successful cyberattack has prompted financial institutions to take a hard look at the security practices of thousands of their vendors who have access to their systems, causing a strain on business relationships as banks try to secure their IT environments.[1]

Rank	United States	Canada
1.	Securing the IT environment	Securing the IT environment
2.	Managing and retaining data	Managing and retaining data
3.	Managing IT risk and compliance	Managing IT risk and compliance
4.	Ensuring privacy	Ensuring privacy
5.	Enabling decision support and analytics	Enabling decision support and analytics
6.	Managing systems implementations	Managing systems implementations
7.	Preventing and responding to computer fraud	Preventing and responding to computer fraud
8.	Governing and managing IT investment/spending	Governing and managing IT investment/spending
9.	Leveraging emerging technologies	Leveraging emerging technologies
10.	Managing vendors and service providers	Managing vendors and service providers

FIGURE 3-1   The AICPA's 2014 top 10 information technologies for the United States and Canada. Source: AICPA.

---

[1] Sidel, R. January 31, 2017. Banks try to thwart hackers, take aim at vendors. *The Wall Street Journal.* Accessed at www.wsj.com.

3.3 INPUT, PROCESSING, AND OUTPUT DEVICES

A computer system includes the computer itself—for example, a microcomputer—as well as the keyboards, printers, hard disks, and similar devices that help the computer perform input and output tasks. These devices are commonly called **peripheral equipment** because they typically surround a computer and help it process data.

One way to classify peripheral equipment is by the tasks they perform. Thus, *input equipment* (such as keyboards) enable users to enter data into a computer system, *output equipment* (such as printers) enable users to see processed results, *secondary storage devices* (such as hard disks) enable users to store data for future reference, and *communications equipment* (such as internal networking cards) enable users to transmit data over data networks. As with any other system, these distinct pieces of computer equipment must work together to accomplish data processing tasks. Figure 3-2 provides examples of these devices and short descriptions of each. Note the many acronyms.

Most accounting transactions are processed in a three-phase operation called the **input–processing–output cycle**. For convenience, we look at technologies that assist AISs in each of these areas in this order.

Input Devices

The starting point of the input–processing–output cycle—especially when processing accounting data—is input. Thus, even where the amount of data is small, most AISs require input methods and procedures that ensure complete, accurate, timely, and cost-effective ways of gathering and inputting accounting data. Usually, there are several ways of capturing accounting data, so systems designers must pick those input procedures and devices that best meet these system objectives.

Source Documents and Data Transcription. The starting point for collecting accounting data in most AISs is a **source document**. Manual examples include time cards, packing slips, employee application forms, patient intake forms, purchase invoices, sales invoices, cash disbursement vouchers, and travel reimbursement forms. Computerized examples include airline reservation screens, bank deposit screens, and Web-based customer-order forms.

Source documents are important to AISs because (1) they are human-readable and (2) they can be completed by the user onsite. Source documents are also important because they provide evidence of a transaction's authenticity (e.g., a signed voucher authorizes a cash disbursement), are the starting point of an audit trail, and (in emergencies) can serve as backup in the event that the computer files created from them are damaged or destroyed.

The greatest disadvantage of manually prepared source documents is that they are not machine-readable. Thus, in order to process source-document data electronically, the data must first be transcribed into machine-readable media. This **data transcription** is mostly an inefficient, labor-intensive, time-consuming, costly, and nonproductive process that has the potential to bottleneck data at the transcription site, embed errors in the transcribed data, and provide opportunities for fraud, embezzlement, or sabotage. Is it any wonder, then, that most AISs capture data that are already in machine-readable formats? The paragraphs that follow describe some devices that overcome these problems.

Type	Device	Description
Input	ATMs	The automated teller machines found at banks and shopping malls.
	Bar code scanners	The scanners that read such bar codes as the UPC code found on products at Wal-Mart or the ISBN codes of books sold on Amazon.com.
	Biometric scanners	Devices such as fingerprint readers, palm readers, retinal scanners, iris scanners, and voice recognition systems.
	Digital pens	Stylus pens with wires that enable you to "write" on a glass screen. Many retailers now ask you to sign for credit card purchases with one.
	Keyboard	Used on computers, tablets, and smart phones.
	Mag strips	The magnetic bands typically found on credit and debit cards.
	MICR	The magnetic ink character recognition used by banks to read the code at the bottom of a personal check.
	Mouse	A handheld device you use to point or click on screen icons and text.
	OCR	Many utility bills and mortgage coupons are read by optical character recognition readers.
	Pointing stick or joy stick	A small, button or directional lever that controls the position of your cursor onscreen.
	POSs	The point-of-sale terminals that resemble cash registers and found in many retail establishments.
	RFID	Radio frequency identification—the ability to interpret the signals reflected by RFID chips.
	Touch screen	A display screen that also allows you to touch icons to make choices. Most cell phones use them.
	Touchpad	The familiar pad found on many microcomputers to control the cursor onscreen.
	Web cam	A real-time video camera that broadcasts your image over the Web.
Processors and primary memory	CPU	The central processing unit or main processor of a computer.
	Cache memory	Fast computer memory that interfaces between the CPU and primary storage.
	Microprocessor	Another term for a CPU.
	Primary memory	The internal memory of a computer, as opposed to secondary storage, and now typically measured in gigabytes.
	Tablet	A small device with a screen for input and output, and a processor that allows the owner to use it. Examples include iPads and Kindle Fires.
Output devices	CRT screens	Older display screens that use cathode ray tubes.
	Ink-jet printer	A printer that creates output by spraying tiny droplets of ink on a page to form characters.
	Laser printer	A printer that creates output using a laser to sensitize portions of the print page, which then attracts toner.
	LCD screens	Flat display screens that use liquid crystal technology to display images.
	LED screens	Computer screens that use light-emitting diodes to display images.
	Voice output	A computer's ability to output spoken language.
Secondary storage devices	CD-ROM drive	A device that reads a compact audio disk.
	DVD drive	A device that reads a DVD (digital video disk).
	Hard disk drive	The hard disks typically found in microcomputers.
	USB drive	A portable device containing flash (solid-state) memory.

FIGURE 3-2 A brief summary of selected computer devices.

1. Clerical errors, such as a salesperson's incorrect reading of a price tag, are detectable and even potentially correctable, automatically.
2. Such standard procedures as the computation of a sales tax, the multiplication of prices times quantities sold, or the calculation of a discount can be performed using the register terminal as a calculator.
3. Processing errors caused by illegible sales slips can be reduced.
4. Credit checks and answers to questions about customers' account balances are routinely handled by using the cash register as an inquiry terminal.
5. The inventory-disbursement data required for inventory control are collected as a natural part of the sales transaction.
6. A breakdown listing of sales by type of inventory item, dollar volume, sales clerk, or store location is possible because the data required for such reports are collected automatically with the sales transaction and may be stored for such use.
7. Sales and inventory personnel levels can be reduced because the manual data processing functions required of such personnel have largely been eliminated.

FIGURE 3-3   Advantages of POS systems.

POS Devices.   Because most of the information required by retailers can be captured at the checkout counter, such businesses now commonly use automated **point-of-sale (POS) devices** to gather and record pertinent data electronically at that time. One example is the **bar code readers** that interpret the *universal product code (UPC)* commonly printed on supermarket and variety store items. POS systems allow retailers to centralize price information in online computers, avoid the task of affixing price stickers to individual items on retail store shelves, and update prices easily when required. With such systems, for example, the sales data obtained at the checkout station of a convenience store can be transmitted directly to a computer where they can be verified for accuracy, reasonableness, and completeness and also stored for later uses—for example, preparing sales reports. Figure 3-3 lists other advantages of POS data collection systems, which are actually growing in use despite the maturity of the technology.

UPC codes are not the only example of business uses of bar codes. Other applications include transportation applications for tracking shipments (e.g., Federal Express), warehousing for logging received or sent merchandise, universities for identifying equipment, airlines for authenticating boarding passes, and publishers for identifying books using ISBN numbers (e.g., see the bar code on the back of this book).

Case-in-Point 3.2   IATA—the International Air Transport Association—standardized its two-dimensional bar-coded boarding pass system for all national and international airlines almost 10 years ago. IATA claims that these codes offer more convenience to passengers, who can now print their own boarding passes on standard stock paper or simply download the bar codes to their cell phones.[2] IATA estimates that these bar codes save the airline industry $1.5 billion annually.[3]

Magnetic Ink Character Recognition.   **Magnetic ink character recognition (MICR)** refers to the odd-looking numbers and symbols magnetically encoded on the bottom

---

[2] No author. 2016. "Bar-Coded Boarding Pass (BCBP)," The International Air Transport Association (IATA) (June 1), accessed at www.iata.org, March 2017.
[3] www.iata.org, accessed March 2017.

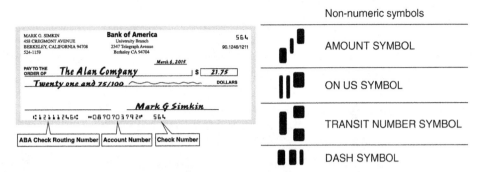

FIGURE 3-4   The MICR symbols of the American Banking Association (ABA).

of bank checks (Figure 3-4)—a standard created by the American National Standards Institute (ANSI). One advantage of the MICR standard is that it is machine-readable by any bank, thus allowing you to write a check anywhere in the United States or Canada. Another advantage is that MICR coding is both machine-readable and human-readable. Yet, a third advantage is that the coding is quite flexible, allowing banks to use documents of varying sizes, thicknesses, or widths. The chief disadvantage of MICR is that the magnetic strength (called the "magnetic flux") of the characters diminishes over time. This makes MICR documents unreliable when they must be input repeatedly.

Optical Character Recognition.   **Optical character recognition (OCR)** uses optical, rather than magnetic, readers to interpret the data found on source documents. Typical OCR devices use light-sensing mechanisms and laser technology to perform the character recognition function required to interpret recorded data. **Mark-sense media** (such as the type used in computerized exams) use simple rectangles or ovals as "characters" that you blacken with a pencil. More sophisticated versions of OCR can read complete character sets of numbers and letters (Figure 3-5) and are therefore more versatile as input.

Accounting uses of OCR include the billing statements of public utility companies, the payment slips of credit card companies, the payment coupons of mortgage companies, and the renewal forms of magazine subscriptions. Most of these are **turnaround documents**—that is, documents that a company sends to individuals and that recipients eventually return for further data processing. As with MICR encoding, the chief advantage of OCR is a source document that is both human- and machine-readable.

Plastic Cards with Magnetic Strips.   Do you own a credit or debit card? Then you own a plastic card that has a magnetic strip attached to one side of it that can store permanent information and therefore provide input data when required. Typically, the "mag strip" stores information for the user—for example, a credit card number, a hotel-room security code, or a security-clearance code for an employee. In the United States, the magnetic strip on these cards has been divided into distinct physical areas, and by agreement, each major industry using these cards has its own assigned space. Thus, the International Airline Transport Association (IATA), the American Banking Association (ABA), and the savings and loan industry each encode information pertinent to their individual needs on such plastic cards without fear that, by accident, these cards will be misused in another application.

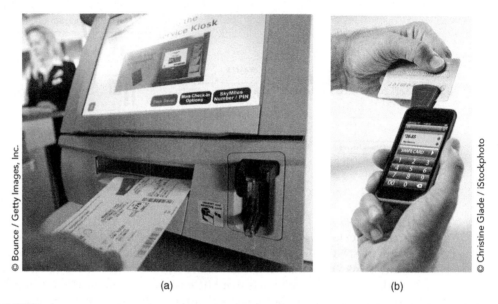

© Bounce / Getty Images, Inc.

© Christine Glade / iStockphoto

(a)   (b)

FIGURE 3-5   Two common input devices. (a) This versatile input device at the airport can read OCR characters, bar codes, or magnetic strips. (b) This credit card reader from Squareup™ allows small business owners such as plumbers or limousine drivers to use their cell phones for customer credit-card payments.

AISs use mag-strip cards to capture data when individuals or employees use them. For example, credit cards can include PIN numbers that automated teller machines (ATMs) can examine every time someone uses the card. This increases the security of the card, facilitates data gathering, and automates the data collection process.

Case-in-Point 3.3   In the United States, many gambling casinos issue mag-strip "club cards" to their customers, who use them as internal credit cards for playing slot machines, poker machines, and so forth. These cards serve to free customers from the task of cashing checks or getting change. But these same cards also enable casinos to gather data on player activities—information that managers can subsequently use to make better decisions about extending credit limits or providing complimentary meals and hotel rooms.[4]

Small-System Input Devices.   Many specialized devices now help users input data to computer systems. *Keyboards* are perhaps the most common. *Computer mice, touch pads, joy sticks,* and similar devices enable users to control a screen cursor, create graphic images, reposition screen objects, or select items from display menus. *Touch screens* such as those on cell phones and computer tablets enable users to make menu choices simply by touching a display screen with a finger or stick. *Computer pens or styluses* permit users to enter data on video screens. See again Figure 3-2.

Video Input.   **Digital video input** includes digital cameras, camcorders, web cams, and similar devices. Although many people only use such devices in recreational settings, accountants also use them for documenting (1) inventories of large assets such as

---

[4] From the authors.

trucks, cranes, and buildings; (2) damage to vehicles or offices due to accidents, vandalism, or natural disasters for insurance purposes; and (3) new or existing employees for identification and security purposes. As with many cell phones, some digital cameras can upload pictures directly to the Internet—an advantage, for example, when instant documentation is useful. As suggested by the following Case-in-Point, the benefits of digital photographs—the ability to store, display, reproduce, and transmit them electronically—must be weighed against their potential social costs.

Case-in-Point 3.4 Red-light cameras automate the process of ticketing motorists who drive through red traffic lights. Such cameras enable municipalities to enforce driving laws at busy or dangerous traffic intersections and often substantially increase revenues from traffic violations. Red-light proponents argue that these cameras reduce accidents and allow government agencies to fund other police work or educational expenses. Critics counter that the cameras are revenue generators and that they are unconstitutional. In a class-action lawsuit in Chicago, a judge in 2016 disagreed and dismissed the lawsuit.[5]

Biometric Scanners. Many accounting applications must verify that a user has legitimate access to a system—for example, can view corporate personnel files. Authentication systems based on *what you know* require you to input codes, passwords, or similar values. These are low-security systems because users can easily forget, lose, or guess such information, making these systems vulnerable to attack and misuse. Systems based on *what you have* require physical keys, magnetic cards, or similar physical media—but suffer many of the same problems as password-based authenticating systems.

    Biometric scanners authenticate users based on *who they are. Behavioral systems* recognize signatures, voices, walking gaits, or keystroke dynamics. *Physiological systems* recognize fingerprints, irises, retinas, faces, and even ears. Most of these devices connect directly to computer USB ports or are integrated into computer keyboards or cell phones. Two of the most common biometric systems use fingerprint or iris scanners to authenticate users (Figure 3-6). While most fingerprints have similar features, experts have yet to discover pairs with the same minute details since 1892 when records were kept. (This uniqueness even applies to identical twins.) Iris and retinal scans record patterns in the colored portion (for irises) or veining patterns (for retinas) of the eye and are even more accurate than fingerprints. This is because of the wider variability in coloration patterns and the fact that these patterns for even the right and left eyes of the same person are not identical.

Case-in-Point 3.5 The AICPA requires the fingerprints of all candidates wishing to take the CPA exam. The system, maintained by Prometric, matches each candidate's fingerprint with other personal identification in order to increase the security and integrity of the exams. According to the National Association of State Boards of Accountancy (NASBA): "During the check-in process, a candidate places his or her finger (generally the finger closest to the thumb on the right hand) on a small electronic device that electronically obtains an image of the fingerprint. For candidates returning from breaks or for candidates returning to re-take a test or a different test section, the stored fingerprint templates are used to confirm that the returning candidate is the same person."[6]

---

[5] Kidwell, D. April 1, 2016. Judge throws out lawsuit challenging Chicago's red light cameras. *Chicago Tribune.* Accessed at www.chicagotribune.com, March 2017.
[6] nasba.org. Accessed March 2017.

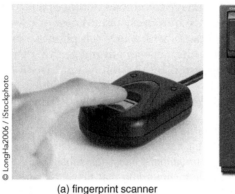
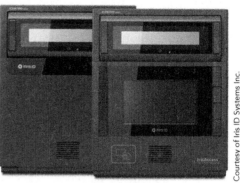

(a) fingerprint scanner   (b) iris scanner

FIGURE 3-6   (a) An inexpensive USB fingerprint scanner. (b) An inexpensive iris scanner. Biometric authentication begins with *enrollment*—the process of creating digital templates for legitimate users. Template files are small, requiring about 256 bytes for a fingerprint and 512 bytes for an iris scan. To authenticate a user, the scanner takes a new sample from the individual and compares it to known templates. Unlike passwords, the new samples will not perfectly match the template, requiring a biometric system to use proprietary mathematical algorithms to determine when the new sample is "close enough."

Central Processing Units

Once data have been captured (and perhaps transcribed into machine-readable formats), they usually must be processed to be valuable to decision-makers. These are the processing tasks of the **central processing unit (CPU)** of a computer system (Figure 3-7). The computer industry often uses the terms *computer* and *CPU* interchangeably.

Computing power starts with the most limited tablets and microcomputers (aka "personal computers" or "PCs") and increases in such capabilities as speed, multiuser support, and peripheral equipment with **minicomputers**, **mainframe computers**, and **supercomputers**. Some people describe computing today as the "post PC era." Electronic readers, **computer tablets** such as the Kindle and iPad, and smart cell phones are examples of devices that help define this vision. Although many people buy these devices for personal uses, commercial applications are now widely available—a trend popularly called **BYOD (bring your own device)**. We provide one example in the following Case-in-Point, and another example in the AIS in Action feature at the end of this chapter.

Case-in-Point 3.6   Professional drivers now have access to a tablet that "does it all" in Rand McNally's android TND(TM) Tablet. While trucking, the tablet offers drivers: (1) trip-planning software and navigation; (2) an eBook of the "Motor Carriers Road Atlas"; (3) a dashboard camera that records the road ahead; (4) tracking of fuel costs and mileage; (5) an accounting system for operators and owners, which includes output for month end tax filings; (6) real-time posting and searching for loads and trucks; and (7) e-mail and submission of documents on the go. The tablet improves the efficiency of operations and cuts down on the use of paper.[7]

---

[7] PR Newswire. February 9, 2015. Rand McNally releases game-changing "TND(TM) tablet" for professional drivers: The first-ever tablet designed for use in the truck, business, and life. New York.

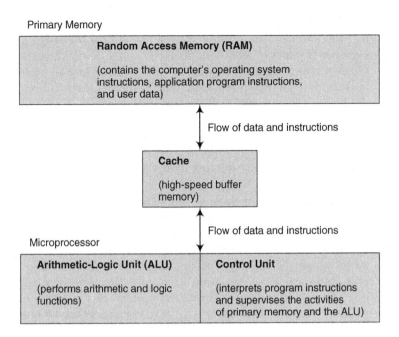

Primary Memory

FIGURE 3-7   A schematic of a central processing unit. In some computers, the "Level 2" (high-speed buffer) cache is part of the microprocessor unit.

The accounting systems of the smallest businesses—for example, a bicycle-repair shop—can often be implemented entirely on a desktop computer. In contrast, the inventory control systems of the nation's largest vendors—for example, Wal-Mart—require multiuser systems that may employ several centralized mainframes working in tandem. One of the biggest challenges facing businesses today is identifying the right combination of computing technologies—that is, computers of various sizes, networks, and related software—that best meet their IT needs. Dollar for dollar, organizations usually get the most processing power and the cheapest software with microcomputers, which helps explain why modern organizations buy so many of them. Reasons to retain older mainframe systems include (1) the need to support multiuser processing capabilities that work best on such systems, (2) the advantages of centralized processing—for example, simplified control over hardware, software, and user accesses to databases, and (3) the huge costs that organizations typically incur when replacing these **legacy systems**.

Primary Memory.   Figure 3-7 indicates that the two main components of a CPU are its primary memory and its microprocessor. *Cache* or buffer memory serves as the interface between these components. The purpose of **primary memory** is to store data and program instructions temporarily for immediate processing and execution. In microcomputers, this primary or *random access memory (RAM)* consists of individual *bytes,* each capable of storing a single character of data—for example, a letter or punctuation mark. RAM capacities are typically measured in *gigabytes* (billions of bytes). Most accounting software requires minimum amounts of primary memory to operate properly, so "RAM size" is often a key concern when matching computer hardware to software requirements for smaller AIS applications.

Microprocessors. Computers cannot manipulate data or execute instructions directly in primary memory. Rather, the CPU's **microprocessor** performs these tasks. An example is Intel Corporation's Core™ i7 chips. The *arithmetic-logic unit (ALU)* portion of the microprocessor performs arithmetic tasks (such as addition and multiplication) as well as logic tasks (such as data comparisons). In contrast, the *control unit* of the processor supervises the actual data processing—for example, transferring data from primary memory to the ALU, performing the required task (adding two numbers together), and transferring the answer back to primary memory. Multicore processors such as Intel's quad-core models integrate more than one processor on the same chip, thus potentially improving processing speeds beyond those of single-core chips.

Computers, Processor Speeds, and AISs. The most important thing to know about processor speeds is that they are rarely important in accounting applications. This is because the input–processing–output cycle characteristic of most accounting tasks requires input and output operations as well as processing procedures in order to perform specific tasks. An example is a payroll application, which must input, process, and output the data from each time card. The speeds of the input/output (I/O) operations involved in this application are much slower than the internal speeds of the processor(s), thus explaining why most computers are **I/O-bound**, not process-bound. What this means to accounting applications is that designers must typically look elsewhere for ways to speed computer *throughput*—that is, the time it takes to process business transactions such as payroll time cards—for example, by employing faster data transmissions.

Output Devices

Accounting data are meaningless if they cannot be output in forms that are useful and convenient to end users. Printed, **hard-copy output** is one possibility, but video or soft-copy output on monitor screens, audio output, and file output to secondary storage devices such as hard disks are other possibilities that we explore here. Outputs are especially important to AISs because "outputs" are usually the basis of managerial decision-making and therefore the goal of the entire system.

Printers. The hope for a *paperless office* has yet to be realized, and most AISs still produce many types of printed outputs—for example, transaction summaries, financial statements, exception reports, spreadsheet-based budget reports, word processing documents, and graphs. Many printers now also perform the functions of fax machines, copiers, and scanners, enabling these devices to serve as input devices, transmission devices, and stand-alone copying devices.

Printers fall into three general categories: (1) dot-matrix, (2) ink-jet, and (3) laser. **Dot-matrix printers** are impact printers that employ tiny wires in a print head to strike an inked ribbon and create tiny dots on a print page. These printers are popular with small-business users because they are inexpensive and can print multipart ("carbon") paper—an important feature commonly used in commercial cash registers to print multiple copies of credit card receipts.

Ink-jet printers create characters by distributing tiny bubbles or dots of ink onto pages. The print resolutions of these printers (commonly measured in *dots per inch* or *dpi*) tend to be higher than those of dot-matrix printers, while the printing speeds (commonly measured in *pages per minute* or *ppm*) tend to be lower than those of laser printers. But most ink-jet printers can print in colors—a capability lacking in many dot-matrix printers—enabling them to print graphics and colored pictures as well as text documents.

Laser printers create printed output in much the same way as duplicating machines. The costs of laser printers are higher than those of dot-matrix or ink-jet printers, but the print quality is usually superior and output speeds are much faster. Laser printers are often the printer of choice for commercial users because of this speed advantage. Many laser printers can now also print in color. Additionally, many of the newer printers can be connected wirelessly to local area networks (LANs), allowing their owners to print documents from both local and remote locations.

Video Output. Because hard-copy outputs clutter offices with paper and take time to print, many AISs use faster, **soft-copy output**, that is, video screen displays instead. Computer monitors are perhaps the most common type of video output, but the airport display screens showing arrivals and departures, stadium scoreboards, highway billboards, and the signage of many private stores are also forms of computerized video outputs.

The monitors of most laptop and desktop computers use flat-panel, *liquid crystal display (LCD), light-emitting diode (LED), or plasma screens* to create video outputs in the same way that televisions do. The **picture elements (pixels)** in these types of screens are tiny, discrete dots of color that are arranged in a matrix. SVGA (super video graphics adapter) refers to a pixel matrix of about 1200 (in width) by 800 pixels (in height). High-definition displays such as found in HD TVs typically use 1280 pixels by 720 pixels. However, the exact dimensions are not standardized and vary with the manufacturer.

Multimedia. **Multimedia** combines video, text, graphics, animation, and sound to produce multidimensional output. By definition, multimedia presentations also require advanced processor chips, sound cards, and fast video cards to work properly. One accounting use of multimedia is storing the pictures of employees in personnel files. Another is recording verbal interviews with audit clients. A third is preparing instructional disks for tax accountants. Accounting uses of multimedia are likely to grow as the cost of producing multimedia applications becomes cheaper and accountants find new applications for this stimulating form of output. Have you watched a video on YouTube? That's multimedia!

3.4 SECONDARY STORAGE DEVICES

Primary memory is **volatile memory**, meaning memory that loses its contents when the computer loses electrical power. In contrast, AISs must store data on permanent media that maintain their accuracy and integrity, yet permit these systems to access and modify information quickly and easily. This is the purpose of **secondary storage** (also called *mass storage* or *auxiliary storage*). As with primary memory, the basic unit of secondary storage is a *byte*, and secondary storage capacities are measured in multiples of these—for example, megabytes or gigabytes. Figure 3-8 provides a table of common storage terms and their meanings.

In this section, we examine several types of secondary storage: magnetic (hard) disks, CD-ROMs, DVD disks, and USB flash disks. Common to all these media is

Term	Approximate Amount	Exact Amount
kilobyte	1 thousand bytes	2^10
megabyte	1 million bytes	2^20
gigabyte	1 billion bytes	2^30
terabyte	1 trillion bytes	2^40
petabyte	1 quadrillion bytes	2^50
exabyte	1 quintillion bytes	2^60

FIGURE 3-8 Units of computer storage.

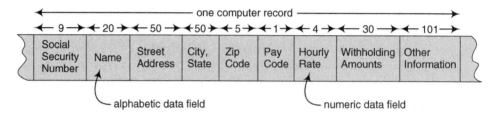

FIGURE 3-9 The format for the computer record of an employee on a payroll file.

the concept of a computer record. As with manual systems, computerized AISs must maintain information about payroll activities, warehouse inventories, and accounts-receivable data in permanent files. In each such file, a **computer record** is a collection of data fields about one file entity—for example, one employee on a payroll file (Figure 3-9).

Magnetic (Hard) Disks

A **magnetic (hard) disk** (Figure 3-10) consists of one or more spinning platters, each surface of which has an iron oxide coating that can be magnetized to record information. The smallest hard disks in laptop computers use only a single, double-sided platter, whereas larger-capacity hard disks use multiple platters. The disk system can access (or write) records from any portion of the platter by moving its read/write heads in toward the center of the disk platters or outward to their outer edges. To avoid contamination from dust or smoke particles, most hard disks are permanently sealed in their boxes.

To further guard against disk failures as well as increase storage capacities, manufacturers now also offer **redundant arrays of inexpensive disks (RAIDs)**. In effect, these are stacks of hard disks, each similar to the disk system shown in Figure 3-10. RAIDs are also commonly used for archiving functions—and therefore critical to AISs in the event of an unforeseen disaster.

One advantage of magnetic disk media is their large storage capacities—now commonly measured in *gigabytes* for microcomputers and *terabytes* or *petabytes* for commercial AISs. Another advantage of magnetic disks is their fast data transfer rates, which now can exceed 100 million characters per second. Finally, perhaps their most important advantage is their ability to directly access any specific record without sequential searching—a capability made possible by the fact that disk records are assigned individual addresses (as with postal addresses). This accessing capability is useful for such online applications as airline reservations or bank account inquiries

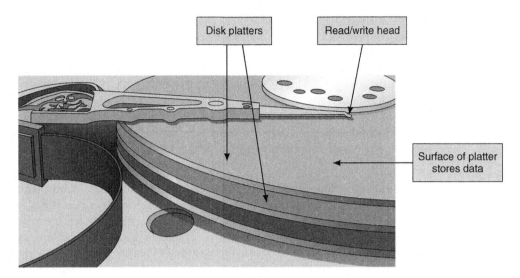

FIGURE 3-10 A schematic of a multiplatter hard disk. The read/write head assembly moves the read/write heads inward (toward the central spindle) or outward as needed, allowing the system to access the data on any portion of any platter.

when users require immediate access to specific records and explains why magnetic disks are also called *direct access storage devices (DASDs)*.

CD-ROMs, DVDs, and Blu-Ray Discs

Three types of secondary storage devices currently popular with microcomputer users are CD-ROMS, DVDs, and Blue Ray Discs. All three media store data digitally and read disk information optically.

CD-ROMs. The term **CD-ROM** is an acronym for "compact disk-read only memory." The name is appropriate because CD-ROMs are the same size and appearance as audio CDs. CD-ROMs contain microscopic pits etched along a spiraling track in their substrate surfaces. Laser beams create or interpret the presence or absence of a pit as the "one" or "zero" of binary codes.

CD-ROMs come in three types. The oldest, prerecorded versions are similar to those on which music or software is distributed. Newer, "CD-R" media are blank CD-ROMs that can be recorded (only once) with inexpensive CD encoding devices. These are **worm (write-once, read-many) media**. Finally, the newest "CD-RW" media are rewritable, allowing AISs to use them as low-capacity hard disks.

One advantage of CD-ROMs is the fact that they are a removable medium with storage capacities in excess of 700 megabytes per disk—the equivalent of 300,000 pages of text! This makes CD-ROMs ideal for storing large amounts of accounting data or reference materials. Because CD-ROMs are read with laser beams, data transfer rates are also very fast and wear and tear is minimal, even with continuous usage. Finally, the worm characteristic of CD-ROMs and CD-rs makes them useful for archiving files securely (i.e., storing files on a medium that cannot be changed). But CD-ROMs suffer from at least one drawback—the fact that worm media cannot be updated (because new information cannot be written on them once they have been encoded).

DVDs. A **digital video disk (DVD)** closely resembles a CD-ROM in that it is also a 5-inch plastic disk that uses a laser to encode microscopic pits in its substrate surface. But the pits on a DVD are much smaller and encoded much closer together than those on a CD-ROM. In addition, a DVD can have two layers on each of its two sides (compared to the single-layered, single-sided CD-ROM). The end result is a medium that can hold as much as 17 gigabytes of data—over 25 times the capacity of a standard CD-ROM disk. The two greatest advantages of DVDs are therefore (1) a storage capacity that enables users to archive large amounts of data and (2) a single, lightweight, reliable, easily transportable medium. Newer DVDs are writeable and even rewriteable.

Blu-Ray Discs. **Blu-ray disc** (BD) writers encode the same-sized disk (disc) medium as CDs and DVDs, but the disks can store more information on them—up to 27 gigabytes of data for a single-layered disk or almost 128 gigabytes for a quad-layer disk. The disks first became commercially available in 2006, and their name comes from the blue color of the shorter-wavelength laser beams used to encode and read the disks. BD-Rs are read-only media that can only be written once, while BD-REs can be erased and rerecorded multiple times. At present, most Blu-ray discs in the United States and Canada store movies and video games, mainly because the standard format for them enables easy recording in high definition and also inhibits illegal copying better than DVD formats. But accounting applications are growing—especially their use as a backup medium.

Flash Memory

Flash memory is solid-state memory that comes in various forms. Examples include the flash drives that use the USB ports of microcomputers, the Personal Computer Memory Card International Association (more commonly known as PCMCIA) memory cards used with laptops, the memory sticks used in digital cameras, and the memory cards used with video games. The term "solid state" means that there are no moving parts—everything is electronic rather than mechanical.

USB drives can store gigabytes of data in an erasable format. Because data transfer rates are high and the devices themselves are compact, they are particularly useful to accountants for creating backups of important files and transporting them offsite. Costs are low—for example, under $20 for the smaller-capacity USB drives.

Image Processing and Record Management Systems

The life cycle of business documents begins with their creation, continues with their storage and use, and ends with their destruction. Two important tools that can help managers with such tasks are image processing systems and record management systems.

Image Processing. **Image processing** allows users to store graphic images of business documents in digital formats on secondary storage media (e.g., the images of digital cameras). Thus, image processing systems are able to capture almost any type of document electronically, including photographs, flowcharts, drawings, and text pages containing handwritten signatures. Commercial users of image processing include: (1) insurance companies that use image processing to store claims forms and accident reports, (2) banks that use image processing to store check images, (3) hospitals that use image processing to store medical-diagnostic scans, and (4) the Internal Revenue Service that uses image processing to capture and store tax returns.

Image processing offers several advantages. One is the fast speeds at which images can be captured—a benefit of special importance to high-volume users such as banks. Another advantage is the reduced amount of physical storage space required (compared to paper storage). A third advantage is the convenience of storing images in computer records, which can then be sorted, classified, retrieved, or otherwise manipulated as needs require. A final advantage is the ability to store images in central files, thus making copies available to many users at once, even at the same time. (This last advantage is an important benefit to business and medical offices, where personnel no longer have to ask "who's got the file?")

Record Management Systems. Simple record management systems enable businesses to systematically capture and store documents. More modern **electronic document and record management systems (EDRMs)** extend such capabilities by helping organizations manage the workflow of electronic documents during their development and use, provide collaborative tools that enable several users to work on the same document, and allow organizations to create and store multiple versions of documents.

It is easy to understand why business and government organizations use EDRM tools. For legal reasons, for example, businesses may need to retain both current and old policy manuals, contracts, or employment records. Similarly, it is convenient to automate the termination of documents when contracts expire, employees quit, or new policies replace them.

3.5 DATA COMMUNICATIONS AND NETWORKS

Data communications refers to transmitting data to or from different locations. Many accounting applications use data communications in normal business operations. For example, banking systems enable individual offices to transmit deposit and withdrawal information to centralized computer locations, airline reservation systems enable travelers to book flights from remote locations, and stock brokerage systems enable brokers to transmit buy and sell orders for their customers. Accountants must understand data communication concepts because so many AISs use them and also because so many clients acquire AISs that depend upon them. In addition, auditors must sometimes audit the capabilities of a network—for example, evaluate its ability to transmit information accurately and to safeguard the integrity of the data during such transmissions.

Communication Channels and Protocols

A *communication channel* is the physical path that data take in data transmissions. Examples include: (1) the twisted-pair wires of older telephone land lines, (2) coaxial cables, (3) optical fibers, (4) microwaves, and (5) radio (cell phone or satellite) waves. Local area networking applications (discussed shortly) typically use the first three of these, while Internet applications often use all five of them.

To transmit data over these communication channels, the digital pulses of the sending computer must be translated into the sound patterns, light pulses, or radio waves of the communications channel. Over voice-grade telephone lines, this translation is performed by a **modem** (an acronym for "modulator–demodulator"). The transmission rates are commonly measured in *bits per second (bps)*.

ISDN (integrated services digital network) is an international data communications standard that transmits data, voice message, or images at a standard rate of 128k bps over the Internet. A similar data transmission service is a **digital subscriber line (DSL)**, which supports data communications rates up to 9 megabits per second. Finally, large data communications installations using fiber optic cables and similar wide-band channels can currently transmit data up to 266 million bps. Future optic fiber transmission rates will transmit data at speeds up to 73.7 terabits per second—nearly the speed of light.[8]

In all data communication applications, the sending and receiving stations must use a compatible transmission format. A **data communications protocol** refers to the settings that provide this format. Two common protocols are *TCP (transmission control protocol)*, which networks commonly use for e-mails, and *HTTP (hypertext transmission protocol)*, which networks commonly use for Web pages.

Local and Wide Area Networks

One important use of data communications is in **local area networks (LANs)**. Figure 3-11 shows that a LAN consists of microcomputers, printers, terminals, and similar devices that are connected together for communications purposes. Most LANs use **file servers** to store centralized software and data files and also to coordinate data transmissions among the other LAN devices and users. Most LANs occupy a single building, although LANs covering several buildings are also common. In the past, installers hard-wired LAN devices together. Today, many LANs are wireless—a convenience to users—who no longer need to worry about where to place computer equipment in their offices—but an added security hazard to network administrators.

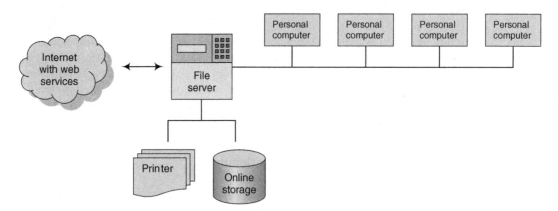

FIGURE 3-11 A local area network with representative devices.

---

[8] Tickle, G. 2013. New fiber network clocks in at 99.7% speed of light, 73.7 terabits per second. Accessed from www.geekosystem.com, March 26.

LANs provide several users access to common hardware, software, and computer files, as well as to each other. Some advantages of LANs are as follows:

1. *Facilitating communications.* The number-one reason why businesses install LANs today is to support e-mail.

2. *Sharing computer equipment.* For example, a LAN can provide users access to the same printers or Internet servers.

3. *Sharing computer files.* LANs enable several users to input or output data to or from the same accounting files.

4. *Saving software costs.* It is often cheaper to buy a single software package for a LAN than to buy individual packages for each of several workstations.

5. *Enabling unlike computer equipment to communicate with one another.* Not all computers use the same operating system (OS) or application software. LANs enable different computers using different software to communicate with one another.

Wide area networks (WANs) are computer networks spanning regional, national, or even global areas. For example, a WAN enables a national manufacturing company to connect several manufacturing, distribution, and regional centers to national headquarters and, therefore, to each other for communications purposes (see Figure 3-12). WANs typically use a multitude of communications channels for this purpose, including leased phone lines, microwave transmitters, and perhaps even satellite transmissions. Rather than developing and maintaining their own WANs, many organizations employ public carriers, the Internet, or third-party network vendors to transmit data electronically.

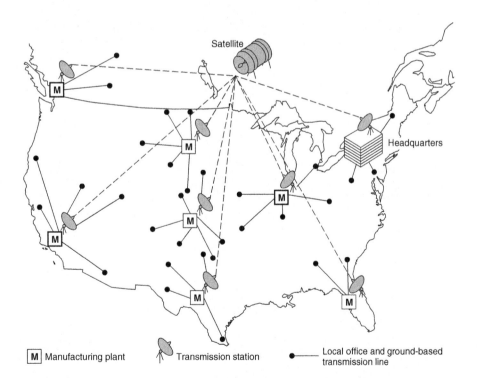

FIGURE 3-12 A wide area network that a large organization might use to connect regional users and computers.

Case-in-Point 3.7 IGT is the world's largest slot machine manufacturer, but nearly half its profits derive from its Megabucks® system—a WAN of progressive slot machines located on the floors of participating casinos. In Nevada, the company links the machines together over private communications lines, enabling the company to both monitor its slot machines and display the growing jackpots in real time as customers play (see https://www.megajackpots.com/games/megabucks-in-nevada.aspx) To date, Megabucks has paid more than $1.0 billion in major jackpots. The world record in slot jackpots was a Megabucks jackpot of $39 million, won in March 2003.[9]

AISs use WANs to gather financial data from remote sites, distribute accounting information to and from headquarters, and support e-mail communications among users. WANs are therefore typically complex, multifaceted systems that serve many users for many purposes. For example, the WANs of large *Internet service providers (ISPs)* such as America Online allow subscribers to access centralized databases over the Internet. Similarly, regional supermarket chains use WANs to gather inventory data, cash receipts data, and sales information from the many stores in their chains. WANs can also be dedicated to specific tasks. For example, most bank ATMs are connected to WANs for the purpose of centralizing customer account information.

Many WANs are organized in a hierarchy, in which the individual microcomputers of a specific branch office are connected to a file server on a LAN, the file servers of several LANs are connected to a regional computer, and several regional computers are connected to a corporate mainframe. This hierarchical approach allows a large company to gather, store, and distribute financial and nonfinancial information at the appropriate geographic level of the company.

A recently developed WAN technology is taking the market by storm. SD-WAN, a simplified, cost-effective alternative to traditional WANs, integrates well with public cloud services and meets the growing requirements of cloud computing. SD-WAN offers enhanced performance and accelerated delivery. So how does SD-WAN differ from traditional WAN? The "SD" stands for software-defined. SD-WAN shifts traffic monitoring from physical devices to the software (hence, the SD prefix). In other words, the software fully automates control of the data and, for example, is more cost-effective by sending low-priority, nonsensitive data over cheaper public networks rather than private networks. SD-WAN also improves network security—the number-one issue for accountants, as identified in the AICPA's top 10 technologies.

Case-in-Point 3.8 Perkins Coie, a worldwide legal advisory service, successfully transitioned from traditional WAN to SD-WAN to accelerate branch office connectivity. With 19 offices and more than 1,000 attorneys in the United States and Asia, Perkins Coie is experienced in navigating the complexities of managing remote offices and the challenges of servicing demanding users. As Perkins Coie's WAN network demands grew, so did the problems. Attorneys faced long wait times and began receiving error messages when checking out documents from the firm's document management system. The IT team could not meet its commitment of a 90-minute recovery time. So, the IT team overhauled WAN with SD-WAN. There was a significant improvement in performance. Users stopped complaining about IT and jobs that previously required hours to complete and were finished in less than 30 minutes.[10]

---

[9] IGT, www.igt.com. Accessed March 2017.
[10] Anonymous. September 29, 2014. Silver Peak Systems, Inc.; Perkins Coie builds software-defined wide area network with Silver Peak. *Network Business Weekly* (Atlanta): 184.

Client/Server Computing

Client/server computing is an alternate technology to mainframe and/or hierarchical networks. Depending on the type of client/server system, the data processing can be performed by any computer on the network. The software application, such as a spreadsheet program, resides on the client computer—typically, a microcomputer, tablet, or cell phone. The database and related software are stored on file servers.

Although mainframe systems normally centralize everything (including the control of the system), client/server applications distribute data and software among the server and client devices on the system. As a result, client/server computing is a way to achieve the overall objective of an **enterprise network**. In so doing, more computing power resides in user devices, yet all online devices link together. The *Internet of things* captures the idea that soon most household appliances will be online clients enables us to check on them or control them from remote locations.

Components of Client/Server Systems. Figure 3-13 shows that a client/server system may be viewed as a set of three interacting components: (1) a presentation component, (2) an application-logic component, and (3) a data-management component. The *presentation component* of a client/server system is the user's view of the system—that is, what the user sees onscreen. This view may resemble the familiar screens of the user's cell phone or home computer or may differ considerably from them. Simple client/server systems that focus on this presentation task are called *distributed presentation systems*. Most Internet applications illustrate this category.

The *application-logic component* of a client/server system refers to the processing logic of a specific application—for example, the logic involved in preparing payroll checks. Thus, client/server computing differs from simple "host/terminal computing" in the user's new ability to (1) query or manipulate the warehoused data on the server, (2) ask what-if questions of the server's data, (3) process a transaction that may affect data stored on both client and server computers, or (4) alter data stored elsewhere on the network. Some systems enable users to write their own data queries (that ask for specific information from the server database) and also to store such queries on local files for later uses.

The processing tasks involved in an application are typically shared unequally between the client device and the server, with the division of labor depending upon the particular application. For example, in a payroll application, the client's

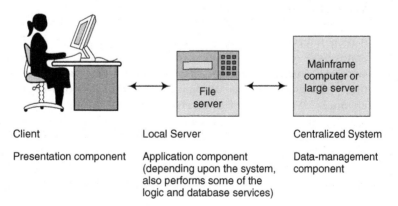

Client
Presentation component

Local Server
Application component
(depending upon the system,
also performs some of the
logic and database services)

Centralized System
Data-management
component

FIGURE 3-13 Components of a client/server system.

contribution may be limited to validating the data entered into the system, while in a word-processing application, the client computer might perform nearly all the computational tasks required.

Finally, the *data-management component* of a client/server system refers to its databases and data-storage systems. Some applications rely on a centralized mainframe for this task. More typically, however, multiple copies of the databases reside on large, regional file servers, thereby speeding user access to the data they contain. These systems are also the most complex and therefore pose the greatest challenges to accountants for control and audit tasks.

Advantages and Disadvantages. One advantage of client/server computing is the flexibility of distributing hardware, software, data, and processing capabilities throughout a computer network. A further advantage can be reduced telecommunications costs—an advantage that enabled Avis Rent-a-Car to save a half-minute on each of its 23 million annual customer calls and therefore $1 million. A third advantage is the ability to install *thin-client systems*, which use inexpensive or diskless microcomputers, instead of more expensive models, to save money on system acquisition and maintenance costs. The managers of Mr. Gatti's, a Texas chain of 300 pizza restaurants, for example, estimate that it will save about 45% on its maintenance costs using such a system.

One disadvantage of a large client/server system is that it must maintain multiple copies of the same databases, which it then stores on its various regional servers. This makes backup and recovery procedures more difficult because multiple copies of the same file (or several parts of a single file) now exist on several different computers. This multiple-copy problem also causes difficulties in data synchronization (i.e., the need to update all copies of the same file when a change is made to any one of them).

Changing from one version of an application program to another is also more difficult in client/server systems because the system usually requires consistency in these programs across all servers. User access and security are also more difficult because access privileges may vary widely among employees or applications. Finally, the need for user training is often greater in client/server systems because employees must not only know how to use the data and application programs required by their jobs but also understand the system software that enables them to access these databases and programs from local work stations.

Wireless Data Communications

A recent survey by Intuit revealed that over 70% of the small businesses in the United States have mobile employees, and by all accounts, that number is growing. The term **wireless communications**, also called **Wi-Fi (wireless fidelity)**, means transmitting voice-grade signals or digital data transmissions over wireless communication channels. Wi-Fi creates a wireless network using access hubs and receiver cards in PCs, cell phones, and tablets, thereby turning them into cordless, multifunction "Web appliances." **Bluetooth** is a transmission standard for short-range wireless communications of cell phones, computers, and similar electronic devices.

Wireless devices have become important tools for business professionals, helping accountants in particular stay in touch with fellow employees, clients, and corporate networks. Early e-mailing uses of wireless communications have now been joined by such job-dependent financial functions as recording sales orders, entering time and billing information, and even preparing the payroll.

> ***Case-in-Point 3.9*** It wasn't until the middle of his son's little league game that Eddie Elizando realized he hadn't prepared the payroll for the employees at his small CPA company. Mr. Elizando was nowhere near his corporate office, but this wasn't a problem. Using his new iPhone, Mr. Elizando called his payroll service, entered data by clicking through the appropriate payroll program, and accomplished the task remotely between innings of the game. An added bonus: one of Mr. Elizando's employees was his wife, who still wanted to be paid![11]

The two key dimensions of Wi-Fi applications are "connectivity" and "mobility." The connectivity advantage means the ability to connect to the Internet, LAN, or WAN without physical wires or cables. To accomplish this, Wi-Fi devices use **wireless application protocol (WAP)**, a set of communications standards and *wireless markup language* (a subset of XML optimized for the small display screens typical of wireless, Internet-enabled appliances). Two important types of wireless communications are Radio frequency identification (RFID) applications and near-field communication (NFC) communications.

RFID. **Radio frequency identification (RFID)** enables businesses to identify pallets and even individual items without unpacking them from shipping crates. *Passive RFID tags* have no power source (and therefore cannot wear out), but can nonetheless respond to inquiries from energized sources. *Active RFID tags* are actually chips with antennas, have their own power source, enjoy ranges of more than 100 meters, and are generally more reliable than passive tags.

Perhaps the most noticeable use of RFID tags is as user identifiers in transportation systems (Figure 3-14). For example, the subway systems of New York City, Moscow, and Hong Kong use them, as do some of the toll roads and parking lots in the states of New York, New Jersey, Pennsylvania, Massachusetts, Georgia, Florida, and Illinois. Similar systems may be found in Paris, the Philippines, Israel, Australia, Chile, and Portugal. To toll-road travelers, RFID systems reduce wait times at tollbooths and represent a convenient way of paying user fees. To their operators, these systems help gather accounting data and update customer accounts.

> ***Case-in-Point 3.10*** RFID applications include employee ID badges, library books, credit cards, and even tire-tread sensors. Wal-Mart and Target are two companies on a growing list of large retailers that now require their major suppliers to include RFID tags in the cases and pallets sent to their distribution centers. The tags are superior to bar codes, which require a line of sight for reading, must appear on the outside of cartons, and can be lost or defaced. Bank of America and Wells Fargo are two of the largest RFID users, with each tagging over 100,000 corporate assets. If your car has a keyless ignition system, you're also using RFID technology.[12]

---

[11] Defelice, A. 2007. Working in a wireless world. *Accounting Technology* 23(10): 30–34.
[12] Desjardins, D. 2005. Implementation easier as No. 2. *DSN Retailing Today* 44(7): 34.

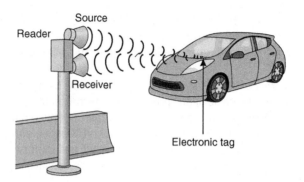

FIGURE 3-14 Reading an RFID tag at a tollbooth.

NFC. **Near-field communication (NFC)** enables mobile devices such as cell phones, credit cards, and even hotel keys to communicate with similar items containing NFC chips (Figure 3-15). With NFC devices, for example, you can make travel reservations on your PC, download airline tickets to your mobile device, and check in at a departure gate kiosk with a swipe of that device—all with no paper or printing. The operating range of NFC devices is limited to about 8 inches—a limitation that helps avoid unintentional uses.

Case-in-Point 3.11   The transit systems in China, Singapore, and Japan now use NFC systems, as do Visa International's credit card system and chip-enabled posters of the Atlanta Hawk's basketball team. Even the door to one of the author's university office building uses an NFC system instead of a key.

NFC technology is a joint product development of Sony, Philips, and Nokia. Three possible communication modes are (1) *active* (bidirectional), (2) *passive* (one way), and (3) *transponder* (batteryless and therefore only powered by an external communication source). NFC-standardized communication speeds are considerably less than the speeds of Bluetooth or Wi-Fi data transmissions. But passive NFC chips cost as little as 20 cents and are currently considerably cheaper than these alternate communications devices.

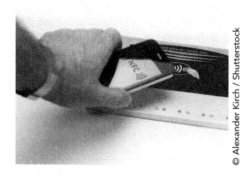

© Alexander Kirch / Shutterstock

FIGURE 3-15 Near-field communication devices.

Cloud Computing

The term cloud computing refers to a range of computing services on the Internet—for example, access to computer software programs, backup and recovery file services, and even Web page development and hosting. The term gets its name from the common use of a cloud symbol to represent the Internet itself—refer back to Figure 3-11. One commercial application of cloud computing is outsourcing—that is, a situation in which one organization hires another to perform a vital service. An accounting application is the use of tax preparation software, which the customer accesses over the Internet from the vendor for a fee—an example of **software as a service (SaaS)**. Many cloud service vendors have familiar names, including Amazon, Google, Yahoo, IBM, Intel, Sun Microsystems, and Microsoft.

3.6 COMPUTER SOFTWARE

As noted in the introduction to this chapter, it is impossible to discuss information technology without also recognizing the importance of computer software. Computer hardware serves as a base, or platform, upon which two types of computer software typically reside: (1) OSs and (2) application software. This chapter concludes by briefly discussing each of these types of software.

It is difficult to overstate the importance of software to AISs. In industry or in personal use, **computer software** helps us create spreadsheets, pay corporate bills, route parcels on conveyor belts, answer telephones, or reserve airline seats. Automated AISs depend on software to function properly. But this dependency also presents important challenges to accountants. For example, every system that influences cash accounts or affects other corporate resources must also contain automated controls to ensure the reliability, completeness, and authenticity of computer inputs, processing, and outputs. Similarly, all AIS software must initially be designed, acquired, and installed by someone. These facts help explain why accountants are often such an integral part of the teams that develop, shop for, test, or audit such systems.

> **Case-in-Point 3.12**   The managers of PepsiCo were surprised to discover that over 90% of those seeking jobs at the $65 billion snack-and-beverage company did so from their mobile phones. Responding to this discovery, the company built a mobile application (app) called Possibilities, and later, a mobile-friendly career site, to help applicants find job openings from their mobile devices. The result: an 800% increase in job applications started on phones. Software from Three Sparks, Jibe, and iMomentous also helps companies such as PepsiCo manage the applications submitted electronically by these job seekers.[13]

Operating Systems

An **operating system (OS)** is a set of software programs that helps a computer, file server, or network run itself and the application programs designed for it. Examples of OSs for microcomputers include macOS, Windows 10, and Linux. OSs

---

[13] Alsever, J. 2014. Objective: Hire top talent. *Fortune Magazine* (February 3): 40.

for larger computers include UNIX, Windows.Net server, and OS2. Some of these OSs are designed as single-user OSs (e.g., Windows 10), while others are designed as multiuser OSs for LANs (e.g., Windows NT Server and Novell Netware). OSs for very small systems such as cell phones include Windows Phone, Android, and Blackberry OS. Most of these OSs combine many convenient software tools in one package and use **graphical user interfaces (GUIs)** with menus, icons, and other graphic elements (instead of instruction commands) to identify system components and launch applications (apps).

On computers of any size, the OS is typically the first piece of software loaded (booted) into primary memory when the computer powers up. System tasks for single-user OSs include testing critical components on boot-up, allocating primary memory among competing applications (i.e., managing the multitasking demands of several Windows sessions), managing system files (such as directory files), maintaining system security, and (in larger computers) gathering system performance statistics. The system tasks for multiuser OSs are even more complicated than for single-user systems because more users are involved and more coordination of system resources is required. These multiuser OSs maintain job queues of programs awaiting execution, create and check password files, allocate primary memory among several online users, apportion computer time in time-sharing (multiprocessing) environments, and accumulate charges for resource usage.

Application (end-user) programs are designed to work with ("run under") a particular OS. An OS helps run application programs by coordinating those programs' input and output tasks, by managing the pieces of an application that are too large to fit entirely in RAM, and by monitoring their execution.

The **utility programs** that come with OSs help users perform such tasks as copying files, converting files from one format to another, compressing files, performing system diagnostics, and building disk directories. Another task is to manage **virtual storage**—disk memory that a computer system uses to augment its limited primary memory. Finally, today's OSs also run antivirus software. A **virus** is a destructive program that, when active, damages or destroys computer files or programs. Today's OSs include **antivirus software** routines that guard against the virus programs a user might accidentally introduce into his or her computer system from external sources. However, because new viruses continue to appear, users should update this software at least monthly.

Application Software

The term **application software** refers to computer programs that help end users such as accountants perform the tasks specific to their jobs or relevant to their personal needs. One category of application software is the **personal productivity software** familiar to most accountants—that is, word processing software (for creating documents and reports), spreadsheet software (for creating worksheets of rows and columns and also for graphing the data), database software (for creating files and databases of personal information), and personal finance software (for paying bills, creating personal budgets, and maintaining investment portfolio data).

Another category of application software is the personal productivity software designed for commercial uses. Examples include *project management software* (for coordinating and tracking the events, resources, and costs of large projects such as construction projects or office moves), *computer-aided design (CAD) software* (for designing consumer products, fashion clothing, automobiles, or machinery), and *presentation graphics software* (for creating slides and other presentations).

A third category of application software is the accounting software that performs such familiar tasks as preparing payrolls, maintaining accounts-receivable files, executing accounts-payable tasks, controlling inventory, and producing financial statements. Often, developers integrate these tasks in complete accounting packages. An example is Quickbooks.

Yet, a fourth type of application software is *communications software* that allows separate computing devices to transmit data to one another. Microcomputer examples include communications packages (for simple data transmissions between computers), Web browsers (for accessing and displaying graphic images on the Internet), backend software (that enables Web servers to communicate with large, commercial databases of customer and product information), and e-mail software (for creating, transmitting, reading, and deleting e-mail messages).

Finally, a fifth type of application software is the **enterprise resource management (ERP) software** that enables businesses and government agencies to transmit and manipulate financial data on an organization-wide basis. An example is SAP. These systems are particularly important to electronic commerce (e-commerce) applications—see Chapter 5.

Most application software are licensed to users, not sold to them. A license's terms of use typically include restrictions on who can use the software, the number of computing devices on which the licensee can install it, and the duration of the licensing agreement. Indiscriminate copying is almost always forbidden. Software licenses are important to accountants for these reasons and also because businesses sometimes ask accountants to audit a department or company for compliance with these restrictions. Figure 3-16 describes various types of software licenses in more detail.

Case-in-Point 3.13 Microsoft Licensing GP is a wholly owned subsidiary of Microsoft Corporation based in Reno, Nevada. Its primary function is to operate and manage Microsoft's licensing activities in North and South America.

Programming Languages

To create application software, developers must write detailed instructions in **programming languages** that computers can understand and execute. FORTRAN,

Type of License	Explanation
Single-user license	Limits the use of the software to one user, perhaps for more than one computing device and perhaps for a limited amount of time.
Network license	Limits the use of the software to those working on the same local area network.
Site license	Limits the use of the software to those working at the same physical location. The license might also allow users working remotely to install the software on their local devices.
Limited-use license	Limits the use of the software to a single session or short time frame.

FIGURE 3-16 Types of application software licenses.

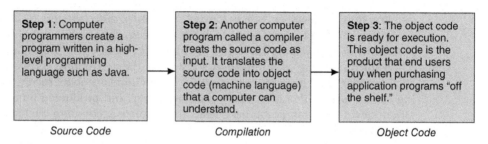

FIGURE 3-17 How computer programmers create application software.

COBOL, and RPG are examples of older programming languages that developers used to create minicomputer and mainframe AISs (i.e., the older but still-viable legacy systems). Newer computer languages include Python (popular for general-purpose programming), C++ (favored for its ability to manipulate data at the bit level), Visual Basic (favored for creating Windows-like user interfaces), HTML (an editing language favored for creating Web pages), and Java (favored for its ability to run on many different types of computers).

Most of the newer programming languages are **object-oriented programming languages**, meaning that they encourage programmers to develop code in reusable modules called *objects*, which are easier to develop, debug, and modify. Both Visual Basic and C++ are **event-driven programming languages**—that is, programming languages whose code responds to events such as a user clicking on a menu item with a mouse.

Figure 3-17 illustrates how developers create application programs using these programming languages. The process begins when computer programmers write instructions in a *source* programming language such as Visual Basic. In a second step, the developers translate this *source code* into the machine language (*object code*) that a computer understands. Yet another computer program called a **compiler** performs this translation in a second step called a *compilation*. The output from the compilation is the object code, which a computer can then load and execute. When end users buy application software packages, they buy compiled computer programs in machine language that are ready to execute on their specific computers.

AIS AT WORK
Using iPads at the Mercedes-Benz Car Dealership[14]

Customers at a Mercedes-Benz dealership are now likely to talk to salespeople armed with iPads when they want to finance or lease their new cars or when they bring their older cars back at lease end. Why an iPad? Simple: An iPad lets dealership employees stay close to the customer on the sales floor when discussing promotional incentives, financing terms, or leasing arrangements.

---

[14] Murphy, C. 2010. 7 Tips for using the iPad in business. *InformationWeek* (November 1): 26.

© svetikd / Getty Images, Inc.

Once a pilot program but now corporate policy, the iPad applications utilize Apple's Safari Web browser and customized MB Financial Advantage programs to allow employees to complete loan applications or the paperwork for end-of-lease turn-ins on the spot—not in some back office. Mercedes Benz considers the iPad a better option than a smart-phone application because the system displays more information on a single screen and both a salesperson and a customer can see the screen at the same time. This makes lease-end check-ins as simple as returning a rental car, for example, and the system can e-mail the customer a copy of the completed form.

Because customers buying cars like to close deals on the spot, perhaps the biggest problem Mercedes had to solve was obtaining customer signatures on completed eletronic loan forms. As suggested by the accompanying picture, MB solved this problem in a particularly innovative way—by allowing customers to sign with their finger!

 ## SUMMARY

✓ It is useful to view an AIS as a collection of hardware, software, data, people, and procedures that work together to accomplish processing tasks.

✓ Information technology will become even more important to accountants as AISs continue to incorporate technological advances and also as they need technology to perform professional tasks.

✓ To achieve their objectives, computerized AISs must input, process, store, and output information and often utilize data communications.

✓ The starting point for most AIS data processing is either an electronic or a manual source document. Automating the data-gathering tasks helps eliminate the errors introduced by human input. POS devices, MICR readers, OCR readers, and magnetic strip readers enable AISs to capture data that are already in machine-readable formats.

✓ Biometric scanners help AISs limit access to legitimate users. Two of the most reliable types of scanners read fingerprints or irises.

✓ The CPU of a computer system performs the data-manipulating tasks required of the system. In order of increasing power, these units are micro- or personal computers, minicomputers, mainframe computers, and supercomputers. New systems include smart phones and computer tablets.

✓ All CPUs have primary memories and microprocessors. Most AISs are I/O-bound, not process-bound.

✓ Three important types of printers are dot-matrix printers, ink-jet printers, and laser printers.

✓ Laser printers are often most preferred because they are the fastest, have the highest print resolutions, and can now also print in color.

✓ Secondary storage devices enable AISs to store and archive data on permanent media. Magnetic disks, CD-ROMs, DVDs, and flash memories are the most common secondary storage devices.

✓ Image processing allows users to capture and store visual graphs, charts, and pictures in digital formats on such media.

✓ Data communications enable AISs to transmit data over LANs and WANs. Many AISs now use LANs or WANs for e-mail, sharing computer resources, saving software costs, gathering input data, or distributing outputs. Wi-Fi technology such as RFID and NFC applications significantly increases our ability to access information accurately as well as to communicate efficiently with others.

✓ Cloud computing refers to the use of service providers over the Internet. Applications include access to computer software programs, backup and recovery file services, and Web page development and hosting.

✓ The software of an AIS performs the specific data processing tasks required. OSs enable computers to run themselves and also to execute the application programs designed for them.

✓ Application software enables end users to perform work-related tasks. Categories of such software include personal productivity software, integrated accounting packages, and communication packages. Programming languages enable IT professionals to translate processing logic into instructions that computers can execute.

KEY TERMS YOU SHOULD KNOW

antivirus software
application software
bar code reader
biometric scanner
Blu-ray discs
Bluetooth
bring your own device (BYOD)

CD-ROM
central processing unit (CPU)
client/server computing
compiler
computer record
computer software
computer tablet

data communications
data communications protocol
data transcription
digital subscriber line (DSL)
digital video disk (DVD)
digital video input
dot-matrix printer

electronic document and record management system (EDRMS)

enterprise network

enterprise resource management (ERP) software

event-driven programming language

file server

flash memory

graphical user interface (GUI)

hard-copy output

I/O-bound computer

image processing

ink-jet printer

input-processing-output cycle

ISDN

laser printer

legacy system

local area network (LAN)

magnetic (hard) disk

magnetic ink character recognition (MICR)

mainframe computer

mark-sense media

microprocessor

minicomputer

modem (modulator/demodulator)

multimedia

near-field communications (NFC)

object-oriented programming language

operating system (OS)

optical character recognition (OCR)

peripheral equipment

personal productivity software

picture elements (pixels)

point-of-sale (POS) device

primary memory

programming language

radio frequency identification (RFID)

redundant array of independent disks (RAIDs)

secondary storage

soft-copy output

software as a service (SaaS)

source document

supercomputer

turnaround document

utility program

virtual storage

virus

volatile memory

Wi-Fi (wireless fidelity)

Wide area networks (WANs)

wireless application protocol (WAP)

wireless communications

worm (write-once, read many) media

TEST YOURSELF

Q3-1. All of the following are reasons why IT is important to accountants *except*:

   a. accountants often help clients make IT decisions

   b. auditors must evaluate computerized systems

   c. IT questions often appear on professional certification examinations

   d. the costs of IT are skyrocketing

Q3-2. Data transcription is best described as:

   a. an efficient process

   b. always necessary in AISs

   c. labor-intensive and time-consuming

   d. an important way to limit fraud and embezzlement

Q3-3. The acronyms POS, MICR, and OCR are examples of:

   a. input devices

   b. processing devices

   c. output devices

   d. communication devices

Q3-4. Purchasing backup services from an Internet vendor is an example of:

   a. OCR

   b. modem services

   c. virtual storage

   d. cloud computing

Q3-5. The term "enrollment" is most closely associated with:

   a. keyboards

   b. biometric scanners

   c. printers

   d. modems

Q3-6. The RAM of a computer is part of:

   a. primary memory

   b. secondary storage

   c. arithmetic-logic unit

   d. modem

Q3-7. The term "I/O-bound" means that:

   a. computers must input and output data when executing accounting applications

    b. AIS are headed for the land of I/O

    c. computers can "think" or process faster than they can read or write

    d. computers are obligated to make inferences and oversights

Q3-8. Video output can also be called:

    a. hard-copy output

    b. soft-copy output

    c. image output

    d. picture output

Q3-9. Which of these devices is capable of storing the most data?

    a. CD-ROM disk

    b. DVD disk

    c. USB (flash memory) drive

    d. Magnetic (hard) disk

Q3-10. All of these are components, or layers, of a client/server computing system *except*:

    a. presentation layer

    b. application/logic layer

    c. client layer

    d. data management layer

DISCUSSION QUESTIONS

3-1. Why is it important to view an AIS as a combination of hardware, software, people, data, and procedures?

3-2. Why is information technology important to accountants?

3-3. Why do most AISs try to avoid data transcription?

3-4. Name several types of computer input devices, and explain in general terms how each one functions.

3-5. How do you feel about red-light cameras? Should cities be allowed to use them? Why or why not?

3-6. Identify the three sections of a CPU, and describe the functions of each component. How are microprocessor speeds measured? Why are such speeds rarely important to AISs?

3-7. Identify several types of printers. What are the advantages and disadvantages of each type?

3-8. What is the function of secondary storage? Describe three types of secondary storage media, and describe the advantages and disadvantages of each type.

3-9. What is image processing? How is image processing used in AISs?

3-10. What are data communication protocols? Why are they important?

3-11. What are local area networks? What advantages do LANs offer accounting applications?

3-12. What is client/server computing? How does it differ from host/mainframe computing? What are some of the advantages and disadvantages of client/server systems?

3-13. What are the names of some current cloud computing vendors other than those discussed in the text? Should all firms use cloud vendors, or are there some reasons why they should be avoided?

3-14. What are windowing operating systems, multi-tasking operating systems, and graphical user interfaces? Why are they useful to AISs?

3-15. Name some general classes of application software. What tasks do each of your software classes perform?

3-16. What are computer programming languages? Name some specific languages, and describe briefly an advantage of each.

3-17. The Business Software Alliance (www.BSA.org) is a nonprofit organization dedicated to fighting illegal software copying (*software piracy*). The organization estimates that one in five software programs is unlicensed and therefore illegal. Is copying a spreadsheet or accounting program for your personal use OK? Is copying software without paying a license fee ever OK? Defend your answer.

PROBLEMS

3-18. Are the following input equipment, output equipment, CPU components, secondary storage devices, or data communications related?

a. CRT screen

b. ALU

c. CD-ROM

d. Keyboard

e. Modem

f. Dot-matrix printer

g. Audio speaker

h. POS device

i. MICR reader

j. Laser printer

k. Bluetooth

l. Flash memory

m. OCR reader

n. Magnetic (hard) disk

o. ATM

p. Primary memory

3-19. All of the following are acronyms discussed in this chapter. What words were used to form each one and what does each term mean?

a. POS

b. CPU

c. OCR

d. MICR

e. ATM

f. RAM

g. ALU

h. MIPS

i. OS

j. MHz

k. Pixel

l. RGB

m. CD-ROM

n. Worm

o. Modem

p. LAN

q. SD-WAN

r. RFID

s. WAP

t. Wi-Fi

u. ppm

v. dpi

w. NFC

3-20. Which of the following holds the most data?

a. 1 DVD disk

b. 1 Hard disk (capacity: 500 gigabytes)

c. 10 CD-ROMs

3-21. An advertisement for a desktop microcomputer says that it includes a 500-gigabyte hard drive. Exactly how many bytes is this? Hint: See the discussions on secondary storage.

3-22. Brian Fry Products manufactures a variety of machine tools and parts used primarily in industrial tasks. To control production, the company requires the information listed as follows. Design an efficient record format for Brian Fry Products. Hint: See Figure 3-9.

a. Order number (4 digits)

b. Part number to be manufactured (5 digits)

c. Part description (10 characters)

d. Manufacturing department (3 digits)

e. Number of pieces started (always less than 10,000)

f. Number of pieces finished

g. Machine number (2 digits)

h. Date work started

i. Hour work started (use 24-hour system)

j. Date work completed

k. Hour work completed

l. Work standard per hour (3 digits)

m. Worker number (5 digits)

n. Foreman number (5 digits)

3-23. Go to the AICPA website at http://www.aicpa.org. What are the top 10 information technologies for the current year? How do these items compare with the list in Figure 3-1? Is it common for new items to appear, or do you think this list is "stable" from year to year?

3-24. Your state has recently decided to install an RFID system for its toll roads. The current plan is to sell nonrefundable transponders for $20 and allow users to deposit up to $1,000 in their accounts. To assist the IT personnel, the system's planners want to develop a list of possible accounting transactions and system responses. Using your skills from earlier accounting classes, what debit and credit entries would you make for each of the following activities? (Feel free to develop your own accounts for this problem.)

a. A user buys a new transponder for $20.

b. A user adds $50 to his account.

c. A user discovers that a data entry clerk charges his credit card $500 instead of $50 when adding $50 to his account.

d. An individual leaves the state, turns in his transponder, and gets a cash refund for the $20.75 remaining in his account.

e. A good Samaritan turns in a transponder that he finds on the side of the road. There is a $10 reward for this act, taken from the owner's account.

3-25. Select a type of computer hardware that interests you and write a one-page report on three possible choices of it. Examples include monitors, USB drives, external hard drives, or computer tablets. Your report should include a table similar to the one shown here that includes: (1) embedded pictures of your choices, (2) major specifications (e.g., storage capacities, pixel sizes, data transfer rates, etc.), (3) the suggested retail price of each item, (4) the likely "street price" of the item, and (5) the name of the vendor that sells the item at the street price.

The major deliverable is a one-page report that includes (1) the table identified earlier, (2) an explanation of why you chose to examine the hardware you did, and (3) an indication of which particular item you would buy of your three choices. The following example is for "USB drives as jewelry."

	(Item)	(Item)
Sushi USB	(Name of item)	(Name of item)
Spec	Spec	Spec
Spec	Spec	Spec

3-26. Assume that you are shopping for a new desktop computer. Log onto the Dell Corporation's website at www.dell.com and develop your own computer system. Include in your system a monitor, keyboard, mouse, and printer, plus whatever additional hardware and software you think you'd need. (a) What is the total price of your system? (b) Can you find a packaged system for less on this site? How about another site? (c) How much will a similar laptop system cost?

3-27. The Accounting Technology website at https://www.accountingtoday.com/technology contains articles on information technology of interest or use to accountants. Examples include "New chatbot uses AI to answer tax inquiries," "The hidden figures behind automation," and "A famous robot wants to ease tax pain." Log onto this website or a similar one as directed by your instructor, select an interesting article you find there, and write a one-page summary of the topic.

3-28. List five examples of personal productivity software. (Hint: one example is a spreadsheet program.) For each example you name, also provide an example of how that particular application can help an accountant perform his or her job better, more easily, or more accurately.

CASE ANALYSES

3-29. Pucinelli Supermarkets (Validating Input Data)

Pucinneli Supermarkets is similar to most other grocery store chains that use the 12-digit UPC code on packages to check out customers. For a variety of reasons, it is important that the computer systems using these codes validate them for accuracy and completeness. To perform this task, UPCs automatically include a "check digit" that can also be computed from the other digits in the code. The system works as follows:

1. The UPC includes all numbers in the bar code. An example is 064200115896. The length is 12 as required.

2. The check digit is the last digit in the code—a "6" for this example.

3. Starting on the left, add the digits up to, but not including, the check digit in the odd-numbered positions (i.e., the numbers in the first, third, fifth position, etc.) together. Multiply this sum by 3.

4. Add the digits up to, but not including, the check digit in the even-numbered positions (i.e., the second, fourth, sixth numbers, etc.).

5. Add the values found in steps 3 and 4.

6. Examine the last digit of the sum. If it is 0, the computed check digit is also 0. If the last digit of the result is not zero, subtract this digit from 10. The answer is the computed check digit and must equal the last number in the UPC code.

To illustrate, suppose that the UPC bar code is 064200115896 as shown. The steps for this example are as follows:

1. The length is 12 as required.
2. The last value is "6," so this is the check digit.
3. Add the odd-position digits: $0 + 4 + 0 + 1 + 5 + 9 = 19$. Multiply this sum by 3: $19 \times 3 = 57$.
4. Add the even-position digits: $6 + 2 + 0 + 1 + 8 = 17$.
5. We add these two values together. The sum is $57 + 17 = 74$.
6. The last digit in this sum is "4," the check digit is not 0, and we therefore subtract 4 from 10 to get "6." The computed value of "6" found in step 5 matches the check digit "6" in step 2, and we therefore conclude that this UPC code is valid.

UPC code:	064200115896
Length test:	Ok
Check digit is:	6
Sum of odd digits:	19
Sum of even digits:	17
Odd digits x 3:	57
Sum:	74
Last digit:	4
Computed check digit:	6
Conclusion:	Valid number

Requirement

Develop a spreadsheet to perform the tests described here and test your model with the following UPC codes. (1) 639277240453, (2) 040000234548, (3) 034000087884, (4) 048109352495, and (5) one UPC value of your own choosing (drawn from something you own or see). For each number, indicate whether the UPC number is valid or invalid. Include a printout of all your work, plus a copy of the formulas for at least one of your tests.

Hints: (1) You should enter your initial UPC code as "text"—not a number. (2) You can use Excel's LEN function to perform the desired length test and Excel's IF function to test whether the entered value passes it. (3) You should use Excel's MID function to parse each digit for these computations. You can use Excel's IF test again to reach the conclusion (e.g., "Valid number").

3-30. Savage Motors (Software Training)

Savage Motors sells and leases commercial automobiles, vans, and trucks to customers in southern California. Most of the company's administrative staff work in the main office. The company has been in business for 35 years, but only in the last 10 years has the company begun to recognize the benefits of computer training for its employees.

The company president, Archer Savage, is thinking about hiring a training company to give onsite classes. To pursue this option, the company would set up a temporary "computer laboratory" in one of the meeting rooms, and the trainers would spend all day teaching one or more particular types of software. You have been hired as a consultant to recommend what type of training would best meet the firm's needs.

You begin your task by surveying the three primary corporate departments: sales, operations, and accounting. You find that most employees use their personal computers for only five types of software: (1) word processing, (2) spreadsheets, (3) database, (4) presentations, and (5) accounting. The accompanying table shows your estimates of the total number of hours per week used by each department on each type of software.

Department (number of employees)	Word Processing	Spreadsheet	Database	Presentation	Accounting
Sales (112)	1,150	750	900	500	700
Operations (82)	320	2,450	650	100	500
Accounting (55)	750	3,600	820	250	2,500

Requirements

1. Create a spreadsheet illustrating each department's average use of each application per employee, rounding all averages to one decimal point. For example, the average hours of word processing for the sales department is 1150/112 = 10.3 hours.

2. Suppose that there were only enough training funds for each department to train employees on only one type of application. What training would you recommend for each department?

3. What is the average number of hours of use of each application for all the employees in the company? What training would you recommend if funds were limited to only training one type of application for the entire company?

4. Using spreadsheet tools, create graphs that illustrate your findings in parts 1 and 2. Do you think that your graphs or your numbers better "tell your story?"

5. What alternatives are there to onsite training? Suggest at least two alternatives, and discuss which of your three possibilities you prefer.

3-31. Backwater University (Automating a Data-Gathering Task)

Backwater University is a small technical college that is located miles from the nearest town. As a result, most of the students who attend classes there also live in the resident dormitories and purchase one of three types of meal plans. The "Full Plan" entitles a student to eat three meals a day, 7 days a week, at any one of the campus's three dining facilities. The "Weekday Plan" is the same as the Full Plan, but entitles students to eat meals only on weekdays—not weekends. Finally, the "50-Meal" plan entitles students to eat any 50 meals during a given month. Of course, students and visitors can always purchase any given meal for cash.

Because the school administration is anxious to attract and retain students, it allows them to change their meal plans from month to month. This, in fact, is common, as students pick plans that best serve their needs each month. But this flexibility has also created a nightmare at lunch times, when large numbers of students attempt to eat at the dining facilities simultaneously.

In response to repeated student complaints about the long lines that form at lunchtime, Lillianna Fiala, the Dean of Students, decides to look into the matter and see for herself what is going on. At lunch the next day, she observes that each cashier at the entrance to the dining facilities requires each student to present an ID card, checks their picture, and then consults a long, hard-copy list of students to determine whether or not they are eligible for the current meal. A cashier later informs her that these tasks are regrettable, but also mentions that they have become necessary because many students attempt to eat meals that their plans do not allow.

The cashier also mentions that, at present, the current system provides no way of keeping a student from eating *two of the same meals* at two different dining facilities. Although Lillianna thinks that this idea is far-fetched, the cashier says that this problem is surprisingly common. Some students do it just as a prank or on a dare, but other students do it to smuggle out food for their friends.

Lillianna realizes that one solution to the long-lines problem is to simply hire more cashiers. She also recognizes that a computerized system might be an even more cost-effective solution. In particular, she realizes that if the current cashiers had some way of identifying each student quickly, the computer system could immediately identify a given student as eligible, or ineligible, for any given meal.

Requirements

1. Suggest two or more "technology solutions" for this problem.
2. What hardware would be required for each solution you named in part 1?
3. What software would be required for each solution you named in part 1? What would this software do?
4. How would you go about showing that your solutions would be more cost-effective than simply hiring more cashiers? (You do not have to perform any calculations to answer this question—merely outline your method.)

3-32. Bennet National Bank (Centralized versus Decentralized Data Processing)

Bennet National Bank's credit card department issues a special credit card that permits credit card holders to withdraw funds from the bank's ATMs at any time of the day or night. These machines are actually smart terminals connected to the bank's central computer. To use them, a bank customer inserts the magnetically encoded card in the automated teller's slot and types in a unique password on the teller keyboard. If the password matches the authorized code, the customer goes on to indicate, for example, (1) whether a withdrawal from a savings account or a withdrawal from a checking account is desired and (2) the amount of the withdrawal (in multiples of $10). The teller terminal communicates this information to the bank's central computer and then gives the customer the desired cash. In addition, the automated terminal prints out a hard copy of the transaction for the customer.

To guard against irregularities in the automated cash transaction described, the credit card department has imposed certain restrictions on the use of the credit cards when customers make cash withdrawals at ATMs.

1. The correct password must be keyed into the teller keyboard before the cash withdrawal is processed.
2. The credit card must be one issued by Bennet National Bank. For this purpose, a special bank code has been encoded as part of the magnetic strip information.
3. The credit card must be current. If the expiration date on the card has already passed at the time the card is used, the card is rejected.

4. The credit card must not be a stolen one. The bank keeps a computerized list of these stolen cards and requires that this list be checked electronically before the withdrawal transaction can proceed.

5. For the purposes of making withdrawals, each credit card can only be used twice on any given day. This restriction is intended to hold no matter what branch bank(s) are visited by the customers.

6. The amount of the withdrawal must not exceed the customer's account balance.

Requirements

1. What information must be encoded on the magnetic card strip on each Bennet National Bank credit card to permit the computerized testing of these policy restrictions?

2. What tests of these restrictions could be performed at the teller window by a smart terminal and what tests would have to be performed by the bank's central processing unit and other equipment?

3-33. Morrigan Department Stores (The Ethics of Forced Software Upgrading)

Morrigan Department Stores is a chain of department stores in Australia, New Zealand, Canada, and the United States that sells clothing, shoes, and similar consumer items in a retail setting. The top managers and their staff members meet once a year at the international meeting. This year's meeting was in Hawaii—a geographical midpoint for them—and several accounting managers participated in a round-table discussion that went as follows:

Roberta Gardner (United States): One of our biggest problems in our Auckland office is the high cost and seemingly constant need to upgrade our hardware and software. Every time our government changes the tax laws, of course, we must acquire software that reflects those changes. But why do we need new hardware too? All this discussion of "64-bit machines" is a mystery to me, but the IT department says the hardware in the old machines quickly become outdated.

Donalda Shadbolt (New Zealand): I'll say! If you ask me, all these upgrades are costly, time-consuming, and even counter-productive. I do a lot of work on spreadsheets, for example, and constantly ask myself: "Why do I have to spend hours relearning how to format a simple column of numbers in the newest version of Excel?" It takes time and effort, it's frustrating, and in the end, I've spent hours relearning skills that I already know how to do in the older version.

Linda Vivianne (Canada): I know what you mean, but the newer hardware is faster, cheaper, and more capable than the old machines. Hard drives have moving parts in them, for example, and they eventually wear out. The newer software runs under the newer operating systems, which are also more competent and have more built-in security such as antivirus software.

Ed Ghymn (Australia): I agree with you, Linda, but I think a lot of these new capabilities are more hype than real. If the security software was competent, we wouldn't need all those patches and upgrades in the first place. And why must we upgrade so often, just to get newer capabilities that most of us don't even need?

Alex McLeod (Australia): I don't think anyone can stop the march of progress. I think the real problem is not the upgrades to new software, but the fact that our company expects us to learn it without proper training. Personally, I don't buy my boss's argument that "you're a professional and should learn it on your own."

Linda Vivianne (Canada): I'm also beginning to realize just what advantages there are in outsourcing some of our accounting applications to cloud service providers. That won't solve all our problems because we all still need word processing and spreadsheet capabilities, but at least we can let cloud providers deal with the software upgrades for our accounting software. Given how dispersed we are, that might also make it easier for us to consolidate our financial statements at year's end too.

Requirements

1. Do you think that Roberta Gardner's description of "64-bit machines" is accurate? Why or why not? Explain your reasons in detail, drawing upon additional Internet discussions to help you answer this question.

2. Summarize some of the arguments *against* upgrading hardware and software at Morrigan Department Stores. It is OK to mention additional, reasonable arguments that are not mentioned in the case.

3. Summarize the arguments *for* upgrading hardware and software at the Morrigan Department Stores. Again, it is OK to mention additional, reasonable arguments that are not included in the case.

4. Do you agree with Ed Ghymn's argument that many upgrades are "more hype than real?" Why or why not?

5. Many software vendors such as Microsoft, Adobe, and Apple ship software packages with both known and unknown defects in them. Do you feel that it is ethical for them to do so? Why or why not?

6. Do you agree or disagree with the argument made in this case that many hardware and/or software upgrades are unnecessary? Why or why not?

7. Do you agree with Alex McLeod's statement that a company should formally train its employees every time it upgrades its software? If not, do you agree with his boss that professionals should learn to use at least some software upgrades on their own? Explain your answer in detail.

8. Do you think it was necessary for the participants to physically meet at one location? Couldn't they simply hold a virtual meeting over the Internet? Explain your answer in detail.

READINGS AND OTHER RESOURCES

Ashley, B. 2013. Tracking physical assets: Barcodes vs. RFID. *ABA Banking Journal* 105(2): 11–12.

Drew, J. 2016. How CPAs can make the most of their tech resources. *Journal of Accountancy* 222(1): 42, 46, 48.

Fowler, J. 2015, March 4. Back up your digital life: The best online services to archive your important files. Personal journal. *The Wall Street Journal*: D1.

Hart, L. 2016. What to know before you commit to the cloud. *Journal of Accountancy* 222(1): 57, 59, 61, 63.

Jackson, L. 2009. Biometric technology: The future of identity assurance and authentication in the lodging industry. *International Journal of Contemporary Hospitality Management* 21(6/7): 894–905.

McConnon, A. 2017, March 13. Why the travel-expense nightmare is getting easier: Technology is removing one of the biggest headaches business travelers endure: The paperwork. Journal Report: Workplace Technology. *The Wall Street Journal*: R8.

Mishler, C. 2015. The future of the Internet of Things. *Strategic Finance* 97(5): 62–63.

Parcells, S. 2016. The power of finance automation. *Strategic Finance* 98(6): 40–45.

Petravick, S. and S. Kerr. 2009. Protect your portable data always and everywhere. *Journal of Accountancy* 207(6): 30–34.

Ritchey, D. 2010. Tracking critical assets. *Security: Solutions for Enterprise Security Leaders* 47(2): 34–33.

Violino, B. 2013. The Internet of things. *Network World* 30(7): 28–30.

Go to www.wiley.com/go/simkin/videos to access videos on the following topics:

Introduction to Cloud Computing
Cloud Computing Explained
What Is Flash Memory?
The Internet of Things
What Is a Local Area Network (LAN)?

ANSWERS TO TEST YOURSELF

1. d **2.** c **3.** a **4.** d **5.** b **6.** a **7.** c **8.** b **9.** d **10.** c

Chapter 4

Accounting and Data Analytics

After reading this chapter, you will be able to:
1. *Discuss* the implications of data analytics on the accounting profession.
2. *Explain* the characteristics of big data.
3. *Describe* the general data analysis process.
4. *Summarize and give examples* of how data analytics are transforming the practice of accounting.

"The full power of analytics can be realized only by continuing the process of maturation and 'moving upstream' to transform in a fundamental way the way audits are approached."

Kress, R. and D. Hildebrand, 2017. How analytics will transform internal audit.
ISACA Journal 2: 18–23

4.1 INTRODUCTION

At its core, accounting is an information discipline. Over the years, the accounting profession has identified key business events and economic exchanges that give rise to data capture, and these data are ultimately aggregated and transformed into information for decision-making purposes. Historically, accounting data has been economic and financial in nature. However, the emergence of big data and the relative ease with which structured and unstructured data are generated has challenged this convention.

In the first chapter of this book, we talked about how IT has fundamentally changed the nature of the profession. The past two decades witnessed significant transformations in accounting as IT and accounting information systems (AISs) have been used as agents to solidify the automation of business processes and facilitate the seamless integration of e-business initiatives with real-time transaction processing. The coming decade will see a variety of accounting and business-related technologies transform the way we generate, aggregate, share, and report accounting and business-related information.

In this chapter, we discuss the changing nature of data, as well as the expectations for accounting professionals regarding data analysis and presentation. We begin by discussing big data and the challenges it presents for decision-making. Next, we will provide an overview of the process typically utilized for data analytics, and cover some of the common tools used for these purposes. We then examine how data analytics are transforming three key areas of the profession: tax accounting, managerial accounting, and assurance and compliance. We conclude with insights from a practicing data scientist to get a glimpse of how data analytics are changing decision processes in the financial services sector.

4.2   BIG DATA

The past few decades have born witness to an almost exponential growth in processing capabilities, storage capacity, and network throughput that have enabled organizations to create, capture, and analyze data at an alarming rate and with far-reaching results. Coupling this rapid growth in technical capability with an ever-increasing universe of Internet-connected devices, many have dubbed this resultant explosion in data as big data. More and more, accounting professionals are beginning to see how big data has the potential to fundamentally challenge how accountants use data for decision-making, and how organizations view us as participants in the decision-making process. Loosely, **big data** is a catch-all term for vast quantities of structured, semistructured, and unstructured data that are often available in real time or near real time. Big data is often characterized by four attributes, collectively known as the 4 V's: volume, velocity, variety, and veracity.

Volume

One of the earliest defining attributes of big data is **volume**, or the sheer quantity and scale of data. While many of us realize that the rate at which data are currently created is astonishing, the pace of that creation is truly staggering. Consider this: 90% of today's data are less than 2 years old. In fact, according to some experts, it would take more than 10 million Blu-ray discs (approximately 2.5 quintillion bytes) to record the new data created on any given day.[1] Facebook, the popular online social media platform, has more users than China, the most populous country in the world, has people. Although the number is changing daily, Facebook stored around 250 billion photographs from its users in 2015 (more on this number in a moment). At the rate of data growth observed in 2016, experts estimate the total of all data in existence will exceed 44 zettabytes, or 44 trillion gigabytes, by 2020. To put that in perspective, the sum total of all data in existence in 2015 was estimated to be roughly 4.4 zettabytes.[2]

In essence, as people and processes become more connected, the amount of data is growing exponentially. The volume of data creates problems for accountants and the tools they use to analyze them. In the past, it was sufficient to train accounting students on spreadsheet and database software packages, such as Excel and Access. However, given the nature and amount of data that we can expect to be used in financial decision-making in the future, these tools are ill-equipped to handle the complex analyses that accountants must now perform.

Velocity

Where is all of this data originating? The simple answer is: everywhere. In 2008, the global population of Internet-connected devices exceeded the global population of

---

[1] "Extracting business value from the 4V's of big data," www.ibmbigdatahub.com, accessed March 2017.
[2] Kanellos, M. "152,000 smart devices every minute in 2025: IDC outlines the future of smart things," www.forbes.com, accessed March 2017.

people. Remember the 250 billion photographs that Facebook users had uploaded as of 2015? That number is grossly understated as you read this chapter, because Facebook users upload, on average, almost 1 billion photos daily! And as **Case-in-Point 4.1** illustrates, organizations are finding novel ways of creating and using data for decision-making.

While the examples provided above are the tip of the iceberg, they succinctly illustrate another characteristic of big data, **velocity**. Simply stated, velocity is the speed at which data are created. As more and more devices connect to the Internet, this velocity, or flow of data, can only grow. Organizations can find it overwhelming to deal with the speed at which data are created and at which it arrives. A useful analogy is to think of "drinking water through a fire hose." The challenge is this: so much water is coming at you so fast, that it's difficult to get anything to drink. You've probably experienced this feeling in some of your classes, and organizations are experiencing this challenge as well. As organizations are inundated with data, it is difficult to quickly and efficiently discern what data are useful for a given decision task.

Case-in-Point 4.1 When the Florida State University Seminoles won the final BCS National Championship game in January 2014, many marveled at how the Seminoles had remained practically immune to injuries throughout the course of the season. It wasn't until Summer 2014 that Head Coach Jimbo Fisher revealed his secret weapon: wearable tech and real-time monitoring in practices. Each of 95 football players wear a tech-enabled harness during practice that captures more than 1,000 unique data points per second, from heart rate and blood pressure to speed and distance ran. Coaches are able to monitor player performance and health in real time, adjusting practice pace and activities on the fly. The Seminoles now employ three full-time data scientists who provide detailed reports to the coaching staff. And the injury bug? The Seminoles saw an 88% decrease in soft tissue injuries (muscle strains and pulls) after implementing the new monitoring system.[3]

Variety

Although volume and velocity once defined big data, many organizations now find that variety is the most challenging aspect. **Variety** deals with the diversity of data that organizations create or collect. Traditionally, data resulted from processing transactions, adhering to a given structure that was easily stored in relational databases or flat files.

Today, organizations now capture and collect unstructured data such as media files (sound, video, image), Twitter feeds and social media posts, scanned documents, Web pages, blogs, and emails. These new data types challenge the traditional database management systems used in organizations and also are incompatible with many of the earlier data analysis tools and software packages that accountants are trained on.

Case-in-Point 4.2 Expected to be a $2.5 billion industry by 2025, wearable tech for farm livestock can perform functions as simple as locating a missing calf to monitoring vital signs as an early indicator of illness, or a heifer coming into estrus. These devices range from Bluetooth-enabled ear tags to collars to ingestible e-pills that permanently reside in the

---

[3] Hale, D. "FSU rides GPS technology to title," www.espn.com, accessed March 2017.

cow's rumen (largest stomach). One device actually serves to ward off predators by emitting a high-pitched noise and flashing lights when a predator approaches. How does it know? Changes in livestock vital signs (blood pressure, heart rate, and body temperature) within a "fear range" are prime indicators of "fight or flight" response. Managing inventory in one of mankind's oldest professions meets precision agriculture.[4]

Although volume and velocity are often cited when we think of big data, variety may be its most challenging aspect. With structured data, accountants and decision-makers are adept at formatting and aggregating these data to gain insights. For example, we know that adding together all sales made on credit and subtracting away all returns and payments yields our Accounts Receivable balance. However, many of us draw a blank when it comes to figuring out how to utilize tweets and retweets to augment product pricing and inventory management decisions.

Veracity

Veracity is the extent to which the data can be trusted for insights. In general, for data to have predictive and/or feedback value, it needs to be objective and representative relative to the question at hand. For example, when we ask for advice from people that only share our worldview, we run the risk of hearing only what we want. This is known as confirmation bias. Similarly, when we utilize data that is inherently biased for an analysis, we run the risk of making decisions that omits relevant facts. Dell learned this early on when it sought to use feedback from its user community website, dubbed Dell IdeaStorm, to make product configuration decisions. The users that were most vocal were not representative of the broader consumer market, and a small but vocal group were able to exert undue influence.[5]

4.3 ANALYZING DATA

The proliferation of data (and the maturation of tools used for data analysis) has the potential to fundamentally change the practice of accounting. Accountants have historically interfaced with an organization's AIS in a limited number of ways: (1) as users to enter data into, or extract information from, these systems, (2) as objective evaluators (auditors) to assess the integrity of data and information provided by these systems, or (3) as investigators assessing the nature and implications of fraud or other malfeasance perpetrated through the AIS. More often than not, the data and information used for accounting purposes has been historical in nature, providing a lookback at how the organization performed financially in a prior period.

More and more organizations expect accountants to challenge these perceptions, which in turn will expand their role within the enterprise. These changing expectations are coming from the top of the organization in many cases. A recent PwC survey of Chief Executive Officers (CEOs) suggests that 85% placed a premium on data analytics

---

[4] Barth, B. "Luddites, beware: These 5 livestock wearables are the future," www.modernfarmer.com, accessed March 2017.

[5] Di Gangi, P. and M. Wasko. December 2009. "Steal my idea! Organizational adoption of user innovations from a user innovation community: A case of Dell IdeaStorm. *Decision Support Systems* 48(1).

initiatives in their organizations, with over 80% ranking data analytics as the second most important technological investment area in the near term (mobile apps and computing was the top ranked strategic technological investment).[6]

Case-in-Point 4.3 The Association to Advance Collegiate Schools of Business (AACSB International) is widely recognized as the most prominent and prestigious accrediting bodies for Schools of Business. In addition to setting standards for business programs, the AACSB also separately accredits accounting programs. One of the newest Accounting Accreditation Standards, Standard A7: Information Technology Skills and Knowledge for Accounting Graduates, requires that separately accredited accounting programs include "data analytics" in their accounting curriculum.[7]

This section provides an overview of the types of data sources that accountants might use in the course of their routine activities, the high level steps necessary to extract and format data from multiple data sources, and finally to analyze the data and present insights in a meaningful and understandable manner. As the various software packages and techniques used in data analytics are well beyond the scope of this textbook, we'll limit our discussion and coverage to a summary level. You should realize that the intersection of big data, data analytics, and accounting are nascent, so many of the tools, techniques, and technologies in these areas are likely to see dramatic shifts in the very short term.

Data Procurement

As previously discussed, data are being generated at a staggering rate from an ever-increasing variety of sources. However, much of this data may not be useful or useable for decision-making in an accounting context. Generally speaking, data relevant for analysis from a budget, control, and accounting perspective would originate from sources that fall into three broad categories: operational, mechanical, or social.

Operational sources include information systems that collect data regarding the business events of an organization and support its day-to-day business data requirements. This category incorporates a broad array of information systems, such as stand-alone transaction processing systems, enterprise systems, and legacy systems. Whether the source is a stand-alone transaction processing system, an enterprise system, or a legacy system, data from these systems almost always conform to a structure that is easily understood and imported into a tool for analysis. `Transaction processing systems` handle the collection, modification, and retrieval of data associated with business events such as making a sale, billing a customer, processing payroll, or depositing cash. They may be either stand-alone systems (such as Micros point-of-sale system or Quickbooks Pro accounting software) or part of a larger enterprise system implementation (such as offerings from SAP, Oracle, Microsoft, or Sage Group).

For many larger organizations, the transaction processing system is folded into their enterprise system implementation. `Enterprise resource planning`

---

[6] PwC. "Data driven: What students need to success in a rapidly changing business world," www.pwc.com, accessed March 2017.

[7] AACSB International. "AACSB International Accounting Accreditation Standard A7: Information Technology Skills and Knowledge for Accounting Graduates: An Interpretation," www.aacsb.edu, accessed April 2017.

(ERP) systems, covered later in this textbook, are comprehensive information systems that integrate front- and back-office business processing functionality and are supported by a single centralized database. In addition to incorporating the AIS, ERP systems may also support customer relationship management, sales force automation, supply chain and logistics, and partner relationship management. The centralized database that enterprise systems utilize to store all data relating to the organization's business events and transactions is often used as a primary source of data for analytics.

Finally, almost all organizations have aging information systems that house historical data that may be of use for decision-makers. **Legacy system** is a catch-all phrase that refers to aging applications and/or hardware that is either outdated or in need of replacement. In many cases, legacy systems were developed and installed a decade or more ago, and interfacing these systems with newer AISs is difficult. This difficulty can arise from the nature of the programming language used to develop the application, or the underlying structure of the data that the legacy system stores. Sometimes, legacy systems in organizations are so termed because the associated applications and data are hosted on hardware that is approaching or beyond its intended useful life. Irrespective of these concerns, legacy systems can be a treasure trove of historical data; data that may be useful inputs into a data analysis exercise.

Case-in-Point 4.4 The U.S. federal government spends approximately $90 billion each year on business information systems. Approximately 80% of that budget funds operating and maintaining legacy systems. A recent study suggests that those federal agencies that spend more on legacy systems, rather than investing in newer information systems, also experience a higher incidence of security breaches.[8]

Mechanical sources include sensors that may be worn, embedded in devices, or ingested. These devices gather different types and quantities of data, which can be stored either internally or uploaded via wireless connections to a server. As mentioned in the first two Case-in-Points in this chapter, sensors can monitor health and location of livestock, adjust athletics practice schedules to optimize game day performance, and much more. The usage of sensor data for accounting and control is increasing in adoption and implementation. Sensor data can be a valuable input into better estimating warranty costs and failure rates on equipment, as well as providing usage statistics on equipment for chargeback and automated billing systems.

Case-in-Point 4.5 Many organizations now utilize wearable tech to drive down health-care costs. Utility giant BP America issued almost 25,000 Fitbits to employees, spouses, and retirees in 2013, with the hope that a healthier workforce would equate to lower costs. Insureds who maintain a healthy lifestyle were eligible for lower premiums, and the Fitbit program was credited as instrumental in lowering BP America's health-care cost below the US average growth rate.[9]

Social sources include vast quantities of unstructured data from social media sites, such as Facebook, Twitter, Pinterest, LinkedIn, YouTube, and Instagram. Social sources

---

[8] Goldstein, P. "Study confirms conventional wisdom: Legacy federal IT breeds cybersecurity risks," www.fedtechmagazine.com, accessed April 2017.
[9] Olson, P. "The quantified other: Nest and Fitbit chase a lucrative side business," accessed from www.forbes.com, April 2017.

create voluminous quantities of data at a staggering rate, and yet we are in the infancy of understanding how to leverage these data to inform financial decisions and resource allocation. To date, retailers are making increased use of social media data to augment traditional methods of anticipating demand for products. Conventional data models may have difficulty accommodating seasonal demand fluctuations, promotional campaigns, and the like; incorporating social media data into the mix allows for more precise modeling that takes into account these factors. Another area where social sources of data have shown promise is in monitoring trend setters and influencers to more quickly move a product to market. For example, Starbucks monitors Twitter feeds and other social media when it releases a new product. Using sentiment analysis, Starbucks is able to identify any issues and then quickly respond by altering price, coffee blend, or other factors.[10] By monitoring social media, agile organizations are better positioned to modify product and service offerings to respond to changing customer demands.

Data Provisioning

Oftentimes, it is necessary to use data from multiple sources to complete an analysis. In these scenarios, a data store may need to be populated with data from various other sources. Going back to Case-in-Point 4.5, an analysis on health-insurance-related claims may require data from the data store hosting the Fitbit data (employee miles per day walked, resting heartbeat, hours slept), current insurance expenses paid, comparable data from industry peers, and historical claims data from legacy systems. In this scenario, specific data relevant to the decision at hand will need to be extracted from their respective data stores, modified and cleansed, and then loaded into a final target data store for analysis. Typically, the final target data store will be another database, a **data mart**, or a data warehouse (discussed later in this chapter). The process of extracting data from similar or disparate data sources, transforming the data into a common format, and loading the harmonized and cleansed data into a final target data store is known as **ETL (Extract-Transform-Load)**.

Extract is the first part of the ETL process and involves identifying and copying relevant data from a source data store to make it accessible for further processing. One of the most critical step in extraction is identifying which data to extract from the source system. It is entirely possible that only a subset of the data will be needed for potential analysis. Because extracting large amounts of data could load the network or the data store, care should be taken to perform extract processes so as to minimize any negative performance hits to the network or other information system components.

Transform is the second part of the ETL process and involves cleaning and converting the data from the source systems so that they can be loaded into the target system. Since data may be coming from several data sources, there is a good chance that field format may be different from data source to data source. For example, gender may be M/F in one data source, MALE/FEMALE in another, and 0/1 in yet another. Similarly, telephone numbers may be stored as "(205) 555-1234" in one system, "205.555.1234"

[10] Muller, O., I. Junglas, S. Debortoli, and J. von Brocke. 2016. Using text analysis to derive customer service management benefits from unstructured data. *MIS Quarterly Executive* (15:4).

in another, and "2055551234" in yet a third system. In both these examples, a standard format must be set. By harmonizing the data, like fields are converted into a uniform format, which will be used in the target data store. Moreover, some data fields may be empty (null values) and may need to be populated with average values (if numeric) or N/A (if alphabetic). In addition to harmonizing the data, there may be a need to perform algebraic or other conversions (date/time, stripping off meta-data tags) prior to loading to the target system.

Load is the final part of the ETL process and involves importing the transformed data into the target system. The target system is the final data store and will be where the actual data analysis occurs. The initial load will typically be a full load, bringing all data into the target data store. Subsequent loads will be incremental, bringing in only those data that have changed since the last (incremental or full) load. The target system may be a data warehouse, data mart, or a database.

Data Analysis

More often than not, decision-makers look to accountants for help answering three basic questions: what happened? what might happen? what should we do? Answering these questions in the past was hindered by the limitations of the tools and technologies necessary to process the vast amount of data, as well as the very nature of the data itself. As the tools mature, accountants will be able to employ sophisticated analyses that take full advantage of the breadth and depth of data available to them. Currently, there are three broad categories of analytics: descriptive, predictive, and prescriptive.

Descriptive analytics are useful in telling us what happened and are historical in nature. They are the most common form of analysis, with some suggesting that descriptive analytics represent more than 80% of business analytics. Examples of descriptive analytics include descriptive statistics (minimum, mean, median, mode, maximum, frequency counts) and key performance indicators (KPIs). By filtering data using geotags or other location identifiers, managers can see descriptive statistics that provide insights into how specific regions are performing and make comparisons that inform resource allocations or identify potential issues. Dashboards make heavy use of descriptive analytics so that decision-makers can quickly assess the health or status of an area under their control. To facilitate monitoring and internal control, continuous monitoring systems utilize descriptive analytics to evaluate transactions against established norms and ranges.

Predictive analytics are useful in telling us what *might* happen in the future and are forward-looking. Predictive analytics describes a set of tools and techniques for analyzing historical data to predict events that may occur in the future. These techniques are useful in identifying relationships and patterns. For example, predictive analytics can be used to identify cellular customers who are at risk of not renewing their contracts, or to analyze past payment patterns to estimate a potential customer's creditworthiness. They can also be used to forecast anticipated demand, promote cross-sell opportunities, and predict the impact of economic swings on product pricing. Regression models, decision trees, and machine learning are three of the more commonly used methods in predictive analytics.

Depending on the nature of the decision, predictive analytics may utilize data sourced from a variety of areas. Personal data includes demographics, opinions, past behaviors, and intentions. Business data includes organizational demographics, financial performance or other publicly available information. Social network data take into account the connections between and within groups, allowing for the influence that group members have on the behaviors and attitudes of others. Web traffic data are useful in determining how much traffic is driven to a website and from what sources, as well as how long a potential customer or employee remains on a Web page.[11]

Prescriptive analytics are useful in telling us what *should be done* by recommending a course of action based on a set of scenarios or inputs. While it's easy to confuse predictive and prescriptive analytics, their goals are different. Predictive analytics are useful in identifying a trend based on historical data. Prescriptive analytics aim to offer a suggested solution (or solutions) that take into account unknowns.

In essence, prescriptive analytics *prescribe* an optimal scenario based on available information. They may take into account the organization's risk appetite, operating and performance thresholds, resource constraints, and other uncertainties to predict possible outcomes based on variations of inputs or consequences of actions. Ultimately, the goal of a prescriptive analytic is to guide the decision-maker to the "best" course of action.

Presentation

For analysis to be effective, the results must be communicated in a meaningful format. The most common means of communicating results will be via reports or some form of data visualization.

A report is a way of presenting and summarizing a view of the data. Decision-makers in organizations consume reports on a daily basis. These reports come in a variety of formats and may be printed out to hard copy, downloaded to an Excel spreadsheet, or saved as a PDF. Common reports may detail monthly performance of budget versus actual sales, travel and expense reports, resource utilization reports, or an account summary (Figure 4-1).

Visualizations (sometimes called dataviz) use graphical representations of the data and results from the analyses. Data visualizations can take the form of charts, graphs, geomaps, or other graphics. Dashboards, discussed earlier in this book, are a type of visualization that aggregates data from multiple sources to provide a succinct snapshot. Much like the instrument cluster on your car, dashboards make heavy use of KPIs so that decision-makers can quickly come up to speed on the health and performance of a given area. Going back to the instrument cluster on your dashboard, a quick glance provides information from a variety of sources that gives you a feel for how your car is performing: how fast is the engine revving, how fast are you going, how cold/hot your coolant is, and how is the lubricating system working (oil pressure). While there are a plethora of other factors that determine the health and performance of your vehicle, your car's engineers determined that these KPIs are sufficient for the average driver.

---

[11] Parr-Rud, O. "Drive your business with predictive analytics," SAS whitepaper, www.sas.com, accessed April 2017.

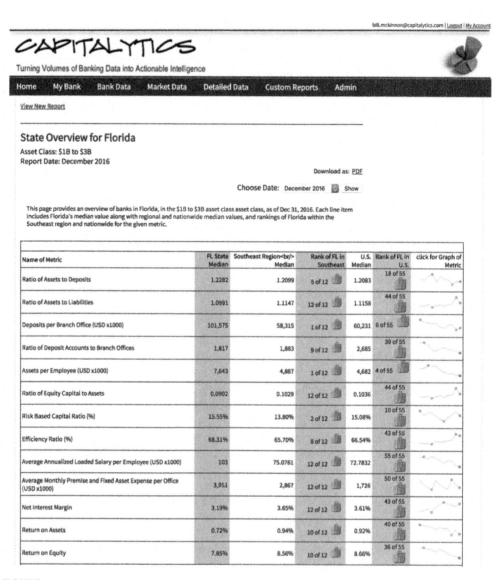

FIGURE 4-1   State of Florida Bank Overview report. Source: www.capitalytics.com, used with permission.

4.4   ENABLING TECHNOLOGIES AND TOOLS

Data Access

Online Analytical Processing (OLAP).   **Online analytical processing (OLAP)** involves using ETL tools to obtain complex information that describes *what* happened and *why* it happened. OLAP is used extensively in firms' business intelligence groups. Several software developers now market OLAP packages. Examples include Essbase (Oracle) and SAS OLAP Services. Some tools only work with specific databases, while others interface with several of them. Most allow end users to perform their own database analyses, including creating pivot tables, which are two-dimensional statistical summaries of database information (and similar to the pivot tables in *Microsoft Excel*). The future of current OLAP systems is not clear because many do not allow enough ad hoc flexibility to deal with big data.

Hadoop. **Hadoop** is an open-source infrastructure for storing and processing large sets of unstructured, semistructured, and structured data. Hadoop is part of the Apache open-source project (http://hadoop.apache.org), and was named after the stuffed elephant belonging to the son of one of Hadoop's developers. It has seen widespread adoption in organizations and environments that utilize big data. Two of the more interesting aspects of Hadoop that lend themselves to big data environments are the manner in which it stores data and the manner in which it processes data.

Hadoop's distributed file system (HDFS, or Hadoop distributed file system) allows it store files that are very large, for example, several terabyte in size. As a point of reference, a 2 terabyte Microsoft Word document would be roughly 86 million pages long.[12] It is entirely possible that a single data file might exceed the storage capacity of a hard drive!

How does HDFS store files this large? By utilizing a name node and a cluster of data nodes, HDFS can split a very large file into smaller pieces, and then store pieces of the single file on servers located throughout the cluster. The name node keeps track of what pieces of the file are stored on specific servers in the cluster and coordinates the reassembly of files when the data are accessed. Because HDFS makes use of clusters of servers and their associated storage, Hadoop is considered a highly fault-tolerant architecture. This is because files are distributed across the cluster (and the data on those servers are replicated to other servers). Thus, if a data node server goes down, the name node simply identifies which other servers store copies of the "lost" data and the data are rebuilt. Figure 4-2 illustrates how HDFS distributes and accesses files.

Hadoop also takes an interesting approach to processing data. In older systems, if data are needed for analysis, the data are moved across the network to a specific application for processing. Moving large files across a network can have serious consequences on load and performance for the infrastructure as a whole.

In contrast, Hadoop uses a program called **MapReduce** that is optimized for processing large data sets in a clustered, distributed environment. MapReduce flips the narrative by loading the processing program on the nodes where the data resides, thereby eliminating the need to move large data sets across the network to the processing program. Processing is also distributed across nodes on the cluster, thereby making more efficient use of processing resources and decreasing processing time. Once MapReduce completes the processing, only the results are transmitted back across the network, thereby virtually eliminating bottlenecks.

Cloud Databases. Shifts toward cloud computing have major implications for modern database systems. **Database-as-a-Service (DAAS)** allows firms to outsource their databases to cloud service providers, and use of DAAS has grown rapidly over the past several years. Many major players in the database, software, and online industries are making large investments in cloud databases (e.g., Amazon, Oracle, SAP, Microsoft, and Google). The databases behind consumer websites like Amazon.com can now be

---

[12] Brown, K. "A terabyte of storage space: How much is too much?" aimblog.uoregon.edu, accessed April 2017.

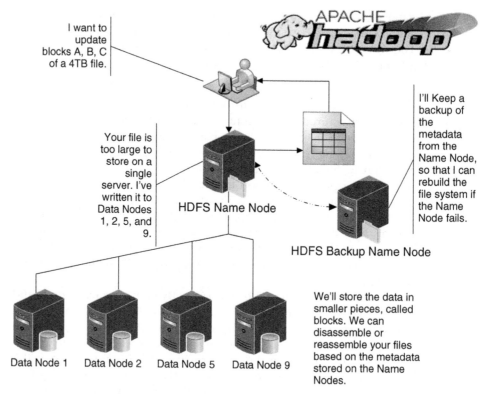

FIGURE 4-2 The Hadoop distributed file system.

outsourced completely to providers that also manage Internet sales systems and Web interfaces. Enterprise systems that contain all of the data for an entire organization can also be outsourced to cloud computing vendors. DAAS systems remove the need for firms to hire their own database administrators, design and maintain database systems, or purchase hardware. Thus, while the basic principles of databases will remain the same, the providers of database systems are changing. As databases move from within firms to "the cloud," new considerations for accountants will emerge. In particular, controls over confidential firm data will be critical in the new cloud environment. Imagine the difficulty involved in protecting firm data that are no longer maintained on private servers within the firm, but are instead being managed on the Web.

Data Warehouses and Data Marts. Where feasible, it often makes sense to pool the data from separate applications into a large, common body of information called a **data warehouse**. The data in a data warehouse are rarely current. Rather, they are typically "older information" that was initially collected for other reasons during the conduct of normal operations and daily activities of an organization. For example, in recording a sale, an AIS collects data about the customer, the product, the timing of the sale, and so on. Extended histories of this information can be helpful in predicting things such as future sales of new products. In order to analyze large volumes of historical data, the data must first be amassed in a central location—the `data warehouse`.

To be useful, the data in data warehouses should have the following characteristics: (1) be error free, (2) be defined uniformly, (3) span a longer time horizon than the company's transaction systems, and (4) allow users to answer complex questions—for example, queries requiring information from several diverse sources.

The primary advantage of a data warehouse is to make organizational information available on a corporate-wide basis. For example, the marketing representatives of a company can gain access to the company's production data and thereby be better able to inform customers about the future availability of desired, but as yet unmanufactured, products. When organizations believe the rewards for building a data warehouse do not outweigh the costs, they can consider a **data mart**. Data marts are smaller than data warehouses, and they typically focus on just one application area, for example, marketing data. However, in most other ways, they are similar to data warehouses.

A data mart acts as the interface between a data warehouse and its end users. Whereas a data warehouse stores data about an entire organization, a data mart is usually designed for a particular subset of users in the organization, for example, a single department or a single functional business area. Some consider it a subset of the data warehouse itself—especially because both the warehouse and its data mart are read-only.

Analysis and Data Visualization Tools

Broadly speaking, data analysis can be viewed as the art and science of identifying and analyzing patterns, trends and anomalies through an examination of data. As we read, there is certainly science and objective methodology associated with data analytics (after all, there's a reason that people who specialize in this field are called data *scientists*), but there is a certain amount of art and creativity associated with presenting the insights gleaned from data analytics in a meaningful and informative way.

Case-in-Point 4.6   The noted 19th century American physician and poet Oliver Wendell Holmes, Sr. wrote: "I would not give one fig for the simplicity this side of complexity, but I would give my life for the simplicity on the other side of complexity." His point gets to the very heart of linking data analytics and data visualization. An effective data visualization finds the simplicity on the far side of complexity; that is, data visualization should simply reveal the insights derived from advanced and sophisticated data analysis.

Data analytics software performs three core functions: enabling data collection, processing data, and communicating insights. Looking at the landscape of data analytics tools in 2017, the market leaders in this crowded field are those that effectively and seamlessly link all three functions while providing robust visualization capabilities. Organizations in the market for data analytics software are looking for solutions with a heavy focus on "visual-based data exploration" and ease of use. Solutions in this sweet spot tend to have leading edge data visualization functionality, require minimal IT support, support sophisticated descriptive/predictive/prescriptive analytics, and move these capabilities out to the business units. Market leaders include Microsoft Power BI, Tableau Desktop, and Qlik Sense. Each of these software solutions meets the requirements listed above and is classified as "Leaders" in Gartner's Magic Quadrant for Business Intelligence and Analytics market report. Figure 4-3 provides

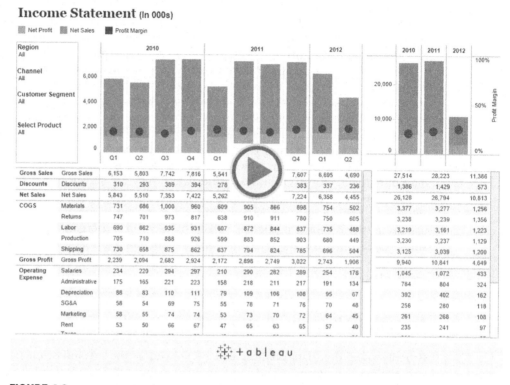

Income Statement (In 000s)

FIGURE 4-3 Data visualization of Income Statement from Tableau Desktop.

an example from Tableau Desktop, while Figure 4-4 lists a few of the software vendors that have mature data analytics offerings.

Case-in-Point 4.7 Gartner's Magic Quadrant is a mainstay in IT market research. The Magic Quadrant has four quadrants: Leaders, Challengers, Niche Players, and Visionaries. Inhabitants of the Leaders quadrant are deemed to have the most complete vision and the highest ability to execute that vision. The Magic Quadrant is typically revised every 2 years to reflect changes in the market as well as maturity of companies' product offerings.[13]

Most of the software in this space can be characterized by drag-and-drop interfaces that are easy to use and master. IBM's Watson Analytics is different. A cloud-based solution, Watson utilizes natural language processing and machine learning to

Google	IBM	Microsoft*
Oracle	Qlik*	SAP
SAS	Tableau*	TIBCO

*"Leaders" in Gartner's 2017 Magic Quadrant for Business Intelligence and Analytics Platforms

FIGURE 4-4 Notable data analytics software vendors.[14]

[13] Gartner Magic Quadrant Research Methodology. www.gartner.com, accessed April 2017.
[14] Gartner. Magic quadrant for business intelligence and analytics platforms. Issued February 2017. www.informationbuilders.com, accessed in April 2017.

interpret and process requests. And, the more requests it receives, the better it is at providing correct answers. If IBM Watson sounds familiar, it might be because you watched the popular television quiz show Jeopardy!

4.5   DATA ANALYTICS AND THE ACCOUNTING PROFESSION

As with any new technology, data analytics has the potential to be a disruptive force in the profession. One concern voiced by accountants is that data analytics will cause a commoditization of accounting services; that is, many tasks that accountants currently perform will be easily routinized and automated as data analytics tools become more sophisticated. While that is almost certain to happen to varying degrees, data analytics also afford accountants the opportunity to replace the value lost to commoditization and automation. In essence, as routine tasks are automated, accountants can leverage this disruptive technology to offer a wider variety of specialized services and to partner in meaningful ways with management and other decision-makers.

In this section, we will look at how data analytics are transforming three sub-disciplines within accounting: tax accounting, managerial accounting, and assurance and compliance. As we'll see, data analytics are driving increased efficiencies in how accountants perform their work, afford quicker access to data for more timely insights, and potentially reposition the accountant's role in the decision-making process.

Tax Accounting

In most organizations, the tax department is one of the largest consumers of data. Every organizational event has some tax implication, and every financial transaction has a tax consequence. To evaluate these implications and consequences, tax accountants must pour over and consume volumes of financial and transactional data. Taxes play a critical role in maximizing shareholder value within an organization: historically, US companies have paid one of the highest corporate tax rates in the world (41%)! While statistics vary, it is estimated that corporate tax accountants spend more than half their time collecting and formatting data from various systems and data sources, and the remainder of their time ensuring compliance with a multitude of tax codes, advising management on tax consequences and strategy, and attending to audit issues.

Big data and data analytics have the potential to transform tax accounting in the coming years. One of the drivers of this transformation is the regulatory nature of tax itself. The current trend is that tax regulators and authorities are requiring more data, and in increasing detail. The rationale for this is pretty clear: just as companies are leveraging big data and data analytics for their strategic and operational objectives, so are the regulators. The US Internal Revenue Service (IRS) is utilizing many of the same tools that companies are to determine which corporate returns to audit.

The complexity and variety of taxes that organizations pay presents challenges as well. Income taxes must be paid at the federal, state, and oftentimes local level. Transaction taxes, such as VAT (value-added tax) and sales tax must be either paid or collected and remitted to taxing authorities. Property taxes, as well as a host of employee taxes, must be paid or collected as well. As mentioned above, most of the data to support calculations associated with these tax determinations are located in disparate systems and data sources throughout the enterprise. Complicating this, much of this data are not in a standard format. As AISs and other information systems are designed and implemented throughout the organization, the needs of the tax department are seldom taken into consideration. As a result, tax accountants must extract data from these systems and manually review, reconcile, and manipulate the data so that they are in a format easily used for their purposes.

One technology that may change this is the tax data hub. A **tax data hub** is a specialized data mart designed to provide a single version of truth for tax-related data. For organizations implementing a tax data hub, this centralized data store automatically extracts data from source systems and loads it in a standard format that lends itself to the needs of the tax department. This approach eliminates many of the manual manipulations currently performed by automating many of these processes. In addition to saving time, tax data hubs increase transparency and enable self-service reporting and analytics.

Data analytics have the potential to more actively engage the tax department in strategic decision-making within the organization. Given more data and the tools necessary to analyze them, tax accountants can provide better insights into reducing the enterprise's effective tax rate (ETR) and protecting and enhancing cash flows. Data analytics can help the tax department more accurately assess the tax consequences of mergers and acquisitions, predict ETR and cash flows associated with taxes, and identify primary drivers of ETR.

Case-in-Point 4.8   Free online tax preparation software sound too good to be true? That's likely because it is. When consumers use free online tax preparation websites to complete their tax returns, they run the risk of having their financial data used for other purposes. These companies are gaining access to consumer data, which is then used to market other financial services, such as mortgages, credit cards, and student loan consolidation loans. As the old adage goes, "There's no such thing as a free lunch."[15]

Managerial Accounting

Historically, management accountants have focused their efforts on three areas: cost management and reporting, performance measurement and analysis, and supporting management's planning and decision-making efforts. The proliferation of internal and external data has been a boon to management accountants. The addition of geotags and other locational data to structured and unstructured data sets has allowed management accountants to provide additional texture to their analyses.

Segment reporting has long been a forte of the management accountant, but this analysis was limited by a lack of granularity in the data. GPS and geotagging allow precise locational data to be associated with transactions, and this new granularity creates opportunities for more nuanced evaluations. For example, at a recent American Accounting Association "Accounting IS Big Data Conference," a consultant recounted a product optimization engagement for one of the Big Three automobile manufacturers. Utilizing Tableau Desktop and the automobile manufacturers' sales and cost data, the consultant was able to overlay these data onto a North America map. This visualization clearly showed which models and option groupings were preferred based on geography. The automobile manufacturer was able to alter their inventory and production models, stocking dealerships with favorably appointed models.

The tasks and responsibilities of a management accountant vary from organization to organization. It is not uncommon for the management accountant to be tasked with special projects aimed at determining the true costs of a course of action, or to develop a budget and control system for a business unit. As data analytics tools mature,

---

[15] Rudegeair, R. and L. Saunders. "The real reason everyone offered you free tax prep this year," www.wsj.com, accessed April 2017.

the speed and efficiency with which these tasks are completed will only increase the management accountant's value to their organization.

Case-in-Point 4.9   After a groundswell of public support, the University of Alabama at Birmingham (UAB) decided to reinstitute several intercollegiate sports programs after shuttering them in 2014 due to financial considerations. UAB's Director of Business Systems Analysis & Special Projects, Andrew Hollis, CPA, developed a series of dashboards to monitor the Athletics Department's financial health. One of the most challenging of these was student financial aid (i.e., scholarship costs). There are many factors to consider when developing this budget: full scholarship versus partial/equivalency scholarships, roster size for each sport, projected number of credit hours taken by student-athletes, room and board obligations, and summer school aid. Using a monthly budget based on historical trend data coupled with anticipated changes in the environment, Hollis created a dashboard that tracks budget versus actual expenses. The dashboard uses a "traffic light" approach, displaying which variances are acceptable (green light), which need monitoring (yellow light), and which need immediate or corrective action (red light). By reviewing these data monthly, the Athletics Department and UAB senior leadership can easily identify positive or negative trends and take appropriate action.[16]

Assurance and Compliance

At their core, assurance and compliance focus on obtaining reasonable assurance that management's assertions are complete, accurate, and truthful, and that the organization is complying with applicable laws, rules and regulations. When senior management issue financial statements, they are implicitly and explicitly claiming ("asserting") that the representations made within the financial statements and accompanying notes are appropriate. Similarly, organizations are subject to a host of laws, regulations, statutes and rules with which they must comply. Sometimes, when organizations are not in compliance with relevant laws, or the financial statements are not a true and accurate representation of the financial position of the organization, fraudulent activity is the cause. It is the role of the auditor to evaluate management's assertions, determine compliance with applicable laws, and evaluate whether any irregularities are the result of fraud.

The audit, whether it be an audit of financial statements or an audit of the controls embedded in an AIS, has always been a labor-intensive effort. In many instances, there are simply too many transactions for a single auditor or even a team of auditors to examine individually. As a result, several decades ago, auditors moved to a sampling approach, whereby only a subset of transactions were examined, with inferences then made to the population as a whole.

Audit data analytics have the potential to reverse this trend and make reviewing the entire population of transaction possible in a relatively short amount of time with minimal effort. Broadly speaking, **audit data analytics** is the art and science of identifying and analyzing pattern, trends and anomalies through an examination of audit-related data. This examination typically entails modeling, visualization and analysis, and informs the planning and execution of an assurance engagement.

Already, the Big Four public accounting firms such as PricewaterhouseCoopers (PwC) and Ernst & Young (EY) have rolled out audit data analytics software that audit

---

[16] Interview with Andrew Hollis, CPA, Director of Business Systems Analysis & Special Projects, Office of the Vice President of Financial Affairs and Administration, University of Alabama at Birmingham, conducted in May 2017.

teams use to enhance the quality and relevance of assurance and compliance engagements. For example, PwC's **Halo** incorporates a journals dashboard that provides a variety of visualizations, such as a graphical frequency distribution that shows which users created the most transactions (by volume and dollar amount), which users created the most or least journal entries, and whether they were manual or automated journal entries. Similarly, EY's **Helix** incorporates a series of visual ledgers that allow auditors to follow the flow of transactions through the various stages of the reporting cycle and flags suspect journal entries. Halo, Helix, and other audit dashboards are fully interactive. For example, by clicking on any of the graphics, an auditor can drill down to the underlying data.[17]

Tools such as Halo (Figure 4-5) and Helix (Figure 4-6) help auditors perform their work faster, cheaper, and better. By utilizing audit data analytics, auditors can better identify areas of the audit that would benefit from more attention, resulting in more focused audits. In addition to gaining deeper insights into traditional audit data, these tools can also integrate external data sources such as benchmarking and competitive analysis metrics to provide greater assurance on the veracity of management's assertions.

The transformation of assurance and compliance activities isn't limited to finding better ways to evaluate financial statements and corporate adherence to applicable regulatory guidance. Auditors are leveraging artificial intelligence and machine learning to develop tools with the ability to read and understand documents. Deloitte's **Argus** tool (developed in partnership with Kira Systems) utilizes artificial intelligence and natural language processing to "read" contracts and extract key information for further analysis. For example, rather than having an auditor or other staff spend time reading a contract and identifying contractual requirements and conditions that must be met, the document is simply uploaded to Argus. In short order, the software extracts key provisions and verbiage.

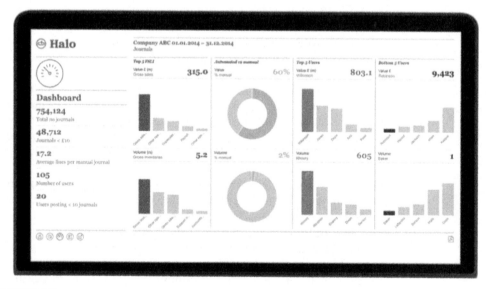

FIGURE 4-5 PwC's Halo.

---

[17] "Data analytics for external auditors: international auditing perspectives," accessed from www.icaew.com/iaae, April 2017.

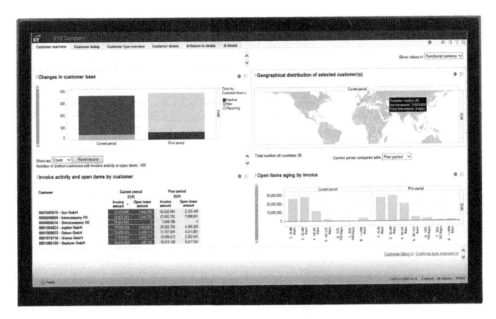

FIGURE 4-6 EY's Helix.

Case-in-Point 4.10 Deloitte took the basic Kira Systems contract analysis software and "taught" it how to recognize the contract parties, revenue recognition and pricing models, and other factors. After initially pilot testing Argus for audit and consulting engagements in 2014, Deloitte decided in 2016 to roll it out to its client base as well.[18]

Fraud investigation and forensic accounting are also leveraging the power of data analytics to transform how fraud is identified and investigated. In addition to fraud tools built into audit data analytics software like Halo and Helix that look for suspicious transactions or account activity, mining and analyzing unstructured data is the wave of the future. Researchers are developing tools that allow for textual analysis of emails and other unstructured data to detect language that potentially signals fraud or deception. Researchers in the communications and information systems fields have long been looking at ways of mining such unstructured textual data to better detect deceptive communications and fraudulent activity. By combining techniques such as textual analysis with social network analysis (which measures the strength of ties within social groups to determine connections and influence), fraud examiners are able to add another tool to their toolbox.[19]

Case-in-Point 4.11 The U.S. Securities and Exchange Commission (SEC) implemented its Accounting Quality Model (AQM), nicknamed RoboCop, in 2013 as part of a broader set of initiatives to identify and combat financial statement fraud by utilizing big data and data analytics tools. Within 24 hours of a company submitting their filings to the SEC's EDGAR online database, AQM analyses the filings for any high-risk activity by comparing the company's filings against other filing from companies in the filer's industry peer group. Based on

---

[18] "Deloitte partners with Kira Systems to bring AI into the workplace," accessed from www.legaltechnology.com, April 2017.
[19] Worrell, J., M. Wasko, and A. Johnston. 2013. Social network analysis in accounting information systems research. *International Journal of Accounting Information Systems* 14(2): 127–137.

an analysis of both quantitative and qualitative factors, AQM is able to assign a risk score to each filing, thereby providing regulators insights into which companies to investigate.[20]

The use of data analytics in assurance and compliance engagements is increasing. However, there are challenges to exploiting these tools to their fullest potential. Besides the technical challenges associated with the tools themselves, one of the most difficult obstacles is cultural: many organizations hesitate to provide auditors direct access to data for fear of security breaches. And while there is wide adoption of data analytics for reviewing journal entries and performing detailed general ledger analyses, its use is still limited in such areas as revenue testing and process analytics.[21]

AIS AT WORK
Conversation with a Data Scientist

Bill McKinnon, Ph.D., is Founder and CEO of Capitalytics (www.capitalytics.com), a boutique data analytics consultancy based in Birmingham, AL. Capitalytics focuses on the financial services industry, specializing in community banks located in the southeastern United States. Dr. McKinnon started his academic and professional career in engineering, specifically electrical and computer engineering. After spending time in academia teaching courses on performance analysis for telecommunication systems at a large research university, he founded Capitalytics in 2008 to respond to the growing need of community banks to manage their risk in the face of increasing banking regulation. One of the authors spent an afternoon with Dr. McKinnon discussing his insights on data analytics and his thoughts on how data analytics were changing business practices.

When asked about the typical focus of a data analytics engagement, Dr. McKinnon's response was pretty straightforward. "Regardless of client size, I'm typically dealing with three types of questions. (1) How do I find new customers? (2) How do I improve profits? (3) How do I manage risks (decrease expenses or losses)? These are universal issues that go to the core of any business and its reason to exist: generating value for its owners." He further elaborated that his clients are generally more focused on issues around driving additional demand (i.e., finding new customers) and managing risk-based capital (i.e., overinvesting in a single category, thereby unnecessarily increasing their exposure).

The conversation shifted to the biggest challenges that organizations face in utilizing analytics for decision-making. Surprisingly, the answer was culture. "Cultural issues seem to regularly turn into the most expensive and most daunting challenges. Convincing stakeholders who are not necessarily experts … when they have an agenda of their own, other obligations and unspoken issues … is an extremely challenging task. Collecting resources to accumulate data, vetting and validating information without bias, and then presenting results in the most palatable manner such that

---

[20] Novack, J. "How SEC's new RoboCop profiles companies for accounting fraud." www.forbes.com, accessed April 2017.

[21] Financial Reporting Council. "Audit quality thematic review: The use of data analytics in the audit of financial statements." Report issued in January 2017, accessed April 2017.

appropriate actions can be taken without implying improper messages can be a chore in and of itself."

We wrapped up our conversation by discussing the role of data visualization and his thoughts on how data analytics might change the accounting profession. Dr. McKinnon noted that "visualization is a necessary portion of the tool suite in order to validate your theories for batches of data and to communicate your information or conclusions to others in meaningful ways." He noted that, in many circles, new opportunities and technologies were characterized as "vitamin," "aspirin," or "condiment". Vitamins strengthen the organization by enabling it to access new revenue streams, aspirin eliminates an organization's headaches by removing expense and mitigating risks, and condiments don't perceptibly help the organization in the end. Based on our discussions, a strong argument can be made that data analytics represent both vitamin and aspirin. Organizations that choose to view data analytics as condiment do so at their peril.

There is a growing demand for accounting students with data analytics skills, and they don't need a Ph.D. in Computer Engineering to get a job. More and more, public accounting firms are either embedding data analytics into their core service delivery methodologies, or creating data analytics practice groups that support core service lines. From PwC's Advanced Risk and Compliance Analytics to KPMG's Audit Data & Analytics, opportunities abound for accounting students looking to marry a passion for accounting and data analysis.

SUMMARY

- ✓ Big data is characterized by its volume, velocity, variety, and veracity.
- ✓ Accountants use data from operational, mechanical, and social sources to complete a variety of analyses.
- ✓ Data analytics allow accountants to answer the following questions: what happened? what might happen? what should be done?
- ✓ Data analytics are driving efficiencies in how accountants perform their work, provide quicker access to data, and have the potential to reposition the role of the accountant within the organization.
- ✓ Data analytics are having a profound impact on tax accounting, managerial accounting, and assurance and compliance.

KEY TERMS YOU SHOULD KNOW

Argus (Deloitte)
data mart
data warehouse
database as a service (DAAS)
descriptive analytics
Hadoop

Halo
Helix
MapReduce
online analytical processing
    (OLAP)
predictive analytics

prescriptive analytics
tax data hub
variety
velocity
veracity
volume

TEST YOURSELF

Q4-1. Which of these is *not* one of the four V's of big data?

    a. velocity

    b. volume

    c. variety

    d. validation

Q4-2. When describing big data, the term "velocity" refers to:

    a. the speed at which data is transmitted over the Internet

    b. the speed at which Internet posts "go viral"

    c. the speed at which new data are created

    d. the speed at which fake news becomes acceptable news

Q4-3. An example of "unstructured data" is:

    a. a purchase amount on credit

    b. a cash payment

    c. a loan for a car

    d. a Twitter feed

Q4-4. In context of big data, the term "veracity" refers to:

    a. trusted data

    b. how widely the data are believed

    c. whether or not the data have been validated

    d. none of these

Q4-5. An example of an ERP system is:

    a. QuickBooks

    b. SAP

    c. a legacy system

    d. all of these

Q4-6. The **process** of extracting data from data sources and storing it in a data store is commonly called:

    a. the SAP process

    b. the AACSB process

    c. the four V process

    d. the ETL process

Q4-7. A pivot table is similar to a:

    a. list of student grades

    b. set of unstructured data

    c. cross tabulation of data

    d. ERP system

Q4-8. A data mart acts as a what for a data warehouse?

    a. data interface

    b. repository

    c. source of data

    d. backup

Q4-9. A tax data hub is an example of:

    a. a data warehouse

    b. a data mart

    c. a computer network

    d. a validation system

Q4-10. Audit data analytics enables auditors to perform audits

    a. only on samples of audit data

    b. only on audit data stored in data warehouses

    c. on complete populations of audit data

    d. on small data—not big data

DISCUSSION QUESTIONS

4-1. What are the four V's that describe big data? What does each "V" mean?

4-2. What do we mean by "unstructured data?" Do you believe that this term is accurate, or would you prefer some other term for it?

4-3. How is big data growing? What new data are now available that were not traditionally used by accounting systems in the past? How is this data growth challenging the way accountants perform their jobs?

4-4. What is the ETL process? What are its steps?

4-5. What is online analytical processing? What are examples of OLAP software?

4-6. What is Hadoop? Why do organizations use it?

4-7. How does Hadoop's data storage system differ from those of traditional system? In what ways are such a system of data storage superior to storing data on a centralized database?

4-8. What is Hadoop's MapReduce? How does it help Hadoop process data? Why is MapReduce's system sometimes superior to the data transmissions of older systems?

4-9. What is a data warehouse? Why do companies use them?

4-10. What is a data mart? How is a data mart related to a data warehouse? Can you have a data warehouse without a data mart?

4-11. How are data analytics helping tax accountants perform their tasks? How is this different from what they did a few years ago?

4-12. How are data analytics helping auditors with assurance and compliance testing? How is this different from what they did a few years ago?

4-13. What are Halo and Helix? How do they help auditors perform their jobs better?

PROBLEMS

4-14. Deceptive Apartments has a policy that requires new tenants to "like" it on Facebook. Some renters don't mind, but others object because it was not a requirement when they moved it. Further, some argue, the policy is unreasonable because it creates a false impression about the complex. However, there is nothing illegal about this requirement. Do you feel this policy is reasonable, or do you object to it? Defend your answer.

4-15. Using your favorite search engine, search for "Gartner Magic Quadrant for Business Intelligence and Analytics Platforms." Pick one of the vendors from the "Visionaries" quadrant. Research their data analytics/data visualization product offering. What do you feel are three strengths of this platform? What do you feel

are three weaknesses of this platform? What do you think is keeping their software from being included in the "Leaders" quadrant (i.e., what does your research suggest is holding the product back regarding ability to execute)?

4-16. IBM's Watson captivated pop culture when it beat two of Jeopardy's most successful champions. Using your favorite search engine, find an example of how Watson is being used in a business context to improve business outcomes.

4-17. As machine learning and artificial intelligence tools become more sophisticated, they are being adopted more and more for detecting fraudulent activity. Using your favorite search engine, find an example of a fraud or other white collar crime that was detected using these tools.

CASE ANALYSES

4-18. Forest Meadows Apartments (Using Social Media for Financial Decisions)

Mattie and Jaime have been friends since grammar school, but they now both attend State University. As agreed, they met under the big tree—a common meeting place for students.

"How did your interview go at Forest Meadows?" asked Mattie as they both sat down on the park bench.

"Well, good and bad" answered Jaime. "On the positive side, they have really nice apartments over there and the rents are reasonable. There is a corner unit available now that looks over a green belt that I especially liked."

"So what's the problem?" asked Mattie.

"The application requires tenants to provide their social media names and passwords, that is, your credentials on Facebook, Instagram, LinkedIn, and Twitter. The manager said they are using new software called "Renter Rater" to evaluate your online comments, analyze your suitability as a tenant, and rate you on such things as your personality, social habits, and even "current financial stress level."

"Is that even legal?" asked Mattie.

"I don't know, but it's certainly an invasion of privacy in my opinion. I asked the manager if most people actually provide their information and he said they did. He also added that 'Most people are willing to compromise their privacy if they want something badly enough.'"

"Are you going to give them your account information?" Mattie asked.

"I'm thinking about it, but I haven't decided. Forest Meadows is not the only apartment complex near campus, and I want to know if this is common practice. I also want to know if it's legal."

Requirements

1. Research the housing and rental laws in your community. Does this renter software violate any housing laws? If so, which ones?

2. Should organizations be allowed to use social media data when making such financial decisions as approving apartment rental applications? How about when a condo board reviews an application from a nonresident to purchase a condominium in its building?

3. Should landlords be allowed to require access to social media platforms as a condition for tenancy? What about employers hiring job applicants?

4. Do you agree with the manager that most people will compromise their privacy for something they want badly?

5. Would you provide your social media account information in order to qualify as a tenant in an apartment complex you liked? Why or why not?

4-19. Blazer Industries (Predictive Maintenance)

Blazer Interactive is a software company that focuses on first-person player video games. In 2013, Blazer's CEO, Alexander James, introduced a revolutionary new gaming console to his company's product line. The z/Station's primary draw was a virtual reality helmet that provided a totally immersive experience for gamers. The z/Helmet not only offered a stunning video and audio experience, as well as vibrations and other movement-simulating feedback that was synced to the action in the game. Additionally, it captured vital statistics data (heart rate, blood pressure, and the like) from the player and, using a complex server-side algorithm, utilized this data to augment the game's action and scenarios. Blazer Interactive upgraded the system in 2015 with other "smart" accessories, and by 2017 the z/System$_2$ had an almost cult following.

However, there were issues. While a new z/System$_3$ was due out later in the Fall, James and his staff were having difficulty estimating demand for the new system. There were also concerns about escalating warranty costs due to component failure. James worried about estimating product failure rates so that the company could properly accruing for warranty cost, and what effect, if any, social media buzz (either positive or negative) would have on demand.

During a brainstorming session, one of Blazer Interactive's new accountants had an idea. "You know, we've captured a ton of data on these systems since we introduced them in 2013. Even though we've innovated our products with regularity every year or so, the underlying hardware—motors and accelerometers and sensors and thingies—well, that hasn't really changed. And don't we have terabytes of data that is granular down to the individual unit level? Stuff like active use time, user vital stats—that junk? What would stop us from pairing that with data from our warranty service center software? We could actually predict *when* a console or z/Helmet was going to fail, couldn't we?"

The head of marketing chimed in as well. "Yeah, that's cool! And we could probably do some analysis on social media buzz … you know, maybe look at the Twitter and Facebook buzz ahead of our previous product launches, and try to use that to extrapolate out what demand might be for the upgraded console?"

Requirements

1. What type of analytics do you feel would be most appropriate for Blazer Interactive to use (descriptive, predictive, prescriptive)? Why?

2. Are there other data sources that the team should be looking to for insights into product failure rates or to anticipate demand for a new console?

3. As an accountant, how comfortable are you with using nonfinancial data (like sentiment analysis from social media) to augment or fine-tune product pricing and demand decisions? Do you think this will become mainstream practice in the short-term?

4. Do you have any concerns about the z/System$_3$ capturing vital statistics on users and storing them on a network? How much privacy are you willing to trade for an enhanced and personalized user experience?

5. What additional service offerings do you thing Blazer Interactive might be able to offer given the data they are collecting? How might these data be monetized into other services or revenue streams?

READINGS AND OTHER RESOURCES

Amana, F. and A. Fadlalla. 2017. Data mining applications in accounting: A review of the literature and organizing framework. *International Journal of Accounting Information Systems* 24: 32–58.

Applebaum, D., A. Kogan, M. Vasarhelyi, and Z. Yan. 2017. Impact of business analytics and enterprise systems on managerial accounting. *International Journal of Accounting Information Systems* 25: 29–44.

PricewaterhouseCoopers. 2015. Data driven: What students need to succeed in a rapidly changing business world. Whitepaper.

PricewaterhouseCoopers. 2017. Investing in America's data science and analytics talent: The case for action. Whitepaper.

ANSWERS TO TEST YOURSELF

1. d **2.** c **3.** d **4.** a **5.** b **6.** d **7.** c **8.** a **9.** b **10.** c

Chapter 5

Integrated Accounting and Enterprise Software

After reading this chapter, you will be able to:

1. *Explain* the meaning, and *list* the advantages and disadvantages of integrated accounting software.

2. *Explain* how integrated accounting software differs from standard accounting software and also from enterprise resource planning (ERP) systems.

3. *Explain* how various functions in enterprise software work together.

4. *Describe* the architecture of enterprise systems, including their use of a centralized database.

5. *Discuss* the relationship between business process reengineering and enterprise system implementation.

6. *Assess* the costs and benefits associated with enterprise systems.

7. *Recognize* when an organization needs a new AIS.

8. *Explain* how organizations go about selecting accounting and enterprise software.

"All too often, companies' accounting departments do not spend enough time or energy planning or designing their systems before purchasing and installing an accounting package. The result is usually a system with a limited ability to capture and report information in a meaningful way."

Laurence, S. 2014. Choosing and configuring accounting software.
The CPA Journal (May): 13.

5.1 INTRODUCTION

This chapter describes various types of integrated accounting and enterprise software. Initially, accounting software packages were simple bookkeeping systems. With advances in hardware and software technology, these packages have become increasingly sophisticated and customized for specific industry needs. Today, they are capable of collecting, storing, processing, and distributing a wide variety of the financial and nonfinancial data needed to support business decisions. Further, specialized accounting software packages can accommodate the specific needs of various industries that have unique business processes (such as those described in Chapter 9).

For many large firms, accounting software has become one or more modules within corporate-wide software called **enterprise resource planning (ERP) systems**. These

ERP systems encompass the informational needs of an entire organization and have large databases at their core. In ERP systems, the accounting functions interface with manufacturing, sales and distribution, human resources (HR), and other systems. Realizing the benefits of integrating their information systems, today's largest enterprises extend their ERP systems throughout their supply chains. This chapter discusses various aspects of integrated accounting software and enterprise-wide systems in some detail, including their functionality, architecture, effects on employees and business processes, costs, and benefits. Because ERP packages are so important to accountants, we also cover this software in more depth.

Knowing when to upgrade to a new accounting information system can be a challenge. In some cases, changes in an organization's external environment, such as increased competition, may force an upgrade. In other cases, management must identify and assess current business processes to determine whether the firm needs new accounting systems to improve processes. Whatever the reason, selecting the right software for an organization is both critical and challenging. The last section of this chapter discusses the topic of software selection.

5.2   INTEGRATED ACCOUNTING SOFTWARE

The term **integrated accounting software** refers to accounting software that bundles several separate accounting processes in the same package. Thus, an integrated package can process most types of accounting transactions—for example, transactions affecting accounts in both general and special journals such as sales and purchases. Integrated accounting software programs organize transaction processing in modules and provide links between these modules. The general ledger module, which includes the chart of accounts, is the foundation for the system. Some additional modules typically found in integrated accounting software are accounts receivable, accounts payable, inventory, and payroll. These modules correspond to the business processes discussed in Chapters 8 and 9.

The journal entries recorded in accounting software modules update the general ledger module on either a periodic or (more often) a real-time basis. An integrated system may also include additional modules such as job costing, purchasing, billing, invoicing, and fixed assets. Figure 5-1 lists several features commonly found in integrated accounting packages.

• Audit trails	• Graphing and charting capabilities
• Budgeting capabilities	• Inventory management
• Cash- and accrual-based accounting options	• Multicompany support
• Check and invoice printing	• Multiple currency handling
• Cloud computing capabilities	• Multiuser support
• Customizable financial reporting	• Recurring journal entry capabilities
• Customizable viewing screens	• Scalability
• E-commerce (Internet) connectivity	• Variance analysis (budget to actual)
• Encryption capabilities	• XBRL reporting capabilities
• Financial analysis tools	

FIGURE 5-1   Some features of integrated accounting software packages (presented in alphabetical order).

Small Business Accounting Software

Integrated accounting software is available to small businesses at low cost or, in the case of Microsoft, free. Two examples are *Quickbooks* by Intuit and various packages of *Peachtree* by Sage Software. Even the most basic accounting software typically includes a chart of accounts and modules for the general ledger, accounts receivable, and accounts payable. The software can produce many kinds of accounting reports, including basic financial statements and budget reports as well as bar graphs and pie charts. In addition, many packages have several sample charts of accounts for different types of organizations, which users can customize to match their organizations' account structures.

Case-in-Point 5.1   If you owned a small hotel, you might want to keep track of different sources of revenue. The prime one is room revenues, of course, but you might also want information on gift-shop sales, restaurant sales, parking fees, laundry services, phone charges, Wi-Fi fees, and room services. The same idea applies to such expenditures as maid services, inventory costs, food costs, and labor expenditures. Do you want reports on a daily, weekly, and monthly basis? Then what you want is an integrated accounting system!

Although the software itself may be inexpensive, the challenge for many small businesses is learning how to use the software and get the greatest value from these products. For example, how many features are there in MS Word that you don't use—or don't even know about? Similarly, to gain the most benefit from any accounting software, a business should consider discussing options with its CPA firm or a local software consultant who can help managers select the software, train employees, identify useful reports, or possibly even help with rescue and recovery needs should a disaster occur.

A trend in low-end and mid-level accounting software has been the consolidation of vendors and the availability of more extensive product lines from the remaining ones. For example, Intuit sells over 20 different versions of its accounting software, and you can select from 10 different Peachtree offerings. The variety of features offered in these software packages also continues to grow. One feature that even low-end packages incorporate today is *Internet connectivity*, which permits small businesses to create websites and engage in electronic commerce. For example, *Peachtree Accounting* has a special link that allows companies to take orders and receive payments over the Internet. Another software feature is the ability to export accounting data in XBRL format (see Chapter 2).

Yet, a third feature now commonly found in many low-end accounting packages is cloud computing capabilities. This feature allows users to store financial data, or even use the accounting software itself, on hosted sites. The advantages of this feature include (1) anytime, anywhere access to accounting information from a variety of Internet access devices, (2) synchronized storage and backup of important accounting data, (3) multiuser access (perhaps from different remote locations), (4) automatic upgrades to newer versions of the software, and (5) the ability to view reports directly from host data sources.

According to a recent article in PC magazine, the top accounting packages for small businesses in 2017 were Freshbooks, Xero, Zoho Books, QuickBooks Online Plus, GoDaddy Bookkeeping, Sage 50c, AccountEdge Pro, FreeAgent, and One UP.[1] Among the features used to rate these packages were time tracking, the availability of

[1] Yakai, K. 2016. The Best Small Business Software for 2017. *PC Magazine*. Accessed online at: http://www.pcmag.com/article2/0,2817,2458748,00.asp.

live support, document management, the availability of employee training, the ability to estimate quarterly taxes, the ability to integrate with customer support management (CRM) systems, and currency options.

Another useful feature of accounting packages for small business is **scalability**—the ability of the software to grow with a business. This allows organizations to include more online users, add modules to the software, or upgrade to more powerful software versions without reinstalling or reconfiguring data. For example, the *Quickbooks* product line includes a low-end package with very basic financial accounting features for about $100, which a company can upgrade to larger and more powerful packages, including an enterprise-wide software package that sells for several thousand dollars. "Scalability" is important because it allows a small business to start small and at low cost and later easily upgrade to more sophisticated software as the business grows.

A feature related to "scalability" is "compatibility with other systems." Each time an organization changes software, for example, it might also need to reformat historical or current transaction data, create new codes for customers, employees, or products, and/or redefine its chart of accounts. Understandably, cost savings occur when software packages allow users to avoid these tasks (e.g., can read file data from other vendors' versions) or provide software tools that make such transitions easier.

Finally, it may be important for a company to be able to customize its software. Some organizations may be willing to use the default screens offered by a software package, but most won't. In fact, the closer a company can make the appearance of new user screens resemble the older ones, the less training employees will need and the easier the transition to a new system.

Small business accounting software is usually adequate for businesses with less than $5 million in revenue and relatively few employees. One factor to consider when choosing a package is "cost." The acquisition costs of new software are likely to be the tip of an iceberg, as transition costs such as as training, implementation, and software modifications can significantly add to total costs. A second factor is the number of transactions that the system can process in a given period of time (e.g., in a month). For example, if a company processes only a few accounts receivable transactions daily, an inexpensive package should be fine. A third factor is the maximum number of online users. Figure 5-2 provides further details about these considerations.

Software Type	Business Characteristics	Cost	Examples
Entry-level	Smaller businesses with less than 10 active users	Free–$1,000	MYOB, Sage Peachtree, Intuit Quickbooks
Small-medium business	Less than 100 active users	$5,000–$100,000	Sage MAS 90, Sage MAS 200, Quickbooks Enterprise
Small-medium business basic enterprise system	Over 100 active users	$20,000–$500,000	Sage MAS 500 ERP, Microsoft Dynamics AX
High-end enterprise system	Over 100 users and capable of handling the volume of Fortune 1000 firms	$500,000–hundreds of millions of dollars	JD Edwards, Oracle, PeopleSoft, SAP
Custom-built	Any size	$5,000–hundreds of millions of dollars	

FIGURE 5-2 Types of accounting and enterprise software.

Mid-Range and Large-Scale Accounting Software

When transaction processing needs grow in volume and complexity, a mid-range or large-scale software package may be necessary. Some examples are *Adaptive Insights*, Microsoft's *Dynamics AX, GP*, and *SL, SAP Business One, Certify, Epicor*, Sage software's *MAS 90* and *MAS200, Everest, Made2Manage, Tagetik*, and *Accpac*. These software packages range in cost from $2,000 to well over $300,000 and offer many of the advanced features needed by larger companies.

One capability required by international companies is the ability to process transactions in multiple currencies. Some software packages can convert transactions from one currency to another and write checks in foreign currencies. Two additional features are the availability of a wide range of reports and the ability to customize them. A third feature is the ability to split commissions among multiple salespersons.

Case-in-Point 5.2 Mid-range and large-scale accounting software may also handle more than just accounting functions. For example, Sage software's *Accpac* product line includes modules for financial accounting, purchasing, sales and receivables, inventory management, project management, and payroll. The software can integrate with other solutions, extending its usefulness for customer relationship management (CRM), business intelligence (BI), e-commerce, human resource management, point-of-sale, management of fixed assets, and supply chain (warehouse) management. Accpac's *Extended Enterprise Suite* now includes dashboards, a fixed asset management module, and other desirable features.[2]

In addition to offering a variety of modules and interfaces, mid-level and large-scale software vendors allow customers to choose from an array of deployment options. One possibility is to avoid purchasing a software package altogether and instead rely on cloud software—i.e., a **hosted solution**. Both *Peachtree* and *Accpac* provide such services.

Specialized Accounting Information Systems

There are literally thousands of vendors that sell accounting software designed to fit a particular industry or niche within an industry. Some examples are accounting software for dental offices, pet retailers, schools, or state tax offices. Many accounting software developers also offer add-on modules for special needs—for example, job-cost modules for manufacturing companies, point-of-sale features for retailers, or reservation systems for car-rental agencies. *Execu/Suite* by Execu/Tech integrates accounting, property management functions, reservation systems, housekeeping management, sales and marketing, online booking, event management, dining reservations, and in-room movie accounting. Similarly, *Rent Centric* offers accounting software for companies that rent cars, motorhomes, motorcycles, and boats.

An interesting category of accounting software are packages designed for non-profit organizations. These include charities, hospitals, churches, private schools, and most state and local government agencies. Captera.com publishes a list of top free accounting software packages for nonprofits at www.captera.com.[3]

---

[2] Sage Software, Inc., accessed at www.sageaccpac.com.
[3] Morpus, N. 2016. The Top 8 Free Accounting Software for Nonprofits. *Captera Nonprofit Technology Blog.* Accessed online at: http://blog.capterra.com/top-free-accounting-software-for-nonprofit/.

Case-in-Point 5.3 *Cougar Mountain Fund Suit*e is an example of accounting software designed for charities. The software allows users to track donations by individuals or track projects and grants needed for governmental reporting purposes. This package can handle transfers among funds, deal with multiple grants with varying year-ends, and keep records about restricted, temporarily restricted, and unrestricted contributions and assets in separate categories.[4]

Another important feature may be customization. Some accounting packages support programs written by independent developers that provide features needed by customers in specialized industries. Other software vendors include the source code with their packages so that businesses can customize the software for themselves. Customizing software is a good business for value-added resellers or consultants who have programming skills and an understanding of the specific needs of specialized businesses.

5.3 ENTERPRISE-WIDE INFORMATION SYSTEMS

An organization's information systems must do more than process accounting data. These systems must also process data from the departments of production, marketing, HR, and finance, all of which must interface with accounting software. One solution to such enterprise-wide requirements is to acquire corporate-wide, integrated software. Examples of such **enterprise resource planning (ERP) systems**, **enterprise software**, or **business application suites** include *Microsoft Dynamics AX, SAP All-in-One, Sage MAS 500, NetSuite Enterprise Solution, Infor Enterprise Solutions, Epicor, and Oracle.*

Because high-end ERP products can cost hundreds of millions of dollars, they are mostly used by the world's largest business organizations. Three important features of ERP systems are (1) integration, (2) centralized databases, and (3) the need for business process reengineering. "Integration" occurs because ERP software integrates the accounting subsystem with CRM, business services, HR, and supply chain management (SCM)—see Figure 5-3. A "centralized database" occurs because the data from the separate functional areas of an organization flow into, and out of, a central repository of corporate-wide data, as opposed to a number of different, nonintegrated databases.

Finally, large-scale ERP software typically forces companies to reengineer or redesign some of their business processes. This is because it is usually not possible, or else very expensive, to customize ERP software for each business. Thus, the joke about low-end software is that the system must accommodate user needs, while for high-end ERPs, users (and business processes) must accommodate the needs of the system.

Case-in-Point 5.4 Such multinational corporations as Eastman Kodak Company, Owens-Corning Fiberglass Corporation, and Procter & Gamble have spent millions of dollars implementing *SAP* for the potential cost savings achieved from streamlining, speeding, or consolidating processes. One study found that the US Department of Agriculture saved $18 million per year by implementing SAP to consolidate its financial management, budget, and purchasing processes.[5]

---

[4] Cougar Mountain Software Inc., accessed at www.cougarmtn.com.
[5] IDC Government Insights, Best Practices: A ProveIT Case Study—Financial Management Modernization at the USDA Positively Impacts Mission by Adelaide O'Brien, accessed from www.government-insights.com in May 2014.

FIGURE 5-3 ERP system integration.

Enterprise System Functionality

Basic ERP Functions. Today's ERP systems integrate many of an organization's major business processes—for example, order processing and fulfilment, manufacturing, purchasing, and HR functions—all of which provide data to each other and to a company's financial system. This integration means, for example, that a salesperson taking an order for a manufacturing company is able to check inventory availability immediately from the same system. If inventory exists, the system notifies shipping to pick the goods and fill the order. If there is insufficient inventory on hand (remember that the customer is important), the ERP system can trigger the manufacturing subsystem to make more product. This can result in a revision to production schedules to accommodate the new orders. HR may also be involved if the new order requires extra workers. The point is that all functional areas of the organization can access and use the same information to meet customer needs, with one centralized database that stores all of the firm's data.

Extended ERP Systems. The business processes in ERP systems that handle **back-office operations** are primarily concerned an enterprise's internal systems. Traditional ERP systems focus on internal data, generated primarily by internal processes (e.g., HR and manufacturing), and an enterprise's own decision-makers. Today's ERP systems also have e-business and other **front-office** capabilities. **Extended enterprise systems** bring customers, suppliers, and other business partners, such as investors and strategic business relations, into the picture.

ERP systems also interface with suppliers and customers through **supply chain management (SCM)** applications. The supply chain for a single enterprise extends from its suppliers to its customers. It includes product development, materials sourcing,

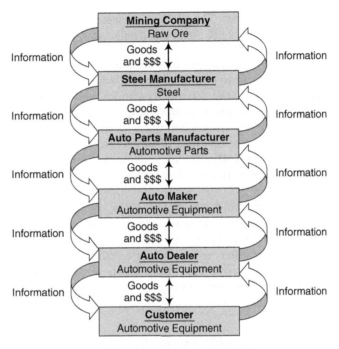

FIGURE 5-4 The supply chain for a component of the automotive industry.

production, and product delivery to the customer. However, the supply chain of one company is only one part of a *linked* supply chain. Figure 5-4 demonstrates this concept for an automotive manufacturer. Note that goods and money are not the only commodities exchanged by partners along the chain. Information flows backward from customers to suppliers. SCM applications provide suppliers with access to the buyer's internal data, including inventory levels and sales orders. These data allow a business to reduce the cycle time for procuring goods for manufacture and sale. At the same time, customers can view the supplier's information related to their orders.

Another tool that helps companies optimize their supply chain is **customer relationship management (CRM)**. CRM is a collection of applications including databases, sales order and customer service systems, and financial packages. The integrated CRM collects the data from these disparate applications and integrates them for decision-making purposes. Businesses also use CRM to analyze customer data—for example, find trends and buying patterns. This analysis can improve customer relations when the business uses the information to meet customer needs.

Business intelligence (BI) tools help managers analyze and report data from their firms' information systems. Combined with BI tools, CRM enables businesses to serve their customers better and to improve their bottom lines. For example, CRM combined with BI can help a company learn which of its customers are most profitable and can direct sales efforts toward those customers. Analysis of buying trends and special customer features can increase sales revenues and cut costs.

Case-in-Point 5.5 Cartridge World is the fastest-growing franchise in the $80 billion printer cartridge industry. Recently, it successfully integrated NetSuite into its operations to oversee hundreds of its 1,650 worldwide franchise locations and manage a rapidly growing business. The company estimates that it saves about $200,000 in annual IT and administrative costs. Their B2B e-commerce capabilities supported a 200% increase in sales across their 1,650 stores worldwide.[6]

Other ERP applications link strategic partners to an organization. Of course, many of these partners are suppliers and customers, but others include investors, creditors, transporters, and other channel partners with whom the enterprise might "team up." **Collaborative business partnerships** are becoming more common as organizations find that there are often advantages to working with other businesses, and even their competitors, to increase their ability to meet customer demands. **Partner relationship management (PRM)** software enhances the working relationship between partners, particularly when they use the Internet.

ERPs for Niche Markets. Some ERPs are designed for specialized markets. For example, ERP software developed specifically for mid-range manufacturing companies include *Infor Distribution A+, SYSPRO, Epicor Prophet 21, and Inform Software. Similar systems catering to wholesale distributors include NetSuite, Sage ERP X3, and Sage 500 ERP.* As you might imagine, these packages differ in price (typically starting at $10,000), maximum number of users (typically less than 1,000), or the ability to work with multiple currencies.

The Architecture of Enterprise Systems

The four major components of an ERP's architecture are the (1) systems configuration, (2) centralized database, (3) application interfaces, and (4) Internet portals. Please refer to Figure 5-5 as we examine each of these components in greater detail.

Systems Configuration. The term "systems configuration" means how the ERP system is deployed. While ERP systems are usually licensed software that companies run on their own computers, some organizations prefer the hosted (cloud) solution discussed earlier. These configurations appeal to managers concerned about the high cost of acquiring an ERP or who are uncertain about their benefits. As with other hosted solutions, the customer saves on purchase or lease costs, hardware costs, and the maintenance and upgrade expenses of an ERP system.

In addition to these cost considerations, there may be security advantages of the hosted option because the vendor assumes the responsibility for encryption, security, and disaster recovery. A business that operates in a region at risk from such natural disasters as hurricanes or earthquakes may find that a hosted solution provides a greater comfort level regarding business continuity because the hardware and software are off-site. However, organizations in some industries where data security is especially important (e.g., health care and banking) may be concerned about a hosted solution because they give up control over their data.

Case-in-Point 5.6 Thermos, Inc., needed better information than it was getting from its current ERP system. However, the IT staff and others had invested heavily in the current system and were reluctant to upgrade. Management therefore decided on a hosted system, *Oracle On Demand.* The switch led to decreased needs for IT staffing, and the company expects benefits from the hosted solution to exceed $6 million.[7]

---

[6] NetSuite Inc., Customer Stories, accessed from www.netsuite.com.
[7] Edwards, J. "Pay-per-view ERP," *CFO Magazine* (February 14, 2006), accessed from ww2.cfo.com.

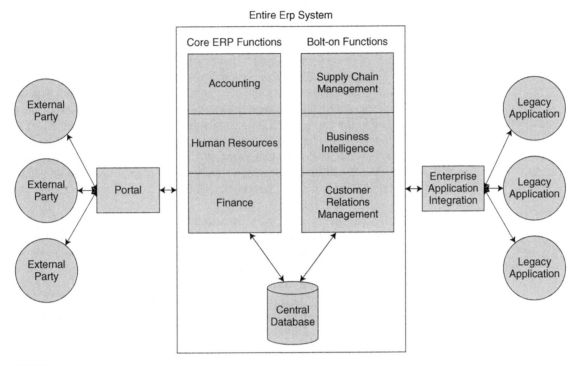

FIGURE 5-5   The architecture of an enterprise resource planning (ERP) system.

A Centralized Database.   To integrate the data from various subsystems, an ERP system uses a **centralized database**. An advantage is that the database stores each data item just once (thus avoiding data redundancy) but makes the information immediately available to all those functions in an organization requiring it. To appreciate the value of this approach, think about the student data at your own university. Many different offices may need your name and address, including the financial aid office, the library, the student health office, the parking office, and of course, the office in charge of student records. If you change your address between semesters, do you really want to visit each of these offices individually to inform them of this change?

Here's a similar example for a business. Most businesses maintain price lists for their products. In firms where there is no centralized database, the price list may be duplicated many times. For example, the marketing department initially sets prices and therefore creates and maintains a price list. Accounts receivable also needs such a price list for invoicing, which the Web master uses to update the selling prices displayed at online. Suppose that the marketing department makes a price change. If the business does not update those prices elsewhere, it might sell products to customers at incorrect prices as well as bill customers for incorrect amounts. The end results can be ugly.

Application Interfaces.   An **application interface** refers to the ability of an ERP system to interact with software from independent vendors. Although an ERP system can integrate data from many business units within an organization, the individual modules within it are not necessarily the best in an industry. The flexibility of choosing the best software in different categories may argue for a **best-of-breed approach**. For instance, a company might implement an ERP system from SAP but want to keep its current

SCM or BI software from other software developers. Some ERP systems support such **bolt-ons**, while others do not.

Case-in-Point 5.7 Virginia Commonwealth University (VCU) in Richmond, Virginia, implemented Banner's ERP system in 2006, which is widely used in higher education. This ERP has modules to support student registrations and payments, course management, financial aid, finance, HR, and development (fund raising). However, when the School of Business moved into its new building in the spring of 2008, university decision-makers determined that the CRM module in Banner did not have the functionality desired. Accordingly, they acquired a bolt-on CRM called Intelliworks Program Management. This CRM helps current and prospective students through the initial exploration and inquiry stages of their searches and allows them to register for courses and submit payments online.[8]

"Cost" might be another reason why an organization might not choose a "one-system solution." For example, a company might run out of money during the implementation of an ERP and decide to complete its system with software from other vendors. Similarly, some companies may have older legacy systems that they wish to retain—for example, a payroll system. Figure 5-5 suggests that it may be possible to connect such applications to their new ERP systems. This conflicts with the general design of a complete, integrated system, but may be the best approach when time or cost constrains become issues. This is **enterprise application integration (EAI)**.

Portals. A **portal** is a gateway through which external users gain access to websites, computer services, or in this case, ERP systems. Portals *within* an organization allow users to access information in an ERP system in order to perform their jobs or to connect with other employees for meaningful collaboration. But why would a company allow *external users* to access its ERP system through Internet portals? One reason is so that customers can view product prices. Another reason is so that suppliers can track the payment status of their invoices. A third reason is so that university students and faculty can access such information as university calendars, course information, and library resources. Two important examples of portals are dashboards and mashups.

Dashboards. Chapter 1 introduced the idea of dashboards and how senior managers use them to monitor corporate performance. Today, such dashboards are essential tools, enabling managers to monitor a wide variety of business processes. For example, a sales dashboard might help marketing managers identify sales trends, best customers, slow-moving products, or high-achieving salespeople (measured by different units such as revenues, units, margins, or sales regions)—refer back to Figure 1-4. Similarly, university deans and department chairs can use dashboards to observe student enrollments or budget statuses. The integrative nature of ERP systems enables the system to access and display the requisite data.

Mashups. **Mashups** are Web pages that can combine the data from two or more sources. In the context of ERP systems, mashups are Web pages that collect data from sources both inside and outside the firm. Two distinguishing features of mashups are (1) their ability to combine the internal data of an organization with external data from elsewhere and (2) the ability of an end user to create such dashboards or Web pages

---

[8] See www.hobsons.com/crm-for-higher-education for more information about Intelliworks.

"on the fly" as needs or interests dictate. This frees managers from predetermined screens and enables them to create dashboards of their own.

Case-in-Point 5.8 In a recent pilot project of a mashup, IBM developed an application for a national home improvement retail chain that merged weather reports with inventory management. For instance, if the weather service predicts a hurricane for a region, it makes sense to transfer inventories of plywood to stores near the area of the storm. Normally, weather forecasts of a possible hurricane would not be an event that would trigger a transfer of inventory in most ERP systems.

Business Processes and ERP Systems

An advantage of an ERP system is that its accounting module can interact with any other subsystem it also supports (see again, Figure 5-3). For example, an accounting module can exchange payroll and tax data with the HR subsystem. Similarly, when a customer places an order, the ERP can check the customer's credit limit in the finance module, check inventory levels in the inventory module, and help the salesperson involved better manage the customer account through the CRM module.

Business Process Reengineering and ERPs. An ERP system often requires organizations to adopt new ways of doing business. This usually requires reengineering operations, hopefully to achieve the best practices of the industry. But implementing an ERP and reengineering business processes is expensive and demanding on employees. Knowing the lessons learned from those who have been through the process is important to implementation success. The respondents to a recent survey of 822 business process reengineering (BPR) leaders identified the following four critical success factors: (1) planning, where scope and roles were decided; (2) high-level reviews of current processes; (3) support from top management; and (4) continuous involvement of key employees.[9] Figure 5-6 lists several additional key aspects that managers should consider to help ensure successful BPR initiatives.

Benefits and Risks of Enterprise Systems

Because ERP systems are so expensive, require extensive training, often involve far-reaching change management, and take so long to implement, the potential benefits and risks associated with these systems are substantial. Here, we briefly examine the benefits and risks of ERP systems (Figure 5-7).

Benefits of ERPs. Despite their high costs, there are many compelling reasons to implement ERP systems. Benefits include the conveniences of an integrated system, increased communication and coordination, reduced data duplication, and reduced labor required to create, distribute, and use system outputs. To make good decisions, most organizations attempt to estimate the expected benefits from a new information system before they actually acquire one. This helps to determine whether the benefits from a new system are likely to exceed its costs. **Spend management** is the ongoing

---

[9] "Prosci Releases 8th Edition of the Best Practices Research Report," February 18, 2014, accessed from www.prosci.com.

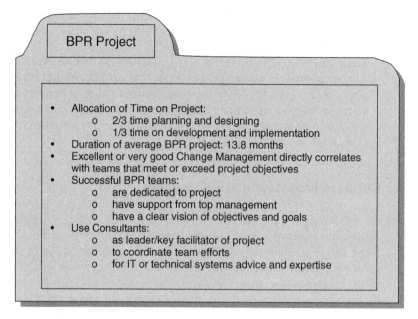

BPR Project

- Allocation of Time on Project:
  - o 2/3 time planning and designing
  - o 1/3 time on development and implementation
- Duration of average BPR project: 13.8 months
- Excellent or very good Change Management directly correlates with teams that meet or exceed project objectives
- Successful BPR teams:
  - o are dedicated to project
  - o have support from top management
  - o have a clear vision of objectives and goals
- Use Consultants:
  - o as leader/key facilitator of project
  - o to coordinate team efforts
  - o for IT or technical systems advice and expertise

FIGURE 5-6 Key aspects of a successful BPR project. Source: ©Prosci 2002. All rights reserved. Reprinted with permission.

Costs	Benefits
• Hardware	• Reduced inventory investment
• Software	• Improved asset management (e.g., cash and receivables)
• Training:	• Improved decision-making
– Technical	• Resolved data redundancy and integrity problems
– business processes	
• Data conversion	• Increased flexibility and responsiveness
• Interfaces and customization	• Improved customer service and satis-faction
• Professional services	
• Reassigned employees	• Global and supply chain integration
• Software maintenance	
• Software upgrades	

FIGURE 5-7 A summary of costs and benefits typically associated with ERP systems.

process of cutting expenses to their bare minimum—for example, by reducing the costs of employee travel, supply procurement, and invoice processing. An ERP system can help a company manage these expenses, and spend management is therefore an oft-cited benefit.

Case-in-Point 5.9   Newell Rubbermaid, a $5 billion international consumer-products company with business units throughout the world, implemented an SAP system to help it collect and interpret data across the entire company. Matt Stultz, Vice President of Information Technology, said the following about the company's ERP system and its spend management capabilities: "Whether it's analyzing our spend data or more efficiently managing our inventory, we have both the historical and up-to-date information we need to move our business forward."[10]

Other benefits of ERP systems include better abilities to: (1) make enterprise-wide decisions, (2) identify trends, (3) understand interrelationships between business units, (4) eliminate redundant data, (5) increase the efficiency of financial reporting, and (6) monitor business processes in new and different ways—for example, with dashboards and mashups.

Finally, there are indirect benefits of ERP systems that are often difficult to identify and even more difficult to quantify. For example, how can you measure the benefits from improved management decision-making or more satisfied customers? Similarly, what is the dollar value of keeping up with, or exceeding, the processing capabilities of your competitors?

Risks and Costs of ERP Systems.   ERP systems have many potential costs and therefore risks. Implementation costs include expenditures for hardware, software, and professional services. There are also costs for employee training, data conversion, and process reengineering. Customers who are inconvenienced during the software implementation may leave—an added risk.

Case-in-Point 5.10   According to a 2015 study by Panorama Consulting Solutions, the typical large company spends almost $400 million implementing an ERP system—an average of almost 6% of its annual revenues. Just as telling: almost 70% of the study respondents indicated that they would not choose the same software vendor if they could do it all again. A key success factor in the study was careful business process reengineering (BPR).[11]

Data conversion can be especially expensive. For example, imagine a multinational corporation that plans to replace more than 100 legacy systems with an ERP system. It is possible that each of the 100 systems uses a different format for an employee number, whereas the new system will use just one uniform employee number. Management must agree on the format of that number, and the staff working on the implementation will have to convert all employee data to the new standard—a massive potential investment of time.

There are also many costs that do not always make it into the cost/benefit equation—for example, the costs of internal staff time. An ERP implementation will require some employee help, even if an organization hires specialized consultants for other aspects of the implementation. Company employees who are dedicated to the project cannot also do their normal jobs, explaining why their salaries should therefore be part of an ERP's implementation costs.

The costs of an ERP system will continue after implementation. These include hardware costs, system maintenance costs, and upgrade costs. One company noted that it had not realized how much it would cost for the highest level of vendor support, staff training on the software, or system upgrades. ERP operating costs can vary from a hundred thousand to millions of dollars.

---

[10] "SAP ERP 6.0 Upgrade Success Stories 1—Matt Stultz on the Impact of Panaya," Panaya Quality Management Cloud, accessed from www.youtube.com in May 2014.
[11] Kimberling, E. 2015. Key Findings from the 2015 ERP Report. *Panorama Consulting Solutions*. Accessed online at: http://panorama-consulting.com/key-findings-from-the-2015-erp-report/.

1. **Waste Management.** Waste Management was looking for a new revenue management system and selected SAP's ERP software. After 2 years and over $100 million in project expenses, it discovered that its ERP software had significant gaps between its functionality and the company's business requirements. Corporate managers decided that the system was a complete failure and sued SAP for fraud, claiming that the system was unstable and lacked promised functionality. SAP settled the lawsuit in 2010 for an undisclosed sum.

2. **The US Air Force.** In November of 2012, the US Air Force decided to pull the plug on an ERP initiative called the Expeditionary Combat Support System. The system began in 2005, used Oracle software, and was intended to replace more than 200 legacy systems. But after 7 years and spending $1 billion, the system allegedly "failed to create any significant military capabilities." Worse yet, the Air Force estimated that the project would require an additional $1.1 billion to complete just 25% of the original project, which would take another 8 years.

3. **The State of California.** In March of 2012 and after spending more than $300 million, the state of California scrapped an ERP system aimed at modernizing the case-management portion of the state's court system. Although officials thought that the software developed so far was "viable," the state felt that it could not afford the additional $343 million needed to complete the project.

4. **Avon, Inc.** In December of 2013 and despite spending more than $100 million, the managers at Avon Products decided to abandon a massive ERP software project designed to integrate its global business operations. Problems included software that disrupted regular operations and modules that were so difficult to use that company reps left the company in "meaningful numbers." Officials expected total write downs to exceed $125 million.

FIGURE 5-8 Four ERP project disasters. Sources: (1) Kanaracus. C. 2010. SAP, Waste Management settle lawsuit. *Computerworld* (May 3). Accessed at www.computerworld.com. (2) and (3) Kanaracus, C. 2012. The scariest software project horror stories of 2012. *Computerworld* (December 10). Accessed at www.computerworld.com. (4) Kepes, B. 2013. Avon's failed SAP implementation: a perfect example of the enterprise IT revolution. *Forbes Magazine* (12/17). Accessed at www.forbes.com.

Finally, ERP projects can have so many unforeseen problems that they result in massive disasters. A recent study by Gartner Research, for example, suggests that between 55% and 75% of all ERP implementations fail.[12] Sometimes, even the entire business fails to survive. Figure 5-8 provides four examples. Unfortunately, these are not isolated cases.

Quantifying the Business Value of an ERP System. The past decade will be remembered for large investments in IT and ERP systems. However, many IT departments have been unable to justify the business value of these huge expenditures, and managers often disagree on how the value of technology is best measured. Trish Saunders, a contributing author to *Customer Insights* (a Microsoft newsletter for mid-size businesses in the United States), claims that whatever methodology a company uses to measure, the value of an ERP should be applied consistently across the organization at specific times after its implementation. Figure 5-9 includes the steps she recommends and suggests that a company that does not establish specific performance metrics will have difficulty gauging how well the ERP meets organizational objectives or how to correct any performance gaps.

[12] Merit Solutions. 2016. Recovering from a failed ERP implementation. *Merit Solutions*. Accessed online at: http://www.meritsolutions.com/business-insights/recovering-failed-erp-implementation/.

---

1. Determine how you will measure success.
2. Set up specific metrics based on your industry.
3. Perform regular postimplementation audits.
4. Analyze your performance numbers.
5. Set up universal processes.
6. Create a continuous learning loop.
7. Prepare for inevitable security failures.

FIGURE 5-9 Methodology for measuring the value of an ERP.

5.4 SELECTING A SOFTWARE PACKAGE

An organization has many choices when selecting accounting information systems. In this section, we briefly discuss how managers and owners can recognize when they might benefit from a new system and how they might select one. You can also find more detail about the general processes of developing or selecting a new accounting system in Chapter 13.

When Is a New AIS Needed?

Some small businesses still keep their accounting records in a shoebox, filing cabinet, or similar manual storage, and their "accounting system" is really their tax preparer. But manual accounting systems do not allow business owners to analyze their data very much, guard against input or clerical errors, automatically generate financial statements or operating reports, or identify trends or opportunities to reduce costs or increase sales. For many businesses, a computerized system has much promise.

For those already using computerized AISs, there are many signals that a new accounting software package, or an upgrade in software, might be a good idea. One example might be new regulations or legislation that requires new reporting documents. Another reason might be the need to comply with new rules or laws. A third reason might be pressures from competitors. Figure 5-10 lists several such signals.

When a business owner or manager recognizes that it is time to purchase new (or more powerful) software, the next question is, "Which software should I select?" Here are some ideas.

Selecting the Right Software

Shopping-mall software retailers rarely sell mid-range or high-end accounting software packages. Instead, business owners and managers working in larger firms are more likely to purchase them from a **value-added reseller (VAR)** or a qualified installer. These companies or individuals make special arrangements with software vendors to sell their programs. They also provide buyers with services such as installation, customization, and training—services necessitated by the complexity of the software. A VAR offers a broader array of services for more software programs than a qualified installer.

1. Late payment of vendor invoices, which means late fees and lost cash discounts.
2. Late deliveries to customers.
3. Growth in inventories, accompanied by an increase in stockouts.
4. Slowdown in inventory turnover.
5. Increased time in collecting receivables.
6. Late periodic reports.
7. Increasing length of time to close out books at the end of a period.
8. Managers concerned about cash flows and financial picture of organization.
9. Manager complaints about lack of information needed for decision-making.
10. Owner worries about cash flows, taxes, and profitability.
11. Preparing reports requires too many time-consuming manual tasks.
12. Current system cannot keep up with data-processing volumes.
13. Data is not secure or is otherwise at risk.
14. Remote access to accounting data is not currently available.

FIGURE 5-10   Indicators that a company might need a new (or upgraded) AIS.

The approach to buying accounting software varies with the complexity of the business and the software. For small businesses, the selection process is usually quicker and less expensive than when a big company needs an ERP system. Chapter 13 elaborates on this selection process and discusses some tools available to help make such decisions.

Large organizations with specialized processing needs can also decide to build a customized AIS from scratch. While custom systems are difficult and expensive to develop, they are becoming less expensive with advances in object-oriented programming, client/server computing, and database technology. Custom systems are often more costly and take longer to develop than management anticipates, which is why most firms retain consultants to help with the selection and implementation of prewritten accounting systems.

Today's accounting software is easy to use and feature-rich. Consultants usually find that packaged software can handle about 80% of a client's processing needs. A company can ignore the other 20%, meet its needs with other vendor software, or develop its own modules to complete its system. Internet research and discussions with other business owners in a similar industry may be enough to help a business owner select a software package. Three helpful Internet sites are (1) www.top10erp.org, (2) www.softwareadvice.com, and (3) www.ctsguides.com, each of which lists important software features, describes these items in detail, and allows individuals to compare software packages. These sites also offer software demos, make software recommendations, and provide detailed online software reviews. Figure 5-11 provides tips for selecting an ERP system.

Finally, because ERP systems can cost millions of dollars and take years to fully implement, it is often advisable to get the help of an expert when choosing one. Consultants can conduct a thorough analysis of an organization's needs and determine which software vendor has the best solution and what customization the buyer might need. Companies should know that some consultants are independent, some work for specific vendors, and some are professionals who work in IT consulting firms or are specialists within large accounting firms. The best way to choose a consultant is to look for someone who has experience with your industry and who is familiar with more

1. **Obtain the support of upper management.** Acquiring an ERP system is as much a strategic decision as it is an operational one. This requires buy-in from top managers.

2. **Document requirements carefully.** The more specific you can be with the functional needs of your company, the better vendors can respond to your request for proposal (RFP).

3. **Carefully evaluate proposed systems.** No system is likely to be perfect, but it is useful to know how imperfect each proposed system is likely to be.

4. **Customization is costly or impossible.** ERP systems try to be a one-size-fits-all. The ability to modify outputs may be difficult or nonexistent.

5. **Don't forget business process reengineering.** The more an ERP requires changes in the way employees perform day-to-day tasks, the more expensive and time-consuming the implementation is likely to be.

6. **Prepare for employee resistance.** Some employees may not understand or appreciate why they need a new system. Companies may benefit from an internal ERP liaison or champion to help overcome fears or dissatisfaction.

7. **Training is both costly and necessary.** Training will take valuable time, especially if the new system differs substantially from the old one.

8. **Remember mobile users.** Employees are more likely to appreciate a new ERP system when they find that they can access it through their smart phone, tablet, or laptop computer.

FIGURE 5-11   Tips for selecting a new ERP system.

than one package. As you would expect, vendor consultants are unlikely to suggest solutions other than the ones offered by their companies.

AIS AT WORK
An ERP Success Story at Mar-Bal[13]

Mar-Bal is a private company that makes composite plastic products and employs 350 people in four locations in North America. The company had all the classic earmarks of an outdated data-management system, including (1) the absence of convenient Electronic Data Interchange (EDI) portals for B2B uses, (2) the inability to create advanced shipping notices for customers, (3) the inability to scan parts production from its shop floors, (4) poor inventory control over vendor-sourced products, (5) manual data entry of inventory data, which introduced data-transcription errors into the system, (6) the inability to meet growing data processing volumes, and (7) limited forecasting and reporting capabilities. In addition, the company took manual counts of its inventory every month. Partially as a result, it took nearly 2 weeks to complete month-end reports, delaying vital information to managers and sometimes responses to customer inquiries.

To address these problems, Mar-Bal managers performed a systems analysis of its processes in order to better understand its system problems and to create a list of requirements for a new system. Given that the company was not in the software business and did not want to develop a customized system, its managers concluded that acquiring a new ERP system was its best course of action. After generating, and then narrowing, an extensive list of software vendors, the company eventually chose

---

[13] More information about the software modules implemented by the company, as well as a detailed list of cost savings attributed to the new system, are available at www.iqms.com/company/mar-bal/.

EnterpriseIQ from IQMS, which it first installed at the company's headquarters in Chagrin Falls, Ohio, and then later implemented companywide.

The new system is a comprehensive solution to Mar-Bal's many problems. For example, the system now provides full EDI capabilities for both customers and suppliers and allows employees to process hundreds of electronic invoices per hour if necessary. Because the production facilities now use a compatible bar-coding system, managers can scan and track every single box or part in its four inventory locations, whether from manufacturing or from external vendors—an improvement that has eliminated its earlier, error-prone data entry system as well as the need to take manual monthly inventories.

Internal communication among employees has also improved with real-time monitoring of inventory—even from remote locations. Floor-level employees now use computer tablets to enter manufacturing data immediately into the system as they complete jobs. Similarly, sales representatives can view available inventory on an up-to-the-minute basis.

In addition to these benefits, the company saves time and money. In total, the company estimates that it saves $270,000 per year across its four plants. This includes $62,000 annually with its real-time production monitoring system, $30,000 in improved inventory control, and $23,000 in month-end reporting costs. The company also estimates that it saves $53,000 each year by eliminating the 2,750 hours of labor it once needed to take monthly physical inventory counts (which it now only performs once a year) and 5,000 hours of machine time (which it lost when making those counts).

 ## SUMMARY

✓ Categories of integrated accounting software include entry-level, small-to-medium business, ERP, special industry, and custom-built software.

✓ Integrated accounting software packages may include modules for general ledger, accounts receivable or sales, accounts payable or purchasing, inventory, and payroll.

✓ Entry level accounting programs usually include a chart of accounts that users can customize, along with the ability to produce a variety of accounting reports, including financial statements and budgets.

✓ Mid-range and large-scale accounting software packages include advanced features and options, such as international currency translation.

✓ Deployment options for accounting software and ERP systems include direct software acquisition, as well as hosted solutions in which users access software as a service from Internet providers. The customer data resides on the vendors' sites in the cloud.

✓ ERP systems integrate both financial and nonfinancial data from the different business processes of an organization, including manufacturing, marketing, and human resources. Traditional ERP systems are therefore termed "back-office systems," while extended ERP systems add front-office features to the traditional systems, helping an organization integrate its supply chain.

✓ The architecture of an ERP system includes (1) its system configuration, (2) a central database that makes information available for corporate-wide decision-making, (3) application interfaces with other corporate systems, and (4) portals that allow both internal and possibly external users to access selected information.

✓ Selecting the right accounting software should follow a formal process that includes (1) obtaining top management support, (2) defining and then documenting system requirements,

(3) understanding the costs of customization and business process reengineering, and (4) evaluating vendor bids carefully. Managers should also be mindful of the possibility of employee resistance, the costs of retraining, and the usefulness of accounting packages that support employee access from such mobile devices as smart phones and tablets.

✓ There are many costs and benefits associated with ERP systems, and managers need to consider all of them when thinking about acquiring one.

✓ ERP systems are large, expensive propositions, usually requiring large-scale business process reengineering. Failed systems can cost over $100 million and bankrupt a company.

✓ There are several warning signals that indicate that a company needs to upgrade its AIS, including dissatisfied suppliers, customers, or employees. Sometimes, the impetus is external, such as with the Sarbanes–Oxley Act or other federal regulations.

✓ The Internet provides many tools to help managers select a new accounting system. The help of a consultant or value-added reseller (VAR) can be useful.

KEY TERMS YOU SHOULD KNOW

application interface
back-office operations
best-of-breed approach
bolt-ons
business application suites
business intelligence (BI) tools
centralized database
collaborative business
  partnerships

customer relationship
  management (CRM)
enterprise application integration
  (EAI)
enterprise resource planning
  (ERP) systems
enterprise software
extended ERP systems
front-office operations
hosted solution

integrated accounting software
mashups
partner relationship management
  (PRM)
portals
scalability
spend management
supply chain management (SCM)
value-added reseller (VAR)

TEST YOURSELF

Q5-1. Low-end accounting software is increasingly complex and sophisticated. However, software costing only a few hundred dollars is not likely to:

a. provide information to multiple stores where a company operates more than one

b. include a chart of accounts that users may customize to suit their industry

c. provide all the information needed to optimize customer and supplier relationships

d. provide information for budgeting decisions

Q5-2. Which of the following reasons might explain why a small business owner would hire a CPA firm or a software consultant to help select accounting software?

a. to train employees to use the software

b. to help the firm identify useful reports for decision-making

c. to help with rescue/recovery needs should a disaster occur

d. all of the above

Q5-3. Which of the following accounting software programs would be appropriate for a small business (e.g., a sole proprietorship with 20 employees)?

a. SAP

b. QuickBooks

c. NetSuite

d. Oracle

Q5-4. Mid-level accounting software:

    a. can only be deployed through a server networked with desktop computers

    b. may be purchased in modules that match various business processes

    c. will not be appropriate for a multinational company because these programs cannot handle foreign currencies

    d. is generally inappropriate for a company operating in a specialized industry, such as retail or not-for-profit

Q5-5. Which of the following is a distinguishing characteristic of an enterprise-wide (ERP) system?

    a. must be a hosted solution

    b. multiple databases

    c. integration of business functions

    d. low cost

Q5-6. An organization will always need to upgrade to a new AIS if:

    a. a major competitor buys a new package

    b. customers complain about late deliveries

    c. the company wants to begin doing business over the Internet

    d. none of the above are necessarily reasons to buy new accounting software

Q5-7. Accounting and enterprise software can be expensive. Which of the following is likely to be the highest cost associated with a new AIS?

    a. the cost of new hardware

    b. the cost of implementing and maintaining the new system

    c. the cost of the software

    d. the cost of converting old data for the new system

Q5-8. In selecting a new AIS, a company's management should:

    a. always hire a consultant

    b. always consult with your accountant during the decision process

    c. never rely on your accountant for help in this decision

    d. always use an Internet software service to make the decision

Q5-9. Components of an ERP's architecture typically include:

    a. a centralized database and application interfaces

    b. Internet portals and multiple databases

    c. a centralized database running on a mainframe computer

    d. business intelligence and multiple databases

Q5-10. Within the context of ERP systems, a mashup is:

    a. a combination of several accounting systems

    b. the mess created when ERP systems fail to interface with legacy systems

    c. a Web page that can combine data from two or more external sources

    d. the informal name given to annual ERP conferences

DISCUSSION QUESTIONS

5-1. What are some important features of integrated accounting software for small businesses? Why are they important?

5-2. How are the integrated accounting systems for small businesses like those for larger businesses? How are they different?

5-3. What features should a small organization look for when thinking about acquiring a new integrated accounting package? Would it make any difference if the organization were a not-for-profit concern?

5-4. What are some of the advantages of the cloud computing feature of integrated accounting software? What are some of the disadvantages of a hosted solution?

5-5. The difference in price for middle-market accounting software versus for an ERP system can be millions of dollars. What can these high-end systems do that the less-expensive enterprise accounting packages cannot?

5-6. Discuss the differences between traditional ERP and extended enterprise systems.

5-7. Discuss some of the basic features of an ERP. How do these features distinguish an ERP from an integrated accounting software program?

5-8. What are the four basic components of an ERP's architecture? How do these components differ from a set of independent accounting systems—for example, separate systems for accounts payable, accounts receivable, inventory control, and payroll?

5-9. What are some of the benefits of a centralized database? What are some of the difficulties in moving from multiple databases or files to a centralized database structure?

5-10. A new company will have no business processes in place. How would the owner go about selecting an appropriate AIS for the new company? Should the owner consider acquiring an ERP package immediately?

5-11. Find an article about a company that has adopted a business application suite. Identify the company and its basic characteristics (such as location, products, number of employees). What are some cost savings realized by the company? Were there specific efficiencies identified as a result of the ERP implementation? Were there problems implementing the system? How long did it take for the company to complete the implementation? Were there cost or time overruns?

5-12. While you are likely to purchase a middle-end accounting software package from a value-added reseller (VAR), why should you be cautious about hiring one to recommend a software package for your business?

5-13. What are some of the consequences to a company that makes a poor decision in selecting a new AIS?

5-14. Why do businesses typically need to engage in business process reengineering when they adopt an ERP? Identify at least four key aspects of a successful BPR project.

5-15. What is a dashboard? What is a mashup? Discuss how these items relate to ERPs and how they might help a business manager in his or her job.

PROBLEMS

5-16. Which accounting software features are likely to be most important for the following businesses? Search the Internet for an example of an accounting information system that you would recommend for each of these owners and include your rationale for that product.

    a. A boutique shop that sells trendy ladies clothing

    b. A small business specializing in custom golf clubs, replacement shafts for clubs, replacement grips for clubs, and similar repairs

    c. A local CPA firm with three partners, five associates, and two administrative employees

    d. A pet breeder that specializes in Burmese kittens

    e. A business that sells and rents Segways in Washington, DC

    f. A high-end men's clothing business that has four stores that are all located in the same large metropolitan city (56 employees), but whose owner is contemplating additional locations for stores in nearby cities

5-17. Visit the software websites of two low-end accounting software package vendors and then two ERP vendors. Analyze the descriptions of the software and then describe the differences you see between the low-end packages and the ERP systems.

5-18. Define the concept of "scalability." Explain why it might be a good idea for owners of small businesses—and managers in larger businesses—to understand this concept.

5-19. Tom O'Neal always wanted to own his own business. When he was in high school, he worked evenings and most weekends at a neighborhood bicycle shop. When Tom went to college at the nearby State University, he still came home in the summers and worked at the bike shop. Upon graduation from college, with his accounting degree in hand, the sole proprietor (Steven Judson) of the bike shop invited Tom to become a full partner in the bike shop. Steven told Tom that he really wanted to grow the business and thought that Tom was just the person to help him do this. Tom decided to join Steven.

Over time, the business grew and they opened two more bike shops in neighboring cities. Sales increased to more than $3.5 million dollars during the past year, and the three bike shops now employ 14 full-time workers and another 6 part-time employees. Although Steven and Tom hired an accountant who was keeping their books for them and producing the financial statements each year, the partners thought they needed much more information to really run their business efficiently. They thought that they might need to make an investment in information technology to take their business to the next level.

a. Would you recommend that Steven and Tom consider an investment in IT?

b. Visit the websites of the vendors that offer the appropriate-sized software packages for this business. What are some of the features of possible software packages that Steven and Tom should consider?

c. Would you advise Steven and Tom to hire a consultant? Support your recommendation with appropriate research citations (e.g., business articles that offer this type of advice—what rationale do they give?).

5-20. B&R, Inc. is one of the world's largest manufacturers and distributors of consumer products, including household cleaning supplies and health and beauty products. Last year, their net sales revenues exceeded $5 billion. B&R has multiple information systems, including an integrated accounting system, a computerized manufacturing information system, and a supply chain management software system. The company is considering using an ERP system to be able to conduct more of its business over the Internet.

B&R hired National Consulting Firm (NCF), and NCF recommended the move to an ERP system, which would have electronic commerce interfaces that will allow B&R to sell its products to its business customers through its website. The cost/benefit justification for the new software, which comes with an estimated price tag of $100 million (including consultant fees and all implementation and training costs) shows that B&R can expect great cost savings from improved business processes that the ERP system will help the company to adopt. NCF implements the ERP, adopting the industry's *best practices* for many of the business processes.

a. What are the likely advantages of an ERP system for B&R?

b. Visit the websites of the major ERP vendors. What are some of the characteristics you notice about their customers?

c. B&R has heard some horror stories from other chief executive officers (CEOs) about ERP implementations. What are some of the concerns B&R should address as they move forward with this project?

5-21. Visit a website such as www.top10erp.org that compares several alternative ERP systems. Select a company with which you are familiar and examine the recommended choices for your company's industry. How do the packages you've selected compare to one another? Which system(s) do you think you'd examine further if you were actually shopping for an ERP system for your company? Do any of the choices offer hosted options? (Hint: You may have to visit the websites of the software developers themselves.)

5-22. Why do ERP systems fail? Perform an Internet search on this topic and identify a new ERP failure not listed in Figure 5-8. Prepare a one-page report describing the failure and providing reasons why it happened. Be sure to include information about the costs or inconveniences caused by the failure.

CASE ANALYSES

5-23. Mar-Bal's New ERP System (Analyzing an ERP Study and Implementation)

Access the full case story of Mar-Bal Company (the AIS-at-Work for this chapter) at www.iqms.com. Then, respond to each of the following requirements:

Requirements

1. Review the items in Figure 5-10, which lists indicators that a company may need a new or upgraded processing system. For each item, provide a specific example from the case description. If the case does not address a particular item or it does not seem to apply, simply state "NA."

2. Review the items listed in Figure 5-9, which lists possible measures of the value of an ERP. For each item, provide a specific example from the case description. If the case does not address a particular item or it does not seem to apply, simply state "NA."

3. What are some of the intangible benefits Mar-Bal appears to enjoy from its new ERP system? Create a list with brief explanations.

4. Mal-Bar's case does not explicitly address the issue of BPR that often happens when organizations install new ERP systems. Would you guess that none took place, or would you argue the opposite? Defend your answer.

5-24. The Retail Cooperative (Creating an Enterprise Portal)

Over the past decade, The Retail Cooperative (TRC) successfully acquired a number of smaller retailers, enabling it to grow significantly. As a result, TRC is now one of the largest retailers in Europe, employing over 230,000 people in 25 countries. The company has three primary business units: department stores, hardware stores, and food stores. TRC has many cross-division service companies in both Europe and Asia to support the three primary business units. These support companies provide a variety of services, such as purchasing, information technology, advertising, and human resources.

In early 2014, the CEO scheduled a full-day strategy session with the vice presidents of the business units. By the end of the day, these senior managers decided on a set of specific strategic objectives to continue the growth of the company. In particular, the CEO and vice presidents of TRC determined that the company needed to: (1) attract well-educated, skilled managers to lead future expansions and (2) optimize distribution channels so that managers at all levels of the organization would have immediate access to information for decision-making. The goal was to link TRC's management expertise with the geographic area of operation so that the company would continue to be dynamic and responsive to customers 24/7. Essentially, the senior managers wanted TRC mid-level managers in each of the business units to have the ability to "Coordinate Globally—Act Locally."

The consensus was that the Human Resources support company would develop and implement appropriate procedures to find the quality of managers that TRC requires. However, the VPs of the business units wanted to be directly involved in the distribution channel optimization. As a result of TRC's rapid growth, the VPs of the business units were encountering a number of recurring problems—such as lapses in customer service, an inability to respond to customer queries, and coordination problems with product availability and delivery dates. In addition, the manager for the travel department of the company noticed a significant increase in travel expenses for each of the business units and sent each of the VPs a memo. Based on these concerns, the VPs decide to meet with the Controller and Chief Information Officer (CIO) to discuss these problems and to identify possible options to resolve these issues.

To prepare for the meeting, Robin Frost (the CIO) talked with several top-level managers to collect their ideas and suggestions of the features that might be required of any new technology solution the firm might purchase. Each of the managers agreed that TRC would need an e-business application(s) that would give its managers a detailed online view of the status of the purchasing process that is shared among TRC's employees, suppliers, and customers. For example, each purchasing agent would like access to all the purchase prices, inventories, and selling prices that are in place in any store, no matter where it is located. He/she should also be able to see TRC's manufacturing prices for its own brands, the bids made by TRC's suppliers, and the comments or complaints made by TRC's customers.

In addition, the new technology would have to link TRC's suppliers, distributors, and resellers with the company's Logistic, Production, and Distribution Departments. The Accounting and Finance Departments would need access to information so they could track the status of TRC's sales, inventory, shipping, and invoicing in any TRC store worldwide. And finally, the Marketing and Sales Departments would also need access to manage and update the company's product catalogs, price lists, and promotional information for any TRC outlet, regardless of its geographic location.

At the meeting with the VPs, Robin made a 10-minute presentation on Internet portals. Her research on this new technology leads her to believe this might help the VPs solve the problem of accessing information that has not been readily available to mid-level managers working with customers. At this point, Robin just knows that software packages exist that can make information available to company employees. She's not able to articulate all the pros and cons of the technology and has not yet called any outside consultants for advice. Robin believes that the primary challenge for this new technology will be to create a real-time "retail connectivity" that will allow vendor collaboration, multichannel integration, and public and private trading exchanges across the globe.

Requirements

Note: Research is required to properly respond to the following case questions, which could include journal articles on enterprise portals, and Internet research that could include online journal articles as well as vendor websites for product information.

1. Assume that you are a consultant with one of the application platform vendors (e.g., IBM, Oracle, SAP, Microsoft) and Robin called you for information regarding Enterprise Portals. Prepare a one-page summary of the advantages TRC might enjoy if it used an Enterprise Portal for each of the business units (and for TRC-wide operations).

2. Prepare a 10-minute PowerPoint presentation on Enterprise Portals, focusing on the advantages for TRC of implementing this technology. (Hint: As a minimum, be sure to address such issues as scalability of the portal, reliability, performance, and fault tolerance.)

3. What sort of implementation schedule would you recommend for TRC, that is, what steps are important in an orderly implementation of this technology? Explain.

4. Based on your research, which system do you recommend for TRC? Prepare a matrix that compares the different features of the different Enterprise Portal solutions that you considered.

5-25. Linda Stanley and State University (Transitioning from a Legacy System to an ERP)

Linda Stanley is the Vice President for Computing and Information Services at State University (SU), a medium-sized, urban university that has experienced a 3% growth in enrollments every year for more than a decade. The university now has almost 22,000 students, just under 12,000 faculty and staff, nearly $1B in revenues, and can currently accommodate 5,000 students in residence halls. In addition, the state legislature has financially supported infrastructure development for SU to help accommodate the sustained growth in enrollments. The campus has significantly and positively impacted the visual appearance and the economy of the city where it is located.

The number of legacy systems across campus has adequately served SU in the past, but with the growth in enrollments, the university has also increased the number of faculty, support staff, and services. Currently, the core applications at SU include Blackboard, Lotus Domino, Web self-service, and legacy administrative applications for all other purposes.

In recent meetings with the Provost of the university, Linda and her staff have responded to a number of concerns and problems from the Deans of academic departments on campus, as well as a number of the support departments, such as payroll, student financial aid, and HR. As Linda pointed out to the Provost and Deans, universities have unique technology challenges, such as an open technology environment 24 hours a day, 7 days a week, and 365 days a year, not just when school is in session. She also mentioned that SU has other factors that impact the effectiveness of IT services—such as their urban location and the rapid growth of the university over the past decade. Linda reminded the Provost that she and her staff were diligently working on a number of major technology initiatives for SU, including network reengineering, e-mail consolidation, telephony modernization, help-desk/customer care redesign, and classroom technology.

Last week, the Provost called Linda and asked her to meet him at the coffee shop in the Student Commons—he wanted to ask her opinion about a technology issue. In the discussion, the Provost reflected on the growth of SU and wondered aloud if the university might be at a stage of maturity where it should consolidate the entire technology infrastructure of the university. He pointedly asked Linda what she thought—should they consider purchasing an ERP?

Of course, Linda was not prepared to discuss this question in great depth and told the Provost that she would do some research and make an appointment in a couple of weeks to have a more meaningful discussion of the issue. When she returned to her office, she scheduled a meeting with her staff for the next day so that she could go over the Provost's request with them and then assign different parts of this research project to them. Linda reminded everyone that they had a limited amount of time to pull the information together—that she needed to deliver the Executive Summary to the Provost in the next few weeks.

Requirements

Note: Some Internet research is required to properly respond to the following case questions.

1. Search the Internet and find ERP solutions that might be suitable for a university such as SU. What are the primary modules for this type of ERP? Briefly describe the functions of each module.
2. What business processes would most likely be affected if SU implemented an ERP?
3. Since this is a state university, the Board of Regents and the State Legislature will need to see a report on the expected costs and benefits of an ERP, both tangible and intangible. Although you don't have any dollar amounts, identify some typical costs and benefits that Linda should include in her executive summary.
4. Should Linda use consultants? If so, what types of support should she expect from them?
5. Search the Internet—can you find an expected timeline for implementation of an ERP at a university? Do you think Linda should include a possible timeline in her report to the Provost? Why or why not?

5-26. Springsteen, Inc. (Planning for an ERP System)

Springsteen, Inc. is a large furniture manufacturer located in Asbury Park, New Jersey. It sells to furniture wholesalers across the United States and internationally. Revenues last year exceeded $500 million. Currently, the company has over 100 legacy information systems. Recently, Wendy Stewart, the CIO, met with Bruce Preston, Chief Financial Officer (CFO), and CEO Patricia Fisher, to discuss some technical problems in these systems. Patricia noted that several competitors have implemented ERP systems and she is wondering if Springsteen should do the same. Wendy and

Bruce agree, with some reservations. Each has heard that Hershey couldn't ship its candy bars one Halloween because of problems with an SAP implementation. They'd heard other horror stories as well. Bruce thought maybe a Best of Breed solution would be less costly. Patricia suggested that they all meet with a consulting team from Warren-Williams (WW), a global consulting firm.

The meeting takes place the next week. Present are: Wendy Stewart—CIO; Bruce Preston—CFO; Patricia Fisher—CEO; Clarence Martin—Analyst with WW; Rosalita Jones—Analyst with WW; and Steve Johnson—Analyst with WW.

Patricia opens the meeting. Her role is to manage the discussion and look for a decision. She talks about what she thinks an ERP might be able to do in terms of providing competitive advantages, particularly with respect to business processes. Bottom line.

Wendy explains the architecture of an ERP and explains the technical issues associated with implementing these systems.

Clarence tries to sell the project any way he can. He also tells the company representatives what his firm will do for them, the expected cost of the system, and the implementation schedule to be expected.

Rosalita explains the potential risks and benefits of such a system for Springsteen, focusing on the benefits.

Steve describes the functionality of an ERP—what the various modules are, its centralized database, and so on. He also talks about options for extending the ERP through the Internet to integrate the supply chain.

Requirement

Note: This case is designed for in-class role play. Each actor and assigned support staff have 20 minutes to prepare for the meeting. The support staffers are the other class members. During the meeting, one support staff member for each role will capture the main points brought out during the meeting, relative to that role. For example, a scribe for Wendy Stewart would make a list of every technical issue brought out in the meeting. The meeting should last approximately one-half hour.

5-27. The Pucini Pediatric Practice (Selecting software for a medical office)

It was Friday afternoon, and Dr. Tammy Pucini had seen her last patient for the day. As she sat in her office, staring at the gloomy afternoon sky, she realized that she was both tired and happy. She thought, for example, about how much she had worried that there wasn't enough demand for another pediatric doctor in town. But not anymore. That first year had been a little difficult, but now her practice included two full-time doctor-partners, and a complete clinic of five nurses, three clerical receptionists, two data entry clerks, and one office manager.

Of all these people, Katie Karr was the newest hire. Katie was bright, personable, genuinely kind, and already a favorite among the office staff. Ironically, this was turning out to be a problem. Katie had suggested that the office needed to upgrade its accounting systems "for all kinds of reasons." A new system, she noted, could handle the higher volume of patients they were now seeing, could produce financial reports both for the individual doctors and for the practice as a whole, and could interface with the software of the many health insurers in town.

Best of all, Katie had noted, she had a friend working in a dental practice in another state, who had just implemented DoctorsFirst—a new medical system that "the staff over there just loved." She heard that it was easy to use, produced both itemized and collective reports, and included an insurance module for third-party billing. It wasn't expensive, Katie added, and was so intuitive to use that little training was required to use it.

Despite these many advantages, Tammy wasn't completely convinced. At a recent conference, for example, she had learned that "acquisition" was only one of the many costs of a complete system, that the medical packages designed for one state did not automatically work well with insurers in another state, and that what was "intuitive" to some people was anything but to others. Most importantly, Tammy realized that she was "out of her element" when it came to picking a good package for her office. She knew pediatric medicine—not computer systems! She also feared that Katie might be too optimistic in her assessment of DoctorsFirst—a natural outcome of her sunny disposition. Tammy feared that the risks were high—a failed system could spell disaster for her small practice.

Tammy felt that she had at least three options. One was to continue to rely on her existing systems. Yes, things were slow, reporting was limited, and third-party insurance interfaces were now mostly faxes and e-mails to insurers. But this option had one huge thing going for it—things worked and the current staff knew how things worked.

Another option was to trust Katie and implement the DoctorsFirst system. She liked this idea because she liked Katie. She realized that she could invite the people at DoctorsFirst to visit the practice and first ask them to make a presentation. That way, the doctors and staff could ask questions and determine just how useful the system might be to them. But the home office of DoctorsFirst was over 1,000 miles away, making an onsite visit expensive. Would she have to pick up the tab for that visit? Also, staff time was valuable and in short supply, and she had no way of knowing just how much she could trust the presenters' answers to their questions. She knew that such people were salespeople first and might promise anything to make a sale.

Then there was a third option: hire a consultant to help them. But who? And where would they find one? Would this person be reliable? Or honest?

Tammy signed. The continuing gloom of the late afternoon did nothing to improve her mood. It was time to go home and feed Tabby-the-cat! Maybe the best choice would come to her while she took a bath. . . .

Requirements

1. The case provides three options. Create a list of them, and for each, itemize the pros and cons. It is fine to list items not mentioned in the case but that are also likely for one or more options.

2. What do you recommend Tammy should do and why?

READINGS AND OTHER RESOURCES

Anonymous. 2016. Nonprofits increasingly adopting cloud-based software services. *Nonprofit Business Advisor.* 2016 (319): 6–9.

Fairkettle, A. 2013. How to choose a payroll system. *Chartered Accountants Journal* 92(1):46–47.

Haynes, R. and C. Li. 2016. Continuous audit and enterprise resource planning systems: A case study of ERP rollouts in the Houston, Tx oil and gas industries. *Journal of Emerging Technologies in Accounting.* 13(1):171–179.

Henri, T., J. Pellinen, and M. Järvenpää. 2013. ERP in action—challenges and benefits for management control in SME context. *International Journal of Accounting Information Systems* 14(4): 278–296.

Hollenbaugh, K. 2016. 5 ERP failure stories and how to avoid becoming one of them. *Datix ERP and CRM Blog.* (July 13). Accessed online at: http://blog.datixinc.com/blog/erp-failure-stories.

Ivancevich, S., D. Ivancevich, and F. Elikai. 2010. Accounting software selection and satisfaction. *The CPA Journal* (January): 66–72.

Johnston, R. 2014. Software strategy: Is your firm doing the right thing? *CPA Practice Adviser* 24(6): 10–11.

Kanellou, A., and S. Spathis. 2013. Accounting benefits and satisfaction in an ERP environment. *International Journal of Accounting Information Systems.* 14(3): 209–234.

Louis, B. 2013. Technology, change, and management control: a temporal perspective. *Accounting, Auditing, and Accountability Journal* 26(1): 48–74.

Macpherson, S. 2015. Choosing the right online accounting software. *In the Black.* (April): 1.

Schiff, Jennifer. 2014. 9 tips for selecting and implementing an ERP system. *CIO* (July 10). Accessed online at: http://www.cio.com/article/2458889/enterprise-resource-planning/9-tips-for-selecting-and-implementing-an-erp-system.html.

She-I, C., D. C. Yen, I-C. Chang, and J. Derek. 2014. Internal control framework for a compliant ERP system. *Information and Management* 51(2): 187–205.

Go to www.wiley.com/go/simkin/videos to access videos on the following topics:

What is an ERP System?
Evaluating Accounting Software (What to Look For)
Introduction to Microsoft Accounting Express
Introduction to Selecting Accounting Software for a Small Business
Total ERP Software Demo

ANSWERS TO TEST YOURSELF

1. c **2.** d **3.** c **4.** b **5.** c **6.** d **7.** b **8.** b **9.** a **10.** c

Chapter 6

Introduction to Internal Control Systems and Risk Management

After reading this chapter, you will be able to:

1. *Discuss* the primary control frameworks commonly used in organizations.

2. *Identify* the components of an internal control system.

3. *Explain* the importance of enterprise risk management and the impact this has on internal controls.

4. *Understand* the importance of Committee of Sponsoring Organizations of the Treadway Commission (COSO) and Control OBjectives for Information and Related Technologies (COBIT) with respect to internal control systems.

5. *Distinguish* between preventive, detective, and corrective controls.

6. *Summarize* the various methods used to analyze internal control decisions.

"Thought leaders have long recognized that strong leadership and ethical culture are foundational building blocks of enterprises with top-performing risk management programs. However, it is only in the past few years that the striking number of operating-risk-related events… have made the consequences of a lack of such leadership conspicuously evident."

Roboff, G. 2016. The tone at the top: Assessing the board's effectiveness. *ISACA Journal, Vol 6*, accessed from www.isaca.org/journal in February 2017.

6.1 INTRODUCTION

The latest advances and pervasive use of IT across organizations significantly impact the internal controls management chooses to protect company assets. This task requires management to develop and implement an effective **internal control system**—a system that can also perform such other functions as helping ensure reliable data processing and promoting operational efficiency across an organization.

The purpose of this chapter is to discuss internal control systems and risk management within organizations. We identify the components of an internal control system, the importance of **enterprise risk management (ERM)** as it relates to internal controls, as well as the different types of internal controls. Finally, we identify methods used in organizations to evaluate controls and to determine which control procedures are cost-effective.

Definition of Internal Control

Internal control describes the policies, plans, and procedures implemented by management of an organization to protect its assets, to ensure accuracy and completeness of its financial information and to meet its business objectives. Usually, the people involved in this effort are the entity's board of directors, the management, and other key personnel in the firm. The reason why this is important is that these individuals want reasonable assurance that the goals and objectives of the organization can be achieved (i.e., effectiveness and efficiency of operations, reliability of reporting, protection of assets, and compliance with applicable laws and regulations).[1]

Figure 6-1 outlines the recent history of key laws, professional guidance, and reports that focus on internal controls and risk management.

In 2001, the AICPA issued **Statement on Auditing Standards (SAS) No. 94**, "The Effect of Information Technology on the Auditor's Consideration of Internal Control in a Financial Statement Audit." This SAS cautions the external auditors that internal controls are both manual and automated. Due to the complexity of IT environments,

Date	Report/Law	Significant Provisions Pertaining to Internal Controls
1992	COSO IC-IF	• Presents criteria to evaluate internal control systems
		• Provides guidance for public reporting of internal controls
		• Offers materials to evaluate internal control systems
2013	COSO IC-IF	• Keeps basic features of 1992 COSO IC-IF (definition, five components, and COSO Cube)
		• Adds 17 principles that inform the five components of internal control
2004	COSO-ERM	• Focuses on enterprise risk management
		• Keeps five components from 1992 COSO IC-IF and adds three new: objective setting, event identification, risk response
2017	COSO-ERM: Aligning Strategy and Performance	• Reconceptualizes enterprise risk management to better align risk management practices with strategy and performance
		• Creates five new components of enterprise risk management
		• Adds 22 principles that inform the five components of enterprise risk management
1992	COBIT	• Provides auditors with guidance on evaluating IT and related controls as part of evaluation of financial statements
2012	COBIT 5	• Provides comprehensive framework of globally accepted principles, practices, analytical tools, and models to help enterprises effectively address critical business issues related to the governance and management of IT
		• Adds 5 principles that inform effective governance and management of enterprise IT
2002	Sarbanes–Oxley Act, Section 404	• Requires publicly traded companies to issue "internal control report" that states management is responsible for establishing and maintaining adequate internal control structure
		• Mandates that management must annually assess effectiveness of internal control structure
		• Requires independent auditor to attest to/report on management's assessment

FIGURE 6-1 Select history of internal controls.

---

[1] Committee of Sponsoring Organizations of the Treadway Commission (COSO), www.coso.org.

especially with the pervasive use of technology, auditors need to use computer-assisted auditing techniques (CAATs) to test the automated controls in an organization.

An important piece of legislation with respect to internal controls is the Sarbanes–Oxley Act (SOX) of 2002. One key provision of this law is Section 404, which reaffirms that management is responsible for establishing and maintaining an adequate internal control structure. At the end of each fiscal year, corporate officers must attest to the effectiveness and completeness of the internal control structure, thus making them personally liable for this structure within the firm. We cover both CAATs and the Sarbanes–Oxley Act in more depth in Chapter 11.

Internal Control Systems

An internal control system consists of the various methods implemented within an organization to achieve the following four objectives: (1) safeguard assets, (2) check the accuracy and reliability of accounting data, (3) promote operational efficiency, and (4) enforce prescribed managerial policies. An organization that achieves these four objectives is typically one with good **corporate governance**, which means managing an organization in a fair, transparent, and accountable manner to protect the interests of all the stakeholder groups.[2]

The COSO Internal Control—Integrated Framework (depicted in the 2013 COSO cube)[3] is widely used by managers to organize and evaluate their corporate governance structure. This framework was developed to improve the quality of financial reporting through business ethics, effective internal controls, and corporate governance.

6.2   COSO INTERNAL CONTROL—INTEGRATED FRAMEWORK

2013 COSO Report[4]

The original **1992 COSO Report** established a common definition of internal control and a standard to assess the design and operating effectiveness of internal control systems. The 2013 COSO Report revised the original to take into consideration the wide-ranging effect of changes that have occurred in technology and the business environment over the intervening two decades—which of course were quite profound.

The **2013 COSO Report** articulates a framework for the establishment and evaluation of internal control within organizations. This framework consists of the following: a *definition* of internal control, a categorization of the broader *objectives* that organizations strive to achieve, *components* that facilitate achievement of those objectives, and the *structure* through which the enterprise is organized and across which internal control must be implemented. Moreover, the 2013 COSO Report establishes a set

---

[2] Governance: The New Strategic Imperative," a white paper from the Economist Intelligence Unit sponsored by KPMG International, 2002, accessed from www.us.kpmg.com in April 2014.onsoring Organizations of the Treadway Commission (COSO), www.coso.org.

[3] Committee of Sponsoring Organizations of the Treadway Commission (COSO), www.coso.org.

[4] Committee of Sponsoring Organizations of the Treadway Commission (COSO), Internal Control—Integrated Framework, Executive Summary, May 2013, accessed from www.coso.org.

of 17 *principles* that inform the five *components* of internal control. These principles apply to the operations, reporting and compliance objectives of the organization.

The 2013 COSO Report defines internal control as "*a process, effected by an entity's board of directors, management, and other personnel, designed to provide reasonable assurance regarding the achievement of objectives relating to operations, reporting and compliance.*" Upon reviewing this definition, it is clear that internal control

- is a *process*, inasmuch as it requires a coordinated series of tasks and activities designed to achieve an intended purpose;
- is *goal-oriented*, inasmuch as it is designed to aid and assist in the achievement of the organization's operations, reporting, and compliance objectives;
- is *effected by people*, in that while its design and implementation are the purview of management, its oversight and execution rest with the board and all members of the organization;
- can only provide *reasonable assurance*, as the design, implementation, and execution of a system of internal controls is subject to trade-offs between costs and benefits; and
- is *applied at any and all levels of the enterprise*, from the entity level down to specific departments and functions.

There are three categories of objectives that organizations attend to with respect to internal control: operations, reporting, and compliance. Operations objectives deal primarily with the efficient and effective utilization of resources and are assessed against financial and performance goals. Reporting objectives deal primarily with the creation and dissemination of financial and nonfinancial information to decision-makers and other stakeholders. Compliance objectives deal primarily with adherence to applicable laws and regulations and will differ based on the external environment within which the organization operates.

The 2013 COSO Report stipulates that an internal control system consists of five components: (1) the control environment, (2) risk assessment, (3) control activities, (4) information and communication, and (5) monitoring activities. Each of these components is discussed next, and the 2013 COSO cube with these components is depicted in Figure 6-2. Figure 6-3 articulates the principles associated with the five components of internal control.

Control Environment. The **control environment** establishes the "tone at the top" of a company. It is the foundation for all the other internal control components and provides discipline and structure. There are a number of factors that are included in the control environment. First, and usually most important, is top management's oversight, integrity, and ethical principles that guide the organization. This includes the attention and direction provided by the board of directors, as well as top management's philosophy and operating style. Equally important are the policies and procedures management develops to assign authority and responsibility across the organization, as well as their policies for developing employees.

Case-in-Point 6.1 In an effort to circumvent various state and national clean air standards, automobile manufacturer Volkswagon installed software on a variety of automobiles equipped with diesel engines that was designed to detect when the vehicle was undergoing an emissions drive cycle test. When the software detected a set of parameters consistent with emissions testing, it would switch into a low-emissions operating mode. In total, more than 11 million Audi, Porsche and Volkswagon diesel vehicles worldwide were equipped with the "cheater" software. When discovered by the U.S. Environmental Protection Agency and the California Air Resources Board in 2014, Volkswagon admitted to the wrongdoing. To date, Volkswagon has agreed to spend up to $22 billion in the United States to settle claims from consumers, regulators, and dealers. In January 2017, six Volkswagon executives were arrested for their part in the scandal.[5]

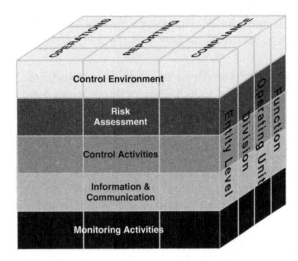

FIGURE 6-2 The 2013 COSO cube with five components of internal control. Used with permission.

Five Components of Internal Control	Principles Associated with Each Component of Internal Control
Control Environment	1. Demonstrates commitment to integrity and ethical values
	2. Exercises oversight responsibility
	3. Establishes structure, authority, and responsibility
	4. Demonstrates commitment to competence
	5. Enforces accountability
Risk Assessment	6. Specifies relevant objectives
	7. Identifies and analyzes risk
	8. Assesses fraud risk
	9. Identifies and analyzes significant change
Control Activities	10. Selects and develops control activities
	11. Selects and develops general controls over technology
	12. Deploys through policies and procedures
Information & Communication	13. Uses relevant information
	14. Communicates internally
	15. Communicates externally
Monitoring Activities	16. Conducts ongoing and/or separate evaluations
	17. Evaluates and communicates deficiencies

FIGURE 6-3 The five components of internal control with associated principles.

[5] "Everything You Need to Know about the VW Diesel-Emissions Scandal," by Clifford Atiyeh, Car and Driver, February 2017, accessed from http://blog.caranddriver.com.

Risk Assessment. It is not possible or even desirable to install controls for every possible risk or threat. The purpose of **risk assessment** is to identify organizational risks, analyze their potential in terms of costs and likelihood of occurrence, and implement only those controls whose projected benefits outweigh their costs. A general rule is: the more liquid an asset, the greater the risk of its misappropriation. To compensate for this increased risk, stronger controls are required. The 2013 COSO Report recommends the use of a *cost–benefit analysis* (discussed and illustrated later in this chapter) to determine whether the cost to implement a specific control procedure is beneficial enough to spend the money.

Control Activities. These are the policies and procedures that the management of a company develops to help protect the different assets of a firm, based on a careful risk assessment. **Control activities** include a wide variety of activities throughout the firm and are typically a combination of manual and automated controls. Some examples of these activities are approvals, authorizations, verifications, reconciliations, reviews of operating performance, and segregation of duties. Through properly designed and implemented control activities, management will have more confidence that assets are being safeguarded and that the accounting data processed by the accounting system are reliable. The next major section describes these activities in more detail.

Information and Communication. Managers must inform employees about their roles and responsibilities pertaining to internal control. This might include giving them documents such as policies and procedures manuals and/or posting memoranda on the company's intranet. This could also include training sessions for entry-level personnel and then annual refresher training for continuing employees. Regardless of the method, all employees need to understand how important their work is, how it relates to the work of other employees in the firm, and how that relates to strong internal controls. It is equally important that employees feel safe communicating any possible problems they may find to management or a company hotline. When this is the case, employees at all levels can actually enhance the effectiveness of good internal controls, which we describe in the following case-in-point.

> *Case-in-Point 6.2* In the 2016 ACFE report on occupational fraud and abuse, the data show that the majority of frauds are detected by tips (39%), much more so than by audits (20%). Anonymous hotlines or Web-based portals, which allow individuals to report misconduct without fear of retaliation or of being identified, can help facilitate this process.[6]

Monitoring Activities. The evaluation of internal controls should be a continuous process. Managers at various levels in the organization must evaluate the design and operation of controls and then initiate corrective action when specific controls are not functioning properly. This could include daily observations and scrutiny, or management might prefer regularly scheduled evaluations. The scope and frequency of evaluations depend, to a large extent, on management's assessment of the risks the firm faces. We include a separate section on this topic later in this chapter.

---

[6] Report to the Nations on Occupational Fraud and Abuse, 2016 Global Fraud Study, Association of Certified Fraud Examiners (ACFE), accessed from www.acfe.com in January 2017.

6.3 ENTERPRISE RISK MANAGEMENT

COSO ERM Introduction

Risk management, from an organizational perspective, is the identification and treatment of those events that may have a negative impact on the achievement of organizational objectives. Given the success and widespread adoption of COSO's Internal Control Framework detailed in the 1992 COSO Report, COSO leveraged and expanded this framework in creating the ERM Framework, which was detailed in the 2004 COSO Report. Although the ERM Framework was well accepted, COSO announced in 2014 an effort to review and revise the ERM Framework.

COSO cited a number of reasons for revising the original ERM Framework. For example, in the intervening decade between the initial issuance and the decision to revise, the landscape of business and associated risks had change dramatically. Moreover, boards of directors had become more active consumers of risk-related information and had taken on a greater role in oversight of risk management activities, likely due to increased scrutiny as a result of the Sarbanes–Oxley Act of 2002. Finally, COSO felt that a stronger linkage between governance, risk management, and enterprise strategy was necessary.

Given that the ERM Framework from the 2004 COSO Report has wide adoption, we cover both the original ERM Framework and the revised ERM Framework in separate sections. As of the writing of this book, COSO has stated that adoption of the revised ERM Frameworkis not mandatory, although some or all of the 2004 ERM Framework may be superseded or retired by the revised version at a later date.

2004 ERM Framework

As we pointed out earlier, the 2013 COSO Report includes risk assessment as one of the five components of internal control. However, COSO determined that organizations needed additional guidance to perform a more comprehensive assessment of risk. The result was the 2004 COSO Report entitled **Enterprise Risk Management—Integrated Framework**, which focuses on ERM. The ERM Framework includes the five components of the original 1992 COSO Report (internal environment (analogous to control environment), risk assessment, control activities, information and communication, and monitoring) and adds three additional components: **objective setting**, **event identification**, and risk response. Figure 6-4 presents the ERM cube with all eight components.

Objective Setting. ERM offers management a process for setting objectives for the firm—that is, the purposes or goals the firm hopes to achieve. ERM helps an organization determine if the objectives are aligned with the organizational strategy and that goals are consistent with the level of risk the organization is willing to take. An enterprise's objectives are viewed from four perspectives: (1) Strategic: the high-level goals and the mission of the firm; (2) Operations: the day-to-day efficiency, performance, and profitability of the firm; (3) Reporting: the internal and external reporting of the firm; and (4) Compliance: adherence to laws and regulations.

Event Identification and Risk Response. Organizations must deal with a variety of uncertainties because many events are beyond management control. Examples include

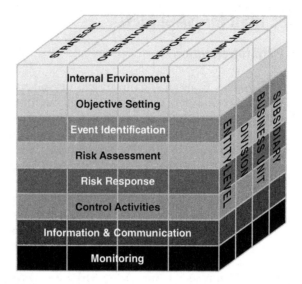

FIGURE 6-4 2004 COSO Enterprise Risk Management—Integrated Framework. Source: COSO Enterprise. Used with permission.

disruptive technologies, natural disasters, wars, unexpected actions of competitors, and changing conditions in the marketplace. However, it is critical for management to identify these external risks as quickly as possible and then consider internal and external factors regarding each event that might affect its strategy and achievement of objectives. Depending on the type or nature of events, management might be able to group some of them together and begin to detect trends that may help with risk assessment.

Case-in-Point 6.3 The responsibility of the Director of the Arkansas Department of Finance and Administration (DFA) is to ensure that state agencies operate uniformly and efficiently. To help the Director achieve these DFA objectives, each state agency is required to perform a risk assessment once every two years and must complete a "Risk Assessment and Control Activities Worksheet." This worksheet (Figure 6-5) helps department managers across the state to think about their operations through a risk-assessment lens.[7]

The objective of risk assessment is to manage and control risk by identifying threats, analyzing the risks, and implementing cost-effective countermeasures to avoid, mitigate, or transfer the risks to a third party (through insurance programs or outsourcing). As they identify and categorize risks, managers will be in a better position to determine the probable effects on the organization. They can then formulate and evaluate possible response options for the organization. In developing risk responses, managers need to consider the level of risk they are willing to assume, as well as the trade-offs between costs and benefits of each choice. A number of computerized governance, risk, and compliance (GRC) tools already exist to help managers with this task.

---

[7] Arkansas Department of Finance and Administration, accessed in April 2014 from www.dfa.arkansas.gov.

Risk Assessment and Control Activities Worksheet

Department: _____   Prepared By: _____

Activity: _____   Date Prepared: _____

Goals & Objectives	Risk Assessment			Actions to Manage Risks/ Control Activities
	Risks	Significance/Impact	Likelihood	
(1)	(2)	(3)	(4)	(5)

(1) List all operations, financial reporting and compliance objectives associated with the activity. Goals should be clearly defined, measurable, and attainable.

(2) List all identified risks to the achievement of each goal and objective. Consider both internal and external risk factors. For each goal and objective, several different risks can be identified.

(3) For each risk, estimate the potential impact on operations, financial reporting or compliance with laws and regulations, assuming that the risk occurs. Consider both quantitative and qualitative costs. Use **Large**, **Moderate**, or **Small**.

(4) For each risk, assess the likelihood of the risk occurring. Use **probable**, **reasonably possible**, or **remote**. Alternatively use **High**, **Medium**, or **Low**.

(5) For each risk with large or moderate impact and probable (high) or reasonable (medium) likelihood of occurrence, list both the actions to mitigate the risk to an acceptable level and the control activities that help ensure that those actions are carried out properly and in a timely manner. If no action is present to manage the risk and/or no control activity is present, an action plan to address the risk and an associated timeline should be included.

FIGURE 6-5 An example of a risk assessment and control activities worksheet. Source: Arkansas Department of Finance and Administration.

Case-in-Point 6.4   GRC software is essential in any organization's risk assessment efforts. GRC software provides tools that support the automation and integration of enterprise, IT, and operational risk management processes. Typically covering areas such as operational and IT risk management, business continuity management, audit management, and corporate compliance/legal management, GRC tools have seen widespread adoption in the post SOX landscape. IT thinktank Gartner Group suggests that these tools will focus more strongly in the future on risks associated with digital business initiatives.[8]

2017 ERM Framework

COSO released an update of its ERM Framework in 2017. The 2017 COSO Report, titled "Enterprise Risk Management—Aligning Risk with Strategy and Performance," incorporates a number of significant changes relative to the 2004 COSO Report. These are discussed below.

First, the revised ERM Framework *adopts a components- and principles-based approach to risk management.* This principles-based approach is akin to the principles-based approach taken in the 2013 update to COSO's Internal Control Framework.[9] In

[8] "What's New on Gartner's Hype Cycle for Risk Management Solutions, 2016," by John Wheeler, Gartner Blog Network, accessed February 2017 from blogs.gartner.com.
[9] Committee of Sponsoring Organizations of the Treadway Commission (COSO), Guidance, accessed in April 2014 from www.coso.org.

addition to revamping the interrelated components from the original ERM Framework from eight (that tightly aligned with COSO's Internal Control—Integrated Framework) to five, a series of 23 principles were developed that inform the components. The 23 principles collectively articulate effective risk management practices. Second, the revised ERM Framework offers *a simplified definition of ERM* and more effectively *aligns risk and value.* In essence, the revised definition of risk is more readily understood by nonaccounting and risk management professionals and more closely aligns risk management with value creation, strategy setting, and business objectives. Third, the revised ERM Framework places an *increased focus on strategy.* Over the past decade, a number of organizations have experienced significant failures when strategy doesn't align with their mission, values, and vision. Finally, an organization's strategy is directly tied to the risks that the organization faces.

The revised ERM Framework defines ERM as "the culture, capabilities, and practices, integrated with strategy and execution, that organizations rely on to manage risk in creating, preserving, and realizing value." COSO elected to change the definition of ERM for the revised ERM Framework for a variety of reasons. As mentioned earlier, the newer definition is easier to read and resonates with a broader audience. COSO received feedback from a wide variety of stakeholders, and the overwhelming message was that the definition from the 2004 COSO report was unwieldy; the new definition is aimed to address this concern.

The revised ERM Framework consists of the following five components: (1) risk governance and culture; (2) risk, strategy, and objective setting; (3) risk in execution; (4) risk information, communication, and reporting; and (5) monitoring ERM performance. Figures 6-6 and 6-7 illustrate the revised ERM framework and associated principles. We summarize the five components of the framework next.

Risk Governance and Culture

Risk governance represents the organization's tone or attitude toward the design, implementation, execution, and oversight of risk management activities. **Culture** represents a shared system of beliefs and norms that informs attitudes and actions within an organization. Collectively, risk governance and culture form the foundation of ERM.

FIGURE 6-6 Revised COSO ERM Framework.[10]

---

[10] Committee of Sponsoring Organizations of the Treadway Commission (COSO), Enterprise Risk Management: Integrating with Strategy and Performance: Executive Summary, accessed in September 2017.

Five Components of Enterprise Risk Management	Principles Associated with Each Component of Enterprise Risk Management
Risk Governance and Culture	1. Exercises board risk oversight
	2. Establishes governance and operating model
	3. Defines desired organizational behaviors
	4. Demonstrates commitment to integrity and ethics
	5. Enforces accountability
	6. Attracts, develops, and retains talented individuals
Risk, Strategy, and Objective-setting	7. Considers risk and business context
	8. Defines risk appetite
	9. Evaluates alternative strategies
	10. Considers risk while establishing business objectives
	11. Defines acceptable variation in performance
Risk in Execution	12. Identifies risk in execution
	13. Assesses severity of risk
	14. Prioritizes risk
	15. Identifies and selects risk responses
	16. Assesses risk in execution
	17. Develops portfolio view
Risk Information, Communication and Reporting	18. Uses relevant information
	19. Leverages information systems
	20. Communicates risk information
	21. Reports on risk, culture, and performance
Monitoring Enterprise Risk Management Performance	22. Monitoring substantial change
	23. Monitors enterprise risk management

FIGURE 6-7 The five components of enterprise risk management with associated principles.

The culture should reflect the core values of the organization and be modeled in the behavior and decision-making processes of the board, management, and employees.

The principles that comprise risk governance and culture serve to ensure that

- the board exercises oversight over strategy and risk management and supports management in achieving organizational objectives;
- the organization displays a commitment to integrity, accountability, and ethical behavior; and
- management prioritizes the recruitment, development, and retention of human capital to support the organization's strategy and objectives.

Risk, Strategy, and Objective Setting

The revised ERM Framework makes a more concerted effort to include discussions on ERM at the strategic planning and objective settings phases. In this way, decision-makers gain additional insights into how the organization's **strategy** drives the risks it faces. In developing strategy and objectives, decision-makers must consider the business context that influences the current and future operational and strategic decisions. The business context is influenced by both the internal (people, processes, and technologies) and external environment (socioeconomic climate, industry, legal and political forces) in which the organization operates.

In setting the strategy and business objectives, decision-makers should consider the organization's risk appetite. **Risk appetite** represents the amount and type of risk that the organization is willing to accept in pursuit of its strategy, objectives, and value creation efforts. Additionally, management should consider alternative strategies to creating value and how these might affect the organization's risk posture. Once a decision is made on which strategy to pursue, management and the board should align the risk appetite to the strategy.

Risk in Execution

Risks that affect strategy execution and value creation need to be identified and assessed. There are a variety of methods to identify risks to the execution of enterprise strategy, including: stakeholder interviews, surveys and questionnaires, process reviews, gap analyses between current and best practices, and benchmarking data. Once these are identified, the severity of the risk is assessed, usually in terms of likelihood (probability that the event will occur) and impact (loss due to the event). Risks are then prioritized, and risk responses are selected. **Risk response** represent a series of actions taken to implement a desired risk management strategy. Risk responses include accepting the risk, avoiding the risk, pursuing the risk, reducing the risk, and sharing the risk. In developing risk responses, management should take a cost–benefit approach; that is, management should weigh the cost of implementing risk responses against the value derived from the perceived benefit.

Risk Information, Communication, and Reporting

For any system to operate effectively, information must be created, aggregated, and disseminated to the right people in a timely manner. Although as accountants we tend to think first of financial statements when we think of reporting, decision-makers use both internal and external, financial and nonfinancial information. Internal sources of information include meeting minutes, financial statements, training and associated documentation, and hotlines (such as whistleblower hotlines). External sources of information include public indices, government reports, marketing reports, and customer satisfaction surveys.

Regardless of source (internal or external) or nature (financial or nonfinancial), quality information is critical to manage the organization's operations and risk management activities. COSO suggests that quality information has the following characteristics:

- Accessibility: information may be obtained by appropriate decision-makers in a timely manner.
- Accuracy: information is correct.
- Appropriateness: information is relevant to the task at hand and is free from bias.
- Currency: information is timely.
- Reliability: information is retrieved from credible sources.
- Integrity: information is complete, accurate, and free from error.

Monitoring Enterprise Risk Management Performance

The performance of the ERM processes must be monitored over time to ensure that they are performing as intended in light of changes to people, process, technologies, and other factors. At its core, risk is uncertainty. Therefore, as changes to the internal and external environment present themselves, decision-makers must re-evaluate the risk management processes to ensure that risk is being managed within the risk appetite, and that the strategies put in place are still relevant and appropriate.

6.4 EXAMPLES OF CONTROL ACTIVITIES

Now that we have introduced you to the control framework that most organizations use, and the guidance management uses to conduct their risk assessments, we move to the topic of the types of controls that can be designed and developed using these tools.

Because each organization's accounting system and business processes are unique, there are no standardized control policies and procedures that will work for every company. This means that each organization designs and implements specific controls based on its particular needs. However, certain control activities are common to every organization's internal control system. The ones that we will examine here are: (1) a good audit trail, (2) sound personnel policies and practices, (3) separation of duties, (4) physical protection of assets, (5) reviews of operating performance, and (6) timely performance reports. We describe each of these in more detail below.

Good Audit Trail

The basic inputs to an Accounting Information Systems (AIS) are usually business transactions that it records and measures monetarily. A good **audit trail** enables auditors to follow the path of the data from the initial source documents (for instance, a sales invoice) to the final disposition of the data on a report. In addition, managers and auditors can trace data from transactions on reports (such as expenses on an income statement) back to the source documents. In both instances, an auditor can verify the accuracy of recorded business transactions. Without a good audit trail, errors and irregularities are more likely to happen and not be detected.

To establish its audit trail, a company needs a *policies and procedures manual* that includes the following items:

- A chart of accounts that describes the purpose of each general ledger account so that employees enter the debits and credits of accounting transactions in the correct accounts.

- A complete description of the types of source documents individuals must use to record accounting transactions. Also, include the correct procedures to prepare and approve the data for these documents.

- A comprehensive description of the authority and responsibility assigned to each individual—for example, the person who sets credit limits for customers.

Sound Personnel Policies and Procedures

Employees at every level of a company are a very important part of the company's system of internal control. This is becoming increasingly obvious as managers downsize and right-size their organizations to streamline operations and cut costs. Consequently, there are fewer employees, and these employees have more responsibility and oversight than in the past. The obvious result is that the opportunity for misappropriation is greater than before.

In addition, the capabilities of a company's employees directly affect the quality of the goods and services provided by the company. In general, competent and honest employees are more likely to help create value for an organization. Employees work with organizational assets (e.g., handling cash, producing products, acquiring and issuing inventory, and using equipment). Competent and honest employees, coupled with fair and equitable personnel policies, lead to efficient use of the company's assets. Most organizations post their personnel policies and procedures on their Intranet so that they are easily accessible to all employees at any time.

Case-in-Point 6.5 Employees at the University of Alabama at Birmingham (UAB) have ready access to a wealth of information regarding the university's personnel policies via the online Human Resources Policies and Procedures Library. The Policies and Procedures Library is easily searchable, and policies can be sorted based on status (student, faculty, staff), keyword, or effective date. The Policies and Procedures Library includes policies on employment, benefits, compensation, employee relations, training and employee development, and additional university policies (e.g., IT acceptable use, conflict of interest, code of research ethics, and others).[11]

In general, little can be done to stop employees who are determined to embarrass, harm, or disrupt an organization. For example, several employees may conspire (collude) to embezzle cash receipts from customers. However, companies can encourage ethical behavior among employees by reviewing the rules and the Code of Conduct, as well as offering annual training. Managers should create an environment that makes a positive contribution to productivity and effectiveness—that is, managers should always lead by example. Figure 6-8 identifies some examples of personnel policies that firms might adopt.

1. Specific procedures for hiring and retaining competent employees.
2. Training programs that prepare employees to perform their organizational functions efficiently.
3. Good supervision of the employees as they are working at their jobs on a daily basis.
4. Fair and equitable guidelines for employees' salary increases and promotions.
5. Rotation of certain key employees in different jobs so that these employees become familiar with various phases of their organization's system.
6. Vacation requirement that all employees take the time off they have earned.
7. Insurance coverage on those employees who handle assets subject to theft (fidelity bond).
8. Regular reviews of employees' performances to evaluate whether they are carrying out their functions efficiently and effectively, with corrective action for those employees not performing up to company standards.

FIGURE 6-8 Examples of personnel policies that firms might adopt.
Source: www.hrarizona.edu.

[11] Human Resources, The University of Alabama at Birmingham, accessed from www.uab.edu/policies, February 2017.

All employees should be required to take their earned vacations (personnel policy 6 in Figure 6-8). This is important for two reasons. First, if an employee is embezzling assets from an organization, the individual will not want to take a vacation—someone else will do the job, increasing the likelihood of detection. Second, required vacations help employees to rest, enabling them to return refreshed and ready to perform their job functions more efficiently.

For employees who handle assets susceptible to theft, such as a company's cash and inventory of merchandise, it is a good personnel policy (number 7 in Figure 6-8) to obtain some type of insurance coverage on them. Many organizations obtain **fidelity bond** coverage (from an insurance company) to reduce the risk of loss caused by employee theft of assets. The insurance company investigates the backgrounds of the employees that an organization wants to have bonded. When an insurance company issues one of these bonds, it assumes liability (up to a specified dollar amount) for the employee named in the bond.

Case-in-Point 6.6   Fidelity bonds are also called employee dishonesty bonds and are intended to cover your company when the unthinkable happens—you have a dishonest employee! For example, if you operate a home cleaning service and have employees in other people's homes, an employee dishonesty bond will cover your company in case one of your employees steals from your customers.[12]

Separation of Duties

The purpose of **separation of duties** is to structure work assignments so that one employee's work serves as a check on another employee (or employees). When managers design and implement an effective internal control system, they must try to separate certain responsibilities. If possible, managers should assign the following three functions to different employees: *authorizing* transactions, *recording* transactions, and maintaining *custody of assets*.

Authorizing is the decision to approve transactions (e.g., a sales manager authorizing a credit sale to a customer). *Recording* includes functions such as preparing source documents, maintaining journals and ledgers, preparing reconciliations, and preparing performance reports. Finally, *custody of assets* can be either direct (such as handling cash or maintaining an inventory storeroom) or indirect, such as receiving customer checks through the mail or writing checks on a company's bank account. If two of these three functions are the responsibility of the same employee, problems can occur. We describe three real-world cases that demonstrate the importance of separating duties. Immediately following each case is a brief analysis of the problem.

Case-in-Point 6.7   As part of a work program for high school students, Rita Humphrey started working for the Dixon, Illinois City Hall in 1970 at the age of 17. She had planned to attend community college after graduating, but instead stayed at City Hall and became a clerk. Humphrey worked her way up over time, and in 1983, when Dixon's previous comptroller retired, she was recommended for the position. In 1983, Dixon had an annual budget of less than $9 million a year. In her new position as comptroller, Humphrey managed all financial aspects of the city funds, including transferring money between accounts, writing checks, and authorizing payments. She also supervised two clerks and managed

---

[12] "Fidelity Bond Insurance," Business Service Reviews, accessed from www.businessservicereviews.com, April 2014.

the finance and accounting departments. Within the next few years, the city experienced several financial shortfalls, but Humphrey always said they were caused because the state owed the city funds. Over time, she started to know more about city financial matters than any of the council members. As a result, they believed her explanations and trusted her. In December 1990, Humphrey opened an account at the Fifth Third Bank of Ohio in the name of the City of Dixon and RSCDA, c/o Rita Crundwell (her married name), known as the RSCDA account. Investigators said that between December 1990 and April 2012, Humphrey used her position as comptroller to transfer funds from Dixon's money market account to various other city bank accounts. Allegedly, Humphrey repeatedly transferred city funds into her RSCDA account and used the money to pay for personal and private business expenses, including horse-farming operations, personal credit card payments, real estate, and vehicles. Although she earned a salary of $80,000 a year, she was known to live lavishly and was a nationally known horse breeder. When a city clerk found a problem in the city's accounts, the mayor contacted the FBI. Agents arrested Humphrey 6 months later. She pleaded not guilty to misappropriating more than $53 million in city funds.[13]

Analysis: The control weakness here is that Humphrey managed all financial aspects of the city funds, including transferring money between accounts, writing checks, and authorizing payments. Humphrey could essentially do all three of the functions: *authorizing* transactions, *recording* transactions, and maintaining *custody of assets*. Consequently, she had total control of almost $9 million (in 1983) and likely many more millions almost 30 years later when her scheme was discovered. Because she was a member of the small community of Dixon and had been a city employee for so many years, she was a trusted employee. Even if there were any controls in place, Humphrey could easily circumvent those controls since there were only two other employees in her office.

Case-in-Point 6.8 The executive assistant (EA) to the president of a home improvement company used a corporate credit card, gift checks, and an online payment account to embezzle $1.5 million in less than 3 years. The EA arranged hotel and airline reservations and coordinated activities for the sales team. She was also responsible for reviewing the corporate credit card bills and authorizing payment. The president gave her the authority to approve amounts up to $120,000. When the EA realized that no one ever asked to look at the charges on the corporate credit card bill, she began making personal purchases with the card.[14]

Analysis: The control weakness here is that the executive assistant was responsible for both *recording* the expenses and then *authorizing* payment of the bills. As a result, she quickly realized that she had nearly unlimited access to a variety of sources of funds from the company—and then found other ways to have the company pay for the things she wanted (i.e., gift checks and a PayPal account that she set up).

Case-in-Point 6.9 Diana L. Farmer-Forston was the sole employee in the bookkeeping department for the law firm of Bennett and Zydron. She was charged with embezzling $567,000 from the law firm over a 4-year period. The case unfolded when law firm partner

[13] "Comptroller, Horse Lady and Crook: How One Woman (Allegedly) Embezzled $53 Million," by Henry C. Smith, III, et al., September/October 2012, Association of Certified Fraud Examiners (ACFE), accessed from www.acfe.com, April 2014.
[14] Sutphen, P. 2008. Stealing funds for a nest egg. *Internal Auditor* (August): 87–91.

John Zydron noticed a shortage in the firm's corporate bank account. He hired outside accountants to conduct an audit, which discovered that 210 checks from the firm's account, totaling $567,000, were forged and deposited into Farmer-Forston's credit union account. The criminal complaint said she used the money to buy a BMW and to fund an investment account.[15]

Analysis: The control weakness here is that the bookkeeper was responsible for all three functions—authorizing transactions, recording transactions, and maintaining custody of assets. As a result of no separation of duties, the bookkeeper could authorize fictitious transactions, record those transactions, and subsequently divert the related payments to her own account.

The *separation of duties* concept is very important. However, the way this concept is applied in IT environments is often different. A computer can be programmed to perform one or all of the previously mentioned functions (i.e., authorizing transactions, recording transactions, and maintaining custody of assets). Thus, the computer replaces employees in performing these functions. For example, the pumps at many gas stations today are designed so that customers can insert their debit or credit cards to pay for their gas. Consequently, the computer performs all three functions: authorizes the transaction, maintains custody of the "cash" asset, records the transaction—and produces a receipt if you want one.

Physical Protection of Assets

A vital control activity that should be part of every organization's internal control system is the physical protection of its assets. Beyond simple protection from the elements, the most common control is to establish accountability for the assets with custody documents. Three application areas for this are (1) inventory controls, (2) document controls, and (3) cash controls.

Inventory Controls. To protect inventory, organizations keep it in a storage area accessible only to employees with custodial responsibility for the inventory asset. Similarly, when purchasing inventory from vendors, another procedure is to require that each shipment of inventory be delivered directly to the storage area. When the shipment arrives, employees prepare a *receiving report* source document (most likely generated on a computer or mobile device). This report, as illustrated in Figure 6-9, provides documentation about each delivery, including the date received, vendor, shipper, and purchase order number. For every type of inventory item received, the receiving report shows the item number, the quantity received (based on a count), and a description.

The receiving report also includes space to identify the employee (or employees) who received, counted, and inspected the inventory items as well as space for remarks regarding the condition of the items received. By signing the receiving report, the inventory clerk (Sarah Thompson in Figure 6-9) formally establishes responsibility for the inventory items. Any authorized employee can request inventory items from the storage area (for instance, to replenish the shelves of the store) and is required to sign the inventory clerk's *issuance report,* which is another source document. The clerk is thereby relieved of further responsibility for these requisitioned inventory items.

---

[15] "Va. Beach woman charged with embezzling from law firm," by Tim McGlone, The Virginian-Pilot, May 26, 2011, accessed from pilotonline.com.

Sarah's Sporting Goods Receiving Report		No. 7824
Vendor: Richards Supply Company		**Date Received:** March 14, 2015
Shipped via: UPS		**Purchase Order** **Number:** 4362

Item Number	Quantity	Description
7434	100	Spalding basketballs
7677	120	Spalding footballs
8326	300	Spalding baseballs
8687	600	Penn tennis balls

Remarks:
Container with footballs received with water damage on outside, but footballs appear to be okay.

Received by: *Sarah Thompson*	Inspected by: *Sarah Thompson*	Delivered to: *Jon Young*

FIGURE 6-9 Example of receiving report (items in boldface are preprinted).

Document Controls. Certain organizational documents are themselves valuable and must therefore be protected. Examples include the corporate charter, major contracts with other companies, blank checks (the following case-in-point), and registration statements required by the Securities and Exchange Commission. For control purposes, many organizations keep such documents in fireproof safes or in rented storage vaults offsite.

Case-in-Point 6.10 The Finance Office in Inglewood, California, did not have adequate controls over important documents. As a result, a janitor who cleaned the finance office had access to blank checks that were left on someone's desk. The janitor took 34 blank checks, forged the names of city officials, and then cashed them for amounts ranging from $50,000 to $470,000.

Organizations that maintain physical control over blank checks may still be at risk of embezzlement by using a method known as a demand draft. For example, if you write a check to your 12-year-old babysitter, he has all the information needed to clean out your account, since all he needs is your account number and bank routing number. **Demand drafts** are often used to pay monthly bills by having money debited automatically from an individual's checking account. Not surprisingly, due to the limited amount of information needed to make a demand draft, the potential for fraud is substantial. The irony of the demand draft system is that it may mean that paper checks are ultimately more risky to use than e-payments.

Case-in-Point 6.11   The Urban Age Institute, a nonprofit organization that focuses on planning new urban sustainability initiatives, received an e-mail from a would-be donor who asked for instructions on how to wire a $1,000 donation into the agency's account. Not thinking anything unusual about the request, the group sent its account numbers. The "donor" used this information to print $10,000 worth of checks, which the "donor" cashed and then used Western Union to wire the money to her new Internet boyfriend in Nigeria. The Director at the Institute later discovered that the "donor" used the Institute's account number and bank routing number to obtain checks at Qchex.com. Fortunately, the Institute discovered the fraud and was able to close its checking account before money was withdrawn to cover the $10,000 in checks, which had already been deposited into the donor's Bank of America account.[16]

Cash Controls.   Probably the most important physical safeguards are those for cash. This asset is the most susceptible to theft by employees and to human error when employees handle large amounts of it. In addition to fidelity bond coverage for employees who handle cash, companies should also (1) make the majority of cash disbursements for authorized expenditures by check rather than in cash and (2) deposit the daily cash receipts intact at the bank.

If a company has various small cash expenditures occurring during an accounting period, it is usually more efficient to pay cash for these expenditures than to write checks. For good operating efficiency, an organization should use a *petty cash fund* for small, miscellaneous expenditures. To exercise control over this fund, one employee, called the *petty cash custodian,* should have responsibility for handling petty cash transactions. This employee keeps the petty cash money in a locked box and is the only individual with access to the fund.

Cash Disbursements by Check.   A good audit trail of cash disbursements is essential to avoid errors and irregularities in the handling of cash. Accordingly, most organizations use prenumbered checks to maintain accountability for both issued and unissued checks.

When paying for inventory purchases, there are two basic systems for processing vendor invoices: *nonvoucher systems* and *voucher systems*. Under a *nonvoucher* system, every approved invoice is posted to individual vendor records in the accounts payable file and then stored in an open invoice file. When an employee prepares a check to pay an invoice, she removes the invoice from the open-invoice file, marks it paid, and moves it in the paid-invoice file.

Under a *voucher* system, the employee prepares a *disbursement voucher* that identifies the specific vendor, lists the outstanding invoices, specifies the general ledger accounts to be debited, and shows the net amount to pay the vendor after deducting any returns and allowances as well as any purchase discount. Figure 6-10 illustrates a disbursement voucher. Like the receiving report (Figure 6-9), we depict paper copies, but both of these processes are electronic in most organizations.

As Figure 6-10 discloses, the disbursement voucher summarizes the information contained within a set of vendor invoices. When the company receives an invoice from a vendor for the purchase of inventory, an employee compares it to the information contained in copies of the *purchase order* and *receiving report* to determine the accuracy and validity of the invoice. An employee should also check the vendor invoice

---

[16] "Easy Check Fraud Technique Draws Scrutiny," by Bob Sullivan, May 24, 2005, accessed from www .nbcnews.com.

Sarah's Sporting Goods Disbursement Voucher				No. 76742	
Date Entered: August 9, 2015				**Debit Distribution**	
Prepared by: *SM*				**Account No.**	**Amount**
Vendor Number: 120				27-330	$750.00

Remit to:
   Valley Supply Company
   3617 Bridge Road
   Farmington, CT 06032
				27-339
				28-019
				29-321
					450.00
					300.00
					425.00

Vendor Invoice			**Returns & Allowances**	**Purchase Discount**	**Net Remittance**
Number	**Date**	**Amount**			
4632 4636	6/28/2015 7/10/2015	$1250.00 675.00	$150.00 0.00	$22.00 13.50	$1078.00 661.50
Voucher Totals:		$1925.00	$150.00	$35.50	$1739.50

FIGURE 6-10   Example of disbursement voucher (items in boldface are preprinted).

for mathematical accuracy. When the organization purchases supplies or services that do not normally involve purchase orders and receiving report source documents, the appropriate supervisor approves the invoice.

A voucher system has two advantages over a nonvoucher system: (1) it reduces the number of cash disbursement checks that are written, since several invoices to the same vendor can be included on one disbursement voucher; and (2) the disbursement voucher is an internally generated document. Thus, each voucher can be prenumbered to simplify the tracking of all payables, thereby contributing to an effective audit trail over cash disbursements.

Cash Receipts Deposited Intact. It is equally important to safeguard cash receipts. As an effective control procedure, an organization should *deposit intact* each day's accumulation of cash receipts at a bank. In the typical retail organization, the total cash receipts for any specific working day come from two major sources: checks arriving by mail from credit-sales customers and currency and checks received from retail cash sales.

When cash receipts are deposited intact each day, employees cannot use any of these cash inflows to make cash disbursements. Organizations use a separate checking account for cash disbursements. When organizations "deposit intact" the cash receipts, they can easily trace the audit trail of cash inflows to the bank deposit slip and the monthly bank statement. On the other hand, if employees use some of the day's receipts for cash disbursements, the audit trail for cash becomes confusing, thereby increasing the risk of undetected errors and irregularities.

6.5 MONITORING INTERNAL CONTROL SYSTEMS

Reviews of Operating Performance

As we discussed at the beginning of this chapter, the **Sarbanes–Oxley Act, Section 404**, reaffirms that management is responsible for establishing and maintaining an adequate internal control structure. This responsibility is typically carried out by the internal audit function of an organization, and the staff in that function makes periodic reviews called **operational audits** of each department or subsystem within its organization. In performing these operational reviews, the internal auditors may find that certain controls are not operating properly. If practice is not according to policy, it is the internal auditor's job to identify such problems and inform management.

COSO Guidance on Monitoring

Since publishing the 1992 COSO Report, COSO observed that many organizations did not fully understand the benefits and potential of effective monitoring. Therefore, organizations were not effectively using their monitoring results to support assessments of their internal control systems. As a result, COSO published **Guidance on Monitoring Internal Control Systems (GMICS)**, which more carefully explains the monitoring component of the 1992 COSO Report.[17]

GMICS, published in 2009, rests upon two principles: (1) Ongoing and/or separate evaluations of internal controls help management determine whether the internal control system continues to function as expected over time. (2) Internal control deficiencies or weaknesses should be identified and communicated promptly to the proper individuals so that management can quickly make corrections. The GMICS suggests that these two principles can be achieved most effectively when monitoring is based on three broad elements (Figure 6-11):

1. Establish a foundation for monitoring (e.g., determine the current baseline).
2. Design and execute monitoring procedures (e.g., collect persuasive information about risks that might affect organizational objectives and the key controls that are intended to mitigate such risks).
3. Assess and report the results of monitoring those key controls.

The following figure shows these broad elements in a graphical format, indicating that they are interconnected and can help management of an organization to effectively monitor the control system and persuasively document that effectiveness.

Operating Performance vs. Monitoring

While "reviews" and "monitoring" might sound like the same thing, there is a subtle difference between them. Organizations rarely have enough time or internal auditors to audit every department or division every year. Consequently, some areas of the

---

[17] Committee of Sponsoring Organizations of the Treadway Commission (COSO), Internal Control—Integrated Framework, Guidance on Monitoring Internal Control Systems, 2009, accessed from www.coso .org.

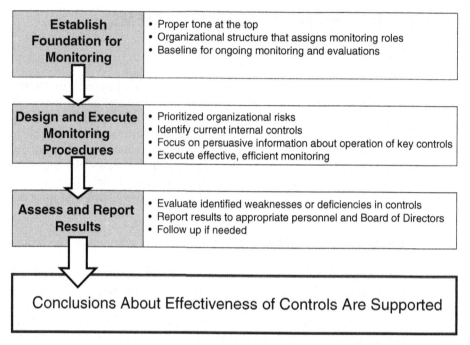

FIGURE 6-11   Overview of 2009 COSO Guidance on Monitoring. Source: COSO Enterprise.

company may only have an internal audit review once every 3 to 5 years. So, an operational audit is a review of the operations of a department or a subunit of the organization and occurs on a regular basis, but not every year. One of the tasks during the operational audit is to test the internal controls that are in place.

On the other hand, effective monitoring within the context of the COSO Framework is both risk-based and principles-based and considers all five components of internal control. Monitoring is a high-level, comprehensive review of firm-wide objectives and risks. With such information, managers can identify critical controls to mitigate identified risks and then develop appropriate tests of those controls to be persuasively convinced that the controls are operating as expected. And as we know, many different types of events can happen in one part of the world that suddenly (and unexpectedly) cause a "risk" for companies in other parts of the world.

COBIT 5[18]

Information is a key resource for all organizations, and due to the pervasive use of technology in organizations, controls around that information is a high priority for management. The professional organization that addresses those concerns is ISACA.[19] This organization issued the first version of **Control OBjectives for Information and related Technology (COBIT)** in 1996. The most current document is COBIT 5 and was published in 2012.

The original COBIT framework (COBIT 1) was released in 1996 by ISACA as guidance for external auditors to evaluate information technology and associated IT-related

---

[18] ISACA, www.isaca.org.
[19] ITGI, http://www.isaca.org/About-ISACA/IT-Governance-Institute/Pages/default.aspx.

controls as they relate to financial statement audits. Subsequent revisions expanded on the original framework by adding guidelines and control procedures for managing and controlling IT, to include IT processes, IT strategy, and value and risk guidance. COBIT 5 incorporates a variety of IT risk and control frameworks and is intended to provide a principles-based, authoritative framework for the management and governance of enterprise information technology. As is the trend with other frameworks and standards, COBIT 5 represents a shift from its prescriptive predecessor (COBIT 4.1) and provides a set of five principles, which guide effective management and governance of information technology within the enterprise (see Figure 6-12).

The first principle, Meeting Stakeholder Needs, is concerned with identifying stakeholders and assessing their needs with respect to value creation. Each stakeholder group likely has subtle differences on their perspectives of value and benefits, and it is up to management and the board to weigh these perspectives when making resource and risk assessment decisions. The second principle, Covering the Enterprise End-to-End, is concerned with the end-to-end governance of the organization as a whole. COBIT identifies a set of enablers (frameworks, structures, principles, processes, and practices), which facilitate the achievement of organizational objectives. The third principle, Applying a Single Integrated Framework, allows COBIT to serve as the overarching governance framework for the enterprise. In other words, COBIT 5 incorporates the guidance from a variety of previously issues ISACA frameworks, such as Val IT, Risk IT, and the Information Technology Assurance Framework (ITAF). The fourth principle, Enabling a Holistic Approach, identifies a series of enablers and links them to the Goals Cascade. As previously mentioned, the enablers facilitate the achievement of organizational objectives, while the Goals Cascade ties stakeholder needs to the enablers. Finally, the fifth principle, Separating Governance from Management, recognizes the distinctness of these two concepts. Governance involves the direction and oversight of management action toward value creation for stakeholders, while Management plans, builds, runs, and monitors activities under direction of the governance body, typically the board of directors.

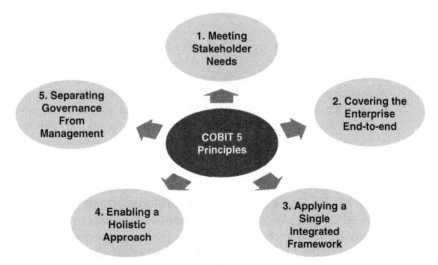

FIGURE 6-12   COBIT 5 Principles.[20]   Source: ITGI.

---

[20] ISACA, COBIT 5 Principles, Figure 2.

COBIT 5 takes into consideration an organization's business requirements, IT processes, and IT resources to support COSO requirements for the IT control environment. This suggests that managers must *first* tend to the requirements outlined in COSO's Internal Control—Integrated Framework and set up an internal control system that consists of these five components: (1) control environment, (2) risk assessment, (3) control activities, (4) information and communication, and (5) monitoring, taking into consideration the 17 principles. The next step managers should take is to work through the principles contained in the ERM Framework. Organizations might use a worksheet like the one in Figure 6-5 to set objectives, identify possible risk events, and consider appropriate risk responses that management would need to take should an event occur.

Once the internal control system is in place, IT managers work with operational managers throughout the organization to determine how IT resources can best support their business processes. To achieve appropriate and effective governance of IT, senior managers of the organization typically concentrate on five areas. First, managers need to focus on strategic alignment of IT operations with enterprise operations. Second, they must determine whether the organization is realizing the expected benefits (value) from IT investments. Third, managers should continually assess whether the level of IT investments is optimal. Fourth, senior management must determine their organization's risk appetite and plan accordingly. Finally, management must continuously measure and assess the performance of IT resources. Here again is an opportunity for managers to consider a "dashboard" to have access to key indicators of these five focus areas to support timely decision-making.

6.6 TYPES OF CONTROLS

We can classify a company's control procedures into three major types: *preventive controls, detective controls,* and *corrective controls.* This section examines each of these types of control procedures in more detail.

Preventive Controls

Preventive controls are controls that management puts in place to prevent problems from occurring. For example, a company might install a firewall to prevent unauthorized access to the company's network, thereby safeguarding the disclosure, alteration, or destruction of sensitive information from external hackers. ERM (discussed earlier in this chapter) helps managers identify areas where preventive controls should be in place. As part of ERM, management must identify possible events that represent a problem to the firm and then identify appropriate safeguards for those problems.

Wise managers engage in a form of brainstorming that is called **scenario planning**, which means that a team identifies various scenarios that range from minor concerns to major disasters that could occur and would disrupt the business of the organization. This team should include a number of informed individuals, such as the IS team, IT auditors, external auditors, and perhaps risk-management consultants. First, management documents each scenario. Then, management must establish preventive controls to minimize the likelihood of each problem they identify.

Even if none of the scenarios ever occur, an organization can still benefit from the contingency plans that were discussed. Through the process, management may see opportunities in other areas of the company that may not have been obvious before the brainstorming sessions. The worst thing management could do is to perform a scenario planning analysis and then never actually use the information to establish preventive controls to prevent a problem that was identified through the process.[21]

Detective Controls

Because preventive controls cannot stop every possible problem from occurring, organizations also need strong **detective controls** that alert managers when the preventive controls fail. As an example, assume that a company's information system prepares daily responsibility accounting performance reports for management that computes variations of actual production costs from standard production costs. If a significant variance occurs, a manager's report signals this problem and the manager can initiate corrective action. Examples of *detective security controls* are log monitoring and review, system audits, file integrity checks, burglar alarms, and motion detection.

Corrective Controls

Corrective controls are procedures a company uses to solve or correct a problem. Organizations can initiate corrective action only if corrective controls are in place. A company establishes corrective controls to remedy problems it discovers by the detective controls. An example of a corrective control procedure might be a change to the company's procedures for creating backup copies of important business files. More than ever before, companies realize the importance of corrective controls, based on the incredible economic and physical impact of natural disasters over the past decade.

Discerning Between Preventive, Detective, and Corrective Controls

Students often struggle discerning the difference between preventive, detective, and corrective controls. Another way of looking at the controls is as follows: preventive controls are designed to stop an instance of noncompliance from occurring in the first place, detective controls are designed to alert someone that an instance of noncompliance has occurred, and corrective controls are designed to resolve an instance of noncompliance once it has occurred or to return the system back to an error-free state.

Consider the following situation at a large urban university. The last class ends at 9:45 pm on Friday evening, with no weekend classes. Due to a series of thefts and acts of vandalism, campus security implements a policy that all classroom and office doors are to be locked by 10:00 pm each night. This policy is a preventive control, as it is designed to prevent an instance of noncompliance, that is, missing or damaged equipment. Now, consider the following two scenarios. In Scenario A, campus security walks into the building starting at 10:30 pm, checking all doors. The campus security officer notes the office number of all unlocked doors and submits this log to campus facilities management at the end of the week. Scenario A describes a detective control. In Scenario B, campus security, upon discovering any unlocked doors, will lock the door. Scenario B represents a corrective control. Generally speaking, detective controls are most valuable when they are performed (and the results are communicated) in a timely manner. In the preceding example, if the security officer notices an unlocked

---

[21] Scenario Planning: Worth the Benefits, by Enterprise Risk Management Staff, September 1, 2009, North Carolina State University, accessed from erm.ncsu.edu, April 2014.

door on Monday but doesn't report it until Friday, an entire week may pass before action can be taken.

6.7 EVALUATING CONTROLS

Once controls are in place, it is a wise practice for management to evaluate them. We introduced several frameworks at the beginning of this chapter that companies might use to evaluate their internal controls, but regardless of *how* management chooses to evaluate their internal controls, it is clear that they *must* do this. Based on requirements contained in SOX, the New York Stock Exchange (NYSE) adopted rules that require all companies listed on this exchange to maintain an internal audit function to provide management and the audit committee ongoing assessments of the company's risk management processes and system of internal controls for financial reporting.

Requirements of the Sarbanes–Oxley Act

As previously discussed, the Sarbanes–Oxley Act of 2002 (SOX) significantly changed the way internal auditors and management view internal controls within an organization. In particular, Section 404 contains very specific actions that the management of a publicly traded company must perform each year with respect to the system of internal controls within the organization. Specifically, the annual financial report of the company must include a report on the firm's internal controls. This report must include the following:

- a statement that management acknowledges its responsibility for establishing and maintaining an adequate internal control structure and procedures for financial reporting;
- an assessment, as of the end of the fiscal year, of the effectiveness of the internal control structure and procedures for financial reporting;
- an attestation by the company's auditor that the assessment made by the management is accurate.

A number of experts believe that some interesting synergies may have happened as a result of companies becoming SOX compliant. Recall that the purpose of SOX was to improve transparency and accountability in business processes and financial accounting. For this to happen, internal auditors and the management of companies had to study their processes very carefully. However, if these same firms already implemented an ERP system, then most likely they already have reengineered some of their business processes to accommodate the ERP. During the evaluation of those processes, it is likely that the appropriate internal controls were considered and included, enabling SOX compliance. In addition, for management to comprehensively consider the requirements of SOX, they most likely used the frameworks we discussed in the opening sections of this chapter.

Cost–Benefit Analysis

Companies develop their own optimal internal control system by applying the cost–benefit concept. Under this concept, employees perform a cost–benefit analysis on each control procedure considered for implementation that compares the expected cost of designing, implementing, and operating each control to the control's expected benefits. Only those controls whose benefits are expected to be greater than, or at least equal to, the expected costs are implemented.

To illustrate a cost–benefit analysis, assume that the West End Boutique sells fashionable high-end ladies' clothing, jewelry, and other accessories. The owner is concerned about how much inventory customers have shoplifted during the last several months and is considering some additional controls to minimize this shoplifting problem. If no additional controls are implemented, the company's accountant estimates that the total annual loss to the boutique from shoplifting will be approximately $120,000. The company is considering two alternative control procedures to safeguard the company's inventory (Figure 6-13).

Based on the owner's goal of reducing shoplifting, alternative #1 (hiring six security guards) is the ideal control procedure to implement. Shoplifting should be practically zero, assuming that the guards are properly trained and perform their jobs effectively.

Even if shoplifting is completely eliminated, however, alternative #1 should not be implemented. Why not? It costs too much. The control's expected cost ($240,000 a year) is greater than the control's expected benefit ($120,000 a year, which is the approximate annual shoplifting loss that would be eliminated).

If the owner implements alternative #2 (hiring two security guards plus installing cameras and mirrors), the boutique's accountant estimates that the total annual loss from shoplifting could be reduced from $120,000 to $25,000. The net benefit is $95,000 ($120,000 − $25,000). Because the second alternative's expected benefit ($95,000 a year reduction of shoplifting) exceeds its expected cost ($80,000 a year), the boutique's owner should select Alternative #2.

The point of this cost–benefit analysis example is that in some situations, the design and implementation of an *ideal control procedure* may be impractical. We are using the term **ideal control** to mean a control procedure that reduces to practically zero the risk of an undetected error (such as debiting the wrong account for the purchase of office supplies) or irregularity (such as shoplifting). If a specific control's expected cost exceeds its expected benefit, as was true with the Alternative #1 control procedure discussed earlier, the effect of implementing that control is a decrease in operating efficiency for the company. From a cost–benefit viewpoint, therefore, managers are sometimes forced to design and implement control procedures for specific

Alternative #1	**Alternative #2**
Hire six plain-clothed security guards to patrol the boutique. Based on the annual salaries that would have to be paid to the security guards, this control would cost West End Boutique an estimated $240,000 a year.	Hire two plain-clothed security guards who would patrol the aisles, and install several cameras and mirrors throughout the company's premises to permit managers to observe any shoplifters. The estimated annual cost of this control would be $80,000.

FIGURE 6-13 Internal control alternatives for West End Boutique.

areas of their company that are less than ideal. These managers must learn to live with the fact that, for example, some irregularities may occur in their organizational system that will not be detected by the internal control system.

Another approach to cost–benefit analysis attempts to quantify the risk factor associated with a specific area of a company. *Risk assessment,* as discussed earlier, is an important component of an internal control system. In general, the benefits of additional control procedures result from reducing potential losses. A measure of loss should include both the *exposure* (i.e., the amount of potential loss associated with a control problem) and the *risk* (i.e., the probability that the control problem will occur). An example of a loss measure is **expected annual loss**, computed as follows:

$$\text{Expected annual loss} = \text{risk} \times \text{exposure per year}$$

The expected loss is based on estimates of risk and exposure. To determine the cost-effectiveness of a new control procedure, management estimates the expected loss both with and without the new procedure. To demonstrate this method of cost–benefit analysis, assume that a company's payroll system prepares 12,000 checks biweekly. Data errors sometimes occur that require reprocessing the entire payroll at a projected cost of $10,000. The company's management is considering the addition of a data validation control procedure that reduces the error rate from 15% to 1%. This validation control procedure is expected to cost $600 per pay period. Should the data validation control procedure be implemented? Figure 6-14 illustrates the analysis to answer this question.

Figure 6-14 indicates that the reprocessing cost expected (= expected loss) is $1,500 without the validation control procedure and $100 with the validation control procedure. Thus, implementing this control procedure provides an estimated reprocessing cost reduction of $1,400. Because the $1,400 estimated cost reduction is greater than the $600 estimated cost of the control, the company should implement the procedure. The net estimated benefit is $800.

A Risk Matrix

Cost–benefit analyses suffer from at least three problems. One is that not all cost considerations can be expressed easily in monetary terms and that *nonmonetary* (or *qualitative*) items are often important in evaluating decision alternatives in a cost–benefit analysis. For example, when an airport contemplates whether or not to install a control that might save lives, it might be difficult to quantify the benefits. Admittedly, this is an

	Without Control Procedure	With Control Procedure	Net Expected Difference
Cost of payroll reprocessing	$10,000	$10,000	
Risk of data errors	15%	1%	
Reprocessing cost expected ($10,000 × risk)	$1,500	$100	$1,400
Cost of validation control procedure (an incremental cost)	$0	$600	$(600)
Net estimated benefit from validation control procedure			$800

FIGURE 6-14 Cost–benefit analysis of payroll validation control procedure.

	Cost to Organization			
	Negligible	**Marginal**	**Critical**	**Catastrophic**
Certain	Busy Street			
Likely		Hit by car		
Possible			Hit by piano	
Unlikely			Burst Dam	
Rare	Locust Swarm			Stampede

(Likelihood of Occurrence — vertical axis label)

FIGURE 6-15   Example of a risk matrix.

extreme example, but the point remains: often qualitative factors exist in a decision-making situation, which requires a degree of subjectivity in the cost–benefit analyses.

Another problem with cost–benefit analyses is that some managers are not comfortable with computations involving probabilities or averages. What does it mean, for example, to state that on average, 2.5 laptops are lost or stolen each year? Finally, a third problem with cost–benefit analyses is that it requires an evaluation of all possible risks and a case-by-case computation of possible safeguards. Typically, companies will run out of money for controls long before they run out of risks to mitigate.

A possible solution to this third problem is to develop a **risk matrix**, which is a tool for prioritizing large risks. As you can see in Figure 6-15, a risk matrix classifies each potential risk by mitigation cost and also by likelihood of occurrence. As a result, highly likely, costly events wind up in the upper-right corner of the matrix, while events with small likelihoods of occurrence or negligible costs wind up in the lower left corner. This helps managers see which events are most important (the upper-right ones) and therefore how to better prioritize the money spent on internal controls.

AIS AT WORK
Separation of Duties is Critical[22]

As we discussed earlier in this chapter in the section on Control Activities, separation of duties is a very important internal control. Unfortunately, the company we describe next had a weak system of internal controls that resulted in a considerable loss to the firm.

The president of a regional home improvement company just hired a new executive assistant. Emily Mason had just graduated from State University as an accounting major and was delighted to have found such a great job. Emily had lots of responsibility and was delighted with her compensation package, which included a generous starting salary. The company was planning an aggressive expansion of operations and was looking for ambitious and eager employees—willing to work hard as team players.

---

[22] Sutphen, P. 2008. Stealing funds for a nest egg. *Internal Auditor* (August): 87–91.

To realize growth, the president knew the company had to be very active in the industry. Thus, the company sponsored booths at trade shows, attended industry conferences, and had morale-building events for its sales team in great vacation spots. Emily's responsibilities included making all the arrangements for these activities. She made hotel and airline reservations and coordinated all of the activities for the sales team.

In addition, Emily was responsible for reviewing the corporate credit card bills and authorizing payments. The president gave her the authority to approve amounts up to $120,000. However, when Emily realized that no one ever asked to look at the charges on the corporate credit card bill, she began making personal purchases with the card. If total charges exceeded $120,000, she simply forged the president's signature on the approval form. When she discovered that the accounts-payable department accepted approvals from the president by e-mail, she would slip into his office when he was at a meeting or out of town, access his computer, and send an approval e-mail to herself.

Unfortunately for Emily, the temptation was so great that she began to find additional ways the company could pay for things she wanted. For example, she soon discovered that she could also purchase gift checks with the corporate credit card, and over a 2-year period, she bought more than $150,000 in gift checks to buy items for herself, her family, and some friends.

Then one day, an employee at the credit card company noticed some questionable transactions involving Emily and the corporate credit card. When the internal auditors investigated the transactions, they discovered that over the 3-year period Emily had been with the company, she had embezzled more than $1.5 million. Emily's standard of living changed overnight as she found herself sitting in jail—pondering her future.

 ## SUMMARY

✓ An organization's internal control system has four objectives: (1) to safeguard assets, (2) to check the accuracy and reliability of accounting data, (3) to promote operational efficiency, and (4) to encourage adherence to prescribed managerial policies.

✓ It is management's responsibility to develop an internal control system.

✓ The control environment, risk assessment, control activities, information and communication, and monitoring are the five interrelated components that make up an internal control system.

✓ Six control activities to include in each organization's internal control system are: (1) a good audit trail, (2) sound personnel policies and practices, (3) separation of duties, (4) physical protection of assets, (5) internal reviews of controls by internal audit subsystem, and (6) timely performance reports.

✓ Within these six activities, specific control procedures should be designed and implemented for each company based on its particular control needs.

✓ There are three types of controls: preventive, detective, and corrective.

✓ To develop an optimal internal control package, management should perform a cost–benefit analysis on each potential control procedure or consider a risk matrix if there are qualitative considerations that cannot be ignored.

✓ A company should only implement those controls whose expected benefits exceed, or at least equal, their expected costs.

KEY TERMS YOU SHOULD KNOW

1992 COSO Report

2004 Enterprise Risk Management—Integrated Framework

2009 COSO Guidance on Monitoring Internal Control Systems (GMICS)

2013 COSO Internal Control—Integrated Framework

2017 Enterprise Risk Management—Aligning Risk with Strategy and Performance

audit trail

control activities

control environment

Control OBjectives for Information and related Technology (COBIT)

corporate governance

corrective controls

culture

demand draft

detective controls

enterprise risk management (ERM)

event identification

expected annual loss

fidelity bond

ideal control

internal control

internal control system

objective setting

operational audits

preventive controls

risk appetite

risk assessment

risk matrix

risk responses

Sarbanes–Oxley Act (SOX), Section 404

scenario planning

separation of duties

Statement on Auditing Standards (SAS) No. 94

strategy

TEST YOURSELF[23]

Q6-1. This term describes the policies, plans, and procedures implemented by a firm to protect the assets of the organization.

   a. Internal control

   b. SAS No. 94

   c. Risk assessment

   d. Monitoring

Q6-2. Which of the following is not one of the four objectives of an internal control system?

   a. Safeguard assets

   b. Promote firm profitability

   c. Promote operational efficiency

   d. Encourage employees to follow managerial policies

Q6-3. Section 404 affirms that management is responsible for establishing and maintaining an adequate internal control structure. This section may be found in which of the following?

   a. The 2013 COSO Internal Control—Integrated Framework

   b. The 2017 COSO Enterprise Risk Management—Aligning Risk with Strategy and Performance Framework

   c. The Sarbanes–Oxley Act of 2002

   d. COBIT

Q6-4. Which of the following would a manager most likely use to organize and evaluate corporate governance structure?

   a. The 2013 COSO Internal Control—Integrated Framework

   b. The 2017 COSO Enterprise Risk Management—Aligning Risk with Strategy and Performance Framework

   c. The Sarbanes–Oxley Act of 2002

   d. COBIT

Q6-5. Which of the following would a manager most likely use for risk assessment across the organization?

   a. The 2013 COSO Internal Control—Integrated Framework

   b. The 2017 COSO Enterprise Risk Management—Aligning Risk with Strategy and Performance Framework

   c. The Sarbanes–Oxley Act of 2002

   d. COBIT

---

[23] Several questions are prior CMA exam questions.

Q6-6. An internal control system should consist of five components. Which of the following is not one of those five components?

a. The control environment

b. Risk assessment

c. Monitoring

d. Performance evaluation

Q6-7. COSO recommends that firms to determine whether they should implement a specific control.

a. Use cost–benefit analysis

b. Conduct a risk assessment

c. Consult with the internal auditors

d. Identify objectives

Q6-8. Which of the following is not one of the three additional components that was added in the 2004 COSO Enterprise Risk Management—Integrated Framework?

a. Objective setting

b. Risk assessment

c. Event identification

d. Risk response

Q6-9. Separation of duties is an important control activity. If possible, managers should assign which of the following three functions to different employees?

a. Analysis, authorizing, transactions

b. Custody, monitoring, detecting

c. Recording, authorizing, custody

d. Analysis, recording, transactions

Q6-10. Which of these is *not* one of the three major types of controls?

a. Preventive

b. Corrective

c. Objective

d. Detective

Q6-11. Which of the following is not one of the components of the 2017 COSO Enterprise Risk Management: Aligning Risk with Strategy and Performance Framework:

a. Risk and Compliance

b. Risk, Strategy, and Objective-Setting

c. Monitoring Enterprise Risk Management Performance

d. Risk in Execution

Q6-12. When management of the sales department has the opportunity to override the system of internal controls of the accounting department, a weakness exists in

a. risk management

b. information and communication

c. monitoring

d. the control environments

Q6-13. Segregation of duties is a fundamental concept in an effective system of internal control. But, the internal auditor must be aware that this safeguard can be compromised through:

a. lack of training of employees

b. collusion among employees

c. irregular employee reviews

d. absence of internal auditing

Q6-14. Which one of the following forms of audit is most likely to involve a review of an entity's performance of specific activities in comparison to organizational specific objectives?

a. Information system audit

b. Financial audit

c. Operational audit

d. Compliance audit

DISCUSSION QUESTIONS

6-1. What are the primary provisions of the 2013 COSO Internal Control—Integrated Framework?

6-2. What were the primary drivers for the redesign of COSO's ERM Framework? Briefly discuss the five components of effective ERM.

6-3. Why are the COSO and COBIT frameworks so important?

6-4. Briefly discuss the interrelated components that should exist within an internal control system. In your opinion, which component is the most important and why?

6-5. Why are accountants so concerned about their organization having an efficient and effective internal control system?

6-6. Discuss what you consider to be the major differences between preventive, detective, and corrective control procedures. Give two examples of each type of control.

6-7. Why are competent employees important to an organization's internal control system?

6-8. How can separation of duties reduce the risk of undetected errors and irregularities?

6-9. Discuss some of the advantages to an organization from using a voucher system and prenumbered checks for its cash disbursement transactions.

6-10. What role does cost–benefit analysis play in an organization's internal control system?

6-11. Why is it important for managers to evaluate internal controls?

6-12. Why did COSO think it was so important to issue the 2009 Report on monitoring?

PROBLEMS

6-13. The Goochland Company manufactures various types of clothing products for women. To accumulate the costs of manufacturing these products, the company's accountants have established a computerized cost accounting system. Every Monday morning, the prior week's production cost data are batched together and processed. One of the outputs of this processing function is a production cost report for management that compares actual production costs to standard production costs and computes variances from standard. Management focuses on the significant variances as the basis for analyzing production performance.

Errors sometimes occur in processing a week's production cost data. The cost of the reprocessing work on a week's production cost data is estimated to average about $12,000. The company's management is currently considering the addition of a data validation control procedure within its cost accounting system that is estimated to reduce the risk of the data errors from 16% to 2%, and this procedure is projected to cost $800/week.

a. Using these data, perform a cost–benefit analysis of the data validation control procedure that management is considering for its cost accounting system.

b. Based on your analysis, make a recommendation to management regarding the data validation control procedure.

6-14. Rogers, North, & Housour, LLC, is a large, regional CPA firm. There are 74 employees at their Glen Allen, SC office. The administrative assistant at this office approached Mr. Rogers, one of the partners, to express her concerns about the inventory of miscellaneous supplies

(e.g., pens, pencils, paper, floppy disks, and envelopes) that this office maintains for its clerical workers. The firm stores these supplies on the shelves at the back of the office facility, easily accessible to all company employees.

The administrative assistant, Sandra Collins, is concerned about the poor internal control over these office supplies. She estimates that the firm loses about $350/month due to theft of supplies by company employees. To reduce this monthly loss, Sandra recommends a separate room to store these supplies and that a company employee be given full-time responsibility for supervising the issuance of the supplies to those employees with a properly approved requisition. By implementing these controls, Sandra believes this change might reduce the loss of supplies from employee misappropriation to practically zero.

a. If you were Mr. Rogers, would you accept or reject Sandra's control recommendations? Explain why or why not.

b. Identify additional control procedures that the firm might implement to reduce the monthly loss from theft of office supplies.

6-15. The Ashland Company recently hired you to review its control procedures for the purchase, receipt, storage, and issuance of raw materials. You prepared the following comments, which describe Ashland's procedures.

- Raw materials, which consist mainly of high-cost electronic components, are kept in a locked storeroom. Storeroom personnel include a supervisor and four clerks. All are well trained, competent, and adequately bonded. Raw materials are removed from the storeroom only upon written or oral authorization from one of the production foremen.

- There are no perpetual inventory records; hence, the storeroom clerks do not keep records of goods received or issued. To compensate for the lack of perpetual records, a physical inventory count is taken monthly by the storeroom clerks, who are well supervised. Appropriate procedures are followed in making the inventory count.

- After the physical count, the storeroom supervisor matches quantities counted against a predetermined reorder level. If the count for a given part is below the reorder level, the supervisor enters the part number on a materials requisition list and sends this list to the accounts-payable clerk. The accounts-payable clerk prepares a purchase order for a predetermined reorder quantity for each part and mails the purchase order to the vendor from whom the part was last purchased.

- When ordered materials arrive at Ashland, they are received by the storeroom clerks. The clerks count the merchandise and see that the counts agree with the shipper's bill of lading. All vendors' bills of lading are initialed, dated, and filed in the storeroom to serve as receiving reports.

a. List the internal control weaknesses in Ashland's procedures.

b. For each weakness that you identified, recommend an improvement(s).

6-16. Listed are 12 internal control procedures or requirements for the expenditure cycle (purchasing, payroll, accounts payable, and cash disbursements) of a manufacturing enterprise. For each of the following, identify the error or misstatement that would be prevented or detected by its use.

a. Duties are segregated between the cash payments and cash receipts functions.

b. Signature plates are kept under lock and key.

c. The accounting department matches invoices to receiving reports or special authorizations before payment.

d. All checks are mailed by someone other than the person preparing the payment voucher.

e. The accounting department matches invoices to copies of purchase orders.

f. The blank stock of checks are kept under lock and key.

g. Imprest accounts for payroll are used.

h. Bank reconciliations are performed by someone other than the one who writes checks and handles cash.

i. A check protector is used.

j. Surprise counts of cash funds are periodically conducted.

k. Orders are placed with approved vendors only.

l. All purchases are made by the purchasing department.

6-17. Ron Mitchell is currently working his first day as a ticket seller and cashier at the First Run Movie Theater. When a customer walks up to the ticket booth, Ron collects the required admission charge and issues the movie patron a ticket. To be admitted into the theater, the customer then presents his or her ticket to the theater manager, who is stationed at the entrance. The manager tears the ticket in half, keeping one half for himself and giving the other half to the customer.

While Ron was sitting in the ticket booth waiting for additional customers, he had a "brilliant" idea for stealing some of the cash from ticket sales. He reasoned that if he merely pocketed some of the cash collections from the sale of tickets, no one would ever know. Because approximately 300 customers attend each performance, Ron believed that it would be difficult for the theater manager to keep a running count of the actual customers entering the theater. To further support his reasoning, Ron noticed that the manager often has lengthy conversations with patrons at the door and appears to make no attempt to count the actual number of people going into the movie house.

- Will Ron Mitchell be able to steal cash receipts from the First Run Movie Theater with his method and not be caught? Explain.

- If you believe he will be caught, explain how his stealing activity will be discovered.

CASE ANALYSES

6-18. Lobs, Love & Lessons Tennis Club

The Lobs, Love & Lessons Tennis Club is a large, regional chain of full-service tennis clubs that cater to the demographics of the region (about 60% of all adults are single in most locations). The clubs each have an indoor swimming pool, exercise equipment, a running track, tanning booths, and a smoothie café for after-workout refreshments. The Midlothian club is open 7 days a week, from 6:00 am to 10:00 pm. Just inside the front doors is a reception desk where an employee greets patrons. Members must present their membership card to be scanned by the bar code reader, and visitors pay a $16 daily fee.

When the employee at the desk collects cash or a check for daily fees, he or she also has the visitor complete a waiver form. The employee then deposits the cash in a locked box and files the forms. At the end of each day, the club accountant collects the cash box, opens it, removes the cash, and counts it. The accountant then gives a receipt for the cash amount to the employee at the desk. The accountant takes the cash to the bank each evening. The next morning, the accountant makes an entry in the cash receipts journal for the amount indicated on the bank deposit slip.

Susan Richmond, the General Manager at the Midlothian club, has some concerns about the internal controls over cash. However, she is concerned that the cost of additional controls may outweigh any benefits. She decides to ask the organization's independent auditor to review the internal control procedures and to make suggestions for improvement.

Requirements

1. Assume that you are the staff auditor for this client. Your manager asks you to identify any weaknesses in the existing internal control system over cash admission fees.
2. Recommend one improvement for each of the weaknesses you identify.

6-19. West End Boutiques

The West End Boutiques company was founded by Libbie Williams in 1990 with a single store in College Station, Texas, and the company now has 21 shops located in the triangle of Dallas, San Antonio, and Austin, Texas. Libbie was an accounting major in college, passed the entire CPA exam in her first attempt with high scores, and worked for one of the large CPA firms for 11 years prior to opening her first store. Based on her work experience, she fully understands the value of strong internal controls. Further, she recently selected a state-of-the-art accounting system that connects all of her stores' financial transactions and reports.

Libbie employs two internal auditors who monitor internal controls and also search for ways to improve operational effectiveness. As part of the monitoring process, the internal auditors take turns conducting periodic reviews of the accounting records. For instance, the company takes a physical inventory at all stores once each year and an internal auditor oversees the process. Chris Domain, the most senior internal auditor, just completed a review of the accounting records and discovered several items of concern. These were:

- Physical inventory counts varied from inventory book amounts by more than 6% at two of the stores. In both cases, physical inventory was lower.

- Two of the stores seem to have an unusually high amount of sales returns for cash.
- In nine of the stores, gross profit has dropped significantly from the same time last year.
- At four of the stores, bank deposit slips did not match cash receipts.
- One of the stores had an unusual number of bounced checks. It appeared that the same employee was responsible for approving each of the bounced checks.
- In seven of the stores, the amount of petty cash on hand did not correspond to the amount in the petty cash account.

Requirements

1. For each of these concerns, identify a risk that may have created the problem.
2. Recommend an internal control procedure to prevent the problem in the future.

6-20. Chesapeake Grocery Store

The Chesapeake Grocery Store is a small local grocery that only carries fresh produce, poultry, and meat that are grown or raised in the 50-mile radius of the grocery. The store also carries other typical grocery items (such as packaged and canned goods). The owner of the grocery, George Lampe, employs about 35–40 people. You are a local CPA with a small firm in the Chesapeake area, and George has retained you as his independent auditor. You are currently reviewing the store's procedures for preparing and distributing the monthly payroll. You've identified the following procedures:

- Each Monday morning, the managers of the various departments (e.g., produce, meat, etc.) turn in their employees' time cards for the previous week and a summary report of the total for each employee to the store's accountant (Charlie Huff).
- Each month, Charlie accumulates the total hours worked by each employee for the month and enters the information in his computer. Charlie uses an Excel spreadsheet.
- Charlie's spreadsheet contains such things as each employee's social security number, exemptions claimed, hourly wage rate, year-to-date gross wages, and FICA taxes withheld.
- Charlie prints out a payroll register indicating each employee's gross wages, deductions, and net pay each month.
- Charlie uses the payroll register to print checks for each employee and distributes the checks on the last day of the month.

To date, you have been unsuccessful in persuading George or Charlie to use a software solution or to outsource the payroll function. You've also recommended that the store consider direct deposit for each employee's pay.

Requirements

1. Assume that the store's management refuses to change its current system of paying the employees. What risks do you see in this situation? Identify any internal controls that might mitigate the risks you identify.
2. Next, search the Web to see if you can find a software solution that you might recommend to George for the grocery store for the payroll. Defend your choice of software.

3. Now assume that George is willing to consider outsourcing the payroll function. What would you recommend? Why?

READINGS AND OTHER RESOURCES

Bollinger, M. 2011. Implementing internal controls. *Strategic Finance* 92(7): 25.

Daugherty, B. 2013. Corporate governance and internal auditing in a state university system. *Internal Auditing* 28(5): 42–45.

Frigo, M., and R. Anderson. 2014. Risk management framework: Adapt, don't adopt. *Strategic Finance* 96(1): 49–53.

Klamm, B., and M. Watson. 2011. IT control weaknesses undermine the information value chain. *Strategic Finance* 92(8): 39–45.

Muglia, K. 2013. Organizational growing pains and managing SOX compliance. *Internal Auditing* 28(5): 19–21.

Oliver, D., and J. Lainhart. 2012. COBIT 5: Adding value through effective GEIT. *EDPACS: The EDP Audit, Control, and Security Newsletter* 46(3): 1–12.

Tsay, B., and R. Turpen. 2011. The control environment in not-for-profit organizations. *The CPA Journal* 81(1): 64–67.

Go to www.wiley.com/go/simkin/videos to access videos on the following topics:

What Are the Benefits of Internal Control
Principles of Internal Control (Fun and Different!)
Implementing Risk Assessment Framework

ANSWERS TO TEST YOURSELF

1. a **2.** b **3.** c **4.** a **5.** b **6.** d **7.** a **8.** b **9.** c **10.** c **11.** a **12.** d **13.** b **14.** c

Chapter 7

Computer Controls for Organizations and Accounting Information Systems

After reading this chapter, you will be able to:

1. *Identify* control objectives related to IT and *explain* how these objectives are achieved.

2. *Describe* enterprise-level controls for an organization and *explain* why they are essential for corporate governance.

3. *Discuss* the importance of general controls for information technology (IT) in the design and implementation of accounting information systems (AISs).

4. *Distinguish between* input controls, processing controls, and output controls and *select* specific examples of control procedures for each of these categories of controls.

"In the digital age, data is business' lifeblood, software is its arms and legs, and hardware holds it all together. Boards and CEOs know about the risks and opportunities of digital transformation, the miracle promises of Big Data, and the threat of cyberattacks. To lift their boats on this rising tide, leadership often approves costly technology-led business transformations that take them into unfamiliar territory."
PwC—Digital Risk Solutions

Risk assurance, PricewaterhouseCoopers, accessed from www.pwc.com, February 2017.

7.1 INTRODUCTION

This chapter continues the discussion of internal controls from Chapter 6 by focusing on controls related to information technology. IT controls can be broadly classified into three categories: function, implementation, and scope. Figure 7-1 presents this classification scheme. When classifying controls based on *function*, we are grouping them based on how they are supposed to act, that is, how they should operate. Information technology (IT)-related controls should either *prevent*, *detect*, or *correct* instances of noncompliance. We introduced this category of controls in Chapter 6.

When classifying IT-related controls based on *implementation*, we are grouping them based on whether they are *automated* or *manual* in nature. Automated controls are those that are programmed or configured within the information systems, operating automatically and without human intervention (e.g., antivirus software that

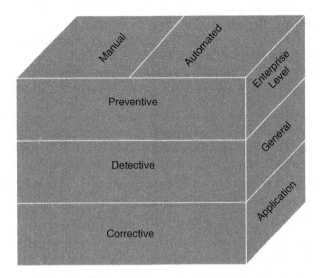

FIGURE 7-1   Classification of IT Controls.

automatically identifies and cleans infected files). Manual controls are those that require human intervention to function (e.g., requiring a manager's signature approval to authorize a software update). In general, automated controls are preferred to manual controls, as information systems tend to do well performing repeatable tasks efficiently and effectively. However, manual controls may be preferred whenever human are necessary to make a decision on a course of action.

When classifying IT-related controls based on *scope*, we are grouping based on the level within the organization at which they operate. *Enterprise-level controls* affect the entire organization, including other IT controls. The next level includes *general controls* for IT, which are controls that involve the entire accounting information system (AIS) and other IT-based systems. Finally, at the third level, *application controls* are designed to protect transaction processing (i.e., to ensure complete and accurate processing of data). These controls are typically programmed into specific modules and applications within the AIS. The remainder of the chapter focuses on the third grouping, scope.

7.2   ENTERPRISE-LEVEL CONTROLS

Enterprise-level controls are those controls that affect the entire organization and influence the effectiveness of other controls. As we discussed in the previous chapter, management's philosophy, operating style, integrity, policies, and procedures are all important characteristics that influence the tone of a company, and these characteristics represent the highest level of enterprise controls. The tone set by management helps to establish the level of security and control consciousness in the organization, which is the basis for the **control environment**. Enterprise-level controls are particularly important because they often have a pervasive impact on many other controls, such as IT general controls and application-level controls.

Auditing Standard No. 2201, "An Audit of Internal Control over Financial Reporting that is Integrated with an Audit of Financial Statements," introduces a framework describing entity-level controls at varying levels of precision (direct, monitoring, and indirect).[1] The external auditor must evaluate these controls, and management must ensure that these controls are in place and functioning. We identified a number of these controls in Chapter 6, such as management's ethical values, philosophy, assignment of authority and responsibility, and the effectiveness of the board of directors. Additional controls that are also very important include the following:

- Consistent policies and procedures, such as formal codes of conduct and fraud prevention policies. For example, a company may require all employees to periodically sign a formal code of conduct stipulating that computer resources are to be used only for appropriate business purposes and any acts of fraud or abuse will be prosecuted.
- Management's risk assessment process.
- Centralized processing and controls.
- Controls to monitor results of operations.
- Controls to monitor other controls, including activities of the internal audit function, the audit committee, and self-assessment programs.
- The period-end financial reporting process.
- Board-approved policies that address significant business control and risk management practices.

Risk Assessment and Security Policies

One level below the tone of the organization is the organization's **security policy**—a comprehensive plan that helps protect an enterprise from both internal and external threats. The policy is based upon assessment of the risks faced by the organization. Figure 7-2 presents issues that organizations should consider when developing this policy.

Designing a Security Policy

In developing its security policies, an organization should consider ISO/IEC 27002, the international information security standards that establish information security's best

---

Designing a Security Policy

1. Determine and identify threats to assets
2. Assess internal and external threats
3. Perform risk assessment
4. Determine if current level of protection of assets is adequate
5. Assemble team of experts to develop security policy
6. Obtain top approval of security policy
7. Develop specifics of the policy
8. Implement security policy throughout organization
9. Develop compliance measures
10. Manage/review policies to consider any new threats to organization

---

FIGURE 7-2 Ten steps to design and maintain an organizational security policy.

---

[1] Public Company Accounting Oversight Board, www.pcaobus.org.

practices. This Standard includes 12 primary sections: risk assessment, security policy, organization of security, human resources security, physical security, communications, access controls, acquisition and development, security incident management, business continuity management, and compliance. ISO certification has become an important consideration with most organizations utilizing e-commerce solutions as part of their broader business strategy. The first step to becoming certified under ISO/IEC 27002 is to comply with the Standard, and one way to measure and manage compliance is to use a risk analysis tool such as the Committee of Sponsoring Organizations of the Treadway Commission (COSO) Enterprise Risk Management (ERM) Framework that we discussed in Chapter 6.

Integrated Security for the Organization

A current trend in security practice is to merge physical security and logical security across an organization. **Physical security** refers to any measures that an organization uses to protect its facilities, tangible resources, or its proprietary data that are stored on *physical* media. **Logical security** uses technology to limit access to only authorized individuals to the organization's systems and information, such as authentication procedures. Figure 7-3 identifies a number of examples of physical and logical security measures that organizations commonly employ. The IT Governance Institute published a document that specifically addresses security called *COBIT 5 for Information Security (2012)*.

Many firms now use an integrated approach to security by combining a number of logical and physical security technologies, including firewalls, intrusion detection systems, content filtering, vulnerability management, and virus protection. An integrated security system, supported by a comprehensive security policy, can significantly reduce the risk of attack because it increases the costs and resources needed by an intruder.

The US government considers computer security a national security issue. The National Institute of Standards and Technology (NIST) has issued guidance, in the form of Special Publications (SPs), on computer and cybersecurity for federal information systems as well as critical infrastructure. NIST SP 800, Computer Security, is a series of approximately 200 documents covering a broad range of guidelines, recommendations, and reference materials for computer security, information security, and cybersecurity topics. NIST SP 1800, NIST Cybersecurity Practice Guides, represents practical guidance on addressing timely cybersecurity challenges in both the public

Physical Security	Logical Security
• Facility monitoring (surveillance systems, cameras, guards, exterior lighting)	• e-IDs and passwords
• Access controls to facilities/data center/computers (biometrics, access cards)	• System authentication
	• Biometrics
• Alarm systems (fire, burglar, water, humidity, power fluctuations) shred sensitive documents	• Logs of logon attempts
	• Application-level firewalls
• Proper storage/disposal of hard drives and other electronic storage media	• Antivirus and antispyware softwares
	• Intrusion detection systems
• Secure storage of backup copies of data and master copies of critical software	• Encryption for data in transit
	• Smart cards

FIGURE 7-3 Examples of physical security and logical security measures.

and private sector. NIST SP 500, Computer Systems Technology, provides guidance on NIST's efforts with respect to computer security.[2] These guidelines, which are mandatory for most federal systems, influence controls for systems at all governmental levels. Security controls (management, operational, and technical safeguards) are critical to protect the confidentiality, integrity, and availability of a computer system and its information.

7.3 GENERAL CONTROLS FOR INFORMATION TECHNOLOGY

IT general controls (ITGCs) protect the IT infrastructure, major components of the IT systems, and data. ITGCs primarily ensure that (1) access to programs and data is granted only to authorized users; (2) data and systems are protected from change, theft, or loss; and (3) development of and changes to computer programs are authorized, tested, and approved before their use. IT general controls affect the integrity of the entire information system. Accordingly, controls at this level are critical for reliance on the application controls that are programmed into specific components of the information system. For example, imagine that an AIS lacks controls over access to financial statement records. If employees can access and change data in the financial statements at will, then the data in the financial statements will be unreliable. Even if there were thousands of application controls that ensured accurate processing of all financial data, the lack of adequate access controls to prevent unauthorized changes to the data makes the financial data unreliable.

Access to Data, Hardware, and Software

Regulating logical access to computers and files is a critical general control in terms of safeguarding sensitive organizational data and software. The ubiquity of network connectivity coupled with an ever-growing population of Internet-connected devices, dubbed the Internet of Things (IoT), has increased the difficulty of safeguarding logical computer access. Part of the strategy to ensure the confidentiality, integrity, and availability of information resources has to be the implementation of robust authentication practices.

Case-in-Point 7.1   In September 2016, French hosting provider OVH was the target of an intense distributed-denial-of-service (DDoS) attack. DDoS attacks occur when hundreds of thousands of compromised machines, termed "bots," are instructed to send connection requests or other traffic to a specific website, thereby overpowering its ability to respond to legitimate requests and shutting down. What made this DDoS attack unique is that most of the more than 150,000 bots in the botnet were IoT devices, such as digital cameras, DVR and Blu-Ray players, and wireless routers. At its height, the botnet was sending nearly 1 terabit per second (Tbps) of traffic to the target server. Security experts blame consumers who failed to change the default passwords on their IoT devices. The OVH attack was, at the time, the largest IoT-based DDoS attempt to date.[3]

Authentication is simply ensuring that a user is who she says she is; stated another way, it is the information system's way of validating the authenticity of a user.

---

[2] National Institute of Standards and Technology, www.nist.gov.
[3] 150,000 IoT Devices Abused for Massive DDoS Attacks on OVH, by Eduard Kovacs, SecurityWeek, www.securityweek.com, accessed March 2017.

Currently, there are three broad strategies by which users are authenticated: "something you know," "something you have," and "something you are."

The most common form of authentication is "something you know," which is typically implemented as either a password, passcode, or personal identification number (PIN). Passwords and the like vary in length and composition, but all have the same intent: to limit logical access to the computer to only those individuals authorized to have it. While passwords and the like are the most common form of authentication, they are inherently the weakest. This is because, at most, the system can only validate that *someone* knows a valid user name and password. It cannot know if the user actually is who she says she is, or if the user has shared her credentials with someone else, or if those credentials have been compromised.

Authentication using "something you have" is typically via a hard or soft token. Hard tokens are tangible devices that store some type of electronic key sequence. They can be used in a variety of ways, such as transmitting the key sequence via Bluetooth connection, displaying an algorithmically generated number that can then be entered at a login prompt, or by plugging the device into a USB port to access data and software. Soft keys usually take the form of cookies or small text files saved on a device's internal storage. In this manner, when a user tries to access a network-connected resource, a cookie's presence on the originating device authenticates the user. More often than not, tokens are used as part of a multifactor authentication scheme, which is discussed shortly.

Authentication via "something you are" is, of the single-factor authentication schemes, the most robust. Also known as `biometric identification` or biometrics, this form of authentication utilizes unique characteristics of the user to validate identity. For example, most smartphones now offer facial recognition as an alternative to swipe patterns or PINs. Fingerprint readers on laptops, voice recognition software, and retinal scanners are all examples of biometric applications currently in use. Biometrics are, all other things being equal, the most robust form of authentication because they do not require a user to do anything other than be herself.

More and more, **multifactor authentication** is used to secure sensitive information resources. Multifactor authentication is when two or more of the aforementioned authentication techniques are used in tandem. For example, access to online banking websites often requires the use of a username and password ("something you know") coupled with accessing the website with a preregistered device that has a cookie soft token saved to the device ("something you have"). In this way, someone accessing your banking account would (1) need to know your username and password, as well as (2) have access to a registered device (such as your laptop or smartphone).

Case-in-Point 7.2   While multifactor authentication has traditionally been implemented as using a username/password combined with some form of soft or hard token, biometrics have become increasingly sophisticated and affordable, giving organizations additional options that are both robust and cost-effective. In early 2017, human interface solutions company Synaptics announced a new multifactor biometric fusion engine specifically targeted to mobile devices. This new biometric engine allows users to choose between facial recognition and fingerprint recognition in implementing a multifactor authentication protocol. The biometric engine is sophisticated enough to discern between fake and real fingerprints and also looks for minute facial movements and eye blinks so as to discern between a photo and real face scan.[4]

---

[4] Synaptics announces multi-factor biometric fusion engine for mobile devices, press release accessed from http://www.synaptics.com/company/news/multi-factor-biometrics, March 2017.

Security for Mobile Devices. The 2010s have seen the rise of mobile devices as a platform for business transactions and connectivity. With the exponential growth of smartphone and tablet adoption in the consumer sector, organizations have been pushed to move many of their applications to the smartphone or tablet form factor. For example, major learning management systems (LMSs) such as Blackboard, Canvas, and Moodle now have mobile apps that allow students to access their coursework on mobile devices. Mobile devices and apps have revolutionized the financial services sector, allowing most home banking needs to be performed from the user's mobile device.

In addition to organizations opening up their networks to access from customers' mobile devices, there is a growing trend of allowing employees to utilize their own mobile devices to access organizational information resources. The "**Bring Your Own Device**" (**BYOD**) trend offers many benefits to organizations. In general, employees are more satisfied when organizations allow BYOD as they can utilize their own devices, rather than being forced to use a company-issued mobile device. Moreover, organizations stand to see substantial cost savings by offloading device and data plan charges to employees, rather than procuring a company-owned device for employees and then assuming responsibility for data plans. Also, BYOD has been attributed to forcing organizations to adopt and adapt to mobile technologies much faster than they would have otherwise.

However, mobile connectivity and BYOD have resulted in a growing list of concerns for organizations, from both employee and outside user access. Chief among these are issues of security, privacy and data protection, administration, and development/support. Mobile devices offer a new vector into the organization for malware, viruses, and hackers. These vectors can include downloading questionable apps, failing to implement a passcode or pattern to lock/unlock the device, or pairing an unsecured mobile device with a laptop containing sensitive information resources or network access. Consider a physician who pairs a personal mobile device to their work laptop that contains clinical and patient medical records. Should the mobile device be compromised, it is possible that the hacker may gain access to sensitive patient health-care records, thereby violating state and federal regulations, as well as doing irreparable harm to the physician's reputation. Finally, administration and app development can be a nightmare for organizations, who must consider multiple operating systems (Windows, iOS, Android), versions of operating systems, and form factors (smartphone vs. tablet) when developing and rolling out mobile device apps.

To address these security concerns, organizations are implementing **mobile device management (MDM)** solutions. MDM software allows an administrator to control and protect data access and configuration settings on a mobile device, thereby reducing risk to organizational information resources. For organizations implementing MDM, an employee is required to download MDM software to their device before being allowed to connect to networked information resources or install corporate apps. The MDM software creates a "container," which is an encrypted and secured location on the mobile device. All resources deemed sensitive by the organization (i.e., e-mail, corporate data, apps using or accessing corporate data) would then be installed in the container, and the apps would run inside the container as well. Should the mobile device be stolen or the employee terminate employment, the administrator can then remotely wipe the container, thereby deleting corporate information resources while leaving the individual's phone otherwise intact. In addition to the container, the MDM could be set to enforce other configuration settings (i.e., require a passcode or pattern to unlock the device) to mitigate risk of unauthorized access.

Case-in-Point 7.3   The MDM marketspace was estimated at almost $1.7 billion in 2016 and expected to grow to well over $5 billion by 2021. While there are several entrants in this growing market space, one of the leaders, according to IT consulting group Gartner, is VMWare's AirWatch. AirWatch was identified as a member of Gartner's "Leaders" quadrant from 2012 to 2016. AirWatch offers a variety of services, such as mobile e-mail management, mobile content management, and various device and application security options.[5]

Security for Wireless Technology.   An important change in today's business environment is the desire for instantly connecting with one another and rapidly exchanging ideas and data. Wireless fidelity (Wi-Fi) technology is based on radio wave transmissions, which makes the transmitted information vulnerable to interception. As a result, organizations that rely on wireless technology must understand the vulnerabilities that exist and explore the various methods of compensating for this risk.

The risk of unauthorized access to data through electronic eavesdropping is minimized by using **data encryption**. It can be used to prevent a company's competitors from electronically monitoring confidential data transmissions. Encryption converts data into a scrambled format prior to their transmission and converts the data back into a meaningful form once transmission is complete. Figure 7-4 shows an example of using encryption keys to scramble accounting data and convert it back into readable form. The encrypted data can be read only by a person with a matching decryption key. Data encryption is relatively inexpensive, which makes it a very efficient control.

Controls for Networks.   Computers are often placed throughout the organization and linked to a centralized computer to form a distributed data processing (DDP) system. The basic objective of each remote computer is to meet the specific processing needs of the remote location and communicate summary results to the centralized (host) computer.

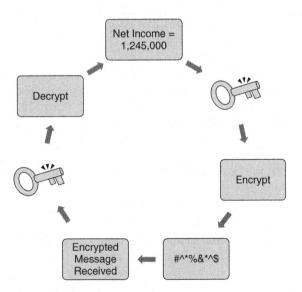

FIGURE 7-4   Data encryption.

---

[5] AirWatch product overview, accessed from www.air-watch.com, March 2017.

DDP systems are still viable in today's business organizations. Large volumes of data are regularly transmitted over long-distance telecommunications technologies. As with wireless technology, the routine use of systems such as DDP and client/server computing increases the potential control problems for companies. These problems include unauthorized access to the computer system and its data through **electronic eavesdropping** (which allows computer users to observe transmissions intended for someone else), hardware or software malfunctions causing computer network system failures, and errors in data transmission. Managers use data encryption to protect information.

To reduce the risk of computer network system failures, companies design their network capacity to handle periods of peak transmission volume. Redundant components, such as servers, are used so that a system can switch to a backup unit in the event of hardware failure. To recover from such a failure, a control procedure, such as a **checkpoint**, helps. Under a *checkpoint control procedure,* which is performed at periodic intervals during processing, a company's computer network system temporarily does not accept new transactions. Instead, it completes updating procedures for all partially processed transactions and then generates an exact copy of all data values and other information needed to restart the system. The system records the checkpoint data on a separate disk file and repeatedly executes this process several times per hour. Should a hardware failure occur, the system is restarted by reading the last checkpoint and then reprocessing only those transactions that have occurred since the checkpoint.

Two control procedures that reduce the risk of errors in data transmission are routing verification procedures and **message acknowledgment procedures**. **Routing verification procedures** help to ensure that no transactions or messages are routed to the wrong computer network system address. They work in the following manner: any transaction or message transmitted over a network should have a *header label* that identifies its destination. Before sending the transaction or message, the system should verify that the transaction or message destination is valid and is authorized to receive data. Finally, when the transaction or message is received, the system should verify that the identity of the receiving destination is consistent with the transaction's or message's destination code.

Message acknowledgment procedures are useful for preventing the loss of part or all of a transaction or message on a computer network system. For example, if messages contain a *trailer label,* the receiving destination (or unit) can check to verify that the complete message was received. Furthermore, if large messages or sets of transactions are transmitted in a batch, each message or transaction segment can be numbered sequentially. The receiving destination can then check whether all parts of the messages or transactions were received and were in the correct sequence. The receiving unit will signal the sending unit regarding the outcome of this evaluation. Should the receiving unit detect a data transmission error, the data will be retransmitted once the sending unit has been signaled about this error.

Controls for Personal Computers. Developing control procedures for an organization's laptops and desktop PCs begin by taking an inventory of them throughout the organization. The various applications for which each PC is used should also be identified. This should be followed by classifying each PC according to the types of *risks* and *exposures* associated with its applications. To discourage outright theft of desktop PCs, many companies bolt them in place or attach monitors to desks with strong adhesives. A control procedure for laptops is to utilize cable locks to secure them to the desk.

As laptops and mobile devices become more sophisticated, people are using them as primary PCs and are saving large amounts of critical data on portable drives. Three simple safeguards are (1) backup important data often, (2) password protect all devices that house or can access critical information resources, and (3) encrypt sensitive files. Organizations can also install antitheft systems in laptops and portable devices—for example, software that uses the integrated Web cam to take a picture of whoever uses it next, or GPS systems can track the equipment itself.

Personnel Policies to Protect Systems and Data

An AIS depends heavily on people for creating the system, inputting data into the system, supervising data processing during computer operations, distributing processed data to authorized recipients, and using approved controls to ensure that these tasks are performed properly. General controls within IT environments that affect personnel include: separation of duties, use of computer accounts, and identifying suspicious behavior.

Separation of Duties. We discussed separation of duties in Chapter 6, but now we want to focus on this topic as it relates to an IT environment. Within IT environments, separation of duties should be designed and implemented by requiring *separate* accounting and IT subsystems or departments and also by *separate* responsibilities within the IT environment.

What do we mean when we say that accounting and information processing should be separate from other subsystems? An organization's accounting and information processing subsystems are *support functions* for the other organizational subsystems. As such, those subsystems should be independent, or separate, from the subsystems that *use data* (accumulated by the accounting function and processed by the information processing subsystem) and *perform* the various operational activities. To achieve this separation, the functional design identified in Figure 7-5 should exist within organizations.

It is equally important that individuals have separate responsibilities within an IT environment. Highly integrated AISs often combine procedures that used to be performed by separate individuals. Consequently, an individual who has unlimited access to the computer, its programs, and live data also has the opportunity to execute and subsequently conceal a fraud. To reduce this risk, a company should design and implement effective *separation of duties* control procedures. Figure 7-6 describes several

---

Methods to Separate Accounting and Other Systems

1. User subsystems initiate and authorize all systems changes and transactions.

2. Asset custody resides with designated operational subsystems.

3. Corrections for errors detected in processing data are entered on an error log, referred back to the specific user subsystem for correction, and subsequently followed up on by the *data control group* (discussed shortly).

4. Changes to existing systems as well as all new systems require a formal written authorization from the user subsystem.

FIGURE 7-5 Functional design to separate accounting and information processing subsystems from other subsystems.

Function	Explanation of Function/Division
Systems analysis function	• Analyze information, process needs, design/modify application programs. • The person performing this function should not perform other related functions. For example, do not allow a programmer for a bank to use actual data to test her program for processing loan payments (she could conceivably erase her own car loan balance).
Data control function	• Use a data control group; maintain registers of computer access codes; help acquire new accounting software (or upgrades); coordinate security controls with specific computer personnel (e.g., database administrator); reconcile input/output; distribute output to authorized users. • Should be independent of computer operations. This function inhibits unauthorized access to computer facility and contributes to more efficient data processing operations.
Programming function	• Require formal authorizations for program changes; submit written description of changes to a supervising manager for approval; test changes to programs prior to implementation.
Computer operations function	• Rotate computer operators among jobs to avoid any single operator always overseeing the same application. • Do not give computer operators access to program documentation or logic. • Two operators in the computer room during processing of data; maintain a processing log and periodically review for evidence of irregularities. • Without these control procedures, a computer operator could alter a program (e.g., to increase his salary).
Transaction authorization function	• For each batch of input data, user subsystems submit signed form to verify that input data are authorized and proper batch control totals are compiled. • Data control group personnel verify signatures and batch control totals before processing data. • These procedures help prevent errors (e.g., a payroll clerk cannot submit unauthorized form to increase pay rate).
AIS library function	• Maintain custody of files, databases, and computer programs in separate storage area called the AIS library. • Limit access to files, databases, and programs for usage purposes to authorized operators at scheduled times or with user authorization; maintain records of all usage. • The librarian does not have computer access privileges.

FIGURE 7-6 Divide certain authority and responsibility functions within an IT environment.

functions within a company's IT environment where it is essential to divide the *authority* and *responsibility* for the functions.

The design and implementation of effective separation of duties control procedures make it difficult for any one employee to commit a successful fraudulent activity. However, detecting fraud is even more challenging when two or more individuals *collude* to override separation of duties control procedures. The 2016 Association of Certified Fraud Examiners (ACFE) Report to the Nations reveals that 47% of fraud cases are committed by two or more individuals who work together to embezzle organizational assets. The median loss in these cases steadily increases as the number of fraudsters involved in the scheme goes up: $150,000 for two in collusion, $220,000 for three in collusion, $294,000 for four in collusion, and $623,000 for five or more in collusion. By comparison, the median loss is $100,000 in fraud cases that involve only one person.[6]

---

[6] 2016 ACFE Report to the Nations, accessed from www.acfe.com, March 2017.

Case-in-Point 7.4 Collusion doesn't just occur between employees; a growing source of fraud in organizations is collusion between employees and third-party vendors, according to PwC Thailand Forensics Partner Vorapong Sutanont. Sutanont reported on the results of a PwC economic crime survey, noting that collusion between employees and vendors often traces its roots to the vendor solution process. Sutanont observed that effective systems-based controls coupled with increased due diligence are crucial to stemming this growing trend.[7]

Use of Computer Accounts. Most computer networks maintain a system of separate *computer accounts*. Each user has an account and each account has a unique password. When the user logs onto the computer, the system checks the credentials against a master list of accounts. Only users with current credentials can access computer resources. Some organizations also use account numbers to allocate computer charges to departments. This control procedure is important to protect scarce computer resources from unauthorized use.

While passwords have been the most used security method to grant users access, IT administrators have a variety of problems with them. Individuals paste their passwords on their monitors, share them with others, or choose simple passwords that are relatively easy for a hacker to guess. As a result, many firms are moving biometric identification and other forms of authentication instead, as discussed earlier.

Identifying Suspicious Behavior. The 2016 ACFE Report to the Nations notes that employees who are defrauding their organizations often display certain behaviors (**red flags**) that can alert coworkers and supervisors to trouble. Examples include lavish spending or becoming very irritable or secretive. In particular, the survey results indicate that in over 45% of the cases of fraud, the fraudsters were living beyond their means, 30% had financial difficulties, 15% had "wheeler-dealer" attitudes, 15% were unwilling to share duties (control issues), and 13% had family problems or were in the middle of a divorce. Sadly, the survey results indicate that the highest percentage of fraud involved employees in the accounting department (21% of all cases reported by survey participants).

While it might be difficult for coworkers or supervisors to know intimate details of coworkers' personal lives, some of these behaviors may be observed without directly confronting the "suspicious" coworker. The threats to an organization by its own employees should never be underestimated. To add emphasis to the need to be alert, PWC's 2014 Global State of Information Security Study estimated that current or former employees (58%), as well as other insiders, are most likely to perpetrate security incidents.[8] Accordingly, it is essential for organizations to safeguard computer files in an AIS from both intentional and unintentional errors.

Additional Policies to Protect Systems and Data

In addition to implementing appropriate personnel policies to protect systems and data, the management of organizations must include a number of additional policies to adequately protect hardware and software resources, as well as to protect data assets.

---

[7] Third-party vendors a major source of corruption, accessed from www.nationmultimedia.com, March 2017.
[8] The Global State of Information Security Survey 2014, PwC, accessed from www.pwc.com, April 2014.

File Security Control	Purpose of File Security Control
External file labels	• Identify contents of a computer file and help prevent an individual from accidentally writing over a disk file.

Internal file labels	• Record name of a file, date file created, and other identifying data on the file medium that will be read and verified by the computer.
	• Internal file labels include *header labels* and *trailer labels*.
	  • Header label is a file description at the beginning of a file.
	  • Trailer label indicates end of a file and contains summary data on contents of file.

Lockout procedures	• Use to prevent two applications from updating the same record or data item at the same time.
Read-only file designation	• Use to earmark data so that it is available for reading only, data cannot be altered by users, nor can new data be stored on the file.

FIGURE 7-7 Examples of file security control procedures.

File Security Controls. The purpose of file security controls is to protect computer files from either accidental or intentional abuse. Protection requires control procedures so that computer programs use the correct files for data processing. Control procedures are also needed for the purpose of creating backup copies of critical files in the event that original copies of a file are lost, stolen, damaged, or vandalized. Figure 7-7 provides examples of file security control procedures to verify that the correct file is being updated and to prevent accidental destruction of files.

Business Continuity Planning (BCP) and Disaster Recovery Planning (DRP). Organizations need the capability to continue operations in the event of disruption to service. In the context of information systems, a **disruption** is any event that causes information resources to be unavailable for a period of time, thereby compromising business operations and processes. Disruptions can be either natural (flood, fire, hurricane, pandemic) or man-made (power outages, civil unrest, security events) and can negatively impact the organization's operations, brand, and reputation. Regardless of the nature of the disruption, an organization that is unable to execute mission critical business processes is soon out of business. To combat these threats, many organizations develop a **Business Continuity Plan (BCP)** and a **Disaster Recovery Plan (DRP)**. Although these plans are complementary and interrelated, there are distinct differences between the two in terms of scope and purpose.

At its core, the BCP is operational in nature and designed to enable the organization to deliver mission critical services and business processes in the event of a disruption. As most business processes have an IT component, a key part of surviving a disruption has to be the re-establishment of information resources and data processing capabilities, and this is where the DRP comes into play. The DRP is technical in nature and designed to ensure that controls are in place to prevent IT outages, as well as to recover from a disruption in IT capabilities should one occur.

In developing and revising a BCP, a **Business Impact Analysis (BIA)** is a major component. The BIA is an exercise to identify and inventory critical business processes and supporting information systems and to establish priorities and time frames for recovery efforts as well as interdependencies between processes and systems. The BCP itself is comprised of various parts, including the BIA, Business Resumption Plan, Emergency Communication Plan, Contact List, and DRP. The Business Resumption Plan provides detailed procedures for recovering business processes immediately after a disruption and will usually provide guidance on the order in which business processes and capabilities are re-established. The Emergency Communication Plan is usually executed by the Public Relations or Communications Department and details procedures to be used for updating employees and the general public on the nature of the disruption and recovery efforts. The Contact List is a prioritized list of key decision-makers, from the operations and IT side of the organization, who should be contacted in the event of a disruption and who will be responsible for authorizing the execution of the BCP and DRP.

An important part of any DRP is the choice and designation of specific backup sites to use for computer processing in the event of a disruption. These backup sites may be other locations owned by the organization or sites that are owned by another organization that can be used for short-term periods. It is a good idea for the various backup sites to be some distance away from the original processing site in case the disruption affects a regional location. For example, selecting a backup site on a different power grid mitigates the risk of a regional power grid failure, while having a backup site several hundred miles away would mitigate risk of disruption due to hurricanes, earthquakes, tsunamis, or other natural calamities. Case-in-Point 7.4 discusses one financial services firm's approach to effective BCP/DRP.

While site selection is important, the nature of the backup site requires much consideration from a resources and capabilities perspective. Mirrored sites are the best option when minimal downtime is a priority. A **mirrored site** is fully redundant with real-time replication of data and transaction processing. Mirrored sites are fully staffed and can take over data processing responsibilities with little to no interruption. **Hot sites** are facilities that have basic communications and IT infrastructure necessary to support critical business operations. Current versions of all operating systems, software, and data are installed on the computers, and enough space is available for a complement of employees to set up shop and begin business operations. **Warm sites** are similar to hot sites in that they are facilities with basic infrastructure in place; however, the IT and communications infrastructure may not be up to the same standard from a processing capabilities perspective as one would see at a hot site, and current backup of data will need to be loaded before processing can commence. **Cold sites** are facilities with basic infrastructure and space, but lacking IT and communications infrastructure. Organizations utilizing a cold site will need to procure computers, network infrastructure, office equipment, software, and data backups necessary for resumption of business operations. **Mobile site** vendors, such as SunGard or Altron, deliver modular data processing facilities that are contained with tractor trailers. Finally, the lowest-cost option is to enter into an agreement with a similar organization to temporarily share their data processing facility. This approach, called a reciprocal agreement, requires that both organizations share similar computing infrastructure.

Case-in-Point 7.5 For Raymond James, a NYSE-member broker-dealer based in St. Petersburg, FL, risk of hurricanes coupled with regulatory requirements for BCP/DRP in the financial services sector encouraged them to pursue a mirrored site for their BCP/DRP solution. Up until 2014, primary data processing and operations were located in the Tampa Bay area, which was highly susceptible to disruptions from storm surge and other hurricane-related threats. As part of their Y2K remediation plan, Raymond James acquired a regional broker-dealer in the Midwest and subsequently set up their mirrored site using high-performance IT capabilities coupled with a sufficient work force capable of handling mission critical business process and IT operations for short-term disruptions. The Midwest location was ideal for BCP/DRP operations, as it was sufficiently distant from the Tampa Bay facilities as to be insulated from weather and power grid issues that might impact the primary site. Testing the BCP/DRP was performed on a regular basis, with lessons learned being incorporated into future BCP/DRP exercises. In 2014, Raymond James moved primary IT processing to a purpose-built facility in Denver, CO, with primary business operations remaining in the Tampa Bay area.[9]

Fault tolerant systems. Organizations use **fault-tolerant systems** to deal with computer errors and keep functioning so that data is accurate and complete. Fault-tolerant systems are often based on the concept of *redundancy*. Computer systems can be made fault-tolerant with duplicate communication paths or processors. Two major approaches are as follows: (1) Systems with **consensus-based protocols** contain an odd number of processors; if one processor disagrees with the others, it is thereafter ignored. (2) Some systems use a second watchdog processor. If something happens to the first processor, the **watchdog processor** then takes over the processing work.

Disks can be made fault-tolerant through a process called **disk mirroring** (also known as **disk shadowing**). This process involves writing all data in parallel to multiple disks. Should one disk fail, the application program can automatically continue using a good disk. At the transaction level, a fault-tolerant system can use **rollback processing**, in which transactions are never written to disk until they are complete. Should there be a power failure or should another fault occur while a transaction is being written, the database program, at its first opportunity, automatically *rolls* itself back (reverts) to its prefault state.

Backup. **Backup** is similar to the redundancy concept in fault-tolerant systems. As an example, if you write a research paper on a computer, you would be wise to back up your work on a flash drive. As we know, a variety of unfortunate events could occur and you might lose all of your work! If you used a computer in a lab on campus, you are probably aware of the fact that the hard drives are automatically "cleaned" every night, so your paper would not be on the hard drive of that computer the next day. And, of course, other events such as a power failure or human error might occur and—your paper is gone. However, if you copied your paper on a flash drive, you created *redundancy* so that a problem will not cause you to lose your work.

Because of the risk of losing data before, during, or after processing, organizations have an even greater need to establish backup procedures for their files. The backup and reconstruction procedure typically used under batch processing is called the grandfather–parent–child procedure. Very large organizations might store more than three such copies (i.e., great-grandfather, great-great-grandfather) and banks typically keep many more copies because of the nature of their business.

Three generations of reference data (i.e., previously processed data stored on master files) are retained with the transaction data used during the general ledger updating process. If the most recent master file, the "child" copy, is destroyed, the data are reconstructed by rerunning the pertinent transaction data against the prior copy of the reference data (the "parent" master file). Should a problem occur during this reconstruction run, there is still one more set of backup data (the "grandfather" master file) to reconstruct the parent. The "parent" master file is then used to reconstruct the "child" master file. Figure 7-8 depicts this procedure.

---

[9] Raymond James and Associates company history, accessed from www.raymondjames.com/about, March 2017.

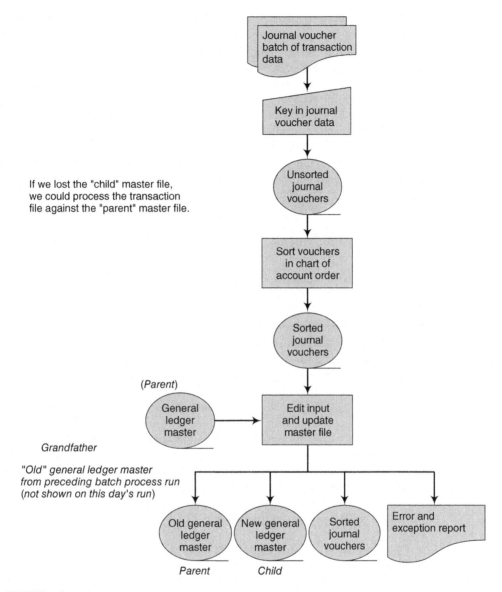

FIGURE 7-8 Grandfather–parent–child procedure under batch processing.

With the sophisticated real-time systems widely used today, online backups are common. A **hot backup** is a backup performed while the database is online and available for read/write, whereas a **cold backup** is performed while the database is off-line and unavailable to its users. During processing, the reference data (master files) are periodically copied on a backup medium. A copy of all transaction data is stored as a *transaction log* as these data are entered into the system. The backup copies are stored at a remote site, which allows data to be recovered in the event a disaster occurs.

The preceding discussion of backup copies and cold sites for disaster recovery is quickly becoming outdated due to the widespread use of cloud computing. Now, if smaller organizations use cloud computing, their operating system, applications, patches, and data can all be contained in a single software bundle or virtual server.

Everything can be copied or backed up to an off-site data center and ready to use in a matter of minutes. Since the virtual server is hardware independent, the operating system, applications, patches, and data can be safely and accurately transferred from one data center to a second data center without reloading each component of the server. As a result, recovery times can be significantly reduced compared to conventional disaster recovery approaches where servers needed to be loaded with the operating systems and application software and patched to the last configuration used in production before the data could be restored.[10]

With regard to electrical power backup, surge protectors provide protection in the case of short, intermittent power shortages or failures. However, large data processing centers may require additional generators for backup power. An **uninterruptible power supply (UPS)** is an auxiliary power supply that can smooth the flow of power to the computer, thereby preventing the loss of data due to momentary surges or dips in power. Should a complete power failure occur, the UPS provides a backup power supply to keep the computer system functioning.

Computer Facility Controls. Physical assets of the data processing center (such as the Web servers, the peripheral devices, and the disk files of the computer library) must also be protected. Perhaps the most important **computer facility controls** (i.e., those that prevent both unintentional and intentional physical harm to systems) include: a safe location of the data processing center, (2) limiting employee access to the center, and (3) purchasing insurance as a corrective control.

Usually, organizations locate data processing centers where the public does not have access. Locations away from public scrutiny and guarded by personnel are obviously preferred. The location of a data processing center should also take natural disasters into consideration. Although it is impossible to protect data processing centers completely from such hazards, advanced planning can minimize exposure to them. For example, companies can increase their protection from fires by locating computer facilities away from boiler rooms, heating furnaces, or fuel storage areas. Similarly, locating computer facilities on high ground or the upper stories of office buildings provides protection from floods. Finally, locating computer facilities in single-story buildings or in heavily reinforced ones can limit earthquake damage.

Case-in-Point 7.6 Fire suppression for data processing centers has long been a challenge. For years, inert gas systems have been a preferred option, as they suppress fires by removing enough oxygen from the hazard area to eliminate the fire, but not so much as to pose a risk of suffocation to people in the vicinity. While inert gas systems are less destructive to sensitive computer equipment than water or dry chemical systems, they aren't without their risks. In the event of a fire, inert gas systems release at speeds up to 450 meters per second, enough pressure to create a shockwave that can destroy server drives and other sensitive components! Clearly, fire suppression nozzle placement is a key design component.[11]

Few people have reason to be inside a data processing center. Thus, another facility control is to limit access to company personnel who wear *color-coded identification badges* with full-face pictures. Security badges typically have embedded magnetic,

---

[10] "Benefits of Disaster Recovery in Cloud Computing," OnlineTech LLC, accessed from www.onlinetech.com, April 2014.

[11] DCD Zettastructure: Improving Fire Suppression through Simulation, by Peter Judge and Max Smolaks, accessed from www.datacenterdynamics.com, March 2017.

electronic, or optical codes that can be read by badge-reading devices. With advanced identification techniques, it is possible to have each employee's entry into and exit from the data processing center automatically recorded in a computer log, which should be periodically reviewed by supervisory personnel.

Another facility control is to place a guard at the entrance to the data processing center. A **man trap** is a small antechamber room between a public corridor and a controlled room. The inner door to the center is self-locking and can be "buzzed" open only by the control person, who permits only authorized personnel to enter. Finally, issuing keys to authorized personnel or using dial-lock combinations limits access to the data processing center. With regard to this last control, it is also a good idea to change locks or lock combinations often and to use keys that cannot easily be duplicated.

Although insurance is usually thought to be an important method of protection for computer systems, it is actually the protection of last resort. Insurance does not protect the purchaser from loss; it merely compensates for losses if they occur. Insurance policies for computer damages are usually limited in coverage, which means that not all instances of loss may be recoverable by the policyholder. Furthermore, compensation usually is restricted to the actual losses suffered by a company. As you might imagine, a fair estimate of the value of data losses is not an easy matter.

7.4 APPLICATION CONTROLS FOR TRANSACTION PROCESSING

The purpose of **application controls** is to prevent, detect, and correct errors and irregularities in processing transactions. IT general controls (ITGCs) and application controls are becoming more integrated because ITGCs support application controls and together they ensure complete and accurate information processing.

Application controls are those controls that are embedded in business process applications. The three major stages of data processing are inputting data, processing the data, and reporting the processed data in some form of output (e.g., a performance report). We discuss various application control procedures for AISs based on these three stages. First, we examine application controls over data input (called *input controls*). Next, we identify application controls that are intended to protect the processing of data (called *processing controls*), and finally, we survey application controls related to data output (called *output controls*).

Figure 7-9 emphasizes the important point that a company's application controls consist of input, processing, and output controls. Since every company's system is somewhat different, each company must consider the risk of errors and irregularities going undetected in processing its accounting data. The company must then design and implement its own cost-effective combination of input, processing, and output application controls.

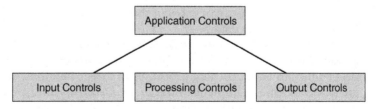

FIGURE 7-9   The composition of a company's application controls.

Input Controls

Although many organizations are now using automated systems to collect data (e.g., bar code scanners), some applications still require employees to manually enter data into the information system. As a result, the risk of undetected errors and irregularities is typically higher in this stage compared to the processing and output stages. In an attempt to reduce this risk factor, the strongest application controls are commonly found in the input stage of data processing.

Input controls help ensure the validity, accuracy, and completeness of the data entered into an AIS. It is usually cost-effective to test input data for the attributes of validity, accuracy, and completeness as early as possible. There are at least four reasons for this:

1. Data that are rejected at the time they are input can be more easily corrected—for example, by reference to a source document.

2. It is not cost-effective to screen accounting data continuously throughout the processing cycles of an AIS. Past some point in the job stream, all data are considered valid and error-free.

3. It is vital that an AIS use accurate data in data processing operations. This protects master files from inaccuracies and safeguards computer processing in subsequent stages of the data processing work.

4. An AIS cannot provide good outputs if it does not start with good inputs.

For discussion purposes, it is useful to divide the topic of input application controls into three categories: (1) observation, recording, and transcription of data; (2) edit tests; and (3) additional input controls.

Observation, Recording, and Transcription of Data. In general, data enter an AIS when business transactions are recorded. An organization often finds it useful to install one or more observation control procedures to assist in collecting data that will be recorded. One such control procedure is the introduction of a *confirmation mechanism*—for example, requiring a customer to sign, and therefore confirm, a sales order.

The data observation process can also make use of *dual observation*. Under this control procedure, the accuracy of the data observation process is enhanced because more than one employee participates in the process. In some organizations, the dual observation control procedure is *supervisory*. Here, the supervisor of the employee (or employees) involved in collecting data is required to confirm the accuracy of the data gathered by the employee.

Once accounting data have been collected, they must be recorded. Data collection and the subsequent recording of these data are areas in which a great deal of automation has taken place. For example, the use of *point-of-sale (POS) devices* has become very common, as we have discussed in the previous chapters. These devices substantially decrease error rates in the recording process and eliminate the expense involved in rekeying data.

In some instances, automated data collection and recording are not feasible, and an initial source document must be prepared manually. To encourage accuracy in the data collection and recording processes in these situations, several control procedures are possible. One example is to use *preprinted recording forms,* such as the inventory receipts form illustrated in Figure 7-10. In general, these forms ensure that all the data required for processing have been collected and also enhance accuracy in the

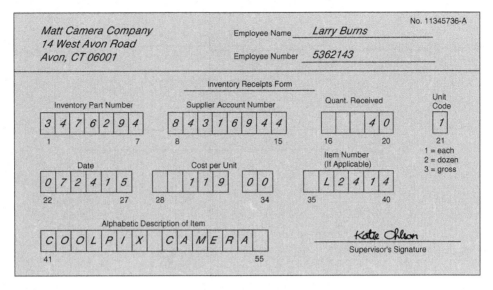

FIGURE 7-10   A preprinted recording from for inventory receipts.

recording process. For example, the exact number of spaces required for such field items as the inventory part number and the supplier account number is clear because a box has been provided for each numerical digit, thus guarding against the loss or addition of digits in these fields. Organizations can use similar controls on Web pages. Additional controls include drop-down lists, check boxes, and radio buttons to limit human errors.

When using transcription, the data on source documents should be organized to facilitate the transcription process. Thus, well-designed, preprinted source-document forms are an important input control because they encourage adherence to the general principle of source-document and computer-input compatibility. Specially designed input forms are the most commonly used method to enter data into a database. Advantages of database forms include: it can be designed to lock certain fields to prevent changes, to control certain fields so that a user cannot enter an unreasonable value, and to limit data values in certain fields.

Edit Tests.   Programs or subroutines that check the validity and accuracy of input data after the data have been entered and recorded on a machine-readable file are called **input validation routines** (or **edit programs**). The specific types of validity and accuracy checks that input validation routines perform are called *edit tests* (or *edit checks*). **Edit tests** examine selected fields of input data and reject those transactions (or other types of data input) whose data fields do not meet the pre-established standards of data quality. Real-time processing systems perform edit tests during the data-entry process. Batch processing systems (illustrated in Figure 7-11) execute edit tests before regular data processing.

Edit tests can also be coordinated in what is called a *redundant data check* to ensure data accuracy. The idea is to encode repetitious data on a file or transaction record, thereby enabling a later processing test to compare the two data items for compatibility. For example, the reason you are always asked for the expiration date of your credit card is because that value is also encoded in the credit card number as well. Examples of edit tests are listed in Figure 7-12.

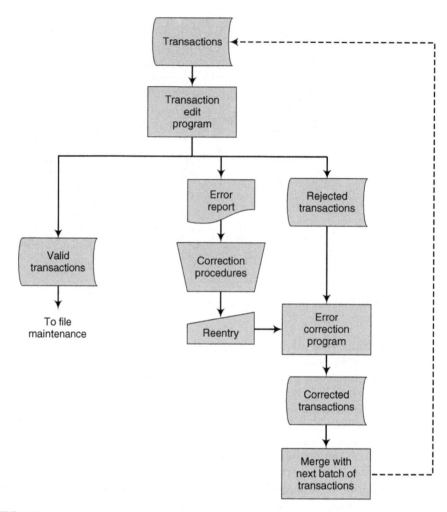

FIGURE 7-11   Use of edit program to execute edit tests under batch processing.

Tests	Purpose
Numeric field content	To make sure that data fields such as Social Security number, sales invoice number, and date contain only numbers
Alphabetic field content	To make sure that fields such as customer name contain only alphabetic letters
Alphanumeric field content	To make sure that fields such as inventory parts descriptions contain letters and/or numbers, but no special characters
Valid codes	For example, 1 = cash sale and 2 = credit sale
Reasonableness	For example, total hours worked by an employee during a weekly pay period does not exceed 50
Sign	For example, paycheck amounts are always positive
Completeness	To check that there are no blanks in fields that require data
Sequence	To make sure that successive input data are in some prescribed order (e.g., ascending, descending, chronological, and alphabetical)
Consistency	For example, all transactions for the same sales office have the same office code number

FIGURE 7-12   Examples of edit tests.

Additional Input Controls. It is possible for a data field to pass all of the edit tests previously described and still be invalid. To illustrate, a bank might use the incorrect account number 537627 (instead of the proper account number 537621) when processing a customer's transaction. When the incorrect account number is keyed into a remote terminal and submitted to edit tests, it will, for example, (1) pass a test of numeric field content ensuring that all digits were numeric, (2) pass a test of reasonableness ensuring that the account number itself fell within a valid range of values (e.g., account number greater than 100,000 and less than 800,000), (3) pass a test of sign (i.e., account number positive), and (4) pass a test of completeness (i.e., no blanks in fields).

Thus, additional control procedures are required for this error to be detected. One control procedure is to incorporate a **validity test** into the data processing routine used to update the master file of bank records. With this approach, any transaction for which there is no corresponding master file record would be recognized as invalid and rejected from the transaction sequence (it would be returned for correction). But what if a master file record did exist for account 537627—the incorrect account number? This would indeed be unfortunate because our "unfound-record" control procedure would not detect the error, and, even worse, the legitimate master file record with account number 537627 would be updated with the transaction data generated by another customer.

Continuing with our bank example, an alternative to this unfound-record test is to expand the six-digit data field of customer bank account numbers to seven digits with *a check-digit control procedure*. Normally, the check digit is computed as a mathematical function of the other digits in a numeric field, and its sole purpose is to test the validity of the associated data. To illustrate, consider the original (correct) account number 537621. The sum of these six digits is $5 + 3 + 7 + 6 + 2 + 1 = 24$. One type of check digit would append the low-order digit of this sum "4" to the account number. The seven-digit value 5376214 would be used instead of the six-digit series 537621 to represent the account number. The computer program would duplicate this computational procedure at the time of data access and therefore validate the accuracy of the data before the transaction data were used to update a master file record.

A check digit does not guarantee data validity. For example, the check-digit procedure described here would be unable to distinguish between the correct account number 5376214 and the transposed number 5736214 because the transposition of digits does not affect the sum. There are, however, check-digit techniques that do include "ordering of digits" in the construction of check-digit values. However, these and other very detailed computer checks are beyond the scope of this textbook, so we'll move on now to processing controls.

Processing Controls

Processing controls focus on the manipulation of accounting data after they are input to the computer system. An important objective of processing controls is to contribute to a good audit trail. A clear audit trail is essential, for example, to enable individual transactions to trace, to provide documentation for changes in general ledger account balances, to prepare financial reports, and to correct errors in transactions. To achieve a good audit trail, some systems require a printed *transaction listing* during each file update by batch processing systems and at the end of every day by online processing systems.

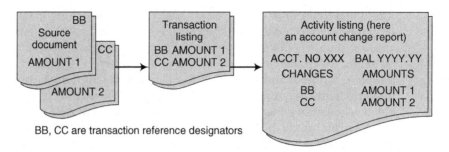

BB, CC are transaction reference designators

FIGURE 7-13 An audit trail for a computer-based system.

Furthermore, use of a unique and sequentially assigned transaction reference designator to identify each transaction in a listing promotes better audit trails. These transaction reference designators should be posted to the general ledger account records and recorded on the specific source documents pertaining to the transactions. Figure 7-13 illustrates an audit trail for a computer-based system, showing how source documents can be easily located by tracing back from an activity (or proof) listing, which is discussed shortly under output controls.

Control Totals. Suppose that you were the data processing manager at a bank that processed over 100,000 bank checks per day. How would you make sure that all these checks are correctly processed by the computer? One procedure is to batch the checks in separate bundles of, say 200 checks, and prepare a special *batch control document* to serve as a control on the contents of each bundle. The information on this document might include the bundle number, today's date, and the total dollar amount for the checks themselves. The total dollar amount represents the **batch control total**.

When computer processing commences, the special information on the lead control record (i.e., the batch control document) is accessed first and the batch control total is stored in computer memory. As the checks are accessed individually, their amounts are also accumulated in computer memory. Once all the checks in the batch are read, the accumulated total is compared with the batch control total. A match signals acceptable processing. A nonmatch signals an error, which may then be traced either to an error in the batch control total or to some difficulty in processing—for example, the inability of the Magnetic Ink Character Recognition (MICR) reader to understand the data on one or more checks.

In fact, MICR readers are themselves a form of control. An original check has a line of magnetic ink with specific information that is recognized by highly reliable MICR readers. Even the best printers do not use this magnetic ink, and copied checks can therefore be detected immediately.[12]

A control total that involves a dollar amount is called a *financial control total*. Other examples of financial control totals include the sum of cash receipts in an accounts-receivable application, the sum of cash disbursements in an accounts-payable application, and the sum of net pay in a payroll application.

AISs also use *nonfinancial control totals,* which compute nondollar sums. For example, controls could compute the sum of the total number of hours worked by employees in a payroll application. A similar control is a *record count*. With this control procedure, the number of transaction items is counted twice: once when preparing

---

[12] www.ehow.com.

transactions in a batch and again when actually performing the data processing. Yet, a third example is the exact byte count of a legitimate computer program, which IT personnel can use to detect tampering.

Control totals do not have to make sense to be useful. For example, when cash receipts from customers are processed, the manual sum of the customers' account numbers in a batch of transactions might be computed to form a **hash total**. This sum is meaningless but is useful as a check against an "internal" tally of this same hash total by the computer at the time of data access.

Data Manipulation Controls. Once data have been validated by earlier portions of data processing, they usually must be manipulated (i.e., processed) in some way by computer programs to produce decision-useful information, such as a report. One processing control procedure is to make sure that the computer programs are complete and thorough in their data manipulation. Ordinarily, this is accomplished by examining *software documentation*. System flowcharts, program flowcharts, data flow diagrams, and decision tables can also function as controls because they help systems analysts do a thorough job in planning data processing functions.

After computer programs have been coded, they are translated into machine language by an error-testing *compiler*. The compiler controls the possibility that a computer program contains programming language errors. A computer program can also be tested with specially designed *test data* that expose the program to the exception conditions likely to occur during its actual use.

Output Controls

Once data have been processed internally by a computer system, they are usually transferred to some form of output medium for storage, screen display, or, in the case of printed output, prepared as a report. The objective of **output controls** is to ensure the output's validity, accuracy, and completeness. Two major types of output application controls within IT environments are (1) validating processing results and (2) regulating the distribution and use of printed output.

Validating Processing Results. The validity, accuracy, and completeness of computerized output in AISs can be established through the preparation of *activity (or proof) listings* that document processing activity. These listings provide complete, detailed information about all changes to master files and thus contribute to a good audit trail. Organizational employees use such activity listings to trace file changes back to the events or documents that triggered these changes and thereby verify current file information or printed information as valid, accurate, and complete output.

Regulating Distribution and Use of Printed Output. One of the more compelling aspects of output control deals with the subject of *forms control*. Perhaps the most interesting situations involve computerized check-writing applications in which MICR forms or perforated printer forms become the encoding media for preparing a company's checks. Usually, these forms are preprinted with the company's name, address, and bank account number. Control over the forms associated with check writing is vital.

The most common type of control used with computer-generated check-writing procedures is the coordination of a preprinted check number on the printer form with a computer-generated number that is printed on the same form at run time. The numbers on these *prenumbered forms* advance sequentially and are prepared by the forms' supplier according to the specifications of an organization.

The computer-generated numbers also run sequentially and are initialized by adding 1 to the check sequence number stored from the last processing run. The numbers on the prenumbered forms and the computer-generated numbers should match during normal processing. Discrepancies should be examined carefully and the causes fully resolved. Other examples of forms that employ prenumbering methods include reports containing sensitive corporate information and computer-generated lottery and athletic event tickets.

Computer reports often contain sensitive information, and it is important that such information be restricted. Thus, for example, a payroll register, indicating the earnings of each employee during a given pay period, is a type of report whose distribution should be restricted. For each output report (hard copy or electronic), distribution is limited to authorized users only. After sensitive reports are no longer needed, it is important to properly destroy them (i.e., use a document shredder). Shredding reports is a stronger control than throwing them away because discarded reports can be retrieved from trash bins.

AIS AT WORK
Biometrics Help Prevent Fraud[13]

Many firms failed in 2009 and 2010 due to the economic crisis. In addition, investors lost billions of dollars as a result of fraud perpetrated by employees and executives. SAP is expanding the use of biometrics in its enterprise systems to better prevent and detect fraud.

The idea is to combine **biometric identification** with passwords such that system users must first be identified with fingerprints and then must supply a password before the user can gain access to any system. In addition, biometric and password combinations are specific to applications and subsets of major systems, which prevents employees from accessing anything that they are not specifically authorized to access.

A recent fraud at Societe Generale Bank could have been prevented with biometric internal controls. One of the bank's traders used his knowledge of the bank's ERP system to engage in secret trading activity. The trader had been trained in using the bank's ERP system prior to becoming a trader, and he used his knowledge of the system to commit fraud.

The trader was able to create e-mails in the system to establish fake authorizations, use his colleagues' log-in passwords to conduct trades in other employees' names, and delete records within the accounting system because he had access to more data within the AIS than he was authorized to have.

Simple changes in IT general controls would have prevented the trader's fraud. For example, biometric identification would have prevented him from logging in as other employees, and biometric identification in combination with password access to only the trading system would have prevented him from changing accounting records to cover his tracks.

---

[13] "Biometric Security for Financial Meltdown Solutions," by Paul Sheldon Foote and Reena Hora, February 24, 2009, SAP, accessed from en.sap.info, April 2014.

In brief, biometric identification systems would have stopped the trader from making secret trades and eliminated his ability to cover his tracks. New versions of SAP emphasize the combination of biometrics and passwords. These systems also solve problems related to lost and stolen passwords. If a hacker is able to steal employees' passwords, the passwords are useless without fingerprint or iris scans.

SUMMARY

✓ IT-related controls can be classified based on scope, function, and implementation.

✓ Enterprise-level controls are so important because they often have a pervasive impact on many other controls, such as ITGCs and application-level controls.

✓ At the organization level, examples of important controls are: management's ethical values, philosophy, assignment of authority and responsibility, and the effectiveness of the board of directors.

✓ An integrated security system, supported by a comprehensive security policy, can significantly reduce the risk of attack because it increases the costs and resources needed by an intruder.

✓ IT general controls are controls that are applied to all IT service activities. These controls are critical for reliance on application controls.

✓ Senior management must have controls over human resources and data resources.

✓ Users authenticate to information resources based on three factors: "something you know," "something you have," and "something you are." A combination of these factors, known as multifactor authentication, is becoming more common and is more robust than utilizing a single-factor alone.

✓ Business continuity planning and disaster recovery planning are essential for surviving business disruptions.

✓ Organizations are increasingly relying on mobile devices and must recognize the need for appropriate policies and controls over BYOD so that users may safely access entity data and other online resources.

✓ Three major types of application controls are: (1) input controls, (2) processing controls, and (3) output controls.

KEY TERMS YOU SHOULD KNOW

application controls	control environment	hot backup
backup	data encryption	hot site
batch control total	data manipulation controls	input controls
biometric identification	disaster recovery plan (DRP)	input validation routines
bring your own device (BYOD)	disk mirroring	IT general controls (ITGCs)
business continuity plan (BCP)	disk shadowing	logical security
business impact analysis (BIA)	disruption	man trap
checkpoint	edit programs	message acknowledgment
cold backup	edit tests	procedures
cold site	electronic eavesdropping	mirrored site
computer facility controls	fault-tolerant systems	mobile device management
consensus-based protocols	hash total	(MDM)

mobile site
multifactor authentication
output controls
physical security
processing controls

red flags
rollback processing
routing verification
 procedures
security policy

uninterruptible power supply
 (UPS)
validity test
warm site
watchdog processor

TEST YOURSELF

Q7-1. A _____ is a comprehensive plan that helps protect the enterprise from internal and external threats.

   a. firewall

   b. security policy

   c. risk assessment

   d. VPN

Q7-2. According to PCAOB Standard No. 5, which of the following is an example of an entity-level control?

   a. Effectiveness of the board of directors

   b. Personnel controls

   c. Access to computer files

   d. All of the above

Q7-3. Fault-tolerant systems are designed to tolerate computer errors and are built on the concept of _____.

   a. redundancy

   b. COBIT

   c. COSO

   d. integrated security

Q7-4. A _____ site is a disaster recovery site that is fully staffed and utilizes real-time replication of data and transaction processing.

   a. hot

   b. cold

   c. mirrored

   d. backup

Q7-5. Disaster recovery plans may not be of much use if _____.

   a. they are not fully documented

   b. the organization does not have a cold site for relocation purposes

   c. the organization does not expect any natural disasters to occur

   d. they are not tested periodically and revised when necessary

Q7-6. Which of the following is not a computer facility control?

   a. Place the data processing center where unauthorized individuals cannot gain entry

   b. Limit access to the data processing center to all employees of the company

   c. Buy insurance to protect against loss of equipment in a computer facility

   d. Use advanced technology to identify individuals who are authorized access to the data processing center

Q7-7. In entering the billing address for a new client in Emil Company's computerized database, a clerk erroneously entered a nonexistent zip code. As a result, the first month's bill mailed to the new client was returned to Emil Company. Which one of the following would most likely have led to the discovery of the error at the time of entry into Emil Company's computerized database?[14]

   a. Limit test

   b. Validity test

   c. Parity test

   d. Record count test

Q7-8. A _____ is a security appliance that runs behind a firewall and allows remote users to access entity resources by using wireless, handheld devices.

   a. data encryption

   b. WAN

   c. checkpoint

   d. VPN

---

[14] Prior CMA exam question, used with permission.

Q7-9. Organizations use _____ controls to prevent, detect, and correct errors and irregularities in transactions that are processed.

    a. specific

    b. general

    c. application

    d. input

Q7-10. A company's management is concerned about computer data eavesdropping and wants to maintain the confidentiality of its information as it is transmitted. The company should utilize[15]

    a. data encryption.

    b. dial-back systems.

    c. message acknowledgment procedures.

    d. password codes.

Q7-11. Which one of the following would most compromise the use of backups as protection against loss or damage of master files?[16]

    a. Use of magnetic tape

    b. Inadequate ventilation

    c. Storing of all files in one location.

    d. Failure to encrypt data

DISCUSSION QUESTIONS

7-1. What is a security policy? What do we mean when we say organizations should have an integrated security plan?

7-2. What do we mean when we talk about multifactor authentication? What are the examples of multifactor authentication in your personal life?

7-3. What guidance or framework would you use to establish IT governance if you were a senior executive in a firm? If you were a mid-level IT manager who was designing IT general controls? A manager who was responsible for identifying the appropriate application controls?

7-4. What controls must be used to protect data that is transmitted across wireless networks?

7-5. Why are business continuity planning and disaster recovery planning so important? How do they complement each other? Identify several reasons why testing these plans is a good idea.

7-6. What is backup, and why is it important when operating an accounting system?

7-7. Discuss the role of cloud computing with respect to backing up files.

7-8. Discuss the different backup site options available to organizations. How does the nature of the business influence which site option is chosen?

7-9. What are some of the unique challenges that mobile devices pose to an organization? What do you see are the trade-offs associated with mobile devices? What are the pros and cons of BYOD?

7-10. Explain how each of the following can be used to control the input, processing, or output of accounting data: (a) edit tests, (b) check digits, (c) passwords, (d) activity listings, and (e) control totals.

7-11. What is the difference between *logical* access to the computer and *physical* access to the computer? Why is the security of both important?

7-12. Discuss the following statement: "The separation of duties control is very difficult in computerized accounting information systems because computers often integrate functions when performing data processing tasks. Therefore, such a control is not advisable for those organizations using computers to perform their accounting functions."

PROBLEMS

7-13. You have been retained as a consultant to the Bentley Company, and the primary reason they think they need your expertise is to help them identify a problem with retaining their best employees. Bentley maintains a very large computer system that supports over 235

---

[15] Prior CMA exam question, used with permission.
[16] Ibid.

networked PCs. The company maintains fairly extensive databases regarding its customers. These databases include customer profiles, past purchasing patterns, and prices charged. Recently, Bentley has been having some major problems with competitors. One competitor in particular seems to be very clever at taking away the company's customers. Apparently, this competitor is offering Bentley's customers identical products at lower prices.

a. In your opinion, what is the possible security problem at Bentley?

b. What can you recommend to the management at Bentley to mitigate this problem?

7-14. Susan Boyd graduated summa cum laude from State University as an accounting major and is now working for a medium-size company. Susan was very clever and quickly realized that she could set up several dummy companies that would direct the company computer to write checks to her dummy companies for fictitious merchandise. Her scheme was discovered when several of the company executives began to wonder how she could afford to live in one of the priciest subdivisions in town and drive a very expensive vehicle. What controls, in your opinion, might have prevented Susan from engaging in this fraud?

7-15. The management of Wiley Coyote Inc. decided that they needed an outside consultant to help them determine which application controls should be implemented for the company's accounting data processing. In one of the workshops, the seminar leader, Margaret, made the following comment: "We can classify all errors in processing accounting data as either accidental or intentional. Controls such as edit tests are primarily aimed at the former type of error whereas personnel controls are primarily aimed at the latter type of error." Do you agree with Margaret? Explain.

7-16. Identify one or more *control procedures* (either *general* or *application* controls, or both) that would guard against each of the following errors or problems.

a. Leslie Thomas, a secretary at the university, indicated that she had worked 40 hours on her regular time card. The university paid her for 400 hours worked that week.

b. The aging analysis indicated that the Grab and Run Electronics Company account was

so far in arrears that the credit manager decided to cut off any further credit sales to the company until it cleared up its account. Yet, the following week, the manager noted that three new sales had been made to that company—all on credit.

c. The Small Company employed Mr. Fineus Eyeshade to perform all its accounts-receivable data processing. Mr. Eyeshade's 25 years with the company and his unassuming appearance helped him conceal the fact that he was embezzling cash collections from accounts receivable to cover his gambling losses at the racetrack.

d. The Blue Mountain Utility Company was having difficulty with its customer payments. The payment amounts were entered directly onto a terminal, and the transaction file thus created was used to update the customer master file. Among the problems encountered with this system were the application of customer payments to the wrong accounts and the creation of multiple customer master file records for the same account.

e. The Landsford brothers had lived in Center County all their lives. Ben worked for the local mill in the accounts-payable department, and Tom owned the local hardware store. The sheriff couldn't believe that the brothers had created several dummy companies that sold fictitious merchandise to the mill. Ben had the mill pay for this merchandise in its usual fashion, and he wrote off the missing goods as "damaged inventory."

7-17. Disgruntled employees can be a significant source of problems for any company as we indicate in this problem. Andi Boyd is a very accomplished computer programmer, but she had a grudge against the company because she did not get a promotion that she thought she deserved. She decided to take out her anger on the company by coding a special routine in the mortgage loan program that erased a small, random number of accounts on the disk file every time the program was run. The company did not detect this malicious code until nearly half of all of the mortgage records were erased. In your opinion, what controls should the company have implemented to mitigate such a problem?

7-18. The Blatz Furniture Company uses an online data input system for processing its sales

Application	Field Name	Field Length	Example
Invoicing	Customer number	6	123456
	Customer name	23	Al's Department Store
	Salesperson number	3	477
	Invoice number	6	123456
	Item catalog number	10	9578572355
	Quantity sold	8	13
	Unit price	7	10.50
	Total price	12	136.50
Salesperson activity	Salesperson number	3	477
	Salesperson name	20	Kathryn Wilson
	Store department number	8	10314201
	Week's sales volume	12	1043.75
	Regular hours worked	5	39.75
	Overtime hours worked	4	0.75
Inventory control	Inventory item number	10	9578572355
	Item description	15	Desk lamp
	Unit cost	7	8.50
	Number of units dispersed this week	4	14
	Number of units added to inventory	4	20
Purchasing	Vendor catalog number	12	059689584996
	Item description	18	Desk pad
	Vendor number	10	8276110438
	Number of units ordered	7	45
	Price per unit	7	8.75
	Total cost of purchase	14	313.75

FIGURE 7-14   Data for the Blatz Furniture Company's applications.

invoice data, salesperson data, inventory control, and purchase order data. Representative data for each of these applications are shown in Figure 7-14. Identify specific edit tests that might be used to ensure the accuracy and completeness of the information in each data set.

7-19. Identify one or more *control procedures* (either *general* or *application* controls, or both) that would guard against each of the following errors or problems.

a. A bank deposit transaction was accidentally coded with a withdrawal code.

b. The key-entry operator keyed in the purchase order number as a nine-digit number instead of an eight-digit number.

c. The date of a customer payment was keyed 2001 instead of 2015.

d. A company employee was issued a check in the amount of $−135.65 because he had not worked a certain week, but most of his payroll deductions were automatic each week.

e. A patient filled out her medical insurance number as 123465 instead of 123456.

f. An applicant for the company stock option plan filled out her employee number as 84-7634-21. The first two digits are a department code. There is no department 84.

g. A high school student was able to log onto the telephone company's computer as soon as he learned what telephone number to call.

h. The accounts-receivable department sent 87 checks to the computer center for processing. No one realized that one check was dropped along the way and that the computer therefore processed only 86 checks.

7-20. To achieve effective separation of duties within a company's IT environment, the company's accounting and information processing subsystems should be separate from the departments that use data and perform operational activities. Discuss some of the ways this "separation of duties" is achieved.

CASE ANALYSES

7-21. Bad Bad Benny: A True Story[17]

In the early twentieth century, there was an ambitious young man named Arthur, who started working at a company in Chicago as a mailroom clerk. He was a hard worker and very smart, eventually ending up as the president of the company, the James H. Rhodes Company. The firm produced steel wool and harvested sea sponges in Tarpon Springs, Florida, for household and industrial use. The company was very successful, and Arthur decided that the best way to ensure the continued success of the company was to hire trusted family members for key management positions—because you can always count on your family. Arthur decided to hire his brother Benny to be his Chief Financial Officer (CFO) and placed other members of the family in key management positions. He also started his eldest son, Arthur Junior (an accountant by training), in a management training program, hoping that he would eventually succeed him as president.

As the company moved into the 1920s, Benny was a model employee; he worked long hours, never took vacations, and made sure that he personally managed all aspects of the cash function. For example, he handled the entire purchasing process—from issuing purchase orders through the disbursement of cash to pay bills. He also handled the cash side of the revenue process by collecting cash payments, preparing the daily bank deposits, and reconciling the monthly bank statement.

The end of the 1920s saw the United States entering its worst Depression since the beginning of the Industrial Age. Because of this, Arthur and other managers did not get raises and, in fact, took pay cuts to keep the company going and avoid lay-offs. Arthur and other top management officials made "lifestyle" adjustments as well—for example, reducing the number of their household servants and keeping their old cars, rather than purchasing new ones. Benny, however, was able to build a new house on the shore of Lake Michigan and purchased a new car. He dressed impeccably and seemed impervious to the economic downturn. His family continued to enjoy the theatre, new cars, and nice clothes.

Arthur's wife became suspicious of Benny's good fortune in the face of others' hardships, so she and Arthur hired an accountant to review the books. External audits were not yet required for publicly held companies, and the Securities and Exchange Commission (SEC) had not yet been formed (that would happen in 1933–1934). Jim, the accountant, was eventually able to determine that Benny had diverted company funds to himself by setting up false vendors and having checks mailed to himself. He also diverted some of the cash payments received from customers and was able to hide it by handling the bank deposits and the reconciliation of the company's bank accounts. Eventually, Jim determined that Benny had embezzled about $500,000 (in 1930 dollars).

If we assume annual compounding of 5% for 84 years, the value in today's dollars would be about $46.67 million! Arthur was furious, and sent Benny "away." Arthur sold most of his personal stock holdings in the company to repay Benny's embezzlement, which caused him to lose his controlling interest in the company and eventually was voted out of office by the Board of Directors.

Jim, the accountant, wrote a paper about his experience with Benny (now referred to as "Bad Bad Benny" by the family). Jim's paper contributed to the increasing call for required annual external audits for publicly held companies. Arthur eventually reestablished himself as a successful stockbroker and financial planner. Benny "disappeared" and was never heard from again.

---

[17] Professor Constance Lehmann, Department of Accounting, University of Houston-Clear Lake. Used with permission.

Requirements

1. Identify the control weaknesses in the revenue and purchasing processes.
2. Identify any general controls Arthur should have implemented to help protect the company.
3. From Chapter 11, identify the internal control activities that Arthur should have considered (or implemented) that would have thwarted Benny's bad behavior.

7-22. Hammaker Manufacturing: Security Controls

Recall, in Chapter 11, the first case was about Hammaker Manufacturing (HM), a company that decided to work with a consultant to computerize much of their operations. HM has grown substantially and must upgrade its information systems. The company is developing a new, integrated, computer-based information system. In conjunction with the design of the new system, the management is reviewing the data processing security to determine what new control features should be incorporated. Two areas of concern are (1) confidentiality of company and customer records and (2) protection of data, computer equipment, and facilities.

The new information system will process all company records, including sales, purchases, budgeting, customer, creditor, and personnel information. The stores and warehouses will be linked to the main computer at corporate headquarters by a system of remote terminals. This will permit data to be communicated directly to corporate headquarters or to any other location from each location within the terminal network. Employees will also be able to access the system with laptops and handheld devices via a secured wireless network.

At the current time, certain reports have restricted distribution because not all levels of management need to receive them or because they contain confidential information. The introduction of remote terminals in the new system may provide access to these restricted data by unauthorized personnel. Management is concerned that confidential information may become accessible and be used improperly.

The company's management is also concerned with potential physical threats to the system, such as sabotage, fire damage, water damage, or power failure. With the new system, a computer shutdown would severely limit company activities until the system is operational again.

Requirements

1. Identify and briefly explain the problems HM could experience with respect to the confidentiality of information and records in the new system.
2. Recommend the measures HM could incorporate into the new system that would ensure the confidentiality of information and records in this new system.
3. What safeguards can HM develop to provide physical security for its (a) computer equipment, (b) data, and (c) data processing center facilities?

7-23. Brazos Valley Inc.

Brazos Valley, Inc. (BVI), a medical device manufacturing firm, has a small systems staff that designs and writes BVI's customized software. Until recently, BVI's transaction data were transmitted to an outside organization for processing on its hardware.

BVI has experienced significant sales growth as the cost of medical devices has increased and medical insurance companies have been tightening reimbursements for cost containment purposes. As a result of these increased sales, BVI has purchased its own computer hardware. The data processing center is installed on the ground floor of its two-story headquarters building. It is behind large, plate-glass windows so that the state-of-the-art data processing center can be displayed as a measure of the company's success and attract customer and investor attention. The computer area is equipped with halon gas fire suppression equipment and an uninterruptible power supply system.

BVI hired a small computer operations staff to operate its data processing center. To handle BVI's current level of business, the operations staff is on a two-shift schedule, 5 days per week. BVI's systems staff and programming staff, now located in the same building, have access to the data processing center and can test new programs and program changes when the operations staff is not available. Because the systems and programming staff is small and the work demands have increased, systems and programming documentation are developed only when time is available. Periodically, but not on a scheduled basis, BVI backs up its programs and data files, storing them at an off-site location.

Unfortunately, due to several days of heavy rains, BVI's building recently experienced serious flooding that reached several feet into the first-floor level and affected not only the computer hardware but also the data and program files that were onsite.

Requirements

1. Describe at least four computer control weaknesses that existed at BVI prior to the flood occurrence.

2. Describe at least five components that should be incorporated in a formal disaster recovery plan so that BVI can become operational within 72 hours after a disaster affects its computer operations capability.

3. Identify at least three factors, other than the plan itself, that BVI's management should consider in formulating a formal disaster recovery plan.

READINGS AND OTHER RESOURCES

Markelevich, A. 2014. Peer benchmarking made easy with XBRL. *Strategic Finance* 96(2): 54–57. (Discusses benchmarking risk analysis.)

Masli, A., G. Peters, V. Richardson, and J. Sanchez. 2010. Examining the potential benefits of internal control monitoring technology. *The Accounting Review* 85(3): 1001–034.

Moldof, A. 2014. The most important internal controls to include in a small company environment. *Internal Auditing* 29(1): 39–42.

Norman, C., M. Payne, and V. Vendrzyk. 2009. Assessing information technology general control risk: An instructional case. *Issues in Accounting Education* 24(1): 63–76.

Peary, E., K. Karim, S. Suh, S. Strickland, and C. Carter. 2013. An examination of SOX's impact on internal control weaknesses. *Internal Auditing* 28(6): 25–31.

Reding, K. 2013. A solid understanding of risk. *Internal Auditor* 70(3): 21–25.

Go to www.wiley.com/go/simkin/videos to access videos on the following topics:

Biometric Security
Data Encryption
Introduction to Business Continuity Planning

ANSWERS TO TEST YOURSELF

1. b **2.** a **3.** a **4.** c **5.** d **6.** b **7.** b **8.** d **9.** c **10.** a **11.** c

Chapter 8

Accounting Information Systems and Business Processes: Part I

After reading this chapter, you will be able to:

1. *List* and *describe* the steps in the financial accounting process.

2. *Explain* and *illustrate* the use of journals and ledgers in processing accounting transactions.

3. *Identify* different types of coding systems used by accounting information systems (AISs).

4. *Explain* why planning an AIS begins with the design of outputs.

5. *Describe* the objectives, inputs, and outputs of the sales and purchasing processes.

6. *Explain* why businesses choose outsourcing and offshoring of business processes.

"[B]usinesses are processes, not buckets of accounting information."

American Accounting Association and American Institute of Certified Public Accountants (AAA/AICPA. 2012. The Pathways Commission—Charting a National Strategy for the Next Generation of Accountants. Sarasota, FL: AAA/AICPA, p. 68.

8.1 INTRODUCTION

In this chapter and in the next chapter, we discuss the fundamentals of business processes and then focus on several core business processes that are common to most businesses. We begin with a brief refresher of the basics of financial accounting because these concepts are at the heart of an accounting information system (AIS). That is, the fundamental elements of accounting are embedded in automated AISs, and they are the basis for a company's financial statements. These fundamental elements include journals, ledgers, accounts, trial balances, and financial statements. We discuss these concepts from the perspective of simple, paper journals and records because this simplifies the discussion of the key business processes.

The nature and types of business processes vary, depending on the information needs of an organization. In this chapter, we examine business transactions related to the sales process (sales and cash collection) and the purchasing process (expenditures for materials and supplies and cash payments for these resources).

Businesses are under tremendous pressure to cut costs, reduce capital expenditures, and become as efficient as possible at their core competencies. As a result, companies search globally to achieve efficiencies—called "**business without boundaries**." In the final portion of this chapter, we give examples of business processes that are commonly outsourced or offshored. We then examine some business process management (BPM) solutions that are available to improve business processes, regardless of their location.

8.2   BUSINESS PROCESS FUNDAMENTALS

An accounting cycle can begin in a number of different ways. For instance, accounting personnel can create a transaction from a source document, or a customer may order products online. Regardless of how the process starts, at the end of the process, we issue annual financial reports and close the temporary general ledger accounts in preparation for a new cycle.

Overview of the Financial Accounting Cycle

An AIS records each transaction or business event affecting an organization's financial condition in journals and ledgers.

Journals.   Accounting transactions are first recorded in a journal. Of course, this is rarely an actual paper journal anymore—it's more likely an electronic entry in an AIS. In many cases, these entries are made directly into database tables. The journal is a chronological record of business events that impact the accounting equation. A journal may be a special journal or a general journal. Special journals capture a specific type of transaction. They are usually reserved for transactions occurring frequently within an organization. In a computerized system, special journals may take the form of special modules with their own files. For example, an accounting clerk would likely record a credit sale in an accounts-receivable module. In an automated system, entries into the accounting system may be entirely electronic, such as scanning a bar code.

Companies can set up a special journal for virtually any type of transaction. Common ones are sales journals, purchases journals, cash receipts journals, and cash disbursements journals. If you think about it, almost all accounting transactions a business organization records fall into one of these categories. Special journals include entries for all but a few types of transactions and adjusting journal entries, such as for depreciation. The general journal records these entries.

Ledgers.   Journal entries show all aspects of a particular transaction. Each entry shows debit and credit amounts, the transaction date, the affected accounts, and a brief description of the event. Once an AIS records a journal entry, it next posts the entry in the general ledger. Within an AIS, a general ledger is a collection of detailed monetary information about an organization's various assets, liabilities, owners' equity, revenues, and expenses. The general ledger includes a separate account (often called a "T account" because of its shape in manual accounting systems) for each type of monetary item in an organization. While journal entries record all aspects of business transactions, an AIS separately posts the monetary amounts in each account to the various accounts in the general ledger. A company's chart of accounts provides the organizational structure for the general ledger. The chart of accounts makes use of a block coding structure (discussed in the next section).

Subsidiary ledgers break down certain general ledger accounts to provide more detailed information to users. For example, the Accounts Receivable Subsidiary Ledger provides the equivalent of a T account for each person or organization owing money to the firm. If you add each of these individual debtor's balances, the total will equal the Accounts Receivable general ledger balance. How else would a firm be able to send out statements each month to those who owe money to the firm? The same applies to the Accounts Payable and Inventory general ledger accounts, for example. A firm would have an Accounts Payable Subsidiary Ledger and an Inventory Subsidiary Ledger.

Trial Balances and Financial Statements. Once an AIS records journal entries and posts them to the general ledger, it can create a trial balance. The trial balance is a listing of all accounts and their debit and credit balances. After debit and credit dollar amounts in this trial balance are equal, an accountant will record any necessary adjusting journal entries. Adjusting entries include journal entries for depreciation and other unrecorded expenses, prepaid expenses, unearned revenues, and unrecorded revenue. Once the debit and credit amounts in this adjusted trial balance are equal, an AIS is ready to produce financial statements.

Financial statements are the primary output of a financial accounting system. These financial statements include an income statement, balance sheet, statement of owners' equity, and cash flow statement. The accounting cycle does not end when an AIS generates financial statements. The computerized system must close temporary accounts, such as revenue and expense accounts, so that a new cycle can begin. This is necessary because users are interested in income information for a specific period of time. Because balance sheet accounts show financial performance at a specific point in time, they are permanent and need not be closed. Thus, an AIS will carry these amounts forward to the next accounting cycle. Figure 8-1 summarizes the steps in an accounting cycle.

Coding Systems

AISs depend on codes to record, classify, store, and retrieve financial data. Although it is possible in a manual system to use simple alphabetic descriptions when preparing journal entries, computerized systems use **numeric codes** (codes that use numbers only) or **alphanumeric codes** (codes that use numbers and letters) to record accounting transactions. For example, a manual journal entry might include a debit to the "Direct Materials Inventory" account. In a computerized system, the debit might be to account "12345." The use of codes instead of account names is important in computerized

```
1.   Record transaction in a journal.
2.   Post journal entries to ledger(s).
3.   Prepare an unadjusted trial balance.
4.   Record and post adjusting journal entries.
5.   Prepare an adjusted trial balance.
6.   Prepare financial statements.
7.   Record and post closing journal entries.
8.   Prepare a post-closing trial balance.
```

FIGURE 8-1 A summary of the steps in the accounting cycle.

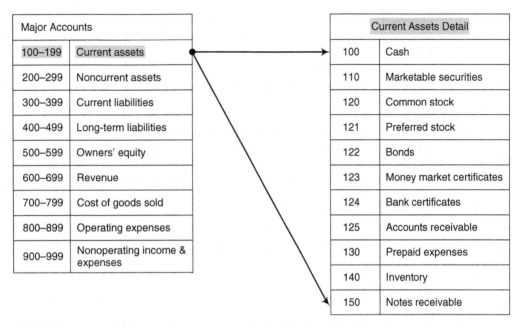

Major Accounts				Current Assets Detail	
100–199	Current assets			100	Cash
200–299	Noncurrent assets			110	Marketable securities
300–399	Current liabilities			120	Common stock
400–499	Long-term liabilities			121	Preferred stock
500–599	Owners' equity			122	Bonds
600–699	Revenue			123	Money market certificates
700–799	Cost of goods sold			124	Bank certificates
800–899	Operating expenses			125	Accounts receivable
900–999	Nonoperating income & expenses			130	Prepaid expenses
				140	Inventory
				150	Notes receivable

FIGURE 8-2 A block code used for a company's chart of accounts.

systems, because they help to ensure uniformity and consistency. Suppose that a clerk entered a debit to "Direct Materials Inventory" one time and another time entered the debit to "Dir. Materials Inventory." A computer would incorrectly set up a new account the second time, rather than recognizing the intended account.

Types of Codes. AISs typically use several types of codes: (1) mnemonic codes, (2) sequence codes, (3) block codes, and (4) group codes. **Mnemonic codes** help the user remember what they represent. The product codes S, M, L, and XL are examples of mnemonic codes describing apparel sizes. As the name implies, a **sequence code** is simply a sequential set of numbers used to identify customer accounts, employee payroll checks, customer sales invoices, and so forth. **Block codes** are sequential codes in which specific blocks of numbers are reserved for particular uses. In a typical application, the lead digit, or two lead digits, in the sequence code acts as the block designator, and subsequent digits are identifiers. AISs use block codes to create a chart of accounts (see Figure 8-2). Combining two or more subcodes creates a **group code**, which is often used as product codes in sales catalogs.

Design Considerations in Coding. There are a number of important factors to consider when designing an accounting code. First, it must serve some useful purpose. For example, if a product code in a manufacturing firm is part of a responsibility accounting system, at least one portion of the code must contain a production department code. Second, it must be consistent. Third, managers must plan for future expansion (e.g., the creation of additional accounts).

8.3   COLLECTING AND REPORTING ACCOUNTING INFORMATION

As you might imagine, most of the accounting data collected by an organization ultimately appear on some type of internal and/or external report. Thus, the design of an effective AIS usually begins with the outputs (reports) that users will expect from the system. Although this might seem counterintuitive, we discuss the reasons for this in Chapter 13.

Among the outputs of an AIS are: (1) reports to management, (2) reports to investors and creditors, (3) files that retain transaction data, and (4) files that retain current data about accounts (e.g., inventory records). Perhaps the most important of these outputs are the reports to management because these reports aid decision-making activities. As you might imagine, the formats of these various reports might be very different. These reports might be hard-copy (paper) reports, soft-copy (screen) reports, e-copy (CD and other electronic media) reports, or audio outputs. If a manager queries a database system, the monitor shows the requested data and the system produces a hard-copy report only upon demand. Graphics enhance reports, and many reports appear on company websites. While Web page design is beyond the scope of this book, it is important to recognize that the rules for preparing good reports apply to Web page reports as well as hard-copy and other multimedia reports.

Designing Reports

Users need many different types of accounting reports—some might be every hour and others not as often. An AIS might issue some reports only when a particular event occurs. For example, an AIS might issue an inventory reorder report only when the inventory for a certain product drops below a specified level. Such an event would probably result in an **exception report**, which is a list of exceptional conditions. As another example, suppose that a purchase order has an authorization signature, but contains some inaccurate or missing information. In this case, the AIS would generate an exception report. The report would include a table that identifies the error or errors and would suggest a possible solution to fix the error. After correcting the error, the purchase order would require a new authorization signature. This signature would clear the exception from the report.

Good output reports share similar characteristics regardless of their type, such as: (1) useful, (2) convenient format, (3) easy to identify, and (4) consistent. For example, summary reports should contain financial totals, comparative reports should list related numbers (e.g., budget vs. actual figures) in adjacent columns, and descriptive reports (e.g., marketing reports) should present results systematically. Sometimes, the most convenient format is graphical, such as a pie chart (Figure 8-3). Other graphical formats include bar charts and trend lines.

Consistency. AIS reports should be consistent: (1) over time, (2) across departmental or divisional levels, and (3) with general accounting practice. Consistency over time allows managers to compare information from different time periods. For example, a manager might want to compare a sales report for June with a similar report for the month of May of the same year. This manager might also look at sales for June of prior years to evaluate whether performance is improving or deteriorating. Similarly, reports should be consistent across departmental levels so that supervisors may compare departmental performance. Finally, report formats should be consistent with general accounting practice so that managers and investors can understand and use these reports.

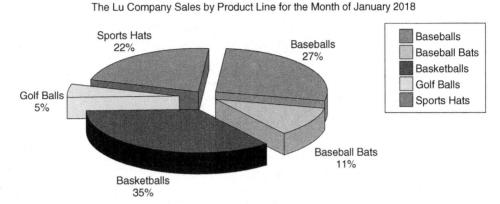

FIGURE 8-3   A pie chart showing the percentage of sales from various product lines.

Date of Report.   Good managerial reports should also contain dates. Balance sheets and similar reports should show the date as of a specific point in time. Reports such as lists of current employees, customers, and vendors should also indicate a specific date. Income statements and similar reports should show a span of dates for the reporting period (e.g., for the month ended January 31, 2018). The reason is clear—a report has no information value if you do not know what the time period is that it covers.

From Source Documents to Output Reports

Companies use a variety of source documents to collect data for the AIS. The primary concerns in the data collection process are accuracy, timeliness, and cost-effectiveness. An example of a source document is the *purchase order* in Figure 8-4. This source document represents a purchase order (number 36551) generated from the BSN Bicycles' database system to purchase goods from the Lu Company, a sporting goods distributor. In a paper-based environment, employees typically prepare several copies of a purchase order for internal use (these may be hard copies or computer images). For instance, the purchasing department keeps one copy to document the order and to serve as a reference for future inquiries. The accounting and receiving departments each would also receive a copy for their records. Purchase orders are normally sequentially numbered for easy reference at a later date.

Based on this purchase order, the Lu Company ships merchandise and sends a sales invoice to BSN Bicycles. Figure 8-5 illustrates the *sales invoice* document. The sales invoice duplicates much of the information on the original purchase order. New information includes shipping address, a reference to the purchase order number, shipping date, due date, sales invoice number, and customer identification number. The Lu Company might produce as many as six copies of the sales invoice. Two (or more) copies are the bill for the customer. The shipping department keeps a copy to record that it filled the order. Another copy goes to the accounting department for processing accounts receivable. The sales department retains a copy for future reference, and the inventory department receives a copy to update its records related to the specific inventory items sold.

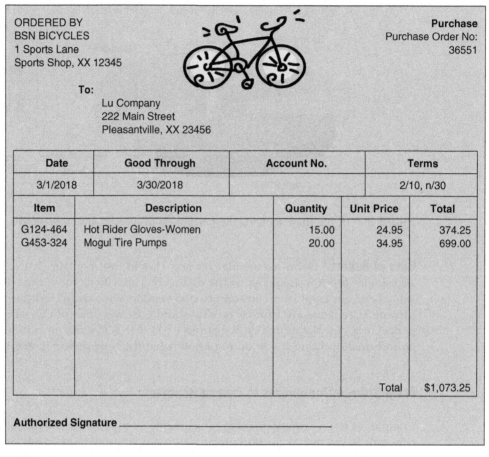

FIGURE 8-4 A sample purchase order.

Source documents of the types illustrated here help manage the flow of accounting data in several ways. First, they dictate the kinds of data to be collected and help ensure consistency and accuracy in recording data. Second, they encourage the completeness of accounting data because these source documents clearly identify the data that needs to be collected and stored. Third, they serve as distributors of information for individuals or departments. Finally, source documents help to establish the authenticity of accounting data. This is useful for such purposes as establishing an audit trail, testing for authorization of cash disbursement checks or inventory disbursements, and establishing accountability for the collection or distribution of money. Many source documents are actually database or Internet-based forms used to input data electronically. Reducing the use of paper forms can create significant efficiencies.

Both manual and computerized AISs use source documents extensively. In many AISs, source documents are still written or printed on paper. However, large companies (such as publicly traded firms) rely heavily on integrated database systems that handle many transactions virtually (i.e., electronically with no paper).

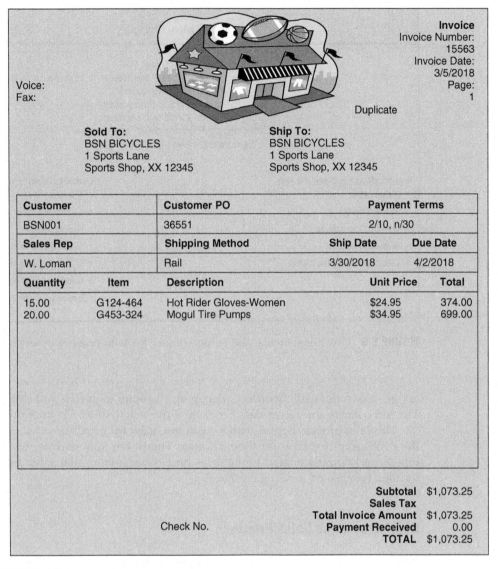

FIGURE 8-5 A sample sales invoice.

8.4 THE SALES PROCESS

A **business process** is a collection of activities and work flows in an organization that creates value. An AIS collects and reports data related to an organization's business processes. The nature and type of business processes might vary from industry to industry, but most businesses and government agencies have some common core processes. Two such business processes are *sales* and *purchasing*. Information processing requires recording, maintaining, grouping, and reporting business and economic activities that make up a business process. For example, the **sales process** includes such activities as

---

The Sales Process

Objectives

Tracking sales of goods and/or services to customers
Filling customer orders
Maintaining customer records
Billing for goods and services
Collecting payment for goods and services
Forecasting sales and cash receipts

Inputs (Source Documents)
- Sales order
- Sales invoice
- Remittance advice
- Shipping notice
- Debit/credit memoranda

Outputs (Reports)
- Financial statement information
- Customer billing statement
- Aging report
- Bad debt report
- Cash receipts forecast
- Customer listing
- Sales analysis reports

FIGURE 8-6 Objectives, inputs, and outputs associated with processing revenue transactions.

taking sales orders, filling orders, managing customer inquiries, and receiving payment. The AIS collects and stores data for each of these activities as part of the sales process.

The sales process begins with a customer order for goods or services and ends with the collection of cash from the customer. Figure 8-6 summarizes the AIS objectives, inputs, and outputs related to the sales process, assuming that sales are on credit and for merchandise or services rendered.

Objectives of the Sales Process

Revenues result from an organization's sale of goods or services. They may also result from donations or gifts, as in the case of charitable organizations. An organization that generates revenues but fails to collect these revenues regularly may find that it cannot pay its bills. Many people unfamiliar with accounting make the incorrect assumption that companies with positive net income cannot go out of business. The reality is that liquidity and ultimately bankruptcy problems result from inadequate cash flow, not from insufficient income, which is accrual-based and not cash-based. A primary objective in processing revenues is to achieve timely and efficient cash collection. To process sales in a timely manner, an organization must be able to track all revenues that customers owe the firm. Once the AIS recognizes these revenues, the system needs to monitor the resulting cash inflows.

Maintaining customer records (i.e., accounts receivable subsidiary ledger information) is an important function of the AIS for the revenue process. This includes validating a customer's bill-paying ability and payment history, assigning credit limits and ratings to customers, and tracking all customers' outstanding invoices. Processing revenue includes filling customers' orders, and this requires an interface with the inventory control function. The AIS should bill customers only for products shipped. The sales process must also allow for certain exceptions—for example, sales returns.

Forecasting is another objective of the AIS to help management in its planning function—a future focus. Predictive analytics, using big data, is increasingly important information that managers need to make these decisions. The AIS must support this need by analyzing sales orders, sales terms, payment histories, and other data. For example, sales orders can predict future revenues, and the terms of sale provide information about likely dates of collection on accounts for cash flow forecast purposes.

Events or Activities in the Sales Process.   First, review the System Flowcharts section in Chapter 12. Then look at how Figure 8-7 illustrates an AIS for the sales process in a system flowchart.[1] This view assumes an online sales order. Notice that e-mails and electronic images replace many of the paper documents. The flowchart also assumes that the AIS uses a centralized database that integrates all data files. The following fictitious example describes the sales process shown in Figure 8-7.

Example.   Hiroshi Ajas needs to purchase books for his classes this semester. He decides to buy the books online. In authorizing the order, Textbooks4U.com's AIS verifies Hiroshi's credit card and checks its inventory to make sure that the books are available. The company then sends Hiroshi an e-mail confirmation, verifying the transaction. Textbooks4U.com's AIS notifies its warehouse via e-mail to pack and ship the books. The warehouse processes the shipment information and creates a packing slip. Warehouse personnel then package the packing slip with the books and send them to Hiroshi. The day that Textbooks4U.com ships the books, it charges Hiroshi's credit card.

The major events in Textbooks4U.com's sales process are the sales order, the shipment of goods, and the customer payment. The company will record information about each of these events. This information allows them to produce a variety of reports—such as book sales by regions of the country. The next two sections describe the information inputs and outputs of the sales process.

Inputs to the Sales Process

First review the section on Data Flow Diagrams in Chapter 12. Figure 8-8 shows a data flow diagram of the sales process, which identifies the data inputs and information outputs of the process. As noted in the example, an AIS typically creates a *sales order* at the time a customer contracts for goods or services. In this example, an accounts-receivable clerk uses this sales order to prepare a sales invoice or the customer might generate one herself using the Web page of an online retailer.

The *sales invoice* reflects the product or products purchased, the price, and the terms of payment. When the customer makes a payment, a *remittance advice* may accompany the payment. When you pay your Visa or MasterCard bill by check, for example, the portion of the bill you return with your check is a remittance advice.

---

[1] The Internet has numerous resources to help draw flowcharts. See, for example, *Basic Flowchart Symbols and Meaning*, at http://www.conceptdraw.com/examples/accounting-symbols-and-meanings, and *How to Create Flowcharts for an Accounting Information System*, at http://www.conceptdraw.com/examples/accounting-information-system-data-flow-diagram, accessed April 30, 2017.

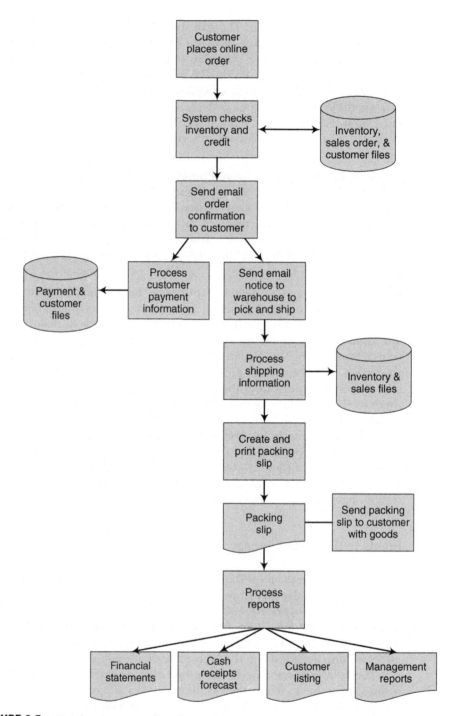

FIGURE 8-7 High-level systems flowchart of the sales process in an online environment.

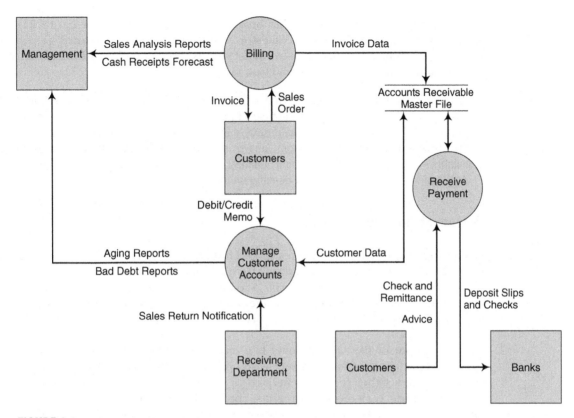

FIGURE 8-8   Data flow diagram of the sales process.

In addition to sales orders, sales invoices, checks, and remittance advices, *shipping notices* are another input to sales processing. When the warehouse releases goods for shipment, the warehouse clerk prepares a shipping notice. A copy of this notice may serve as a *packing slip* and would be included in the package with the goods. A copy of this document is also sent to the accounts-receivable department and is used as a prompt for the department to bill the customer, because at this point an accounting transaction has occurred.

Debit/credit memoranda are source documents affecting both the sales and purchasing processes. An organization issues these memoranda to denote the return of damaged goods or discrepancies in the amount owed. For example, assume that Hiroshi's package with the textbooks arrived, but two of the books were damaged and two were the wrong textbooks. Hiroshi would return the four books (worth $400) to Textbooks4U.com. However, Hiroshi must wait until the company receives the books and processes the return (this is when an accounting transaction occurs) before he will be issued a *credit* to his account (credit card) for the $400.

If a company finds that it has charged a customer too little for goods sold, the company would issue a *debit* memorandum. This debit memorandum signifies a debit to the customer's account receivable with the company to reflect the amount not charged originally. The customer now owes more to the company.

Business organizations use the data they collect about their customers and sales transactions to improve customer satisfaction and increase profitability. As a result, firms are purchasing or developing **customer relationship management (CRM)** software to gather, maintain, and use customer data to provide better customer service and enhance customer loyalty. Think broadly here about potential uses of CRM software. For example, Amazon uses Salesforce's cloud-computing software—a platform powered by artificial intelligence—to qualify leads, predict when customers are ready to make a purchase, and help them close more sales.

Case-in-Point 8.1 "It's fortunate that with technological developments, 'more firms are starting to mine the gold they have in their CRM systems,' observes Jim Dickie, a research fellow at CSO Insights. For decades, he says, managers have told sales people to enter data into CRM, and now with more options, users can analyze that wealth of Big Data to glean insights into prospect profiling, pricing optimization, fact-based forecasting, proactive churn identification, and other areas that demand attention."[2]

Outputs of the Sales Process

Processing sales transactions creates several outputs. An AIS uses some of these outputs to produce external accounting reports (such as financial statements) as well as internal reports (such as management reports). Management reports can be in any format and contain any type of information managers need for decision-making. In this and the following sections of the chapter, we discuss a few of the many reports that may be created by AISs.

One output of the sales process is a *customer billing statement*. This statement summarizes outstanding sales invoices for a particular customer and shows the amount currently owed. Other reports generated by the sales process include aging reports, bad debt reports, cash receipts forecasts, approved customer listings, and various sales analysis reports. The *aging report* shows the accounts-receivable balance broken down into categories based on time outstanding (see Figure 8-9). The *bad debt report* contains information about collection follow-up procedures for overdue customer accounts. In the event that a customer's account is uncollectible, the account is written off against an allowance account for doubtful accounts.

All of the data gathered from source documents in processing sales transactions serve as inputs to a *cash receipts forecast*. Data such as sales amounts, terms of sale, prior payment experience for selected customers, and information from aging analysis reports and cash collection reports are all inputs to this forecast.

Accounts-Receivable Aging Report

Customer #	A/R Balance ($)	Current ($)	Current 0–30 days ($)	31–60 days ($)	Past Due 61–90 days ($)	91–120 days ($)	over 120 days ($)
1106	15,460.00		10,000.00	5,460.00			
1352	6,453.00	6,453.00					
1743	18,684.00	13,454.00			5,230.00		
1903	2,349.00						
2258	6,530.00			6,530.00			
4378	5,434.00	2,400.00	1,235.00			1,799.00	
4553	173.00	173.00					
4623	389.00						389.00
5121	4,189.00			2,356.00			1,833.00

FIGURE 8-9 A sample accounts-receivable aging report.

[2] Smilansky, O. (2017). 10 CRM trends to watch in 2017. *CRM Magazine* (Spring), p.25.

Recall that maintaining customer records is an important function of the AIS in the sales process. The billing or accounts-receivable function should approve new customers, both to ensure that the customers exist and to assess their bill-paying ability. This may require obtaining a credit report from a reputable credit agency. The billing function assigns each new customer a credit limit based on credit history. From time to time, the AIS produces an *approved customer listing* report. This report is likely to show such information as customer ID numbers (for uniquely identifying each customer), contact name(s), shipping and billing addresses, credit limits, and billing terms.

If an AIS captures (or converts) appropriate sales data electronically, it can also produce various *sales analysis reports*. These include sales classified by product line, such as type of sale (cash, credit, or debit card), or sales region. However, the sales process can only produce effective sales analysis reports if the AIS captures appropriate sales data. A CRM solution can help managers take advantage of this data to maximize revenue and to provide better customer service.

8.5 THE PURCHASING PROCESS

The **purchasing process** begins with a request (or an order) for goods or services and ends with payment to the vendor. Figure 8-10 shows the objectives, inputs, and outputs associated with purchasing events. Our discussion assumes that credit purchases are for goods rather than for services. But in general, purchases may be for either goods or services and for cash or on credit.

Objectives of the Purchasing Process

Credit transactions create accounts payable (a liability). Accounts-payable processing closely resembles accounts-receivable processing; it is the flip side of the picture. With accounts receivable (an asset), companies keep track of amounts owed *to* them from

---

The Purchasing Process

Objectives
Tracking purchases of goods and/or services from vendors
Tracking amounts owed
Maintaining vendor records
Controlling inventory
Making timely and accurate vendor payments
Forecasting purchases and cash outflows

Inputs (Source documents)	**Outputs (Reports)**
• Purchase requisition	• Financial statement information
• Purchase order	• Vendor checks
• Vendor listing	• Check register
• Receiving report	• Discrepancy reports
• Bill of lading	• Cash requirements forecast
• Packing slip	• Sales analysis reports
• Debit/credit memoranda	

FIGURE 8-10 Objectives, inputs, and outputs associated with the purchasing process.

their customers. An accounts-payable application tracks the amounts owed *by* a company to vendors. The objective of accounts-payable processing is to pay vendors at the optimal time. Companies want to take advantage of cash discounts offered and also avoid finance charges for late payments.

Maintaining vendor records is as important to the purchasing process as maintaining customer records is for the sales process. The purchasing department is responsible for maintaining a *list of authorized vendors* to ensure the authenticity of vendors as well as finding reputable vendors who offer quality goods and services at reasonable prices. Vendor shipping policies, billing policies, discount terms, and reliability are also important variables in the approval process. Businesses today are strengthening their relationships with their vendors or suppliers, recognizing that they are partners in a **supply chain**.

Case-in-Point 8.2   The supply chain partnership between Airbus SE, an airplane manufacturer, and engine maker Pratt & Whitney is having significant supply chain issues. While Airbus has committed to building 200 A320neo jets using Pratt engines in 2017, it delivered only 26 jets to its customers in the first quarter. The intricate supply chain, involving very sophisticated components, is experiencing difficulties in keeping up with production needs.[3]

The purchase of goods affects *inventory control*. The objective of inventory control is to ensure that an AIS records all goods purchased for and dispensed from inventory. The inventory control component of the purchasing process interfaces with production departments, the purchasing department, the vendor, and the receiving department.

A final objective of the purchasing process is forecasting cash outflows. The addition of outstanding purchase requisitions, purchase invoices, and receiving reports provides an estimate of future cash requirements. With the forecast of cash receipts produced by the sales process, this estimate allows an organization to prepare a cash budget.

Events in the Purchasing Process. Figure 8-11 shows a systems flowchart that describes the purchasing process. As with the sales process, the flowchart assumes a centralized database and a mix of paper documents and electronic images. The following fictitious example describes the purchasing process shown in Figure 8-11.

Example. Benjamin Controller is an employee at a large state university. He needs to purchase a new computer, so he pulls up the purchase requisition form on the university's website and fills in the appropriate information. He sends the completed form to his supervisor for approval, who approves the request and clicks the "Submit" button to forward the request electronically to the purchasing department. A purchasing agent creates an electronic purchase order based on the information provided. The agent consults the vendor file to locate an authorized vendor for the requested computer. The AIS then sends an electronic version of the order to the receiving department and another copy to the vendor. When the computer arrives from the vendor, a receiving clerk consults the AIS system to verify that a purchase order exists for the goods received. The clerk then enters information about the receipt (e.g., date, time, count, and condition of merchandise) to create an electronic receiving report. Upon receipt

---

[3] Page, P. 2017. Today's Top Supply Chain and Logistics News (April 28). *The Wall Street Journal*. Accessed online at www.wsj.com, April 28, 2017.

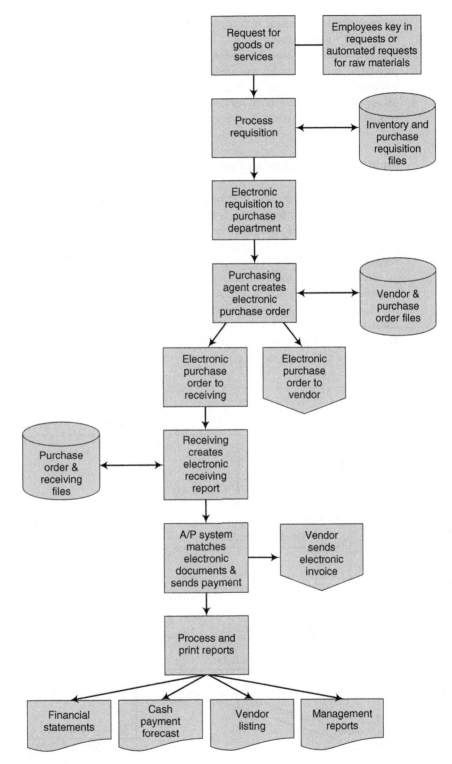

FIGURE 8-11 High-level systems flowchart of the purchasing process in an online environment.

of an electronic vendor invoice and the receiving report, the accounts-payable system remits payment to the vendor.

The economic and business events in the university's purchasing process are the purchase request, purchase order, receipt of goods, and payment to the vendor. The university's AIS records information about each of these events and produces a variety of reports. The next two sections describe the information inputs and some of the reports associated with the purchasing process.

Inputs to the Purchasing Process

As explained earlier, the purchasing process often begins with a requisition from a production department for goods or services. Sometimes, an AIS triggers purchase orders automatically when inventories fall below prespecified levels. The *purchase requisition* shows the item(s) requested and may show the name of the vendor who supplies the goods.

In Figure 8-12, the accounts-payable system matches *three source documents* before remitting payment to the vendor: the purchase order, the receiving report, and the purchase invoice. A *purchase invoice* is a copy of the vendor's sales invoice. The purchasing organization receives this copy as a bill for the goods or services purchased. The purpose of matching the purchase order, receiving report, and purchase invoice is to maintain the best possible control over cash payments to vendors. For example, the

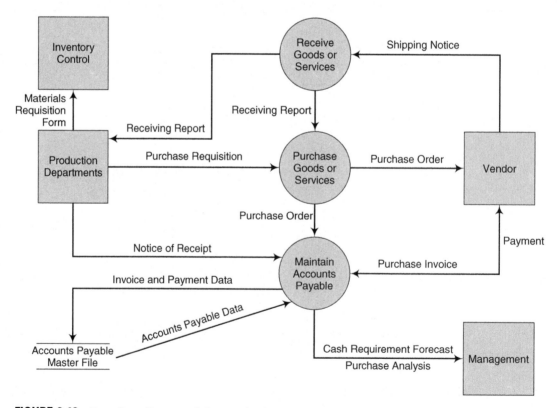

FIGURE 8-12 Data flow diagram of the purchasing process.

absence of one of these documents could signify a duplicate payment. A computerized AIS can search more efficiently for duplicate payments than a manual system.

For example, auditors can search for intentional (or unintentional) errors by instructing an AIS to print a list of duplicate invoice numbers, vendor checks for like dollar amounts, and similar control information.

The *purchase requisition* initiates the purchase order. Besides the information on the requisition, the purchase order includes vendor information and payment terms (see Figure 8-4). The purchasing department typically prepares several copies (or images) of the purchase order. In a paper-based system, the purchasing clerk sends one copy of the purchase order to the receiving department to serve as a receiving report or, preferably, to prompt the receiving department to issue a separate receiving report. This copy of the purchase order is specially coded (or color-coded) to distinguish it from other copies of the purchase order if there is no separate receiving report. The receiving department *copy should leave out the quantities ordered* that are identified in the purchase order. This is done for internal control purposes, so that workers receiving the goods must do their own counts, rather than simply approving the amounts shown on the purchase order.

Another source document, a bill of lading, accompanies the goods sent. The freight carrier gives the supplier a bill of lading as a receipt, which means that the carrier assumes responsibility for the goods. It may contain information about the date shipped, the point of delivery for freight payment (either shipping point or destination), the carrier, the route, and the mode of shipment. The customer may receive a copy of the shipping notice with the purchase invoice. This is important to the accounts-payable subsystem, since accounts-payable accruals include a liability for goods shipped free on board (FOB) from the shipping point. Goods shipped this way have left the vendor, but the customer has not yet received them. Another source document, the packing slip, is usually included in the merchandise package. This document indicates the specific quantities and items in the shipment and any goods that are on back order. The next time you order goods through a catalog or over the Internet, look for a packing slip, such as the one shown in Figure 8-13, in the container with your merchandise.

Outputs of the Purchasing Process

Typical outputs of the purchasing process are vendor checks and the accompanying check register, discrepancy reports, and a cash requirements forecast. The check register lists all checks issued for a particular period. Accounts payable typically processes checks in batches and produces the *check register* as a by-product of this processing step. **Discrepancy reports** are necessary to note any differences between quantities or amounts on the purchase order, the receiving report, and the purchase invoice.

The purpose of a discrepancy report is to ensure that no one authorizes a vendor check until the appropriate manager properly reconciles any differences. For example, assume that a receiving report indicates the receipt of 12 units of product, whereas the purchase order shows that a company ordered 20 units and the purchase invoice bills the company for all 20 units. The accounts-payable function records the liability for 20 units and notes the situation on a discrepancy report for management. This report would trigger an investigation. For example, it is possible that the vendor made two shipments of merchandise, and one shipment has yet to be received. If this is the case, receipt of the second shipment clears this discrepancy from the next report. However,

BlueBooks

http://www.bluebooks.com
orders@bluebooks.com

BlueBooks.com
1100 Industrial Drive, #44
Mountaintown, IL 55005
USA

Toll–Free: (800) 555-5555
Voice: +1 (305) 655-6890
FAX: +1 (305) 655-1245

Dumont Jones
100 Lakeview Drive
Summerville, MI 02187

Your order of July 26, 2018 (Order ID 678-134568-9504123)

Qty	Item	Description	Format	Our Price	Total
	In This Shipment				
1	Betty Crocker Cookbook: 1500 Recipes for the Way You Cook Today, 12th Edition	Betty Crocker	Hardcover	$29.99	$29.99
1	Weight Watchers in 20 minutes	Weight Watchers	Hardcover	$29.95	$29.95
			Subtotal:		$59.94
			Shipping & Handling:		5.67
			Order Total:		65.61
			Paid:		65.61
			Balance Due:		0.00

This shipment completes your order.

You can always check the status of your orders from the "Your Account" link on our homepage.

FIGURE 8-13 A sample packing slip.

if this is not the case, it is important for management to determine the cause of the discrepancy as soon as possible.

The purchasing process produces a *cash requirements forecast* in the same manner that the sales process produces a cash receipts forecast. By looking at source documents such as outstanding purchase orders, unbilled receiving reports, and vendor invoices, an AIS can predict future cash payments and their dates.

Information Technology (IT) Used in the Sales and Purchasing Processes. Most of the inputs and outputs related to business processes are now electronic. For instance, inputs (sales order or purchase requests) can be voice inputs, touch-tone telephone signals, bar codes, video signals, magnetic ink characters (as on checks), scanned images, or key strokes from a computer. Sales people in the field typically use laptop computers, handheld devices, portable bar code scanners, or other types of input devices to enter data. With wireless capability, they can enter information in real time.

> *Case-in-Point 8.3*   If you have moved lately, you probably watched a moving company representative walk through your home with a bar code scanner and a sheet of paper with various bar codes for different pieces of furniture and other items in your home. After the walk through, the representative can quickly download the information to a laptop, print out an estimate of the cost of your move, and discuss the estimate with you—all in the same visit!

Automated data-entry technology helps companies reduce costs and provide better customer service. For example, bar code scanners that are commonly used in most retail stores gather essential inventory data (and help to avoid human error) for the retailer, and they also help expedite the checkout process for customers. Automated data-entry technology is also very important for efficient government operations as we describe in the following case-in-point.

> *Case-in-Point 8.4*   The Hickam Air Force base in Hawaii uses bar code scanning technology in a system that also meets federal guidelines for managing expendable medical supplies for tracking, restocking, and maintaining inventory and assets valued at millions of dollars. An automated inventory and tracking system that ensures the availability of assets and supplies when needed is crucial to the national security of the United States at such a strategically important location.[4]

IT supports the purchasing process in a variety of ways. As we previously discussed, an organization might determine that some inventory items can be reordered automatically and electronically when the company reaches a predetermined minimum quantity of those inventory items. An automatic reorder can be generated by the computer system, sent electronically to the vendor, and the vendor can be paid electronically by using EDI. We discussed this aspect of E-commerce more in depth in Chapter 2.

After purchases arrive, our next concern is inventory management, an important element of supply chain management. To effectively manage inventory, we might use different technologies. Next, we describe how a company uses **RFID tags** (a computer chip with a tiny antenna) in the manufacturing process. The interesting point

---

[4] "Case Study: ASAP Passport Helps Hickam Air Force Base Track High-Valued Assets and Inventory. Accessed at https://www.slideshare.net/asapsys/hafb-casestudy on April 28, 2017.

about RFID tags, unlike bar codes, is that they can contain information and then additional information can be added or deleted from the tag as the part moves through the process.

Case-in-Point 8.5   General Motors puts RFID tags in the bolts used on engine assembly lines, turning simple hardware into tracking devices that make sure that everything gets assembled properly. That bolt has a (2kb) brain! Inside the head of GM's "data bolt" are an RFID memory tag and a coiled antenna. The brainy bolts are installed on each engine block and cylinder head at the beginning of the machining process. Scanners check the bolts during nearly 50 separate machining processes, ensuring that the previous steps were completed successfully and marking the current step as completed. If an RFID scanner detects a part that was improperly machined, it's kicked off the assembly line for inspection.[5]

8.6   CURRENT TRENDS IN BUSINESS PROCESSES

Organizations frequently divide business processes into "core processes" and "other processes." In the past, management accountants focused on cost management, while internal auditors primarily focused on improving core processes. In all cases, the goal was typically to make these processes as efficient as possible. However, in the past several decades, organizations have been examining their processes to determine which ones to keep and which ones to outsource. And it appears that companies outsource for strategic advantages as much as for cost savings, as we highlight in the following case-in-point.

Case-in-Point 8.6   A survey by Deloitte suggests that there are a variety of reasons their firms choose to outsource:

- Reduce costs (59%)
- Enable more focus on core business processes (57%)
- Solve capacity issues (47%)
- Enhance service quality (31%)
- Critical to business needs (28%)
- Gain access to intellectual capital (28%)
- Better manage business environment (17%)
- Drive broader transformational change (17%)[6]

Business Process Outsourcing (BPO)

Companies outsource such business processes as human resources (HR), finance and accounting, customer services, learning services and training, and information technology. According to the CFO survey above, **business process outsourcing (BPO)** is mostly driven by an organization's need to cut operating costs. Logically they would

---

[5] "GM's RFID Engine Bolts Prevent Assembly Line Screw-Ups," by Robert Sorokanich, January 3, 2014, gizmodo.com, accessed on April 28, 2017.
[6] Deloitte's 2016 Global Outsourcing Survey, May 2016, accessed from www.deloitte.com on April 28, 2017.

do so by outsourcing noncore processes. Research firm Gartner estimates that global market for BPO will reach $199 billion by 2020.[7]

Case-in-Point 8.7   At Microsoft, cost savings were expected when outsourcing the accounting and finance function, but the main reason was to create a world-class financial organization. Microsoft partnered with Accenture. The initial agreement spanned 90 countries and 450 individual roles—resulting in a 35% reduction in costs. So, Microsoft controllers are now able to focus on more strategic activities. The contract—now worth $330 million—was extended to 2018.[8]

The combination of networked enterprises and globalization has given rise to a business model called "business without boundaries." Companies no longer have all of their employees in one location, working on various business processes such as HR, accounting, production, customer service, and others. Employees may be located anywhere in the world, and they are. This version of outsourcing is called **offshoring**—moving jobs offshore—to countries such as India, Indonesia, the Philippines, China, Canada, Mexico, and Malaysia.

Of course, not all outsourced business processes are accomplished by employees in foreign countries. Many of these processes are still accomplished by businesses in the United States. Nevertheless, all business processes are under a great deal of scrutiny by managers and management accountants as companies become more strategically oriented toward revenue generation and more vigilant about managing costs.

Some experts suggest that we will see more BPO movement onshore and nearshore. Factors cited for this movement include (1) the rising costs of doing business in other countries, (2) language barriers and the demands from American consumers for better customer service, and (3) the desire of US firms to work with outsourcers who are geographically close.[9] In addition, US President Donald Trump has a political agenda that discourages outsourcing to other countries in order to make more jobs available for Americans. A 2016 survey by consulting firm AlixPartners indicates that the number of firms considering reshoring is growing. Almost 70% of American and European manufacturing and distribution companies said that they were considering moving production closer to home, up from 40% in 2015.[10]

The important point for accountants is that, at some point, you will most likely be on a team of professionals in your organization that will study the costs and benefits of either keeping a business process in-house or outsourcing the function. If the team decides that the organization should keep the process, then the next task might be to decide what BPM software the company should use to automate that process. Software companies are developing a wide variety of business process solutions to help managers integrate their existing data and applications into efficient and effective business systems. If the decision is to outsource the process, then accountants will most certainly be involved in analyzing the many costs and benefits associated with the decision.

---

[7] Gartner. 2016. "Predicts 2017: The Future State of Business Process Services and Outsourcing." November 18, 2016. Accessed April 28, 2017 at www.gartner.com.
[8] Mastering High-Performance BPO: Keys to the Kingdom by Mary Lacity and Leslie Willcocks, Microsoft Sponsored by Accenture, The Outsourcing Unit, London School of Economics and Political Science, 2012. Accessed from www.accenture.com.
[9] "Top Outsourcing Trends of 2016," by DATAMARK, July 13, 2016, accessed from www.datamark.met on April 29, 2017.
[10] Simon, R. and V. Monga. 2017. "Small U.S. Manufacturers Struggle to Bring Jobs Back Home," April 13, 2017, *The Wall Street Journal*, accessed from www.wsj.com on April 29, 2017.

Case-in-Point 8.8   "As outsourcing sweeps through almost every industry in the U.S., the videogame business looks a lot like the workplace of the future. It has become standard in the $75 billion industry for a lean core of in-house employees to focus on the most important jobs, with the rest hired out to layers of contractors and subcontractors. Of the 120 people who work on the hit game 'Rocket League,' 40 or 50 are contractors. 'Rocket League,' created by Psyonix, has amassed more than 29 million players in less than two years. The industry's contractor-heavy model resembles Hollywood studios, though longtime work practices and unions in the movie business provide a safety net for many actors and writers. People who make videogames are often hired quickly—and then let go just as fast."[11]

Business Process Management Software

Business Process Management (BPM) software packages help companies collect corporate knowledge, data, and business rules into a business system to improve core business processes. Think of BPM as a combination of software tools and management practices that enables entities to accomplish business processes more efficiently. As a result, managers have timely access to performance data related to clients, projects, financials, and people to improve company performance—and these benefits are available even to smaller businesses, as the following case-in-point describes.

Case-in-Point 8.9   The Sleeter Group is a nationwide community of experts who provide QuickBooks consulting services to small business owners—and they also announce their Annual Award List of "Awesome Add-ons for QuickBooks." For 2016, this list includes **TSheets** (employee time-tracking software); **Workato** (integrates many applications to automate business processes); **Expensify** (automates and integrates real-time expense reporting); and a number of other very innovative BPM solutions.[12]

AIS AT WORK
Is Outsourcing the Answer?[13]

Although BPO is now very common, the momentum for this type of business decision started in the 1990s due to the rapid changes in technology. As we moved to a more globalized marketplace, many managers became aware of the costs and benefits of "giving" their noncore business processes to companies who could do the same job more quickly, more efficiently, and more cost-effectively. Many jobs associated with those functions were moved to other countries, especially India, China, and the Philippines. Management of the US firms claimed that such business decisions were necessary for their companies to remain competitive and to generate value for shareholders.

Experts now suggest that offshoring may have reached a plateau. Companies are beginning to reconsider earlier decisions to offshore—and are bringing jobs back to

[11] Baker, G. 2017. "The 10-Point," April 11, 2017, *The Wall Street Journal,* accessed from www.wsj.com on April 29, 2017.
[12] "2016 Awesome Application Award Winners," The Sleeter Group, accessed from www.accountexnetwork.com in April 29 2017.
[13] McClatchy, J. 2008. Hundreds of jobs returning. Tribune Business News (July 16); "Study: Could onshoring become the new offshoring?" by Denise Dubie, August 17, 2007.

the United States or choosing not to offshore new jobs. One such company, DESA Heating Products (DHP) of Bowling Green, Kentucky, announced in 2008 that the company would move their manufacturing production from China back to Bowling Green. Although DHP had outsourced hundreds of manufacturing jobs to China, management decided to reverse that decision and bring those jobs back to its Kentucky factory. The rationale for this decision focuses on two factors: quality and cost. And when you think about it, these are both critical factors for a company's success because today's customers demand the best-quality products at the lowest price.

According to the Governor of Kentucky, DHP's decision to bring their production back to the United States is a strong indicator of evolving outsourcing trends in the global economy. So, what exactly are these trends? A recent report from a global consulting firm contains a number of clues: transportation costs, wage inflation, currency fluctuations, and quality issues.

If we examine DHP's experience with offshoring, perhaps we can understand the Governor's claim. First, Chinese workers are now demanding higher wages for their labor, which means that Chinese workers are no longer an economical solution to labor costs in the United States. Second, significant fluctuations in oil prices cause great difficulty in budgeting the costs of transportation of goods produced in China—especially for the large, heavy products that DHP produces.

Also, Kentucky's central location in the United States means that DHP is only one day's drive from 70% of the population in the United States. That translates to products in the hands of DHP's customers in 12 hours instead of the 6–8 weeks to ship from China. And finally, DHP expects to save money in warranty repairs and replacement costs—manufacturing costs that tripled on the products made in China.

 SUMMARY

- ✓ The fundamentals of any business process include journals, ledgers, accounts, trial balances, and financial statements.
- ✓ When planning a new AIS, developers usually start by designing the outputs that are needed from the system.
- ✓ The fundamental instrument for collecting data in a typical AIS is the source document, which can be paper or electronic.
- ✓ Two business processes that are common to many business organizations are the sales process and the purchasing process.
- ✓ The sales process begins with a customer order and ends with the collection of cash from the customer.
- ✓ Important source documents associated with the sales process are sales orders, sales invoices, remittance advices, shipping notices, and customer checks.
- ✓ The primary outputs of the sales process are reports, such as a cash receipts report, a bad debt report, and a customer listing report.
- ✓ For the purchasing process, managers rely upon the AIS to ensure timely payment for purchased goods and services.
- ✓ Source documents common to the purchasing process include purchase requisitions, purchase orders, receiving reports, purchase invoices, and bills of lading.
- ✓ Although companies still outsource to better manage costs, they now outsource and offshore business processes for strategic advantages.

✓ Some of the business processes that are most likely to be outsourced or offshored are human resources, finance and accounting, customer services, learning services and training, and information technology.

KEY TERMS YOU SHOULD KNOW

alphanumeric codes
block codes
business process
Business Process Management
  (BPM) software
business process outsourcing
  (BPO)

business without boundaries
customer relationship
  management (CRM)
discrepancy reports
exception report
group code
mnemonic codes

numeric codes
offshoring
purchasing process
RFID tags
sales process
sequence code
supply chain

TEST YOURSELF

Q8-1. Which of the following provides the organizational structure for the general ledger?

   a. Special journals

   b. A source document

   c. General journals

   d. The chart of accounts

Q8-2. AISs often depend on codes to record, classify, store, and retrieve financial data. Which of the following codes is a group of numbers reserved for particular uses?

   a. Block codes

   b. Mnemonic codes

   c. Alphanumeric codes

   d. Numeric codes

Q8-3. AIS reports should be consistent in at least three ways. Which of the following is NOT one of those ways?

   a. Over time

   b. Across firms

   c. Across departmental or divisional levels

   d. With general accounting practice

Q8-4. A(n) _____ is a collection of activities or flow of work in an organization that creates value.

   a. economic event

   b. accounting transaction

   c. business process

   d. chart of accounts

Q8-5. Which of the following is NOT an objective of the sales process?

   a. Controlling inventory

   b. Tracking sales of goods and/or services to customers

   c. Billing customers for goods and services

   d. Forecasting sales and cash receipts

Q8-6. Which of the following reports includes data from both the sales and the purchasing processes?

   a. Cash receipts forecast and cash requirements forecast

   b. Financial statements

   c. Discrepancy reports and bad debt report

   d. None of the above

Q8-7. Which of the following source documents is common to both the sales and the purchasing processes?

   a. Debit/credit memoranda

   b. Financial statements

   c. Discrepancy reports and bad debt report

   d. None of the above

Q8-8. Which of the following business processes is most often targeted for offshoring?

   a. Janitorial services

   b. Landscaping maintenance

   c. Information technology

   d. Employee training

Q8-9. If a manager wanted to sort out any differences between quantities or amounts on the purchase order, the receiving report, and the purchase invoice, which of the following AIS reports would be most useful?

a. A purchase analysis report

b. An inventory control report

c. A check register report

d. A discrepancy report

Q8-10. Which of the following would be most helpful for a university to manage admissions, grading, attendance, student messaging, and alumni?

a. A supply chain report

b. CRM software

c. BPO

d. BPM software

Q8-11. Which of the following is a relatively new way to manage inventory?

a. A purchase analysis report

b. RFID tags

c. BPM software

d. An inventory register

Q8-12. Which of the following is (are) often cited as the primary reason(s) to outsource a function?

a. Cut costs

b. Strategic advantage

c. a and b

d. None of the above

DISCUSSION QUESTIONS

8-1. The chart of accounts for a manufacturing firm would be different from that of a service firm. Not surprisingly, service firms differ so much that software now exists for almost any type of firm that you could name. Think of yourself as an entrepreneur who is going to start up your own business. Now, search online to find at least two different software packages that you might use for the type of firm you are going to start up. What does the chart of accounts include? What are the differences between the software packages?

8-2. What are the purposes of accounting codes? How are they used? Bring to class some examples of codes used by manufacturing firms, accounting firms, and merchandising firms.

8-3. What are some typical outputs of an AIS? Why do systems analysts concentrate on managerial reports when they start to design an effective AIS? Why not start with the inputs to the system instead?

8-4. What are some criteria that systems designers should consider when developing managerial reports for an AIS? How do system designers know what to include on reports?

8-5. Visit a local business or search online and collect some examples of source documents used in an AIS. For each source document you collect, discuss its purpose(s). Are different source documents required for manufacturing firms versus merchandising organizations? Are all the business' source documents paper-based?

8-6. This chapter discussed many inputs to an organization's sales process. What are the specific data items needed to add a new customer and record a sales order?

8-7. How does a data flow diagram for the sales process differ from a system flowchart describing that process?

8-8. How are the inputs and outputs of the purchasing process likely to be different for a restaurant versus an automobile manufacturer?

8-9. Explain the term "business-without-boundaries." How is this changing the nature of organizations?

8-10. What do we mean when we say companies are offshoring business processes?

8-11. Some businesses choose offshoring to solve the issue of expertise, especially for IT personnel. These companies claim they simply cannot find enough qualified employees in the United States to do certain technology jobs. Do you agree with this assessment? Why or why not?

8-12. Search the Web for unusual and interesting uses of RFID tags. Find at least two that are unusual and share those in class.

8-13. Discuss the privacy issues created by the use of RFID tags. Do you support the use of RFID tags for personal ID, customer relationship management, and inventory tracking? Why or why not?

8-14. When companies think about outsourcing a function, many questions need to be answered. Search the Internet for answers to the following questions:

   a. What are some of the "pros" associated with outsourcing?

   b. What are some of the "cons" associated with outsourcing?

8-15. Since the accounting and finance function is a target for outsourcing for some firms, how does that make you feel about your choice of accounting as a major? How can you protect your future job security?

8-16. Do individuals engage in outsourcing? If you answered yes, give some examples.

PROBLEMS

8-17. Listed below are several types of accounting data to be coded. For each data item, recommend a type of code (mnemonic, sequence, block, or group) and support your choice.

   a. Employee identification number on a computer file

   b. Product number for a sales catalog

   c. Inventory number for the products of a wholesale drug company

   d. Inventory part number for a bicycle manufacturing company

   e. Identification numbers on the forms waiters and waitresses use to take orders

   f. Identification numbers on airline ticket stubs

   g. Automobile registration numbers

   h. Automobile engine block numbers

   i. Shirt sizes for men's shirts

   j. Color codes for house paint

   k. Identification numbers on payroll check forms

   l. Listener identification for a radio station

   m. Numbers on lottery tickets

   n. Identification numbers on a credit card

   o. Identification numbers on dollar bills

   p. Passwords used to gain access to a computer

   q. Zip codes

   r. A chart of accounts for a department store

   s. A chart of accounts for a flooring subcontractor

   t. Shoe sizes

   u. Identification number on a student examination

   v. Identification number on an insurance policy

8-18. Novelty Gadgets is a marketer of inexpensive toys and novelties that it sells to retail stores, specialty stores, and catalog companies. As an accountant working for the company, you have been asked to design a product code for the company. In analyzing this problem, you have discovered the following:

   a. The company has three major product lines: (1) toys and games, (2) party and magic tricks, and (3) inexpensive gifts. There are major subproducts within each of these product lines, and the number of these categories is 25, 18, and 113, respectively.

   b. The company has divided its selling efforts into five geographic areas: (1) the United States, (2) the Far East, (3) Europe and Africa, (4) South America, and (5) International (a catchall area). Each major geographic area has several sales districts (never more than 99 per area). Between 1 and 20 sales people are assigned to each district.

   c. As noted earlier, there are three major categories of customers, and certain customers can also purchase goods on credit. There are five different classes of credit customers, and each rating indicates the maximum amount of credit the customer can have. Design a group code that Novelty Gadgets could use to prepare sales analysis reports. Be sure to identify each digit or position in your code in terms of both use and meaning.

8-19. Figure 8-14 is a system flowchart for P. Miesing and Company's purchase order preparation. Prepare a narrative to accompany the flowchart describing this purchase order preparation process. Include in your narrative the source documents involved, the computerized data processing that takes place, data inputs used to

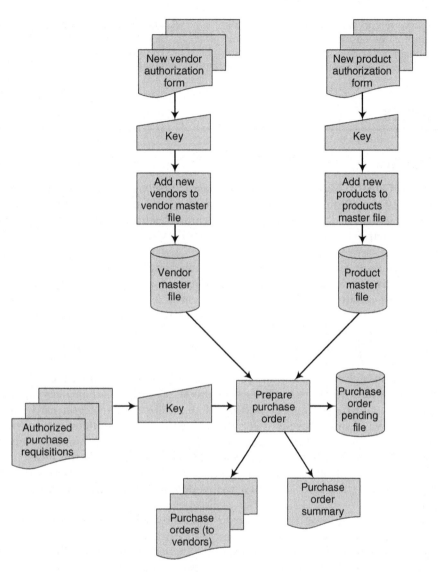

FIGURE 8-14   System flowchart illustrating the preparation of purchase orders for P. Miesing and Company.

prepare purchase orders, and the outputs prepared from the processing function.

8-20. SaveToday is a national discount retail store chain with annual revenues of more than $1 billion. It's a typical bricks-and-mortar operation with accounting software that records sales transactions in real time and tracks inventories on a perpetual basis. Management is considering an online store and will sell the same products as in the stores. Customers will be able to use credit cards only for online payments

(vs. cash, credit card, or debit card in the stores). The marketing manager is interested in learning about customers and using the information to improve both in-store and online sales.

a. Contrast the sales process of their retail store operation with the sales process in an online store environment. Would any of the events in the process change?

b. At what points do you collect data about customers and sales transactions in the retail store? In the online environment?

c. What data might you collect about retail store and online customers to improve your profitability? What data might you collect to improve customer satisfaction?

d. How is the sales process different for a public accounting firm? What data can they collect to improve customer relationships and grow revenues?

CASE ANALYSES

8-21. Food Court Inc.

Food Court Inc. (FCI) is a business in Boston, Massachusetts, that offers meal plans to college students. Students, or their families, buy debit cards with fixed amounts that they can use to purchase food at more than 50 local restaurants. FCI sells the cards to students using an online storefront and in several locations near major college campuses. The following paragraph describes the online card sale process.

A customer enters their credit card information online and then the amount of purchase. FCI's software automatically checks the card number to determine that it is a valid credit card number; for instance, there are certain digits that indicate Visa cards. The software displays an error message if the number is not valid. The usual cause of these errors is typographical. Once the customer completes the card order screen, the software sends the data in an encrypted form to FCI's host computer. Periodically, the FCI accountant retrieves transactions from the server. This is done by clicking on the "Get Transactions" screen button.

For each online transaction, the accountant then manually copies down the credit card number on a scrap of paper, walks across the office to the credit card machine, and keys in the credit card number, the amount, and the numerical portion of the address. The credit card software checks to see if the card is valid and charges it for the amount. The accountant next writes down the validation number, returns to the host computer, and enters it. The accountant prints a receipt for the transaction and puts it in a file. The customer database now reflects the new customer. When a customer purchases a card off-line with a credit card, the accountant swipes the card directly, checks its validity, charges the card, and then writes down the validation number, and enters it in the host computer.

FCI is considering the purchase of credit card software that can reside on the host computer and interact with their accounting software. The credit card software costs about $700. The credit card company rates are likely to increase by about 0.75% because cards could no longer be swiped directly—all credit card purchases would need to go through the online software. The rate FCI has to pay the credit card company is based on this mix. Credit card companies typically charge more if card numbers are punched rather than swiped because they have more chance of invalid transactions due to theft. It's easier to steal a number than a card. Currently, about half of FCI's sales transactions arise from online sales; the other half result from sales through the office.

Requirements

1. Should FCI buy the credit card software?

2. Develop a flowchart for FCI's online sales process.

3. What are the business risks associated with this process?

8-22. The Caribbean Club

The Caribbean Club is one of the Virgin Island's hottest night spots. It's a great place for locals to meet after work and relax with friends, it's a popular destination for tourists who stay on the island,

and it's always on the list of fun entertainment choices for the crowds from the cruise ships that dock in the harbor.

The reason why the Club is so popular with such a variety of customers is because the founder of the club, Ross Stewart, always has such innovative and visionary ideas that delight the patrons. For example, every night of the week, the Club features different activities or shows, including beach volleyball, Caribbean shows with calypso singers, world-class musicians who play steel drums, and other island entertainment.

Since Ross was a former accountant and auditor with one of the largest public accounting firms in New Zealand, he is very accustomed to brainstorming sessions to generate ideas and surface concerns. He brought this practice with him to the Caribbean and holds brainstorming sessions with his "club associates" (which is what he calls all of the employees at the club) once every month to identify new and novel ideas to increase the popularity and profitability of the club.

As you might imagine, the patrons of a night club are there to relax and enjoy themselves. So, the associates thought it would be a great idea to somehow be able to recognize their regular patrons so that they wouldn't have to trouble them with a bill every time a server came to their table with another round of drinks. After all, if the Club wanted these people to "feel like they were at home with friends," the patrons shouldn't have to bother with trying to decide who owed what to pay the bill. What a nuisance!

So, Ross and his associates came up with the idea to implant their regular customers with an implantable microchip. The idea was to make the chip "fun"—to give it an elite status so that their regular patrons would want to be implanted. To dramatize the elite status of the chip, Ross decided that the Club would have a special area where only those with chips, the "VIPs," would be admitted. And, of course, this area would have various exclusive services for these members. The chip would allow the VIPs to be "recognized" and to be able to pay for their food and drinks without any ID—they would simply pass by a reader and the Club would know who they are and their credit balance. Ross also wanted the information system supporting the chip to be a customer relationship management (CRM) tool.

Requirements

1. What do you think of this idea? That is, what are the advantages and disadvantages of this idea for the Caribbean Club?
2. If you were Ross, what information would you want the CRM to collect? Search the Internet to see if you can find a CRM software package that seems appropriate for the Club. Why did you select this particular software?
3. What are the advantages and disadvantages for the patrons?
4. If you were a passenger on a cruise ship, or staying at a resort on the island, would you get the chip implanted? Why or why not?

8-23. Mount Pleasant Community College

Mount Pleasant Community College (MPCC) is a medium-sized academic institution that employs about 200 full-time faculty and 250 staff personnel. There are 11,439 students enrolled at the college for the 2017–2018 school year.

The Purchase Process. The college's budget for purchases of equipment and supplies is about $20,000,000 annually. Allen Lee is in charge of the Purchasing Department. He reports directly to the Vice President of Finance for the university. Allen supervises four purchasing clerks and three receiving personnel. The office is responsible for purchases of all equipment and supplies except for computer equipment and software and plant purchases or additions.

The Payment Process. The various departments across campus manually fill out hard-copy purchase requisition forms when there is a need for equipment/supplies. Each department forwards these forms to the Purchasing Department. If the request is for computer equipment or software, the requisition is forwarded to the Department of Information Technology for action.

Purchase requisitions are assigned to one of the three purchasing clerks by department. For instance, one purchasing clerk makes purchases for all university departments beginning with the letters A through H (Accounting–History). Purchasing clerks check the requisition to make sure that it is authorized and then consult the Approved Vendor Listing to find a supplier. The clerk may contact a supplier for pricing and product specification. Once this task is complete, the purchasing clerk enters the purchase requisition and vendor and price information into the computer system, which prints out a multiple part purchase order. Clerks send copies of the purchase order to Central Receiving, to the vendor, and to the Accounts-Payable Department. (The university considered using EDI for its purchases, but chose not to adopt it due to the large number of vendors used.)

When Central Receiving receives an order, a receiving clerk consults the Purchase Order file to make sure that the correct product and quantity have been delivered. The clerk also checks the product for damage. Central Receiving does not accept any overshipments. Receiving clerks forward accepted shipments to the adjacent warehouse for distribution to the appropriate department. Clerks file one copy of the Receiving Report, send one copy to the Purchasing Department, and forward a third copy to Accounts Payable.

Eric Hammer is the Supervisor of Accounts Payable. Two accounting clerks report to him. He assigns invoices to them for payment based on vendor name. One clerk processes payments for vendors A–M and the other clerk handles payments to all vendors with names beginning with letters N–Z. The clerks match each vendor invoice with a copy of the receiving report and purchase order before entering it into the computer for payment by due date. There are often discrepancies among the three documents. This requires frequent phone calls to the vendor, the Receiving Department, or Purchasing for resolution. As a result, the company frequently makes payments late and forfeits cash discounts.

Requirements

1. Identify the important business events that occur within MPCC's purchase/payment process.
2. What changes would you suggest to the current process to take advantage of information technology?

READINGS AND OTHER RESOURCES

Bradford, M., S.B. Richtermeyer, and D.F. Roberts. 2007. Systems diagramming technologies: An analysis of methods used in accounting education and practice. *Journal of Information Systems* 21(1): 173–212.

Brewer, B., B. Ashenbaum, and J. Carter. 2013. Understanding the supply chain outsourcing cascade: When does procurement follow manufacturing out the door? *Journal of Supply Chain Management* 49(3): 90–110.

Lennon, G. 2013. Signaling Credibility. *Strategic Finance* 95(11): 64.

Stambaugh, C., and F. Carpenter. 2009. RFID: Wireless innovations in inventory monitoring and accounting. *Strategic Finance* 91(6): 35–40.

Tueffel, H. 2016. Boost the bottom line with accounts payable best practices. *Journal of Accountancy* 222(5): 1–4.

Wang, M. 2013. Implementing CRM in nursing homes: The effects on resident satisfaction. *Managing Service Quality* 23(5): 388–409.

Go to www.wiley.com/go/simkin/videos to access videos on the following topics:

Introduction to CRM (this site graphically depicts advantages and features of CRM)
Introduction to Outsourcing
Key Steps of the Purchasing Process
RFID Tags and Inventory Management

ANSWERS TO TEST YOURSELF

1. d **2.** a **3.** b **4.** c **5.** a **6.** b **7.** a **8.** c **9.** d **10.** b **11.** b **12.** a

Chapter 9

Accounting Information Systems and Business Processes: Part II

After studying this chapter, you should be able to:
- *Explain* the ways technology is changing management's ability to monitor and control business processes across the organization.
- *Describe* the objectives, inputs, and outputs of the resource management, production, and financing processes.
- *Explain* how business strategy affects the data collected in the firm's accounting information system (AIS) and how that affects performance measures.
- *Explain* why some organizations have special accounting information needs.
- *Discuss* the special information needs of several different types of organizations.
- *Explain* how companies use business process reengineering (BPR) to cut costs and improve their operational efficiency.

"Understanding the opportunities and risks allows companies to incorporate digital into their strategy and into the delivery of the strategy. CFOs can then help the business to deliver the right digital capability at scale, be it by striking a balance between near-term targets and long-term potential or by building the business case for significant technology investments."

Vollmer, S. 2017. How a CFO Can Become Great.[1]

9.1 INTRODUCTION

In Chapter 8, we discussed the sales process and the purchasing process, two processes that are common to most organizations. This chapter continues the discussion of business processes by exploring three additional processes: resource management, production, and financing. The resource or management process includes human resources (HR) and fixed assets. The production (or manufacturing) process entails the conversion of raw materials into finished goods available for sale. Finally, the financing process involves the ways that organizations fund their operations.

Many organizations, such as government agencies, have specialized information needs, apart from the typical accounting information system (AIS) requirements

---

[1] "How a CFO Can Become Great," by S. Vollmer, April 1, 2017, accessed from www.journalofaccountancy.com on April 30, 2017.

for information about revenues, purchases, production, and resources. The second section of this chapter considers some unique accounting information needs of these organizations.

Maximizing the efficiency of every business process is critical to business success in today's "business without boundaries" operating environment. Sometimes, managers decide that a current business process isn't working and must be reengineered. This is usually the case, for example, when a firm decides to implement a new enterprise-wide IT system. As a result, they turn to business process reengineering (BPR), which is the topic of the final section of this chapter.

9.2   THE RESOURCE MANAGEMENT PROCESS

Two resources that managers must closely manage are an organization's HR and its fixed assets. Because the inputs, processing, and outputs for HR and fixed assets are so different, we examine them separately.

Human Resource Management

An organization's **human resource (HR) management** activity includes the personnel function, which is responsible for hiring and terminating employees. HR must properly maintain the personnel and payroll records for employees, as well as handle the many actions associated with employee terminations. Nevertheless, the primary objective of the personnel function is to hire, train, and employ qualified people to do an organization's work (see Figure 9-1).

Today, many **business process management (BPM) software** packages are available to automate the core processes that normally occur in an HR office. For example, HR departments are increasingly turning to technology to help with such diverse responsibilities as recruitment, oversight of legal and regulatory compliance, benefits

---

HUMAN RESOURCE MANAGEMENT PROCESS

Objectives

Hiring, training, and employing workers
Maintaining employee earnings records
Complying with regulatory reporting requirements
Reporting on payroll deductions
Making timely and accurate payments to employees
Providing an interface for personnel and payroll activities

Inputs (Source Documents)

- Personnel action forms
- Time sheets
- Payroll deduction authorizations
- Tax-withholding forms

Outputs (Reports)

- Financial statement information
- Employee listings
- Paychecks
- Check registers
- Deduction reports
- Tax (regulatory) reports
- Payroll summaries

FIGURE 9-1   Objectives, inputs, and outputs for the human resource management process.

administration, training, performance evaluation, and safeguarding confidential employee information.

Case-in-Point 9.1 Jennifer Wilson, partner and cofounder of leadership consulting and coaching firm ConvergenceCoaching.com, has an interesting perspective on the HR function and the seemingly "impatient" next-generation leaders in firms, who want change, and want it now. One strategy to retain this talent, according to Jennifer, is to "form a Next Gen technology and process committee and let them loose on reengineering your firm's business processes. Have them prioritize the top five system, process, or technology changes they want to make—the what and the how—and then invest in their ideas and make these changes happen. This one should be easy because it is likely to increase efficiency and save money and time."[2]

Although the main purpose of **payroll processing information systems** is to pay employees for their work, such systems also maintain employee earnings records (a payroll history), comply with various government tax and reporting requirements, report on various deduction categories (e.g., retirement funds and group insurance), and interact with other personnel functions. Figures 9-2 and 9-3 show sample system flowcharts for the personnel function and for the payroll function.

Inputs to Human Resource Management Processing. The source documents used in payroll processing are personnel action forms, time sheets, payroll deduction authorizations, and tax-withholding forms. The personnel department sends *personnel action forms* to payroll that document the hiring of new employees or changes in employee status. For example, payroll receives a personnel action form when an employee receives a salary increase. This document is very important for control purposes. As an

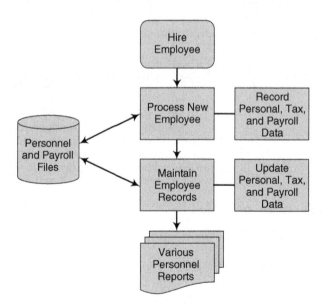

FIGURE 9-2 Systems flowchart of the AIS for the personnel function.

---

[2] "Want to keep your Next Gen leaders? Make these changes ASAP," by Jennifer Wilson, June 6, 2016, accessed from www.journalofaccountancy.com on April 30, 2017.

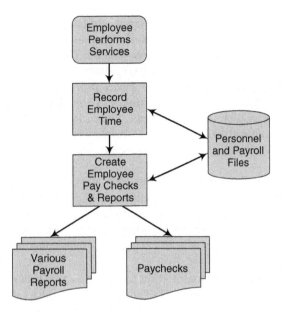

FIGURE 9-3   Systems flowchart of the AIS for the payroll function.

example, auditors will detect an employee who increases his or her own salary when they fail to find a personnel action form authorizing the increase.

Many companies use *time sheets* to track the hours that employees work. The source of information for these time sheets varies widely with the level of sophistication of the technology that the organization uses. Some companies use a time clock that requires employees to "punch in" (on time cards) when they arrive for work. Others use picture ID cards or radio-frequency identification (RFID)-enabled ID cards that serve to verify the identity of an employee and record the time when employees enter and leave the workplace or a specific location within the firm. To guard against employees having their friends punch in for them, some organizations now use various biometric devices (e.g., fingerprints or iris scans) to identify employees and capture their entry and departure from workplaces.

At the end of the pay period, the employee's supervisor verifies the number of hours worked and authorizes payment. Next, either a payroll clerk or an internal control embedded in the payroll processing information system checks for the appropriate authorization before processing these hours. Companies that use a job cost information system can cross-reference employee time sheets with time recorded on individual jobs.

Employees fill out *payroll deduction authorizations* that direct the payroll processing system to deduct amounts from gross pay for items such as health and life insurance, parking fees, retirement plan contributions, and union dues. An authorization form should document each deduction. In the United States, every employee must also complete tax-withholding forms, which authorize the payroll system to reduce gross pay by the appropriate withholding tax. The information system uses each employee's W-4 withholding form to calculate the correct withholding for federal income taxes.

Outputs of Human Resource Management Processing.   The outputs of HR management processing include employee listings, check registers, paychecks, deduction reports, tax reports, and payroll summaries. As you might imagine, the processing of paychecks should include very strict internal control procedures. *Employee listings* show current employees and may contain addresses and other demographic information. *Check registers* list gross pay, deductions, and net pay. In the past, payroll clerks used the check register information to make journal entries for salary and payroll-tax expenses—a task that is mostly automated now. *Deduction reports* can contain summaries of deductions for all employees in a department, a division, or company-wide. Finally, the payroll function issues various *payroll summaries* that help managers analyze expenses. A typical payroll summary report might classify payroll expenses by department or job or show the total overtime hours worked in each department.

Case-in-Point 9.2   The city of Reno, Nevada, is one of the many cities in the United States seeking ways to lower its expenditures. Recently, the issue of overtime pay for firemen came to the attention of the city council because reports indicated that there were excessive amounts of overtime. Apparently, the number of firemen that the city could hire was limited, but not the amount of overtime pay these individuals could earn.

The US government requires various *tax reports* for income tax, Social Security tax, and unemployment tax information. Employees pay some taxes in their entirety, but employers share others. For instance, both the employee and the employer pay equal amounts of Social Security taxes. The payroll system allocates shared taxes to the appropriate accounts. Taxes paid by employees are allocated to payroll expense, but employer taxes are part of the employer's tax expense.

Because manual payroll processing can be tedious, repetitive, and error-prone, the payroll function was one of the first accounting activities to be computerized in many organizations. Today, many companies find it cost-effective to outsource the process for paychecks and payroll reports.

Case-in-Point 9.3   Automatic Data Processing, Inc., or ADP, is the world's largest payroll service provider. More than 650,000 companies in 110 countries outsource their payroll processing and, in some cases, their human resource administration to ADP. The company has been in business for over 60 years.[3]

Fixed-Asset Management

Even small organizations generally own many fixed assets, which management must track as they are purchased and used. The objective of the **fixed-asset management (FAM)** function is to manage the purchase, maintenance, valuation, and disposal of an organization's fixed assets (also called "long-term assets" because they last more than 1 year).

In thinking about how complex it might be to track fixed assets, imagine the endless number of fixed assets that are owned by a large, publicly traded firm such as Boeing (which has about $12,807 million in net property, plant, and equipment on its 2016 balance sheet). A firm must record each fixed asset on its books when it purchases the asset. In addition, the firm must maintain depreciation schedules for its fixed assets. Many large firms will calculate depreciation using five or more different depreciation methods because of different calculation requirements for GAAP financial statements,

---

[3] One World, One ADP, A Message from President and CEO Carlos Rodriguez, accessed from www.adp.com on April 30, 2017.

federal income tax reporting, state tax reporting, and so forth. Employees often move fixed assets around within an organization, and an effective AIS should keep track of all asset locations. Bar codes affixed to physical assets make this job easier.

Because fixed assets often require repairs, an AIS should also track repair costs and distinguish between revenue expenditures and capital expenditures. Revenue expenditures are ordinary repair expenses, whereas capital expenditures add to the value of assets. Finally, the AIS calculates the amount of gain or loss upon disposal of individual fixed assets. By comparing the amount received for the asset with the asset's book value, the AIS can compute a gain or loss. Fortunately, software companies offer a variety of solutions to help managers and automate these processes.

Case-in-Point 9.4   BNA Software offers a fixed-assets system that manages, depreciates, and tracks fixed assets. "BNA Fixed Assets™ enables tax and accounting professionals in companies of any size to automate and manage the complete fixed assets lifecycle—from construction and acquisition through disposal."[4]

BNA provides a case study of how First Bankers Trust Company, a bank in Quincy, Illinois, used its FAM software to automate the management and reporting of moveable fixed assets. Prior to using the BNA software, the staff accountant found it time-consuming and difficult to reconcile the physical fixed assets with the bank's accounting records. Once the decision was made to switch to the new system, the bank conducted an inventory of all fixed assets. They attached a bar-coded asset label to each fixed asset. A handheld device then scanned the bar codes for input into the system. Corresponding invoices were matched, scanned, and attached to the asset records. This new system allowed the bank to track the physical location and condition of assets for an accurate assessment of insurance payments. Now, when an item is disposed of, the bank can immediately update its records and avoid paying unnecessary insurance. The accounting records also reconcile with the physical assets.[5]

Inputs to Fixed-Asset Management Processing.   Fixed-asset processing begins with a request for a fixed-asset purchase. The individual making the request enters the appropriate information on a purchase requisition form (typically an e-form). *Fixed-asset requests* usually require approval by one or more managers, especially where purchases require substantial investments. Other documents associated with fixed-asset purchases are receiving reports, supplier invoices, and repair and maintenance records. The receiving department typically scans in the information electronically to the AIS, which produces a *receiving report* upon receipt of a fixed asset. The asset's supplier sends an *invoice* when it ships the asset. Sometimes, a company builds a fixed asset, for example, a warehouse, rather than acquiring it from an outside vendor. Here, processing fixed assets requires a *work order* detailing the costs of construction.

Those responsible for a particular fixed asset should complete a *fixed-asset change form* when transferring fixed assets from one location to another. The fixed-asset change form also records the sale, trade, or retirement of fixed assets. FAM requires maintaining repair and maintenance records for each asset individually or for categories of fixed assets. The department performing this service should record these activities on a *repair and maintenance form*. This form notifies the AIS to update expense or

---

[4] www.bnasoftware.com, accessed on April 30, 2017.
[5] Streamline Asset Management Tracking with BNA Asset Inventory, accessed from www.bnasoftware.com on April 30, 2017.

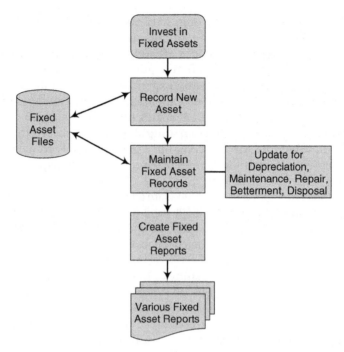

FIGURE 9-4 Systems flowchart of the AIS for the fixed-asset management function.

asset accounts. Figure 9-4 is a systems flowchart that shows fixed-asset acquisition, maintenance, and disposition.

Outputs of Fixed-Asset Management Processing. One output of the fixed-asset processing system is a listing of all fixed assets acquired during a particular period. A *fixed-asset register* lists the identification number of all fixed assets held by a company and each asset's location at a point in time. The *depreciation register* shows depreciation expense and accumulated depreciation for each fixed asset. *Repair and maintenance reports* show the current period's repair and maintenance expenses, as well as each fixed asset's repair and maintenance history. Finally, a *report on retired assets* reflects the disposition of fixed assets during the current period. Figure 9-5 summarizes the objectives, inputs, and outputs of the FAM process.

9.3 THE PRODUCTION PROCESS

The **production process**, sometimes called the conversion process, begins with a request for raw materials and ends with the transfer of finished goods to warehouses.

Objectives of the Production Process

The objective of a manufacturing organization's production process is to convert raw materials into finished goods as efficiently as possible. Today's production of goods and services often requires expensive factory machinery, such as computer-assisted design technology or robotics.

FIXED ASSET MANAGEMENT PROCESS

Objectives
Tracking purchases of fixed assets
Recording fixed asset maintenance
Valuing fixed assets
Allocating fixed asset costs (recording depreciation)
Tracking disposal of fixed assets

Inputs (Source Documents)

- Purchase requisition
- Receiving reports
- Supplier invoices
- Construction work orders
- Repair and maintenance records
- Fixed asset change forms

Outputs (Reports)

- Financial statement information
- Fixed asset register
- Depreciation register
- Repair and maintenance reports
- Retired asset report

FIGURE 9-5   Objectives, inputs, and outputs for the fixed-asset management process.

Accounting for the acquisition and use of production machinery is part of the FAM process described in the previous section of this chapter. Another important objective of an AIS's production process is collecting cost accounting data for operational managers, who then can make informed decisions with respect to the products produced in their departments. Figure 9-6 identifies the objectives, inputs, and outputs associated with the production of goods and services.

Accounting Subsystem.   Because the cost of goods sold is likely to be the largest expense on a manufacturing firm's income statement, a critical part of the production process is an AIS's cost accounting subsystem. The **cost accounting subsystem**

PRODUCTION PROCESS

Objectives
Track purchases and sales of inventories
Monitor and control manufacturing costs
Control inventory
Control and coordinate the production process
Provide input for budgets

Inputs (Source Documents)

- Materials requisition form
- Bill of materials
- Master production schedule
- Production order
- Job time cards

Outputs (Reports)

- Financial statement information
- Material price lists
- Periodic usage reports
- Inventory status reports
- Production cost reports
- Manufacturing status reports

FIGURE 9-6   Objectives, inputs, and outputs commonly associated with the production process.

provides important control information (e.g., variance reports reflecting differences between actual and standard production costs) and varies with the size of the company and the types of product produced. As you might guess, a bakery producing baked goods would collect very different data in its AIS compared to an automobile manufacturer. Cost accounting subsystems for manufacturing organizations are commonly job costing, process costing, or activity-based costing systems.

A **job costing information system** keeps track of the specific costs for raw materials, labor, and overhead associated with each product or group of products, called a "job." This type of costing system is most appropriate for manufacturers of large-scale or custom products, such as home builders or book publishers. Manufacturers of homogeneous products (such as soft drinks or toothbrushes) that are produced on a regular and continuous basis use a **process costing information system**. In this system, it is not feasible or practical to keep track of costs for each item or group of items produced. Instead, process costing systems use averages to calculate the costs associated with goods in process and finished goods produced.

Activity-based costing systems help managers describe processes, identify cost drivers of each process, and then determine the unit costs of products created in each process. By studying their business processes, managers are in a better position to recognize opportunities to improve those processes. Thus, activity-based costing gives managers a better understanding of their processes, an improved ability to allocate indirect costs to those processes, and a better understanding of the true cost of each product. The systems flowchart in Figure 9-7 shows a typical information flow for production in a manufacturing firm.

Just-in-Time (JIT) Inventory Systems. Inventory control ensures that the production process handles inventory transactions appropriately so that the financial statements correctly state the value of the inventory and cost of goods sold. Carrying inventory has a number of costs associated with it, including storage, obsolescence, shrinkage, or reduction in sales value.

Toyota (of Japan) popularized the use of **just-in-time (JIT) inventory systems**. Some managers refer to a JIT system as a "make-to-order inventory system." This phrase indicates that the organization produces goods to fill an order rather than to fill inventory. The objective of a JIT system is to minimize inventories at all levels. Each stage in the production operation manufactures (or acquires) a part just in time for the next process to use it. While the best possible JIT system would maintain zero inventory balances, this is often not practical in real-world applications. Manufacturing organizations need some inventories to protect against interruptions in supply from manufacturers and fluctuations in demand for their finished goods that are beyond the manufacturer's control.

A JIT system requires a reliable and high-quality AIS. If the AIS does not process transactions timely and accurately, manufacturing processes may lack the raw materials necessary to maintain a constant work flow. Inefficient processing of transactions can also lead to shortages of finished goods that in turn translate into lost sales. While JIT is a great concept for a company that is intent on efficiently managing stock, it can make life difficult for the accounts-payable department that is responsible for paying many JIT invoices. This leads some organizations to be proactive and reengineer the process, as the following case-in-point describes.

Case-in-Point 9.5 Dell Computer Company found itself ordering certain parts as frequently as 12 times a day. The A/P department was inundated with paper invoices. GE

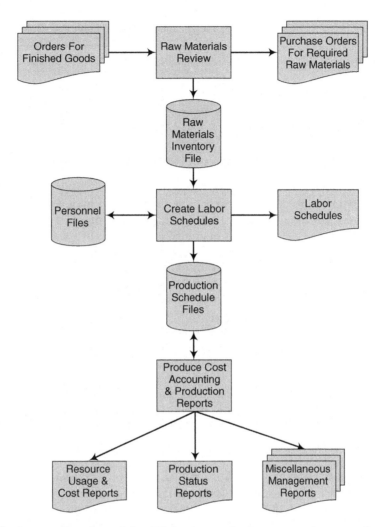

FIGURE 9-7   Systems flowchart of the AIS for the production process in a manufacturing organization.

Capital dispatched several of its Six Sigma analysts to Dell to analyze its A/P process. The consultants mapped out the entire process and then recommended that Dell change to an Internet-based electronic filing process. The move saves Dell over $2 million each year.[6]

Lean Production/Manufacturing.   Although JIT inventory systems are an important step for manufacturing companies to control costs associated with inventory, the truth is that companies must learn to eliminate waste throughout the manufacturing process—indeed, throughout the organization—if they hope to become a world-class organization. **Lean manufacturing** involves making the commitment to eliminate waste throughout the organization (not just in production), which is a philosophy that is often attributed to the *Toyota Production System (TPS)*. The TPS essentially focuses on elimination or reduction of **non-value-added waste** to improve the overall customer value and to increase the profitability of the products or services that the

---

[6] "What is Six Sigma?" General Electric Company, Our Company, accessed from www.ge.com in April 2014.

Types of Non-Value-Added Waste	
• Human potential	• Processing
• Defects	• Transportation
• Motion	• Waiting
• Inventory	• Overproduction

FIGURE 9-8 Categories of waste that are the focus of lean operations management.
Source: Burton, T., and S. Boeder, The lean extended enterprise: Moving beyond the four walls to value stream excellence (2003), Boca Raton, FL: J. Ross Publishing.

organization offers. So, we might say that lean manufacturing developed as a result of the concepts of JIT and Total Quality Management.

Figure 9-8 depicts eight different categories of waste that companies hope to reduce or eliminate. In the figure, *overproduction* means producing more than your customers want to purchase. *Waiting* refers to the time that is lost when employees, products, services, or machines wait for the next step in a process to occur.

Transportation identifies the unnecessary movement of materials or information around a firm or organization. Excessive *processing* can be the result of an organization that has poor products, defective inputs, or an inefficient business process. From JIT principles, we know that it is wasteful to store more *inventory* than the minimum required to produce the goods or services of the company. Excess (or unnecessary) *motion* of people, materials, products, or anything should be avoided. Whenever substandard products are produced, companies end up with *defects*, scrap, rework, and/or paperwork errors. Finally, when organizations do not fully engage the skills, talents, and abilities of their employees, they lose some of the *human potential* that is available to the firm.

Lean Accounting. Accountants are quick to point out that you cannot have lean manufacturing without lean accounting. A company that follows lean manufacturing concepts must identify value from the perspective of their customers, organize production (and data collection) in value streams, empower employees to make decisions, and then continually pursue excellence in all areas of the organization. Thus, you can't use the same old performance measures—you need new ones. Why is that the case? The reason is that the goal of performance measures is to communicate, motivate, clarify, and evaluate. Management accountants use performance measures to give managers information and feedback for decision-making. Traditional performance measures typically support only top managers as decision-makers. Lean manufacturing requires that many leaders (i.e., employees other than high-level managers) be empowered as decision-makers, which means that they also need timely information to be effective.

While reengineering the traditional performance measures would be ideal, this is often not possible. However, management accountants, managers, and empowered team members can work together to identify critical data that the AIS must collect to support lean production. At a minimum, these data should include metrics that will help managers and team members make wise decisions regarding methods to reduce or eliminate waste that is identified in Figure 9-8.

Lean accounting means measuring and evaluating results by **value stream management** rather than by *traditional departments* (such as customer service, purchasing, etc.). For instance, an order fulfillment value stream includes all metrics from the sales/order entry point, through manufacturing, all the way to after-sales support. Each value stream has a leader who is responsible for coaching and profitability of the specific metrics identified for that value stream. Standard costs, variances, and overhead allocations are not the drivers of decisions—only directly incurred costs are used for decision-making.

Lean accounting has many implications throughout organizations. There are two areas that may need to be evaluated by management accountants—the collection of data in the AIS and the chart-of-accounts that the company uses. Fortunately, AISs that are built upon a relational database (see Chapters 14–16) can be modified to support lean accounting. Regarding the chart-of-accounts (covered in Chapter 8), the accountants at each organization will need to work with managers and team leaders to determine the most appropriate coding system to use, based on the value streams that are identified.

Inputs to the Production Process

When a production manager needs raw materials, she issues a *materials requisition form* to acquire more material from a storeroom or warehouse where the raw materials are kept. If the level of inventory falls below a certain predetermined level, the inventory control clerk issues a purchase requisition to the purchasing department (probably an e-form—but this could be an automatic determination that is transmitted electronically to the vendor). Finished goods consist of a complex array of parts or subassemblies. For example, an armchair consists of four legs, a seat, two arms, and a back. The *bill of materials* shows the types and quantities of parts needed to make a single unit of product.

An important input to the production process is the *master production schedule*, which shows the quantities and timing of goods needed to meet quantities required for anticipated sales. The marketing department's sales projections, combined with desired inventory levels, are inputs to the production order, which authorizes the manufacture of goods and dictates the production schedule. Tracking labor time is important to a job costing system because one employee may work on many jobs and one job might require the work of many employees. An input to a job costing system is the *job time card.* This card shows the distribution of labor costs to specific jobs or production orders. Each worker completes a job time card (usually daily or weekly), detailing the hours worked on specific operations and jobs.

Typically, large- and medium-sized firms use enterprise resource planning (ERP) systems to collect essential data about their production operations so that they can better manage these processes. ERPs are multimodule software packages backed by large databases that help a manufacturer effectively track, monitor, and manage product planning, parts purchasing, maintaining inventories, interacting with suppliers, providing customer service, and tracking orders. We discuss ERP software in more depth in Chapter 5.

In conjunction with ERPs, manufacturers have replaced manual data entry with such automated technologies as bar code readers, radio frequency (RF) technology, RFIDs, handheld devices, GPS locators, and other advanced technologies. These input technologies can be used individually or combined in innovative ways to significantly reduce input errors (compared to human data entry) and support fast, accurate, real-time production and data collection.

Case-in-Point 9.6 Manufacturing companies that use SAP can use RFID to track their products along the supply chain. This means that items can be identified during the inbound delivery process, when the items are in inventory, and then during the outbound delivery process. Customers have access to track their items during the shipping process by the RFID tags on the items. When deliveries reach the customer with RFID, the tagged items can be processed using automated goods receipt and validation of the advanced shipping notice (ASN). The goods receipt process also identifies incorrect items and quantities sent by the vendor.[7]

Other technologies are being combined in innovative ways to improve management's ability to track and monitor production and processes. For example, United Parcel Service (UPS) uses combinations of technology to manage the efficiency of their deliveries and to control costs.

Case-in-Point 9.7 UPS deployed a new fleet tracking system in 2010. The system combines GPS technology, telematics, and Bluetooth technology to record data about trucks. The system analyzes information such as the number of times a truck is put into reverse, the number of minutes a truck idles, whether or not the driver wears a seatbelt, and over 200 other pieces of information. Using this information, UPS has already found methods for reducing fuel usage by over 1.4 million gallons per year.[8]

Outputs of the Production Process

Examples of output reports for the production process include materials price lists, periodic usage reports, inventory reconciliation reports, detailed inventory status reports, production cost reports, and manufacturing status reports. The *materials price list* shows the prices charged for raw materials. The purchasing department updates this list. Cost accountants use price lists to determine the standard costs needed to budget production costs. *Periodic usage reports* show how various production departments use raw materials. Managers scrutinize these reports to detect waste by comparing raw material usage to output (finished goods) produced.

A company using a perpetual inventory system issues an inventory reconciliation report. When auditors take a physical inventory, the accounting subsystem compares the physical inventory results with book balances and notes discrepancies in this *inventory reconciliation report*. Another report important for inventory control purposes is the periodic detailed *inventory status report*. This report allows purchasing and production managers to monitor inventory levels.

Cost accountants use *production cost reports* to calculate budget variances. Some manufacturing organizations use standard costing systems that allow them to compare standard costs with actual costs and compute variances for materials, labor, and overhead. The production cost report details the actual costs for each production operation, each cost element, and/or each separate job. *Manufacturing status reports* provide managers with information about the status of various jobs. Because manufacturing a product usually requires coordination of many operations, it is important to report on production status regularly.

Of course, as more companies move to lean production and manufacturing methods, some of these production reports will be replaced with value stream management metrics that would be more useful for decision-making.

---

[7] "RFID and SAP," by Martin Murray, About.com Logistics/Supply Chain, accessed April 2014.
[8] "Telematics Sensor-Equipped Trucks Help UPS Control Costs," by Shelley Mika, July 2010, Automotive Fleet, accessed at www.automotive-fleet.com on April 30, 2017.

9.4   THE FINANCING PROCESS

The **financing process** describes how a company acquires and uses such financial resources as cash, other liquid assets, and investments. Cash and liquid assets are an organization's working capital. The financing process interfaces with the revenue, purchasing, fixed asset, and HR processes. Much of the capital available in an organization comes from sales revenue and is used to pay expenses and personnel and to buy fixed assets.

Besides obtaining financial resources through the sales of goods and services, most organizations acquire funds by borrowing cash or selling ownership shares. The financing process includes managing these activities. Figure 9-9 is a data flow representation of the financing process.

Objectives of the Financing Process

The financing process has a number of objectives. These include managing cash effectively, minimizing the cost of capital, investing for maximum returns, and projecting cash flows. Effective cash management requires collecting cash as soon as possible and spending it carefully. To collect cash quickly, an organization's AIS can provide useful information about how quickly customers pay their bills. An AIS can also show trends in cash collections.

Organizations can use **lock-box systems** to reduce the float period during which checks clear the bank. A lock-box system is an effective cash management tool because

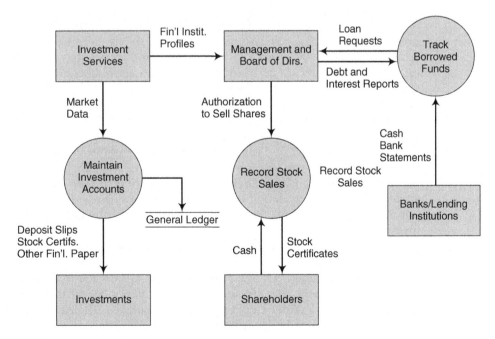

FIGURE 9-9   A data flow diagram of the financing process. This data flow diagram does not include cash management related to sales revenue, purchases, payroll, or fixed assets.

BENEFITS OF A LOCK-BOX SYSTEM

- Better-managed large-volume deposit customers
- Capture market share with lock-box services
- Process any coupon payment format
- Reduce operating costs
- Increase efficiencies
- Cross-selling opportunities through daily access

- Online home page marketing capabilities
- Flexible implementation options
- Archive all check payment information online
- Research images for all lock-box transactions
- Capture greater share of wallet

FIGURE 9-10 Additional benefits firms may realize by using a lock-box system. Source: Website for Image Way® Payment Processing.

banks typically require several days, and sometimes a full week, to provide an organization with credit for out-of-state checks. With a lock-box system, a company directs its customers to mail their checks on account to a lock-box in their home state. A local bank collects the checks in the lock box, clears the checks, sends the customer payment data in an electronic format, and deposits the cash into the company's account. In this way, cash is available for use more quickly. Figure 9-10 identifies additional benefits that companies might realize by using a lock-box system.

Electronic funds transfer (EFT), or electronic payment, is another cash management technique that is very common. Using EFT, business organizations eliminate paper documents and instead transfer funds electronically. Similarly, most companies today pay their employees electronically by directly depositing the funds to each employee's bank account rather than issuing a paper check.

Managing cash on the expenditure side means paying cash as bills come due and taking advantage of favorable cash discounts. While an organization wants to make sure that there is cash available for timely payments to vendors and employees, it is also possible to have too much cash on hand. Idle cash is an unproductive asset, and short-term investments often earn less return compared to long-term investments. Effective cash management means cash balances are not unreasonably high and managers invest excess cash wisely. Managers in large companies monitor excess cash and invest it for very short time periods.

Minimizing the cost of capital (i.e., the cost of obtaining financial resources) requires management to decide how much cash to borrow and how many shares of ownership (stock) to sell. Borrowed funds require interest payments. While businesses do not pay interest to shareholders, they do pay dividends. Financial managers frequently use **financial planning models** to help them select an optimum strategy for acquiring and investing financial resources. These models require an information system that can make complex calculations and consider alternative investment, borrowing, and equity (sale of stock) strategies.

A final objective of the financing process is to project cash flows—here again we see the value of understanding predictive analytics. An output of the revenue process is a cash receipts forecast, and the purchasing and HR processes contribute to a forecast of cash disbursements. The financing process makes use of these forecasts to invest excess funds and determine debt and equity strategies. The AIS for the financing process contributes to cash flow predictions through estimates of interest and dividend payments and receipts. Figure 9-11 summarizes the objectives, inputs, and outputs of this process.

FINANCING PROCESS

Objectives
Effective cash management
Cost of capital optimization
Earn maximum return on investments
Project cash flows

Inputs (Source Documents)	Outputs (Reports)
• Remittance advices	• Financial statement information
• Deposit slips	• Cash budget
• Checks	• Investment reports
• Bank statements	• Debt and interest reports
• Stock market data	• Financial ratios
• Interest data	• Financial planning model reports
• Financial institution profiles	

FIGURE 9-11   Objectives, inputs, and outputs associated with the financing process.

Inputs to the Financing Process

Many inputs to the financing process originate outside an organization. Externally generated data or source documents might include remittance advices, deposit slips, checks, bank statements, stock market data, interest data, and data about financial institutions. Chapter 10 explained that a *remittance advice* accompanies a customer's payment on account. Banks provide *deposit slips* to document account deposits. For example, you receive a deposit slip when you make a cash deposit to your account through an automated teller machine and a credit slip when you purchase gasoline with your debit card.

Regardless of whether companies transfer funds electronically or receive/issue paper checks, accountants use the company's *bank statements* to reconcile any account discrepancies and as proof of payment. Accountants use bank statements to reconcile the cash account balance in the company's ledger against the cash balance in the bank account. Discrepancies between these two accounts arise from outstanding checks, deposits in transit, and various other transactions. Sometimes, of course, discrepancies are due to errors or even fraud. Because cash is a company's most liquid asset, AISs use control procedures to help protect against misappropriations.

Outputs of the Financing Process

Like all other business processes, the financing process provides general ledger information to help an AIS produce periodic financial statements. Examples include interest revenue and expense, dividend revenue and expense reports, and summaries of cash collections and disbursements. It also provides information about balances in debt, equity, and investment accounts. Besides providing general ledger information, the financing process of an AIS produces a *cash budget* showing projected cash flows.

The AIS for the financing process can produce a variety of reports about investments and borrowings. Investment reports may show changes in investments for a period, dividends paid, and interest earned. Reports on borrowings could show new

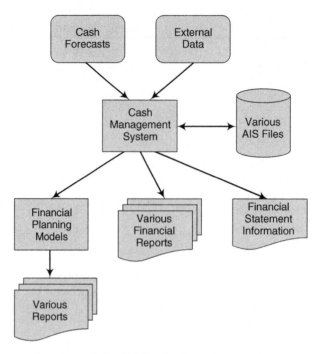

FIGURE 9-12 Systems flowchart of the AIS for the financing process.

debt and retired debt for a period. These reports should list the lending institutions, interest rates charged, and payments of principal and/or interest for the period.

Managers perform *ratio analyses* to manage an organization's capital effectively. Significant ratios, such as return on investment and debt to equity, help management make decisions regarding investment and borrowing strategies. A company's financial planning model calculates and reports these ratios. The planning model also prepares recommendations regarding the appropriate mix of debt versus equity financing, and short- versus long-range investments. Figure 9-12 is a sample systems flowchart for the financing process.

9.5 BUSINESS PROCESSES IN SPECIAL INDUSTRIES

The term vertical market refers to markets or industries that are distinct in terms of the services they provide or the goods they produce. When you think about it, most organizations fit into a vertical market category. For example, an accounting firm is a professional service organization while a grocery store is in the retail industry. However, large conglomerates may operate in several different **vertical markets**—for instance, many large manufacturers have branched out to also provide professional and financial services. The same is true of retail firms. Consider, for example, Sears, Roebuck and Co. While still known primarily as a retailer, a large share of the company's profit comes from providing consumer credit.

Vertical markets with specialized AIS-related needs include professional services, not-for-profit, health care, retail, construction, government, banking and financial services, and hospitality. This section describes a few of these types of organizations in terms of their unique characteristics and AIS needs.

Professional Service Organizations

Professional service organizations are business establishments providing a special service to customers such as accounting, legal services, engineering, consulting, and architectural services. Compared with organizations that provide tangible goods (such as automobile manufacturers), professional service organizations have several unique operating characteristics: (1) no merchandise inventory, (2) emphasis on professional employees, (3) difficulty in measuring the quantity and quality of output, and (4) small size. These are common characteristics, although not every organization in this industry segment has all of them. For instance, some accounting and consulting firms are relatively large. They have hundreds of partners and international offices in cities throughout the world.

Because professional service organizations do not maintain a product inventory, they do not need an AIS that tracks inventory levels. Instead, the primary accounting information needed by professional service organizations relates to time and billing for their professional staff. **Time and billing information systems** are similar to job order costing systems—they track hours and costs associated with each job (i.e., each client) and each employee (i.e., professional staff). There are two major outputs of the time and billing system: (1) the client bill and (2) the professional staff member's record of billable hours (hours actually spent working on client business).

Figure 9-13 shows an example of a software consulting firm's client bill. The client bill may detail the number of hours worked by every professional staff member and the rate charged by each. For example, an audit client might incur charges for audit staff, supervisors or seniors, managers, and partners. An AIS multiplies the hours worked by each staff member by his or her respective billing rate to compute the total charge. Time and billing systems can also show other charges on the bill or client invoice—for example, charges for overhead and detailed charges for phone, fax, mail, support staff, and copy costs.

Billable hours are important in a professional service organization. Law firms, for example, stress the importance of accumulating an accurate accounting of the number of billable hours. Nonbillable hours are hours spent on training, marketing, and general research. While these latter activities are important, they do not directly generate revenue for a law firm. A time and billing system can track each staff member's hours in many ways. The increments of time recorded vary by firm. Some professional service firms record every 15 minutes spent working on a client job. Some law firms even record time in 6-minute increments. Because time is literally money, it is important to keep records that are as detailed and accurate as possible.

Automation helps professional service organizations keep accurate records of billable hours. For example, phone systems can record the amount of time spent on calls to and from clients, and the phone system can enter values directly into the time and billing system. A copy machine in which users enter client numbers for each job is another tool that helps assign copy costs to client accounts. Finally, as professional staff members rely increasingly on their computers for their work, special computer programs can automatically record the time spent on each job as the staff member logs on to different programs with client-oriented passwords.

Not-for-Profit Organizations

Not-for-profit organizations provide resources and services for the protection and betterment of society. Examples include public schools, museums, churches, and governmental agencies. Not-for-profits differ from for-profit businesses in that they: (1) are

Smith & Smith Partners
8888 Newbury Rd.
Glenwood, NC 00301
Office: 634/344-9845
Fax: 634/344-5468

Mr. Bob Townsend
234 Bayberry St.
Rocktown, NC 12093

Invoice #:	2309
Invoice Date:	July 26, 2018
Terms:	Net 15 Days
Due Date:	August 26, 2018
Customer #:	12088

FOR SERVICES RENDERED

Work Type	Date	Description	Employee	Time
Chargeable	3/17/18	Planning	MAS	0.60
No Charge	3/19/18	Issues/Resolves	SBC	0.25
Chargeable	3/20/18	Processing Error & Corrections	MAS	0.60
			Total Hours:	**1.20**
			Not Charged Hours:	**0.25**
			Chargeable Hours:	**1.20**
			Invoice Dollar Total:	**$240.00**

FIGURE 9-13 A sample client bill for a software consulting firm.

usually staffed by volunteers as well as professional employees, (2) do not emphasize maximizing net income (and do not have owners/shareholders), (3) are usually not as affected by market forces as are for-profit organizations, and (4) sometimes have a political emphasis.

As with other organizations in vertical markets, not-for-profit organizations have special accounting information needs that reflect their unique characteristics. For example, public schools (such as a university) must keep records of students' schedules, grades, health records, and so on. Charitable organizations, on the other hand, must keep track of its donors' personal information and giving history while properly accounting for current donations. The federal government (certainly the largest not-for-profit organization) must value various unique assets that are not traded in a public market. How much, for instance, is the Lincoln Memorial or Interstate 95 worth, and how would you determine the annual depreciation for these assets?

In general, it is the need for proper stewardship of organizational resources that most influences the special AIS needs of not-for-profit organizations. The reporting systems of not-for-profit organizations must be equipped to handle fund accounting. Funds can be seen as separate pots of money and resources for the various programs/objectives of a nonprofit, which presents unique challenges as it relates to AIS. For example, each fund has its own asset/liability balances, revenue and expenditure accounts, and equity (or fund) balances. Properly functioning fund accounting systems show the resources available for carrying out an organization's objectives, both individually and in the aggregate. Funds may be restricted by donors for special purposes (e.g., funds donated to a university for student scholarships) or unrestricted in nature and available for general use.

Although the effectiveness of not-for-profit organizations cannot be evaluated using traditional profit measures, some mechanism for performance evaluation is still desirable. A frequently used mechanism is a budgetary AIS. By comparing actual performance against planned activity, the managers in not-for-profit entities can determine how well they met their goals. Many not-for-profit entities (especially governmental organizations) use formal long-range budgetary techniques, though the main focus of budgetary systems is a short-term (1–2 year) focus. These budgets include projections of current-year expectations (approved by governing bodies, including legislative bodies in the case of governmental entities) or future activity that may serve as performance measures when compared with actual data.

One difficulty often encountered in not-for-profit budgetary systems is the lack of a monetary measure of performance output. Consequently, managers must often use process measures (i.e., nonmonetary measures) to measure performance. In a police department, for example, the process measures might be number of arrests, number of homicides, or burglary rates. Public universities might use the number of students graduating each academic year or retention rates.

A good short-range budgetary planning and controlling system is typically more important to a not-for-profit entity (particularly for governmental entities) than to a profit-oriented company. The reason is the fixed, rather than flexible, nature of these organizations' annual budgets. For example, at publicly financed state universities, biannual state legislators approve annual operating budgets years in advance that cannot be changed in off years. Thus, in those not-for-profit organizations subject to fixed or static budgets, good short-range planning is necessary to obtain accurate budget projections for the coming year.

Health Care Organizations

The dollars spent on health care make this vertical market segment the target of considerable controversy and concern as the United States struggles to contain health-care costs. With the implementation of the Affordable Health Care Act, the technology supporting health care will remain at the center of the controversy. Paperwork has been a bottleneck in delivering efficient health care, and it is also an important cost. Figure 9-14 shows examples of the many subsystems in a health-care organization's AIS.

Health-care entities share many characteristics with professional service organizations and not-for-profit institutions. Like these entities, health-care organizations do not provide tangible goods to their customers (except for drugs). In addition, health-care organizations also count professional staff as their most important asset resource. Some health-care organizations are public and operate on a not-for-profit basis. Finally, output is exceptionally difficult to measure for this industry. For example, a patient may get well due to the quality of health care received, or the patient may simply get well due to his body's ability to overcome an illness. On the other hand, some patients die despite excellent health-care and heroic measures.

The special AIS needs of health-care organizations primarily relate to **third-party billing**. Health-care organizations usually do not bill their customers directly for services received. Rather, they bill insurance companies or government agencies who in turn reimburse these service providers. Typically, bills to third-party payers (insurance companies) use standardized codes for both the medical diagnosis and the procedures

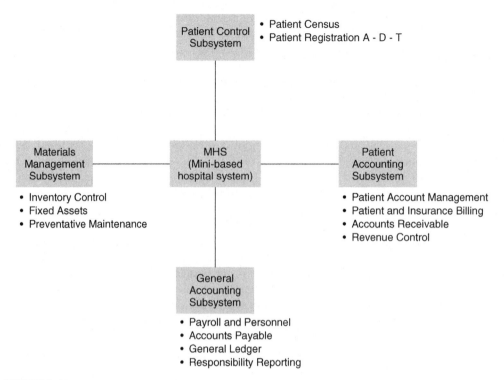

FIGURE 9-14 Mini-based hospital system.

performed by medical personnel. Although standardized codes promote efficiency in processing information, coding can still be difficult. For example, sometimes a diagnosis is hard to pinpoint, and medical personnel often do procedures for multiple purposes. Reimbursement from an insurance company depends on the codes used. In addition, one plan may cover a particular procedure, and another may not. Because doctors often have discretion in making a diagnosis or prescribing a procedure, the accounting staff needs to understand the nuances of the codes and general classifications. Errors in coding can be costly and not just in terms of the processing costs associated with them. Errors can lead to a patient's inability to obtain coverage for charges and also potentially be viewed as fraud by insurance carriers.

Payment policies and filing forms may vary among third-party insurers. Government insurance (Medicare and Medicaid) presents another problem in terms of claim forms. These health-care programs are state administered and each state has special filing requirements. The several hundred medical insurance carriers in the United States all use the same coding base. However, clerical personnel and AISs do not uniformly apply these codes. As previously mentioned, special AIS needs for the health-care industry relate mostly to third-party billing, but other features of the industry also require special processing.

Health-care AISs generally need to maintain patient information. Hospitals, doctors' offices, and nursing homes all need systems to efficiently schedule patients. Home health-care services need to keep track of travel costs for employees. Information needs may be unique to very specific industry segments. For example, physical therapy offices, chiropractic practices, ophthalmologists, and dental offices each have very special information needs. Physical therapy offices are different from other medical offices in that a patient may spend an hour in therapy on many different kinds of equipment. An AIS might charge differently for 10 minutes spent in the whirlpool versus 10 minutes on exercise equipment. The following case describes a specialized health-care software solution—that is strictly online.

Case-in-Point 9.8   Managing an optometry practice doesn't require a software solution these days—according to one software vendor. Vision2020online offers optometrists a new way to manage their practice. It's a pay-as-you-go online service—right over the Internet. And it's scalable. The service allows the optometrist to start with one location and add multiple locations later. And the optometrist, salespeople, and office employees can all work simultaneously on the system. Typical technology support for optometrists includes: patient scheduling, electronic billing, patient registration and reporting, and HIPAA compliant patient portal.[9]

9.6   BUSINESS PROCESS REENGINEERING

Business process reengineering (BPR) is about redesigning business processes that are no longer efficient or effective. BPR is a continuous process that involves the analysis of an existing process to find areas for improvement (see Figure 9-15). As an example, consider an order process that begins with inquiries from a customer about the products available for sale and ends when the customer pays cash to complete a sale. In many organizations, several individuals handle the order process. Each person has responsibility for a particular function: a receptionist may handle inquiries, a sales person follows up on product inquiries, warehouse personnel assume responsibility for filling the order, an accounts-receivable clerk bills the customer, and so on. This division of responsibility can make it difficult for some organizations to fill customer orders quickly. The result: dissatisfied customers. Through BPR, inefficient processes such as the one described earlier are identified and then either improved or replaced with a new process.

Reengineering the order process may result in an integration of functional activities so that one specified individual handles customers from start to finish. This redesign means a customer knows whom to talk to when an order is late so that the customer is not passed around from one person to another when problems occur. As we discussed

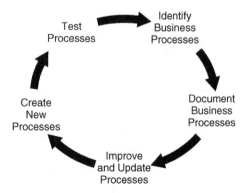

FIGURE 9-15   The business process reengineering cycle.

---

[9] Vision2020online, www.vision2020online.com, accessed on April 30, 2017.

earlier in this chapter, this might be an opportunity for the firm to evaluate the possibility of *value stream management.*

Case-in-Point 9.9 Prior to BPR, an insurance application at Mutual Benefit Life included 30 steps performed by 19 people in five departments—approval took from 5 to 25 days. Rather than simply automating the paper/people intensive process, the insurance company reengineered its system, abolishing existing job descriptions and departmental boundaries. Instead, the company created the position of "case manager" and gave each manager the authority to perform all application approval tasks for insurance policies, supported by IT. Now, cycle times are dramatically reduced, 20% of new applications are issued automatically by an expert system, and the company has a 20% increase in business volume![10]

Why Reengineering Sometimes Fails

While employee resistance is often fatal to BPR efforts, management support can help overcome some of the obstacles. BPR needs champions in top management. Successful BPR efforts also need top managers who are good communicators and are willing to give employees both good and bad news. Managers who try to mask the downside of change are likely to run into difficulty. Because of these concerns, managers could consider the professional help of **change management consultants** to facilitate this complex process and overcome potential negative reactions.

AIS AT WORK
Reengineering Medical Records

A key provision of the American Recovery and Reinvestment Act of 2009 (commonly referred to as the "stimulus bill") is that all public and private health-care providers must use electronic medical records (EMR) to maintain their Medicaid and Medicare reimbursement levels. The goal of EMR is to make medical records more secure and less expensive. This provision of the law went into effect on January 1, 2014. The purpose of this mandate is to:

- Improve quality, safety, efficiency, and reduce health disparities
- Engage patients and family
- Improve care coordination
- Maintain privacy and security of patient health information

Not surprisingly, there are penalties for noncompliance. As a result, many health-care providers were forced to reengineer their business processes to comply with the law—which required professionals with the skills and knowledge necessary to develop, implement, and manage IT software and applications in a medical environment.

But you might be asking yourself the question: "With technology so pervasive these days, how can it be possible that health care providers are so far behind?" That's a very

---

[10] "Mutual Benefit Life" by Davis Li Minyong, Novita, and Daryl See Zhi Xiang, accessed from leedavis83.wordpress.com on May 1, 2017.

insightful question. For example, when was the last time you went to your favorite clothing store and the salesperson had to manually enter the price of your garment? Similarly, when was the last time you went to the grocery store and the clerk at the register had to manually enter the price of every item you purchased? Maybe your answer is *never*! And that's because most retail stores now use bar code scanners that electronically capture the price.

The American Recovery and Reinvestment Act of 2009 requires health-care providers to use technology to capture patient information. EMR should improve the collection, organization, accuracy, and accessibility of information and hopefully improve health care and reduce costs. However, many health-care providers still do not efficiently use technology or EMR. Instead, at almost every visit, you are handed a clipboard with a form (or several forms) and you had to fill out the exact same information you did the last time you came for an appointment.

Imagine, for example, that your personal physician has prescribed a medication that must not be taken with many other common medications because of dangerous interactions. If you are admitted to the emergency room because of an accident, EMR will prevent emergency-room doctors from giving you medications that might interact with your current prescription. And what if a particular drug is pulled off the market? A doctor could quickly and easily identify her patients who need to be notified. These are some of the many possible advantages that can be realized by reengineering procedures for collecting and recording patient information.

 ## SUMMARY

- ✓ This chapter discusses three additional business processes: resource management, production, and financing.
- ✓ The resource management process includes two areas of interest: human resource (HR) management and fixed-asset management. HR management encompasses both the personnel activities in an organization and the payroll events.
- ✓ The production process includes the events related to converting raw materials into finished goods inventories.
- ✓ The concept of lean manufacturing is a commitment to eliminate waste throughout the organization (not just in production).
- ✓ A company that follows lean manufacturing concepts must identify value from the perspective of their customers, organize production (and data collection) in value streams, empower employees to make decisions, and then continually pursue excellence in all areas of the organization.
- ✓ To support lean manufacturing concepts, the firm must also adopt lean accounting concepts, which means measuring and evaluating results by value stream management rather than by traditional departments.
- ✓ The financing process overlaps all the other processes since it is concerned with the acquisition and use of funds needed for operations.
- ✓ The financing process also includes investing, borrowing, and stock-selling activities.
- ✓ Cash management is an important part of the financing process. Sound cash management requires companies to constantly monitor cash balances, investing any excess and covering temporary shortfalls with bank loans.
- ✓ There are many other business processes unique to specific industries. Each industry, or vertical market segment with specialized processes, has associated custom AIS needs.

✓ Current technology, combined with management scrutiny of business processes, provides opportunities to reengineer business processes in ways that help organizations achieve their objectives.

✓ Business process reengineering (BPR) is the practice of examining business processes and redesigning them from scratch.

✓ Many companies today are engaged in BPR as a way to improve customer service and satisfaction, increase profitability, and decrease costs.

KEY TERMS YOU SHOULD KNOW

activity-based costing systems
business process management (BPM) software
business process reengineering (BPR)
change management consultants
cost accounting subsystems
electronic funds transfer (EFT)
financial planning models
financing process

fixed-asset management (FAM)
human resource (HR) management
job costing information systems
just-in-time (JIT) inventory systems
lean accounting
lean manufacturing
lock-box systems
non-value-added waste

payroll processing information systems
process costing information systems
production process
third-party billing
time and billing information systems
value stream management
vertical markets

TEST YOURSELF

Q9-1. All of the following activities are common to the Human Resource Management function except:

a. hiring, training, and employing workers

b. reporting on payroll deductions

c. maintaining employee earnings records

d. providing certified financial planning for employees

Q9-2. Which of the following two resources are common to the Resource Management Process?

a. Human resources and payroll processing

b. Business processes and payroll procession

c. Fixed assets and human resources

d. Business processes and fixed assets

Q9-3. Which of the following outputs (reports) is common to all of the processes described in this chapter?

a. Financial statement information

b. Deduction reports

c. Supplier invoices

d. Budget reports

Q9-4. What is the objective of the fixed-asset management function?

a. To track purchases of fixed assets

b. To manage the purchase, management, valuation, and disposal of an organization's fixed assets

c. To record maintenance and depreciation of fixed assets

d. To keep a current listing of approved vendors

Q9-5. All of the following attributes are true for not-for-profit organizations, except:

a. they do not emphasize maximizing net income

b. they have special accounting needs

c. they do not use fund accounting

d. they include the federal government

Q9-6. The special AIS needs of health-care organizations typically include the following, except for:

a. third-party billing

b. standardized billing codes

c. master production schedules

d. HIPAA compliant patient portals

Q9-7. Which of the following automated systems help minimize inventory costs?

a. JIT systems

b. ABC systems

c. Job order costing systems

d. Process costing systems

Q9-8. Which of the following reports is common to the Fixed-Asset Management Process?

a. Bill of materials report

b. Periodic usage report

c. Depreciation report

d. All of the above

Q9-9. Automated point-of-sale (POS) technology offers many advantages to retailers as well as customers. Which of the following is the most commonly used POS technology?

a. Cell phones

b. RFID

c. Bar code scanners

d. None of these

Q9-10. The concept of lean production or manufacturing includes all of the following, except:

a. commitment to eliminate "waste" throughout the manufacturing process

b. eliminate or reduce non-value-added waste

c. improve overall customer value and the profitability of products or services

d. there are 12 categories of waste that companies hope to reduce or eliminate

Q9-11. Lean accounting is:

a. an AIS that is generally considered low cost (i.e., an entry-level system)

b. designed to support traditional financial performance measures

c. new performance measures that support decision-making by managers and operational improvement leaders

d. none of these

Q9-12. Business process reengineering:

a. is an incremental approach to redesigning business processes

b. involves redesigning business processes from scratch

c. is rarely successful in cutting an organization's costs

d. is usually welcomed by an organization's employees

DISCUSSION QUESTIONS

9-1. The resource management process includes events associated with both personnel and payroll functions. Describe four data items that could be used by both functions. Describe two data items for each function that would not necessarily be needed by the other (e.g., spouse name for personnel but not payroll).

9-2. Why are accounting transactions associated with payroll processing so repetitive in nature? Why do some companies choose to have payroll processed by external service companies rather than do it themselves?

9-3. In this chapter, we discussed many data inputs to an organization's production process. What are the specific data items to input into a system when adding a new raw materials inventory item? What specific data items need to be input when a worker records the time spent on the production line?

9-4. What nonfinancial information would be important for an AIS to capture about a manufacturing firm's production process?

9-5. What are the basic concepts of lean manufacturing? What concepts are the "root" of lean production and lean manufacturing?

9-6. Find an example of a firm that is using lean manufacturing concepts. Has the company realized any improvements? What are they?

9-7. Can you find an example (other than the one described in Case-in-Point 9.6) of a firm that is using lean production concepts that are supported by lean accounting? How are they doing?

9-8. Are the inputs and outputs of a production process likely to be different for a home builder than for a cement company? How?

9-9. There are many vertical market industries with special accounting information needs apart from the industries discussed in this chapter. Identify three additional vertical market industries. What are the unique characteristics of these industries that affect their AISs?

9-10. Assume for the moment that you are the controller for Dr. Lazik & Associates, which is a full-service ophthalmology practice with 10 locations in a large metropolitan area. The president of the company just asked you to take charge of the task of automating the practice due to the new mandate for electronic medical records (EMR). Search the Internet for a software solution that you would recommend for the company. Identify the vendor, the name of the software package, and the features that you believe would be most beneficial to your company.

9-11. Discuss specific steps you would take as a manager to ensure that a business process reengineering effort is successful.

PROBLEMS

9-12. Choose an industry described in this chapter and find out what vertical market accounting software is available for that industry. You may use resources such as the Internet, trade associations, interviews with organizations within the industry, or interviews with software consultants.

9-13. Literally thousands of business process management (BPM) solutions are available to help managers accomplish tasks in a more effective, efficient manner. Assume that you work in a payroll processing function and your supervisor asked you to select a BPM solution for your company. Which BPM software would you select and why? Identify the vendor, the name of the software package, and several of the features that you thought would be most beneficial to your company.

9-14. Now, assume that you work in the internal audit function at a large hospital that is considering a software package to automate the process of complying with the requirements of the American Recovery and Reinvestment Act of 2009 (commonly referred to as the "stimulus bill")—that all public and private health-care providers must use electronic medical records (EMR) to maintain their Medicaid and Medicare reimbursement levels. Which BPM software would you select and why? Identify the vendor, the name of the software package, and several of the features that you thought would be most beneficial to your company.

9-15. Assume that you started your own law practice 10 years ago, specializing in estate planning, and you currently employ five attorneys, two legal assistants, one legal secretary, and a bookkeeper/receptionist. The firm has always used a manual accounting system, which includes procedures for time and billing. How could an automated time and billing system help your firm? Search the Internet for a specific technology to automatically capture a professional employee's time spent on a particular client engagement. What is the name of the software package, and what are the primary features of this BPM software?

CASE ANALYSES

9-16. Hammaker Manufacturing: Selecting an AIS

Dick Hammaker has been fascinated with Corvette cars, especially convertibles, since he was a teenager. Dick grew up in Michigan and worked part-time through his high school and college years at a car manufacturer, so he knew the business well. Not surprisingly, when he graduated from college, he bought his first car, a used Corvette convertible, and became a member of the local Corvette Club of America.

As an accounting graduate, Hammaker was hired by one of the large automobile manufacturers in Michigan and was selected for the "fast-track" management training program. After 5 years,

Hammaker decided to leave Michigan and start a specialty parts manufacturing company strictly for Corvettes. Before he even left Michigan, a potential customer contacted him—the repair shop was replacing the black convertible top on a 1967 Corvette that the owner was going to sell for $76,995! Hammaker decided to locate his company, Hammaker Manufacturing Co. (HMC), in Northern Virginia since this is the site of the oldest Corvette Club of America. Dick knows that he will need the appropriate technology to support his company, so he decided to focus on this aspect of his company prior to starting any production activities. His first action was to hire a CFO (Denise Charbonet) who could work with Lloyd Rowland (a software consultant) to determine the inputs and outputs needed for an AIS for the new company. Of particular concern is the data the AIS will need to collect regarding inventories. As Dick, Denise, and Lloyd know, inventory management will be a key factor for the success of HMC since Corvette cars are unique—parts are needed for these cars since the 1960s!

Dick believes that an AIS will give him the data and information needed for good decision-making—especially to manage inventory investments. HMC's customers are primarily Corvette specialty repair shops and they typically demand parts only as needed, but exactly when needed. Inventory can be very costly for HMC if they must stockpile many specialty parts to be able to quickly meet customer orders.

Hammaker knows from his work experience in Michigan that there are a number of costs associated with holding inventories (warehousing, obsolescence, and insurance costs)—money that could be put to better use elsewhere. Dick knows that he will need to buy raw materials from suppliers and hold raw materials inventories plus make-to-stock parts, or customers will find other parts suppliers.

Denise and Lloyd meet to discuss the issues. They decide that they need to do two things. First, they need to determine what AIS software package would be best for the new company, one that is particularly focused on inventory control (or one with an inventory control module that would be well-suited for HMC). Second, they need to decide what data elements they need to capture about each inventory item to optimize inventory management and control. Denise notes that while some inventory descriptors are easy to determine, such as item number, description, and cost, others are more difficult. For instance, inventory on hand and inventory available for sale could be two different data items since some of the inventory on hand might be committed but not yet shipped.

Requirements

1. Explain how an AIS could help HMC optimize inventory management and control.
2. What data elements should HMC include in the new AIS to describe each inventory item?

9-17. Hammaker Manufacturing: Reengineer or Outsource

Implementation of a new AIS went smoothly, for the most part. It is 15 years later, and now HMC is interested in mapping a variety of their business processes to determine whether improvements can be made and whether business process reengineering should be considered. Hammaker asked Denise to work with the consulting firm analysts to determine the feasibility of these two options and also to consider the possibility of outsourcing. Denise does not know much about outsourcing and she is not sure which process (or processes) Dick might want to outsource.

Denise discovers that a number of developing countries have the capacity and the labor to make the parts that HMC is currently producing and at much cheaper prices. Further, Denise discovers that many companies are outsourcing and offshoring a number of processes that used to be accomplished by company employees. Denise makes a note to herself to check the number of employees in each of the following departments: HR, computer support, accounting, and janitorial services. She also decides to query the AIS to determine what performance measures are available to assess the efficiency and effectiveness of each of these departments. Denise places a call to Lloyd Rowland to discuss this issue with him.

HMC is not unionized, but Denise ponders the legal and social issues associated with outsourcing jobs, since many of the 365 employees at Hammaker Manufacturing have been with the company for well over a decade.

Requirements

1. Identify tools that would help Denise and Rowland map HMC's business processes. Which processes do you think they should work on first? Why those processes?

2. Identify at least six reasons why companies choose to outsource a business process. Which of these reasons might Dick use to make his decision to outsource or to attempt BPR?

3. Is producing automotive parts a "core" business process for Hammaker manufacturing? Explain.

4. Do companies ever outsource "core" business processes? Search the Internet to see if you can find an example of a company or an industry that outsources core business processes. What are they? Why are they doing this?

5. What social or legal issues might Denise consider? Be specific and explain why these issues might be important to Hammaker manufacturing.

6. What would you recommend if you were one of the analysts at the consulting firm? Explain.

9-18. Hammaker Manufacturing: Lean Production/Lean Accounting

HMC continues to be profitable. Although Denise and Lloyd Rowland mapped several business processes 5 years ago to determine whether HMC should work on process improvements or consider business process reengineering, they never really finished that effort nor did HMC decide whether to outsource any processes. Hammaker still thinks that HMC could be more efficient and more profitable, but he's not really sure how the company can achieve this "next level" of excellence. About a year ago, Denise started reading books and trade journals on the topics of business strategy, lean production, and lean manufacturing. So, when Dick approached her regarding his intent to improve the company, she began to share with him some of the insights she had gained over the past year on business strategy and how their current AIS might not be capturing the most useful metrics for optimal decision-making. Denise mentioned that the next Lean Accounting Summit will be in September and suggested that she and her three financial analysts go to the 4-day conference to gain a better understanding of lean production and accounting concepts to determine how they might be able to better support HMC and Dick's goal of improving the company.

Requirements

1. If Dick decided to adopt the business strategy of lean production, what changes might he and his managers consider?

2. Explain how HMC might benefit from implementing lean production/manufacturing concepts.

3. Why would it be important for Denise and her financial analysts to attend the Lean Accounting Summit? What benefits would you expect them to acquire from this conference that would be useful at HMC?

READINGS AND OTHER RESOURCES

Frigo, M.L. 2017. Managing healthcare costs and value. *Strategic Finance* 98(7): 24.

Merrill, K. 2017. The importance of the CMA. *Strategic Finance* 98(9): 72.

Murphy, M.L. 2016. Best practices that not-for-profits can't afford to overlook. *Journal of Accountancy* 221(5): 42–47.

Ovaska-Few, S. 2017. What large firms expect from new accounting grads. *Journal of Accountancy* 223(3): 1–4.

Page, B. 2013. Should we change the system or the process? *Strategic Finance* 95(11): 46–51.

Smith, D., and C. Smith. 2013. What's wrong with supply chain metrics? *Strategic Finance* 95(10): 27–33. (Opinions on supply chain accounting and management.)

Snyder, H. 2017. Nonprofit fraud: How good are your internal controls? *Strategic Finance* 98(9): 54.

Wiatt, R.G. 2016. Manufacturing enters the third dimension. *Strategic Finance* 98(6): 46–54.

Go to www.wiley.com/go/simkin/videos to access videos on the following topics:

Basics of Activity-Based Costing
Business Process Reengineering (five videos)
Change Management Example

ANSWERS TO TEST YOURSELF

1. d **2.** c **3.** a **4.** b **5.** c **6.** c **7.** a **8.** c **9.** c **10.** d **11.** c **12.** b

Chapter 10

Cybercrime, Fraud, and Ethics

After reading this chapter, you will be able to:

1. *Explain* the differences between cybercrime and fraud.
2. *Discuss* the various components of the fraud triangle.
3. *List* examples of cybercrime and fraud, as well as the proper controls and procedures for preventing them.
4. *Describe* the profile of cyber criminals.
5. *Illustrate* the importance of ethical behavior within accounting information system (AIS) environments.

"Adversaries have more tools at their disposal than ever before. They also have a keen sense of when to use each one for maximum effect. The explosive growth of mobile endpoints and online traffic works in their favor. They have more space in which to operate and more choices of targets and approaches."

Cisco Systems, Inc.[1]

10.1 INTRODUCTION

Managers, accountants, and investors use computerized information to control valuable resources, sell products, authenticate accounting transactions, and make investment decisions. But the effectiveness of these activities is compromised when the underlying information is incorrect, incomplete, or falsified. This is why digital information is a valuable asset that must be protected. The more managers and accountants know about cybercrime and fraud, the better they are able to assess risks and implement controls to protect organizational assets.

Fraud is estimated to cost US businesses nearly $1 trillion each year, and understanding how to leverage accounting systems to detect and prevent fraud and cybercrime is valuable and essential for today's accounting and auditing practitioners. Compared to manual accounting systems, the widespread use of complex technology and networks allow fraud perpetrators to steal more, in much less time, with much less effort, and leave less evidence of their actions. Consequently, cyber fraud is often more difficult to detect than other types of fraud. Accounting information systems (AISs) help control financial resources and are often the favored targets of computer abusers and criminals. Also, AISs are prized targets for disgruntled employees seeking to compromise computer systems for revenge. Today's accountants are responsible for

---

[1] 2017 Annual Cybersecurity Report, Cisco Systems, Inc., access from www.cisco.com in February 2017.

designing, selecting, and/or implementing the control procedures that protect AISs and use data collected by AISs to detect and prevent fraud.

This chapter describes common cybercrimes, frauds, and other irregularities in order to inform readers of the important threats to AISs and firm resources. In the first section, we take a closer look at cybercrime and fraud and explain the differences between them. In the second section, we examine three specific cases involving cybercrime and fraud. The third section of this chapter identifies actions organizations can undertake to protect themselves from cybercrime and fraud—that is, what they can do to recognize potential problems and what they can do to control them.

Not all computer-related offenses are illegal—some are just unethical. Because of the importance of ethical behavior within the environment of computerized AISs, we also discuss key issues related to the intersections of AISs and ethics. Finally, the last section of our chapter addresses the importance of privacy and identity theft. The dramatic increase in the number of individuals, companies, and organizations using the Internet draws our attention to the question of privacy. What information is collected about us and how much of it is authorized? Also, how much of it is freely provided by individuals who do not realize that others will store and use the information for purposes other than what was intended? Accordingly, we focus on the issue of collection and protection of information.

10.2   CYBERCRIME AND FRAUD

Articles in *Fortune, BusinessWeek, Wall Street Journal, Computerworld, Security Focus,* and *WIRED* all testify to the high level of public interest in computer crime. At least three reputable organizations conduct surveys that help us understand the breadth and depth of cybercrime. First, the **Computer Security Institute (CSI)** conducts an annual survey to help determine the scope of cybercrime in the United States. The respondents to this survey are computer security practitioners in US corporations, government agencies, financial institutions, medical institutions, and universities.

Second, KPMG, a global network of professional firms providing audit, tax, and advisory services, conducts surveys on fraud and business integrity. Survey participants are business professionals who work for one of the top 2,000 companies listed in Dun and Bradstreet. Third, the **Association of Certified Fraud Examiners (ACFE)**—an international professional organization committed to detecting, deterring, and preventing fraud and white-collar crime—conducts a biannual survey and publishes the results in its *Report to the Nation on Occupational Fraud and Abuse*. The participants in this survey are its members, each of whom provides detailed information on one occupational fraud case he or she had personally investigated within the past 2 years.

Distinguishing between Cybercrime and Fraud

Cybercrime is a general term that refers to any criminal activity that involves computers or networks. Cybercrime can involve direct attacks on computers or networks, using such methods as viruses or **denial of service (DOS) attacks**, or cybercrime can employ computers or networks to commit a crime. Computers may be used, for example, to steal identities, harass an individual, or commit fraud.

Fraud can be defined as an intentional act of deceit or concealment in which the victim suffers some form of loss and/or the fraudster benefits. More often than not,

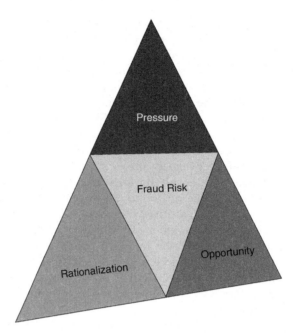

FIGURE 10-1 The Fraud Triangle.

a computer or some form of technology is used to either execute the fraud or to record the consequences or benefits of the fraud. Irrespective of the nature of the fraud, the following must occur:

1. An intentional, dishonest misrepresentation of fact.
2. An intentional attempt to cause another person or business to do or refrain from doing something that causes loss.

One of the more well-known frameworks for understanding the nature of fraud is the Fraud Triangle. The **Fraud Triangle** suggests that three "root causes" or drivers must be present for fraud to occur: pressure, opportunity, and rationalization. The Fraud Triangle is presented in Figure 10-1.

Pressure represents the perceived **need** that motivates someone to commit the fraud. Pressures come in many forms and from a variety of sources. For example, financial pressures can include the need to sustain an extravagant lifestyle, resulting from living beyond one's means, credit issues, or sudden financial needs. Vices also can serve as a pressure to commit fraud. Drug addiction, gambling debts, and extramarital affairs are often the inducements that create a strain on existing resources, thereby serving as the lever to commit fraud. Finally, work-related pressures can lead someone to commit fraud. Unobtainable sales or bonus goals, feeling personally tied to the success or failure of a business venture, or being overlooked for promotion can all trigger fraud.

Opportunity exists when a reasonable expectation exists that the fraud will go undetected, or there will be no consequences. Weak or ineffective internal controls, especially those embedded in the AIS, often present the chance someone needs to commit a fraud. A guest speaker in one of the authors' classes sums it up best: "An effective system of internal controls is in place to protect people from themselves." His

Asset Class	Type of Fraud	Example
Cash	Larceny Skimming	Direct theft or removal from bank deposit Nonreporting or underreporting of sales Write-offs of legitimate receivables as bad debts Lapping schemes
	Fraudulent disbursements	Payments to ghost companies or employees Payments for fictitious goods or services Multiple payments for the same bill Forged checks Altered payee on legitimate check False refunds
Inventory and all other assets	Misuse Larceny	Use of corporate limousine or jet for personal travel Theft of raw materials or finished goods Fictitious inventory adjustments Nonreporting or underreporting of received goods

FIGURE 10-2 Examples of asset misappropriation.

point is simple: everyone, at some point, will arrive at a place where their conscience fails them. An effective system of internal controls should remove the expectation that the fraudulent act will go undetected.

In essence, **rationalization** allows fraudsters to overcome their consciences. It can be viewed as a coping mechanism to allow them to believe that they've done nothing wrong or that the fraudulent act was justified. Fraudsters often rationalize embezzlement by convincing themselves that they'll pay the money back. In white-collar settings, fraudsters may rationalize falsifying financial statements by convincing themselves that not meeting analysts' expectations (and the resulting drop in stock price) would unduly burden too many good people. At the end of the day, fraudsters have to convince themselves that what they're doing is justifiable.

The American Institute of Certified Public Accountants (AICPA) tends to view fraud in a narrower context, especially as it relates to financial statements and the external audit. Statement on Auditing Standards No. 99 identifies two types of accounting-related fraud: (1) fraudulent financial reporting and (2) misappropriation of assets.[2] *Fraudulent financial reporting* (sometimes called "cooking the books") occurs when corporate officials such as senior-ranking executives intentionally falsify accounting records to mislead analysts, creditors, or investors. As a result, the annual financial statements do not fairly represent the true financial condition of the firm. Corporate scandals discussed in Chapter 1 are examples of this type of fraud.

Misappropriation of assets involves stealing assets from a company and is usually committed by employees within an organization or through collusion of employees and outside conspirators. The ACFE calls this type of crime *occupational fraud* and has developed a "fraud tree" to describe the many ways that employees can misappropriate assets from an organization. Examples include skimming, larceny, payroll tampering, and check tampering. Figure 10-2 gives several examples of asset misappropriation. Many of these activities directly involve AISs.

Individuals can also use computers and networks to conduct unethical activities that do not violate criminal law or involve fraud. **Computer abuse** means that someone, who does not have permission, uses or accesses someone else's computer or causes

---

[2] AICPA. 2003. Statement on Auditing Standards No. 99, *Consideration of Fraud in a Financial Statement Audit.*

1. A graduate student infected a campus computer network with a virus that eventually disrupted over 10,000 different systems. The student did not realize how quickly the virus would get out of control.

2. In a fit of resentment and anger, a data entry clerk shattered the screen of her computer with her shoe.

3. Some employees of a credit bureau sent notices to individuals listed in its files as "bad credit risks." For a fee, the employees would withhold damaging information, thereby improving the credit-worthiness of the individuals who paid the fee.

4. A programmer changed a program that calculated dividends paid to shareholders such that the dividends of selected stockholders were reduced and the remaining dividends were paid into an account owned by the programmer. The programmer was able to pay himself over $100,000 using this scheme.

FIGURE 10-3 Examples of computer crimes.

damage without intention to harm. Computer abusers can be considered mischievous pests with motives such as "revenge" or "challenge." Of course, individuals seeking revenge or challenge through computer abuse can violate criminal laws, and their actions then become cybercrimes.

Case-in-Point 10.1 In an effort to draw attention to high school football players who were under arrest for assaulting a fellow student, a pair of Winchester, KY, men hacked into the local high school's athletics fan website. In addition to posting a video of one of the perpetrators wearing a mask and reading a manifesto, the pair used social media to hawk their hack in an attempt to gain notoriety. They also downloaded the administrator's private e-mails and posted false claims on the website that the administrator was engaged in salacious illegal activity. The pair subsequently entered a guilty plea and are now enjoying an extended vacation at one of the Federal Bureau of Prison's all-inclusive resorts. These charming extended-stay destinations include luxurious semiprivate accommodations, gourmet meals, and breathtaking vistas of cinder-block walls and razor-band topped fences. No need to pack a bag; clothing and toiletries are provided.[3]

Figure 10-3 provides several examples of cybercrime, fraud, or abuse. Consider the examples in the figure and see if you can classify each before reading further.

In the first example, the primary objective was to disrupt a computer network, but there is no clear evidence of misrepresentation that creates a loss. Thus, this example would be a cybercrime, but not fraud. In the second case, a computer screen was damaged, and there is clear abuse, but the loss would likely not be considered a criminal offense. In the third example, the attempt to sell credit information would be a criminal offense, but it would not constitute fraud because there is no misrepresentation of fact. Finally, the fourth case involved a misrepresentation and losses to stockholders, and this is an example of a crime that is classified as fraud.

Cybercrime Legislation

Formal definitions of cybercrime and fraud can be found in law. Such definitions are important because they determine what law enforcement officials can prosecute as

---

[3] U.S. Department of Justice press release. "Winchester Man Sentenced to 24 Months for Illegally Hacking into Website and Lying to Federal Agents." www.justice.gov, accessed in March 2017.

Fair Credit Reporting Act of 1970. This act requires that an individual be informed why he or she is denied credit. The act also entitles the individual to challenge information maintained by the credit-rating company and to add information if desired. Seven years after this law was put into effect, the annual number of complaints filed under it exceeded 200,000.

Freedom of Information Act of 1970. This is a federal "sunshine law" guaranteeing individuals the right to see any information gathered about them by federal agencies.

Federal Privacy Act of 1974. This act goes further than the Freedom of Information Act of 1970 by requiring that individuals be able to correct federal information about themselves, by requiring that agency information not be used for alternate purposes without the individual's consent, and by making the collecting agency responsible for the accuracy and use of the information. Under this act, an individual may ask a federal judge to order the correction of errors if the federal agency does not do so.

Small Business Computer Security and Education Act of 1984. This act created an educational council that meets annually to advise the Small Business Administration on a variety of computer crime and security issues affecting small businesses.

Computer Fraud and Abuse Act of 1986. This act makes it a federal crime to intentionally access a computer for purposes such as (1) obtaining top-secret military information or personal financial or credit information; (2) committing a fraud; or (3) altering or destroying federal information.

Computer Fraud and Abuse Act (1996 amendment). This act prohibits unauthorized access to a protected computer and illegal possession of stolen "access devices," which includes passwords and credit card numbers.

Computer Security Act of 1987. This act requires more than 550 federal agencies to develop computer security plans for each computer system that processes sensitive information. The plans are reviewed by the National Institute of Standards and Technology (NIST).

USA Patriot Act of 2001. This act gives federal authorities much wider latitude in monitoring Internet usage and expands the way such data is shared among different agencies. However, a judge must oversee the FBI's use of an e-mail wiretap, and the FBI must disclose what was collected, by whom, and who had access to the information that was collected.

Cyber Security Enhancement Act of 2002. This act permits the United States Sentencing Commission to review and, if appropriate, amend guidelines and policy statements applicable to persons convicted of a computer crime to reflect the serious nature of (1) the growing incidence of computer crimes, (2) the need for an effective deterrent, and (3) appropriate punishment to help prevent such offenses.

CAN-SPAM Act of 2003. This act requires unsolicited commercial e-mail messages to be labeled, to include opt-out instructions, and to include the sender's physical address. It prohibits the use of deceptive subject lines and false headers in messages. This law took effect on January 1, 2004.

FIGURE 10-4 Federal legislation affecting the use of computers.

well as how statistics on crimes are accumulated. Both federal and state statutes govern cybercrime.

Federal Legislation. Figure 10-4 lists some important federal legislation governing activities involving computers. Of these acts, the most important is probably the **Computer Fraud and Abuse Act of 1986** (CFAA), which was last amended in 2008. The CFAA defines cybercrime as any illegal act for which knowledge of computer technology is essential for its perpetration, investigation, or prosecution. The following paragraphs identify the criminal acts found in the CFAA and give examples of each type of crime. The CFAA has been revised eight times between 1988 and 2008, with most of these revisions focusing on the nature and severity of penalties. There are fierce and continuing debates about its effectiveness because much of its language was developed before the Internet boom and the creation of modern communications devices. Many worry that the act is outdated and classifies noncriminal activities as serious crimes.

1. ***Unauthorized Theft, Use, Access, Modification, Copying, or Destruction of Software or Data.*** The PC manager at a King Soopers supermarket in Colorado was called repeatedly to correct computer errors that were thought to be responsible for a large number of sales voids and other accounting errors. Eventually, the company discovered that this manager was in fact the cause of these problems. Over the course of 5 or more years, officials estimate that he and two head clerks used a number of simple methods to steal more than $2 million from the company—for example, by voiding sales transactions and pocketing the customers' cash payments.

2. ***Theft of Money by Altering Computer Records or the Theft of Computer Time.*** To commit an inventory fraud, several employees at an East Coast railroad entered data into their company's computer system to show that more than 200 railroad cars were scrapped or destroyed. These employees then removed the cars from the railroad system, repainted them, and sold them.

3. ***Intent to Illegally Obtain Information or Tangible Property through the Use of Computers.*** One case of industrial espionage involved Reuters Analytics, whose employees were accused of breaking into the computers of their competitor, Bloomberg, and stealing lines of programming code. These instructions were supposedly used in software that provides financial institutions with the capability to analyze historical data on the stock market.

4. ***Use or the Conspiracy to Use Computer Resources to Commit a Felony.*** Paul Sjiem-Fat used desktop publishing technology to perpetrate one of the first cases of computer forgery. Sjiem-Fat created bogus cashier's checks and used these checks to buy computer equipment, which he subsequently sold in the Caribbean. He was caught while trying to steal $20,000 from the Bank of Boston. The bank called in the Secret Service, which raided his apartment and found nine bogus checks totaling almost $150,000. Sjiem-Fat was prosecuted and sent to prison.

5. ***Theft, Vandalism, or Destruction of Computer Hardware.*** A disgruntled taxpayer became enraged over his tax bill. He was arrested for shooting at an IRS computer through an open window of the building.

6. ***Trafficking in Passwords or Other Login Information for Accessing a Computer.*** Two former software developers of Interactive Connection (now known as Screaming Media) were arrested for breaking into Interactive's computer system one night. They allegedly stayed on the system for about 4 hours and copied proprietary files and software.

7. ***Extortion That Uses a Computer System as a Target.*** A disgruntled employee of a European company removed all of the company's tape files from the computer room. He then drove to an off-site storage location and demanded half a million dollars for their return. He was arrested while trying to exchange the data files for the ransom money.

State Legislation. Every state now has at least one computer-crime law. Most of the laws have provisions that (1) define computer terms (many of which vary from state to state), (2) define some acts as misdemeanors (minor crimes), and (3) declare other acts as felonies (major crimes). These laws require willful intent for criminal convictions. Thus, words such as *maliciously, intentionally,* or *recklessly* often appear in the wording of the computer-crime laws, and willful intent must be established for a successful prosecution.

Cybercrime Statistics

No one really knows how much is lost each year as a result of cybercrime. One reason for this is the fact that a large proportion of cybercrime takes place in private companies, where it is handled as an internal matter. We have no laws that require private organizations to report all computer offenses. But the most important reason we know so little about computer offenses is because most of it is likely not discovered. Recently, for example, the FBI estimated that only 1% of all cybercrime is detected. Other estimates of cybercrime detection are between 5% and 20%. Computer criminals are primarily caught as a result of luck, chance, or accident. This is why experts believe the cybercrime that is detected is only the tip of the iceberg.

Despite our lack of complete statistics, there are several reasons why experts believe cybercrime is growing. One reason is the exponential growth in the use of computer resources (e.g., computer networks, the Internet, smart devices, and cloud systems). As more people become knowledgeable about how to use devices and networks, more people are in a position to compromise systems.

Another reason why experts believe cybercrime is growing is because of continuing lax security. There are countless computer and wireless device users in the world, but many of them are not aware of, or conscientious about, computer security. In addition, many websites now give step-by-step instructions that detail how to perpetrate cybercrimes. For example, an Internet search by the authors found more than 50 million matches for "denial of service," and there are many thousands of websites that detail how to break into computer systems or disable Web servers.

Case-in-Point 10.2 Shortly after the 2016 US presidential election, the hacker group "Anonymous" posted detailed instructions on how to break into President-elect Donald Trump's personal smartphone. The instructions, which went out to Anonymous' almost 2 million Twitter followers, named a specific malware that would compromise the phone. In commenting on the ease with which the device could be compromised, Anonymous quipped that it would be "the sort of project I would assign as homework for my advanced undergraduate classes."[4]

The FBI, in partnership with the National White Collar Crime Center, established the Internet Fraud Complaint Center (IFCC) in May 2000 to provide cybercrime victims a point of contact for reporting computer crime and abuses. The IFCC changed its name in December 2003 to the Internet Crime Complaint Center (IC3) to reflect the broad nature of complaints that it handles, including international money laundering, online extortion, intellectual property theft, identity theft, online scams, and computer intrusions. In 2015, there were over 288,000 fraud complaints filed that represent a dollar loss of $1,070,711,522. This is compared to only 75,000 complaints in 2002. The majority of the complaints in 2015 were received from individuals in California (14.5%), Florida (8.5%), and Texas (7.7%), and some of the most common crimes reported involved nonpayment/nondelivery, identity theft, and online auction fraud.[5]

---

[4] Hamil, J. "Anonymous Hacktivists Publish Guide on How to Hack Donal Trump's Smartphone," www.thesun.co.uk, accessed in March 2017.
[5] Internet Crime Complaint Center, 2015 Internet Crime Report, ic3.gov, accessed in March 2017.

10.3 EXAMPLES OF CYBERCRIME

Cybercrime is perhaps best understood by studying selected cases. As one reads the fascinating accounts of different crimes, a pattern begins to emerge. Crimes related to accounting systems often involve the falsification of data or unauthorized access to data and files. This section of the chapter examines several cases of cybercrime that exemplify specific threats.

Compromising Valuable Information

A major class of accounting-related cybercrime involves illegal access to, or misuse of, the information stored in AISs. In the TRW Credit Data case, the information involved was credit data. TRW (now called Experian) was one of several large credit-rating companies in the United States. When the fraud was discovered, the company was collecting and disseminating credit information on approximately 50 million individuals. Clients of TRW included banks, retail stores, and credit-conscious concerns such as Diner's Club, American Express, MasterCard, and Visa.

TRW advised its clients of bad credit risks on the basis of the information maintained in its databases. However, this information could be changed. The fraud began when six company employees, including a key TRW clerk in the consumer relations department, realized this fact and began selling good credit to individuals with bad credit ratings. The names and addresses of the bad credit risks were already on file. It merely remained to contact these individuals and inform them of a newfound method of altering their records. Accordingly, the perpetrators approached individuals with bad credit ratings and offered them a clean bill of health in return for a "management fee." Those people who decided to buy good credit ratings paid TRW employees "under the table," and the clerk in the consumer relations department then inserted into TRW's credit files whatever false information was required to reverse the individual's bad credit rating. In some cases, this required deleting unfavorable information that was already stored in the individual's credit record. In others, it required adding favorable information. Fees for such services varied from a few hundred dollars to $1,500 per individual. Ironically, the TRW clerk who input the false information to the computer system received only $50 for each altered record. However, the losses resulting from these activities were not so inconsequential. Independent estimates have placed this figure at close to $1 million.

The principal victims of the fraud were TRW's clients who acted on credit information that was inaccurate. Exactly how many file records were altered is difficult to determine. Lawyers for the prosecution documented 16 known cases of altered file records, but had reason to believe the number exceeded 100 cases. Paradoxically, the prosecution had difficulty acquiring testimonies because the buyers of good credit ratings as well as the TRW sellers were also in violation of the law by conspiring to falsify credit-rating information.

Analysis. **Data diddling** refers to changing data before, during, or after they are entered into a computer system. The change can delete, alter, or add important system data, especially data stored in corporate databases. This is a problem because these data (1) are often proprietary, (2) may give a firm a competitive advantage, and (3) are sometimes an organization's most valuable asset (think eBay, for example). Finally, because the data processing tasks in most computerized AIS job streams are automated, data that are input manually to a system are particularly vulnerable to compromise.

The TRW case involves two key issues: (1) the accuracy of the inputs used to update a specific AIS and (2) the protection of users of credit information and protection of the individuals whose credit information is gathered by a private company. With regard to the first point, it is clear that the fraud was successful only because the perpetrators were able to enter false information into the accounting system. This observation points to the importance of control procedures (e.g., the authorization and validation of credit changes) that safeguard the accuracy and completeness of information. As with many cases of cybercrime, the six TRW employees involved in the fraud were caught only by chance: an individual approached with an offer to buy a good credit rating for $600 became angry and called the FBI. Later, the TRW clerk in the consumer relations department decided to confess.

The second point, which involves protection of individuals' credit information and protection of the users of this credit information, encompasses a much larger issue. In 1970, Congress passed the Fair Credit Reporting Act, which requires that an individual be told why he or she is denied credit. The consumer also has the right to contest the information maintained by the credit-rating company, although there is clearly a vast difference between the right to *challenge,* versus the right to *change,* credit information.

Shortly after the Fair Credit Reporting Act went into effect, TRW reported consumer inquiries increased 100-fold, and at the time the fraud was detected, approximately 200,000 consumers annually were complaining about their credit ratings. The fact that, by TRW's own admission, fully one-third of these inquiries resulted in a file change or update is unsettling. Moreover, it is not known how much more information collected by TRW is still inaccurate but simply not challenged—for example, because an individual is not aware of an inaccuracy, or because the consumer does not know his or her rights under the law.

Hacking[6,7]

In one of the most widely publicized hacks of this decade, **hackers** stole credit and debit card information from more than 40 million customers of Target stores. Customers who purchased goods from Target stores during the Christmas shopping season were targeted by malware called BlackPOS, which was written by a Russian teenager who sold his malware to hackers. The malware was installed onto credit card reading machines in Target stores. The stolen data allowed cyber criminals to create replica credit cards, withdraw funds from ATMs, and use stolen credit card information to make purchases.

While the Target attack can be viewed as a watershed moment with respect to credit card information being compromised, the frequency with which credit card information finds its way into the hands of hackers is alarming. In March 2017, a US District Judge sentenced Iranian national Milad Kalantari to 10 years in prison for selling stolen credit card information online. Kalantari was arrested upon re-entry into the United States and ultimately pleaded guilty to conspiracy to commit identity theft and access device fraud

---

[6] Wallace, G. Target credit card hack. What you need to know. *CNNMoney* (money.cnn.com) (December 23, 2013).

[7] U.S. Department of Justice Press Release. "Iranian Member of International Cybercrime Conspiracy Sentenced to 10 Years in Prison for Selling Stolen Credit Card Information." www.justice.gov, accessed in March 2017.

and substantive access device fraud. Kalantari operated a global network of websites that sold approximately 2.5 million stolen credit and debit card numbers. Discover and American Express alone accounted for more than $30 million of the estimated $1.2 billion intended loss value.

Analysis. Hacking is a widespread problem. This is due, in part, to the fact that many computer applications now involve cloud, local, and wide area networks, where computer files become accessible to unauthorized users. With the widespread use of cloud-based and Internet-based services, users are able to log onto a vast array of systems from remote sites, again increasing vulnerability to hacking.

Case-in-Point 10.3 At the University of Central Missouri, investigators traced a hacking scheme to two students and then raided the dorm room where the plot was hatched—only to find a Post-It note stuck to a computer monitor that read "too late!" with a smiley face on it. However, the students were apprehended and were charged with computer intrusion causing damage, computer intrusion to further a fraud scheme, computer intrusion to obtain information, intercepting electronic communication, and two counts of aggravated identity theft.[8]

Many hackers brag that they can compromise any type of information once they have successfully logged into a computer system. One way they achieve this is to elevate their system status to that of a "super user" or "network manager," which are security levels that gain the hackers access to password files, system control data, and other high-security information. These activities are thwarted by using system programming routines that test for and deny such techniques and that also immediately communicate such attempts to computer supervisors as possible security violations.

One of the most useful protections against hacking is **encryption**, which protects transmitted data that might be intercepted en route and also stored data, which are rendered useless to a hacker even if he or she manages to gain access to files that are protected by other means. Encryption is also useful in networking situations because a properly encrypted password further ensures that an authentic user sent it. Lawsuits have recently been initiated against Target stores after a hacking attack because of claims that Target failed to adequately encrypt credit card data.

Organizations can also test their vulnerability to hacking by hiring **ethical hackers**. These are network and computer experts who purposefully attack a secured system to help its owners find any vulnerabilities that could be exploited by a malicious hacker. Ethical hackers use the same methods as malicious hackers to test a security system, but instead of taking advantage of these vulnerabilities, they report them to management. Ethical hacking is also referred to as **intrusion testing**, **penetration testing**, and red teaming. There is even a certification for this line of work, called a Certified Ethical Hacker.[9]

Another helpful practice is "user education"—that is, making potential hackers aware of the ethics of computer usage and the inconvenience, lost time, and costs incurred by victim organizations. **Strong passwords** are also helpful, but passwords are not foolproof mechanisms because, at present, many systems cannot distinguish

[8] "Joseph Camp and Daniel Fowler indicted for computer hacking at University of Central Missouri," Posted by Justin Kendall, November 23, 2010, The Pitch Blogs (www.pitch.com).
[9] Ethical Hacking and Countermeasures to Become a Certified Ethical Hacker, EC-Council Certification (www.eccouncil.org).

between authorized employees using their own passwords and unauthorized users entering compromised passwords. Thus, until biometric authentications such as retina scans or other cost-effective intrusion detection systems become widely available, protecting passwords is paramount. We will review some methods for this in a later section of the chapter.

Denial of Service[10,11,12]

On October 21, 2016, a sophisticated distributed denial of service (DDoS) attack was launched against domain name system (DNS) provider Dyn. Utilizing the Mirai malware and countless IoT devices, hackers were able to create a sizeable botnet that "broke the Internet." Before the dust settled, such popular websites as Twitter, Spotify, Paypal, Pinterest, Netflix, and a host of companies utilizing Amazon Web Services were crippled or unreachable for large blocks of time.

How did this happen? DNS servers are the backbone of the Internet, as they resolve domain names to IP addresses for servers. For example, when you type www.cnn.com into a Web browser, a DNS server somewhere resolves that domain name to the network address (151.101.64.73) assigned to the server hosting the website. Since most people can remember an URL easier than they can a seemingly random series of numbers, DNS providers and their servers play a critical role in Internet traffic and e-mail. Hackers used the Mirai malware tool to take advantage of unsecured **Internet of Things (IoT)** devices where the owners hadn't changed the default passwords, and created a botnet of countless devices. A **botnet** is a network of Internet-connected devices that are infected with malware; botnets are controlled by a hacker or group of hackers and are used for malicious intent without the true owners' knowledge or consent. The person behind Mirai directed the botnet to simultaneously and continuously send junk network traffic to Dyn's DNS servers, thereby making them unreachable to legitimate traffic and blocking a who's who of websites.

Ultimately, the person behind the Mirai malware was discovered. Numerous online outlets and noted information security blogger Brian Krebs reported that Mirai author "Anna-Senpai" worked for a company that sold DDoS protection services for *Minecraft,* a best-selling online sandbox video game. "Anna-Senpai" ultimately released the code for Mirai into the wild, allowing numerous copycats to perpetrate similar attacks in subsequent weeks.

Analysis. DOS attacks can take multiple forms and often involve malware. **Malware** is a term for many types of malicious or damaging software. Common examples are viruses, worms, and Trojan horses. A **virus** is code that attaches itself to other innocent files or programs and replicates itself. At some point, the code activates and destroys computer files, disrupts operating system activities, damages software, or initiates DOS attacks.

Computer **worms** also replicate themselves repeatedly like a virus, and they can consume internal memory, disk space, and Internet bandwidth. Unfortunately, the

---

[10] Waterman, S. "2016: The Year IoT Broke the Internet," accessed at www.cyberscoop.com in March 2017.
[11] Wawro, A. "Report: Internet-breaking DDoS work traced to Chief of *Minecraft*-focused DDoS Guard Firm," accessed at www.gamasutra.com in March 2017.
[12] Krebs, B. "Who is Anna-Senpai, the Mirai Worm Author?," accessed at www.krebsonsecurity.com in March 2017.

Internet facilitates the spread of viruses and worms from one system to another, making them a popular form of computer crime and also abuse. In DDoS attacks, a single virus or worm program enlists the aid of innocent Internet-connected devices (botnet), which then send e-mail messages to, or request services from, the target system. The barrage of incoming mail or service requests then overwhelms the target system, typically requiring its owners to disable it.

Viruses often reside on secondary storage media, where they hide until finding an opportunity to execute. There are several variations of these viruses. **Boot-sector viruses** hide in the boot sectors of a disk, where the operating system accesses them every time it accesses the disk itself. **Trojan horse programs** reside in the disk space occupied by legitimate copies of computer programs, for example, spreadsheet programs. **Logic bomb** programs are similar to Trojan horse programs, except that they remain dormant until the computer system encounters a specific condition, such as a particular day of the year or a particular Social Security number in a file. Trojan horse and logic bomb programs are termed "programs" rather than "viruses" because they sometimes contain code to defraud users, while viruses are more likely to destroy or disrupt computer resources.

The Internet is a perfect environment for computer viruses because of its widespread use for e-mail, conducting research, and downloading files or software. For example, a virus might be stored in a java **applet** (i.e., a small program stored in a Web page file and designed to run by Web browser software). Friendly applets animate Web pages, allow users to play games, or perform processing tasks. But unfriendly applets contain viruses that can infect computers and cause damage.

A computer virus that is lodged on a file server can affect thousands of other computers or servers before it is detected and eliminated. Estimating the business costs of recovering from a virus infection is difficult. The costs can be small—for example, limited to the inconveniences of reformatting a hard disk and reloading a few software programs, or the costs can be huge—by some estimates, billions of dollars annually.

There are a number of ways to prevent computer viruses. These include: (1) **firewalls**, which limit external access to company computers; (2) antivirus software; and (3) antivirus control procedures. **Antivirus software** are computer programs that scan inputs for malware and virus-like coding, identify active malware already lodged in computer systems, clean infected systems, or perform some combination of these activities. Recent versions of Microsoft's Windows operating system incorporate software of this type. Generally speaking, however, antivirus programs provide less than complete protection because misguided individuals continuously write new, more powerful malware that can avoid current detection schemes. Even worse, some antivirus programs have themselves contained viruses and other malware.

Perhaps one of the most vulnerable areas is e-mail. Consider the number of e-mails you send and receive every day, and then multiply that by the number of people at your university, and you can understand why the risk of passing a virus around is very high. Unfortunately, viruses can hide in e-mails from friends and colleagues because their computer systems have been infected. To help mitigate this problem, many organizations most likely uses an antispam software solution in addition to antivirus software.

For many, antivirus control procedures are often better safeguards. These include: (1) buying software from reputable sources, (2) avoiding illegal software copying, (3) not downloading suspicious files from the Internet, (4) deleting e-mail messages from unknown sources before opening them, and (5) maintaining complete backup files in the event you must rebuild your system from scratch. Additional safeguards include being wary of public-domain software available on the Internet and being suspicious of unusual activity on your computer system—for example, spontaneous disk writing that you did not initiate.

In organizational settings, effective control procedures against computer viruses include educating users about viruses and encouraging computer users to follow the virus prevention and detection techniques just discussed. Additional control procedures include (1) adopting policies that discourage externally acquired computer programs, (2) requiring strong passwords that limit unauthorized access to computing resources, and (3) using antivirus filters on networks.

10.4 PREVENTING AND DETECTING CYBERCRIME AND FRAUD

What can organizations do to protect themselves against cybercrime and fraud? Experts note that, for all their intricacy and mystique, we can protect computer systems from crimes, abuses, and fraud just as well as we can manual systems and sometimes better. For example, systems can be programmed to automatically search for anomalies and to print exception conditions on control reports. These computerized monitoring systems are often superior to manual surveillance methods because they are automatic and can screen 100% of transactions and processes, instead of merely a sample of the target population data. The New York Stock Exchange now uses an **Integrated Computer-Assisted Surveillance System (ICASS)** to search for insider trading activities. This section of the chapter discusses several methods for preventing and detecting cybercrime.

Enlist Top-Management Support

Most employees do not automatically follow organizational security policies and procedures—they are rarely rewarded for it and understanding security can take time away from the activities for which they are directly rewarded. This is why experts agree that computer security begins (or ends) with top management and security policies. Without such policies, for example, organizations can only expect limited employee compliance with security procedures, sensitivity to potential problems, or awareness of the importance of computer abuse. Unfortunately, many top managers are not fully aware of the dangers of cybercrime, abuse, and fraud themselves, and they are therefore not sufficiently concerned about this type of offense. This is why security safeguards are only effective if top management takes cybercrime seriously and chooses to financially support and enforce control procedures to stop, or at least minimize, cybercrimes. The complaint of many mid-level security managers is that they must be able to justify their funding requests for investments in appropriate levels of security for a firm. In fact, the importance that top managers place on computer safeguards can potentially be measured by the level of funding they allocate to IT security.

Increase Employee Awareness and Education

Ultimately, controlling cybercrime means controlling people. But which people? Many computer abusers are the employees of the same companies at which the crimes take place. Many retail firms have clear prosecution policies regarding shoplifting.

In contrast, prosecution policies associated with other types of employee fraud are notable for their absence in many organizations. Yet, the evidence suggests that prosecuting cybercrimes may be one of the most effective restraints.

In fairness, employees cannot be expected to automatically understand the problems or ramifications of cybercrime. Thus, another dimension of preventing cybercrime is employee education. Informing employees of the significance of crime and abuse, the amount it costs, and the disruptions they create can help employees understand why computer offenses are a serious matter. Studies suggest that informal discussions, periodic departmental memos, and formal guidelines are among the most popular educational tools for informing employees about crime and abuse. Requiring new hires to sign security statements indicating that they have received, read, and understand policy statements can also be beneficial.

One final idea regarding employee conduct comes from the 2016 ACFE *Report to the Nations*. This survey revealed that almost half of all the fraud reported by the survey's respondents was not detected by internal controls or audits, but rather from tips obtained from fellow employees, customers, or vendors. Given the value of such information, a prudent managerial policy is to provide channels that employees can use to report suspicious activity—for example, by allowing them to communicate with management anonymously through company websites. Indeed, public companies are now required to provide anonymous whistle-blowing channels to their employees. This and rewarding employees for providing information may be two of the most effective things that organizations can do to curb fraud and embezzlement.

Assess Security Policies and Protect Passwords

Common sense dictates that organizations should regularly survey their computer and mobile device security measures and assess potential areas of vulnerability. Nearly all organizations use firewalls, antivirus software, and access controls, but many are not as conscientious about performing periodic security reviews. An important security process that organizations should consider is evaluating employee practices and educating users to protect their own devices. Figure 10-5 provides a list of 10 recommended steps for safeguarding personal computers. Similar safeguards apply to laptop computers, tablets, and mobile devices.

Protecting passwords is an important dimension of computer security because passwords are the "keys to the kingdom" (of valuable corporate data). Hackers use a variety of tactics to steal passwords, including posing as a legitimate user and "borrowing" them from unsuspecting employees, creating phishing websites that ask users to input their passwords "for security purposes," or using simulation programs that try all the words in a standard dictionary as potential passwords. To help foil these tactics, users should be trained to not "loan" their passwords to others or tape them to their monitors, understand that most businesses will not ask for their passwords via the Internet, and use strong passwords—that is, passwords that are difficult to guess. Examples of strong passwords are long, nonsense words (e.g., words not found in dictionaries) or words with embedded capitals or random numbers. Another control is to install password-checking software on file servers that tests passwords for such requirements. A third control is to require employees to change their passwords periodically.

Hackers often use a tactic called **social engineering** to gain access to passwords. Sometimes, this means posing as bona fide employees and convincing network administrators to give them passwords over the phone. In other cases, the social engineer

1. **Keep your firewall turned on.** Firewalls help protect your computer from hackers who might try to gain access to it, delete information, or steal passwords or other sensitive information.

2. **Install or update your antivirus software.** Antivirus software helps protect your computer from malicious code such as viruses or worms and can be set to update automatically.

3. **Install or update your antispyware technology.** Spyware is just software that is secretly installed on your computer and that allows others to observe your activities on it. Inexpensive antispyware software is readily available for download on the Internet or at local computer stores.

4. **Keep your operating system up to date.** Software developers regularly update their operating systems to stay current with technology requirements and fix security holes.

5. **Do not provide personal information online.** Hackers create phishing websites to lure visitors into providing their personal information and therefore steal their identity. Many people share too much information on social media websites; much of this can be used for social engineering purposes.

6. **Be careful what you download.** Downloading e-mail attachments can thwart even the most vigilant antivirus software. Never open an e-mail attachment from someone you don't know, and be wary of forwarded attachments from anyone. For links embedded in e-mails, always pass your cursor over the link to ensure that the target destination matches the text on the hyperlink.

7. **Change default passwords.** Most Internet-enabled devices (routers, Blu-ray players, cameras, and the like) come with a default password or PIN number (usually ADMIN or 0000). These defaults are well-known among hackers and allow easy access to your device and files. Always change the default password to something easy to remember but difficult to guess or compromise.

8. **Create backups often.** Computers are not infallible, and all hard disk drives eventually fail. Creating duplicate copies of your important files and storing them offsite enables you to easily recover from such problems. The authors recommend the automated backup services of a cloud service provider.

9. **Use surge protectors.** Power surges can "fry" your computer, but even the least expensive surge protector can guard against most such events.

10. **Protect passwords.** Many websites and computer systems now require logon names and passwords, but writing them on sticky notes stuck to your computer's monitor or keyboard is not a good idea. Try to find safer places to store the ones you can't commit to memory. Using mnemonics and a "special character/letter substitution pattern" makes easy work of this (i.e., JameyWorrell becomes J@m3yW0rr311).

FIGURE 10-5   Ten simple steps to safer personal computers.

poses as a new, helpless employee who appears desperate and "borrows" a password from a fellow worker in order to accommodate a fictitious "emergency." While it is advisable to distribute new passwords through external channels rather than through computer systems themselves, the practice of giving passwords to unknown employees compromises standard security procedures and should never be allowed.

Implement Controls

Most cybercrime and abuse succeed because of the *absence* of controls rather than the *failure* of controls. There are many reasons why businesses do not implement control procedures to deter cybercrime. One is the all-too-common belief of those managers who have not suffered a cybercrime that they have nothing to fear. Further, charities and not-for-profit organizations often believe that their mission somehow insulates them from crime. Also, businesses that do not have a specific computer security officer have no one to articulate this concern or to argue for specific control procedures. Finally, at least some businesses do not feel that security measures are cost-effective—until they incur a problem!

Case-in-Point 10.4   To execute a disbursement fraud, one man used a desktop publishing package to prepare fictitious bills for office supplies that he then mailed to companies across the country. He kept the dollar amount on each bill less than $300 and found that an amazingly large percentage of the companies paid the bills without question—probably because many organizations automatically pay vendor invoices for small amounts.

The solution to the computer-security problems of most organizations is straightforward: design and implement controls. This means that organizations should install control procedures to deter cybercrime, managers should enforce them, and both internal and external auditors should test them. Experts also suggest that employee awareness of computer controls and the certainty of prosecution may also act as deterrents to cybercrime. Certainly, the enactment of the Sarbanes–Oxley Act of 2002 has placed a much greater emphasis on strong internal controls, including criminal offenses for senior executives who knowingly disregard such precautions.

Identify Computer Criminals

To prevent specific types of crimes, criminologists often look for common character traits with which to screen potential culprits. What are the characteristics of individuals who commit cybercrimes or abuse, and what can be done to create a composite profile that organizations can use to evaluate job applicants?

Nontechnical Backgrounds.   A company's own employees—not external hackers—perpetrate a significant amount of cybercrime and abuse. How technically competent are such employees? Figure 10-6 identifies the job occupations of computer criminals and abusers from a survey performed by Hoffer and Straub. Although this figure suggests that some computer offenses are committed by those with strong technical backgrounds, this study found that almost as many computer offenses are perpetrated by clerical personnel, data-entry clerks, and similar individuals with limited technical skills. A similar study by the US Sentencing Commission (USSC) found that most of the computer criminals convicted under the Computer Crime and Abuse Act of 1986 were corporate insiders with only "pedestrian levels" of computer expertise. There is good reason for this. It is usually easier and safer to alter data before they enter a computer than midway through automated processing cycles. In addition, input data can often be changed anonymously, whereas most computerized data cannot. These facts explain why many computer criminals are not highly computer literate and also why computer security must extend beyond IT personnel. While computer criminals often lack significant technology skills, large-scale hacking incidents and cybercrimes committed against large corporations and governments are often committed by very sophisticated criminal organizations, foreign governments, and market competitors.

Noncriminal Backgrounds.   The USSC study also found that most of the convicted computer criminals had no prior criminal backgrounds. In addition, most computer criminals tend to view themselves as relatively honest. They argue, for example, that beating the system is not the same as stealing from another person—or that they are merely using a computer to take what other employees take from the supply cabinet.

Programmers and systems analysts	27%
Clerical, data entry, and machine operators	23%
Managers and top executives	15%
Other system users	14%
Students	12%
Consultants	3%
Other information processing staff	3%
All others	3%
Total	100%

FIGURE 10-6 Occupations of computer-abuse offenders.

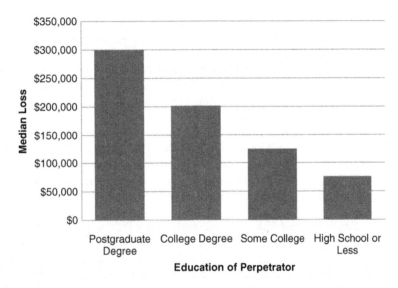

FIGURE 10-7 Median fraud losses, classified by the education level of the perpetrator. Source: *2016 ACFE Report to the Nations.*

Furthermore, many perpetrators think of themselves as long-term borrowers rather than thieves, and several have exercised great care to avoid harming individuals when they committed their computer offenses.

Education. Although most media reports suggest that computer offenders are uniformly bright, motivated, talented, and college-educated individuals, the average computer criminal often does not fit this profile. In the ACFE 2016 *Report to the Nations*, for example, nearly half of the perpetrators did not have a college degree. But, according to the report, highly educated fraudsters steal more when they do commit cybercrimes—see Figure 10-7. However, because we believe that most cybercrime and abuse are not detected—or prosecuted when it is detected—we do not know how representative these observations are for the general population of computer offenders.

Maintain Physical Security

An old adage in the computer security industry is that "a good hammer beats a strong password every time." What this means is that physical safeguards can be even more important than logical ones in deterring computer crime and abuse. For example, did you know that the most common security problem with laptop computers and mobile devices is simple theft? Other examples of physical security include protecting servers and work stations, enforcing "clean-desk policies" for employees, and protecting employee laptops and other mobile devices against theft (see again Figure 10-5).

Case-in-Point 10.5 The administrators at one university believed that their desktop computers were safe as long as employees locked their individual office doors at night. But the university usually kept the buildings unlocked. The folly of this thinking became clear one morning when officials discovered that thieves had simply brought a ladder that allowed them to climb through the false ceiling of a building to steal over 30 PCs from one of the computer labs on campus.

Organizations must also be able to recover from computer security breaches or losses when they do occur. One safeguard is to implement backup procedures. Another safeguard is to develop and test a disaster recovery plan that enables a business to replace its critical computer systems in a timely manner. As suggested by the aforementioned case-in-point, monitoring cameras, motion detectors, and insurance are also important security measures.

Finally, organizations should be careful about how they dispose of outdated electronic devices and computers. While state and federal environmental laws affect such disposals, our primary concern is the sensitive data stored on the hard drives of these devices. Reformatting these drives is usually not enough—the data may still be retrieved with readily available software tools.

Case-in-Point 10.6 As solid-state drives (SSDs) overtake traditional platter-based hard disk drives (HDDs) in laptops and desktop computers, conventional wisdom on wiping the drive goes out the window. HDDs utilize magnetic charges on platters to store data, so placing these next to a strong magnetic field will normally do the trick. Alternatively, drilling holes in the disk destroys the platters, rendering data recovery efforts futile. Not so with SSDs. Since the data is stored on microchips (similar to a USB thumbdrive), they are generally impervious to damage from magnetic force. Similarly, drilling the device could leave some microchips undamaged. Low-level formatting (overwriting all sectors with garbage data), a technique commonly used with HDDs, is not as effective on SDDs. The best bet if you're selling or recycling an SDD-equipped device? Encrypt the drive first, and then low-level format. That way, unless the purchaser has the encryption key, they are unable to recover the data stored on the drive.[13]

Recognize the Symptoms of Employee Fraud

The clues reveal that some computer offenses can be subtle and ambiguous, but many are rather obvious. Although recognizing the symptoms of computer offenses will not prevent cybercrime, knowing the telltale signs may help individuals detect and report it, which can help limit the potential damage to the victim organization.

Case-in-Point 10.7 The Comfortable Shoe (TCS), a fashionable, high-end retail chain, created its own health-care plan for its employees. The plan was self-insured for medical claims

---

[13] Allen, D. "Selling an old SSD? Be Careful How You Deal with Wiping the Drive," accessed at TechRadarPro (www.techradar.com) in March 2017.

under $30,000, which it handled internally, but plan administrators forwarded claims for larger amounts to an independent insurance company. The managers of TCS believed that the company had excellent control procedures for its system, which included both internal and external audits. Yet, over a period of 4 years, the manager of the medical claims department was able to embezzle more than $12 million from the company!

Although the name of the company has been changed, the events just described actually happened at a large company. However, you may be asking yourself how such a huge fraud could occur if the company had an excellent internal control system. Chapter 13 discusses a number of practices and procedures that firms should use to protect against employee wrong-doing in more detail. The following internal control weaknesses were present at TCS and are typical warnings of **computer fraud**.

Accounting Irregularities.   To embezzle funds successfully, employees commonly alter, forge, or destroy input documents, or perform suspicious accounting adjustments. An unusually high number of such irregularities are cause for concern. At TCS, no one noticed that payments to 22 of the physicians submitting claims to the company were sent to the same two addresses. While it is not uncommon for several physicians to form a group practice, it still should have caused TCS management concern that such a large number of doctors were receiving mail at only two addresses.

Internal Control Weaknesses.   At TCS, the medical claims manager had not taken a vacation for years, those employees submitting claims were never sent confirmation notices of the medical payments made in their behalf, and the physicians receiving these payments were never first investigated or approved. Here again, we recognize obvious internal control problems! Managers should require all employees to take vacations. Similarly, management should require reports for all employee claims, and they should require payment confirmation notices to employees—who would almost certainly report erroneous payments that were made on their behalf. TCS, and all firms, should also have an approved list of vendors (i.e., physicians) for payments.

Anomalies.   An important clue that can reveal computer fraud is the presence of anomalies that somehow go unchallenged. Examined critically, such anomalies are unreasonable and require observers to suspend common sense. At TCS, for example, why were 100% of the medical payments to the 22 physicians all paid from the self-insured portion of the company program? Why were checks to those 22 physicians always endorsed by hand and deposited in the same two checking accounts? And why did some of the medical claims include hysterectomies for male employees? Exception reports may have highlighted these unusual items.

Lifestyle Changes.   Employees who miraculously solve pressing financial problems or suddenly begin living extravagant lifestyles are sometimes broadcasting fraud. At TCS, why did the medical claims manager announce that she had inherited a lot of money but never took a vacation? And why did she treat her employees to lunches in chauffeured limousines? An alert supervisor should have recognized such behavior as a red flag.

Behavioral Changes.   Employees who experience guilt or remorse related to their crimes, or who fear discovery, often express these feelings through unusual behavior. At TCS, employees joked that the medical claims manager had developed a "Jekyll and Hyde personality," including intense mood swings that were unusual even for her.

Use Data-Driven Techniques

Organizations collect overwhelming quantities of data with modern accounting and database systems. These data can be employed to seek out indicators of crime and fraud. Two of the current and developing techniques are described as follows.

Query and Spreadsheet Skills. The most basic spreadsheet and database query skills can be valuable fraud detection tools. Imagine, for example, that you are an internal auditor, and you have access to all of your company's sales and credit memo records. You can develop queries or spreadsheet manipulations to look for red flags related to revenue recognition. Such tests would not rely on samples of sales invoices, but would instead involve analyses of all sales records. Potential indicators of fraud that could be detected would include items such as end-of-year sales that are reversed by credit memos at the beginning of the next year, sales or credit memos that are not properly authorized, sales made after hours or during holidays, and sales made at amounts just below requirements for authorization.

Data and Text Mining. Big data has become a hot topic in the AIS community. Big data refers to the fact that many organizations now capture nearly endless quantities of data (transactions, locations from cell phones, e-mail text, social network activity, Internet traffic, GPS data from corporate cars, and the list goes on and on). The huge volumes of data have created a new problem—companies are losing the ability to interpret the data they have collected. Data and text mining are tools that allow for meaningful patterns to be detected in massive data sets. These techniques are rapidly becoming powerful tools for detecting fraud and computer crime. As one example, new software is able to analyze corporate e-mails and identify language patterns that are indicative of employee intent to commit fraud within the organization. Other data mining tools can identify anomalies in accounting data, such as salespeople whose history of phone GPS locations do not match information from travel reimbursement forms.

Employ Forensic Accountants

When an organization suspects an ongoing computer crime or fraud, it can hire forensic accountants to investigate its problem, document findings, and make recommendations. Many such individuals are professional accountants who have passed the 2-day certified fraud examiner (CFE) examination administered by the ACFE. Forensic accounting is one of the fastest-growing areas of accounting, and there are now more than 60,000 members of the ACFE working in organizations such as the FBI, CIA, law firms, and CPA firms. For more information about forensic accounting, visit the ACFE website: www.acfe.org.

Forensic accountants have the required technical and legal experience to research a given concern, follow leads, establish audit trails of questionable transactions, document their findings, organize evidence for external review and law enforcement bodies, and (if necessary) testify in court. Most use specialized software tools to help them perform their tasks—for example, **Audit Control Language (ACL)** for auditing tasks, and **EnCase** for file copying, custody documentation, and other forensic activities.

10.5 ETHICAL ISSUES, PRIVACY, AND IDENTITY THEFT

Fighting cybercrime, abuse, or fraud is sometimes more dependent on ethical behavior than observing legal restrictions. Ethics is a set of moral principles or values. Therefore, ethical behavior involves making choices and judgments that are morally acceptable and acting accordingly. Ethics can govern organizations as well as individuals. In the context of an organization, an underlying ethical principle is that each individual in the organization has responsibility for the welfare of others within the organization, as well as for the organization itself. For example, the managers of a company should make decisions that are fair to the employees as well as beneficial to the organization.

Ethical Issues and Professional Associations

Ethical concerns are often an issue in instances of computer abuse. In cases involving hacking, for example, ignorance of proper conduct or misguided playfulness may be the problem. To some, the challenge of defrauding a computer system and avoiding detection is irresistible because success brings recognition, notoriety, and even heroism. In these cases, ethical issues are overlooked and the costs of recovering from the abuse are ignored. The acceptability of these motives involves issues of morality.

Some argue that "morality" in corporate cultures is a relative term. But is it? In one case, for example, a man named Fred Darm stole a computer program from a rival firm through his computer terminal. At his trial, the defense argued that it was common practice for programmers of rival firms to "snoop" in each other's data files to obtain competitive information. Thus, when he was apprehended for his offense, Darm was not only surprised, he was quite offended! Similarly, some claim the Ethics Code of the Pharmaceutical Research and Manufacturers of America (PhRMA) isn't working, as explained in the following case-in-point.

> *Case-in-Point 10.8*   While the PhMRA Code promises that marketing practices will comply with the highest ethical standards, whistle-blower lawsuits in the past 3 years have totaled $7 billion. Apparently, PhMRA has been using prominent physician speakers to push their drugs for uses that are not approved by the FDA.[14]

The accounting profession has a number of associations, such as the Institute of Management Accountants (IMA), the American Institute of Certified Public Accountants (AICPA), the Institute of Internal Auditors (IIA), and the Information Systems Audit and Control Association (ISACA) that have had codes of ethics or codes of professional conduct in force for a number of years. These professional accounting and audit association codes are self-imposed and self-enforced rules of conduct. One of the most important goals of a code of ethics or conduct is to aid professionals in selecting among alternatives that are not clear-cut. Included within professional association codes are rules pertaining to independence, technical competence, and proper practices during audits and consulting engagements involving information systems. The certification programs of these associations increase awareness of the codes of ethics and are essential in developing professionalism.

In recent years, professional accounting associations at both the national and state levels have established ethics committees to assist practitioners in the self-regulation

---

[14] Verschoor, C. 2011. Pharma ethics code isn't working! *Strategic Finance* 92(8): 17–19.

Ethical Issue	Example in Computer Usage
Honesty	Organizations expect employees to perform their own work, to refrain from accessing unauthorized information, and to provide authentic results of program outputs.
Protecting computer systems	Examples include tying up network access ports with multiple log-ins, sending voluminous (but useless) e-mails and computer files to others, complaining to system administrators about fictitious hardware or software failures, introducing computer viruses into networks, or giving unauthorized users access to private computer systems.
Protecting confidential information	Allowing unauthorized individuals to view private information—for example, financial data on a mortgage loan application or the results of diagnostic medical tests stored in the files of local area networks.
Social responsibility	Sometimes, social responsibility conflicts with other organizational goals. For example, suppose that a programmer discovers a possible error in a software program that controls a missile guidance system. His boss tells him to ignore it—the design team is already over budget and this is only a possible error.
Acceptable use	The availability of computer hardware and software in workplaces does not automatically convey unrestricted uses of them. At universities, for example, ethical conduct forbids downloading microcomputer software for personal applications or using free mainframe time for personal gain.
Rights of privacy	Do organizations have the right to read the personal e-mail of their employees? Do employees have the right to use their business e-mail accounts for personal correspondence? In 2002, the state of Montana decided that monitoring computer activity on state-owned computers at state universities is legal. Officials at colleges and universities in Montana are hoping to decrease the incidence of illegal activity by individuals who are using campus property.

FIGURE 10-8   Examples of ethical issues in computer usage.

process. These ethics committees provide their members with continuing education courses, advice on ethical issues, investigations of possible ethics violations, and instructional booklets covering a variety of ethics case studies. Some of the ethics committees provide their members with a hotline to advise them on the ethical and moral dilemmas experienced in the workplace. These committees also encourage the instruction of ethics in accounting curricula at colleges and universities.

Professional computer associations, such as the Association of Information Technology Professionals (AITP) and the Association for Computing Machinery (ACM), have developed codes of ethics, ethics committees, and certification programs. The codes of these professional computer associations examine such issues as obligations to their professional associations, clients, and society. Figure 10-8 presents a few examples of ethical issues related to computer usage.

Meeting the Ethical Challenges

Because a significant amount of business activity and data communications now takes place on the Internet, it is not surprising that an increasing amount of computer crime involves the Internet. Examples include thieves supplying fake credit card numbers to online retailers in order to buy everything from investment securities to Internet access time itself, copying Web pages without permission, denying legitimate users Internet access, harassment, stalking, and posing as someone else for any number of illegal or dishonest purposes.

How we respond to the aforementioned ethical issues is determined not so much by laws or organizational rules as by our own sense of "right" and "wrong." Ethical standards of behavior are a function of many things, including social expectations, culture, societal norms, and even the times in which we live. More than anything else, however, ethical behavior requires personal discipline and a commitment to do the right thing.

How can organizations encourage ethical behavior? Some argue that morals are only learned at an early age and in the home—they cannot be taught to adults. However, others suggest that it helps to (1) inform employees that ethics are important, (2) formally expose employees to relevant cases that teach them how to act responsibly in specific situations, (3) teach by example, that is, by managers acting responsibly, and (4) use job promotions and other benefits to reward those employees who act responsibly.

Case-in-Point 10.9 Are you familiar with the student code of conduct at your school? Some universities have very lengthy and detailed codes of conduct, while others, such as Texas A&M University, have a very short, direct one: An Aggie does not lie, cheat, or steal, or tolerate those who do.[15]

Privacy

Although Americans are concerned and aware of various privacy issues, the events of September 11, 2001, changed our focus in some respects. For example, we are willing to accept less privacy at airports and to submit to increased security measures at various points in airport terminals. On a day-to-day basis, we freely give our name, address, phone number, and similar information to receive **value cards** at grocery stores, shoe stores, sporting goods stores, greeting card stores, and other retail establishments. In some cases, we receive discounts; in other cases, we receive points that may be exchanged for goods or services; and in some instances, we simply receive advance information for upcoming sales before the general public.

Privacy also affects our use of the Internet. For example, when we order a book from Amazon.com, future visits to the site involve greetings by name and marketing tailored to our purchase histories. A remarkable marketing tool, but how do they know? They know because most commercial websites deposit a **cookie** on your computer, which is a small text file that stores information about your browsing habits and interests, as well as other information that you may supply by logging onto the site. Of course, cookies are not necessarily bad. If you frequently purchase items from a particular online vendor, it is very convenient to have your credit card and shipping information automatically recalled so that you are not required to enter this information for every purchase.

Some individuals even claim that the Internet and privacy are mutually exclusive—that you can't have both. A critical issue is whether the invasion of our privacy is with or without our permission. That is, did we agree or authorize the information to be collected? For example, few object to Amazon.com tracking their browsing habits on their website; but if we ordered a book or other item from that website, we would most certainly object to unauthorized uses of our credit card information.

---

[15] "Aggie Code of Honor (Revised: 2003)," Texas A&M University, Student Rules (student-rules.tamu.edu).

Company Policies with Respect to Privacy

Because of the widespread use of computers in business, coupled with the fact that many employees travel and use portable devices, employers should develop and distribute a company policy with respect to privacy. The Fair Employment Practices Guidelines suggest that these policies cover such issues as: (1) who owns the computer and the data stored on the computer, (2) how may the computer be used (e.g., primarily for business purposes), and (3) what uses are unauthorized or prohibited. Further, employers should specifically identify the types of acceptable and unacceptable uses, with some examples. Another idea is to have a screen pop-up each time an employee signs on that reminds the employee of the company policy. In general, companies would benefit from legal counsel on this topic.

Most commercial websites have a privacy policy, although they are sometimes difficult to find. For example, at Amazon.com, you need to click on "help" and then scroll down to the bottom of the page to find the section on policies. However, your search is rewarded with a comprehensive list of information that is covered by their **privacy policy**—including information you give them, cookies they use, e-mail communications, and information Amazon.com receives about you from other sources. Another online merchant, Lands' End, provides an easy-to-find link to its privacy policy on its home page. Its privacy policy states the information it does and does not collect and offers advice about managing cookies.

An important point to remember is that companies typically are very careful about protecting your personal information. They understand that their future viability depends, in part, on the security of both your information and their proprietary data. Of course, recent events such as the massive theft of credit card data from Target stores indicates that corporations need to remain vigilant and always take steps to protect their data and their customer' data from sophisticated hackers.

Identity Theft

Identity theft refers to an act in which someone wrongfully obtains and uses another person's personal data for fraud or deception. Unlike your fingerprints, which are unique to you and cannot be used by someone else, your personal data can be used by other individuals to their advantage. Your personal data may be any one or a combination of the following pieces of information: your Social Security number, your bank account, your debit card number, your credit card number, your birth date, or your mailing address. It was not until 1998 that Congress passed legislation making identity theft a crime.

Thieves steal identities in a number of ways including **dumpster diving** (stealing personal information from garbage cans), taking delivered or outgoing mail from house mail boxes, or making telephone solicitations that ask for personal information. **Phishing** scams use e-mail or websites that claim to be legitimate but that ask you to provide or update your personal information such as account number, credit card number, or password. **Smishing** is a similar scam using text messages on cell phones.

Case-in-Point 10.10 Stolen identities can often be purchased on the cheap, sometimes for as little as $10 each. A Tampa man tried to sell a confidential informant the names, dates of birth, and social security numbers of 86 victims, more than a third of which were children.

Method	Examples
Shoulder surfing	• Watching you from a nearby location as you punch in your debit or credit card number
	• Listening to your conversation if you give your debit or credit card number over the telephone to a hotel or rental car company
Dumpster diving	• Going through your garbage can or a communal dumpster or trash bin to obtain copies of your checks, credit card or bank statements, or other records that typically have your name, address, and telephone number
Applications for "pre-approved" credit cards	• If you discard them without tearing up the enclosed materials, criminals may retrieve them and try to activate the cards
	• If your mail is delivered to a place where others have access to it, criminals may simply intercept and redirect your mail to another location
Key logging software	• Loading this type of software on computers in general use areas, such as university computer labs or public libraries to obtain your personal data and other identifying data, such as passwords or banking information
Spam and other e-mails	• Many people respond to unsolicited e-mail that promises some benefit but requests identifying data, which criminals use to apply for loans, credit cards, fraudulent withdrawals from bank accounts, or other goods

FIGURE 10-9 Examples of methods used by criminals to obtain your personal data.

After investigation by the U.S. Secret Service and Florida Department of Law Enforcement, the fraudster was arrested and sentenced to a mandatory 2 years in federal prison.[16]

In the United States and Canada, many people have reported that unauthorized persons have taken funds out of their bank or financial accounts. Even worse, some unscrupulous individuals have gone so far as to take over an individual's identity, incurring huge debts and committing numerous crimes. Victims can incur enormous costs attempting to restore their reputation in a community or correcting erroneous information. Figure 10-9 identifies a number of ways you can become a victim of identity theft if you are not careful.

AIS AT WORK
The Greatest Threat[17]

PwC's latest survey of global information security tapped the collective expertise of over 10,000 business and IT executives to garner their views on cybersecurity and privacy. Survey results suggest that organizations will be focusing future efforts on cybersecurity initiatives in four key areas: threat intelligence and information sharing, IoT security, geopolitical threats, and digital business model safeguards.

More and more organizations are taking a page from cybercriminals' playbook: they are sharing information on threats with industry groups, governmental agencies, and peer organizations. In fact, 55% actively collaborate with these stakeholders in an effort to gain valuable intelligence and improve their overall cybersecurity postures.

---

[16] U.S. Department of Justice Press Release, "Tampa Man Pleads Guilty to Selling Stolen Identities," accessed from www.justice.gov in March 2017.
[17] PwC. 2017. *Global State of Information Security Survey 2017.* Accessed from www.pwc.com in March 2017.

Likely, a result of recent IoT-based malware and DDoS attacks, many survey respondents indicated that their organizations were ramping up efforts at securing corporate infrastructure against these threats, revising data governance policies, and increasing efforts around employee awareness and education. Augmenting this increased threat exposure is a dynamic geopolitical climate that is seeing an increase in state-sponsored cyberattacks and growing hactivism by loosely affiliated groups such as Anonymous.

Finally, the digital nature of modern business has created a pivot point between information-enabled business processes and products and threats from increased network connectivity and openness. More and more organizations are moving IT infrastructure (63%), operations (36%), customer service (34%), and other key processes to the cloud.

Across the business landscape, surveys such as this one suggest that there is a shortage of employees with information security skills. Accountants who understand technology and security may have a great opportunity to position themselves in this growing market.

 ## SUMMARY

✓ We know very little about cybercrime because few cases are reported and many more cases go undetected.

✓ Cybercrime is growing and is likely to be expensive for those organizations that suffer from it.

✓ For fraud to occur, three things must be present: opportunity, rationalization, and need.

✓ Three examples of real-world cybercrime included compromising valuable information, hacking, and denial of service.

✓ Organizations can use the following methods to protect themselves against computer offenses: (1) enlist top management support, (2) educate users about computer crime and abuse, (3) conduct a security assessment and protect passwords, (4) design and implement control procedures, (5) identify criminals, (6) maintain physical security, (7) recognize the symptoms of crime and abuse, (8) use data-driven techniques, and (9) employ forensic accountants.

✓ Managers should implement programs that focus on ethical behavior. Examples of ethical behavior include protecting confidential information, being socially responsible, respecting rights of privacy, avoiding conflicts of interest, and understanding unacceptable uses of computer hardware and software.

✓ Organizations can encourage ethical behavior by educating employees, rewarding employees, and encouraging employees to join professional associations with ethical codes of conduct.

✓ Identity theft is a growing problem, and individuals must adopt reasonable precautions to protect their personal data.

KEY TERMS YOU SHOULD KNOW

antivirus software	Audit Control Language (ACL)	computer fraud
applet	boot-sector virus	Computer Fraud and Abuse Act
Association of Certified Fraud	botnet	of 1986
Examiners (ACFE)	computer abuse	Computer Security Institute (CSI)

cookie	hacker	phishing
cybercrime	identity theft	privacy policy
data diddling	Integrated Computer-Assisted	rationalization
denial of service (DOS) attack	Surveillance System (ICASS)	smishing
dumpster diving	Internet of Things (IoT)	social engineering
EnCase	intrusion testing	strong passwords
encryption	logic bomb	Trojan horse programs
ethical hacker	malware	value cards
firewall	need	virus
forensic accountants	opportunity	worm
Fraud Triangle	penetration testing	

TEST YOURSELF

Q10-1. Which of the following is NOT an example of computer fraud?

   a. Entering invoices in the AIS for services that were not provided and depositing the check in a private bank account.

   b. Sending an e-mail to everyone in your address book asking for a $1 donation.

   c. Programming a change to decrease the dividend payment to stockholders of a firm and issuing a check to your friend for the total change.

   d. Using a university computer to set up a realistic looking virtual "store front" to sell toys, although you don't have any—you just don't have time to get a real job and need some money to cover the rent.

Q10-2. Which of the following pieces of computer legislation is probably the most important?

   a. Cyber Security Enhancement Act of 2002

   b. Computer Security Act of 1987

   c. The Computer Fraud and Abuse Act of 1986

   d. Federal Privacy Act of 1974

Q10-3. What is it called when someone intentionally changes data before, during, or after they are entered into the computer (with the intent to illegally obtain information or assets)?

   a. Trojan horse

   b. Logic bomb

   c. Data diddling

   d. A cookie

Q10-4. The TRW Case is notable because:

   a. the amount of dollars involved was not significant

   b. no one got caught

   c. the fraud was detected by a surprise audit

   d. the real victims were TRW customers

Q10-5. Which of these is not helpful in attempting to thwart computer crime and abuse?

   a. Enlist the support of top management

   b. Keep employees in the dark so that they cannot perpetrate them

   c. Use strong passwords

   d. Design and test disaster recovery programs

Q10-6. A local area network administrator receives a call from an employee requesting his password. The person calling is not a real employee. This is an example of:

   a. a DOS system

   b. security Trojan horse

   c. a worm

   d. social engineering

   e. a security policy

Q10-7. Most computer criminals:

   a. have nontechnical backgrounds

   b. have noncriminal backgrounds

   c. have little college education

   d. are young and bright

   e. have probably not been caught, so we don't really know much about them

Q10-8. Which of these is a software tool often used by forensic accountants?

 a. MS-DOS

 b. ACFE

 c. Computer Spy

 d. Logic bomb

 e. EnCase

Q10-9. Smishing is a form of:

 a. fishing

 b. local area network

 c. computer worm

 d. identity theft

DISCUSSION QUESTIONS

10-1. The cases of cybercrime that we know about have been described as just "the tip of the iceberg." Do you consider this description accurate? Why or why not?

10-2. Most cybercrime is not reported. Give as many reasons as you can why much of this crime is purposely downplayed. Do you consider these reasons valid?

10-3. Why have most computer experts suggested that cybercrime is growing despite the fact that so little is known about it?

10-4. Does a company have the right to collect, store, and disseminate information about your purchasing activities without your permission?

10-5. What enabled the employees at TRW to get away with their crime? What controls might have prevented the crime from occurring?

10-6. Consider the number of IoT devices you own. Have you taken appropriate steps to secure them from becoming compromised? Do you believe that consumers have an obligation to secure these?

10-7. What is a computer virus?

10-8. How can educating employees help stop cybercrime?

10-9. What cybercrimes are committed on the Internet? What assets are involved? What can be done to safeguard these assets?

10-10. How would you define "ethics"? What types of ethical issues are involved in computerized accounting information systems? How can organizations encourage their employees to act ethically?

10-11. The Rivera Regional Bank uses a computerized data processing system to maintain both its checking accounts and its savings accounts. During the last 3 years, several customers have complained that their balances have been in error. Randy Allen, the information systems bank manager, has always treated these customers very courteously and has personally seen to it that the problems have been rectified quickly, sometimes by putting in extra hours after normal quitting time to make the necessary changes. This extra effort has been so helpful to the bank that this year, the bank's top management is planning to select Mr. Allen the Employee-of-the-Year Award. Mr. Allen has never taken a vacation. Comment.

PROBLEMS

10-12. Comment on each of the following scenarios in light of chapter materials. Hint: Use the references at the end of this chapter to help you.

 a. A legitimate student calls the computer help desk from her cell phone because she has forgotten her password to the university system. The "tech" on duty refuses to give it to her as a matter of university policy. The student is unable to complete her assignment and proceeds to file a formal complaint against the university.

b. An employee at a building supply company is caught downloading pornographic materials to his office computer. He is reprimanded by his boss, asked to remove the offending materials, and told never to do it again. The employee refuses on the grounds that (1) there is no company policy forbidding these activities, (2) he performed all his downloads during his lunch breaks, (3) his work reviews indicate that he is performing "above average," and (4) the discoveries themselves were performed without a search warrant and therefore violate his right to privacy.

c. The local community college installed a new, campus-wide local area network that requires all staff members to enter a login name and password. Users can choose their own passwords. Some pick the names of their pets or spouses as passwords, while others tape their passwords to their computer monitors to help remember them.

d. An employee in a hospital was hardly ever at his desk, but almost always reachable through his cell phone. When the department replaced his old computer with a new one, his boss scanned the old hard drive and made the startling discovery that this employee had a full-time second job as a beer distributer.

e. A routine audit of the computer payroll records of the local manufacturing plant reveals that the address of over 20 employees in different departments is the same empty lot in the city.

f. An analysis of online bidding on eBay reveals that one seller has bid on several of his own items in an effort to increase the final sales price of his items.

g. A retailer sues a Web hosting company when it discovers that the employees of the Web company have been visiting sites on which the retailer advertises. The retailer pays a fee of $1 every time someone clicks on these advertising links.

10-13. The U.S. Department of Justice, Office of the U.S. Attorney press release site (www.justice .gove/usao/pressreleases) is a good source for current cybercrimes and fraud. Find a description of a cybercrime not already discussed in this chapter and prepare an analysis of the crime similar to the analyses in the second section of this chapter.

10-14. What company policies or procedures would you recommend to prevent each of the following activities?

a. A clerk in the human relations department creates a fictitious employee in the personnel computer file. When this employee's payroll check is received for distribution, the clerk takes and cashes it.

b. A clerk in the accounts-receivable department steals $250 cash from a customer payment, then prepares a computer credit memo that reduces the customer's account balance by the same amount.

c. A hacker manages to break into a company's computer system by guessing the password of his friend—Champ, the name of the friend's dog.

d. An accounts-receivable clerk manages to embezzle more than $1 million from the company by diligently lapping the accounts every day for three consecutive years.

e. A computer virus on the company's local area network is traced to an individual who accidentally introduced it when he loaded a computer game onto his computer.

f. A clerk at a medical lab recognizes the name of an acquaintance as one of those whose lab tests are "positive" for an infectious disease. She mentions it to a mutual friend, and before long, the entire town knows about it.

10-15. Download a copy of the Association of Certified Fraud Examiners Fraud Prevention Checkup, which is available at: www.acfe .com/uploadedFiles/ACFE_Website/Content/ documents/Fraud_Prev_Checkup_DL.pdf.

On a separate piece of paper, list the seven areas and the maximum number of points suggested for each one. An example is:

1. Fraud Risk Oversight (20 points)
Do you think that this checklist is likely to enable organizations to prevent most types of fraud? Why or why not?

CASE ANALYSES

10-16. Find-a-Fraud

Download the following Excel spreadsheet from the textbook website: www.Findafraud.xls. These data include sales transactions and credits for a retail store. You are concerned that the store is attempting to manipulate its revenue. Use your spreadsheet skills and knowledge of revenue recognition to identify red flags that could indicate fraud related to revenue recognition. Alternatively, convert this spreadsheet into an Access table and use the query skills described in Chapter 8 to analyze this data using queries.

Requirements

1. Document each red flag that you identify.
2. Explain the potential implications of each red flag.
3. Discuss the fraud or frauds that you believe are most likely.

10-17. The Resort

The Mountain Top Resort Community is an elegant, thriving four-season resort and community of over 1,200 single family homes, 1,000 time-share units, and a multimillion-dollar ski business. Guests visiting the resort can enjoy the indoor/outdoor water park, play golf on one of the two 18-hole championship golf courses, ski, snowboard, or snow tube in the winter on 14 trails that are all lighted for night skiing, or relax at the full-service spa. There are also three dining rooms, card rooms, nightly movies, and live weekend entertainment.

The resort uses a computerized system to make room reservations and bill customers. Following standard policy for the industry, the resort also offers authorized travel agents a 10% commission on room bookings. Each week, the resort prints an exception report of bookings made by unrecognized travel agents. However, the managers usually pay the commissions anyway, partly because they don't want to anger the travel agencies and partly because the computer file that maintains the list of authorized agents is not kept up-to-date.

Although management has not discovered it, several employees are exploiting these circumstances. As often as possible, they call the resort from outside phones, pose as travel agents, book rooms for friends and relatives, and collect the commissions. The incentive is obvious: rooms costing as little as $100 per day result in payments of $10 per day to the "travel agencies" that book them. The scam has been going on for years, and several guests now book their rooms exclusively through these employees, finding these people particularly courteous and helpful.

Requirements

1. Would you say this is a computer crime? Why or why not?
2. Is this fraud? Why or why not?
3. What internal controls would you recommend that would enable the resort's managers to prevent such offenses?
4. Classify the controls that you just identified as either preventive, detective, or corrective controls.
5. How does the matter of "accountability" (tracing transactions to specific agencies) affect the problem?

10-18. The Department of Taxation

The Department of Taxation of one state is developing a new computer system for processing state income tax returns of individuals and corporations. The new system features direct data input and inquiry capabilities. Identification of taxpayers is provided by using the Social Security numbers of individuals and federal identification numbers for corporations. The new system should be fully implemented in time for the next tax season. The new system will serve three primary purposes:

- Data will be input into the system directly from tax returns through data entry workstations located at the central headquarters of the Department of Taxation.

- The returns will be processed using the main computer facilities at the central headquarters. The processing includes (1) verifying mathematical accuracy; (2) auditing the reasonableness of deductions, tax due, and so forth, through the use of edit routines (these routines also include a comparison of the current year's data with previous years' data); (3) identifying returns that should be considered for audit by revenue agents of the department; and (4) issuing refund checks to taxpayers.

- Inquiry service will be provided to taxpayers on request through the assistance of Tax Department personnel at five regional offices. A total of 50 kiosks will be placed at the regional offices.

A taxpayer will be able to determine the status of his or her return or to get information from the last 3 years' returns by calling or visiting one of the department's regional offices. The state commissioner of taxation is concerned about data security during input and processing over and above protection against natural hazards such as fires or floods. This includes protection against the loss or damage of data during data input or processing and the improper input or processing of data. In addition, the tax commissioner and the state attorney general have discussed the general problem of data confidentiality that may arise from the nature and operation of the new system. Both individuals want to have all potential problems identified before the system is fully developed and implemented so that the proper controls can be incorporated into the new system.

Requirements

1. Describe the potential confidentiality problems that could arise in each of the following three areas of processing and recommend the corrective action(s) to solve the problems: (a) data input, (b) processing of returns, and (c) data inquiry.

2. The State Tax Commission wants to incorporate controls to provide data security against the loss, damage, or improper input or use of data during data input and processing. Identify the potential problems (outside of natural hazards such as fires or floods) for which the Department of Taxation should develop controls, and recommend possible control procedures for each problem identified.
   (CMA Adapted)

READINGS AND OTHER RESOURCES

Holtfreter, R., and A. Harrington. 2014. Will hackers win the battle. *Strategic Finance* (February): 27–34.

Lightle, S., B. Baker, and J. Castellano. 2009. The role of Boards of Directors in shaping organizational culture. *The CPA Journal* 79(11): 68–72.

Liu, C., L. Yao, and N. Hu. 2012. Improving ethics education in accounting: Lessons from medicine and law. *Issues in Accounting Education* 27(3): 671–690.

Thomas, S. 2012. Ethics and accounting education. *Issues in Accounting Education* 27(2): 399–418.

Ugrin, J., M. Odom, and R. Ott. 2014. Examining the effects of motive and potential detection on the anticipation of consequences for financial statement fraud. *Journal of Forensic & Investigative Accounting* 6(1): 151–180.

Weber, J. 2010. Assessing the "Tone at the Top": The moral reasoning of CEOs in the automobile industry. *Journal of Business Ethics* 92(2): 167–182.

Go to www.wiley.com/go/simkin/videos to access videos on the following topics:

Cybercrime: What You Can Do About It
Hacking: Massive Theft of Credit Card Numbers
Ethics: Business Leader Ethics

ANSWERS TO TEST YOURSELF

1. b **2.** c **3.** c **4.** d **5.** b **6.** d **7.** e **8.** e **9.** d

Chapter 11

Information Technology Auditing

After reading this chapter, you will be able to:

1. *Discuss* the role of information technology (IT) auditing on an internal and external audit context.
2. *Describe* the IT audit process and nature of careers in information technology auditing.
3. *Summarize* the software and people skills needed by IT auditors.
4. *Evaluate* the effectiveness of internal controls over specific information systems.
5. *Recognize* various techniques auditors use to evaluate computerized information systems.
6. *Explain* how auditors can use IT to prevent and discover fraudulent activities.
7. *Explain* how the Sarbanes–Oxley Act of 2002 and AS 2201 influence the role of IT auditors.
8. *Identify* the various Information Systems Audit and Control Association (ISACA) and the Institute of Internal Auditors (IIA) guidance available to the IT auditor.

" …dependence on complex computing and large-scale data schemes has led organizations around the globe to recognize how IT auditors can help them understand the constantly shifting risks of the information age."

Donathan, C. 2012. So You Want to Be an IT Auditor? *Internal Auditor.*[1]

11.1 INTRODUCTION

Chapters 6 and 7 stressed the importance of control procedures in the effective operation of an accounting information system (AIS). To make sure that these controls are functioning properly and that additional controls are not needed, organizations perform examinations or audits of their accounting systems. Auditing is usually taught in one or more separate courses within the typical accounting curriculum, and a single chapter of a book is not sufficient to cover the spectrum of topics involved in a complete audit of an organization. This chapter will be introductory and limited to areas of immediate consequence to AISs and the information technology (IT) audit.

We begin our discussion with introductory comments about the nature of auditing and the distinction between internal and external auditing. We then describe the relationship between an IT audit and a financial audit. Next, we discuss tools an IT auditor uses, and the various approaches for evaluating internal controls in a computerized AIS.

---

[1] The Institute of Internal Auditors, www.theiia.org.

We conclude with several topics related to IT auditing today: IT governance, fraud auditing, the effect of Sarbanes–Oxley (SOX) and AS 2201 on IT audits, and resources and guidance for IT auditors.

11.2   THE AUDIT FUNCTION

To audit is to examine and assure. An audit is an objective assessment of a set of assertions. The hallmark of an audit is that it provides an unbiased view of the area under review. The nature of auditing differs according to the subject under examination. Many times, students are confused over the distinction between internal and external auditing and how IT auditing fits into these two broad categories.

Internal versus External Auditing

Conventionally, we distinguish between two types of audits: internal auditing and **external auditing**. The Institute of Internal Auditors (IIA) defines **internal auditing** as *"an independent, objective assurance and consulting activity designed to add value and improve an organization's operations. It helps an organization accomplish its objectives by bringing a systematic, disciplined approach to evaluate and improve the effectiveness of risk management, control and governance processes."*[2] The scope of internal audit activities covers three broad areas: efficiency and effectiveness of operations, reliability of internal and external reporting, and compliance with applicable laws and regulations. Within this broad scope, internal audit activities can include such diverse activities as auditing for fraud, ensuring that employees are not copying software programs illegally, or providing assurance to a company's top management and board of directors regarding the efficiency and effectiveness of almost any aspect of the organization.

Internal auditors usually are employees of the organization that they audit (hence *internal* to the organization) and report through a **Chief Audit Executive (CAE)** to the Audit Committee of the Board of Directors. The CAE is a senior management position that has a dual reporting structure, answering to the Chief Executive Officer (CEO) of the organization on administrative issues and the Chairperson of the Audit Committee on more strategic issues (i.e., which areas to audit, funding of the internal audit function, and the like). This dual reporting structure preserves the independence of the internal audit function by insulating it from influences that the departments being audited might try to exert.

In contrast to the broad perspective of internal auditors, the chief purpose of an external audit is the attest function—that is, rendering an opinion on the accuracy and fairness of financial statements. The external audit is conducted by independent auditors working for a public accounting firm. These auditors are *external* to the organization being audited. Their efforts at determining the fairness and accuracy of the financial statement are conducted in the context of generally accepted accounting principles (GAAP) and require application of generally accepted auditing standards (GAAS). Recently, the external auditor's role has expanded with respect to auditing for fraud. *Statement on Auditing Standards (SAS) No. 99 Consideration of Fraud in a Financial Statement Audit* requires auditors working for public accounting firms

---

[2] The IIA International Professional Practices Framework (IPPF), accessed at www.theiia.org in March 2017.

to undertake a number of specific actions to ensure that an organization's financial statements are free of erroneous or fraudulent material misstatements. Similarly, AS 2201 emphasizes the importance of evaluating controls designed to prevent fraud.

Outside of employment considerations, perhaps a cleaner and easier way of understanding the difference between the two is as follows. When we look at the scope of internal audit activities, internal auditors are concerned with efficiency and effectiveness of operations, reliability of internal and external reporting, and compliance with applicable laws and regulations. Looking specifically at reliability of reporting and compliance with laws and regulations, *financial reporting is a small sliver* of the overall (external) reporting and compliance efforts within an organization. The external audit will focus on that small sliver, ensuring that the financial statements are a true and accurate representation of the financial position of the organization as of a point in time and that internal controls over financial reporting are in place and support this assessment. The internal auditor is charged with examining the *entirety* of reporting and compliance within the organization, as well as the added responsibility of providing assurance that the organization's processes are making efficient and effective use of resources. As you can see, the scope of internal auditing is much broader.

Despite the differences in purpose between internal and external audits, internal and external auditors perform a number of similar functions related to computerized AISs. Therefore, most of the following discussion applies to both internal and external auditors. We use the term *auditor* broadly to encompass both types of auditors. A large degree of cooperation and interaction often exists between an organization's internal auditors and a public accounting firm's external auditors. For example, external auditors frequently review, and often rely upon, the work of internal auditors as they assess an organization's financial statements.

Information Technology Auditing

Information Technology (IT) auditing is, at its core, the evaluation and assessment of an organization's IT infrastructure, processes, and practices to provide assurance on the confidentiality, integrity, and availability of information systems. In addition to evaluating the design and operating effectiveness of internal controls embedded in and around an organization's information systems, IT auditing includes evaluating the efficiency and effectiveness of processes performed by the IT function and their services delivered to the various business units within the organization.

The assurance aspect of IT auditing involves ensuring that data and information are reliable, confidential, secure, and available as needed. Traditional financial audit objectives are also present in IT auditing. These include attest objectives such as the safeguarding of assets and data integrity and management objectives such as operational effectiveness.

IT auditing is a relatively new area of focus within the audit domain, truly coming into its own as a subdiscipline in the early 1990s. Starting out as electronic data processing (EDP) auditing in the late 1960s, significant changes in the business and accounting landscape influenced the evolution of IT auditing. Arguably, the impetus for IT auditing was the convergence of three factors: adoption of computerized accounting systems, migration of business processes to computerized platforms, and enforcement of data security.

Starting with the introduction of computerized accounting systems in the 1950s, more and more organizations began to realize the efficiencies gained by implementing computerized accounting systems. While computerized payroll systems were the first adopted, it was not long before other accounting-related modules followed suit. Other business processes soon began utilizing computerized systems, such as materials and inventory management. These systems created and collected large amounts of data, which were stored in databases on mainframe computer systems. As centralized mainframe computing models gave way to distributed computing, organizations (and auditors) found that databases were scattered throughout the IT infrastructure. This distribution of data, combined with the explosive growth in the 1990s of network connectivity and the Internet, made gaining access to data much easier, while simultaneously complicating effective data security practices. In sum, the aforementioned factors combined with increased network connectivity and the rise of the "hacker generation" were the final catalysts necessary to cement IT auditing as an in-demand audit specialization.

The Information Technology Audit Process. As illustrated in Figure 11-1, the IT audit function encompasses all components of a computer-based AIS: people, processes, hardware, networks, software, and databases.

External auditors often ask IT auditors to examine an organization's computer-based AIS primarily to evaluate how the organization's control procedures over computer processing affect the financial statements (attest objectives). The controls in place will directly influence the scope of the audit. For instance, if computer controls are weak or nonexistent, auditors will need to do more substantive testing—that is, detailed tests of transactions and account balances. An example of substantive testing is the confirmation of accounts receivable with customers. If the control procedures over a company's computerized financial accounting system are strong, the auditors may limit the scope of their audit by examining fewer transactions underlying accounts receivable account balances. For our example, this would mean contacting fewer customers to confirm accounts receivable than would be the case if little or no reliance could be placed on the computer-based controls.

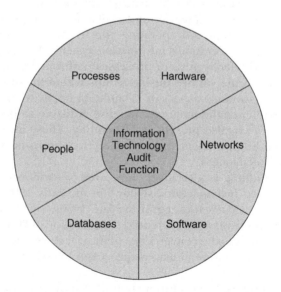

FIGURE 11-1 The six components of a computer-based AIS examined in an information technology audit.

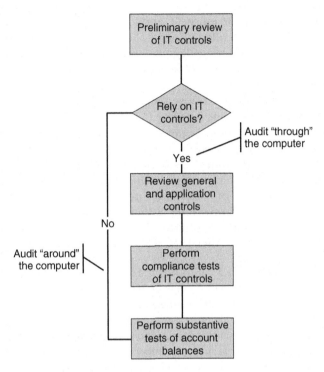

FIGURE 11-2 Flowchart of information technology audit process.

Figure 11-2 shows a flowchart of the steps that generally take place when IT auditors are engaged as part of an external audit of financial statements. These steps are
similar to those performed in any financial audit. What is different is that the auditor's
examination in this case concerns a *computer-based* AIS. In Figure 11-2, the process
begins with a preliminary evaluation of the system. The auditor will first decide if computer processing of accounting data is significant or complex enough to warrant an
examination of the computer-based information system itself. Sometimes, if the system
is neither large nor complex, the audit might proceed as it would in a manual data processing environment. Most often, computer-based processing warrants a preliminary
review by the IT auditor to make an assessment of the control environment.

Typically, an auditor will find enough computer-based controls in place to warrant
further examination. In this situation, an auditor will want to make a more detailed
analysis of both *general* and *application controls*. After examining these controls in
some detail, the auditors will perform **compliance testing** to ensure that the controls are in place and working as prescribed, that is, they are operating effectively.
This may entail using some **computer-assisted audit techniques (CAATs)** to audit
the computerized AIS. These involve the use of computer processes or controls to perform audit functions, such as sorting data to detect duplicate accounts-payable invoice
numbers. Finally, the auditor will need to substantively test some account balances. As
explained earlier, the results of the previous analysis and testing affect the scope of
this testing.

Careers in Information Technology Auditing. As organizations increasingly rely on
computer-based AISs and as these systems become more technologically complex,
the demand for IT auditors is growing. The passage of the Sarbanes–Oxley Act also

created a need for more IT auditors. IT auditing requires a variety of skills. Some IT auditors have college degrees in computer science or information systems, while others have accounting degrees and general audit experience. The ideal background includes a combination of accounting, auditing, and information systems or computer science skills.

IT auditors may choose to obtain a professional certification, with the **Certified Information Systems Auditor (CISA)** being the most widely recognized among information systems audit, control, and assurance professionals. Applicants achieve this certification by successfully completing an examination given by the Information Systems Audit and Control Association (ISACA) and meeting experience requirements. Maintaining this certification requires staying current on IT audit trends by attaining at least 120 hours of continuing professional education every 3 years, complying with ISACA's Code of Professional Ethics, and adhering to ISACA's Information Technology Audit and Assurance Standards. Figure 11-3 describes the content areas covered on the CISA and selected other ISACA IT audit, control, and security certifications.

Case-in-Point 11.1 ISACA is the leading professional association for IT audit and governance professionals, with over 140,000 members in over 215 chapters across more than 92 countries worldwide. Full-time college students are eligible for student membership at a reduced rate. In addition to complimentary or reduced-rate access to the *ISACA Journal,* eLibrary, COBIT, IT audit guidance, and various publications, many local ISACA chapters allow student members to attend monthly meetings and seminars at reduced rates. It is a great way for students interested in IT auditing to learn about the profession and network with IT audit professionals.[3,4]

IT auditors may be employed as either internal or external auditors. Evaluating controls over information systems hardware and various AIS applications requires a high level of expertise. As an example, an IT auditor evaluating controls that limit access to certain information needs to be familiar with the way a particular application organizes its access security. Compared to external auditors, internal auditors can more easily specialize in knowledge about their particular organization's hardware, operating system platform, and application programs.

An external auditor is likely to audit the information systems of many different client organizations. The external IT auditor may or may not be part of the regular financial audit team. In some cases, the financial audit team only calls on external IT auditors when a special risk assessment appears warranted. The Big Four public accounting firms all employ IT auditors and perform a variety of assurance-related IT services for clients.

Case-in-Point 11.2 Big Four public accounting firm PricewaterhouseCoopers' (PwC) Process Assurance group offers many opportunities for IT auditors to develop their skills. In addition to documenting and testing the operating effectiveness of IT controls, external IT auditors within the Process Assurance group often evaluate IT governance and strategy, assess IT services delivery and back-office process performance, and provide an objective assessment of IT project planning and execution. Process Assurance associates may also work with IT professionals from other practice groups to deliver integrated IT governance, risk, and compliance solutions. [5]

---

[3] ISACA Fact Sheet, www.isaca.org, accessed in March 2017.
[4] ISACA Student Membership, www.isaca.org/membership, accessed in March 2017.
[5] PwC Risk Assurance services, www.pwc.com, accessed in March 2017.

	Job Practice Areas (Coverage on Exam)	Target Market and Experience Requirements
CISA (Certified IS Auditor)	• Process of Auditing Information Systems (21%) • Governance and Management of IT (16%) • Information Systems Acquisition, Development and Implementation (18%) • Information Systems Operations, Maintenance and Service Management (20%) • Protection of Information Assets (25%)	• IT audit and control professionals responsible for assessing and monitoring an organization's information technology and business information systems. • Experience Requirement • 5 years of work experience in information systems audit, control, or security fields
CRISC (Certified in Risk and IS Control)	• IT Risk Identification (23%) • IT Risk Assessment (28%) • Risk Response and Mitigation (23%) • Risk and Control Monitoring and Reporting (22%)	• IT professionals responsible for identifying IT-related risks and linking those risks to overall business risks. • Experience Requirement • 3 years of work experience across 2 of the 4 job programs, of which 1 must be either IT Risk Identification or IT Risk Assessment
CISM (Certified Information Security Manager)	• Information Security Governance (24%) • Information Risk Management (30%) • Information Security Program Development and Management (27%) • Information Security Incident Response Management (19%)	• IT audit and security professionals responsible for designing, implementing, and assessing enterprise information security programs. • Experience Requirement • 5 years of work experience in information security field, with at least 3 being in information security management
CGEIT (Certified in Governance of Enterprise IT)	• Framework for the Governance of Enterprise IT (25%) • Strategic Management (20%) • Benefits Realization (24%) • Resource Optimization (15%)	• IT and business professionals responsible for aligning IT capabilities with business goals and objectives. • Experience Requirement • 5 years of work experience in IT governance field, with at least 1 being in "definition, establishment and management of a Framework for the Governance of IT"

FIGURE 11-3 Job practice domains and experience requirements covered on select ISACA certifications. Sources: CISA/CRISC/CGEIT/CISM Certification Job Practice domains, accessed from www.isaca.org in March 2017.

Evaluating the Effectiveness of Information Systems Controls

The more confidence auditors have (as a result of strong controls) that data are input and processed accurately in a computer-based system, the less substantive testing they perform. On the other hand, if a computer-based system has weak controls over data input and processing, there is more need for detailed testing of financial transactions.

Risk Assessment. An external auditor's main objective in reviewing information systems control procedures is to evaluate the *risks* (associated with any control weaknesses) to the integrity of accounting data presented in financial reports. Control strengths and weaknesses will affect the scope of the audit. A second objective of the external auditor's review is to make recommendations to the client about improving these controls. Improving controls is also an objective of internal auditors.

The following four steps provide a logical framework for performing a risk-based audit of a company's AIS:

1. Determine the threats (i.e., errors and irregularities) facing the AIS.
2. Identify the control procedures that should be in place to minimize each of these threats and thereby prevent or detect the errors and irregularities.
3. Evaluate the control procedures within the AIS. The process of reviewing system documentation and interviewing appropriate personnel to determine whether the necessary control procedures are in place is called a *systems review*. In addition, auditors investigate whether these control procedures are satisfactorily followed. The tests include such activities as observing system operations; inspecting documents, records, and reports; checking samples of system inputs and outputs; and tracing transactions through the system.
4. Evaluate weaknesses (i.e., errors and irregularities not covered by control procedures) within the AIS to determine their effect on the nature, timing, or extent of auditing procedures. This step focuses on the *control risks* and whether a company's control system as a whole adequately addresses the risks. If a control deficiency is identified, the auditor should determine whether there are compensating controls or procedures that make up for the deficiency. Control weaknesses in one area of an AIS may be acceptable if control strengths in other areas of the AIS compensate for them.

The **risk-based audit** approach provides auditors with a good understanding of the errors and irregularities that can occur in a company's AIS environment and the related risks and exposures. This understanding provides a sound basis for the auditors' development of recommendations to the company's management regarding how its controls can be improved.

The value of an internal control procedure is a function of its ability to *reduce business risk*. Internal control systems are designed to protect the business from risk. For example, natural disasters such as floods or earthquakes pose a risk to an organization's ability to continue its business without interruption. Developing, implementing, and testing a *business continuity plan* and a *disaster recovery plan* are internal control procedures designed to reduce this risk. Focusing on business risk focuses attention on those controls that are necessary and also cost-effective. One method by which an auditor can evaluate the desirability of IT-related controls for a particular aspect of business risk is through an **information systems risk assessment**.

In addition to the risk of fraud or intentional manipulation, auditors must also consider risk with respect to errors or accidents. For instance, inputting asset purchases incorrectly could lead to financial statement misrepresentations in the form of incorrect asset valuations. The loss of company secrets, unauthorized manipulation of company files, and interrupted computer access are also important risks in accounting systems with significant IT components. Auditors must assess the probability of data losses and recommend the implementation of control procedures to reduce threats to the integrity and security of data. In cases where the costs of protection are greater than potential losses, the auditor may recommend against implementing costly controls.

Sometimes, companies assess their information systems risks by employing ethical hackers to conduct penetration testing. While unauthorized hacking is a computer crime, when an IT auditor employs "white hat" hacking techniques, the purpose is to evaluate risk and design controls to protect against unauthorized access. We call this type of ethical hacking **penetration testing** because the auditor is trying to penetrate the system to gain access to resources or sensitive information.

Chapters 6 and 7 pointed out that the Information Systems Audit and Control Foundation developed the **Control Objectives for Information and related Technology (COBIT)** framework. This framework provides auditors and business with guidance in managing and controlling for business risk associated with IT environments. COBIT includes control objectives and control outcomes tests for evaluating the effectiveness of IT controls. Using this framework, management and auditors can design a cost-effective control system for IT resources and processes. COBIT benefits business and IT managers, as well as auditors. For auditors, the model helps in advising management on internal controls and can provide substantive support for audit opinions.

Case-in-Point 11.3 ISACA has an online COBIT Self-Assessment Tool to assist organizations in performing self-assessment on IT process maturity and IT service delivery capabilities.[6]

11.3 THE INFORMATION TECHNOLOGY AUDITOR'S TOOLKIT

Auditors can use *computer-assisted audit techniques (CAATs)* to help them in various auditing tasks. In an automated AIS, **auditing with the computer** (i.e., using the computer itself as an audit tool) is virtually mandatory because data are stored on computer media and manual access is impossible. However, there are many reasons for auditing with the computer beyond the need to access computerized accounting data. One of the most important is that computer-based AISs are rapidly increasing in sophistication. Another is that CAATs save time. Imagine footing and cross-footing large spreadsheets or schedules without using a computer.

Auditing Software

Auditors can use a variety of software when auditing with the computer. Examples include *general-use software* such as word processing programs, spreadsheet software, and database management systems. Other software that we discuss, such as *generalized audit software (GAS)* and *electronic workpaper (EWP) software*, are more specifically oriented toward auditor tasks.

General-Use Software. Auditors employ **general-use software** as productivity tools that can improve their work. For instance, word processing programs improve effectiveness when writing reports because built-in spell checks can significantly reduce spelling errors. Similarly, an auditor can write a customer confirmation letter with a word processing program and mail-merge it with an address file so that each letter appears to have been individually prepared.

---

[6] COBIT, cobitonline.isaca.org, accessed in March 2017.

Spreadsheet software allows both accountants and auditors to make complex calculations automatically. It also allows the user to change one number and update all related numbers at the click of a mouse. One of the most common uses of electronic spreadsheets by accountants and auditors is for making mathematical calculations, such as interest and depreciation. Spreadsheet software can also be used to perform analytical procedures, such as computing ratios. Different presentation formats for data contained in spreadsheets contribute to the usefulness of these data for management decision-making and other managerial functions.

Accountants and auditors can use a *database management system (DBMS)* to perform some of the same functions as spreadsheet software. For instance, DBMSs can sort data and make certain mathematical computations. However, they are distinguished from spreadsheet software by their ability to manipulate *large* sets of data in fairly simple ways. As a general rule, accountants and auditors use spreadsheet software to make complex calculations with relatively small sets of data, whereas they will use DBMSs for simpler calculations or manipulations, such as sorting, on large data sets.

A DBMS is the backbone of almost all organizational accounting systems. The auditor can select subsets of a client company's data for manipulation purposes. This can be done either on the client's computer system or on the auditor's computer after the data are downloaded. A valuable tool for retrieving and manipulating data is **Structured Query Language (SQL)**, a popular data manipulation language. Auditors can use SQL to retrieve a client's data and display these data in a variety of formats for audit purposes. As an example, an auditor may use the SELECT command to retrieve inventory items meeting certain criteria, such as minimum dollar amount. Other data manipulation capabilities of SQL include: (1) selecting records matching specified criteria, (2) deleting records from a file based on established criteria, (3) generating customized reports based on all or a subset of data, and (4) rearranging file records in sequential order.

Generalized Audit Software. **Generalized audit software (GAS)** packages enable auditors to review computer files without continually rewriting processing programs. Large CPA firms have developed some of these packages in-house, and many other programs are available from various software suppliers. GAS programs are capable of the basic data manipulation tasks that spreadsheet or DBMS software might also perform. These include mathematical computations, cross-footing, categorizing, summarizing, merging files, sorting records, statistical sampling, and printing reports. One advantage GAS packages have over other software is that these programs are specifically tailored to audit tasks. Auditors can use GAS programs in a variety of ways in specific application areas, such as accounts receivable, inventory, and accounts payable. Figure 11-4 shows some of the ways auditors might use GAS to audit inventory applications.

Two popular GAS packages used by auditors are *Audit Command Language (ACL)* and *Interactive Data Extraction and Analysis (IDEA)*. These programs allow auditors to examine a company's data in a variety of formats. They include commands such as STRATIFY, EXTRACT, and JOIN. Each of these commands provides an auditor with a different view of the data. For example, the STRATIFY command lets an auditor group data into categories. This is useful, for example, in sorting inventories into various classes based on their cost. Stratification lets an auditor concentrate on high-dollar-value inventory items.

Another example of data stratification is related to auditing accounts receivable. Auditors will want to verify large receivable balances in greater proportion than

- Merge last year's inventory file with this year's, and list those items with unit costs greater than a certain dollar amount and that have increased by more than a specified percentage.
- List inventory quantities on hand in excess of units sold during a specified period, and list those inventory items with a last sales date prior to a specified date to identify possible obsolete inventory items.
- Select a sample of inventory tag numbers, and print the sample selection.
- Scan the sequence of inventory tag numbers, and print any missing or duplicate numbers.
- Select a random sample of inventory items for price testing on a dollar-value basis, and list all items with an extended value in excess of a specified amount.
- Perform a net-realizable-value test on year-end inventory quantities, and list any items where inventory cost exceeds net-realizable value.

FIGURE 11-4 Various ways to use generalized audit software packages to audit inventory.

small accounts-receivable balances. Most GAS packages allow auditors to *extract* data according to some specification. Auditors can extract data to detect a variety of exception conditions, such as duplicate invoice numbers, inventory items that have not been sold in more than 1 year, and customers with negative accounts-receivable balances. By *joining* files, auditors can compare data. For example, combining the employee file with the vendor file may show that an employee has perpetrated a fraud by creating a fictitious vendor. The following case describes how Stanford University used ACL to detect errors and improve security.

Case-in-Point 11.4 Stanford University uses ACL to analyze data from many different systems and its large Enterprise Resource Planning (ERP) system. Stanford recently analyzed its payment transactions and identified $480,000 in annual duplicate payments to vendors. The university also detected a programming error in its ERP system that created a data security threat.[7]

Electronic Workpapers. **Electronic workpaper** software (EWPs) allow internal and external auditors to automate and standardize specific audit tests and audit documentation. Some of the capabilities of EWPs are to: (1) generate trial balances, (2) make adjusting entries, (3) perform consolidations, (4) conduct analytical procedures, and (5) document audit procedures and conclusions. One advantage of using EWPs is the automation of footing, cross-footing, and reconciliation to schedules. Auditors can use this software to prepare consolidated trial balances and financial statements (that combine accounts of multiple companies). EWPs can also help auditors create common-size income statements and balance sheets that show account balances as percentages. In addition, EWPs can easily calculate financial statement ratios and measurements, such as the current ratio, working capital, inventory turnover rate, and price-earnings ratio.

The Internet can also be a valuable resource for IT auditors. There are many websites that offer useful advice and guidance. These include software vendor sites with patches for software security holes, sites with alerts about security threats, and websites that have special tools that may be used free of charge or purchased.

---

[7] ACL Services Ltd., www.acl.com/customers.

Case-in-Point 11.5   AuditNet[8] describes itself as a "global resource for auditors." Registered users can subscribe to download audit programs for a variety of application areas, such as accounts payable. These programs include detailed audit procedures. There is also a Sarbanes–Oxley resource center, a discussion forum, a virtual library, and a list of audit terminology and definitions.

People Skills

Arguably the most important skills that auditors require are people skills. After all, auditors must work as a team and be able to interact with clients. For example, to understand the organizational structure of the IT function, the IT auditor will need to interview the Chief Information Officer (CIO). Interviews are a mainstay of IT auditing. Similarly, IT auditors are also likely to find that many of the audit steps in their evaluation of internal controls have more to do with human behavior than technology. For example, one of the best protections against programmed threats such as viruses and worms is regularly updated antivirus software. While it may be important to understand the capabilities of the software, it is even more important to see if the security administrator is checking for virus updates and patches on a regular basis.

11.4   AUDITING COMPUTERIZED ACCOUNTING INFORMATION SYSTEMS

When computers were first used for accounting data processing functions, the typical auditor knew very little about automated data processing. The basic auditing approach, therefore, was to follow the *audit trail* up to the point at which accounting data entered the computer and to pick these data up again when they reappeared in processed form as computer output. This is called **auditing around the computer**. It assumes that the presence of accurate output verifies proper processing operations. This type of auditing pays little or no attention to the control procedures within the IT environment. Auditing around the computer is not generally an effective approach for auditing in a computerized environment, in part because it tests normal transactions but ignores exceptions. It is the exceptions that are of primary interest to the auditor.

When auditing a computerized AIS, an auditor should follow the *audit trail* through the internal computer operations phase of automated data processing. This approach, **auditing through the computer**, attempts to verify that the processing controls involved in the AIS programs are functioning properly. It also attempts to verify that the accounting data processed are accurate. Because this type of auditing tests the existence and functioning of control procedures, it normally occurs during the compliance phase of the flowchart in Figure 11-2.

Auditing through the computer usually assumes that the CPU and other hardware are functioning properly. This leaves the auditor the principal task of verifying processing and control logic as opposed to computer accuracy. Five techniques that auditors use to audit a computerized AIS are: (1) use of test data, integrated test facility (ITF), and parallel simulation to *test programs*; (2) use of audit techniques to *validate computer programs*; (3) use of logs and specialized control software to *review systems software*; (4) use of documentation and CAATs to validate user accounts and access privileges; and (5) use of embedded audit modules to achieve *continuous auditing*.

---

[8] AuditNet, LLC, www.auditnet.org.

Testing Computer Programs

In testing computer programs, the objective is to ensure that the programs accomplish their goals and that the data are input and processed accurately. Three techniques that auditors may employ to test computer programs are: (1) test data, (2) integrated test facilities, and (3) parallel simulation.

Test Data. It is the auditor's responsibility to develop a set of transactions that tests, as completely as possible, the range of exception situations that might occur. Conventionally, these transactions are called **test data**. Possible exception situations for a payroll application, for example, include out-of-sequence payroll checks, duplicate time cards, negative hours worked, invalid employee numbers, invalid dates, invalid pay rates, invalid deduction codes, and use of alphabetic data in numeric codes.

To conduct audit testing, an auditor will compare the results obtained from processing test data with a predetermined set of answers on an audit worksheet. If processing results and worksheet results do not agree, further investigation is necessary. A sample set of program edit tests and test data appears in Figure 11-5.

Integrated Test Facility. Although test data work well in validating an application's *input controls*, they are not as effective for evaluating integrated online systems or complex programming logic. In these situations, it may be better to use a more comprehensive test technique such as an **integrated test facility (ITF)**. The purpose of an ITF is to audit an AIS in an operational setting. This involves: (1) establishing a fictitious entity such as a department, branch, customer, or employee; (2) entering transactions for that entity; and (3) observing how these transactions are processed. For example, an auditor might create a number of fictitious credit customers and place appropriate accounts-receivable master records in the company's accounts-receivable computer files. From the standpoint of the auditor, of course, the information contained on these records is for test purposes only. To most of the employees of the company, however, these records represent bona fide customers entitled to purchase company merchandise inventory or services on credit.

To use an ITF, an auditor will introduce *artificial transactions* into the data processing stream of the AIS and have the company routinely handle the business involved. In a truly ITF, this may mean actually shipping merchandise (not ordered by anyone) to designated addresses or billing customers for services not rendered. Because of the amount of work involved, however, it may be necessary to intercept the ordered merchandise at the shipping department and reverse the billing transactions at the managerial level.

Parallel Simulation. With **parallel simulation**, the auditor creates a second system that duplicates a portion of the client's system. The auditor's system runs at the same

Program Edit Test	Required by Program	Test Data
Completeness	6 characters required	12345
Numeric field	Numeric characters only	123C45
Sign	Positive numbers only	−123456
Reasonableness	Hours worked should not exceed 80 per week	110
Valid code	Accept only I (invoice), P (payment), M (memo)	C
Range	Accept only dates between 01/01/10 and 12/31/11	02/05/13

FIGURE 11-5 Program edit tests and test data.

time as the client's system, and the auditor processes *live* data, rather than test data. The auditor can compare the processing and outputs from their own system to the client's system. Differences between the processing and outputs of the client system, relative to the auditor's duplicate (or parallel) system, indicate problems with the client's system.

In order for this method to be effective, an auditor must thoroughly understand the audited organization's computer system and know how to predict the results. As you might imagine, it can be very time-consuming and thus cost-prohibitive for an auditor to write computer programs entirely replicating those of the client. For this reason, parallel simulation usually involves replicating only certain critical functions of a program. For example, a program that replicates payroll processing might just calculate net pay for employees rather than making all the payroll calculations in the entire payroll program.

Validating Computer Programs

A clever programmer can thwart the use of test data by changing programs just before an auditor asks for the processing routine(s) required for the audit. Therefore, an auditor must validate any program that he or she is given by a client. Although there is no 100% foolproof way of validating a computer program, several procedures may be used to assist in this task, including tests of program change controls and program comparisons.

Tests of Program Change Controls. The process by which a newly developed program or program modification is put into actual use should be subject to **program change controls**. These are internal control procedures developed to protect against unauthorized program changes. Sound program change control practices require documentation of every request for application program changes. It also requires computer programmers to develop and implement changes in a separate environment rather than a live processing environment.

Depending on the size of an organization, the change control process might be one of many duties performed by one individual. Alternatively, responsibility might be assigned to more than one individual. The basic procedures in program change control include testing program changes and obtaining proper authorizations as programs move from a testing stage to actual production (live) use. The auditor's responsibility is to ensure that a company's management establishes and executes proper authorization procedures and that the company's employees observe these procedures.

A test of program change controls begins with an inspection of the documentation maintained by the information processing subsystem. Many organizations create flowcharts of their change control processes. The organization should also have special forms that authorize changes to existing programs or the development of new programs. Included on these *program authorization forms* should be the name of the individual responsible for the work and the signature of the supervisor responsible for approving the final programs. Similarly, there should be forms that show that the work has been completed and a signature authorizing the use of the program(s) for data processing. These authorizing signatures affix responsibility for the data processing routines and ensure accountability when problems arise. We call this a **responsibility system of computer program development and maintenance**. Figure 11-6 describes the processes that an auditor should validate.

The chief purpose of a responsibility system at the computer center is not to affix blame in the event of program failures but to ensure accountability and adequate supervisory controls in the critical area of data processing. Tighter control over both

- Programmers document all program changes on the proper change-request forms.
- Users and accountants properly cost all program change requests and the planning committee reviews high-cost projects.
- Both computer development committee personnel and users sign the outline specification form, thereby establishing authorization for the programming work.
- Program changes match those in the programs in the production load library (where currently used programs are stored).
- Documentation matches the production version of a computer program.
- Information systems personnel properly carry out librarian functions, especially a review of the paperwork involved with the documentation of program change requests.

FIGURE 11-6 Each of the aforementioned processes is checked by an auditor in reviewing a responsibility system of computer program development and maintenance.

the development of new programs and changes to existing programs is likely to result in better computer software, since individuals tend to exert more effort when they are held responsible for a given piece of work.

Program Comparison. To guard against unauthorized program tampering, such as the insertion of malicious code, it is possible to perform certain *control total tests* of program authenticity. One is a *test of length*. To perform this test, an auditor obtains the latest version of an accounting computer program to be verified and compares the number of bytes of computer memory it requires with an entry in a security table of length counts of all valid accounting programs. If the accounting program's length count fails to match its control total, the program is then further scrutinized. This process is similar to comparing the word count in two similar documents produced by *Microsoft Word*.

Another way to ensure consistency between the authorized version of an accounting computer program and the program version currently in use is to compare the code directly on a line-by-line basis using a *comparison program*. A comparison program will detect any changes that a programmer might have made, even if the programmer has been clever enough to ensure that the program length for the two versions is the same. Auditors must evaluate the trade-off between efficiency and effectiveness in choosing whether to use control totals, perform detailed program comparison, or rely on general controls over program changes to prevent unauthorized tampering with computer programs.

Review of Systems Software

Systems software controls include: (1) operating system software, (2) utility programs that do basic "housekeeping" chores such as sorting and copying, (3) program library software that controls and monitors storage of programs, and (4) access control software that controls logical access to programs and data files.

When auditing through the computer, auditors will want to review the systems software documentation. In addition, auditors will request management to provide certain output or runs from the software. For instance, the auditor, in reviewing how passwords within the system are set, will ask the information systems manager for a listing of all *parameters* or password characteristics designated in the system. Figure 11-7 lists some of the characteristics of passwords that the auditor typically examines.

Parameter	Definition	Sample Setting	Risk
Minimum password length	Minimum number of characters required	6 digits	Short passwords are more easily guessed
Required password change	Require users to change passwords at specific intervals	60 days	Compromised passwords can be used forever
Minimum interval before password change	Minimum number of days before user can change password	1 day	If a user believes someone has learned the password, how much time must pass before it can be changed?
Maximum number of repeating characters allowed	Specifies how many characters may be repeated within the password	2 characters	Passwords such as "AAAAAA" are easily guessed
Alphabetic characters	Passwords may not consist of only numbers	Alpha	Protects against use of birthdates or other easily guessed numbers
Dictionary entries	Passwords cannot be dictionary words	ROOTTOOT	Hackers use standard dictionaries to find passwords
Assignment	Only bona fide users are given passwords	Employee	Passwords ensure accountability in addition to providing access

FIGURE 11-7 Examples of parameters that might be set to control passwords.

Auditors may choose to use software tools to review systems software. A number of tools are available, ranging from user-written programs to commercial packages such as *CA-Examine*. There are also general analysis software tools, such as *SAS*, *SPSS*, and *FOCUS*. These software tools can query operating system files to analyze the system parameters.

Systems software usually generates automatic outputs that are important for monitoring a company's computer system. In auditing the company's system, an auditor will want to inspect these outputs, which include logs and incident reports. The company's management uses *logs* for accounting purposes and for scheduling the use of computer resources efficiently. Auditors will make use of these logs to evaluate system security. Unusual occurrences, such as programs run at odd times or programs run with greater frequency than usual, are noted and subsequently investigated. Management may manually maintain *incident reports*, or systems software may automatically generate these reports. The reports list events encountered by the system that are unusual or interrupt operations. Examples of incidents commonly recorded are security violations (such as unauthorized access attempts), hardware failures, and software failures.

Validating Users and Access Privileges

An IT auditor needs to make sure that all computer-system users are valid and that each has access privileges appropriate to his or her job responsibilities. Systems software generally includes access control software that determines how the system administrator sets up and controls user IDs, user profiles, and passwords. The IT auditor should verify that the software parameters are set appropriately and that IT staff are using them appropriately. For example, one audit task is to make sure that employee accounts are closed immediately after someone leaves the organization. To accomplish this, the IT auditor might request a list of current personnel from human resources. Another approach would be to obtain a current phone directory and compare names with those in the listing of user accounts.

IT auditors should also look at user listings to see if there are any Group IDs assigned. For example, there may be an ID named AP_Clerk. Sometimes, managers decide to issue these IDs to cut down on paperwork when making personnel changes. However, this type of ID prevents assigning responsibility to an individual. If one AP clerk were to make a mistake or commit fraud, the use of a Group ID would make it difficult to identify which of the accounts-payable clerks was responsible.

An IT auditor can visually inspect printouts from databases and software documentation to verify users, appropriateness of passwords, and spot Group IDs. However, a variety of auditor software tools are available to make the work more efficient. As an example, such software might examine login times. If a user has not logged in for several months, it may be that the account should have been deleted. Users logging on at odd hours may also provide information that something is not right. As we noted earlier in the chapter, IT auditors need to identify exception conditions and irregularities.

Continuous Auditing

Some audit tools can be installed within an information system itself to achieve continuous auditing or real-time assurance. **Continuous auditing** is increasingly important as we move toward real-time financial reporting. There is also increasing pressure to reduce the time span between the production of financial information and the audit of the information, known as the audit cycle. Stakeholders want audited information quickly. Many businesses already report some information in real time using the Internet, and public firms report financial information to the Securities and Exchange Commission (SEC) using Extensible Business Reporting Language (XBRL). As more reporting becomes electronic and the demand for the supply of real-time information increases, the demand for more continuous auditing of information is also growing.

Five specific approaches for continuous auditing are: (1) embedded audit modules or audit hooks, (2) exception reporting, (3) transaction tagging, (4) the snapshot technique, and (5) continuous and intermittent simulation. These tools allow auditing to occur even when an auditor is not present. With *embedded audit modules*, application subroutines capture data for audit purposes. These data usually are related to a high-risk area. For example, an application program for payroll could include program code that causes transactions meeting prespecified criteria to be written to a special log. Possible transactions that might be recorded in a log include those affecting inactive accounts, deviating from company policy, or involving write-downs of asset values. For payroll applications, these transactions could reflect situations where, for instance, employees worked more hours than are allowed. Another example might be recording related transactions occurring in a particular sequence.

The practice of *exception reporting* is also a form of continuous auditing. If the information system includes mechanisms to reject certain transactions that fall outside predefined specifications (such as an unusually large payment to a vendor), then the ongoing reporting of exception transactions allows the system to continually monitor itself.

Using *transaction tagging*, auditors can tag certain transactions with special identifiers such that the transactions can be traced through processing steps in the AIS and logged for review. For example, if a large payment is tagged by the AIS, the auditor will be able to review how this transaction entered the system, how it was processed, and what output it produced. Tagging in this instance could also check to see that controls within the system are operating. Suppose that a control procedure requires rejection of vendor payment if it exceeds a predetermined level. Auditors can review tagged transactions to make sure that the control procedure is functioning properly or determine if someone is overriding the control.

The *snapshot technique* examines the way transactions are processed. Selected transactions are marked with code that triggers the snapshot process. Audit modules in the computer program record these transactions and their master file records before and after processing activities. Snapshot data are recorded in a special file and reviewed by the auditor to verify that all processing steps have been properly performed.

Continuous and intermittent simulation (CIS) embeds an audit module in a database management system (DBMS). The CIS module examines all transactions that update the DBMS. If a transaction has special audit significance, the audit module independently processes the data (in a manner similar to *parallel simulation*), records the results, and compares them with those results obtained by the DBMS. If any discrepancies exist, the details of these discrepancies are written to an audit log for subsequent investigation. If serious discrepancies are discovered, the CIS may prevent the DBMS from executing the update process. A challenge for continuous auditing is that the data in complex organizations may be located in multiple DBMS. To effectively conduct real-time assurance, auditors may need to create a data mart or subset of the data warehouse specifically for audit purposes.

An example of continuous auditing on a smaller scale is embedding audit modules in spreadsheets. For example, the *Excel* payroll spreadsheet in Figure 11-8 computes the regular and overtime earnings for the employees of a construction company. Most

	A	B	C	D	E	F	G
1			**Choi Construction Company**				
2			**Payroll for Week Ending: 3/15/XX**				
3							
4		**Payrate**	**Regular Hours**	**Overtime Hours**	**Regular Pay**	**Overtime Pay**	**Total**
5	Adams	8.90	40	3	356.00	40.05	396.05
6	Baker	12.55	35	0	502.00	0.00	502.00
7	Carlton	9.60	40	2	384.00	38.80	422.80
8	Daniels	10.20	35	0	408.00	0.00	408.00
9	Englert	9.60	40	5	384.00	72.00	456.00
10	Franklin	11.55	40	0	462.00	0.00	462.00
11	Griffin	10.80	35	0	432.00	0.00	432.00
12	Hartford	9.90	40	10	396.00	148.50	544.50
13							
14	Totals:		305	20	$3,324.00	$ 299.35	$3,623.35
15							
16	Totals:						
17	Counts:	8	8	4			
18	Maximums:	12.55	40.00	10.00			
19	Sum: Reg + O'time						$3,623.35
20	Max Regular Pay:				$4,016.00		
21	Max Overtime Pay:					$ 753.00	

FIGURE 11-8 This simple spreadsheet to compute regular and overtime payments contains several errors.

spreadsheets of this type would only include the first few lines shown in the figure, plus perhaps the "Total" line in row 11. But this spreadsheet includes an auditing module that can help an accountant audit the application and check its validity and accuracy. The figure in the "Counts" row uses *Excel's* COUNTIF function to count the number of positive values in columns B, C, and D of the spreadsheet. An auditor can compare the largest of these numbers to the total number of employees known to work for the company. If we assume that this company has upper limits for the pay rate ($13), regular hours (40), and overtime hours (10), an auditor can also compare the values in the "Maximums" row against these upper limits to determine if any entries are too large.

11.5 INFORMATION TECHNOLOGY AUDITING TODAY

In this section, we discuss IT governance, important regulations that affect IT auditing, and additional guidance on performing IT audit services.

Information Technology Governance

IT governance is the process of using IT resources effectively to meet organizational objectives. It includes using IT efficiently, responsibly, and strategically. The IT Governance Institute, an ISACA affiliate, was created to help organizations ensure that IT resources are properly allocated, that IT risks are mitigated, and that IT delivers value to the organization.

There are two primary objectives of IT governance. The first set of objectives focus on using IT strategically to fulfill the organizational mission and to compete effectively. Top management and the Board of Directors are responsible for ensuring these IT governance objectives are achieved. The second set of IT governance objectives involves making sure that the organization's IT resources are managed effectively and that management controls IT-related risks. Meeting these objectives is the concern of the CIO, the auditors, and top management.

Case-in-Point 11.6   In 2014, the Texas A&M University System conducted a massive overhaul of its IT governance structure. A&M's universities expect to save $200 million over 10 years as a result of changes to IT infrastructure and a new, system-wide IT governance structure.[9]

The Sarbanes–Oxley Act of 2002

In 2002, Congress passed the **Sarbanes–Oxley Act**, the most sweeping piece of legislation to affect financial reporting and the accounting profession since the SEC Acts of 1933 and 1934. SOX was a response to the wave of corporate accounting scandals that took down many long-time business icons, including Enron and Arthur Andersen. Figure 11-9 describes several of the major provisions of the act. For example, *Section 201: Services Outside the Scope of Practice of Auditors; Prohibited Activities* prohibits public accounting firms from offering nonaudit services to a client at the same time

---

[9] Government Technology magazine, www.govtech.com.

Section 201: Services Outside the Scope of Practice of Auditors: Prohibited Activities

- Bookkeeping or other services related to accounting records of financial statements
- Financial information systems design and implementation
- Appraisal or valuation services, fairness opinions, or contribution-in-kind reports
- Actuarial services
- Internal audit outsourcing services
- Management functions or human resources
- Broker or dealer, investment adviser, or investment banking services
- Legal services and expert services unrelated to the audit
- Any other service determined by the Public Company Accounting Oversight Board as unallowable

Section 302: Corporate Responsibility for Financial Reports

The CEO and CFO of each public company issuing financial reports must prepare a statement that accompanies the audit report to certify the "appropriateness of the financial statements and disclosures contained in the periodic report, and that those financial statements and disclosures fairly present, in all material respects, the operations and financial condition of the issuer." The CEO and CFO must knowingly and intentionally violate this requirement in order to be liable.

Section 404: Management Assessment of Internal Controls

Public company annual reports must contain an internal control report, which should state the responsibility of management for establishing and maintaining an adequate internal control structure and procedures for financial reporting and contain an assessment, as of the end of the issuer's fiscal year, of the effectiveness of the internal control structure and procedures of the issuer for financial reporting. Each issuer's auditor must attest to, and report on, management's assessment.

FIGURE 11-9 A summary of key provisions of the Sarbanes–Oxley Act of 2002.

they are conducting an audit. This means that, for example, one Big Four firm might be the external auditors of Company A and a different Big Four firm could be the outsourced internal auditors for Company A. (They may, however, provide these services to nonaudit clients.)

SOX has four basic groups of compliance requirements: (1) audit committee/corporate governance requirements; (2) issues regarding certification, disclosure, and internal controls; (3) rules about financial statement reporting; and (4) regulations governing executive reporting and conduct. However, Sections 302 and 404 of the Act are sometimes called full-employment acts for IT auditors! The cost of complying with the legislation, particularly the requirement to document and attest to internal controls, runs into millions of dollars for large public companies.

When Jeffrey Skilling, Enron's Chief Executive Officer (CEO), testified before the Senate Banking and Commerce Committee in 2002, he claimed ignorance with respect to Enron's accounting. Later, Bernie Ebbers, CEO of WorldCom, claimed a similar lack of knowledge about his company's financial records. Shocked that corporate leaders might not understand the financial activities of their own companies, lawmakers included Section 302. This SOX provision requires both Chief Financial Officers (CFOs) and CEOs to certify personally that their company's financial statements are accurate and complete and also that internal controls and disclosures are adequate. Thus, SOX requires top management in public companies to understand their internal controls and makes them legally liable if they knowingly misrepresent the condition of these controls.

Section 404 of SOX requires both the CEO and CFO to assess their organization's internal controls over financial reporting and attest to them. They do so in an internal control report that is filed with the annual report. This section also requires that the external auditors report on management's internal control assessment. This is the work that is keeping management and a company's internal and external auditors the busiest.

To assess internal financial controls requires documenting business processes and internal controls. Large public companies are likely to make heavy use of IT in their processes and financial reporting, which means that they'll need an IT auditor to document the processes and controls. This can be a daunting task, but useful for companies to undertake. Consider that you may have a large financial services firm, for example, with literally hundreds of software applications and very complex business processes. Who has the big picture? Probably no one, unless the internal audit staff takes the time to fit the pieces together and create a "map" of the entire company's processes and applications.

The auditors can use this map to examine the internal controls in general and for each application. For example, one general type of internal control is separation of duties. Employees' duties should be clearer after the documentation of processes. Various applications will each have internal controls unique to them as well, such as a control over a procurement application concerning who may enter invoices.

An interesting by-product of SOX is the emergence of software to facilitate compliance with the new rules. The main uses of software for SOX are for managing communication, workflow, and documentation. Many accounting software packages include features to document internal controls. However, there are also specialized programs designed specifically to adhere to the requirements of Sarbanes–Oxley.

SOX regulations do not require companies to automate their controls or processes in order to be compliant. So, a company may have many manual processes and manual controls over those processes, in addition to the computerized processes and controls that are of primary interest to the IT auditor. IT auditors must work closely with financial auditors to complete the thorough internal control review mandated by Section 404.

Auditing Standard No. 2201 (AS 2201)

As a result of the substantial burdens created by Section 404 and the uncertainty surrounding the specific requirements of Section 404, the Public Company Accounting Oversight Board provided guidance in Auditing Standard No. 2201 (AS 2201)[10] that helps internal and external auditors reduce control testing and focus on the most critical controls.

One of the major changes that has resulted from AS 2201 is what has been called a rebalancing of internal auditors' work. Decreasing the volume of control testing allows internal auditors to spend more time on issues such as advising the board of directors and ensuring compliance with laws and regulations. AS 2201 also allows external auditors to increase their reliance on the test performed by internal audit functions, which reduces redundant tests.

---

[10] Note that the PCAOB renumbered the Auditing Standards in December 2016. AS 2201 was previously AS 5.

ISACA Information Technology Assurance Framework

In 2014, ISACA released the third edition of its Information Technology Assurance Framework (ITAF), which it bills as a "professional practices framework for IS audit and assurance." The purpose of the ITAF is to (1) set forth standards that inform the practice of IT auditing, defining roles and responsibilities, applicable knowledge, skills and abilities, and professional conduct; (2) define key terms and concepts applicable to the practice of IT auditing; and (3) guide the planning, design, execution, and communication of IT audit engagements.

ISACA's Code of Professional Ethics are included as part of the ITAF and is mandatory for all ISACA members and certification holder. The Code of Professional Ethics requires, among other things, that IT audit professionals:

- support standards and procedures conducive to effective governance, risk management, control and security practices;
- perform their duties in an objective and professional manner, adhering to applicable laws and doing nothing to discredit the profession;
- maintain the privacy and confidentiality of all information obtained during the course of an engagement;
- maintain and advance their repertoire of knowledge, skills, and abilities relevant to the profession;
- report their findings in a complete and objective manner; and
- educate stakeholders on IT audit, governance, security, and control issues.

IT auditors who fail to comply with the Code of Professional Ethics are subject to investigation and subsequent disciplinary action.

In addition to the Code of Professional Ethics, IT auditors who hold ISACA certifications or are ISACA members are required to comply with the Audit and Assurance Standards. The Standards are divided into three broad groupings: General Standards, Performance Standards, and Reporting Standards. The General Standards (1000 series) provide guidance on the attributes of the IT auditing profession, dealing primarily with the practitioner's ethics, knowledge, and abilities, and the auditor's ability to perform her duties with integrity and objectivity. The Performance Standards (1200 series) provide guidance on the planning and execution of IT assurance activities, as well as advising the IT auditor on the exercise of professional judgment and due care. Finally, the Reporting Standards (1400 series) provide guidance on the nature of communications issued by the IT auditor, include the types of reports, the audience, and the nature of information communicated.

The ITAF also includes a set of Guidelines that provide additional information on complying with the Standards. The Guidelines align with the Standards, such that there is a series of guidelines for the General Standards, Performance Standards, and Reporting Standards. The Guidelines often provide clarification on how to implement the associated Standard or may provide current thought leadership on best practices related to the implementation of a Standard. While the Guidelines are not mandatory, it is advisable for IT auditors to review them and be prepared to justify any departure.

Lastly, the ITAF also incorporates a series of Tools and Techniques. These are intended to provide examples to IT auditors on how to perform specific engagements, as well as technical guidance on frameworks (such as COBIT) and whitepapers. As with the Guidelines, use or implementation of Tools and Techniques is not mandatory.

IIA's Global Technology Audit Guides and Guide to the Assessment of IT Risk series

As previously mentioned, oftentimes IT auditors are employed as internal auditors for large organizations. Accordingly, the IIA, as the professional association of internal auditors, has provided a substantial set of guidance for IT auditors who perform internal audit services. As with ISACA's ITAF, this guidance is incorporated into the broader framework of the IIA's International Professional Practices Framework (IPPF). Similar to ISACA's ITAF, the IPPF provides a Code of Ethics, a set of Standards, and Recommended Supplemental Guidance. While a discussion of the IPPF is outside the scope of this chapter, suffice it to say that it is not at conflict with the ITAF or other standards from audit-related professional associations.

Perhaps the most useful set of guidance related to IT auditing in the IPPF are the Global Technology Audit Guides (GTAGs). These Practice Guides are part of the IPPF's Supplemental Recommended Guidance and are designed to inform the auditing practice on a diverse array of technology-related areas. Many of the GTAG publications provide an overview of the risks and associated controls related to the technology, guidance on planning the engagement, and a sample audit plan that auditors can customize for their specific audit needs.

In addition to the GTAGs, the IPPF's Supplemental Recommended Guidance also includes a series of publications that comprise the Guide to the Assessment of IT Risk (GAIT). The purpose of the GAIT publications is to better explain the complex relationship between business risks, controls embedded within business processes, and their interplay with associated IT general and application controls. The GAIT Methodology publication articulates a methodology for assessing the scope of implementation and operating effectiveness of IT general controls that are relevant to internal control over financial reporting. The GAIT Methodology is designed to be complimentary in nature with the guidance espoused in AS 2201. A second publication, *GAIT for IT General Control Deficiency Assessment*, is useful in identifying and remediating any IT general control deficiencies identified as part of the organization's annual risk assessment process. Also known as GAIT 2, this publication provides guidance on mapping IT general control weaknesses to weaknesses in internal control over financial reporting. Finally, a third publication, *GAIT for Business and IT Risk* (GAIT-R), provides additional guidance in linking business risks to IT risks. GAIT-R focuses auditors and managers on those IT risks that directly translate to a risk in achieving business objectives.

AIS AT WORK
Future of Information Technology Auditing[11, 12]

One of the author's graduate accounting students recently visited her former professor after working for several years with a Big Four public accounting firm. She indicated that her work involved much more IT auditing than she ever expected. In fact, her very

---

[11] Protivi. Arriving at Internal Audit's Tipping Point Amid Business Transformation: Assessing the Results of the 2016 Internal Audit Capabilities and Needs Survey—and a Look at Key Trends over the Past Decade. www.protiviti.com. Accessed in March 2017

[12] Robert Half. Everything You Need to Know about IT Auditor Jobs. Accessed in March 2017.

first assignment in public accounting was to audit the passwords and access controls of an operating system. The former student was amazed that most of her work during the first year involved both the use and analysis of sophisticated technology. Recent research of the audit profession suggests that IT auditing will only continue to grow in importance.

The pervasiveness of IT audit needs is not limited solely to the Big Four public accounting firms and the external audit space. A 2016 survey by global risk and business consulting firm Protiviti suggested that internal audit departments had reached a tipping point with respect to IT audit needs. For example, survey respondents identified several areas of concern associated with technology-enabled initiatives: increased Board awareness of cybersecurity concerns, increased coverage of IT risks as a permanent component of the annual internal audit plan, threat of Internet of Things (IoT) and other emerging technologies, and an increasing need for data analytics and technology-enabled continuous auditing. In fact, nearly half of the priorities identified in the 2016 survey by internal audit leadership are associated with better utilizing technology in the audit, as well as more fully incorporating data analytics into audit activities.

Financial recruiting firm Robert Half's 2016 Salary Guide for Accounting and Finance listed IT auditor among the top 10 positions in greatest demand. The average starting salary for an IT auditor with 1 to 3 years of experience rose by almost 4% in 2016. The results of these and other recent studies reveal that there is a growing need to recruit auditors with IT skills, as well as a need to increase spending on IT training. Thus, we should expect to see increased demand for students with both IT and audit skills and knowledge.

 ## SUMMARY

✓ Although both the internal and external auditors are concerned with computerized systems, there are important differences in the goals of each type of auditor.

✓ IT auditing may complement the financial audit, by providing a basis for determining the appropriate scope of the financial audit.

✓ Auditors today have some special tools available to them for designing and evaluating internal controls in IT environments, including general-use software and generalized audit software (GAS).

✓ People skills, including team-building and interpersonal skills are important for an IT auditor.

✓ IT auditors use a risk assessment approach in designing their audit programs to ensure that the costs of control procedures do not outweigh their value.

✓ Auditing through the computer involves both testing and validating computer programs, as well as review of systems software and validating user accounts and access privileges.

✓ Embedded audit modules are an example of one tool available to perform a continuous audit.

✓ Proper IT governance mandates that managers not only control risks associated with IT, but that they also use IT strategically.

✓ An increase in attention to fraud and internal controls, as mandated by SAS No. 99 and the Sarbanes–Oxley Act of 2002 has increased the need for the type of work done by IT auditors.

✓ IT auditors have a variety of resources available to them.

KEY TERMS YOU SHOULD KNOW

auditing around the computer

auditing through the computer

auditing with the computer

Certified Information Systems
Auditor (CISA)

Chief Audit Executive
(CAE)

compliance testing

computer-assisted audit
techniques (CAATs)

continuous auditing

Control OBjectives for
Information and related
Technology (COBIT)

electronic workpaper

external auditing

general-use software

generalized audit software (GAS)

information systems risk
assessment

information technology (IT)
auditing

integrated test facility (ITF)

internal auditing

IT governance

parallel simulation

penetration testing

program change control

responsibility system of
computer program
development and maintenance

risk-based audit

Sarbanes–Oxley Act

Structured Query Language (SQL)

test data

TEST YOURSELF

Q11-1. An IT auditor:

a. must be an external auditor

b. must be an internal auditor

c. can be either an internal or external auditor

d. must be a certified public accountant

Q11-2. In determining the scope of an IT audit, the auditor should pay most attention to:

a. threats and risks

b. the cost of the audit

c. what the IT manager asks to be evaluated

d. listings of standard control procedures

Q11-3. Auditing around the computer:

a. is the approach to auditing that is recommended in most cases to reduce IT audit costs

b. focuses on computerized control procedures

c. assumes that accurate output is sufficient evidence that processing operations are appropriate

d. follows the audit trail through internal computer operations

Q11-4. COBIT is:

a. a control framework developed by the Institute of Internal Auditors

b. a control framework developed specifically for organizations involved in e-business

c. an internal control model that covers both automated and manual systems

d. an internal control framework and model that encompasses an organization's IT governance and information technologies

Q11-5. Which of the following is NOT true with respect to generalized audit software (GAS)?

a. They require auditors to rewrite processing programs frequently while reviewing computer files

b. They are specifically tailored to auditor tasks

c. They may be used for specific application areas, such as accounts receivable and inventory

d. They allow auditors to manipulate files to extract and compare data

Q11-6. Which of the following is NOT an audit technique for auditing computerized AIS?

a. Parallel simulation

b. Use of specialized control software

c. Continuous auditing

d. All of the above are techniques used to audit computerized AIS

Q11-7. In auditing program change control, the IT auditor will:

a. make sure that only computer programmers have tested the changes they made to programs

b. ensure an organization is following the process described in their documentation for program change control

c. not need to inspect program authorization forms for signatures

d. make sure that only computer programmers move their own changes into a production environment

Q11-8. Continuous auditing:

a. has been talked about for years but will never catch on

b. will become more necessary as investors demand more real-time information

c. does not include techniques such as embedded audit modules

d. will never allow IT auditors to provide some types of assurance on a real-time basis

Q11-9. With respect to changes in IT auditing today, which of the following is NOT true?

a. IT governance, which ties IT to organizational strategy, is increasingly important

b. Section 404 of the Sarbanes–Oxley Act of 2002 created an increase in demand for both IT auditors and internal auditors

c. IT auditors are concerned only with supporting financial auditors and should not investigate fraud cases

d. third-party assurance seals may provide some comfort to e-business customers regarding the security of online transactions

Q11-10. Of the following, the primary objective of compliance testing is to determine whether[13]

a. procedures are regularly updated

b. financial statement line items are properly stated

c. controls are functioning as planned

d. collusion is taking place

DISCUSSION QUESTIONS

11-1. Distinguish between the roles of an internal and an external auditors. Cite at least two examples of auditing procedures that might reasonably be expected of an internal auditor but not an external auditor. Which type of auditor would you rather be? Why?

11-2. How does information technology auditing differ from financial auditing? Make a list of the skills you think are important for financial auditors and for IT auditors. Do you think all auditors should have all the skills on both lists? Why or why not?

11-3. Describe the differences between general-use software and generalized audit software. How might you use spreadsheet software, database software, and word processing software in conducting an audit of fixed assets?

11-4. IT auditors need people skills as well as technical skills. One such skill is the ability to interview effectively. Discuss some techniques or tools that might help an interviewer get the best information from an interviewee, including sensitive information.

11-5. Describe how an auditor might use through-the-computer techniques such as test data, an integrated test facility, parallel simulation, or validation of computer programs to accomplish audit objectives relative to accounts payable.

11-6. Jose Rodriguez was the only internal auditor of a medium-sized communications firm. The company used a computer for most of its accounting applications, and recently, several new software packages had been implemented to handle the increased volume of the company's business. To evaluate the packages' control capabilities, Jose performed a cost–benefit analysis and found that many of the control procedures were potentially useful but not clearly cost-effective. The problem, therefore, was what to say in his report to management. After pondering this question for some time, he decided to recommend almost all the controls based on the idea that a company was "better to be safe than sorry." Comment on the wisdom of this idea.

11-7. Discuss the historical drivers for the development of IT auditing as a profession. What factors do you foresee influencing the field of IT auditing in the next decade? What do you feel are the greatest challenges facing IT auditors?

---

[13] Prior CMA exam question.

PROBLEMS

11-8. The Espy Company recently had an outside consulting firm perform an audit of its information systems department. One of the consultants identified some business risks and their probability of occurrence. Estimates of the potential losses and estimated control costs are given in Figure 11-10.

   a. Using the Figure 11-10 information, develop a risk assessment for the Espy Company.

   b. If you were the manager responsible for the Espy Company's information processing system, which controls would you implement and why?

11-9. Visit www.isaca.org, the website for the Information Systems Audit and Control Association. Investigate the Certified Information Systems Auditor (CISA) credential. Describe the purpose of the credential and the types of auditing CISAs perform.

11-10. Information systems auditors sometimes use tools or information they can download from the Internet. These tools or information may include software, audit guides, or computer security advisories. Locate some examples from the Internet of audit tools, audit guides, or computer security advisories that you would find useful in conducting an audit of a client's computer system.

11-11. Continuous auditing has the potential to reduce labor costs associated with auditing. It also can provide audit assurance closer to the occurrence of a transaction, which improves the reliability of frequent or real-time financial reports. Using an Internet search engine, find an example of an organization's usage of continuous auditing.

| Hazard | Probability that Loss will Occur | Losses ($) | | Estimated Control Costs ($) |
		Low Estimate	High Estimate	
Equipment failure	0.08	50,000	150,000	2,000
Software failure	0.10	4,000	18,000	1,400
Vandalism	0.65	1,000	15,000	8,000
Embezzlement	0.05	3,000	9,000	1,000
Brownout	0.40	850	2,000	250
Power surge	0.40	850	2,000	300
Flood	0.15	250,000	500,000	2,500
Fire	0.10	150,000	300,000	4,000

FIGURE 11-10   A risk analysis for the Espy Company.

CASE ANALYSES

11-12. Basic Requirements (Systems Reliability Assurance)

Kara and Scott Baker own a small retail company, Basic Requirements, with one store located in a small college town and a website through which customers can make purchases. The store sells traditional but up-to-date clothing for young women such as tee-shirts, jeans, chinos, and skirts. The store has been open for 10 years, and the owners added the online shopping capability just last year. Online business has been slow, but Kara and Scott believe that as student customers graduate from the university, they will use the online site to continue to have access to their favorite store from their college days.

The store's website has many features. It classifies clothing by type, and customers can view items in various colors. To purchase an item, the user clicks on the icon depicting the desired product and adds it to an individual online shopping basket. The customer can view the basket and make a purchase at any time while browsing the site. When checking out at the site, a new customer must first register, providing billing and shipping information, as well as credit card data. Returning customers log in with the identification code and password they created when they registered. They also use that method to check on an order status. If a customer forgets their login information, they can simply click on a link to have it e-mailed to them. Once a user registers, Basic Requirements' system will automatically add their e-mail address to a file that they use to regularly send out e-mails about sales and other promotions.

Kara and Scott are concerned about internal controls in their business. They especially worry because they know that their Web access creates some special risks. They have asked one of their customers who is an accounting student at the university to evaluate the reliability of their information system with respect to security, availability, and privacy.

Requirements

1. Identify two security, availability, and privacy risks that Basic Requirements faces.

2. For each risk identified earlier, describe two internal controls Basic Requirements should use to protect against these risks.

3. The accounting student who is evaluating the reliability of Basic Requirements' information system is interested in becoming an IT auditor. Describe some of the specific actions an IT auditor would take to verify that Kara and Scott have adequate controls in place concerning privacy.

11-13. Tiffany Martin, CPA (Information Technology Audit Skills)

Tiffany Martin is an audit manager in a medium-sized public accounting firm. Tiffany graduated from college 7 years ago with a degree in accounting. She obtained her CPA certification soon after she joined the firm where she currently works. Tiffany is a financial auditor; she has had little training in auditing computerized information systems.

The current engagement Tiffany is working on includes a complex information processing system with multiple applications. The financial accounting transactions are processed on a server. The IT department employs 25 personnel, including programmers, systems analysts, a database administrator, computer operators, technical support, and a director. Tiffany has not spoken with anyone in the department because she is fearful that her lack of technical knowledge relative to IT will cause some concern with the client.

Because Tiffany does not understand the complexities of the computer processing environment, she is unable to determine what risks might result from the computerized system's operations. She is particularly worried about unauthorized changes to programs and data that would affect the reliability of the financial statements.

Tiffany has spoken to Dick Stanton, the partner who has responsibility for this audit client, about her concerns. Dick has suggested that Tiffany conduct more substantive testing than she would undertake in a less complex processing environment. This additional testing will hopefully ensure that there are no errors or fraud associated with the computer processing of the financial statements.

Requirements

1. Do you think that Dick Stanton's suggested approach is the most efficient way to control risks associated with complex computer environments?

2. How should Tiffany respond to Dick's suggestion?

3. What can a public accounting firm, such as the one in which Tiffany works, do to ensure that audits of computerized accounting information systems are conducted efficiently and effectively?

4. Should Tiffany be allowed to conduct this audit given her limited skill level? How might she acquire the necessary skills?

11-14. Consolidated Company (Audit Program for Access Controls)

Jason Saving is an IT auditor for a large, public accounting firm. His manager has assigned him to the Consolidated Company audit. The IT auditors must complete several evaluating and testing procedures in order to help determine the scope of financial audit. The IT auditors also need to evaluate IT controls to provide the financial auditors with information in order to form an opinion on internal controls as part of Sarbanes–Oxley compliance.

Consolidated Company manufactures automotive parts and supplies them to the largest automakers. The company has approximately 1,500 employees and has manufacturing operations and offices in three locations. Consolidated uses a mid-sized Enterprise Resource Planning (ERP) software program for manufacturers that they acquired and implemented 2 years ago.

You need to develop an audit program to examine logical access to the ERP system. According to the Security Administrator at Consolidated, each employee is assigned a unique User ID and password when they join the company. The company is very concerned about security, so there is no remote access to the ERP system. The ERP system requires that users change their passwords every 6 months. System and group settings assigned to each User ID determine what parts of the ERP systems are available to each user.

Requirements

1. Explain how a deficiency in controls over User IDs and passwords might affect the financial statements.
2. Why is it necessary to examine User IDs and passwords?
3. Describe at least four control procedures that Consolidated should have in place to ensure that only authorized users access the system and that user access is limited according to their responsibilities.

READINGS AND OTHER RESOURCES

Debreceny, R. 2013. Research on IT governance, risk, and value: Challenges and opportunities. *Journal of Information Systems* 27(1): 129–135.

Kuhn, J., and S. Sutton. 2010. Continuous auditing in ERP system environments: The current state and future directions. *Journal of Information Systems* 24(1): 91–112.

Steinbart, P., R. Raschke, G. Gal, and W. Dilla. 2013. Information security professionals' perceptions about the relationship between the information security and internal audit functions. *Journal of Information Systems* 27(2): 65–86.

Go to www.wiley.com/go/simkin/videos to access videos on the following topics:
  Introduction to Continuous Auditing
  IT Auditing: Where Companies Are Falling Short

ANSWERS TO TEST YOURSELF

1. c **2.** a **3.** c **4.** d **5.** a **6.** d **7.** b **8.** b **9.** c **10.** c

Chapter 12

Documenting Accounting Information Systems

After studying this chapter, you will be able to:

1. *Explain* why documenting an accounting information system (AIS) is important.

2. *Draw* simple data flow diagrams and document flowcharts, and explain how they describe the flow of data in AISs.

3. *Draw* simple system flowcharts and process maps, and interpret these diagrams.

4. *Explain* how program flowcharts, decision tables, and decision trees help document AISs.

5. *List* software available for documenting AISs and helping companies comply with the Sarbanes–Oxley Act and Auditing Standard 2201.

6. *Explain* the importance of end-user documentation.

"Efforts by the Public Company Accounting Oversight Board to ensure that audits of public companies adhere to the provisions of Auditing Standard No. 5 [now No. 2201]... have prompted audit firms and internal audit departments to improve their understanding and documentation of business processes and controls."

Borthick, A. F., and G.P. Scneider. 2016. Detecting errors in and making inferences from business process representation. *Journal of Emerging Technologies in Accounting* 13(2): 185–194

12.1 INTRODUCTION

Documentation explains how accounting information systems (AISs) operate and is therefore a vital part of any accounting system. For example, documentation describes the tasks for recording accounting data, the procedures that users must perform to operate computer applications, the processing steps that AISs follow, and the logical and physical flows of accounting data through systems. This chapter explains in greater detail why accountants need to understand documentation and describes tools for diagramming complex systems.

Accountants can use many different types of logic charts to trace the flow of accounting data in an AIS. Although we live in the electronic age, a surprising number of accounting systems continue to depend upon physical order forms, employee application documents, or requisition slips to transmit information from one place to another. *Document flowcharts* describe the *physical* flow of such documents through an AIS. These flowcharts pictorially represent data paths in compact formats and save pages of narrative description. *System flowcharts* are similar to document flowcharts, except that **system flowcharts** usually focus on the electronic flows of data in computerized AISs. Other examples of documentation include process maps, data flow diagrams (DFDs), program flowcharts, decision tables, and decision trees. This chapter describes these documentation aids, as well as some computerized tools for creating them.

Today, many end users develop computer applications for themselves. This end-user programming is very helpful to managers, who consequently do not require information technology (IT) professionals to develop simple word processing, spreadsheet, or database applications. But end-user programming can also be a problem because many employees do not know how to document their work properly or simply don't do so. The final section of this chapter examines the topic of end-user programming and documentation in greater detail.

12.2 WHY DOCUMENTATION IS IMPORTANT

Accountants do not typically write complex computer programs. Nonetheless, it is important for them to understand the documentation that describes how the processing of financial information takes place. Documentation includes the flowcharts, narratives, and other written communications that describe the inputs, processing, and outputs of an AIS. Documentation also describes the logical flow of data within a computer system and the procedures that employees must follow to accomplish application tasks. Here are 10 reasons why documentation is important to AISs.

1. **Depicting how the system works.** Observing large AISs in action is an impractical way to learn about them, even if they are completely manual. In computerized systems, it is impossible to understand systems without thorough documentation because the processing is electronic and therefore invisible. Examining written descriptions and diagrams of the inputs, processing steps, and outputs is an efficient way to understand key components of systems. This is one purpose of documentation: to help explain how an AIS operates. Documentation facilitates this understanding, assists accountants in designing controls, demonstrates to managers how AISs will meet their information needs, and assists auditors in understanding the systems that they test and evaluate.

    The Internet contains many examples of flowcharts or logic diagrams that help individuals understand unfamiliar tasks or processes. For example, some universities use them to show students what classes to take and when they should take them to complete their majors in a timely manner. The University of Washington has flowcharts that show how to obtain grants and other types of funding. The University of Illinois at Urbana-Champaign uses elaborate diagrams to depict what happens when a faculty member's employment terminates. Figure 12-1 is a logic diagram from the University of Arizona website that shows employees how to file a claim for reimbursement. If the employee would like additional information for any step in the process, a click of the mouse on the appropriate flowchart symbol reveals additional information. The charts are intended to simplify long narratives describing how to file reimbursements.

2. **Training users.** Documentation also includes user guides, manuals, and similar operating instructions that help people learn how an AIS operates. Whether

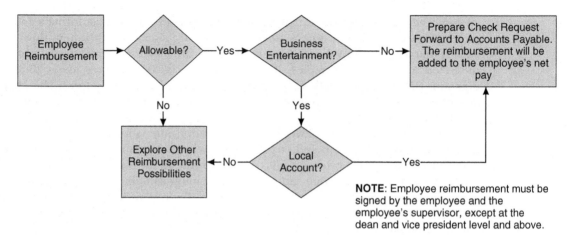

FIGURE 12-1 Example of a flowchart used at the University of Arizona to help employees file a reimbursement claim. For additional information, individuals simply click on the appropriate symbol.

distributed manually in hard-copy format or electronically in Help files or "get-started tours" of microcomputer applications, this documentation helps train users to operate AIS hardware and software, solve operational problems, and perform their jobs better.

> **Case-in-Point 12.1** One task of the US Internal Revenue Service (IRS) is to help tax filers understand when their home mortgage interest payments or closing costs are deductible and, if so, for how much. Figures A and B of IRS Publication 936 (2016 version) contain flowcharts that provide step-by-step decisions to help tax filers answer these questions.[1]

3. **Designing new systems.** Documentation helps system designers develop new systems in much the same way that blueprints help architects design buildings. Professional IT personnel commonly hold **structured walkthroughs** in which they review system documentation to ensure the integrity and completeness of their designs or to identify design flaws. Well-written documentation and related graphical systems-design methodologies play key roles in reducing systems failures and decreasing the time spent correcting "emergency errors." Conversely, poorly designed systems often lead to large-scale errors and expensive write-offs.

4. **Controlling systems development and maintenance costs.** Personal computer applications typically employ prewritten, off-the-shelf software that is relatively stable, reliable, and inexpensive. In contrast, custom-developed business systems can cost millions of dollars and can be less reliable. Good documentation helps systems designers develop **object-oriented software**, which is software that contains modular, reusable code. This object-orientation helps programmers avoid writing duplicate programs and facilitates changes when programs must be modified later. If you have ever replaced a specialized part in your car, you have some idea of how frustrating, time-consuming, and expensive "nonstandardization" can

---

[1] IRS publication 936 Home Mortgage Interest Deduction can be accessed online at www.irs.gov/pub/irs-pdf/p936.pdf.

be and therefore how useful object-oriented programming might be to business organizations.

5. **Standardizing communications with others.** The usefulness of narrative descriptions can vary significantly, and a reader can interpret such descriptions differently from what the writer intended. Documentation aids such as document flowcharts, entity–relationship (E–R) diagrams, or DFDs are standardized tools that are more likely to be interpreted the same way by all parties viewing them. Thus, documentation tools are important because they help describe an existing or proposed system in a "common language" and help users communicate with one another about these systems.

6. **Auditing AISs.** Documentation helps depict audit trails. When examining an AIS, for example, the auditors typically focus on internal controls. In such circumstances, documentation helps auditors determine the strengths and weaknesses of a system's controls and therefore the scope and complexity of the audit itself. Similarly, auditors may want to trace sample outputs to the original transactions that created them (e.g., tracing inventory assets back to original purchases). Finally, Auditing Standard 2201 requires auditors to understand a client's system of internal controls before conducting an audit. System documentation helps auditors with these tasks.

7. **Documenting business processes.** Understanding business processes can lead to better systems and better decisions. Documentation helps managers better understand how their businesses operate, what controls are involved or missing from critical organizational activities, and how to improve core business activities.

8. **Complying with the Sarbanes–Oxley Act.** Section 404 of the Sarbanes–Oxley Act of 2002 (SOX) requires publicly traded companies to identify the major sources of business risks, document their internal control procedures, and hire external auditors to evaluate the validity and effectiveness of such procedures. Documentation is crucial for analyzing the risks of errors, frauds, omissions, and problems with important business processes, as well as helping auditors evaluate the controls used to mitigate such risks.

> ***Case-in-Point 12.2*** In addition to passing the Sarbanes–Oxley Act, Congress established the Public Company Accounting Oversight Board (PCAOB) to help protect the interests of investors and the general public. At one time, the board was satisfied with written descriptions of the internal financial controls of a company. Now, it asks for flowcharts to better understand these complicated financial processes.[2]

Almost everyone acknowledges that the costs of complying with SOX are enormous, and many also believe that SOX gave documentation "a new life." To save money, many companies now use software packages to help them automate SOX documentation tasks. We describe some examples of such software in a later section of this chapter. While Auditing Standard 2201 has reduced some of the documentation burdens created by SOX, the documentation requirements for internal controls and risk assessments remain much more substantial than during the pre-SOX era.

---

[2] Swan, H. 2012. How flowcharts help companies save money, get accurate audits, and satisfy the government, accessed at mapthink.blogspot.com.

9. **Establishing accountability.** Manual signatures on business and government documents allow employees and government agents to execute their responsibilities, create audit trails, and establish accountability for their actions. An example is a **signed checklist** that outlines the month-end journal entries an accountant must perform. Such checklists verify that an accountant performed these tasks, that a supervisor approved them, and that both individuals are accountable for the accuracy of the work. Similar comments apply to the checklists for preparing financial statements, tax returns, auditing working papers, budgets, and similar accounting documents. Including such checklists with the statements themselves documents the work that the employees performed as well as the procedures and controls *involved* in the work. Signed approvals (e.g., manager-approved purchase requests) create similar levels of accountability for large expenditures.

> **Case-in-Point 12.3** Quality documentation, evidence of proper authorization, and clear accountability can yield benefits in addition to improved systems design and better internal control. During recent economic times, employee layoffs were high and wrongful-termination lawsuits also rose. Lawyers suggest that an employer's best defense in these lawsuits is clear documentation of employee duties and the procedures they should follow. When managers document employee responsibilities and their inability to meet them, organizations have an easier time defending termination decisions.[3]

10. **Saving Money.** Because documentation takes time to create, it costs organizations money. But adequate documentation can also save money. To illustrate, imagine a new AIS with no documentation, but that employees must now use to perform their jobs. In such cases, employees will typically first try to figure things out for themselves by trial and error (sometimes with disastrous consequences) and then look for answers from online forums or call the Technical Support desk. By this time, they are angry, frustrated, and unforgiving. But tech support is also expensive, and the ability to minimize the costs of providing tech support can save money.

> **Case-in-Point 12.4** Blogging on Writing Assistance, Inc., Jacquie Samuels includes a calculator that shows how much a business can save with "great documentation." For the example shown—an illustration for a small-to-medium-sized company—the total savings was over $2 million.[4]

12.3 PRIMARY DOCUMENTATION TOOLS

Despite the many reasons why documentation is important, most organizations find that they document less than they should. One explanation for this deficiency is that organizations often create or implement large AISs under tight deadlines. In such cases, the urgency to develop "a system that works" overrides the need for "a system that is well documented." Another reason is that most IT professionals much prefer creating systems relative to documenting them. Thus, many developers actively resist it, arguing that they will "get around to it later" or that documenting is a job for somebody else.

---

[3] Bresler, J. L. 2009. Proper Documentation Is Your Best Legal Defense. Accessed at www.TheLedger.com
[4] Samuels, J. Great Documentation Can Save You Big Bucks When It Comes to Support. Accessed at www.writingassistant.com/resources/articles.

Insufficient and/or deficient documentation costs organizations time and money, and good documentation can be as important as the software it describes. We next describe several documentation methods that are available to document AISs. Four common documentation methods are DFDs, document flowcharts, system flowcharts, and process diagrams.

Data Flow Diagrams

System designers primarily use **data flow diagrams (DFDs)** in the systems development process—for example, as a tool for analyzing an existing system or as a planning aid for creating a new system. Because documented data flows are important for understanding an AIS, many of the chapters of this book use DFDs to illustrate the flow of data in the AISs under discussion.

Different types of diagrams give different views of systems, which is why reviewers may need multiple diagrams to fully understand a complete process. A DFD describes the sources of data stored in a database and the ultimate destinations of these data.

Data Flow Diagram Symbols. Figure 12-2 illustrates the four basic symbols used in DFDs. A rectangle or square represents an external data source or data destination—for example, a customer. To show this, a DFD would include the word "customer" inside a data source or destination symbol. In Figure 12-2, the term "external entity" means "an entity outside the system under study," not necessarily an entity that is external to the company. Thus, for example, a "customer" might be another division of the same company under study.

Data flow lines are lines with arrows that indicate the direction that data flow in the system. For this reason, every data source symbol will have one or more data flow lines leading away from it, and every data destination symbol will have one or more data flow lines leading into it. For clarity, you should label each data flow line to indicate exactly what data are flowing along it.

A circle or "bubble" in a DFD indicates a system entity or process that changes or transforms data. (Some authors prefer to use squares with rounded corners for this symbol.) In physical DFDs (discussed shortly), the label inside a bubble typically contains the title of the person performing a task—for example, "cashier." In logical DFDs (also discussed shortly), the label inside the bubble describes a transformation process—for example, "process cash receipts."

Finally, DFDs use a set of parallel lines or an open rectangle to represent a store or repository of data. This is usually a file or database table. If data are permanently

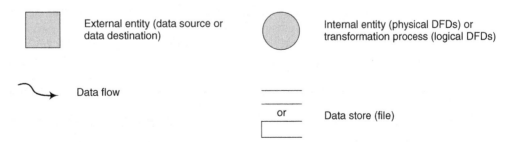

FIGURE 12-2 Symbols for data flow diagrams.

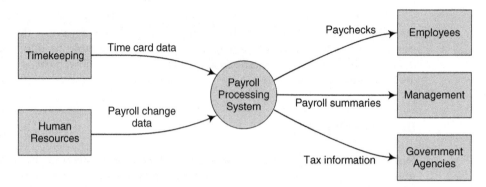

FIGURE 12-3 A context diagram for a payroll processing system.

stored, a data store symbol is mandatory. If data are collected over time and stored in some temporary place, you are not required to use a file symbol for this (although experts recommend including one for clarity).

Context Diagrams. We typically draw DFDs in levels that show increasing amounts of detail. Designers first prepare a high-level DFD called a **context diagram** to provide an overview of a system. Figure 12-3 is an example of a context diagram for payroll processing.

The DFD in Figure 12-3 shows the inputs and outputs of the application (payroll processing) as well as the data sources and destinations external to the application. Thus, this context diagram uses rectangles to identify "Timekeeping" and "Human Resources" as external entities, despite the fact that these departments are internal to the company. This is because these entities are external to the payroll processing system under study. The data flow lines connecting these entities to and from the system (e.g., time card data) are "system interfaces."

Physical Data Flow Diagrams. A context diagram shows very little detail. For this reason, system designers usually elaborate on the elements in context DFDs by decomposing them into successively more detailed levels. These subsequent DFDs show more specifics, such as processing details or the inputs and outputs associated with each processing step.

The first level of detail is commonly called a **physical data flow diagram**. Figure 12-4 is an example for our payroll illustration. The bubbles in the physical DFD of Figure 12-4 identify the data-entry clerk who enters payroll information into the computer, the payroll cashier who distributes paychecks to employees, and the tax accountant who sends tax information to the Internal Revenue Service.

Figure 12-4 illustrates several important characteristics of physical DFDs. First, we observe that each bubble contains a unique number and title. Including a number in each bubble makes it easier to reference it later. This also assists designers in the decomposition tasks discussed shortly. Second, we notice that a physical DFD includes the same inputs and outputs as its predecessor context diagram in Figure 12-3—that is, the context DFD and the physical DFD are balanced. This *balancing* is important because unbalanced DFDs are inconsistent and likely contain errors. Third, we find that all bubbles in the physical DFD contain the names of system entities (i.e., the titles of employees). These titles should correspond to the titles in an official organization chart.

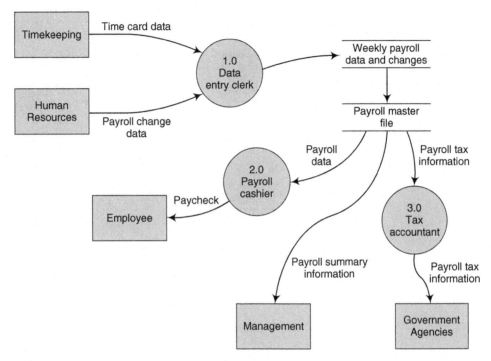

FIGURE 12-4 A physical data flow diagram.

Finally, we see that a physical DFD lists the job title of only one typical employee in an entity symbol, despite the fact that several employees may perform the same task—for example, several data-entry clerks or payroll cashiers. This last characteristic also applies when several employees perform the same task at different locations—for example, a company has several payroll cashiers who distribute paychecks at each of its manufacturing facilities. Representing types of employees, rather than individual employees, keeps DFDs simple and makes them easier to interpret.

Logical Data Flow Diagrams. A physical DFD illustrates the internal and external entities that participate in a process, but does not give the reader a good idea of what these participants do. For this task, we need **logical data flow diagrams**.

Figure 12-5 is a logical DFD for the payroll illustration in Figure 12-4. In Figure 12-5, note that each bubble no longer contains the name of a system entity, but instead contains a verb that indicates a task the system performs. For example, instead of a single bubble with the title "data-entry clerk," as in Figure 12-4, the logical DFD in Figure 12-5 shows two bubbles with the titles "process employee hours worked" and "process payroll change data"—because these are separate data processing tasks that clerks perform.

From the standpoint of good system design and control, describing system processes is important because understanding how a system performs tasks can be more important than knowing what tasks the system performs. For example, all payroll systems prepare paychecks, but not all payroll systems do this exactly the same way.

The differences may require different hardware, software, procedures, or controls. Logical DFDs help designers decide what system resources to acquire, what activities

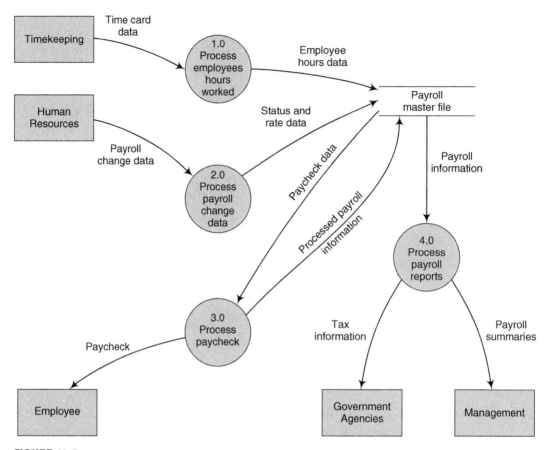

FIGURE 12-5 A logical data flow diagram for a payroll processing system.

employees must perform to run these systems, and how to protect and control these systems after they are installed.

Figure 12-5 is called a **level 0 data flow diagram** because it shows only in broad terms what tasks a system performs. Most systems are more complex than this and therefore require more detail to describe them completely. The task of creating such detail is called **decomposition**, which becomes necessary because DFD designers try to limit each level diagram to between five and seven processing symbols (bubbles).

Figure 12-6 shows an example of a **level 1 data flow diagram**—an "explosion" of symbol 3.0 (in Figure 12-5) with the caption "process paycheck." Here, we see that "process paycheck" entails computing gross pay, determining payroll deductions, and calculating net pay. If necessary, you can also show ancillary computer files at this level.

To fully document the system, you would continue to perform these decomposition tasks in additional DFDs. For example, you might decompose the procedure "compute payroll deductions" in bubble 3.2 of Figure 12-6 into several additional processes in lower-level DFDs—for example, create separate DFDs for "compute medical deductions," "compute savings plan deductions," "compute tax deductions," and so forth. In this way, a set of DFDs become linked together in a hierarchy.

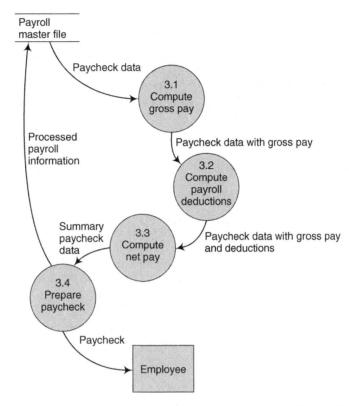

FIGURE 12-6   An exploded view of the "process paycheck" bubble of Figure 12-5.

Guidelines for Drawing Data Flow Diagrams.   Creating DFDs is as much art as science. The following guidelines can help you avoid errors and make your diagrams easier to interpret:

1. Avoid detail in high-level DFDs (i.e., in levels 0 and 1). Where appropriate, combine activities that are performed at the same place or same time or that are logically related. In short, use the keep-it-simple (KIS) approach to enhance understanding.

2. As a general rule, each logical DFD should contain between five and seven processing bubbles. This guideline helps you simplify the diagrams and avoid showing too much detail in high-level DFDs. A context diagram should fit on one page.

3. Do not cross lines and do use a unique reference number and name for each process symbol.

4. Different data flows should have different names to avoid confusion about the data produced and used by different processes.

5. Unless they are outside the system or used for archiving, all data stores should have data flow lines both into and out of them. Thus, an internal file symbol that lacks both of these data flow lines is usually a diagramming error.

6. Even if a file is temporary, it is usually desirable to include it in a DFD.

7. Classify most of the final recipients of system information as external entities.

8. Classify all personnel or departments that process the data of the current system as internal entities.

9. Display only normal processing routines in high-level DFDs. Avoid showing error routines or similar exception tasks.

10. Where several system entities perform the same task, show only one to represent them all. This rule also applies when system personnel perform the same task at different locations of the organization—for example, at different plants.

11. Obtain user feedback, where possible, to verify the accuracy and completeness of your diagrams.

Document Flowcharts

A **document flowchart** traces the physical flow of documents through an organization—that is, the flow of documents from the departments, groups, or individuals who first created them to their final destinations. Document flowcharts provide more details about documents than do DFDs. Figure 12-7 illustrates common document flowcharting symbols, and the following examples illustrate how to use them to create basic document flowcharts.

Constructing a document flowchart begins by identifying the different departments or groups that handle the documents for a particular system. The flowchart developer then uses the symbols in Figure 12-7 to create the document flows. Let us first examine two simple cases and then discuss the general flowcharting guidelines.

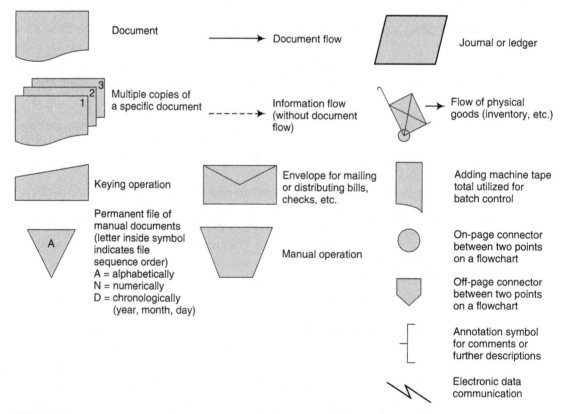

FIGURE 12-7 Common document flowcharting symbols.

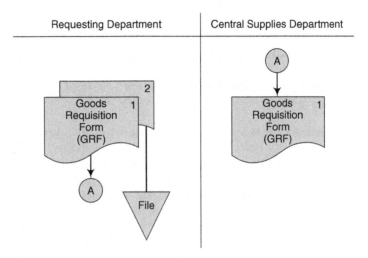

FIGURE 12-8   A simple document flowchart.

Example 1. Your boss asks you to document the paperwork involved in acquiring office supplies from your company's Central Supplies Department. Your administrative assistant explains the process as follows:

> *Reordering supplies requires a requisition request. When I need more stationery, for example, I fill out two copies of a goods requisition form (GRF). I send the first copy to central supplies and file the second copy here in the office.*

There are two departments involved in this example—your department (which we will call the Requesting Department) and the Central Supplies Department. Thus, you should begin by naming these departments in the headings on your document flowchart (Figure 12-8). Next, draw two copies of the GRF under the heading for the Requesting Department because this is the department that creates this form. Number these copies 1 and 2 to indicate two copies.

Finally, indicate where each document goes: copy 1 to the Central Supplies Department and copy 2 to a file in the Requesting Department. A document's first appearance should be in the department that creates it. A solid line or the on-page connectors shown here indicate its physical transmittal from one place to another. Then redraw the transmitted document to indicate its arrival at the department that receives it. Figure 12-8 illustrates the completed flowchart for this narrative.

Example 2. Now consider a slightly more complex example—the task of hiring a new employee at your company. The process begins when a department develops a vacancy. The Human Resources (HR) director explains the process as follows:

> *The department that develops a vacancy must first complete a job vacancy form, which it forwards to my department. We then advertise for the position and, with the help of the requesting department, interview applicants. When the vacancy is filled, the HR Department prepares a position hiring form (PHF) in triplicate. We file the first copy in a manual file, which is organized by employee Social Security number. We staple the third copy to the job vacancy form and return it to the Requesting Department, where clerks file it alphabetically by employee last name.*

The HR Department forwards the second copy of the PHF to the Payroll Department. The Payroll Department uses the form as an authorization document to create a payroll record for the new employee. Thus, the information on the form is keyed directly into the company's computer system using an online terminal located in the payroll office. This copy of the PHF is then filed numerically for reference and also as evidence that the form has been processed.

Figure 12-9 is a document flowchart for this example. To draw it, your first step is the same as before—to identify the participants. In this case, there are three of them: (1) the department with the job vacancy (i.e., the Requesting Department in Figure 12-9), (2) the HR Department, and (3) the Payroll Department. You identify each of these departments in separate columns at the top of the document flowchart.

Your next step is to identify the documents involved. There are two major ones: (1) the Job Vacancy form, which we presume is prepared as a single copy, and (2) the Position Hiring form, which we are told is prepared in triplicate. In practice, multiple-copy forms are usually color-coded. However, in document flowcharts, these are simply numbered and a separate page is attached to explain the color–number equivalencies.

Your third step is to indicate where the documents are created, processed, and used. This is probably the most difficult task, and a document flowchart designer must often use considerable ingenuity to represent data flows and processing activities accurately. Figure 12-9 illustrates these flows for the hiring procedures just described. Where there are a large number of document transmittals, you can use on-page connectors

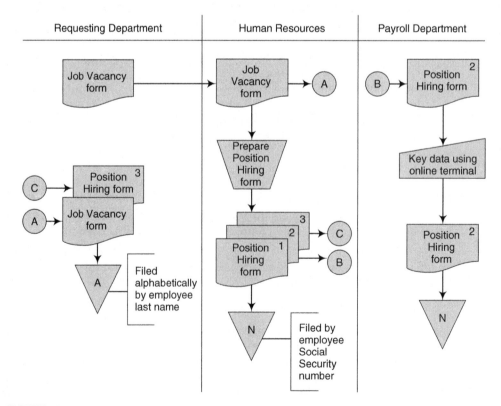

FIGURE 12-9 A document flowchart illustrating the flow of documents involved in the hiring of a new employee.

(circles) to connect document flows from one place on a page to another and avoid complicated flow lines. Thus, Figure 12-9 uses several on-page connectors (with letters A, B, and C) to avoid cluttering the chart. You should use a unique identifier in each connector (such as a letter) for identification purposes. You can also use off-page connectors (to connect data flows to other pages) if necessary.

When constructing document flowcharts, some analysts also include the movement of physical goods—for example, moving inventory from a receiving department to an inventory storeroom. Document flowcharts typically use hand-truck symbols for this task. Some document flowcharts also illustrate information flows that do not involve documents (e.g., a sales clerk telephoning to check a customer's account balance before approving a credit sale). Thus, the term "document" broadly includes all types of organizational communications and data flows. It is also important to recognize that document flowcharting symbols are not standardized across all firms.

Guidelines for Drawing Document Flowcharts.   You can use the following guidelines to help you create good document flowcharts:

1. Identify all the departments that create or receive the documents involved in the system. Use vertical lines to create "swim lanes" to separate each department from the others.

2. Carefully classify the documents and activities of each department, and draw them under their corresponding department headings.

3. Identify each copy of an accounting document with a number. If multiple-copy documents are color-coded, use a table to identify the number–color associations.

4. Account for the distribution of each copy of a document. In general, it is better to overdocument a complicated process than to underdocument it.

5. Use on-page and off-page connectors to avoid diagrams with lines that cross one another.

6. Each pair of connectors (a "from" and a "to" connector in each pair) should use the same letter or number.

7. Use annotations if necessary to explain activities or symbols that may be unclear. These are little notes to the reader that help clarify your documentation.

8. If the sequence of records in a file is important, include the letter "A" for alphabetical, "N" for numeric, or "C" for chronological in the file symbol. As indicated in guideline 7, you can also include a note in the flowchart.

9. Many flowcharts in practice use acronyms (e.g., GRF or PHF in the preceding examples). To avoid confusion, use full names (possibly with acronyms in parentheses) or create a table of equivalents to ensure accuracy in identifying documents.

10. Consider using automated flowcharting tools. See the section of this chapter on computer-assisted software engineering (CASE) tools for more information.

Case-in-Point 12.5   Some accountants disagree about the usefulness of document flowcharts relative to other documenting tools, but one manuscript reviewer of this book wrote: "Flowcharting is one of the most essential skills, in my opinion, for a student to learn in a systems course. During my tenure at a CPA firm, I had the opportunity to document several accounting information systems and document flowcharting was the key skill. When word got around the office that I was a good flowcharter, I got placed on more important clients, furthering my career."

System Flowcharts

Whereas document flowcharts focus on tangible documents, system flowcharts concentrate on the computerized data flows of AISs. Thus, a system flowchart typically depicts the electronic flow of data and processing steps in an AIS. Figure 12-10 illustrates some common system flowcharting symbols. Most of these symbols are industry conventions that have been standardized by the National Bureau of Standards (ANSI Standard X3.5), although additional symbols are now necessary to represent newer data transmission technologies—for example, wireless data flows.

Some system flowcharts are general in nature and provide only an overview of the system. These *are high-level system flowcharts*. Figure 12-11 is an example. The inputs

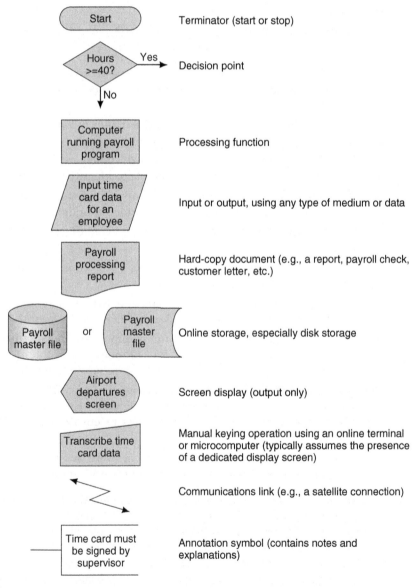

FIGURE 12-10 Some common system and programming flowcharting symbols.

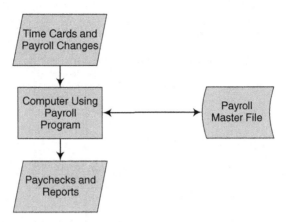

FIGURE 12-11   A high-level system flowchart for payroll processing.

and outputs of the system are specified by the general input and output symbol—a parallelogram. In more detailed system flowcharts, the specific form of these inputs and outputs would be indicated—for example, by magnetic disk symbols.

Figure 12-11 refers to only one process—processing payroll. A more detailed system flowchart would describe all the processes performed by the payroll program and the specific inputs and outputs of each process. At the lowest, most-detailed level of such documentation are **program flowcharts** that describe the processing logic of each application program. We will examine program flowcharts later in this chapter.

Like document flowcharts, the process of drawing system flowcharts is probably best understood by studying an illustration. Figure 12-12 is a system flowchart for the following example.

> *The Sarah Stanton Company is a magazine distributor that maintains a file of magazine subscribers for creating monthly mailing labels. Magazine subscribers mail change-of-address forms or new-subscription forms directly to the company, where input personnel key the information into the system through online terminals. The computer system temporarily stores this information as a file of address-change or new-subscription requests. Clerical staff key these data into computer files continuously, so we may characterize it as "daily processing."*
>
> *Once a week, the system uses the information in the daily processing file to update the subscriber master file. At this time, new subscriber names and addresses are added to the file, and the addresses of existing subscribers who have moved are changed. The system also prepares a Master File Maintenance Processing Report to indicate what additions and modifications were made to the file. Once a month, the company prepares postal labels for the magazine's mailing. The subscriber master file serves as the chief input for this computer program. The two major outputs are the labels themselves and a Mailing Labels Processing Report that documents this run and indicates any problems.*

The system flowchart in Figure 12-12 documents the flow of data through the company's computerized system. Thus, it identifies the sources of the data, the places where the data are temporarily stored, and the outputs on which processed data appear. In Figure 12-12, for example, the system flowchart begins with the subscriber request forms and documents the flow of data on these forms through the keying phase, master file-maintenance phase, and finally, the monthly mailing phase.

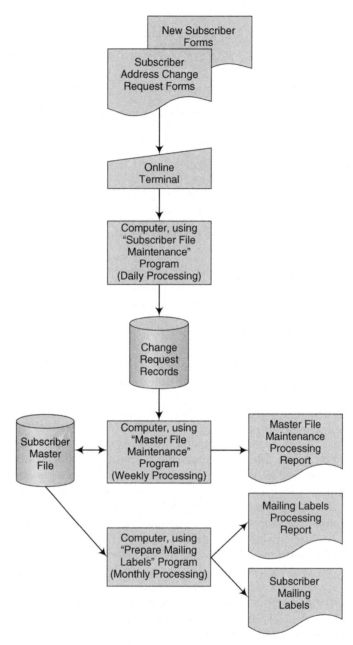

FIGURE 12-12 A system flowchart illustrating the computer steps involved in maintaining a subscriber master file and creating monthly mailing labels.

Indirectly, system flowcharts also indicate processing cycles (daily, weekly, or monthly), hardware needs (e.g., disk drives and printers), areas of weak or missing application controls (can online clerks give free subscriptions to their friends?), and potential bottlenecks in processing (e.g., manual data entry). In Figure 12-12, we can also identify the major files of the system (a temporary log file of change-request records and a subscriber master file) and the major reports of the system. Finally, note that each processing phase of a system flowchart usually involves preparing one or more control reports. These reports provide processing-control information (e.g., counts of transactions processed) for control purposes and exceptions information (e.g., the identity of unprocessed transactions) that helps employees correct the errors detected by the system.

System flowcharts depict an electronic **job stream** of data through the various processing phases of an AIS and therefore also illustrate audit trails. Each time the records of a file are sorted or updated, for example, a system flowchart should show this in a separate processing step. Recognizing the usefulness of system flowcharts, both the American Institute of Certified Public Accountants (AICPA) and the Institute of Management Accountants (IMA) consistently include test questions in their professional examinations that require a working knowledge of system flowcharts.

Guidelines for Drawing System Flowcharts. Although no strict rules govern exactly how to organize or draw a system flowchart, the following list provides some guidelines:

1. System flowcharts should read from top to bottom and from left to right. In drawing or reading such flowcharts, you should begin in the upper-left corner.

2. Because system flowcharting symbols are standardized, you should use these symbols when drawing your flowcharts—do not make up your own.

3. A processing symbol should always be found between an input symbol and an output symbol. This is called the **sandwich rule**.

4. Use on-page and off-page connectors to avoid crossed lines and cluttered flowcharts.

5. Sketch a flowchart before designing the final draft. Graphical documentation software tools (discussed shortly) make this job easier.

6. Add descriptions and comments in flowcharts to clarify processing elements. You can place these inside the processing symbols themselves, include them in annotation symbols attached to process or file symbols, or add them as separate notes in your systems documentation.

Process Maps. A *business process* is a natural group of business activities that create value for an organization. **Process maps** document business processes in easy-to-follow diagrams. Did you understand the logic diagram in Figure 12-1 at the beginning of the chapter? It's an example of a process map. Studies suggest that process maps are among the easiest to draw and are also among the easiest for novices to follow.

In businesses, a major process is usually the sales or order fulfillment process. A process map for this process (Figure 12-13) shows such business activities as customers placing orders, warehouse personnel picking goods, and clerks shipping goods. Managers can create similar maps that show just about any other process—for example, how an organization processes time cards for a payroll application, how a business responds to customer returns, or how a manager deals with defective merchandise.

Case-in-Point 12.6 Increased competition and tighter profit margins have forced companies to look for places where they might be able to save money. One large accounting firm uses process mapping software to assist clients in evaluating and redesigning their business processes. For example, the firm's business reengineering practice helped a financial services company cut its costs and become more efficient. The company was able to cut in half the time it took to approve a loan—and it needed 40% fewer staff to do it.

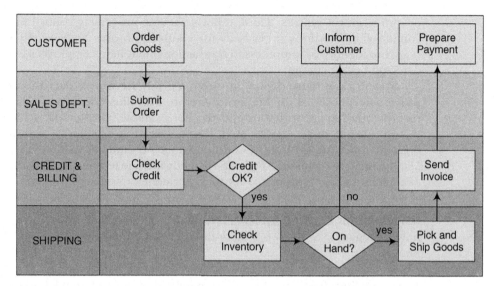

FIGURE 12-13 A process map for the order fulfillment process (created with Microsoft Word).

Internal and external auditors can use process maps to help them learn how a department or division operates, document what they have learned, and identify internal control weaknesses or problems in existing operations. An additional benefit is to use such maps as training aids. Consultants frequently use process maps to help them study business processes and redesign them for greater productivity. Accountants and managers can also use this tool to help them describe current processes to others.

Case-in-Point 12.7 The approval process at Software Contracts—a software development company—was so complicated that it took weeks to complete. When the company created a process map to examine its own system, it found that it could combine three separate approval forms into one, cutting the approval time to less than 1 week. The process map cost the company $1,600 to create. The company estimates that the changes it made as a result of that exercise will save it over $68,000 *annually.*[5]

Like most other types of documentation, you can draw process maps in multilevel versions called *hierarchical process maps* that show successively finer levels of detail. Such maps are especially popular on the Web because viewers can click on individual symbols to drill down and see more information for any given process or decision. Figure 12-14, for example, illustrates a secondary-level process map for checking credit that might link to the "Check Credit" box in Figure 12-13.

Guidelines for Drawing Process Maps. Process maps vary considerably across firms, and the symbols found in Web versions are remarkably inconsistent. Nonetheless, it is possible to use the flowchart symbols that you already know to create process maps, including: (1) a rectangle (to represent a process), (2) a diamond (to represent a decision), (3) an oval (to depict the starting or ending point for a process), (4) an off-page

---

[5] How to Save Money with Process Mapping from Software Contracts home page (www.softwarecontracts .co.nz) accessed March 2014.

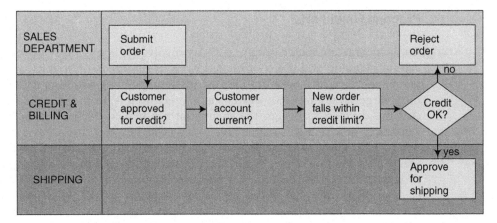

FIGURE 12-14 A second-level process map for the credit approval process of Figure 12-13.

connector, and (5) a document symbol. Creating a good process map requires a blend of art, science, and craftsmanship, all of which mostly comes with practice. Here are some guidelines to use when drawing process maps:

1. Identify and define the process of interest. The goal is to stay focused on the scope of the process you are trying to map.

2. Understand the purpose of each process map. Is it to identify bottlenecks? Discover redundancies? Train employees? Inform users?

3. Meet with employees to get their ideas, suggestions, and comments. Don't hesitate to ask challenging or probing questions.

4. Remember that processes have inputs, outputs, and enablers. An example of an input is an invoice; an output could be a payment check to a supplier, and an enabler helps a process achieve results. In AISs, information technology is a common enabler.

5. Show key decision points. A process map will not be an effective analytical tool without decision points (the intellectual or mental steps that employees perform in a process).

6. Pay attention to the level of detail you capture. Did you capture enough detail to truly represent the process and explain it to others?

7. Avoid mapping the "should-be" or "could-be." Map the process that is in place.

8. Practice, practice, practice.

12.4 OTHER DOCUMENTATION TOOLS

There are many other tools for documenting AISs besides DFDs, document flowcharts, system flowcharts, and process maps. Three of them are (1) program flowcharts, (2) decision tables, and (3) decision trees. Because these tools are used mostly by consultants and IT professionals rather than accountants, we will describe them only briefly. Accountants should have some familiarity with these tools, however, because they may see them—for example, when reviewing the design for a revised accounting system.

Program Flowcharts

Because large computer programs today involve millions of instructions, they require careful planning and the coordinated work of hundreds of systems analysts and programmers. Typically, organizations use **structured programming** techniques to create these large programs in a hierarchical manner, that is, from the top down. This means that the developers design the main routines first and then design subroutines for subsidiary processing as major processing tasks become clear.

To help them plan the logic for each processing routine, IT professionals often create program flowcharts (Figure 12-15) that outline the processing logic of computer programs as well as the order in which processing steps take place. After designing such program flowcharts, the developers typically present them to colleagues in a structured walkthrough or formal review of the logic. This process helps the reviewers assess the soundness of the logic, detect and correct design flaws, and make improvements. Upon approval, the program flowcharts then become blueprints for writing the instructions of a computer program as well as documenting the program itself.

Program flowcharts use many of the same symbols as system flowcharts (refer back to Figure 12-10). A few specialized symbols for program flowcharts are the diamond symbol (which indicates a decision point in the processing logic) and the oval symbol (which indicates a starting or stopping point).

Like system flowcharts and DFDs, program flowcharts can be designed at different levels of detail. The highest-level program flowchart is sometimes called a **macro program flowchart**, which provides an overview of the data processing logic.

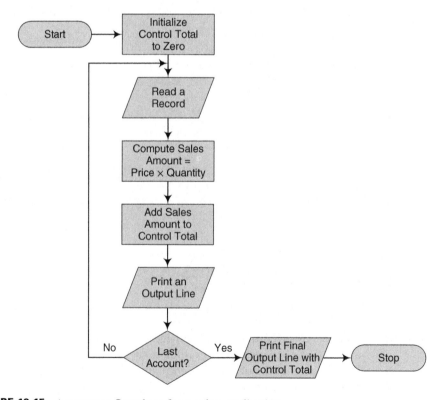

FIGURE 12-15 A program flowchart for a sales application.

A lower-level program flowchart contains the detailed programming logic necessary to carry out a processing task. Figure 12-15 is a detailed (lower-level) program flowchart for a sales report application.

Decision Tables and Decision Trees

When a business process involves a substantial number of conditions and subsequent courses of action, a decision table or decision tree can document these items and increase understanding. We briefly review both types of documentation aids here.

Decision Tables. A **decision table** (Figure 12-16) is a table of conditions and processing tasks that indicates what action to take for each possibility. Sometimes, decision tables are used as an alternative to program flowcharts. More commonly, they are used in conjunction with flowcharts. To illustrate a decision table, consider the following scenario:

A credit union pays interest to its depositors at the rate of 5% per year. Accounts of less than $5 are not paid interest. Accounts of $1,000 or more that have been with the credit union for more than 1 year get paid the normal 5%, plus a bonus of 0.5%.

Figure 12-16 presents a decision table for the credit union that shows how much interest to pay each account. Note that the decision table consists of four parts: (1) the condition stub outlines the potential conditions of the application, (2) the action stub outlines the available actions that can be taken, (3) the condition entries depict the possible combinations of conditions likely to occur, and (4) the action entries outline the action to be taken for each combination of conditions.

The rules at the top of the decision table set forth the combination of conditions that may occur and the action entries show what to do for each condition. For the illustration at hand, three conditions affect the data processing of each account: an account balance less than $5, (2) an account balance less than $1,000, and (3) an account that is 1 year old or less. As defined, each of these conditions can now be answered "yes" or "no." Figure 12-16 is a decision table for the illustration at hand, in which Y stands for "yes" and N stands for "no." The combination of Ys and Ns in each

		Rules				
		1	2	3	4	
	Conditions					
Condition stub	Account balance less than $5	Y	N	N	N	Condition entries
	Account balance less than $1,000	*	Y	*	N	
	Account 1 year old or less	*	*	Y	N	
	Actions					
Action stub	Pay no interest	X				Action entries
	Pay 5 percent interest		X	X		
	Pay 5.5 percent interest				X	

FIGURE 12-16 This is a decision table to help a credit union decide how much interest to pay each account. An asterisk (*) means that the condition does not affect the course of action.

column of the table illustrates each possible set of conditions that the system might encounter. Using Xs, the decision table also shows what course of action should be taken for each condition (i.e., how much interest should be paid to each account).

The major advantage of decision tables is that they summarize the processing tasks for a large number of conditions in a compact, easily understood format. This increases system understanding and results in fewer omissions of important processing possibilities. Decision tables are also useful when new conditions arise or when changes in organizational policy result in new actions for existing conditions. This advantage is particularly important to AISs because of organizational concern for accuracy and completeness in processing financial data.

One drawback of decision tables is that they do not show the order in which a program or employee tests data conditions or takes processing actions, as do program flowcharts. This is a major deficiency because the order in which a person or computer tests or processes accounting data is often as important as the tests or processes themselves. A second drawback is that decision tables require an understanding of documentation techniques beyond flowcharting. Finally, decision tables require extra work to prepare, and this work may not always be cost-effective.

Guidelines for Developing Decision Tables. Follow these guidelines to develop clear, easy-to-follow decision tables:

1. Identify all the conditions that might affect the outcomes (actions).
2. Identify all the actions that are possible for the process (e.g., three actions in Figure 12-16).
3. For a Y–N decision table, the maximum number of *combinations* of conditions (and therefore the number of columns you will need) is 2^n, where n is the number of conditions. For example, if you have three possible conditions, you will need a maximum of 2^3 or 8 columns or rules. Usually, you can eliminate some of these, resulting in a smaller number. For example, if an account balance is less than $5 in Figure 12-16, it does not matter how old the account is—the bank will pay no interest on the balance.
4. Check your resulting table for impossible situations or repetitive logic. For example, in Figure 12-16, it is impossible for an account balance to be less than $5 (a "Y" for a given rule) and also *not less than* $1,000 (an "N" for the same rule). Eliminating such impossibilities will result in yet fewer rules, again simplifying your table.
5. Check your resulting table for contradictions. For example, although it is possible for two different sets of rules to require the same course of action, it should be impossible for the *same set of conditions* to require different actions.
6. Check that the decision tree recommends each action at least once. If this does not happen, the table itself probably contains an error.

Decision Trees. A **decision tree** graphically depicts business processes that usually contain several steps. Figure 12-17 is a decision tree for the decision table in Figure 12-16. Figure 12-17 shows that we usually draw decision trees on their "sides," with the starting point or tree trunk on the left and branches extending to the right and ending with the 4 rules, A, B, C, and D. Circles represent decisions (asking a question beginning with "if") and squares represent actions (beginning with the word "then"). It is not necessary for a circle (node) to have only two choices, nor is it necessary for each branch to be the same length.

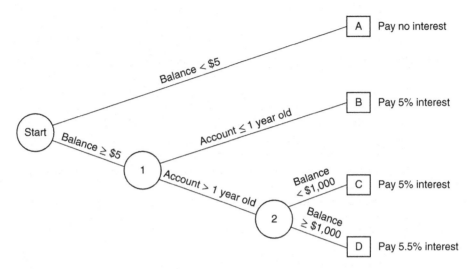

FIGURE 12-17 A decision tree representing the logic of the decision table in Figure 12-16.

One advantage of a decision tree over a decision table is that it is graphic—a feature that usually aids human understanding. A second advantage is that decision trees also capture the *order* in which employees or computers should make decisions as well as the actions for each sequence. A third advantage is that decision trees easily identify "holes" in process logic (see the following guidelines 6 and 7).

Guidelines for Developing Decision Trees. Some guidelines for drawing decision trees are as follows:

1. Begin on the left and draw branches to the right.
2. If the order of decisions is important, make sure that you capture this order in your decision tree.
3. Use numbers for circles and letters for squares. This does not improve the logic of the tree, but does help viewers identify particular aspects of the tree in group discussions.
4. Capture all possible conditions and include an action for each one.
5. If a node represents a subset of conditions (e.g., "does an employee qualify for a 401k plan?"), the tree can represent this as one node, but provide additional details in a separate decision tree.
6. A tree node (circle) that lacks at least two alternate branches is usually an error.
7. A branch in a decision tree that does not eventually lead to an action is usually an error or perhaps indicates the absence of a control.

Software Tools for Graphical Documentation and SOX Compliance

Accountants, consultants, and system developers can use a variety of software tools to create **graphical documentation** of existing or proposed AISs. The simplest tools include presentation software, such as Microsoft PowerPoint, as well as word processing and spreadsheet software such as Microsoft Word and Excel. The advantages of using such tools closely parallel those of using word processing software instead of typewriters (e.g., easily revised documents, advanced formatting capabilities and coloring options, and a variety of reproduction capabilities). For example, the authors used Microsoft Word to create the process maps in Figures 12-13 and 12-14.

Microsoft Word, Excel, and PowerPoint. Using the "AutoShapes" option in the Drawing Toolbar of Microsoft Word, Excel, or PowerPoint, you can reproduce most of the graphics symbols and logic diagrams in this chapter. (The connectors in Excel are different from, as well as better than, simple lines because they adjust automatically when you reposition symbols in your charts.) Two additional advantages of using Excel to create graphical documentation are the ability to create large drawings (that exceed the margins of word processing documents) and the option to embed computed values in flowcharting symbols. Problem 12-21 at the end of the chapter describes how to use Excel to create such graphical documentation.

CASE Tools. The capabilities of specialized graphical documentation software exceed those of word processing or spreadsheet packages. These **CASE (computer-assisted software engineering) tools** automate such documentation tasks as drawing or modifying flowcharts, drawing graphics and screen designs, developing reports, and even generating code from documentation. Thus, CASE tools are to flowcharts what word processors are to text documents. Figure 12-18 is an example of a CASE package being used to draw a DFD.

Most CASE products run on personal computers. Examples include *iGrafx* (Micrografx, Inc.), *allCLEAR* (Proquis, Inc.), *SmartDraw* (SmartDraw LLC), and *Visio*

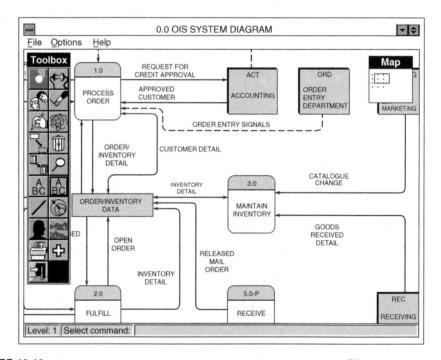

FIGURE 12-18 This CASE tool is a software program called Excelerator™, which is used here to create a data flow diagram. The toolbox on the left contains symbols that the user can select for his or her diagram.

(Microsoft Corp.). These products are especially popular with auditors and consultants, who use them to document AISs using the techniques discussed, as well as to analyze the results. Graphical documentation software enables its users to create a wide array of outputs, including DFDs, system flowcharts, program flowcharts, process maps, and even computer network designs.

Front-end CASE tools focus on the early tasks of systems design—for example, requirements-design activities. *Backend CASE tools* automate the detailed design tasks required in the later stages of a project—for example, developing detailed program flowcharts. Integrated CASE (I-CASE) packages enable users to perform both types of tasks and can even generate computer code directly from logic diagrams. As a result, these tools support **rapid application development (RAD)** and help organizations reduce development costs.

Graphical documentation software tools enable their users to generate documentation quickly and consistently, as well as to automate modifications to this documentation later when changes are required. They include templates and models that allow users to document almost any business and system environment. But these packages only create what they are told to create. Like word processors, they lack imagination and creativity, and they also require training to use them effectively.

SOX and AS 2201 Compliance. Many businesses now use specialized software packages to automate the tasks required by Section 404 of the Sarbanes–Oxley Act of 2002 and standards of the Public Company Accounting Oversight Board (PCAOB). Since the adoption of Auditing Standard 2201 by the PCAOB, companies now place more emphasis on entity-level controls (such as the tone at the top, management override of internal controls, and the overall control environment) than in the previous years. Just as word processing software makes document revisions easier, these "compliance software packages" enable businesses to reduce the time and costs required to satisfy legal requirements.

Symantec Control Compliance Suite (Symantec Corporation), for example, automates processes required by SOX that are intended to reduce IT risks. *OpenPages FCM* (OpenPages, Inc.) and *BizRights* (Approva Corp.) provide somewhat similar capabilities. *OpenPages FCM* includes a compliance database, workflow management tools, and a software dashboard that enables executives to verify that specific managerial controls are in place as well as to identify control deficiencies that might affect financial reports. *BizRights* software enables firms to reduce the risk of fraud by continuously testing and monitoring controls.

12.5 END-USER COMPUTING AND DOCUMENTATION

End-user computing refers to the ability of non-IT employees to create computer applications of their own. Today, we take much of this "computing" for granted—for example, when employees manipulate data with word processing, spreadsheet, database management systems, or tax packages—because all of these programs were developed to allow end users to develop applications for themselves.

The Importance of End-User Documentation

End-user applications often perform mission-critical functions for busy organizations. In many cases, the outputs of user-developed budgets, other financial spreadsheets, and database applications find their way into financial systems and ultimately influence an organization's strategic decisions or financial statements. Thus, end users should document their applications for many of the same reasons that professionals must document applications. Managers, auditors, and other system users need to understand how user-developed systems work in order to prevent errors and use system outputs. In addition, if an employee leaves an organization, other employees may need to maintain these systems, use these applications, and correctly interpret their outputs.

Unfortunately, documentation of end-user applications is often overlooked or is performed so poorly that it might as well be overlooked. Such oversight can be costly. For example, time is wasted when other employees must alter the system but lack the basic documentation to accomplish this task. Thus, even if the developer is the only one in the office who uses a particular application, managers should insist that he or she document it.

Case-in-Point 12.8 The Institute of Internal Auditors (IIA) released a white paper in 2010 that guides internal auditor's evaluations of end-user applications. Because nearly all organizations use employee-developed software such as spreadsheets, the IIA observes that such software may pose threats to organizations (including honest mistakes, noncompliance with regulations, and fraud). As a result, the IIA states that it is critical to evaluate and document these systems.[6]

The specific items that should be used to document any particular end-user application will, of course, vary with the application. For example, businesses often find it convenient to use systematic file names to identify word processing documents and to embed these file names within the reports to help others find them later. Figure 12-19 provides some guidelines for documenting spreadsheet applications.

1. Name of the developer.
2. Name of the file where the application is stored.
3. Name of the directories and subdirectories where the application is stored.
4. Date the application was first developed.
5. Date the application was last modified, and the name of the person who modified it.
6. Date the application was last run.
7. Name and phone number of person to call in case of problems.
8. Sources of external data used by the system.
9. Important assumptions made in the application.
10. Important parameters that must be modified in order to change assumptions or answer "what-if" questions.
11. Range names used in the application and their locations in the spreadsheet.
12. List of approval signatures required.

FIGURE 12-19 Examples of information to include when documenting spreadsheets.

---

[6] The Institute of Internal Auditors, 2010. Global Technology Audit Guide (GTAG) 14: Auditing User-Development Applications.

Policies for End-User Computing and Documentation

To avoid redundant or ineffective systems, businesses should follow these guidelines to control end-user applications development:

1. *Formally evaluate large projects.* Employees should be allowed to create a large application only after it has withstood the scrutiny of a formal review of its costs and benefits. When projects are large, higher-level management should be involved in the go-ahead decision.

2. *Adopt formal end-user development policies.* Employees usually do not develop poor applications because they wish to do so, but because no organizational policies exist that restrict them from doing so. Policy guidelines should include procedures for testing software, examining internal controls, and periodically auditing systems.

3. *Formalize documentation standards.* At this point in the chapter, the importance of formal documentation should be self-evident. What may be less obvious is the need to create procedures for ensuring that employees meet these documentation standards.

4. *Limit the number of employees authorized to create end-user applications.* This restricts applications development to those employees in whom management has confidence or perhaps who have taken formal development classes.

5. *Audit new and existing systems.* The more critical an end-user system is to the functioning of a department or division, the more important it is for organizations to require formal audits of such systems for compliance with the guidelines outlined previously.

AIS AT WORK
Better System Documentation Helps Protect Minnesota's Environment[7]

The Minnesota Pollution Control Agency is charged with protecting Minnesota's environment. The agency realized that it has collected vast amounts of data for nearly 40 years, but it still did not have reliable methods for assessing many of its functions and their effectiveness. To enhance the agency's effectiveness, the CIO decided that the agency needed detailed business process mapping and documentation. The purpose of the new documentation was to help the agency better understand its existing business processes and identify the current bottlenecks.

The agency undertook four main steps in its documentation efforts. First, it identified the critical business processes and defined these processes. Next, the agency gathered information about the processes by interviewing key personnel and performing walkthroughs of processes. Third, processes were graphically mapped using the forms of documentation described in this chapter. Finally, experts within the agency analyzed the existing processes in order to identify opportunities for improvement.

---

[7] Adapted from: "Effective Business Process Management," Copyright © 2010 Studio One Networks. All rights reserved. Accessed from www.theusdaily.com.

Some of the initial benefits of the new documentation were a reduction in the percentage of backlogged permits from 40% to 9%, streamlined reporting processes to the federal government, and better understanding of the key risks involved in business processes.

SUMMARY

✓ Ten reasons to document an AIS are: (1) to explain how the system works; (2) to train others; (3) to help developers design new systems; (4) to control system development and maintenance costs; (5) to standardize communications among system designers, company personnel, and auditors; (6) to provide information to auditors; (7) to document a business's processes; (8) to help a company comply with the Sarbanes–Oxley Act of 2002 and AS 2201; (9) to establish employee accountability for specific tasks or procedures; and (10) to save money.

✓ Data flow diagrams provide both a physical and a logical view of a system, but concentrate more on the flow and transformation of data than on the physical devices or timing of inputs, processing, or outputs.

✓ A document flowchart describes the physical flow of documents through an AIS, for example, by providing an overview of where documents are created, sent, reviewed, and stored and what activities they trigger.

✓ A system flowchart describes the electronic flow of data through an AIS, indicates what processing steps and files are used and when, and provides an overview of the entire system.

✓ Process maps also describe the flow of information through an organization, use only a few symbols, and (to many) are among the easiest to draw and understand.

✓ Three additional documentation tools are program flowcharts, decision tables, and decision trees. Accountants should understand in general terms how these tools work.

✓ A variety of software tools exist for documenting AISs. These include standard personal productivity tools such as word processing and spreadsheet software, specialized CASE tools, and software packages designed to help companies comply with SOX and AS 2201.

✓ End-user computing is important because it is used extensively and also because such applications often contribute significantly to the efficiency of specific departments or divisions. But many employees do not document their applications very well, and this often costs time and money.

KEY TERMS YOU SHOULD KNOW

CASE (computer-assisted software engineering) tools
context diagram
data flow diagrams (DFDs)
decision table
decision tree
decomposition
document flowchart
documentation
end-user computing

graphical documentation
job stream
level 0 data flow diagram
level 1 data flow diagram
logical data flow diagram
macro program flowchart
object-oriented software
physical data flow diagram
process map
program flowcharts

rapid application development (RAD)
sandwich rule (system flowcharts)
signed checklists
structured programming
structured walkthrough
system flowchart

TEST YOURSELF

Q12-1. The first three questions refer to this diagram:

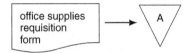

The diagram here is most likely taken from a:

a. document flowchart

b. system flowchart

c. data flow diagram

d. program flowchart

Q12-2. In the diagram here, the symbol with the letter A represents:

a. an on-page connector

b. an off-page connector

c. a file

d. an answering machine

Q12-3. In this diagram, the arrow represents:

a. a wireless transmission

b. a telephone call

c. an information flow

d. a management order to a subordinate

Q12-4. Document flowcharts would not be able to represent:

a. the flow of information when ordering office supplies

b. the flow of information when hiring new employees

c. the flow of information when creating orders for new magazine subscriptions

d. the logic in performing payroll processing

Q12-5. Which of the following is *not* true about system flowcharts?

a. They can depict the flow of information in computerized AISs

b. They use standardized symbols

c. They cannot show how documents flow in an AIS

d. They often document an audit trail

Q12-6. Which of the following is *not* true about process maps?

a. They depict the flow of information in computerized AISs

b. They use standardized symbols

c. Government agencies as well as businesses often use them

d. Web pages often depict hierarchical versions of them.

Q12-7. The *sandwich rule* states that:

a. you should only create logic diagrams that have some "meat" in them

b. every diagram should have a cover page and a summary page

c. a processing symbol should be between an input and an output symbol

d. in DFDs, there should always be data flow lines leading to and from files

Q12-8. Which of these is *not* a good guideline to follow when creating DFDs?

a. Avoid detail in high-level DFDs

b. Avoid drawing temporary files in DFDs

c. Classify most of the final recipients of system outputs as external entities

d. Avoid showing error routines or similar exception tasks

Q12-9. A data flow diagram helps reader to understand:

a. the data structure of tables

b. the resources involved in transactions

c. the destinations of important reports

d. the logical operations of programs

Q12-10. A decision table shows:

a. the possible conditions and processing alternatives for a given situation

b. who sat where at a board meeting

c. the rules for drawing DFDs

d. the local outsourcing vendors in the area for documentation tasks

DISCUSSION QUESTIONS

12-1. Why is documentation important to accounting information systems? Why should accountants be interested in AIS documentation?

12-2. Distinguish between document flowcharts, system flowcharts, data flow diagrams, and program flowcharts. How are they similar? How are they different?

12-3. What are document flowcharts? How does a document flowchart assist each of the following individuals: (1) a systems analyst, (2) a systems designer, (3) a computer programmer, (4) an auditor, and (5) a data security expert?

12-4. Flowcharting is both an art and a science. Guidelines can be used to make better flowcharts. What are these guidelines for document, system, and data flow diagram flowcharts?

12-5. What are the four symbols used in data flow diagrams? What does each mean?

12-6. Why are data flow diagrams developed in a hierarchy? What are the names of some levels in the hierarchy?

12-7. Look at the process map in Figure 12-13. Trace the steps in the order fulfillment process. Do you think this figure is more helpful than a narrative would be in understanding the flow of events in the process?

12-8. What is the purpose of a decision table? How might decision tables be useful to accountants?

12-9. What are CASE tools? How are they used? How do CASE tools create documentation for AISs? If you were a systems analyst, would you use a CASE tool?

12-10. What is end-user computing? Why is documentation important to end-user computing? What guidelines should companies develop to control end-user computing?

PROBLEMS

12-11. To view the flowchart shapes in Microsoft Excel, select the following options from the main menu: Insert\Shapes. There should be many of them (using Excel 2016), including many flowcharting symbols. If you allow your mouse to hover over a specific symbol, its title and meaning will appear in a tool-tip box. Finally, if you click on a specific symbol, your mouse icon will change to a cross-hair, and you will be able to draw this symbol on your spreadsheet. Create a list with items similar to the following one that contains all the flowchart symbols in your version of Excel.

Predefined Process

12-12. Draw a document flowchart to depict each of the following situations.

a. An individual from the marketing department of a wholesale company prepares five copies of a sales invoice, and each copy is sent to a different department.

b. The individual invoices from credit sales must temporarily be stored until they can be matched against customer payments at a later date.

c. A batch control tape is prepared along with a set of transactions to ensure completeness of the data.

d. The source document data found on employee application forms are used as input to create new employee records on a computer master file.

e. Delinquent credit customers are sent as many as four different inquiry letters before their accounts are turned over to a collection agency.

f. Physical goods are shipped back to the supplier if they are found to be damaged upon arrival at the receiving warehouse.

g. The data found on employee time cards are keyed onto a hard disk before they are processed by a computer.

h. The data found on employee time cards are first keyed onto a floppy diskette before they are entered into a computer job stream for processing.

i. A document flowchart is becoming difficult to understand because too many lines cross one another. (Describe a solution.)

j. Three people, all in different departments, look at the same document before it is eventually filed in a fourth department.

k. Certain data from a source document are manually copied into a ledger before the document itself is filed in another department.

12-13. Develop a document flowchart for the following information flow. The individual stores in the Mark Goodwin convenience chain prepare two copies of a goods requisition form (GRF) when they need to order merchandise from the central warehouse. After these forms are completed, one copy is filed in the store's records and the other copy is sent to the central warehouse. The warehouse staff gets the order and files its copy of the GRF form in its records. When the warehouse needs to restock an item, three copies of a purchase order form (POF) are filled out. One copy is stored in the warehouse files, one copy goes to the vendor, and the third copy goes to the accounts-payable department.

12-14. The Garcia-Lanoue Company produces industrial goods. The company receives purchase orders from its customers and ships goods accordingly. Assuming that the following conditions apply, develop a document flowchart for this company:

a. The company receives two copies of every purchase order from its customers.

b. Upon receipt of the purchase orders, the company ships the goods ordered. One copy of the purchase order is returned to the customer with the order, and the other copy goes into the company's purchase order file.

c. The company prepares three copies of a shipping bill. One copy stays in the company's shipping file, and the other two are sent to the customer.

12-15. The data-entry department of the Ron Mitchell Manufacturing Company is responsible for converting all of the company's shipping and receiving information to computer records. Because accuracy in this conversion is essential, the firm employs a strict verification process.

Prepare a document flowchart for the following information flow:

a. The shipping department sends a copy of all shipping orders to the data-entry department.

b. A data-entry operator keys the information from a shipping order onto a diskette.

c. A supervisor checks every record with the original shipping order. If no errors are detected, the diskette is sent to the computer operations staff and the original shipping order is filed.

12-16. Amanda M is a regional manufacturer and wholesaler of high-quality chocolate candies. The company's sales and collection process is as follows. Amanda M makes use of an enterprise-wide information system with electronic data interchange (EDI) capability. No paper documents are exchanged in the sales and collection process. The company receives sales orders from customers electronically. Upon receipt of a sales order, shipping department personnel prepare goods for shipment and input shipping data into the information system. The system sends an electronic shipping notice and invoice to the customer at the time of shipment. Terms are net 30. When payment is due, the customer makes an electronic funds transfer for the amount owed. The customer's information system sends remittance (payment) data to Amanda M. Amanda M's information system updates accounts-receivable information at that time.

Draw a context diagram and a level 0 logical data flow diagram for Amanda M's sales and collection process.

12-17. The order-writing department at the Winston Beauchamp Company is managed by Alan Most. The department keeps two types of computer files: (1) a customer file of authorized credit customers and (2) a product file of items currently sold by the company. Both of these files are direct-access files stored on magnetic disks. Customer orders are handwritten on order forms with the Winston Beauchamp name at the top of the form, and item lines for quantity, item number, and total amount desired for each product ordered by the customer.

When customer orders are received, Alan Most directs someone to input the information at one of the department's computer terminals. After the information has been input, the computer program immediately adds the information to a computerized "order" file and prepares five copies of the customer order.

The first copy is sent back to Alan's department; the others are sent elsewhere. Design a system flowchart that documents the accounting data processing described here. In addition, draw a data flow diagram showing a logical view of the system.

12-18. The LeVitre and Swezey Credit Union maintains separate bank accounts for each of its 20,000 customers. Three major files are the customer master file, the transaction file of deposits and withdrawal information, and a monthly statement file that shows a customer's transaction history for the previous month. The following lists the bank's most important activities during a representative month:

   a. Customers make deposits and withdrawals.

   b. Employers make automatic deposits on behalf of selected employees.

   c. The bank updates its master file daily using the transaction file.

   d. The bank creates monthly statements for its customers, using both the customer master file and the transactions file.

   e. Bank personnel answer customer questions concerning their deposits, withdrawals, or account balances.

   f. The bank issues checks to pay its rent, utility bills, payroll, and phone bills.

   Draw a data flow diagram that graphically describes these activities.

12-19. The Jeffrey Getelman Publishing Company maintains an online database of subscriber records, which it uses for preparing magazine labels, billing renewals, and so forth. New-subscription orders and subscription renewals are keyed into a computer file from terminals. The entry data are checked for accuracy and written on a master file. A similar process is performed for change-of-address requests. Processing summaries from both runs provide listings of master file changes.

Once a month, just prior to mailing, the company prepares mailing labels for its production department to affix to magazines. At the same time, notices to new and renewal subscribers are prepared. These notices acknowledge receipt of payment and are mailed to the subscribers. The company systems analyst, Bob McQuivey, prepared the system flowchart in Figure 12-20 shortly before he left the company. As you can see, the flowchart is incomplete. Finish the flowchart by labeling each flowcharting symbol. Don't forget to label the processing runs marked "Computer."

12-20. The Bridget Joyce Company is an office products distributor that must decide what to do with delinquent credit-sales accounts. Mr. Bob Smith, the credit manager, divides accounts into the following categories: (1) accounts not past due, (2) accounts 30 days or less past due, (3) accounts 31 to 60 days past due, (4) accounts 61 to 90 days past due, and (5) accounts more than 90 days past due. For simplicity, assume that all transactions for each account fall neatly into the same category.

Mr. Smith decides what to do about these customer accounts based on the history of the account in general and also the activity during the account's delinquency period. Sometimes, for example, the customer will not communicate at all. At other times, however, the customer will either write to state that a check is forthcoming or make a partial payment. Mr. Smith tends to be most understanding of customers who make partial payments because he considers such payments acts of good faith. Mr. Smith is less understanding of those customers who only promise to pay or who simply ignore follow-up bills from the company.

Mr. Smith has four potential actions to take in cases of credit delinquency. First, he can simply wait (i.e., do nothing). Second, he can send an initial letter to the customer, inquiring about the problem in bill payment and requesting written notification of a payment schedule if payment has not already been made. Third, he can send a follow-up letter indicating that a collection agency will be given the account if immediate payment is not forthcoming. Fourth, he can turn the account over to a collection agency. Of course, Mr. Smith prefers to use one of the first three actions rather than turn the account over to a collection agency because his company only receives half of any future payments when the collection agency becomes involved.

   a. Create a decision table for the Bridget Joyce Company and provide a set of reasonable decision rules for Mr. Smith to follow. For now, ignore the influence of a customer's credit history.

   b. Expand the decision table analysis you have prepared in question "a" to include the credit history of the customer accounts. You are free to make any assumptions you wish

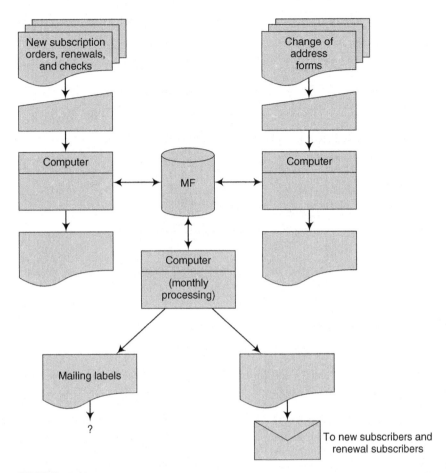

FIGURE 12-20 System flowchart for processing the subscription orders and changes for the Jeffrey Getelman Company.

about how this history might be evaluated by Mr. Smith.

12-21. Follow the directions in Problem 12-11 to access Excel's drawing tools, and then re-create the two program flowcharts shown in Figure 12-21. Draw each flowchart on a separate work sheet. Rename the first sheet "Main" and the second sheet "Sub." To embed text inside a symbol, right-click on that symbol with your mouse and then choose "Edit Text" from the dropdown menu that appears. To center the text inside a symbol, highlight the text and then click on the centering icon in the main toolbar.

Create the words "Yes" and "No" that appear in this flowchart using the Text Box selection from the Insert menu. To eliminate the black (default) borders around these words, right-click on a Text Box and select Format Shape. Select the line color option and choose "No line" from the "Line Color" options on the right. Finally, you can fine-tune the position of any object by clicking on its border, holding the left button and dragging the text box.

Linking Flowcharts

After drawing these two flowcharts, we want to link them together. In this case, we want the user to click on the "Process Record" symbol in the main flowchart and then be able to view the second spreadsheet you've created on the alternate sheet. To create this link, right-click on the "Process Record" symbol, and then select Hyperlink from the main menu.

When the Hyperlink dialog box appears, first select "Place in this Document" from the choices on the left side of the box, and then click on the name of the sheet in which you've drawn the second flowchart ("Sub") in the

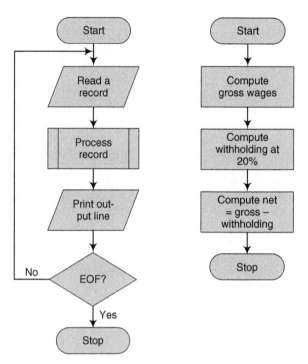

FIGURE 12-21 Draw the flowchart on the left on one Excel sheet and the flowchart on the right on a second sheet.

lower box on the right. If you wish, you can also select a particular cell for linking in the top box—a handy feature if you've drawn your flowchart in a lower portion of the Sub sheet. That's it! Now, when you move your mouse over the "Process Record" symbol in the "Main" sheet, your mouse icon should turn into a hand, indicating that clicking on this symbol links you to the supporting document's sheet.

Using Excel software and the skills described earlier, recreate the documents from the following list or the ones required by your instructor:

a. The context diagram in Figure 12-3.

b. The physical DFD in Figure 12-4.

c. The logical data flow diagram shown in Figure 12-12.

d. Link the DFD in Part c to a new DFD similar to Figure 12-6.

e. The document flowchart in Figure 12-8.

f. The system flowchart in Figure 12-11.

g. The process map in Figure 12-13.

h. The program flowchart shown in Figure 12-15.

12-22. Visit the website "How Flowcharts Help Companies Save Money, Get Accurate Audits, and Satisfy the Government" at: http://mapthink .blogspot.com/2012/10/how-flowcharts-help -companies-save.html. According to this site, how do flowcharts help save companies in these three areas? Can you think of any additional ways that flowcharts can help?

CASE ANALYSES

12-23. Big Fun Toys (Data Flow Diagrams)

Big Fun Toys is a retailer of children's toys. The accounts-payable department is located at the company headquarters in Boston, Massachusetts. The department consists of two full-time clerks and one supervisor. They are responsible for processing and paying approximately 2,000 checks each month. The accounts-payable process begins with receipt of a purchase order from the purchasing department. The purchase order is held until a receiving report and the vendor's invoice have been forwarded to accounts payable.

At that time, the purchase order, receiving report, and invoice are matched together by an accounts-payable clerk, and payment and journal entry information is input to the computer. Payment dates are designated in the input, and these are based on vendor payment terms. Company policy is to take advantage of any cash discounts offered. If there are any discrepancies among the purchase order, receiving report, and invoice, they are given to the supervisor for resolution. After resolving the discrepancies, the supervisor returns the documents to the appropriate clerk for processing. Once documents are matched and payment information is input, the documents are stapled together and filed in a temporary file folder by payment date until checks are issued.

When checks are issued, a copy of each check is used as a voucher cover and is affixed to the supporting documentation from the temporary file. The entire voucher is then defaced to avoid duplicate payments. In addition to the check and check copy, other outputs of the computerized accounts-payable system are a check register, vendor master list, accrual of open invoices, and a weekly cash requirements forecast.

Requirement

Draw a context diagram and data flow diagram similar to those in Figures 12-3 and 12-4 for the company's accounts-payable process, using the symbols in Figure 12-2.

12-24. The Berridge Company (Document Flowcharts)

The Berridge Company is a discount tire dealer that operates 25 retail stores in a metropolitan area. The company maintains a centralized purchasing and warehousing facility and employs a perpetual inventory system. All purchases of tires and related supplies are placed through the company's central purchasing department to take advantage of the quantity discounts offered by its suppliers. The tires and supplies are received at the central warehouse and distributed to the retail stores as needed. The perpetual inventory system at the central facility maintains current inventory records, which include designated reorder points, optimum order quantities, and balance-on-hand information for each type of tire or related supply.

The participants involved in Berridge's inventory system include (1) retail stores, (2) the inventory control department, (3) the warehouse, (4) the purchasing department, (5) accounts payable, and (6) outside vendors. The inventory control department is responsible for maintenance of the perpetual inventory records for each item carried in inventory. The warehouse department maintains the physical inventory of all items carried by the company's retail stores.

All deliveries of tires and related supplies from vendors are received by receiving clerks in the warehouse department, and all distributions to retail stores are filled by shipping clerks in this department. The purchasing department places every order for items needed by the company. The accounts-payable department maintains the subsidiary ledger with vendors and other creditors. All payments are processed by this department. The documents used by these various departments are as follows:

Retail Store Requisition (Form RSR). The retail stores submit this document to the central warehouse whenever tires or supplies are needed. The shipping clerks in the warehouse department fill the orders from inventory and have them delivered to the stores. Three copies of the document are prepared, two of which are sent to the warehouse, and the third copy is filed for reference.

Purchase Requisition (Form PR). An inventory control clerk in the inventory control department prepares this document when the quantity on hand for an item falls below the designated reorder point. Two copies of the document are prepared. One copy is forwarded to the purchasing department, and the other is filed.

Purchase Order (Form PO). The purchasing department prepares this document based on the information found in the purchase requisition. Five copies of the purchase order are prepared. The disposition of these copies is as follows: copy 1 to vendor, copy 2 to accounts-payable department, copy 3 to inventory control department, copy 4 to warehouse, and copy 5 filed for reference.

Receiving Report (Form RR). The warehouse department prepares this document when ordered items are received from vendors. A receiving clerk completes the document by indicating the vendor's name, the date the shipment is received, and the quantity of each item received. Four copies of the report are prepared. Copy 1 is sent to the accounts-payable department, copy 2 to the purchasing department, and copy 3 to the inventory control department. Copy 4 is retained by the warehouse department, compared with the purchase order form in its files, and filed together with this purchase order form for future reference.

Invoices. Invoices received from vendors are bills for payment. The vendor prepares several copies of each invoice, but only two copies are of concern to the Berridge Company: the copy that is received by the company's accounts-payable department and the copy that is retained by the vendor for reference. The accounts-payable department compares the vendor invoice with its file copy of the original purchase order and its file copy of the warehouse receiving report. Based on this information, adjustments to the bill amount on the invoice are made (e.g., for damaged goods, for trade discounts, or for cash discounts), a check is prepared, and the payment is mailed to the vendor.

Requirements

1. Draw a document flowchart for the Berridge Company using the symbols in Figure 12-7.

2. Could the company eliminate one or more copies of its RSR form? Use your flowchart to explain why or why not.

3. Do you think that the company creates too many copies of its purchase orders? Why or why not?

12-25. Classic Photography Inc. (Systems Flowcharts)

Jenny Smith owns Classic Photography Inc., a company that restores photos for its clients and creates electronic images from the restored photos. The company also frames restored photos and creates sophisticated custom artworks. Artworks include materials such as glass and frames that are purchased from local suppliers. In addition to supplies for displays, the company purchases office supplies and packaging materials from several vendors.

Classic Photography uses an off-the-shelf accounting software package to prepare internal documents and reports. As employees note a need for supplies and materials, they send an e-mail to Jenny, who acts as the office manager and company accountant. Either Jenny or her assistant Donna enters order information into the accounting system and creates a purchase order that is faxed to the supplier. Jenny or Donna may also call the supplier if there is something special about the product ordered.

When ordered materials and supplies arrive, either Jenny or Donna checks the goods received against a copy of the purchase order and enters the new inventory into the computer system. Jenny pays bills twice each month, on the first and the fifteenth. She checks the computer system for invoices outstanding and verifies that the goods have been received. She then enters any information needed to produce printed checks from the accounting system. Classic Photography mails checks and printed remittance advices (portions of the vendor bill to be returned) to suppliers.

Requirements

1. Create a systems flowchart for the purchase and payment processes.
2. Comment on the value, if any, that a systems flowchart describing this process would have to Jenny.

12-26. Filzen Company (Process Maps and Decision Tables)

The Filzen Company sells construction supplies to building contractors, mostly on a wholesale basis. The company has been in business for over 30 years. The current owner is Joshua Filzen, although the company was originally founded by his father, James Filzen. When he retired in 2014, the elder Filzen handed the business over to his son, who has run it ever since.

The company operates in Small County—a rural area where most people in the building trades know each other well. For this reason, the company extends credit to its regular customers, many of whom have done business with it for years. Most settle their accounts about once a month.

You work for a small CPA firm, whom Joshua has hired to look at its accounting procedures and to make recommendations based on its findings. You've been assigned to the consulting team, and your first job is to document the company's authorization procedures for credit purchases. The rules are as follows. (1) Purchases of less than $100 that are made by known customers in good standing are approved automatically. (2) Purchases between $100 and $500 require authorization by a supervisor. Purchases over $500 must be approved by Jason Bergner, the accounts-receivable manager. Credit purchases attempted by new customers not yet approved for credit or by customers not in good standing are denied.

Requirements

1. Create a process map for this task, using the symbols in Figure 12-13.
2. Create a decision table for this task. Hint: see Figure 12-16.
3. Create a decision tree for this task. Hint: see Figure 12-17.
4. Which documentation aide do you prefer and why?
5. Do any of these documents suggest control problems with the current system? If so, what controls do you recommend?

12-27. Stingy Upstate University (Process Maps, Decision Tables, and Decision Trees)

The approval rules for reimbursing those faculty members at Upstate University who attend professional conferences are somewhat complicated and, in the opinion of most, "hardly generous." For example, the maximum allowed for breakfast, lunch, or dinner is $8, $10, and $12, respectively. In addition, no reimbursements are made for breakfast if the traveler leaves home after 10 am, for lunch if the traveler leaves home after 2 pm, or for dinner if the traveler leaves home after 8 pm. Finally, no reimbursements are made for "business lunches" or similar meals if their costs are included as part of the conference registration fee.

When Upstate University faculty file for travel reimbursements, they must file a form that requests the time they left home and the time they left the hotel to return home. They must also provide a copy of their conference registration receipt, showing what meals were included in the program.

Requirements

1. Develop a process map that displays the logic for deciding whether or not a given meal should be reimbursed.

2. Develop a decision table for these same reimbursement rules.

3. Develop a decision tree for these same reimbursement rules.

4. Which documentation method do you most prefer and why?

5. Marsha Tightfist approves or denies travel reimbursements at Upstate University. She gets paid $50,000 a year, reviews all requests for travel reimbursements, and denies those that violate these rules. What calculations would you make to determine whether or not her salary is money well spent?

12-28. The Dinteman Company (Document Analysis)

The Dinteman Company is an industrial machinery and equipment manufacturer with several production departments. The company employs automated and heavy equipment in its production departments. Consequently, Dinteman has a large repair and maintenance department (R&M department) for servicing this equipment.

The operating efficiency of the R&M department has deteriorated over the past 2 years. For example, repair and maintenance costs seem to be climbing more rapidly than other department costs. The assistant controller has reviewed the operations of the R&M department and has concluded that the administrative procedures used since the early days of the department are outmoded due in part to the growth of the company. In the opinion of the assistant controller, the two major causes for the deterioration are an antiquated scheduling system for repair and maintenance work, and the actual cost to distribute the R&M department's costs to the production departments. The actual costs of the R&M department are allocated monthly to the production departments on the basis of the number of service calls made during each month.

The assistant controller has proposed that a formal work order system be implemented for the R&M department. With the new system, the production departments will submit a service request to the R&M department for the repairs and/or maintenance to be completed, including a suggested time for having the work done. The supervisor of the R&M department will prepare a cost estimate on the service request for the work required (labor and materials) and estimate the amount of time for completing the work on the service request. The R&M supervisor will return the request to the production department that initiated the request. Once the production department approves the work by returning a copy of the service request, the R&M supervisor will prepare a repair and maintenance work order and schedule the job. This work order provides the repair worker with the details of the work to be done and is used to record the actual repair and maintenance hours worked and the materials and supplies used.

Production departments will be charged for actual labor hours worked at a predetermined standard rate for the type of work required. Parts and supplies are charged to the production departments at cost. The assistant controller believes that only two documents will be required in this new system—a Repair/Maintenance Service Request initiated by the production departments and a Repair/Maintenance Work Order initiated by the R&M department.

Requirements

1. For the Repair/Maintenance Work Order document:

    a. Identify the data items of importance to the repair and maintenance department and the production department that should be incorporated into the work order.

    b. Indicate how many copies of the work order would be required, and explain how each copy would be distributed.

2. Prepare a document flowchart to show how the Repair/Maintenance Service Request and the Repair/Maintenance Work Order should be coordinated and used among the departments of

Dinteman Company to request and complete the repair and maintenance work, to provide the basis for charging the production departments for the cost of the completed work, and to evaluate the performance of the repair and maintenance department. Provide explanations in the flowchart as appropriate.

(CMA Adapted)

READINGS AND OTHER RESOURCES

Araulo, B., R. F. Marcello, B. Amado, F. Goncalves. 2016. Business process management notation for a costing model conception. *Brazilian Journal of Operations and Production Management* 13(3): 244–251.

Best, B. 2011. The Whys and Hows of Flowcharting. *Quality* 50(4): 23–25.

Borthick, A. F., and G.P. Scneider. 2016. Detecting errors in and making inferences from business process representation. *Journal of Emerging Technologies in Accounting* 13(2): 185–194.

Bradford, M., S. Richtermeyer, and D. Roberts. 2007. System diagramming techniques: An analysis of methods used in accounting education and practice. *Journal of Information Systems* 21(1): 173–212.

Chartier, Tim. 2017. Graphic stories. *Journal of Corporate Accounting and Finance* 28(3): 82–83.

Indulska, M., J. Recker, M. Rosemann, and P. Green. 2009. Business process modeling: current issues and future challenges. *Lecture Notes in Computer Science* 5565: 501–514.

Lehman, M. W. 2000. Flowcharting made simple. *Journal of Accountancy* 190(4): 77–88.

Nellen, A., S. J. Cereola, and D. A. Riordan. 2011. Learning tax with flowcharts. *Tax Adviser* 42(2): 124–127.

Go to www.wiley.com/go/simkin/videos to access videos on the following topics:

Creating Data Flow Diagrams (DFDs)
Creating a Flowchart Using Microsoft Word
Creating Process Maps with TaskMap
Using Visio to Create Process Maps
Creating Decision Tables
Creating Decision Trees in Excel

ANSWERS TO TEST YOURSELF

1. a **2.** c **3.** c **4.** d **5.** c **6.** b **7.** c **8.** d **9.** c **10.** a

Chapter 13

Developing and Implementing Effective Accounting Information Systems

After studying this chapter, you should be able to:

1. *Discuss* the roles of accountants, analysis teams, and steering committees in systems studies.

2. *Explain* why systems analysts must identify the strategic and operational goals of an accounting information system.

3. *Identify* the deliverables in systems analysis work, especially the systems analysis report.

4. *Plan* and *describe* the analysis and design phases of a systems study.

5. *Describe* and *conduct* a feasibility evaluation.

6. *Identify* costs, benefits, tools, and techniques associated with systems design work.

7. *Evaluate* alternative systems proposals and make a selection or choose to outsource.

8. *Discuss* the activities required to implement and maintain a large information system.

"[M]odel defects can lead to misinterpretation of user requirements and to erroneous system designs and can ultimately be a root cause of system failure. Erroneous models may lead to the formulation of incorrect queries against a database, reliance on incorrect information obtained by these queries, and costly decision-making errors. Because of the deleterious outcomes that can occur when conceptual models contain defects, those who build them should evaluate their quality carefully."

Dunn, C. L., G. J. Gerard, S. V. Grabski, and S. R. Boss. 2017. Asymmetry in identification of multiplicity errors in conceptual models of business processes. *Journal of Information Systems* 31(1): 23.

13.1 INTRODUCTION

Developing effective accounting information systems (AISs) requires the collaboration of a wide range of individuals, including systems analysts, system designers, and managers. Accountants, both as auditors and as general information users, should be part of all information technology (IT) studies involving AISs.

This chapter is about systems studies—the planning, analysis, design, implementation, and maintenance of AIS applications. As you might imagine, sometimes an organization might choose to design some of its applications in-house, and at other times, it might decide to purchase, lease, or outsource the work to others. Selecting the best choice from among these alternatives is part of the **systems study** process.

13.2 THE SYSTEMS DEVELOPMENT LIFE CYCLE

Acquiring, implementing, and training people to use a large AIS is a difficult task. A systems study (also called *systems development work*) begins with a formal investigation of an existing AIS to identify strengths and weaknesses.

Who actually performs a systems study? This varies from organization to organization as well as from project to project. Many large organizations have IT professionals to perform this work. In contrast, smaller organizations with limited technical expertise as well as larger organizations with other priorities are more likely to hire outside consultants for this work. (Note: The Sarbanes–Oxley Act of 2002 expressly forbids a CPA firm from performing such systems work for a client with whom it already has an audit relationship.) Our discussion assumes that a generic "study team" of experts, who may or may not be outside consultants, perform this work.

Four Stages in the Systems Development Life Cycle

The **Systems Development Life Cycle (SDLC)** model (also known as the waterfall approach) is a systematic and orderly approach used to guide systems development. This sequential development process, with each step having a downstream effect on the next step, is one of the oldest software development approaches and yet remains the most common one in use.[1] Traditionally, we can identify four major steps or phases of a systems study:

1. **Planning and investigation.** This stage involves investigating how to use information architecture to implement a strategic plan. It involves organizing a systems study team, performing a preliminary investigation of the existing system, and developing plans for the remainder of the study.
2. **Analysis.** This step involves analyzing the company's current system to identify the information needs, strengths, and weaknesses of the existing system. Analysts try to understand the business by drawing "pictures" or models of the business and its workings, including narrative descriptions of policies, procedures, and controls. These models represent the business processes of the firm, depicting the business activities (or business events) and the data about these business activities that the firm wants to capture in its database. For example, in an Accounts-Receivable process, for the business activity, "customer buys goods on credit," the firm would want to collect data such as customer name, date of sale, amount of sale, and inventory items and quantity purchased.
3. **Design and acquisition.** In this step, an organization designs changes that eliminate (or minimize) the current system's weak points while preserving its strengths. The organization also decides what system is best and how to acquire it.

---

[1] Vijayasarathy, L. R. and C. W. Butler. 2016. Choice of software development methodologies: Do organizational, project, and team characteristics matter? *IEEE Software* 33(5): 90.

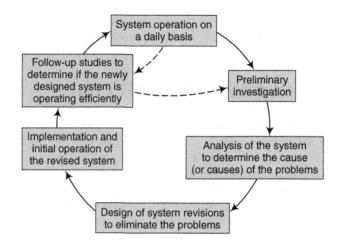

FIGURE 13-1 Systems development life cycle of a business information system.

4. Implementation, follow-up, and maintenance. This phase includes installing resources for the new system as well as training new or existing employees to use it. Companies conduct follow-up studies to determine whether the new system is successful and, of course, to identify any new problems with it. Finally, organizations must maintain the system, which means that they must correct minor flaws and update the system as required.

These four phases are the SDLC of a business information system. Logically, the activities in these phases flow from stage to stage in only one direction, like water flowing in a stream. This is why the SDLC is also called the **waterfall model**. In practice, there is usually much overlap between phases in the life cycle and the steps in a systems study don't necessarily occur in sequence. Instead, system developers often perform two or more stages in parallel with one another.

Figure 13-1 illustrates that this life cycle spans the time during which a company's system is operating normally and is subsequently revised as a result of some problem(s). Each time a newly revised system takes over the company's daily operating activities, a new life cycle begins.

The dashed arrows in Figure 13-1 emphasize that follow-up studies of a system should be a continuous process. An organization reevaluates systems regularly to confirm that they are still working well. If follow-up studies indicate that previous problems have recurred or new ones have developed, an organization should begin a new systems study.

Case-in-Point 13.1 This case illustrates that the SDLC remains a reliable approach for software acquisition and development. By following the stages of the SDLC for the acquisition of software for the Home Health subsidiary of a hospital, the development team achieved a highly successful IT implementation in a twenty-first century environment. Home Health's old system was not scalable and could not cope with changes in the health-care environment, such as patient health records, medical billing practices, and Medicare requirements. The reason for the change in the information system was to modernize Home Health's operations and to integrate with the hospital's state-of-the-art information system. The new system achieved the team's objectives. It provided electronic health records that doctors and patients could access electronically at all times. The software also included special billing and Accounts-Receivable modules, real-time reports, dashboards for business intelligence outputs, and the ability to optimize scheduling.[2]

Systems Studies and Accounting Information Systems

A systems study looks at all systems in an organization's **applications portfolio**. This portfolio may include an integrated enterprise resource planning (ERP) system, along with other specialized information systems, or it may consist of many separate systems for functional areas such as accounting, marketing, and human resources. AISs are prime targets for systems studies—for example, because older ones may not comply with new governmental regulations. But in general, a systems study means more than just replacing or modifying existing information systems. Typically, altering an AIS also affects work flows, data gathering and recording tasks, employee responsibilities, and even the way an organization rewards its managers. Thus, one reason why organizations perform systems studies is because such studies are part of the greater task of **business process reengineering (BPR)**—that is, the task of making major modifications to one of an organization's core systems. Because the accommodation involves so many changes, employee resistance is common and often quite strong—especially where jobs are at stake. This is also one reason why so many new systems fail. We discussed BPR in more depth in Chapter 9.

Case-in-Point 13.2   One of the most public IT project failures was the US Healthcare.gov website, developed to implement the US Affordable Care Act. The purpose of the website was to allow US taxpayers to find out whether they qualified for government subsidies for health-care insurance, compare prices of health insurance plans, and enroll in health-care plans. Shortly after the launch in 2013, users experienced significant issues. They were unable to log in to the website, or they received cryptic error messages, incorrect quotes, or refusal of coverage. Insurers also received incorrect and incomplete information. It was a mess. There were serious development issues. Around 250,000 users attempted to access the website simultaneously in the week after the launch, but the website slowed down significantly after only 1,100 users. Subsequently, almost 600 other defects were identified.[3]

13.3   SYSTEMS PLANNING

The first phase of a systems study involves systems planning and an initial investigation. Think you can skip this phase? Think again. Just as you would not build a house without first determining what rooms you'd need *in* that house, organizations are well advised to plan carefully.

Planning for Success

In large organizations, system redesigns (or new development work) typically involve millions of dollars, making mistakes very costly. In smaller organizations, major

---

[2] McMurtney, M. 2013. A case study of the application of the systems development life cycle (SDLC) in 21st century health care: Something old, something new? *Journal of the Southern Association for Information Systems* 1(1): 14–25.

[3] McConville, D. 2016, January 13. An Exploration of Information Systems (IS) and IT Project Failures. *CPA Ireland*. Accessed from www.cpaireland.ie on May 3, 2017.

errors can be catastrophic, leading a firm to bankruptcy—or embarrassment for a government. What else can happen when organizations do not plan carefully? Here are some examples:

- Systems do not meet users' needs, causing employee frustration, and resistance.
- Systems are not flexible enough to meet the business needs for which they were designed and are ultimately scrapped.
- Project expenditures significantly overrun what once seemed like very adequate budgets.
- The time required to complete the new system vastly exceeds the development schedule—often by years.
- Systems solve the wrong problems.
- Top management does not approve or support the new systems.
- Systems are difficult and costly to maintain.

Studies of unsuccessful information systems projects suggest that mistakes made at the outset of a systems study are a common reason why such projects ultimately fail. Careful systems planning and an initial investigation can avoid critical missteps that lead to disaster. "Planning for success" means beginning a systems study with a focused investigation that: (1) approaches specific organizational problems from a broad point of view, (2) uses an interdisciplinary study team to evaluate an organization's information systems, and (3) makes sure that the company's study team works closely with a steering committee (described next) and end users in all phases of the work.

Broad Viewpoint in a Systems Study.   When performing a systems study, the participants should use a **systems approach**—that is, a broad point of view. This approach aligns the systems study with the organization's mission and strategic planning goals and objectives. For example, if a company plans to consolidate divisions or discontinue unprofitable product lines, new IT systems will need to reflect these plans. In another scenario, a company that is embarking on a growth strategy through mergers and acquisitions should think twice about implementing a new enterprise system that might not be compatible with newly acquired companies. Also, management should think strategically about whether a potential new system could accommodate acquired businesses operating in different industries.

Case-in-Point 13.3   One common justification for airline mergers has been "cost savings"—for example, from eliminating flights on duplicate routes or consolidating back-office personnel. But airline executives must also worry about the compatibility of their computer systems and how much it will cost to merge them. Sometimes, the answer is "a lot."[4]

The Study Team and the Steering Committee.   Using an interdisciplinary study team follows from the need for a broad viewpoint when performing a systems study. It also serves to correct the thinking that the system belongs only to the IT staff. Because most accounting and computer professionals are specialists, it is unlikely that any one or two people will have the broad background and experience necessary to understand

---

[4] Caldwell, J. 2010. The good, bad, and ugly of airline consolidation. *Business Travel News* 27(15): 15.

and change a large AIS. For this reason, the recommended approach is to form (or hire) a team of specialists—a "study team"—to perform the system's study.

It is important that the study team communicate closely and meaningfully with the company's top managers. To provide this continuous interface, the company's top management should also appoint a **steering committee** to work with each study team as it performs its tasks. Ideally, the committee will include top management personnel—for example, the controller, the vice president of finance, the chief information officer (CIO), internal audit representation, and (for very important projects) even the chief executive officer (CEO) of the company. The rationale for such involvement is straightforward: *top management commitment is critical to the ultimate success of a new or revised system.*

Investigating Current Systems

Systems study includes constant monitoring of current systems. When any appear to have problems, the systems study team performs a **preliminary investigation** of the system in question and advises the steering committee of its findings. One important part of this work is *to separate symptoms from causes*. In its deliberations, the study team may consider alternatives to the current system, attempt to estimate the costs and benefits of its proposed solutions, or make recommendations for desired alternatives. In this phase of the project, the study team enjoys wide latitude in what it can choose to examine, and it is usually encouraged to "think outside the box" (i.e., consider vastly different and innovative approaches to address current problems).

The duration of a preliminary investigation is comparatively brief—typically, a matter of a few weeks. The deliverable from this phase of the systems study is a preliminary investigation report describing the problems or objectives the study team identified, the solutions or alternatives it investigated, and the course(s) of action it recommends. The study team submits this report to the company steering committee for a final determination. The steering committee may decide to: (1) disband the study team and do nothing, (2) perform additional preliminary investigations, or (3) proceed to the formal systems analysis stage of the systems study.

13.4   SYSTEMS ANALYSIS

The basic purpose of the **systems analysis** phase is to examine a system in depth. The study team will familiarize itself with the company's current accounting system, identify specific inputs and outputs, identify system strengths and weaknesses, and eventually make recommendations for supplementary work. Figure 13-2 shows the logical procedures that the team should follow.

In performing its work, the study team should avoid overanalyzing a company's system. Instead, the team should try to identify and understand the organization's goals for the system, perform a systems survey, and prepare one or more reports that describe its findings.

Understanding Organizational Goals

For the study team to do an adequate job—for example, determine the real problems within a company's information system—its members must first understand the

Understand the systems goals

↓

Perform a survey to acquire sufficient information
relating to current system's problems

↓

Suggest possible solutions to solve the system's
problems through a systems analysis report

FIGURE 13-2   Systems analysis procedures.

system's goals. Of special importance is determining which goals are not being achieved under the present system and why this happens. Organization goals include: (1) general systems goals, (2) top management systems goals, and (3) operating management systems goals.

General Systems Goals.   General systems goals apply to most organization's information systems and help an AIS contribute to an efficient and effective organization. Principles contributing to these goals are: (1) awareness that the benefits of a new system should exceed its costs, (2) concern that the outputs of the system help managers make better decisions, (3) commitment to a system that allows optimal access to information, and (4) flexibility so that the system can accommodate changing informational needs.

The study team must determine whether the current information system helps to achieve these general systems goals. For example, if an AIS has excessive costs associated with using traditional paper documents (e.g., purchase orders, receiving reports, and vendor invoices), this will violate goal number one (cost awareness), and the study team might recommend that the company use an online system instead.

Top Management Systems Goals.   AISs typically play key roles in satisfying top management goals. For instance, AISs usually provide top managers with long-range budget planning data so they can make effective strategic decisions about future product-line sales or similar business activities. Similarly, periodic performance reports provide top management with vital control information about corporate operations— for example, how sales of new product lines are doing. Finally, top management needs to know about the short-range operating performance of its organization's subsystems—for example, summary information about individual department operating results and how these results compare with budgetary projections.

Operating Management Systems Goals.   Compared to top management, the information needs of operating managers (e.g., department heads) are normally easier to determine. This is because the decision-making functions of operating managers typically relate to well-defined and narrower organizational areas. In addition, the majority of operating managers' decisions are for the current business year (in contrast to top management's long-range decision-making functions). As a result, operating managers need information that helps them meet daily, weekly, or monthly operating targets.

Systems Survey Work

The objective of a **systems survey** is to enable the study team to obtain a more complete understanding of the company's current operational information system and its environment. Of special importance is identifying the strengths and weaknesses of the current system. The overall objective of any new system is to retain the system's strengths while eliminating the system's weaknesses, especially those weaknesses causing problems in the current system. These weaknesses will likely relate to specific goals that the current system does not now accomplish.

Understanding the Human Element and Potential Behavioral Problems. Since the appearance of a study team on the work scene usually signals change, employees are often resistant to help. Unless the study team deals directly with this problem at the beginning, there is a good chance that employees will oppose the changes that the team recommends. Thus, a systems study must gain the full cooperation and support of those employees who are crucial to the success of a new system.

Data Gathering. A systems survey requires the study team to gather data about the existing system. There are several ways of doing this, including:

- **Review existing documentation or create new materials.** This documentation includes descriptive data such as organizational charts, strategic plans, budgets, policy and procedure manuals, job descriptions, and charts of accounts, as well as technical documentation such as flowcharts, process maps, and training manuals (see Chapter 12 to refresh your memory on flowcharts and process diagrams).

- **Observe the current system in operation.** Visiting various parts of the operation on a surprise basis and asking employees questions about their jobs can help team members learn whether the system works as described, the morale of employees, the amount of downtime, and workload cycles.

- **Use questionnaires and surveys.** These can be anonymous so that respondents share their views openly about sensitive issues. *Open-ended questionnaires* provide an unstructured free flow of ideas that may bring new issues to light. *Close-ended questionnaires* (Figure 13-3), on the other hand, are efficient and allow for easy tabulation of results.

Example of an open-ended question on a systems study questionnaire:

1. Please use the space in this box to explain why you are either satisfied or dissatisfied with the current general ledger system.

> *The system is ok, but finding the right account requires a lot of drill down. Some account definitions are also unclear to newbies.*

Example of a closed-ended question on a systems study questionnaire:

2. Please indicate your level of satisfaction with the current general ledger system by checking the appropriate button:

Very satisfied	Somewhat satisfied	Neither satisfied nor dissatisfied	Somewhat dissatisfied	Very dissatisfied
○	○	○	○	◉

FIGURE 13-3 Sample questions and illustrative answers on a systems survey questionnaire. Note that such a questionnaire could be conducted on the Web.

- **Review internal control procedures.** Unit 2 of this book discusses the importance of internal control systems. Weaknesses in these procedures can cause major problems for a company. The study team should identify high risk areas, strengths, and weaknesses of the specific procedures.
- **Interview system participants.** Face-to-face interviews allow the study team to gather system information in the greatest depth and can sometimes reveal surprises. For example, an interview might reveal that a manager's decisions don't really require input from several existing reports.

Data Analysis

Once the study team completes its survey work, it must analyze the results. Often, this means nothing more than creating summary statistics, but it can also involve developing flowcharts and/or process maps that can highlight bottlenecks in information flows, redundant reporting, and missing information links.

Systems analysis work necessarily takes longer than a preliminary investigation, typically months. Where required, the study team will provide interim reports to the steering committee about its progress. The most important deliverable from the analysis portion of the systems study, however, is the *final systems analysis report*, which signals the end of the analysis phase of the system study. Like other reports, the study team submits this report to the steering committee, which then considers the report's findings and debates the recommendations it contains.

As representatives of top management, the steering committee has, within limits, the ability to do whatever it wants. It could abandon the project, ask for additional analyses and a set of revised recommendations, or vote to proceed to the systems design phase of the project.

Evaluating System Feasibility

After obtaining a positive response from the steering committee, the design team must perform a detailed investigation of different potential systems. Figure 13-4 shows that this work involves five major procedures or activities. The first of these is a **feasibility evaluation** in which the design team determines the practicality of alternative proposals. Only after this step is completed can the design team tackle the other steps. For each system alternative, the design team must examine five feasibility areas: (1) technical feasibility, (2) operational feasibility, (3) schedule feasibility, (4) legal feasibility, and (5) economic feasibility.

Technical Feasibility. The **technical feasibility** of any proposed system attempts to answer the question, "What technical resources are required by a particular system?" Hardware and software are obvious components. A proposed system that can interface with critical existing software is more desirable than one requiring the organization to buy new software. Computer experts typically work on this phase of the feasibility evaluation because a thorough understanding of IT is essential.

In addition to developing a preliminary hardware or software configuration for a proposed system, the design team must also determine whether current employees have the technical skills to use it. If a specific computerized system is too sophisticated for a company's employees, it is unlikely that requiring employees to use it in subsequent daily operations will be very successful.

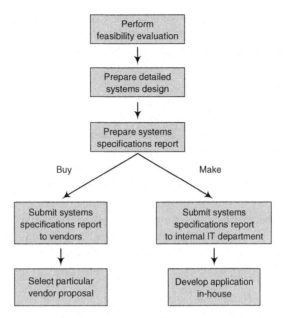

FIGURE 13-4   Steps in the systems design phase of a systems study.

Operational Feasibility.   The **operational feasibility** of a proposed system examines its compatibility with the current operating environment. This means determining how consistent the tasks and procedures required by the new system will be with those of the old system. The design team must also analyze the capabilities of current employees to perform the specific functions required by each proposed system and determine to what extent employees will require specialized training.

Case-in-Point 13.4   Operational feasibility hit a snag at Delta Air Lines in April 2017. The systems meltdown began with thunderstorms in Atlanta and subsequently resulted in 4,000 cancelled flights and hundreds of thousands of stranded and very frustrated passengers. An internal investigation led to a puzzling conclusion in today's sophisticated IT environment: the airline's business process for scheduling its 13,000 pilots and 20,000 flight attendants involved dialing in via telephone for new assignments after the thunderstorm. They could not get through to the employees responsible for the rescheduling due to overloaded circuits. Flights had still not taken off days after the thunderstorm had passed.[5]

Operational-feasibility analysis is mostly a human relations study because it is strongly oriented toward "people problems." For this reason, human-relations specialists participate heavily in it. As noted earlier, employees commonly have negative attitudes toward changes that can affect their organizational duties. Encouraging employees to attend briefing sessions, suggest changes, and understand how a new system will enable them to perform their jobs more easily can help limit employee resistance.

Case-in-Point 13.5   When a prominent, mid-sized CPA firm decided to install a new "paperless office" system to expedite workflows, the "really hard part" turned out to be employee obstacles, not technology. Ms. I. M. Notwilling in the trust and estates department

---

[5] McCartney, S. 2017. At Delta, busy signals, then delays. *The Wall Street Journal*, May 4, 2017, pp. A1, A13.

was a notable holdout, continuing to use paper-based documents and other workarounds because she believed the new system hindered her ability to perform her work. Using both rewards and penalties, top management convinced her otherwise. As a result, her billing rate of 85% improved to 94% the following year.[6]

Schedule Feasibility. Timeliness is important. **Schedule feasibility** requires the design team to estimate how long it will take a new or revised system to become operational and to communicate this information to the steering committee. For example, if a design team projects that it will take 16 months for a particular system design to become fully functional, the steering committee may reject the proposal in favor of a simpler alternative that the company can implement in a shorter time frame.

Legal Feasibility. Are there any conflicts between a newly proposed system and the organization's legal obligations? **Legal feasibility** requires a new system to comply with applicable federal and state statutes about financial reporting requirements as well as the company's contractual obligations.

Case-in-Point 13.6 Nevada is one of five states in the United States that does not have a state income tax. You would think, therefore, that any payroll system a Nevada company chose to implement would not need a module to withhold state income taxes from employee paychecks. But Reno, Nevada, is only 10 miles from the California border, California does have a state income tax, and California residents must pay state income taxes even if they work in Nevada. Thus, Reno, Nevada, corporations must have state withholding modules in their payroll systems for such employees.

Economic Feasibility. **Economic feasibility** seeks assurance that the anticipated benefits of the system exceed its projected costs. This requires accountants to perform a cost–benefit analysis. This analysis takes into account all costs, including indirect costs such as time spent by current employees on implementing the new system. It also considers benefits, which are sometimes difficult to foresee or estimate. A common mistake is underestimating the costs of implementation and continuing operations. The accountants conducting the analysis need to separately identify one-time costs versus recurring ones. The point of the economic feasibility analysis is to get a "best estimate" of the worthiness of a project.

13.5 DETAILED SYSTEMS DESIGN AND ACQUISITION

Once the steering committee approves the feasibility of a general system plan (project), the design team can begin work on a **detailed systems design**. This involves specifying the outputs, processing procedures, and inputs for the new system. Just as construction blueprints create the detailed plans for building a house, the detailed design of a new system becomes the specifications for creating or acquiring a new information system. Figure 13-5 provides examples of the detailed requirements that the design team must create, and these requirements in turn explain specifically what the proposed system must produce.

---

[6] Dykman, C. A., and C. K. Davis, 2012. Addressing resistance to workflow automation. *Journal of Leadership, Accountability, and Ethics* 9(3): 115–123.

Requirements	Discussion
Processes	Descriptions of the various processes to be performed in the revised system, stressing what is to be done and by whom.
Data elements	Descriptions of the required data elements, including their name, size, format, source, and importance.
Data structure	Preliminary data structure that indicates how the data elements will be organized into logical records.
Inputs	Copies of system inputs and descriptions of their contents, sources, and who is responsible for them.
Outputs	Copies of system outputs and descriptions of their purpose, frequency, and distribution.
Documentation	Descriptions of how the revised system and each subsystem will operate.
Constraints	Descriptions of constraints such as staffing limitations and regulatory requirements.
Controls	Controls to reduce the risk of undetected errors and irregularities in the input, processing, and output stages of data processing work.
Reorganizations	Necessary changes such as increasing staff levels, adding new job functions, and terminating certain existing positions.

FIGURE 13-5   Examples of detailed requirements for a system proposal.

From an accounting standpoint, one of the most important elements in a new system is its control requirements. In this matter, the design team should have a "built-in mentality" when designing control procedures for a system. In other words, rather than adding controls after a system has been developed and installed, the team should design cost-effective general and application control procedures into the system as integrated components. The Committee of Sponsoring Organizations (COSO) of the Treadway Commission (see Chapter 6) emphasizes the importance of this view:

Whenever management considers changes to its company's operations or activities, the concept that it's better to "build-in" rather than "build-on" controls, and to do it right the first time, should be the fundamental guiding premise.[7]

Designing System Outputs, Processes, and Inputs

Once the design team determines that a system is feasible and creates a general design, it can focus on developing the system's input, processing, and output requirements. When performing design tasks, it is perhaps curious that the design team first focuses on the outputs—not the inputs or processing requirements—of the new system.

The reason for this is that the most important objective of an AIS is to satisfy users' needs. Preparing output specifications first lets these requirements dictate the inputs and processing tasks required to produce them.

During the analysis phase and general system design, the study team must develop boundaries for the new system that define the project's scope. Failing to do so causes **scope creep**—that is, expands the scope of a project and costs money. Outside consultants often handle these requests by drafting proposals showing the additional costs associated with them. These costs can include delays in meeting the schedule for delivering the project.

Case-in-Point 13.7   Universities are large, complex organizations with many specialized processes. These entities are good candidates for enterprise systems, but scope creep and

[7] The Committee of Sponsoring Organizations of the Treadway Commission (www.coso.org).

other problems can send project costs spiraling upward. The North Dakota University System had troubles as they worked to implement *PeopleSoft ERP*. The software project cost was $49 million ($14 million over budget) and over 3 years behind planned rollout. Extensive customized computing was one, but not the only, source of the cost overruns for North Dakota's ERP. According to a study by the Standish group, over 75% of all ERP implementations fail.[8]

System Outputs. The design team will use the data gathered from the prior systems analysis work to help it decide what kinds of outputs are needed as well as the formats that these outputs should have. Although it is possible for the design team to merely copy the outputs of an older system, this would make little sense—the new system would be just like the old one. Instead, the team will attempt to create better outputs—that is, design outputs that will better satisfy their users' information needs than did the old system.

Outputs may be classified according to which functional area uses them (e.g., marketing, human resources, accounting, or manufacturing) as well as how frequently they must be produced (e.g., daily or weekly). Where a specific report is not needed on a regular basis, the system should be able to provide it when requested (a *demand report*) or triggered when a certain condition is met (an *exception report*). For example, an accounts-receivable report on a specific customer's payment history might be issued on demand or generated automatically when a customer owes more than a specified amount. Although many organizations still rely heavily on hard-copy (printed) reports, systems designers should also consider the possibility of creating soft-copy (screen) reports as an alternative, which use less paper and, of course, do not require a printer for viewing.

Process Design. Until now, the system designers have focused on *what the system must provide* rather than *how the system can provide it*. After designing the outputs, their next step is to identify the processing procedures required to produce them. This involves deciding which application programs are necessary and what data processing tasks each program should perform.

There are a large number of tools for modeling computer processes. Among them are the system flowcharts, data flow diagrams, program flowcharts, process maps, and decision tables discussed in Chapter 12. Another popular tool is the entity–relationship (E–R) diagram discussed in Chapter 14. Common to all these design methodologies is the idea of **structured, top-down design**, in which system designers begin at the highest level of abstraction and then "drill down" to lower, more detailed levels until the system is completely specified.

Designing System Inputs. Once the design team has specified the outputs and processing procedures for a new project, its members can think about what data the system must collect to satisfy these output and processing requirements. Thus, the team must identify and describe each data element in the systems design (e.g., "alphabetic," "maximum number of characters," and "default value") as well as specify the way data items must be coded. This is no easy task, because there are usually a large number of data items in even a small business application. Chapter 14 discusses the subject of data modeling in detail.

---

[8] Songini, M. 2006. PeopleSoft apps vex N.D. colleges, Computerworld, accessed at www.computerworld .com; and Garg, P., and A. Garg, 2013. An empirical study on critical failure factors for enterprise resource planning implementation in Indian retail sector. *Business Process Management Journal* 19(3): 496–514.

After the design team identifies and describes the input data, it can determine the source of each data element. For example, customer information such as name, address, and telephone numbers may be gathered directly from Web screens, while the current date can be accessed from the computer system itself. Wherever possible, the design team will attempt to capture data in computer-readable formats. As noted in Chapter 3, this avoids costly, time-consuming data transcription as well as the errors such transcription typically introduce into the job stream.

Prototyping. **Prototyping** means developing a simplified model of a proposed AIS. The prototype is therefore a scaled-down, experimental version of a nonexistent system that a design team can develop cheaply and quickly for user-evaluation purposes. The prototype model does not run, but presents users with the "look and feel" of a completed system. By allowing users to experiment with the prototype, the designers can learn what users like and dislike in the mockups. They can then modify the system's design in response to this feedback. Thus, prototyping is an iterative process of trial-use-and-modification that continues until users are satisfied. Prototyping has four steps, as illustrated in Figure 13-6.

Case-in-Point 13.8   A company hired a consulting firm to develop a large-scale student information system to manage its training and continuing education programs. The firm developed a prototype that showed the primary input screens and reports and used it to obtain user feedback on how to modify the system. For example, users experimented with the screens and considered how easy it would be to input data through them. Users also decided whether the reports would give them the information they needed, such as a listing of all students in a class and all classes taken by a student. The programming to activate the screens and enable the processing, along with the database functionality, came later. This prototyping approach ensured that the completed system would satisfy user needs.

Prototyping has several advantages. For example, it is useful when (1) end users do not understand their informational needs very well, (2) system requirements are hard

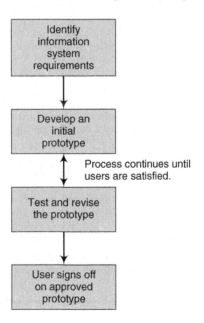

FIGURE 13-6   Steps in prototyping an accounting information system.

to define, (3) the new system is mission-critical or needed quickly, (4) past interactions have resulted in misunderstandings between end users and designers, and/or (5) there are high risks associated with developing and implementing the wrong system.

However, prototyping is not always the best design approach. One problem is that both managers and IT professionals can distrust it—the managers if they perceive prototyping as "too experimental" and the IT professionals if they harbor fears that the results lead to poor design solutions. Then, a design team can also be misled if it relies on a small portion of the user population for developing its models and thus satisfies only some employees. For this reason, prototyping is not normally appropriate for designing large or complex information systems that serve many users with significantly different information needs. Finally, IT professionals do not recommend prototyping for developing traditional AIS applications such as accounts receivable, accounts payable, payroll, or inventory management, where the inputs, processing, and outputs are known and further design specifications are unnecessary.

The System Specifications Report

After the design team completes its work of specifying the inputs, outputs, and processing requirements of the new system, the members will summarize their findings in a (typically large) systems specification report. Figure 13-7 provides some representative information in such a report. The design team submits this report to the steering committee for review, comment, and approval.

---

1. **Historical background information about the company's operating activities.** Included here would be facts about the types of products manufactured and sold by the company, the financial condition of the company, the company's current data processing methods, the peak volume of data processing activities, and the types of equipment currently being used in the company's data processing system.

2. **Detailed information about the problems in the company's current system.** By understanding the present systems problems, the computer vendors should have a better idea of what type of specific computer application will eliminate the company's system weaknesses. The design team may also include information about how soon they would like to receive the vendors' recommendations and the approximate date that the final decision will be made by their client regarding which computerized system will be purchased (or leased).

3. **Detailed descriptions of the systems design proposals.** For every design proposal, information should be included about things such as the data input and output of specific computer processing runs, the types of master files needed and the approximate volume of each file, the frequency of updating each master file, the format of each output report, the approximate length of each output report, the types of information included in each report and how often the various reports will be prepared, the organizational managers to whom every report will be distributed, and the company's available space for computer facilities.

4. **Indication of what the vendors should include in their proposals to the company.** This section of the systems specifications report, in effect, tells the vendors how detailed they should make their proposals. The company might request information regarding the speed and size of the central processing unit needed, the type of PCs needed for the company's local area network, the type and quantity of input and output devices as well as the capabilities of these devices, the availability of prewritten software packages for specific processing activities, the training sessions offered by the vendors on the operating details of the new system, the help provided by the vendors in implementing and testing the new system, the maintenance services available from the vendors, and the vendors' provisions for backup data processing facilities.

5. **Time schedule for implementing the new system.** This final section of the report will request the computer vendors to estimate the number of weeks, months, or years that will be necessary to implement their recommended computer system within the company.

FIGURE 13-7 Systems specifications report information.

The Make or Buy Decision. The project is now at a critical juncture. If the steering committee approves the detailed design work, it now faces a **make-or-buy decision**. In large organizations, one possibility is to use internal IT staff to develop the system. This choice offers the tightest control over project development, the best security over sensitive data, the benefits of a custom product that has been tailor-made for the exact requirements of the application, the luxury of replacing the old system piecemeal as modules become available, and a vote of confidence for the organization's IT staff. But this choice also uses valuable employee time and can divert the organization's resources from its main objectives—for example, manufacturing products.

Another possibility is to outsource the project's development to a contractor. This choice is useful when an organization lacks internal expertise to do the work or simply wishes to avoid the headaches of internal project development. Finally, the steering committee can purchase prewritten software (commonly called **canned software**) and perhaps modify it to suit the organization's needs. If the organization requires both hardware and software, the committee may also choose to shop for a complete, "ready-to-go" **turnkey system**. The steering committee can ask the computer vendors to submit bid proposals for such a complete system or, alternatively, can ask each vendor to provide separate bids for hardware and software.

Choosing an Accounting Information System

Because internal project management and systems development are beyond the scope of this text, we'll assume here that the steering committee opts to acquire most of its system resources from outside vendors. This is the most common choice today. If the committee takes this course of action, the systems specifications report can help them create a **request for proposal (RFP)** outlining the specific requirements of the desired system. Upon finalizing the systems specifications, the committee (with the help of the design team and perhaps outside consultants) will send a copy to appropriate vendors. Typically, the RFP also contains a deadline for bidding, the length of which varies—for example, just a few weeks for hardware and longer periods of time for systems requiring custom development tasks.

After the deadline has passed, an evaluation committee supervised by the steering committee will review vendor submissions and schedule separate meetings with those vendors who provide viable system proposals. The participants at each meeting include representatives from the vendor, representatives from the steering committee, and representatives from the evaluation team. The vendor's role is to present its proposal and to answer questions from the other participants. The evaluation committee's role is to listen to the vendor proposals, ask questions, provide input to the steering committee about the pros and cons of each one, and perhaps make a recommendation for a preferred provider.

Selection Criteria. The steering committee's responsibility is to make a final selection and is not restricted in its choices. It can accept one bid totally or spread its purchases among two or more providers. Here are five key factors that a steering committee might consider, listed in order of importance according to a survey of 160 international financial officers[9]:

---

[9] Ivancevich, S. H., D. M. Ivancevich, and F. Elikai, 2010. Accounting software selection and satisfaction. *CPA Journal* 80(1): 66–72.

1. **The functionality and performance capabilities of each proposed system.** An accounting system must be able to process an organization's data and provide users with the outputs they need. Examples of performance measures include the types of normal and customizable information the system can provide, response time, and maximal number of simultaneous online users supported.

2. **Compatibility of each proposed system with existing systems.** The new system must interface and work with existing computer hardware, software, and operating procedures. In some instances, this comes down to hardware issues—for example, it may not be possible to run the new software on the company's older local area networks, which will consequently have to be upgraded. But compatibility issues can also involve the operating system, existing application software, or operational concerns—for example, requiring employees to learn new procedures for inputting data or generating reports.

3. **Vendor stability and support.** Vendor support includes such things as (1) training classes that familiarize employees with the operating characteristics of the new system, (2) help in implementing and testing the new system, (3) assistance in maintaining the new system through a maintenance contract, (4) backup systems and procedures, and (5) telephone assistance for answering user questions. The availability of "business-hours-only" versus "round-the-clock" support and the availability of domestic versus offshore customer support are other considerations. Most vendors charge extra for enhanced services. Although a vendor's reputation is relative, a buyer can also check with the Better Business Bureau or speak with some of the vendor's other clients.

4. **Costs and benefits of each proposed system.** The accountants on the design team will analyze the costs of every vendor's proposed system in relation to the system's anticipated performance benefits. They will also consider the differences between purchasing and leasing each vendor's system. If the steering committee elects to purchase a system, the accountants should then advise the committee on a realistic depreciation schedule for the new system.

5. **Maintainability of each proposed system.** Maintainability means the ease with which a system can be modified. For example, a flexible system enables a firm to alter a portion of a payroll system to reflect new federal tax laws. Because the costs of maintaining large systems are typically five times as much as the costs of initially acquiring or developing a system, evaluators should emphasize this dimension in its deliberations for custom-built systems.

Making a Final Decision. If a company finds several software packages that appear to satisfy its needs, how should it decide on the best one? Two methods for this are (1) point scoring analysis and (2) hands-on testing.

Point-Scoring Analysis. Figure 13-8 illustrates an example of a **point-scoring analysis** for an accounts-payable system. Here, an organization finds three independent vendors whose packages appear to satisfy current needs. Since the cost to lease each vendor's software package is about the same, "cost" is not an issue in this selection process.

To perform a point-scoring analysis, the evaluation committee first assigns potential points to each of the selection criteria based on its relative importance. In Figure 13-8, for example, the committee feels that "adequate controls" (10 possible points) is more important than whether users are satisfied with the software (8 possible points). After developing these selection criteria, the evaluation committee proceeds to rate each

Software Evaluation Criteria	Possible Points	Vendor A	Vendor B	Vendor C
Does the software meet all mandatory specifications?	10	7	9	6
Will program modifications, if any, be minimal to meet company needs?	10	8	9	7
Does the software contain adequate controls?	10	9	9	8
Is the performance (speed, accuracy, reliability, etc.) adequate?	10	7	8	6
Are users satisfied with the software?	8	6	7	5
Is the software well documented?	10	8	8	7
Is the software compatible with existing company software?	10	7	9	8
Is the software user friendly?	10	7	8	6
Can the software be demonstrated and test driven?	9	8	8	7
Does the software have an adequate warranty?	8	6	7	6
Is the software flexible and easily maintained?	8	5	7	5
Is online inquiry of files and records possible?	10	8	9	7
Will the vendor keep the software up to date?	10	8	8	7
Totals	123	94	106	85

FIGURE 13-8 A point-scoring analysis for evaluating three independent vendors' accounts-payable software packages.

vendor or package, awarding points as it deems fit. The highest point total determines the winner. In Figure 13-8, the evaluation indicates that Vendor B's accounts-payable software package has the highest total score (106 points) and the committee should therefore acquire this vendor's system.

Although point-scoring analyses can provide an objective means of selecting a final system, many experts believe that evaluating software is more art than science. There are no absolute rules in the selection process, only guidelines for matching user needs with software capabilities. This is one reason why user input in the selection process is so important.

Hands-On Testing. Even after selecting a finalist, an organization might still be hesitant to commit. With hands-on testing, potential buyers "test drive" a software package to further evaluate the system. Figure 13-9 provides a list of tests that AIS shoppers can use for this purpose. Note especially **benchmark testing**.

Method	Description
Benchmark testing	The new system performs a standardized data processing task (e.g., preparing a payroll). Managers then examine the outputs for accuracy, completeness, consistency, and efficiency.
Documentation testing	This test makes sure that the system includes all necessary documentation—for example, documentation for programs, systems, backup and recovery, operations, and users. Training manuals, videos, and online tutorials may also be important here.
Integration testing	Evaluators test how well the inputs and outputs of the new software link to, or integrate with, existing software.
Pilot testing	Managers install the new software in an experimental site, often called the *beta site*, for evaluation purposes.
System testing	As an extension of integration testing, evaluators assess the entire set of features, capabilities, compatibilities, and limitations of a new software package.
Unit testing	Managers test individual modules of a complete software package with the objective of identifying errors, abnormal execution problems, and logic errors.

FIGURE 13-9 Testing strategies for evaluating new software, listed in alphabetical order.

Selecting a Finalist. After each vendor presents its proposal and perhaps additional hands-on testing, the steering committee must make its final selection. If a clear winner emerges from these activities, the organization can commence to the implementation stage. But it is also possible that none of the proposed systems is satisfactory. At this point, the organization's steering committee can (1) request the design team to obtain additional systems proposals from other vendors, (2) abandon the project, or (3) consider outsourcing needed services—discussed in the following section.

Outsourcing

An alternative to developing and installing AISs is to outsource them. As we also explain in Chapter 5, outsourcing occurs when a company hires an outside organization to handle all or part of the operations for a specific business function. Accounting tasks have long been a target for outsourcing, including accounts payable, accounts receivable, payroll, general ledger, accounting for fixed assets, and financial reporting. Even preparation of US income tax returns is outsourced, typically to English-speaking countries such as India. Two popular types of outsourcing are business process outsourcing (BPO) and knowledge process outsourcing (KPO).

Business Process Outsourcing (BPO). **Business process outsourcing (BPO)** means contracting with outside firms to perform such normal tasks as preparing payrolls. Companies commonly sign such contracts for 5- to 10-year periods. The annual costs depend on the amount of processing work required and range from "thousands" to "millions" of dollars. However, "outsourcing" does not necessarily mean "offshoring" as much of such business goes to domestic consultants or data-processing concerns.

Case-in-Point 13.9 Financial and accounting outsourcing (FAO) includes routine payroll and accounts-payable processing, as well as more complex tasks such as month-end closings, variance analysis, budgeting, forecasting, and even mergers-and-acquisition work. Xerox Corporation, for example, employs over 7,000 FAO professionals in its global operations. A study by HfS Research and KPMG indicated that, although most companies continue to perform accounting work in-house, the global market for FAO is now $25 billion annually and growing.[10]

Knowledge Process Outsourcing (KPO). Businesses have been outsourcing such processes as sales order processing for years. With **knowledge process outsourcing (KPO)**, a business contracts with an outside company to perform research or other knowledge-related work. Four examples are (1) intellectual property research related to developing and filing a patent application, (2) data mining of consumer data, (3) preparing US tax returns, and (4) research related to medical drugs and biotechnology. The growth of KPO has been high, with companies in countries such as India and Ireland doing much of the work.

Advantages and Disadvantages of Outsourcing. Making a decision to outsource a process or knowledge activity is not an easy one. One advantage of outsourcing is that an organization can focus on its core competencies while "experts" in the outsourced company do the other work. For example, hospitals often outsource their

---

[10] Caruso, J. 2013. The value proposition of finance and accounting outsourcing. *Pennsylvania CPA Journal* 84(4): 1–2.

data processing functions so they can focus on better patient care. Outsourcing also frees managerial time, financial assets, and related resources for other purposes, and an organization doesn't need to worry about keeping up with technology.

Another advantage of outsourcing is "cost savings." These savings often come from economies of scale where the process-provider is able to spread such costs as software leasing or personnel benefits among several clients. Another cost savings comes from moving selected operations to areas where real-estate prices, building rents, or labor costs are low—for example, to offshore sites. Yet additional cost savings can come from (1) shifting data risks to the contracting company and (2) depending upon the contractor to adjust personnel levels caused by large swings in monthly processing volumes. All these advantages enable a company to reduce its own labor force, save money, and remain competitive.

Outsourcing is not always the best alternative. One disadvantage is inflexibility. The typical outsourcing contract requires a company to commit to services for an extended period of time—for example, 10 years. Should the contracting company become dissatisfied with the services it receives during this period of time, however, it is usually difficult to break the agreement. Even with a termination clause, the company may still be locked into outsourcing—for example, because it has already terminated its software leases and some of its IT staff.

Loss of control is another potential disadvantage. When an outsourcing vendor performs a significant portion of an organization's data processing, that organization loses control of its information systems. For example, the contracting company can no longer control its data, data errors, or other processing irregularities that occur from the outsourcer's processing work. Finally, outsourcing can cause an organization to lose competitive advantage. This happens when a company loses a basic understanding of how its information systems helps it compete in the marketplace.

13.6 IMPLEMENTATION, FOLLOW-UP, AND MAINTENANCE

Systems implementation is often called the "action phase" of a systems study because the recommended changes from the prior analysis, design, and development work are now put into operation. Alternatively, the organization commits to, and now must implement, a new system.

Systems implementation can be a stressful time. As the time draws near for installing the new software, end users and clerical personnel become nervous about their jobs, middle managers wonder if the new system will deliver the benefits as promised, and top managers become impatient if installations run longer than anticipated or go over budget. Even if an organization does a perfect job of analyzing, designing, and developing a new system, the entire project can fail if its implementation is poor.

Implementation Activities

Implementing a new AIS involves many tasks that will vary in number and complexity depending on the scale of the system and the development approach. Some of the steps that may be involved are the following:

a. **Prepare the physical site.** An organization must have physical space for any new hardware and personnel.

b. **Determine functional changes.** Whenever a company makes changes to a major accounting system, it must also consider the effects of such changes on its reporting structure and personnel relationships.

c. **Select and assign personnel.** Since the design team has developed detailed specifications for the new system, the organization should now have a firm idea about the job descriptions of system users.

d. **Train personnel.** Both the implementation team and computer vendors can help train company employees to work with the new system, while seminars can acquaint other employees with the new system's advantages and capabilities. Vendors may provide technical training for free, or at reduced costs, to corporate users as incentives to use their products.

e. **Acquire and install computer equipment.** After preparing the physical site location for the new computer system, the company must acquire computer equipment such as microcomputers, Web servers, routers, modems, and printers from outside vendors.

f. **Establish internal controls.** Chapters 6 and 7 describe why an organization must install control procedures that safeguard its assets, ensure the accuracy and reliability of accounting data, promote operating efficiency, and encourage employee compliance with prescribed managerial policies. Again, these controls should be built into a system rather than added later.

g. **Convert data files.** When converting to a new system, an organization may have to convert its data files to alternate, more-useful formats. This activity is also common when merging two systems—for example, when consolidating formerly separate divisions of a company or merging the systems from two separate companies into one.

h. **Acquire computer software.** The implementation team must also install the software that was acquired or developed for the project. The software from independent vendors sometimes comes bundled with hardware in complete turnkey systems. In general, the process of acquiring (and possibly making modifications to) computer software from an independent vendor takes considerably less time than developing the programs in-house.

i. **Test computer software.** Programs must be tested regardless of where they came from to ensure day-to-day processing accuracy and completeness. See again Figure 13-9 for a list of possible tests.

j. **Convert to the new system.** In switching to the new system, the firm may choose to make a **direct conversion** by immediately discontinuing use of the old system and letting the new system "sink or swim." An alternative is **parallel conversion**, where the organization operates both the new and the old system for some period of time. Another choice is **modular conversion**, where the new system is implemented in stages, one process or module at a time. An example would be first implementing the inventory module, then order processing, and so on.

The most difficult issue in implementing a new system is **change management**. The new system will bring with it changes to employee job descriptions and, in some cases, new jobs and no jobs. Members of the implementation team and steering committee should communicate openly with affected workers about how the new system will impact them. Organizations should give those employees whose jobs are either eliminated or materially altered an opportunity to apply for the new jobs and obtain retraining, if necessary. Similarly, terminated employees should receive ample notice to enable them to apply for other jobs before their employment ends. Some companies even set up internal outplacement offices for displaced employees or create early retirement plans for qualified employees.

Managing Implementation Projects

An organization cannot perform implementation tasks randomly, but rather must complete them in a logical sequence. A good analogy is the process of building a house, which requires completing the foundation, subfloors, and load-bearing walls before putting on the roof. Similarly, if an organization does not plan its systems implementation in an orderly manner, the project's coordination is almost sure to suffer, and its completion may be prolonged unreasonably.

There are many tools available to help manage projects. Two of these, **Program Evaluation and Review Technique (PERT)** and Gantt charts, help managers schedule and monitor the activities involved in large projects, such as the implementation of a large-scale information system. There are also software solutions that managers can use for project management, which we also discuss here.

Program Evaluation and Review Technique. With **PERT**, a project leader first prepares a list of systems implementation activities, identifies the prerequisite activities that must be completed before others can start, and estimates (or obtains estimates of) the amount of time required to complete each activity. Figure 13-10 shows a PERT diagram for the implementation tasks outlined earlier. The lines with arrows in this diagram conventionally flow from left to right and represent the activities required to implement the system. Thus, for example, Activity A takes 17 weeks, and the diagram indicates that it must be completed before Activity E. The circles (called *nodes*) in the diagram represent project milestones—that is, the starting points or completions of specific activities—and therefore do not require any time.

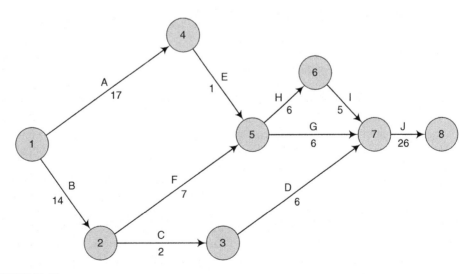

FIGURE 13-10 PERT network diagram for a systems implementation project.

Top managers may not be interested in PERT analyses, but they are usually very concerned about the time required to complete the entire implementation. The project leader can estimate this completion time by examining the various paths in the PERT network. For example, the activities A-E-H-I-J together would take 55 weeks. Since all activities must be completed before the project is done, the answer to the question "when will this project be finished" is equivalent to finding the longest path—termed the **critical path**—through the network. By examining all the possibilities, this is path B-F-H-I-J, which takes 58 weeks. This is why some prefer to call PERT analysis *critical path method (CPM)*.

Because PERT diagrams in actual practice are so large (often covering entire walls when drawn on paper), project leaders normally use computer software to identify the critical path. The project leader will closely monitor the work on each critical-path activity to avoid setbacks. **Slack time** describes the amount of delay time that can occur in each noncritical activity and still not delay the project. Thus, slack time is the extra time that noncritical activities have before they start. By definition, the slack time for each activity along the critical path is zero. There is no extra time for any of them, and any delays will automatically extend the completion time of the entire project.

PERT helps project managers identify critical paths and areas where slack time occurs. For example, can you understand why activity J (on the critical path) has no slack time, while activity D (not on the critical path) has 4 weeks of slack? Hint: subtract the earliest start time from the latest start time of this activity.

As the implementation team performs specific activities, it also provides feedback reports to the steering committee that compare actual implementation times with planned times. These reports enable both parties to focus on delays in completing specific activities and to estimate what effect these delays may have on the entire installation project. If a specific critical activity is behind schedule, the project leader may allocate additional resources to speed its completion. Alternately, if another activity is ahead of schedule, the project leader may reduce the resources assigned to it and use them elsewhere.

Gantt Charts. Another tool that an organization can use in planning and controlling a systems implementation project is a **Gantt chart** (Figure 13-11). Gantt charts are useful for both scheduling and tracking the activities of systems implementation projects because actual progress can be indicated directly on the Gantt chart and contrasted with the planned progress.

Case-in-Point 13.10 When it ran 15 months late on completion of a construction project, a building company incurred extensive penalty charges that eventually led to its closure. The original contract for the construction of a block of flats did not include a dated project plan showing the critical path. When the customer made changes to the specification, the contractor failed to also create plan revisions to show how these changes would affect the project's completion date. If it had created a Gantt chart at the contract stage, it also would have had a baseline plan against which to monitor progress.[11]

Gantt charts are straightforward, easy to understand, and can be used with PERT to compare estimated completion times against actual ones. A disadvantage of Gantt charts is that they do not indicate the precedence of activities for the project, as do PERT charts. Rather, a Gantt chart treats each activity as if it were independent of

---

[11] Russell, L. 2014. How Gantt Charts Can Help Avoid Disaster, accessed at www.projectsmart.co.uk.

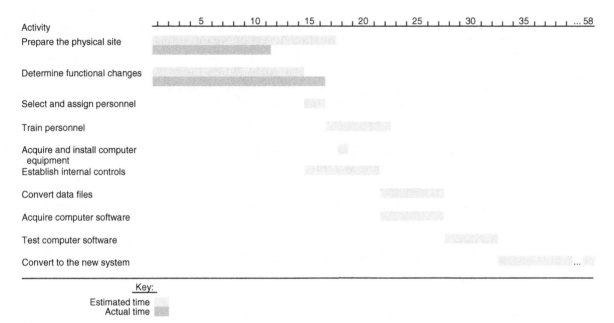

Activity	5	10	15	20	25	30	35	... 58

Prepare the physical site

Determine functional changes

Select and assign personnel

Train personnel

Acquire and install computer
  equipment
Establish internal controls

Convert data files

Acquire computer software

Test computer software

Convert to the new system

Key:
Estimated time
Actual time

FIGURE 13-11   A Gantt chart depicting systems implementation activities.

the others, which of course is not really the case. For this reason, Gantt charts are better suited for systems implementation projects that are not highly complex and have relatively few interrelationships among implementation activities.

Project Management Software.   As noted earlier, PERT diagrams can be complicated, making the calculations required to compute and recompute critical paths and slack times difficult. **Project management software** that runs on desktop or notebook computers can perform these tasks easily and quickly, enabling a project leader to plan and control implementation tasks and helping a team install a new system on time and within budget.

Project management software requires users to break down large projects into smaller, simpler activities and to estimate the time, cost, and other resources required for each of them. The project leader then enters these estimates into the computer running the software, along with the precedence relationships of the various activities of the project. The software can then schedule tasks, identify critical and noncritical activities, compute slack times, and so forth. Project management software also allows the project leader to perform **what-if analyses**—for example, to experiment with different systems implementation work schedules or determine how delays in specific activities are likely to affect other project tasks.

Probably because "project management" is such a common activity, users can choose from more than 100 software packages. Examples include *Microsoft Project, Comindware Project, Unanet Project Management*, and *Wrike*. You can find a comparison of project management software at: en.wikipedia.org/wiki/Comparison_of_project_management_software.

Postimplementation Review

Regardless of which conversion method is used, the new system will eventually become the sole system in operation. This brings us to the final, **follow-up and maintenance**

phase of our SDLC. The purpose of this phase is to monitor the new system and make sure that it continues to satisfy the three levels of organizational goals discussed at the beginning of this chapter: (1) general systems goals, (2) top management systems goals, and (3) operating management systems goals. When these goals are not adequately satisfied, problems normally occur and the system requires further modifications.

After the new system has been in operation for a period of time, the implementation team should reevaluate the new system's effectiveness by:

- Talking with top management and operating management personnel about their satisfaction with the new system.
- Talking with end users to determine their satisfaction.
- Evaluating the control procedures of the system to verify whether they are functioning properly.
- Observing employee work performance to determine whether they are able to perform their job functions efficiently and effectively.
- Evaluating whether computer processing functions, including data capture and preparation, are performed efficiently and effectively.
- Determining whether output schedules for both internal and external reports are met with the new computer system.

At the conclusion of the initial follow-up study, the team will prepare a *postimplementation review report* for the steering committee that summarizes the implementation team's findings. If the team is satisfied that the new system is working satisfactorily, no further revisions are required. If follow-up studies reveal that problems still exist in the new system, the team will communicate these findings to the steering committee and perhaps recommend further systems studies. Upon receiving approval from the steering committee, the organization will then perform the systems study steps again with the objective of making revisions to the system.

A postimplementation review is also beneficial to the implementation team. At this point in the SDLC, the team members are now in a position to evaluate their own work, learn from the mistakes they made or successfully avoided, and become more skilled "systems people" in future engagements.

System Maintenance

In practice, implementation teams do not normally perform follow-up studies of their company's new information system. Instead, the team turns over control of the system to the company's IT department, which then shoulders the responsibility for maintaining it. In effect, **system maintenance** continues the tasks created by the initial follow-up study, except that experts from the company's IT subsystem now perform the monitoring and perhaps modifications. For example, when users complain about errors or anomalies in the new system, it becomes the IT subsystem's responsibility to respond to these needs, estimate the cost of fixing them, and (often) perform the necessary modifications—or communicate with the vendor to perform needed modifications. The IT departments of even medium-size companies typically have forms for such requests, policies for prioritizing maintenance tasks, and formulas for allocating maintenance costs among the various user departments.

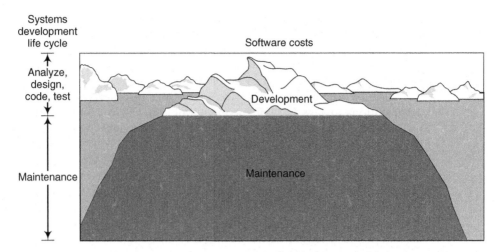

FIGURE 13-12 In the systems development life cycle, the costs of analysis, design, development, and implementation are often just the tip of the iceberg: software maintenance costs are the most expensive part.

It is common for business systems to require continuous revisions. Some reasons for this include competition, new governmental laws or regulations, or the changing information needs of top management. Studies show that, over the life of a typical information system, organizations only spend about 20% to 30% of the total system costs developing or acquiring and implementing it. They spend the remaining 70% to 80% maintaining it, typically on further modifications or software updates. In other words, although "maintenance" may not be the most glamorous part of an SDLC, it is almost always the most expensive part (Figure 13-12). For this reason, organizations try to develop or acquire scalable systems (that can handle larger volumes of transactions in the future) as well as ones that are easily modified. Such systems save businesses money in the long run, even if they cost more in the short run.

AIS AT WORK
Agile software development[12]

One Common criticism of the waterfall method of the SDLC analysis is its rigid, linear progression. **Agile software development** is a popular, alternate set of methodologies that stress user participation, developer collaboration, and software-that-works over strict development protocols. It acknowledges, for example, that many system requirements cannot be known or fully understood at the start of a project, but emerge slowly over time. Thus, agile software development stresses mindful team responses, flexible adaption, and continuous improvement as teams better understand system requirements.

---

[12] Verheyen. 2012, December. ING: Capturing agility via Scrum at a large Dutch bank. Accessed from scrum.org on May 4, 2017.

Most agile methodologies divide software into smaller pieces that teams can analyze, design, code, and test in time frames ("timeboxes") of a month or less. Team members present their results in short daily stand-ups to report progress, discuss problems, identify unanswered questions, and outline the day's work. Depending upon the environment, "documentation" can be of secondary importance.

Because "agile" is itself a collection of over 15 different development systems that organizations always implement in unique venues, its overall success is difficult to measure. It appears to work best in smaller projects and to fail most often when teams do not have sufficient training.

ING is a leading bank in the Netherlands. The IT department was tasked with improving daily customer contact for millions of ING customers via the Internet, telephone, e-mail, and branch offices. The CIO knew that the department needed a significant improvement in IT services to remain competitive. He decided to adopt the agile systems development approach, rather than the costly traditional waterfall approach used in the past. This initiative was highly successful. Cycle time for projects decreased from 3–6 months to 6–9 weeks. Cost savings in software delivery ranged from 30% to 50%. Technical incidents were sometimes reduced by over 30%. To top off these successes, employee satisfaction and collaboration improved and management and employees worked closer together. These improvements positively impacted the company's bottom line.

SUMMARY

- ✓ The four stages in a systems development life cycle are (1) planning and investigation; (2) analysis; (3) design and acquisition; and (4) implementation, follow-up, and maintenance.

- ✓ Planning requires creating a team to investigate the current system and make recommendations to a steering committee.

- ✓ Systems analysis requires identifying general systems goals, top management systems goals, and operating management systems goals.

- ✓ A systems survey uses a variety of data gathering techniques to understand and document the system.

- ✓ The systems analysis report contains the study team recommendations.

- ✓ The components of a feasibility evaluation are technical, operational, schedule, legal, and economic feasibility.

- ✓ Detailed systems design begins with the design of outputs and then inputs and processes.

- ✓ Designers may choose a prototyping approach to create the new system.

- ✓ A systems specification report contains detailed information about the organization and its desired system.

- ✓ Choosing a system requires evaluating system performance capabilities, costs and benefits, system maintainability, system compatibility with other systems, and vendor support.

- ✓ An organization may choose to outsource its IT operations, accounting processes, or research-related (knowledge) tasks.

- ✓ Organizations use PERT, GANTT charts, and project management software to manage the implementation of complex information systems.

- ✓ Organizations need to follow up to find out if new systems are working as planned.

KEY TERMS YOU SHOULD KNOW

agile software development
applications portfolio
benchmark testing
business process outsourcing
 (BPO)
business process reengineering
 (BPR)
canned software
change management
critical path
detailed systems design
direct conversion
economic feasibility
feasibility evaluation
follow-up and maintenance phase
Gantt chart

knowledge process outsourcing
 (KPO)
legal feasibility
make-or-buy decision
modular conversion
operational feasibility
parallel conversion
point-scoring analysis
preliminary investigation
Program Evaluation and Review
 Technique (PERT)
project management software
prototyping
request for proposal (RFP)
schedule feasibility
scope creep

slack time
steering committee
structured, top-down design
system maintenance
systems analysis
systems approach
systems development life cycle
 (SDLC)
systems study
systems survey
technical feasibility
turnkey system
waterfall model
what-if analyses

TEST YOURSELF

Q13-1. Which of the following statements is NOT true?

 a. A preliminary investigation of a current system is conducted by the steering committee

 b. Implementation, follow-up, and maintenance of it includes acquiring resources for the new system

 c. In designing an AIS, the design team will begin with outputs

 d. The more work done during planning and analysis, the less likely the new system will fail

Q13-2. The feasibility evaluation:

 a. is completed prior to detailed systems design

 b. includes economic, schedule, technical, legal, and operational feasibility

 c. both a and b are true

 d. neither a nor b is true

Q13-3. In developing and implementing a new system, the study team and steering committee must consider organizational goals. These include:

 a. general, technical, and top management goals

 b. general, operating management, and technical goals

 c. top management, operating management, and economic goals

 d. top management, operating management, and general systems goals

Q13-4. Prototyping, as an IT development approach, has both advantages and disadvantages. In general, prototyping is most appropriate when:

 a. the design team is not pressed for time in creating a new system

 b. users have a thorough understanding of their information needs

 c. there are high risks associated with developing and implementing an ineffective system

 d. system requirements are easily defined

Q13-5. In selecting a new accounting information system, the steering committee should consider:

 a. all expected costs and benefits of the new systems, including maintenance and operating costs

 b. support that a vendor can provide, including training, maintenance, and backup

 c. compatibility of a new system with existing systems

 d. all of the above are considerations in selecting a new system

 e. only a and b are important considerations in selecting the new system

Q13-6. A point-scoring analysis:

    a. is a useful tool in conducting a feasibility analysis

    b. helps the systems study team to decide whether or not to outsource their AIS

    c. provides a systems study team with an objective means for selecting a final AIS

    d. is a tool used for managing IT projects

Q13-7. Which of the following statements is *not* true with respect to managing IT projects?

    a. Program evaluation and review technique (PERT) allows management to determine the shortest time it will take to implement a new system and any slack time that might exist between implementation activities

    b. An advantage of PERT is that it allows managers to identify the critical path in implementation

    c. Both PERT and Gantt charts are manual techniques used in managing IT implementations

    d. Gantt charts are useful in scheduling and implementing IT because they allow you to indicate actual progress versus planned progress directly on the chart

Q13-8. When converting to a new system, which of the following conversion alternatives would be the most risky for a financial services firm?

    a. Direct conversion

    b. Modular conversion

    c. Parallel conversion

    d. Turnkey conversion

Q13-9. Which one of the four stages in the systems development life cycle is likely to be the most costly for a new system?

    a. Planning and investigation

    b. Analysis

    c. Design

    d. Implementation, follow-up, and maintenance

Q13-10. Which of the following would be most helpful to managers of a project where the precedence of activities is important?

    a. Outsourcing

    b. PERT

    c. A Gantt chart

    d. A turnkey system

DISCUSSION QUESTIONS

13-1. Discuss the major differences between the planning, analysis, and design phases of a systems study.

13-2. What is a steering committee? Discuss its role in a systems study performed by a consulting firm.

13-3. A systems study team should understand three levels of corporate goals: general systems goals, top management systems goals, and operating management systems goals. If you had to select one of these categories of systems goals as the most important to the effective operation of an organization's information system, which one would you choose? Explain the reasons for your choice.

13-4. What is the purpose of a systems feasibility evaluation? Should this activity precede or follow the preparation of a systems specifications report for computer vendor evaluation? Explain.

13-5. Discuss some of the annual cash benefits and annual cash costs that a company might have when it creates an online ordering system on the World Wide Web.

13-6. What is prototyping? Under what circumstances should prototyping be used? Under what circumstances should it not be used?

13-7. What is the purpose of a systems specifications report? In what ways, if any, do the data included in this report differ from the data accumulated by the design team during their feasibility evaluation work?

13-8. When implementing a new computer system, two activities required are to (1) establish controls and (2) convert data files. What is the rationale for performing activity 1 before activity 2?

13-9. Three methods for implementing a new system in an organization are direct conversion, parallel conversion, and modular conversion.

Discuss the advantages and disadvantages of using each of these three systems implementation methods.

13-10. What is a PERT chart? What is a Gantt chart? Discuss the advantages and disadvantages of using PERT network diagrams versus Gantt charts for planning and controlling the activities involved in implementing an information system.

13-11. What is the purpose of follow-up in a systems study? Describe some of the specific activities that the management implementation team would perform in their follow-up work.

13-12. Discuss the two major ways that a company's software can be acquired. Which of these ways for acquiring software do you recommend? Explain your reasoning.

13-13. What is the difference between business process outsourcing (BPO) and knowledge process outsourcing (KPO)? Why do many organizations outsource at least some of their accounting functions?

13-14. What is the difference between "outsourcing" and "offshoring?" Why might this difference be important to managers?

PROBLEMS

13-15. The Chris Hall Company manufactures and distributes low-priced bottled wines to retailers. You are hired as a management consultant to help this company solve some of its systems problems. Describe the types of decision-making information that probably would be needed by the company's (a) supervisor of the production plant, (b) top management, and (c) marketing manager.

13-16. Use your Internet browser and preferred search engine to find a company that provides financial and accounting outsourcing (FAO) services. What services does this company provide? Find a second company and compare its services with those of the first company. Which company would you choose if you were interested in outsourcing the payroll processing for your own company? Would you change your mind if you needed accounts-payable processing instead?

13-17. Stevenson Apparel is a manufacturer of fashion apparel that has just opened its first large retail store for selling in-season clothes at regular prices. The company's competitive strategy depends on a comprehensive point-of-sale (POS) system supporting online, up-to-the-minute sales totals, day-to-day tracking of stock information, and quick checkout of customer purchases. Since cashiers were already familiar with electronic cash registers, management decided that only minimal training was required. Cashiers enter four-digit stock tracking numbers (STNs) into one of the POS terminals that retrieves price and description data, computes the tax and total amount due,

accepts the type of payment, and controls the cash drawer. A unique STN identifies each of the 9,500 pieces of merchandise. The central microcomputer server maintains stock information.

In the first month of operation, new cashiers were awkward using the new system. They eventually became proficient users but were frustrated with the slow printing of sales tickets and the unpredictable action of their cash drawers. Each checkout stand has a telephone that cashiers use to call for approval of credit-card transactions. Customers became impatient when credit approvals delayed the checkout process or when the microcomputer was down, thus stopping all sales, including cash sales. Identify four problems with the system and describe how you would remedy each of them.

13-18. Jay Beck works for the AAZ Consulting Firm. His friend, Hank Henley, is the general manager and majority stockholder of the Pacific Worldwinds, a professional football team. Hank asked Jay to design an online, real-time computer system for "the efficient operation of the football franchise." Jay was quite confused because he could not think of any possible uses for an online, real-time system within the operational activities of a football team (or any other type of athletic team). Assume that you are also employed at the AAZ Consulting Firm. Provide several suggestions to Jay concerning specific areas of athletic teams' (football teams, base-ball teams, etc.) information systems where an online, real-time system might be useful for managerial decision-making.

13-19. GuessRight Consultants is a New Zealand business that helps clients with financial planning—especially preparing wills, creating trusts, and allocating funds among competing investment categories. It's not an unusual business, but the company has not been able to find the billing software it needs. Accordingly, the company has hired Superior Software Solutions, your company, to help it develop a custom system. The owner, David Cutler, is thoughtful and visionary, but not particularly well-versed in systems development methodology. To help him imagine what a new billing system might look like, you believe that a prototype might help. Develop a set of presentation slides that address the following items:

a. Explain the purpose(s) of prototyping, and why it is useful.

b. Explain why a prototype might never become a real system.

c. Identify the different advantages and disadvantages of prototyping from the perspectives of (1) end users, (2) managers, and (3) system developers.

13-20. Cook Consultants is currently in the process of completing the systems implementation activities for converting Samuel Company's old system to a new one. Because of unexpected delays in performing specific implementation activities, Jerry Hazen, the project manager, is concerned about finishing the project on time. The one remaining activity is testing the new computer system and subsequently eliminating the old one. Jerry's assistant, Gary Fong, suggests that they can still meet their completion deadline if they use "direct conversion" rather than "parallel conversion." Assuming that you are the CIO of the company, how would you react to Gary Fong's suggestion? Discuss.

13-21. Are software developers cheap or expensive? That's important because developing custom software for your accounting system depends in part on how much such labor will cost. To find out, access government statistics from the Bureau of Labor Statistic's Occupational Outlook Handbook at www.bls.gov/ooh. Select the category "Business and Financial." What is the current median pay for "accountants and

auditors?" How does this pay compare to that of software developers (whose pay you can also find on this site)?

13-22. Identify a particular information system that is not working very well and perform a preliminary investigation of it. In your work, be sure to talk to (1) at least one external "customer" who is affected by the system, (2) one employee who uses the system daily, and (3) one person who manages this type of employee. For example, at a university, you might study the student parking information system. The "customers" are those car owners who purchase parking permits (e.g., students, faculty, and university staff members), data input clerks are the employees who use the system daily, and the parking manager is the person who supervises these employees. Ask each such person what he or she feels are the problems of the system and what they think should be done to address these problems.

Prepare a preliminary investigation report that describes your system and outlines the following items: (a) the problems that each person experiences with the system, (b) the actions that each person thinks might solve the problems, and (c) your opinion of which difficulties are the "real problems" and which are just symptoms of these problems. Also include some recommendations. Should the present system be replaced, or are just minor modifications required?

13-23. Do you understand PERT charts? Refer back to Figure 13-10 and answer the following questions:

a. Which activity or activities must be completed before activity C can begin?

b. Which activity or activities must be completed before activity G can begin?

c. Which activity or activities must be completed before activity J can begin?

d. What are the five paths through the network? Which one is the critical path?

e. What is the earliest projected start time for activity F?

f. What is the earliest projected start time for activity G?

g. What is the latest time that activity J can begin without delaying the entire project?

h. What is the latest time that activity G can begin without delaying the entire project?

   i. What is the slack time for activity G? (Hint: It's the difference between the early and late start times.)

13-24. Do you understand Gantt charts? Use Figure 13-11 and test your understanding by answering the following questions. (Hint: You might also want to look at the PERT chart in Figure 13-10.)

   a. When is the activity "convert data files" scheduled to begin and end?

   b. When is the activity "test computer software" scheduled to begin and end?

   c. How much time did it actually take the company to complete the task "Prepare the physical site location?" Was this more or less time than planned?

   d. How much time did it actually take the company to complete the task "Determine the functional changes in the system?" Was this more or less time than planned?

   e. Given what has happened so far, when can the activity "Acquire and install computer equipment" actually begin?

   f. Given what has happened so far, when can the activity "Select and assign personnel" actually begin?

CASE ANALYSES

13-25. Prado Roberts Manufacturing (What Type of Computer System to Implement?)

Prado Roberts Manufacturing is a medium-sized company with regional offices in several western states and manufacturing facilities in both California and Nevada. The company performs most of its important data processing tasks, such as payroll, accounting, marketing, and inventory control, on a mainframe computer at corporate headquarters. However, almost all the managers at this company also have personal computers, which they use for such personal productivity tasks as word processing, analyzing budgets (using spreadsheets), and managing the data in small databases.

   The IT manager, Tonya Fisher, realizes that there are both advantages and disadvantages of using different types of systems to meet the processing needs of her company. While she acknowledges that many companies are racing ahead to install microcomputers and client/server systems, she also knows that the corporate mainframe system has provided her company with some advantages that smaller systems cannot match. Tonya knows that American companies annually purchase over $5 billion in used computers, primarily mainframes.

Requirements

1. Identify several advantages and disadvantages of operating a mainframe computer system that are likely to be present at Prado Roberts Manufacturing. Are these advantages and disadvantages likely to parallel those at other manufacturing companies?

2. Identify at least two factors or actions that companies experience or do to prolong the lives of their legacy systems. Are these factors or actions likely to apply to Prado Roberts Manufacturing?

3. Identify several advantages and disadvantages of microcomputer/client server systems. Would these advantages apply to Prado Roberts Manufacturing?
   (CMA Adapted)

13-26. Wright Company (Analyzing System Reports)

Wright Company employs a computer-based data processing system for maintaining all company records. The current system was developed in stages over the past 5 years and has been fully operational for the last 24 months.

When the system was being designed, all department heads were asked to specify the types of information and reports they would need for planning and controlling operations. The systems department attempted to meet the specifications of each department head. Company management specified that certain other reports be prepared for department heads. During the 5 years of systems development and operation, there have been several changes in the department head positions due to attrition and promotions. The new department heads often made requests for additional reports according to their specifications. The systems department complied with all of these requests. Reports were discontinued only on request by a department head and then only if it was not a standard report required by top management.

As a result, few reports were discontinued. Consequently, the information processing subsystem was generating a large quantity of reports each reporting period. Company management became concerned about the quantity of report information that was being produced by the system. The internal audit department was asked to evaluate the effectiveness of the reports generated by the system. The audit staff determined early in the study that more information was being generated by the information processing subsystem than could be used effectively. They noted the following reactions to this information overload:

- Many department heads would not act on certain reports during periods of peak activity. The department heads would let these reports accumulate with the hope of catching up during subsequent lulls.

- Some department heads had so many reports that they ignored the information or made incorrect decisions because of misuse of the information.

- Frequently, actions required by the nature of the report data were not taken until the department heads were reminded by others who needed the decisions. These department heads did not appear to have developed a priority system for acting on the information produced by the information processing subsystem.

- Department heads often would develop the information they needed from alternative, independent sources, rather than use the reports generated by the information processing subsystem. This was often easier than trying to search among the reports for the needed data.

Requirements

1. Indicate whether each of the foregoing four reactions contributes positively or negatively to the Wright Company's operating effectiveness. Explain your answer for every one of the four reactions.

2. For each reaction that you indicated as negative, recommend alternative procedures the Wright Company could employ to eliminate this negative contribution to operating effectiveness. (CMA Adapted)

13-27. Viva Vacations (A Systems Study for a Time Share Rental Agency)

Viva Vacations operates in Tampa, Florida. The company sells time shares and also manages residential properties that it rents to vacationers. Due to the large dip in the real-estate market the last few years, most of its recent income has come from its rental business.

Until now, Viva has maintained its reservation records manually. To do this, the company maintains a separate manila folder for each rental property. The information in a folder includes reservations for the coming 6 months, maintenance and repair records, and receipts for other expenses that it collects for the property owner.

The company charges a client 30% of short-term rental income and 10% of long-term rental income (rentals of 3 months or more). The company's rental business has grown steadily, and Chad Anderson, the owner, thinks it may be time to computerize this portion of its business. The problem is that he knows little about computers and has hired you as a consultant to study his situation and make recommendations.

Requirements

1. How would you explain to Chad why you would like to perform a systems analysis to study this system? What information do you think you would gather in the analysis phase of your study? Do you think it might be important that Chad is thinking about listing rental units on a new website to increase his business?

2. You are familiar with several software packages that might automate Viva's rental business processes. You estimate that the best package comes from Global Adventures. It is the most expensive and will probably cost about $100,000 to implement. This includes the lease costs of the package itself, plus the costs of computerizing the company's manual files. Assume that there are no benefits from the system the first year. You estimate that the system will save the company a net of $20,000 the second year (after costs) and then $30,000 per year for the next 3 years. What is the net present value of the system? What recommendation will you make, based upon your calculations?

3. An alternate software package is also available from your friend, Mark Johnston. You don't think it's as good as the one from Global Adventures, but (1) it costs $20,000 less and (2) Mark is willing to pay a finder's fee of $10,000 to you if you convince Chad to go with this system. Is it ethical for Mark to pay such a fee? Why or why not? Is it ethical for you to recommend this system instead of the Global package? Why or why not?

4. Discuss the role of an RFP for this situation. How might issuing an RFP help solve the ethical dilemma you might experience in number 3 above?

13-28. Stephen Kerr Cosmetics (Point Scoring Analysis)

Kerr Cosmetics distributes cosmetic products to large retailers across the country. The firm was started in 1975 by its first president, Stephen Kerr, who still serves as chairman of the board. Over the years, the company has grown in size and complexity. As the company has prospered, Richard Mason, the controller, has acquired and installed new accounting software to accommodate the increasing demands on the firm's accounting systems.

This year, Richard has convinced Stephen that it is time to upgrade their payroll system, which is now 7 years old. The company hires an outside consultant, who examines their situation and concludes that either one of two systems can meet their requirements. Richard therefore asks two of his most competent employees, Fritz Grupe and Meg Chrisman, to help him perform a point-scoring analysis and make a final choice.

The three individuals meet as a study team and agree upon five qualities for rating the two vendors: (1) need for further modifications, (2) ease of use, (3) strength of internal controls, (4) flexibility for updating and Internet options, and (5) vendor support. To help them rate the two vendors on these five criteria, the committee invites representatives from each vendor to visit the company and make a presentation. Fritz makes arrangements for the presentation team from Vendor A to present on a Friday morning and a similar team from Vendor B to visit that same afternoon. Unfortunately, an emergency makes it impossible for Richard to attend either presentation. Meg and Fritz attend both sessions, but come away with very different impressions of the competing software. The following table provides some relevant data.

Requirements

1. To start their analysis, Meg and Fritz decide to use their own ratings to perform separate point-scoring analyses. For this part, use equal weightings of 0.2 for each category. Perform similar analyses using a spreadsheet. Which vendor does each person prefer?

2. Both Meg and Fritz decide that using equal weight for each category doesn't make sense. After some discussion, they agree to the "compromise weights" shown in the table. They again perform their analyses. Which vendor does each person prefer now?

3. Fritz and Meg show their results to Richard, who suggests that they use their "compromise weights" but use combined averages for their "grades" for each vendor. They perform yet a third analysis. Which vendor receives the highest total now?

4. What do these exercises suggest about point scoring analyses? Does this method still seem "objective" to you? Why or why not?

	Equal Weights	Compromise Weights	Fritz's Weights		Meg's Weights	
			Vendor A	Vendor B	Vendor A	Vendor B
Required Modifications	0.2	0.2	3	2	3	3
Ease of Use	0.2	0.3	8	3	4	6
Internal Controls	0.2	0.1	3	4	2	4
Flexibility	0.2	0.1	4	5	3	7
Vendor Support	0.2	0.3	7	5	3	9

READINGS AND OTHER RESOURCES

Ahlemann, F. 2009. Towards a conceptual reference model for project management information systems. *International Journal of Project Management* (January): 19–30.

Ahmad, M. M., and R. P. Cuenca. 2013. Critical success factors for ERP implementation in SMEs. *Robotics & Computer-Integrated Manufacturing* 29(3): 104–111.

Cerpa, N., and J. Verner. 2009. Why did your project fail? *Communications of the ACM* 52(12): 130–134. Conboy, K., and L. Morgan. 2011. Beyond the customer: Opening the agile systems development process. *Information & Software Technology* 53(5): 535–542.

Coyne, J.G, E.M. Coyne, and K.B. Walker. 2017. Accountants and tech: a game changer? To be successful in the future, management accountants must understand and be able to use the latest technology and information systems. *Strategic Finance* 98(9): 41–47.

Kless, E. 2010. Project management for accountants. *Journal of Accountancy* 209(4): 38–42.

Longinidis, P., and G. Katerina. 2009. ERP user satisfaction issues: insights from a *Greek industrial giant Industrial Management & Data Systems* 109(5): 628–645.

Marks, G. 2013. Are cloud-based accounting apps ready for prime time? *Accounting Today* 27(9): 72–73.

Premuroso, R., F. W. S. Hopwood, and B. Somnath. 2011. Tasteless tea company: A comprehensive revenue transaction cycle case study. *Issues in Accounting Education* 26(1): 163–179.

Sadler, I., and S. Watts. 2013. Disrupting the status quo. *Accountancy* 150(1438): 50–51.

Wood, M. and S. Brown. 2013. The fast track to better, more profitable IT. *Financial Management* 42(2): 50–53.

Go to www.wiley.com/go/simkin/videos to access videos on the following topics:

Best Practices for Evaluating and Selecting Accounting Software
How to Write a Request for Proposal (RFP)
How Software Prototyping Can Help You
What Is a Systems Analyst?
PERT and Critical Path Analysis
The Pros and Cons of Outsourcing
Using Excel to Draw a Gantt Chart

ANSWERS TO TEST YOURSELF

1. a **2.** c **3.** d **4.** c **5.** d **6.** c **7.** c **8.** a **9.** d **10.** b

Chapter 14

Database Design

After reading this chapter, you will be able to:

1. *Describe* the importance of databases to accounting information systems (AISs).

2. *Describe* the concepts of the data hierarchy, record structures, and keys.

3. *Explain* why design concerns such as processing accuracy, concurrency, and security are important to multiuser databases.

4. *Model* a database with resources, events, and agents (REA).

5. *Normalize* database tables.

"Although any given database is tested … to make sure it is doing what the database is designed to do, very few checks are made to check the database is not doing things it should not be doing."

Osborne, C. 2013. The top ten most common database security vulnerabilities. ZDNet. Accessed online at: http://www.zdnet.com/article/the-top-ten-most-common-database-security-vulnerabilities/.

14.1 INTRODUCTION

Civilizations have collected and organized accounting data for at least 6,000 years. The ancient Babylonians, for example, stored clay tablets in their temples that recorded information such as inventory, payroll records, and real-estate transactions. Modern accounting information systems (AISs) use computers rather than clay tablets, but many of the same basic requirements remain—the systematic recording of data, convenient and useful organizations of data, the ability to create useful reports from data, and easy access to required information. This chapter examines how to *design* a database that is efficient and effective, while the next two chapters examine how to *build* and *use* a database. We begin by describing some database concepts and then discuss database design and data modeling techniques in more depth.

14.2 AN OVERVIEW OF DATABASES

Many of the data requirements from the ancient Babylonian days remain today. For example, even the most basic AIS needs to record accounting data systematically and organize accounting records in logical ways. Often, accountants achieve these objectives by storing relevant data in a database. For this reason, it is essential for accountants to understand the basic principles of database-driven systems.

What Is a Database?

A database is a collection of organized data that multiple users often access and that help accounting systems store data. In many large firms, enterprise databases store all of the data used by almost every function in the organization. Data in databases are manipulated by specialized software packages called **database management systems** (DBMSs). You can find databases in nearly all accounting systems—for example, inventory systems, general ledger systems, and production-scheduling systems. Most accounting systems involve complex combinations of data stored in databases, processing software, and hardware that interact with one another to support specific storage and retrieval tasks. Most accounting databases are **relational databases**, which are groups of related, two-dimensional tables.

Technically, not every collection of data is a database. For example, a payroll system might store the time-card data in one or more Excel files, but this is generally too simplistic to be called a "database." Most commercial databases are large and complex collections of proprietary data that developers carefully design and protect. These complex databases form the core of AISs.

Significance of Databases

It is difficult to overstate the importance of computerized databases to AISs. Nearly every accounting system that influences financial reports involves the extensive use of databases. For example, accounts receivable applications require information about customers' accounts, accounts payable applications require information about suppliers, and payroll applications require information about employees. In many publicly traded firms, the databases needed to support accounting systems cost hundreds of millions of dollars to design and maintain, and firms rely on these databases to make key business decisions and conduct their day-to-day operations. The extensive use of databases in accounting systems makes it important to understand issues that databases can raise for companies and accounting professionals. These issues include:

- **Critical information.** The information stored in an organization's databases is oftentimes its most valuable asset. Equifax, for example, is one of the nation's largest credit bureaus, maintaining credit information about millions of Americans. Its credit files *are* its business.

- **Volume.** Many databases are truly enormous. For example, the United States maintains a database of visitors, each of whom must complete a standard online entry form (ESTA) that the U.S. Customs and Border Protection office uses. In 2015, there were over 77 million visitors to the United States. Similarly, Sprint keeps records on over 50 million customers and inserts about 70,000 records to its database every second. Amazon.com has a database with more than 40 terabytes of data, and YouTube visitors watch more than 6 billion hours of video clips from its database every month. Designing, using, and maintaining databases of such great size requires substantial resources.

> *Case-in-Point 14.1*   One of the world's biggest databases is the list of books maintained by the US Library of Congress, which requires 20 terabytes of storage and increases by about 10,000 items per day.

- **Distribution.** The databases of some organizations are centralized (i.e., the system stores the database in a single location). Many other databases, however, are distributed (i.e., duplicated in local or regional computers as processing needs dictate). Distributing data can make it difficult to (1) ensure data accuracy, consistency, and completeness and (2) secure information from unauthorized access.

- **Privacy.** Databases often contain sensitive information—for example, employee payrates or customer credit card numbers. This information must be protected from those unauthorized to access it. Experts suggest that the procedures for protecting databases from unwarranted access are among the most critical controls in an organization.

   Case-in-Point 14.2   In 2013, hackers illegally accessed 40 million credit card and debit card accounts from Target stores' databases in what was one of the largest breaches of credit and debit card data in history. Federal officials called for a Federal Trade Commission probe, stating "it appears that Target may have failed to employ reasonable and appropriate security measures to protect personal information."[1]

- **Irreplaceable data.** The information contained in most accounting databases is unique to the organization that created it and is typically priceless. Many organizations would fail shortly after losing the information contained in their accounting databases. For this reason, the security of databases is critical to the organization.

- **Need for accuracy.** The data stored in databases must be complete, comprehensive, and accurate—and there can be severe consequences for small data errors. For example, consider the tax payer who forgot to tell his accountant he had moved. His tax return was completed on time, but sent to his old address, compromising his privacy and costing him several sleepless nights.

- **Internet uses.** Databases are critical components of both internal and external corporate Web systems. Databases store information related to product information for online catalog sales, product registration data, employment opportunities, stock prices, and so on. Internet applications often store customer-entered data such as online product orders, credit card numbers, subscription information, airline reservations, and university-student registration data.

- **Big data.** The term **big data** refers to data that are of such great volume that they cannot be captured, stored, and analyzed by traditional databases and existing hardware. Big data create new opportunities for accountants and auditors because analyzing such data can reveal meaningful patterns and produce information from data that were previously unknown.

   Case-in-Point 14.3   At 220 terabytes, the largest database in the world is the World Data Centre for Climate (WDCC) at the Max Planck Institute for Meteorology and German Climate Computing Centre. It uses a supercomputer worth about $37 million USD. The center maintains an additional 6 petabytes of data offline.[1,2]

Big data consist of structured data (e.g., in databases) and unstructured data (e.g., CEO conference calls, press releases, social media entries, and multimedia files).

---

[1] Atlantadarpan. Ten largest databases in the world. *Atlanta Darpan*. Accessed online at http://www.atlantadarpan.com/news-detail/top-10-largest-databases-in-the-world.htm.

[2] Moffitt, K., and M. Vasarhelyi, 2013. AIS in an age of big data. *Journal of Information Systems* 27(2): 1–19.

Historically, the unstructured data were difficult or impossible to analyze. With declines in the costs of storage and processing, such analysis is now possible. Today, firms often combine the information from traditional databases with such unstructured data in order to gain competitive advantages.

Storing Data in Databases

To be useful, the data in an organization's databases must be stored efficiently and organized systematically. In order to understand how databases store information, it is important to understand three concepts: (1) the data hierarchy, (2) record structures, and (3) database keys.

The Data Hierarchy. Storing accounting data in databases involves organizing the data into a logical structure. In ascending order, this **data hierarchy** is:

data field → record → file → database

The first level in the data hierarchy is a **data field**, which is information that describes a person, event, or object in the database. In a payroll file, for example, data fields would include employee names, employee identification numbers, and pay rates for the employees. Other names for a data field are "attribute," "column," or simply "field."

The second level of the data hierarchy combines data fields to form a complete record. A database **record** (also called a *tuple*) stores all of the information about one file entity—for example, one inventory item (in an inventory file), one customer (in a customer file), or one employee (in a payroll file). It is helpful to liken the structure of a record to how you might store it in a spreadsheet—see Figure 14-1. In a spreadsheet, each row contains the information about one employee and each column describes a characteristic about an employee—for example, his or her last name.

At the third level of the data hierarchy, a set of common records forms a file, or using database and Microsoft Access terminology, a *table*. Thus, a file or table contains a set of related records—for example, a set of customer records or inventory records. **Master files** typically store permanent information—for example, part numbers and part descriptions for the individual records in an inventory parts master file. **Transaction files** typically store information about business activities—for example, inventory disbursements and replenishments for a specific time period.

Finally, at the highest level, several tables create a complete database (i.e., a collection of tables that contains all of the information needed for an accounting application). In an inventory application, for example, the database might contain an inventory table, a supplier table, a products table, and an order transaction table, as well as several other tables that would help users organize, store, access, or process inventory information efficiently.

Employee Number	Last Name	First Name	Dept. Code	Pay Rate	Date of Hire	Overtime OK?	Other information
E677542	Barfar	Ari	A	12.85	10-15-2017	yes	....

FIGURE 14-1 Examples of data fields in an employee record.

Record Structures. The specific data fields in each record of a database table are part of the **record structure**. In many accounting applications, this structure is fixed, meaning that each record contains the same number, same type, and same-sized data fields as every other record in the file. This would likely be the case for the employee record illustrated in Figure 14-1. In other applications, the number of data fields in each record might vary, or the size of a given data field in each record might vary. For example, in a file of customer complaints, the memo field in each record might vary in length to accommodate different-length descriptions of customer problems.

Database Keys. The **primary key** is the data field in each record that uniquely distinguishes one record from another in a database table. Primary keys are required for every record in a database, and they are unique. For the employee record in Figure 14-1, the primary key would be the employee number. End users and computer programs use primary keys to find a specific record—for example, the record for a particular employee, inventory item, or customer account. It is also possible for a record to have a primary key that consists of more than one data field.

Some accounting records contain data fields called **foreign keys** that enable them to reference one or more records in other tables. The term **referential integrity** means in part that the foreign key in one table always matches the primary key of the related table. For example, in addition to the employee table in Figure 14-1, a firm might have a department table with the data fields shown in Figure 14-2. The primary key for the department table is the department code (e.g., "A" and "B"). With this arrangement, the department code field in the employee record of Figure 14-1 would be a foreign key that the database system could use to reference the appropriate department record from the department table. These foreign keys enable a database system to combine the information from both tables to produce a report such as the one in Figure 14-3.

Note that each line of this report contains information from the records in two tables: the employee records in Figure 14-1 and the department records in Figure 14-2.

Department code (primary key)	Manager	Number of employees	Location	Secretary phone	Other information
A	B. Wright	45	Bldg. 23	x8734	...

FIGURE 14-2 A sample record from a department table.

Employee Roster
Friday, July 28, 20XX

Last Name	First Name	Dept.	Manager	Location	Administrative Asst. Phone
Barfar	Arii	A	Wright	Bldg. 23	ext. 8741
Garadis	Sue	B	Garadis	Bldg. 23	ext. 9330
Gold	Karen	A	Wright	Bldg. 23	ext. 8792
Hale	Lois	C	Hale	Bldg. 24	ext. 8655
Wright	Barbara	A	Wright	Bldg. 23	ext. 8734

FIGURE 14-3 A formatted report that uses the data from two tables.

Additional Database Issues

Small databases such as those used in small businesses or sole proprietorships tend to be fairly straightforward and manageable. However, large, multiuser databases pose special challenges for their designers and users because of their complexity. Here, we describe some database design concerns that are of special importance to accounting applications.

Cost. Although databases are only one part of complete computer systems, they are often one of the largest cost component of them. AISs are textbook examples of such systems. Can you imagine, for example, an accounts-payable, accounts-receivable, or payroll system that did not have a database as one of its components?

Administration. Without an overall supervisor, a large commercial database is somewhat like a rudderless ship—that is, an entity without cohesion or direction. Similarly, it does not make sense to permit database designers to work unsupervised or to develop large databases without also creating accountability for subsequent changes. A **database administrator** supervises the design, development, and installation of a large database system and is also the person responsible for maintaining, securing, and changing the database. As a result of the administrator's many duties and powers, it is essential that the administrator be both skilled and trustworthy.

> *Case-in-Point 14.4* A database administrator for an oil and gas production firm created secret users in a database system that allowed him to access the system after he stopped working for the firm. When the firm terminated his contract, he sabotaged the firm's systems, which could have resulted in a serious environmental disaster. The case highlights the powers of the database administrator and the critical importance of hiring highly qualified and trustworthy employees for this position.[3]

Documentation. Databases undergo changes throughout their design, development, and use. This makes documentation critical. Descriptions of database structures, contents, security features, and password policies are examples of important documentation materials. A **data dictionary** is a critical component of database documentation that describes the data fields in a specific type of database record. Thus, a data dictionary is **metadata**—that is, data about other data.

Figure 14-4 provides examples of the information that a data dictionary might contain (listed in the "Entry" column) and an example for the employee number data field in Figure 14-3. In this figure, the data dictionary indicates that the employee number must be seven characters, is a "text" data field (rather than a "number" data field because it is not manipulated mathematically), has no default value, and so forth. Entries in the data dictionary describe each data field in each record of each table (file) of an AIS database. When developers add a new data field to the record structure of an existing table, they also should add the appropriate information about the new field to the data dictionary.

---

[3] Vijayan, J. 2009. "IT contractor indicted for sabotaging offshore rig management system," *Computerworld*, March 18, 2009. Accessed from www.computerworld.com, April 2014.

Item	Entry	Example
1	Field name	Employee number
2	Field size	Seven characters
3	Type of data field	Text
4	Default value	None
5	Required?	Yes
6	Validation rule(s)	All digits must be numeric characters
7	Range	None
8	Source document	Employee hiring form
9	Programs used to modify it	Payroll X2.1
10	Individuals allowed access	Payroll personnel
11	Individuals not allowed access	Nonpayroll personnel

FIGURE 14-4 Examples of information that might be stored in a data dictionary for the employee number data field of a payroll table.

Data dictionaries enjoy a variety of control uses. One use is as a documentation aid for those who develop, correct, audit, or enhance either the database or the computer programs that access it. As suggested in items 10 and 11 of Figure 14-4, an organization can also use a data dictionary for security purposes—for example, to indicate who can or cannot access sensitive data fields in a database.

Accountants can also make good use of a data dictionary. For example, a data dictionary can help establish an audit trail because it identifies the input sources of data items, the potential computer programs that use or modify particular data items, and the management reports that use the data. When accountants help design a new computer system, a data dictionary can help them trace data paths in the new system. Finally, a data dictionary can serve as a useful aid when investigating or documenting internal control procedures.

Data Integrity and Authenticity. IT professionals estimate that it costs about 10 times as much to correct information that is already in a database than it does to enter it correctly initially. Even simple errors in databases can lead to costly mistakes, bad decisions, or disasters (think about air traffic controllers as an example). For these reasons, the software used to create databases should include edit tests that protect databases from erroneous data entries. Database administrators or developers design these **data integrity controls** and customize them for different applications. Examples include tests for data completeness, conformance to the data type required for the data field, valid code tests (e.g., a state code such as "CA"), and reasonableness tests (e.g., regular payroll hours worked must be between "0" and "40").

Data integrity controls do not safeguard a database from entries that are mechanically correct but unauthorized. This is why most databases also use **authenticity controls**—for example, require passwords that limit access to approved users and protect databases from external hacks. In some applications, entries for new records or modifications to existing records must also be approved—for example, when adding new employee names to payroll tables.

Case-in-Point 14.5 In 2015, it came to light that, over 5 years, selected employees at Well's Fargo bank created over 2 million fictitious checking, savings, and credit-card accounts over 5 years. Why? Those same employees received bonuses for opening new accounts, and (apparently) no one examined the new business for authenticity.[4]

---

[4] Scudder, V. 2016. Anatomy of a scandal at Wells Fargo. *Public Relations Strategist* 22(4): 22–23.

Processing Accuracy and Completeness. Within the context of database systems, *transaction processing* refers to the sequence of steps that a database system uses to accomplish specific processing tasks. AISs need **transaction controls** to ensure that the system performs each transaction accurately and completely.

To illustrate, imagine an inventory application with two types of inventory records: raw materials records and work-in-process records. An inventory manager wishes to subtract 200 units from a particular raw materials record and add the same number of units to a corresponding work-in-process record. Now suppose that the database system executes the first part of this transaction (i.e., subtracts 200 units from the raw materials record) and then stops operating for some reason. This is a problem because the transaction has not been executed completely and the balance-on-hand field in the current work-in-process record is incorrect. To overcome this problem, databases should either process a transaction entirely or not process at all. Database systems maintain an auditable log of transactions to help achieve this goal. When a system only partially executes a specific transaction, it can recover by verifying that a problem has occurred, reversing whatever entries it made, and starting anew. This is why the ability to audit any particular transaction to ensure processing accuracy and completeness is critical.

Concurrency. In multiuser systems, it is possible for more than one user to access the same database at the same time. Without **concurrency controls**, it is possible for two or more users to access the same record from the same table at the same time. This creates problems. To illustrate, suppose that "User A" and "User B" access the same inventory record at the same time. The initial balance-on-hand field for this record is 500 units. When User A accesses this record, the system transfers the entire record to A's work area. User A wants to add 100 units to the balance-on-hand field. The result is a new balance of 600 units. User A completes this transaction, the system writes the new record back to the disk, and the new balance on hand in this record is now "600 units."

When User B accesses this same record at the same time, the system also transfers the same initial record to B's work area. User B wants to decrease the balance on hand by 200 units. This results in a balance of 300 units because this user also starts with an initial balance on hand of 500 units. Assuming that B completes this transaction after A is done, the system updates to reflect the transaction completed by B. The end result is an inventory record with a balance on hand of 300 units, not the correct value of 400 (= 500 + 100 − 200). To guard against this problem, database systems include **lockout controls** that do not allow multiple users to access the same record at the same time. Rather, databases require that the system completes one user's transaction before allowing the next user to make further changes to the database.

Backup and Security. As noted earlier, the information in many accounting databases is critical to the day-to-day operations of a company and is typically irreplaceable. Thus, databases require careful protection. A key security feature of any database is the set of backup procedures that enables the organization to restore data if the original copies are lost or damaged.

Case-in-Point 14.6   A 2014 report from the Disaster Recovery Preparedness Council found that three out of four companies surveyed are not adequately prepared for disasters that could threaten company data. In addition, nearly half of the companies who had experienced a disaster found that their backup plans were inadequate when they needed to use these plans.[5]

---

[5] Disaster Recovery Preparedness Council, 2014. *The State of Global Disaster Recovery Preparedness*, (drbenchmark.org).

In addition to backup security, an organization must also protect databases from unauthorized access, especially if an organization grants access from remote users. A system should have the ability to assign, maintain, and require employees to use passwords and guard against unwarranted intrusions. Similarly, database systems can use encryption techniques to scramble data into unintelligible formats, thereby protecting file data even if an unauthorized user obtains access to a company's databases. This is especially important when database information resides on laptops, which can easily be lost or stolen.

Case-in-Point 14.7 On January 29, 2017, the entire computer system of Delta Airlines crashed, requiring the company to delay or cancel almost 300 flights. Upset passengers vented their frustrations on social media as the company struggled to restore its system to working order. The estimated cost of the 5-hour outage: $300 million.[6]

A final database security feature involves the use of **view controls** that limit each user's access to information on a need-to-know basis. For example, a defense contractor will limit its employees' access to many files that contain sensitive information. We cover intrusion detection systems and controls in Chapter 2.

14.3 STEPS IN DEVELOPING A DATABASE USING THE RESOURCES, EVENTS, AND AGENTS (REA) APPROACH

At a state department of social services, the director wants to know how many inquiries were made for a certain type of medical assistance last month. At the headquarters of a department store chain, a vice president wants to know how many credit customers made partial payments on their accounts last week. At a local university bookstore, a manager wants to know how many book orders went unfilled last year.

In each aforementioned case, a decision-maker needs information that an AIS must gather and store in convenient formats. The challenges involved in creating large, useful databases include determining what data to collect and how to gather, record, organize, and store the data in ways that satisfy multiple objectives. Key goals include: (1) identifying the reports desired by users of the system; (2) finding hardware and software solutions that can adequately perform the data-gathering, storage, and reporting tasks involved; (3) keeping the databases from becoming too large, complex, and unwieldy; (4) protecting the privacy of sensitive information; and (5) avoiding data redundancy (i.e., avoiding the storage of the same data repeatedly in different tables). To accomplish these and other goals, databases must be carefully designed to serve their intended uses.

Case-in-Point 14.8 How much does the design of a database cost? It depends upon the size and complexity of the database itself. The cost may be as little as $10,000 for small systems and $500,000 or more for larger ones.[7]

When a company wants to create a database, it often utilizes the services of a database architect to help design a database that meets its needs. Based on the information

---

[6] Mclean, R. and J. Mullen. 2017. Computer outage grounds Delta flights in U.S. *CNN Money*. Accessed online at http://money.cnn.com/2017/01/29/news/delta-system-outage/.
[7] CostOwl.com. 2017. How much does a database design service cost? Accessed online at http://www.costowl.com/b2b/design-services-database-cost.html.

obtained from managers and end users, the database architect employs a process called **data modeling** to design the database. This can be the most challenging step in the process of creating a database because the designer must collect a considerable amount of information through investigation and interviews and must then determine the needs of all stakeholders as accurately and completely as possible. This process is both an art and a science.

The **REA model** is one approach for designing the databases in accounting systems. REA is an acronym for resources (R), events (E), and agents (A). The basic assumption of this model is that business events affect firm resources and involve agents (i.e., people) who participate in the event. Many describe the REA model as event-driven, meaning that it focuses on the important business events that managers must understand to make decisions.

REA databases store data about objects of interest called **entities**. These entities include business and economic events plus information about "who" and "what" were involved in those activities. **Agents** are the "who" associated with events. Internal agents work within the firm for which a database is designed (e.g., salespeople), while external agents such as customers are outside the firm. Most events involve both internal and external agents. For example, both a salesperson and a customer participate in a merchandise sale.

Economic **resources** are the "what" that databases store—that is, things of economic value. For example, a merchandise sale will transfer an inventory resource to a customer and generate a cash resource for the firm. Common examples of resources are cash, raw materials, and inventory.

Using the REA model involves the following steps: (1) identify business and economic events, (2) identify entities, (3) identify relationships among entities, (4) create entity–relationship diagrams, (5) identify the attributes of data entities, and (6) create database tables and records. We discuss each of these steps in greater detail next, using the sales process as an example.

Step 1—Identify Business and Economic Events

Chapters 8 and 9 discuss key business processes in most organizations and describe the events involved in these processes. There are two main types of events: economic events and business events. **Economic events** typically affect an organization's financial statements—for example, a sale on account. This event increases an entity's accounts receivable (balance sheet) and increases a sales revenue account (income statement).

Critics of traditional financial accounting systems note that AISs often ignore organizational activities and events that are important to managers, investors, and creditors. These **business events** may not affect financial statements but can affect important aspects of an organization. One example is the discovery that a construction project will cost far more than originally budgeted. While there is no journal entry for this event, the fact would certainly be important information to managers. Other examples are (1) hiring a new CEO or (2) making a valuable discovery during research and development. Again, these events do not require journal entries, but the information will affect critical decisions made by the firm. When creating a database using an REA approach, a system designer will try to record all events that are relevant for management decision-making in the database, whether they are business or economic events.

Resources	Events	Agents
Cash	Sales	Customer (external)
Equipment	Purchase	Employee (internal)
Inventory	Receive goods	Manager (internal)
Plant facilities	Hire an employee	Vendor (external)

FIGURE 14-5 Examples of resource, event, and agent entities.

Step 2—Identify Entities

The REA model helps designers identify database entities because each resource, event, or agent represents an entity in a relational database. Figure 14-5 provides several examples. You may notice that Figure 14-5 does not list accounts receivable as a resource. This is because the REA model does not recognize "receivables" as resources. Rather, receivables represent *claims* to resources rather than resources themselves. Similarly, the REA model does not treat "billing" as a business or economic event because creating a paper bill replicates information about an economic event such as a sale.

Step 3—Identify Relationships

Entities are related to other entities. For instance, a sale involves the exchange of merchandise inventory to a customer for cash, and the relationship between them is a *direct relationship*. Inventory and customer also share a relationship, but it is an *indirect relationship*. The REA model helps database designers define the relationships between entities. In the REA model, events typically have direct relationships with resources and agents and also with other events. The links between resources and agents are *through* events. Reports can logically combine data from any entities that are linked, either directly or indirectly.

Data modelers need to know about entity relationships in order to create links between database tables. Without these links, database users could not access data from more than one table at a time. Before we can determine the best way to link database tables, we must first understand the nature of the relationships among entities. We describe relationships in terms of **cardinalities**. Cardinality describes how entities are related, and we often abbreviate the description of the cardinality between two entities as *one-to-one (1:1), one-to-many (1:N),* or *many-to-many (N:N)*. This terminology refers to the maximum number of one entity that can occur given its relationship to another entity.

We must examine the relationship between two entities in two directions because each direction of the relationship can yield a different maximum cardinality. For example, consider the relationship between a "customer" and a "sale"—a one-to-many cardinality. This is because, a given customer can have many sales events, but any given sale is to only one customer. Figure 14-6 depicts this relationship graphically, where | represents a maximum of 1, and ⎯< represents a maximum of many.

FIGURE 14-6 Maximum cardinality example.

FIGURE 14-7 A one-to-many maximum and minimum cardinality example.

Cardinalities also have minimums. In our sales example, one customer can be involved in many sales transactions, but some customers may have never purchased anything. Thus, we say that the minimum number of sales for a customer is 0, which is indicated with a ○. Reading this relationship in the other direction, a sale cannot be made unless there is a customer, so the minimum number of customers is "1." Figure 14-7 depicts the relationship with both minimum and maximum cardinalities.

To read this relationship, we start on one side of the relationship and assume that the initial entity is singular. Then, we read the minimum and maximum cardinalities of the related entity. Thus, we interpret the cardinalities in Figure 14-7 as: (1) one sale is made to a minimum of one customer and a maximum of one customer and (2) one customer has a minimum of zero sales and a maximum of many sales.

Three other points about cardinalities are as follows. First, you will often find that events involve single agents, but that agents are involved in events many times. As a result, agent–event relationships are often one-to-many relationships. Second, in the case of a sequence of events, you will typically notice that the first event must occur before the next event can occur. Thus, the minimum cardinality for the first event will be 1. This would be the case between a Sale and a subsequent Cash Receipt (see Figure 14-8). The Cash Receipt cannot occur unless there was first a sale. From the other direction, the cardinality says that a sale relates to a minimum of zero cash receipts (because some customers will not pay) and a maximum of many cash receipts (because some customers may pay in installments). Again, plainly stated, this means that you cannot have a cash receipt without a sale, and you could receive several cash receipts for a sale.

Finally, cardinalities can also say something about the controls for a given business event. Notice that Figure 14-8 tells us, for example, that this firm allows installment payments. Otherwise, the maximum cardinality for the cash receipts would be 1.

Step 4—Create Entity–Relationship Diagrams

Database designers use a graphical documentation technique called the **entity–relationship (E-R) diagram**, sometimes called an ERD, to depict entities and their relationships. We have already introduced you to the basic elements of E-R diagrams

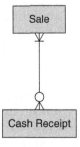

FIGURE 14-8 A many-to-many cardinality example for business events.

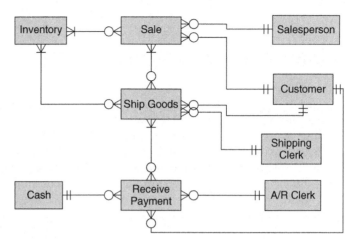

FIGURE 14-9 Sample E-R diagram for a sale process.

in the preceding figures related to cardinalities. The diagram consists of three items: rectangles, connecting lines, and cardinality notations. Rectangles represent entities and connecting lines depict relationships. E-R diagrams depict all of the entities and the relationships graphically. In addition, the diagrams are arranged as events that occur in temporal sequence when using the REA modeling approach. Therefore, a reader can quickly see the main business events and the order in which events occur. In addition, the resources are arranged on the left, and the people (agents) appear on the right (i.e., the diagram is ordered from left to right as Resources, Events, and Agents). Recall that each event will be related to at least one resource, internal agent, and external agent. Figure 14-9 provides an example of an E-R diagram for a simple sales process.

Step 5—Identify Attributes of Entities

Eventually, the database designer must create a database table for every entity in the E-R diagram. The tables consist of records, each containing data fields that describe the entity's **attributes**. Figure 14-10 shows four database tables for our merchandise sale example: (1) an event table (Sale), (2) a resource table (Inventory), (3) an external agent table (Customer), and (4) an internal agent table (Salesperson).

Entities have characteristics or attributes that describe them. For example, a salesperson is an agent entity, and the attributes for a salesperson are the data fields that describe each salesperson. What data should you collect about a salesperson? First, it is necessary to include an attribute that uniquely identifies each salesperson within the Salesperson table. This is the primary key discussed earlier. The salesperson's employee identification number is a good choice for the primary key.

Other attributes to include might be last name, middle name, first name, work phone number, cell phone number, address, e-mail, date of birth, date hired, department assignment, salary code, and so on. You do not want to include attributes that the system can calculate or that require manual updates. For example, you would not store the "number of years worked" because you would need to update it every year. It is better to store the date hired and to use a formula that *calculates* the current number of years of service based upon today's date.

Customer Order Table (Event)

Order #	Employee #	Customer #	Date	Comments
1003	M24SP	B104	01/03/2011	
1004	R63SP	P202	01/03/2011	Ship ASAP
1005	M24SP	S200	01/03/2011	
1006	W11SP	C100	01/03/2011	

Inventory Table (Resource)

Item #	Description	Unit Cost	Sales Price	Beg QOH
1400	Goodie Bar	$0.20	$0.40	13025
1500	Almond Delight	$0.25	$0.45	5010
1600	Gummy Lions	$0.60	$0.95	20109
1700	Pecan Bar	$0.70	$1.09	4508
1800	Milky Bars	$0.18	$0.30	2207

Customer Table (Agent)

Customer #	Name	Address	City	State	Zip Code	Credit Limit
A101	Amanda Wills	22 Yellow Ln.	Charlotte	NC	79803	$20,000.00
B104	Boris Bailey	321 Church St.	Oxford	OH	45056	5,000.00
C100	Carly Riccardi	1899 Green St.	Dayton	OH	43299	10,000.00
P202	Peggy Martin	1260 Main St.	Columbus	OH	43320	10,000.00
S200	Bill Safer	860 Broad St.	Fairfax	VA	22030	5,000.00

Salesperson Table (Agent)

Employee #	Name	Address	City	State	Zip Code	Dept ID	Date Hired
A06SP	Sally Anderson	3026 Skye Ln.	Columbus	OH	43213	247	1/31/1989
M24SP	Randy Merit	262 Main St.	Bexley	OH	43209	182	7/2/1999
R63SP	Barry Rogers	80 N. Long St.	Gahanna	OH	43215	247	1/16/2001
R73SP	Jim Rudolph	64 Lantern Ave.	Columbus	OH	43213	76	8/15/2000
W11SP	John Walker	1028 Fields Ln.	Lancaster	OH	43307	182	9/1/1992

FIGURE 14-10 Four sample tables in a relational database.

Three guidelines for deciding which entities to store in a database are as follows: (1) When possible, "keep it simple" and do not store data that are not needed. Instead, let the outputs (e.g., reports) from the system dictate the data requirements. (2) The attributes should describe one entity and that entity only. For example, if you have an inventory table, you would not include information about the vendor in this table. You can reference the vendor, but the name, address, and other information about the vendor belong in a separate Vendor table. (3) Finally, you should only include entities that are singular. In other words, do not create attributes that contain lists of other data—for example, the children's names for an employee. The database would not be able to store this attribute because there could be many names, but there is only space for one child's name in the database table. We will discuss how to deal with such problems in this chapter's section on Normalization.

Step 6—Convert E-R Diagrams into Database Tables

Each entity in the E-R diagram becomes a table in the completed database. However, a database is likely to contain more tables than the total number of entities in the E-R diagram. This can occur because linking tables together sometimes requires the creation of additional tables. In databases, tables are linked using foreign keys as previously described. For example, in Figure 14-10, the Customer Number in the Sales table is a foreign key that references the primary key of a particular customer in the Customer table. The relationship between the primary key and foreign key enables the database software to link the two tables together. If you wanted to create a sales report that shows the *name of the customer* associated with each sale, the links allow the creation of this report.

Creating links between tables is simple when the relationship between the entities is one-to-one or one-to-many. In one-to-one relationships, the foreign key can be in either table. If the entities are events that occur in sequence, the foreign key will usually be in the second event. In one-to-many relationships, the foreign key will be on the many side of the relationship. Looking at the sample E–R diagram for a sales process in Figure 14-9, for example, we see that the cardinality between a Salesperson and Sale is one-to-many. To create a foreign key, we would use the primary key from the Salesperson table as the foreign key in the Sale table. Looking at Figure 14-10, this is the case. The primary key for the Salesperson table, Employee #, appears in the Sale table as an attribute. This is the link between the two tables.

Linking tables with foreign keys becomes problematic when there is a many-to-many relationship between two entities. New **relationship tables** are necessary when you have many-to-many relationships. The reason for this is that without relationship tables, there would be fields in a database table that could contain many possible values. For example, there is a many-to-many relationship between Sale and Inventory in Figure 14-10. If we placed the inventory item number in the Sale table as a foreign key, it would not be possible to input the value for the inventory item number, because there can be many items related to a single sale. Similarly, an item can be sold many times, making it impossible to input a single sale number for a given item. Figure 14-11 shows the relationship table that is necessary to join the Sales and Inventory Item entities.

How many tables, including relationship tables, will we have for a complete database and the Sales process described in Figure 14-9? Looking at the diagram, we see that there are nine entities, but only seven tables are needed because three of the entities represent employees, and one table can be created for all employees. There are also four many-to-many relationships: (1) Inventory and Sale, (2) Inventory and Ship Goods, (3) Sales and Ship Goods, and (4) Sales and Receive Payment. Therefore, we would have 11 tables in the finished database: 7 tables for entities and 4 additional relationship tables.

Figure 14-12 lists all the database tables and their attributes for our Sales example. Because data modeling is a creative process, there are other possible sets of database tables and other attributes that you might include in a database for a sales process. Figure 14-12 is one example.

Sale #	Item #	Quantity
1003	1400	230
1004	1400	430
1005	1600	180
1005	1800	200
1005	1900	360
1006	1400	80
1006	1800	100

FIGURE 14-11 A relationship that joins the Sale and Inventory tables.

Inventory Table
Item#, Description, Quantity on Hand

Cash Table
Account#, Account Type, Bank Name, Balance

Sale Table
Sale#, [Employee#], [Customer#], Date

Ship Goods Table
Shipment#, [Employee#], [Customer#], Date

Receive Payment table
Cash Receipt#, [Employee#], [Customer#], Date, Amount Received

Employee Table
Employee#, First Name, Last Name, Address, City, State, Zip Code, Date of Birth, Hire Date

Customer Table
Customer#, Company Name, Address, City, State, Zip Code, Current Credit Limit

Inventory/Sale Table
[Sale#], [Item#], Quantity Sold, Sales Price

Inventory/Ship Goods Table
[Shipment#], [Item#], Quantity Shipped

Sale/Ship Goods Table
[Sale#], [Shipment#]

Ship Goods/ Receive Payment Table
[Shipment#], [Cash Receipt#]

FIGURE 14-12 Database tables and attributes for the sales process in Figure 14-10.

14.4 NORMALIZATION

Normalization is another methodology for ensuring that a database stores data in the most appropriate tables and that the design of the database promotes data integrity, data accuracy, and nonredundant data storage. There are multiple levels of normalization, but we shall only examine the first three: first normal form, second normal form, and third normal form. These three normal forms address the vast majority of problems when designing database tables.

First Normal Form

A database is in **first normal form (1NF)** if all of a single record's attributes (data fields) are singular. That is, each attribute has only one value. Figure 14-13 shows a set of university parking ticket data with repeating groups in its rightmost four columns. Real parking tickets will contain many more data fields than shown here, but we will keep things simple to focus on normalization tasks. Databases cannot store more than one value in the same data (i.e., column) of the same record, so we must do something to overcome this limitation.

A solution to this problem is to use a separate record to store the information for each parking ticket. Figure 14-14 illustrates the results. For this file, the ticket number

Student ID Number	Last Name	First Name	Phone Number	License Plate State	License Plate Number	Ticket Number	Date	Code	Fine
S123456	Curry	Dorothy	(916)358-4448	CA	123 MCD	10151	10/15/10	A	$10
						10152	10/16/10	B	$20
						10121	11/12/10	B	$20
S323176	Mason	Richard	(916)563-7865	CA	253 DAL	10231	10/23/10	C	$50
						12051	12/5/10	A	$10

FIGURE 14-13 A set of unnormalized parking ticket data.

Ticket Number	Student ID Number	Last Name	First Name	Phone Number	State	License Plate Number	Date	Code	Fine
10151	S123456	Curry	Dorothy	(916)358-4448	CA	123 MCD	10/15/2010	A	$10
10152	S123456	Curry	Dorothy	(916)358-4448	CA	123 MCD	10/16/2010	B	$20
10121	S123456	Curry	Dorothy	(916)358-4448	CA	123 MCD	11/12/2010	B	$20
10231	S323176	Mason	Richard	(916)663-7865	CA	253 DAL	10/23/2010	C	$50
12051	S323176	Mason	Richard	(916)663-7865	CA	253 DAL	12/5/2010	A	$10

FIGURE 14-14 The data from Figure 14-13 in first normal form.

serves as the primary key. There are no repeating groups for any one column, and there is no longer a violation of the first normal form.

Although we now have corrected the problem associated with nonsingular attributes, several problems remain. One difficulty is a large amount of *data redundancy* (i.e., the fact that much of the information in this table is repetitive). Another problem is that we have created an *insertion anomaly,* which is a situation where desired data cannot be entered into the database. In particular, the current version of this database reveals that it only stores information about students with parking tickets. Students with registered cars but no parking tickets will have no records in this file—a difficulty if school administrators also want to use this file for car registration purposes. A third problem is a *deletion anomaly,* which occurs when more data is deleted than is desired by the database user. When we delete records after students pay their tickets, we will no longer have a car registration record on file for anyone who has paid all of his or her tickets.

Second Normal Form

To solve the problems described earlier, we now consider **second normal form (2NF)**. A database is in second normal form if it is in first normal form and all the attributes in each record depend entirely on the record's primary key. To satisfy this requirement for our student-parking ticket example, let us split our student information into two files—a "Car Registration File" and a "Ticket File"—as shown in Figure 14-15. This approach results in a more efficient design and also eliminates much of the first file's data redundancy. Notice that the solution to both the insertion and deletion anomalies is the same—make more tables.

In our new Car Registration table, what should serve as the primary key? At first glance, you might guess "Student ID number." If students are only able to register one car, then this choice might be satisfactory. If students can register more than one car, then it makes more sense to use the license plate number as the primary key.

```
┌─────────────────────────────────────────────────────────────────────────────────┐
│  ┌──────────────────────┐                                                         │
│  │ Car Registration File │                                                        │
│  └──────────────────────┘                                                         │
│                                                                                   │
│                                                          (primary key)            │
│    Student ID      Last        First         Phone        License Plate           │
│    Number         Name        Name         Number      State    Number            │
│    S123456        Curry       Dorothy      (916)358-4448  CA     123 MCD           │
│    S323176        Mason       Richard      (916)563-7865  CA     253 DAL           │
│       .             .            .              .          .        .             │
│       .             .            .              .          .        .             │
│                                                                                   │
│  ┌────────────┐                                                                   │
│  │ Ticket File │                                                                  │
│  └────────────┘                                                                   │
│                                                                                   │
│  (primary key)              (foreign key)                                         │
│    Ticket                  License Plate                                          │
│    Number     State        Number          Date       Code      Fine             │
│    10151      CA           123 MCD          10/15/10    A        $10              │
│    10152      CA           123 MCD          10/16/10    B        $20              │
│    10231      CA           253 DAL          10/23/10    C        $50              │
│    10121      CA           123 MCD          11/12/10    B        $30              │
│    12051      CA           253 DAL          12/5/10     A        $15              │
│       .        .              .                .         .         .             │
│       .        .              .                .         .         .             │
└─────────────────────────────────────────────────────────────────────────────────┘
```

FIGURE 14-15   The data of Figure 14-14 in second normal form.

Remember: The primary key must uniquely identify a record, and this would not be possible if one person (with one student IS number) had two records in this table.

What about a primary key for our new Ticket file? In this table, the "ticket number" serves this purpose, while the student's license plate number serves as the foreign key. The foreign key enables a database to link appropriate records together—for example, to trace a particular parking ticket to the car's registered owner. It also enables database users to answer such questions as "Does a particular student have any outstanding parking tickets?"

Third Normal Form

Although we are making headway in our database design, our goal is to create a database that is in **third normal form (3NF)**. A database is in third normal form if it is in second normal form and contains no **transitive dependencies**. This means that the same record does not contain any data fields where data field *A* determines data field *B*. The Ticket file in Figure 14-15 suffers from this problem because the ticket code data field (e.g., a code of "A") determines the description of the type of ticket (e.g., "meter expired"), which results in unnecessary repetition of the long descriptions of violations.

One way to solve this problem is to store the data for parking code violation types in a new "Parking Violations Code Table" as shown in Figure 14-16. This enables us to eliminate the redundant information (the Description data field) in the Ticket table of Figure 14-16 and streamline our data. Figure 14-16 illustrates the results.

```
┌─────────────────────────────────────────────────────────────────────┐
│  ┌──────────────────────┐                                             │
│  │ Car Registration File │                                            │
│  └──────────────────────┘                                             │
│                                                                       │
│    Student ID      Last      First         Phone                      │
│    Number          Name      Name          Number          State      │
│    S123456         Curry     Dorothy       (916)358-4448   CA         │
│    S323176         Mason     Richard       (916)563-7865   CA         │
│       .              .          .             .             .         │
│       .              .          .             .             .         │
│       .              .          .             .             .         │
│                                                                       │
│  ┌──────────────┐                                                     │
│  │ Ticket File  │                                                     │
│  └──────────────┘                                                     │
│                                                                       │
│  (primary key)                  (foreign key)                         │
│    Ticket                     License Plate                           │
│    Number        State         Number        Date          Code      │
│    T10151        C             123 MCD        10/15/17       A         │
│    T10152        C             123 MCD        10/16/17       B         │
│    T10231        C             253 DAL        10/23/17       C         │
│    T10121        C             123 MCD        11/12/10       B         │
│    T12051        C             253 DAL        12/5/10        A         │
│       .          .                .             .           .         │
│       .          .                .             .           .         │
│                                                                       │
│  ┌──────────────────┐                                                 │
│  │ Parking Violations│                                                │
│  │ Code File         │                                                │
│  └──────────────────┘                                                 │
│                                                                       │
│  (primary key)                                                        │
│    Code                       Explanation                   Fine      │
│     A                         meter expired                 $20       │
│     B                         parking in no-parking zone    $30       │
│     C                         no parking sticker            $50       │
│       .                              .                                │
│       .                              .                                │
└─────────────────────────────────────────────────────────────────────┘
```

FIGURE 14-16 The data of Figure 14-15 in third normal form.

The ticket codes (A, B, and so forth) in the Ticket table serve as a foreign key that links the information in the Ticket table to an entry in the Parking Violations Code table. We now have a database in third normal form.

Large databases tend to become very complicated, with multiple tables that are linked together with foreign keys. The database in Figure 14-16, for example, is more complex than our original file in Figure 14-13, but it is also more efficient. For example, this database design will allow its users to (1) store the car registration information of all students, even if they do not have any parking tickets; (2) alter a student's name, phone number, or license plate by altering only one record in the Car Registration file—not several of them, as would be required using the file in Figure 14-13; and (3) delete a ticket without deleting a student's registration. Finally, this database design eliminates redundant information and therefore makes data storage more efficient.

AIS AT WORK
The SEC and Big Data[8]

The Securities and Exchange Commission (SEC) accumulates large amounts of data from publicly traded companies. In 2013, the SEC initiated a new program where it will use data drawn from Extensible Business Reporting Language (XBRL) tagged data (discussed in more detail in Chapter 2) to detect potential financial fraud. The system is called the Accounting Quality Model (AQM), and the popular press has named the new tool "Robocop." The SEC designed AQM to look for patterns in the XBRL data submitted by filers and then to identify deviations from the patterns. The system focuses on discretionary accruals and evidence of earnings management. If a firm's disclosures deviate too far from expected patterns identified in the XBRL-tagged data, the system will initiate further investigations of the firm. The common tags for all financial data have made it possible to detect patterns that were not previously observable.

Many believe that the next step for the SEC is to integrate big data within its fraud-finding tools. Currently, the system only analyzes XBRL-tagged data in the SEC's databases. In the future, the SEC and others interested in detecting fraud (such as internal and external auditors) could detect anomalies by combining XBRL-tagged financial data with unstructured data such as corporate e-mail, social networking activities, customer complaints, and numerous other sources. The result will be sophisticated tools that take advantage of databases, unstructured data, the structure of accounting data (e.g., XBRL), and contemporary software.

SUMMARY

✓ Most AISs use databases to store accounting data.

✓ Primary keys and foreign keys enable database systems to identify database records uniquely as well as link records to one another.

✓ Large, multiuser accounting databases pose several concerns for accounting professionals. These include the administration and supervision of database development and maintenance; the need for documentation; the importance of data integrity, data processing accuracy, and data completeness; database security and backup; and the need for concurrency controls to safeguard data when two users wish to access the same record.

✓ The REA model is a database design methodology that focuses upon resources, events, and agents.

✓ E-R diagrams graphically depict the entities needed for a database and the types of relationships between them. The ultimate goal is to determine what data to store and how to organize it.

✓ The process of normalization enables designers to minimize data redundancy, eliminate insertion and deletion anomalies, and remove transitive dependencies. The goal is a database that is at least in third normal form.

---

[8] Jones, A. 2013. SEC to roll out Robocop against fraud, *Financial Times* (February).

KEY TERMS YOU SHOULD KNOW

agent
attributes
authenticity controls
big data
business event
cardinalities
concurrency controls
data dictionary
data field
data hierarchy
data integrity controls
data modeling
database administrator

database management system
economic event
entities
entity–relationship (E-R) diagram
first normal form (1NF)
foreign keys
lockout controls
master files
metadata
normalization
primary key
REA model
record

record structure
referential integrity
relational database
relationship tables
resources
second normal form (2NF)
third normal form (3NF)
transaction controls
transaction files
transitive dependencies
view controls

TEST YOURSELF

Q14-1. Which of these does *not* characterize a typical database?

a. Large number of records

b. Irreplaceable data

c. High need for accuracy

d. Simple systems

Q14-2. The part of the data hierarchy that represents one instance of an entity is a:

a. field

b. record

c. file

d. database

Q14-3. Which of these would *not* be a good primary key for a file of employee records?

a. Phone number

b. Last name

c. Company employee number

d. All of these would make equally good primary keys

Q14-4. In the REA model, the "A" stands for:

a. agents

b. additions

c. accounts

d. associations

Q14-5. In the REA model, which of these would *not* be classified as an event?

a. Cash sale

b. Credit sale

c. Hiring a new chief executive

d. Date of the office picnic

Q14-6. Which of these is *not* a cardinality between two database entities?

a. One-to-one

b. None-to-none

c. One-to-many

d. Many-to-many

Q14-7. What is the typical cardinality between a customer and a purchase event?

a. One-to-one

b. Many-to-many

c. One-to-many

d. None-to-one

Q14-8. An insert anomaly occurs when the database user cannot:

a. delete data

b. modify data

c. view data

d. add new data

Q14-9. To link the records in a many-to-many relationship within a relational database:

a. you must create an intermediate "relationships" table

b. you must create a new database

c. you must use foreign keys and a spreadsheet system

d. you cannot link records together under these circumstances

Q14-10. Within the context of databases, the term "concurrency" refers to the possibility that:

a. a customer of one store might also be a customer of another store

b. two database users might want to access the same record at the same time

c. a credit entry for a customer requires a debit entry for a matching account

d. none of these

Q14-11. A database is in third normal form (3NF) if it is second normal form and:

a. all the data attributes in a record are well defined

b. all the data attributes in a record depend upon the record key

c. the data contain no transitive dependencies

d. the data can be stored in two or more separate tables

DISCUSSION QUESTIONS

14-1. Why are databases important for accounting information systems? Describe some concerns, and explain why each one is important.

14-2. What is the hierarchy of data in databases? Provide an example for a particular accounting application.

14-3. What are primary keys in accounting databases and what purpose(s) do they serve?

14-4. Name some specific accounting files and a potential primary key for each one.

14-5. Describe each of the following database issues that are relevant to accounting systems, and give an example of each: (1) data integrity, (2) transaction accuracy and completeness, (3) concurrency processing, and (4) security.

14-6. What is the REA model? How does REA differ from more traditional accounting views of data collection and storage? Hint: Would a traditional accounting database store data about personnel matters?

14-7. What are database cardinalities? Give some examples of cardinalities for an accounting application other than sales.

14-8. What is an entity–relationship (E-R) diagram? What can you determine about an organization from examining an E-R diagram?

14-9. Suppose that a data modeler creates a database that includes a Sales table and a Salesperson table. Would you be likely to need a relationship table to link these two entities? Why or why not?

14-10. What is the process of normalization? What levels are there, and why do database developers seek to normalize data?

14-11. Amazon designed its Echo devices to listen, and respond to, voice commands. But in December of 2016, police in Arkansas sought the audio recordings of Victor Collins for another reason—to help them solve his murder. As the case unfolded, it because clear that the device listens to, and uploads to cloud servers, a wide variety of audio inputs, including (the police hoped) incriminating evidence that might help them solve the case.

Amazon refused to provide the recordings, arguing that "personal privacy" was more important. For example, defense attorney Kimberly Weber stated "You have an expectation of privacy in your home, and I have a big problem that law enforcement can use the technology that advances our quality of life against us." Additional issues were the reliability of what might have been recorded, who recorded it, and the accuracy of the information on it.

Ultimately, the situation involved issues involving personal privacy, the workings of an Internet of Things, and the question of who should have final control over the audio logs made by an Internet listening device used in a private home. At the time of this writing, the police decided that they had enough incriminating evidence without the audio tapes and decided not to pursue their acquisition.

Obtain additional information about this case—for example, at: https://www.engadget.com/2016/12/27/amazon-echo-audio-data-murder-case/. Based on this information, do you think Amazon should be forced to provide Echo recordings, or are "Privacy rights" more important? Defend your position with arguments to support it.

PROBLEMS

14-12. An internal auditor should have a sound understanding of basic data processing concepts such as data organization and storage in order to adequately evaluate systems and make use of retrieval software.

    a. Define the following terms as used in a data processing environment (all are nouns): (1) field, (2) record, and (3) file.

    b. (1) Define a database. (2) List two advantages and two disadvantages of a database system.
(CIA adapted)

14-13. What attributes (i.e., table columns) would you be likely to include in a Cash table and in a Cash Receipts table?

14-14. Describe the meaning of each of the entity–relationship diagrams shown in Figure 14-17.

14-15. Draw an entity–relationship diagram for the following: Sales of inventory are made to customers by salespeople. After the sale, cash is received by cashiers.

14-16. Draw an entity–relationship diagram for the following: An accounting firm holds recruiting events for college students. At these events, recruiters are seeking students with particular skills.

14-17. Give some examples of attributes you would include in a Customer table. Would you use one data field or two for the customer name? Why?

14-18. Design tables to store the following attributes (make sure that all tables are in third normal form): Customer name, customer address, customer phone, and names of customers' children.

14-19. The quotation at the beginning of this chapter suggested that "… *very few checks are made to check the database is not doing things it should not be doing.*" What are some things that accounting databases should not do? Compile a list of items, and for each one, explain why it is a problem.

14-20. Design tables to store the following attributes (make sure that all tables are in third normal form). Student name, student phone, classes taken by student, student address, class number, class time, class room, students' grades for each class.

14-21. Bonadio Electrical Supplies distributes electrical components to the construction industry. The company began as a local supplier 15 years ago and has grown rapidly to become a major competitor in the north central United States. As the business grew and the variety of components to be stocked expanded, Bonadio acquired a computer and implemented an inventory control system. Other applications such as accounts receivable, accounts payable, payroll, and sales analysis were gradually computerized as each function expanded. Because of its operational importance, the inventory

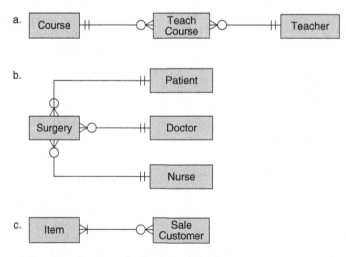

FIGURE 14-17 Entity–relationship diagrams for Problem 14-14.

system has been upgraded to an online system, while all the other applications are operating in batch mode. Over the years, the company has developed or acquired more than 100 application programs and maintains hundreds of files. Bonadio faces stiff competition from local suppliers throughout its marketing area. At a management meeting, the sales manager complained about the difficulty in obtaining immediate, current information to respond to customer inquiries. Other managers stated that they also had difficulty obtaining timely data from the system. As a result, the controller engaged a consulting firm to explore the situation. The consultant recommended installing a database management system (DBMS), and the company complied, employing Jack Gibbons as the database administrator.

At a recent management meeting, Gibbons presented an overview of the DBMS. Gibbons explained that the database approach assumes an organizational, data-oriented viewpoint as it recognizes that a centralized database represents a vital resource. Instead of being assigned to applications, information is more appropriately used and managed for the entire organization. The operating system physically moves data to and from disk storage, while the DBMS is the software program that controls the data definition library that specifies the data structures and characteristics. As a result, both the roles of the application programs and query software and the tasks of the application programmers and users are simplified. Under the database approach, the data are available to all users within security guidelines.

a. Explain the basic difference between a file-oriented system and a database management system.

b. Describe at least three advantages and at least three disadvantages of the database management system.

c. Describe the duties and responsibilities of Jack Gibbons, the database administrator. (CMA Adapted)

14-22. In 2016, the *Journal of Accountancy* published an article by James Long et al., entitled "New database provides free access to audit research." Access this database at: http://commons.aaahq.org/groups/e5075f0eec/summary. What does this database contain? Would you describe it as a conventional database or is it really a list? If you were an auditor, would you find this information helpful? Why or why not?

CASE ANALYSES

14-23. Ian's Place (The REA Model and E-R Diagrams)

Ian's Place sells pet supplies to dog and cat owners. To sell its products, the marketing department requires sales personnel to call on the pet store retailers within their assigned geographic territories. Salespeople have an application on their mobile phones that allows them to record sales orders and send these sales orders directly to the company network for updating the company's sales order file.

Each day, warehouse personnel review the current sales orders in its file, and where possible, pick the goods and ready them for shipment. (Ian's Place ships goods via common carrier, and shipping terms are generally FOB from the shipping point.) When the shipping department completes a shipment, it also notifies the billing department, which then prepares an invoice for the customer. Payment terms vary by customer, but most are "net 30." When the billing department receives a payment, the billing clerk credits the customer's account and records the cash received.

Requirements

1. Identify the resources, events, and agents involved in the revenue process at Ian's Place.

2. Develop an E-R diagram for this process.

3. Design the tables for this revenue process. Note that you will need tables for each resource, event, and agent, as well as tables for each many-to-many relationship.

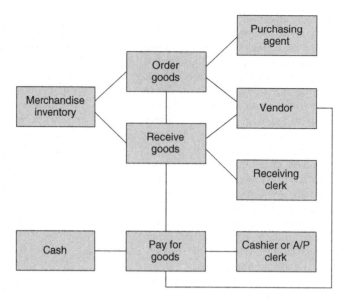

FIGURE 14-18 An E-R diagram for the purchasing system of Clooney and Bullock Manufacturing.

14-24. Clooney and Bullock Manufacturing (Data Modeling with REA)

Clooney and Bullock is large manufacturer of trophies that is headquartered in Boston, Massachusetts. The Entity–Relationship diagram in Figure 14-18 shows a simplified version of the company's process for purchasing and paying for equipment and supplies.

Requirements

1. Insert appropriate cardinalities for the relationships in the Entity–Relationship model developed with the REA data modeling approach.
2. Describe the attributes for each database table that would be created using this model. You will need a table for each entity, as well as one or more relationship tables. Identify the table name, and then include all attributes within parentheses. Next, indicate the primary key by underlining it. Show any foreign keys by framing them in brackets (e.g., [Vendor#]). Include at least three fields in each table. Following is an example for the Vendor table and the Order Goods table.

   Vendor (Vendor#, Name, Street Address 1, Street Address 2, City, State, Zip Code, Phone, e-mail, Fax, Contact, Comments)
   Order Goods (Order#, Date, [Vendor#], [Employee#], Shipping Instructions, Comments)

14-25. Quick Jolt Electronics (Understanding Relational Databases)

Quick Jolt Electronics manufactures and sells specialized electronic components to customers across the country. The tables in Figure 14-19 illustrate some of the records in its accounting databases. Thus, for example, the "Sales by Inventory Number" records show detailed sales data for each of the company's inventory items, and the "Customer Payments" records indicate customer cash payments, listed by invoice number. Use the information in these tables to answer the following questions.

Sales by Inventory Number

Item Number	Invoice Number	Quantity	Price Each
I-1	V-1	1	2,000
	V-3	1	2,000
	V-6	3	1,575
I-2	V-5	2	3,000
	V-6	10	3,500
I-3	V-3	6	1,000
I-4	V-1	2	600
	V-5	2	300
I-5	V-3	2	4,000
	V-7	3	3,000
I-6	V-2	2	5,000
	V-4	2	5,000
	V-5	2	5,000
	V-7	2	7,000

Sales by Invoice Number

Invoice Number	Amount	Customer Number	Date	Salesperson Number
V-1	7,200	C-1	July 1	S-12
V-2	10,000	C-2	July 12	S-10
V-3	16,000	C-5	July 22	S-10
V-4	10,000	C-2	July 26	S-10
V-5	16,600	C-5	July 31	S-10
V-6	35,000	C-3	August 1	S-10
V-7	23,000	C-4	August 2	S-11

Sales by Salesperson

Salesperson Number	Quarterly Sales	Commission Rate
S-10	?	0.10
S-11	?	0.10
S-12	?	0.12
S-78	0	0.08

Customer Payments

Invoice Number	Remittance Advice Number	Amount
V-1	R-3	7,200
V-2	R-1	1,666
V-2	R-5	1,666
V-3	R-4	16,000
V-4	R-2	10,000
V-5	R-4	16,600

Customer Data

Customer Number	Customer Name	Accounts Receivable Amount	Salesperson
C-1	Dunn, Inc.	?	S-12
C-2	J. P. Carpenter	?	S-10
C-3	Mabadera Corp.	?	S-10
C-4	Ghymn and Sons	?	S-99
C-5	D. Lund, Inc.	?	S-10

FIGURE 14-19 Sample of some of the records in the Quick Jolt accounting database.

Requirements

1. In the "Sales by Invoice Number," what is the total amount of sales on invoice V-2? What was the name of the customer that made this purchase? What specific inventory items did this customer purchase? How much did this customer pay for each item?

2. Customers can choose among one of three payment options: (1) 5% discount if immediate cash payment, (2) 2% discount off list amount if total invoice paid by the 15th day of the month following purchase, or (3) deferred payment plan, using 6 monthly payments. Which option does J. P. Carpenter appear to be using for invoice V-2?

3. Using just the information provided, what are the quarterly sales amounts for salespeople S-10, S-11, and S-12?

4. Assume that customers C-1 through C-5 began this quarter with net accounts-receivable balances of zero. What are their balances now?

14-26. Kick and Swing, Inc. (Normalization Rules)

Kick and Swing Inc. is a wholesaler of sporting goods equipment for retailers in a local metropolitan area. The company buys sporting goods equipment direct from manufacturers and then resells them to individual retail stores in the regional area. The raw data in Figure 14-20 illustrate some of the

Purchase Order Number	Date	Customer Number	Customer Name	Customer Phone Number	Item Number	Item Description	Unit Cost	Unit	Quantity Ordered
12345	01/03/2011	123-8209	Charles Dresser, Inc.	(752)433-8733	X32655	Baseballs	$33.69	dozen	20
					X34598	Footballs	53.45	dozen	10
					Z34523	Bball Hoops	34.95	each	20
12346	01/03/2011	123-6733	Patrice Schmidt's Sports	(673)784-4451	X98673	Softballs	35.89	dozen	10
					X34598	Footballs	53.45	dozen	5
					X67453	Soccer balls	45.36	dozen	10

FIGURE 14-20 Some purchasing data for Kick and Swing.

information required for the company's purchase order system. As you can see, this information is characteristic of accounting purchase order systems but is not well organized. In fact, because of the repeating groups in the right-most columns, it cannot even be stored in a database.

Requirements

Store this data in a spreadsheet to make it easy to manipulate. Then perform each of the following tasks in turn:

a. Reorganize the data in first normal form. Why is your data in first normal form?

b. Reorganize the data from part 1 into second normal form. Why is your data in second normal form?

c. Reorganize the data from part 2 into third normal form. Why is your data in third normal form?

READINGS AND OTHER RESOURCES

Caserio, C., L. Marchi, and G. Pulcini. 2013. Hierarchical and relational database accounting systems: Critical aspects and trade-offs. *Lecture Notes in Information Systems and Organisation* 3: 221–231.

Geets, G. L., and O'Leary, D. E. 2015. A note on an architecture for integrating cloud computing and enterprise systems using REA. *International Journal of Accounting Information Systems* 19: 59–67.

Hunka, Frantisek. 2014. Managing Processes in the REA Framework. *Journal of Emerging Technologies in Accounting* 11(1): 27–39.

Long, J., MuellerPhillips, J., and Stefaniak, C. 2016. New database provides free access to audit research. *Journal of Accountancy* 222(5): 1–1.

Microsoft Corporation. 2017. Description of database normalization basics. Accessed online at: https://support.microsoft.com/en-us/help/283878/description-of-the-database-normalization-basics.

Moffitt, K., and M. Vasarhelyi. 2013. AIS in an age of big data. *Journal of Information Systems* 27(2): 1–19.

Go to www.wiley.com/go/simkin/videos to access videos on the following topics:

Create an ER Diagram with Visio
Introduction to Databases
Introduction to Normalization

ANSWERS TO TEST YOURSELF

1. d **2.** b **3.** b **4.** a **5.** d **6.** b **7.** c **8.** d **9.** a **10.** b **11.** c

Chapter 15

Organizing and Manipulating the Data in Databases

After reading this chapter, you will be able to:

1. *Create* tables, records, and relationships using Microsoft Access.

2. *Describe* important data-field properties as validation rules and how a database system uses them to test data inputs.

3. *Explain* "referential integrity" and how it helps ensure valid database information.

4. *Explain* the importance in extracting data from databases.

5. *Construct* multitable queries using Microsoft Access.

"Big Data is here with a vengeance.... [but] beware of the dangers. Big Data is here, but it must not permit you to be distracted from your primary task: take care of the little data."

Lyon, L. 2014. Big data: Integration with little data. *Database Journal* (February 17). Accessed at www.databasejournal.com.

15.1 INTRODUCTION

In theory, system developers should first design databases, using the techniques described in Chapter 14, and then construct them afterward, based on these designs. In practice, organizations create many commercial databases from collections of preexisting manual files, nonintegrated computerized files, personal or informal files, or the databases of acquired companies. Thus, the key databases of a company are often in a state of continuous evolution, reevaluation, and revision. While the use of big data is a hot topic, it is important to remember that the databases containing transaction data and internally generated data (i.e., the normal "little data") are vital to organizations and their success.

The previous chapter introduced the concept of databases and discussed data modeling—the process of designing database tables. This chapter focuses on how to construct a functioning database in Microsoft Access. We begin with a discussion of the software used to create databases (i.e., database management systems) and then describe how to create Access 2016 database tables in practice. After that, we discuss how to retrieve and manipulate the data in database tables using queries.

15.2 CREATING DATABASE TABLES IN MICROSOFT ACCESS

After you have normalized your database data, you are ready to create database tables and input records. Typically, you complete these tasks with a database management system.

Database Management Systems

A **database management system (DBMS)** is a software that enables users to create, delete, query (i.e., select subsets of records for viewing or analysis), alter the information stored in records, and reorganize records as needed. This section explains how to perform some of these tasks in greater detail.

A DBMS is not a database. Rather, a DBMS is a separate computer system that enables users to create, modify, and utilize database information efficiently, thus allowing businesses to separate their database system operations from their accounting applications. This enables organizations to change record structures, queries, and report formats without also having to reprogram the accounting software that accesses these database items. It also enables businesses to upgrade either system independently of other systems.

Examples of DBMS packages include Microsoft Access, Cloudera, Datameer, and Toad. Examples of DBMSs that run on client/server systems or mainframes include Microsoft SQL Server, DB2, Oracle, MySQL, and Sybase. Most DBMSs are single-user systems, whereas others (for larger applications) are multiuser systems. Each system is limited in how many concurrent users it can support, the maximum number of transactions per hour it can process, and so forth. Also, not every accounting package can interface with every database, so managers should make sure that any new accounting software they acquire can also work with their existing databases, and vice versa.

Using Microsoft Access

Microsoft Access is a popular database that many businesses and individuals use for small database applications. The procedures for creating tables and entering records in several alternative database systems are similar to those used in Access, so Access is a good software package to know. Employers prefer accounting students with database skills, so hands-on familiarity with a DBMS package is vital. This chapter illustrates database concepts using Access 2016.

After launching Access 2016, click on the "Blank desktop database" icon on the top portion of the screen, and you will launch the option to open a new blank database (Figure 15-1). The panel in Figure 15-1 asks you to name your database. The default name is "Database1," but you should rename your database something more meaningful—for example, "My First Database" (blanks are permitted in Access database names).

Your next task is to decide where to store the database. To do this, click on the file-folder icon to the right of the filename textbox. Clicking on this icon will in turn display Microsoft's "Save As" dialog box that enables you to select where to store your database. After you have done this, click on the "Create" button at the bottom of the dialog box in Figure 15-1 to finish creating your database.

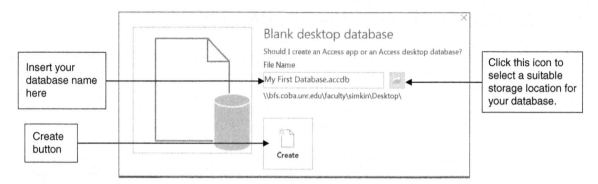

FIGURE 15-1   The dialog box for creating, naming, and storing a database in Access.

Creating Database Tables

You use database tables to store data about specific entities—for example, customers, vendors, or employees. To illustrate how to create tables in Access, we will create a table of employee records similar to the one we previously described in Figure 14-1.

Defining a Record Format.   After defining your database name and indicating where to store it (from Figure 15-1), Access will display a screen similar to Figure 15-2. This Home screen has several other menu tabs: File, Home (the one selected), Create, External Data, Database Tools, Fields, and Table. Because you can customize these menus choices, yours may differ. Each tab setting has several choices as well. Within the Home tab in Figure 15-2, for example, there are options for Views, Clipboard, Sort & Filter, Records, Find, and Text Formatting.

Your first task is to create a new table. When you begin to create a new database, Access will normally provide you with one at the start. If not, you can click on the "Create" tab and then click "Table." Access supplies the default name "Table1," as shown in Figure 15-3.

Figure 15-3 also illustrates the **navigation pane** on the left, which lists the tables, queries, forms, and reports for a database. Figure 15-3 also shows the **navigation bar** at the bottom, which enables you to navigate from record to record.

Before you enter data in a new database table, you must first define the **record structure** for that table. *It is much easier to spend time developing this format prior to entering data than to spend hours changing it later.*

Figure 15-4 displays the form for defining the record fields and field properties for the tables in your database. To get to this screen, click on the View menu option in Figure 15-3 and select "Design View" from the set of choices. Access may first ask you

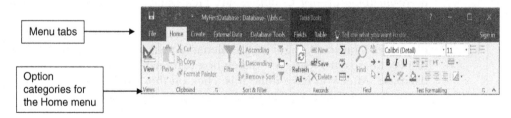

FIGURE 15-2   The Home menu for Microsoft Access 2016.

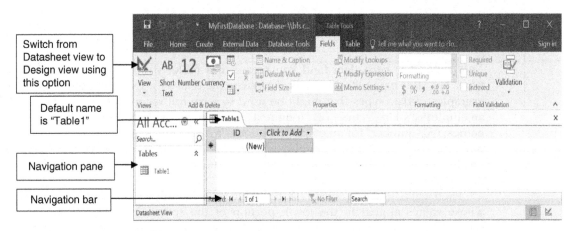

Switch from Datasheet view to Design view using this option

Default name is "Table1"

Navigation pane

Navigation bar

FIGURE 15-3   Opening screen for creating a table.

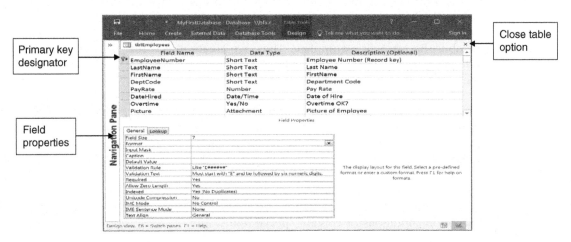

Primary key designator

Field properties

FIGURE 15-4   Defining the data structure of an employee table. For each data field, you must provide the field name (e.g., EmployeeNumber), data type (Short Text), and a description (optional).

to name and save your table. Name the table "tblEmployees" or some similar name. (The prefix "tbl" is the conventional naming prefix for a table.)

A screen similar to the one in Figure 15-4 will appear—the template for creating the data fields of your records. There are three columns that you need to complete for each data field: (1) Field Name (which is required), (2) Data Type (also required), and (3) Description (optional). Let's look at each of these items separately.

Field Name.   To define a record format, begin by typing the name of the first data field you wish to create—for example, the term "EmployeeNumber" (without spaces)—in the top row of the first column in Figure 15-3. It is best not to embed blanks in field names. Two other rules to follow when naming data fields are: (1) use mnemonic names (that help you remember their use such as "ZipCode") and (2) do not use long names (which are cumbersome to type). Although it isn't obvious from Figure 15-4, you can use the same field names in different tables because the field names in different tables are completely independent of one another. In fact, using the same field names for the same data—for example, "VendorNumber"—in both a Vendor table and a Vendor

Invoices table often makes sense because this makes it easy to identify the data field that can link the tables together. We'll look at this shortly.

Data Type. For each data field you create in a table, you must also specify a **data type**. The data type tells Access how to store the data—for example, as a date. Several examples of data types that might be used in a payroll record are: (1) "short text" for an employee's First Name, (2) "long text" for memos, explanations, and other lengthy entries, (3) "number" for an employee's hours worked, (4) "currency" for an employee's pay rate, (5) "date" for an employee's date of hire, (6) "Yes/No" for an employee's qualifications to earn overtime pay, and (7) "attachment" for attaching pictures, word documents, and spreadsheet files.

Each data field you specify for a table also includes a set of **field properties**, whose values appear in the lower portion of the screen in Figure 15-4. These are settings for such items as the "field size" (e.g., a maximum length of 7 characters), "format" (e.g., a number with a percent sign for a number data field), and "input mask" (e.g., an input template for entering a phone number in a specific format). Figure 15-4 shows the field properties for the EmployeeNumber field in our table. We define this as a "short text" data field rather than a "number" because it is a code rather than a number that we will manipulate. Thus, we create it as a text field and limit its Field Size property to 7 characters (see the bottom portion of Figure 15-4). We shall examine these settings in greater detail shortly.

Finally, if you use a "number" data type, you may also wish to select the type of number you wish to use—for example, Integer, Long Integer, Single (a small decimal value), or Double (a large decimal value). These choices are important when using numeric data fields to link tables together—the data-type fields must match for the link to work.

Description. The description is an optional field. However, as you can see from the figure, data field descriptions help document the table itself and can also describe exception conditions or contain special notes.

Identifying a Primary Key. The **primary key** is the data field that uniquely identifies each record. After you have defined the data fields in your table, you should designate a primary key—for example, the Employee Number here. One way to designate the primary key is to right click on a field name and then select the "Primary Key" (🔑) choice from the drop-down menu that appears. Another way is to select the primary key icon from among the icons in the Design menu at the top of the screen. The end result in either case will be the same—a little key icon appearing in the first column opposite the data field you selected, designating the primary key for the table (see Figure 15-4).

Saving a Table. You can save your current work at any time using Ctrl+S or by selecting "Save" from the File Menu tab. If you attempt to close your table at this point (by clicking on the X on the upper-right portion of the screen), Access will also prompt you to save the table.

Creating Relationships

After creating your tables, it is important to know how to create relationships between the tables. Chapter 14 explains that these relationships link tables together. Links also

	Field Name	Data Type	Description (Optional)
🔑	DepartmentCode	Short Text	Department Code
	Manager	Short Text	Manager
	Location	Short Text	Building Number
	DepartmentPhone	Short Text	Phone Number of Administrative Assistant

tblDepartments

FIGURE 15-5 The record structure for the Departments table.

enable users to create multitable reports, such as the one in Figure 14-3. To illustrate how to create relationships in Access, assume that you have created a department table with records similar to the one in Figure 14-2. Figure 15-5 illustrates the record structure for this table, which we named "tblDepartments." The department code is the primary key for this table.

You now have two tables—"tblDepartments" and "tblEmployees." They are related in a one-to-many relationship because each department has many employees, but each employee is in only one department. The department code is common to both tables, although its data-field name differs slightly from one table to another. (We purposely used different names to demonstrate the fact that the field names do not have to match in order to link tables.) This field will act as the foreign key in the Employees table. To create a relationship between the two tables, follow these steps:

Step 1: Select the Tables You Wish to Use. Click on the "Database Tools" tab (refer back to Figure 15-2) and then click on the "Relationships" choice within this menu. A dialog box of possible tables should automatically appear. If not, click the "Show Table" option from the Design menu. Now, from the tables listed in the "Show Tables" dialog box, click on the tables you wish to link (i.e., the tblEmployees and tblDepartments tables). In the relationships window, boxes for both tables should appear as shown in Figure 15-6A.

Step 2: Link the Tables. To link the two tables together, drag and drop the department code name from either table to the similar name in the other table. When you do, you

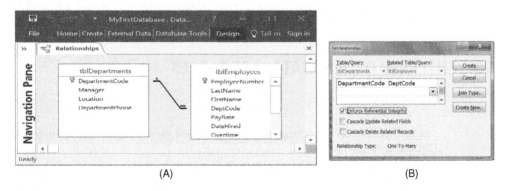

(A)   (B)

FIGURE 15-6 Linking tables and enforcing referential integrity. (A) A relationships window for linking records. (B) Enforcing Referential integrity.

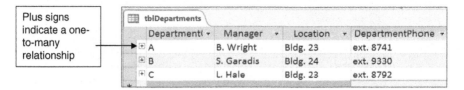

FIGURE 15-7 The departments table with expansion (+) symbols, indicating a one-to-many relationship between "Departments" and "Employees."

should also see the Edit Relationships dialog window of Figure 15-6B. This window enables you to enforce **referential integrity**. Check the "Enforce Referential Integrity" box. In the context of this example, referential integrity is a control that prohibits users from creating employee records with references to nonexistent departments. (However, it does not affect your ability to create a department with no employees.)

If you follow these steps successfully, you should end up with a Relationships window with linked tables as shown in Figure 15-6(A). The line with symbols "1" and "∞" identifies the one-to-many relationship of the two tables. What you've done is link the tables together, using the department code as a foreign key in the Employees table. One dramatic way to see this linkage is to open the Departments table in run view (Figure 15-7). Note that there are now plus signs to the left of each department, indicating linked records. If you click on one of these plus marks with your mouse, you'll be able to see these records. Although it isn't obvious, the relationship you've created for your two tables will also enable you to create multitable reports. We explain how to do that in Chapter 16.

The database tables that we have constructed are simple, text-based files, but it is important to recognize that databases can handle a wide variety of data formats. For example, database records can also store hypertext links (to websites), graphics files, video files, audio files, spreadsheet files, and so on. For example, real-estate brokers store pictures and narrated tours of listed properties, police departments store "mug shots" and voice prints of prisoners, and publishing houses store descriptions of their books. Your employer could use a database to store your picture in an employee file or even your current location using a GPS locator in your mobile device.

Case-in-Point 15.1 Did you know that when you post pictures to sites like Facebook or Google+, you may be revealing your location? Picture files taken with phones or other devices with GPS contain metadata that identify the exact location where the picture was taken. If you do not want this information posted with your photos, use a metadata editor to remove it or turn off the GPS function on your phone or camera before taking pictures.

15.3 ENTERING DATA IN DATABASE TABLES

Creating Records

After specifying the names, data types, sizes, descriptions, and primary key for the data fields in your tables, you can enter individual records for it. To do so, you must switch to "datasheet" (or run) view. An easy way to do this is select the "Datasheet" view from the "View" menu on the upper-left portion of the Access screen in Figure 15-3. After making these choices, you should see a screen similar to this figure. This is a table in *datasheet view*, and you are now free to input the data for individual records. Begin by entering data in the row with the asterisk (*), and use the tab key to transition from data field to data field. Every time you complete the data entry for a new record, Access will save the record in the appropriate table automatically.

If you make a mistake while entering data, you can use your backspace key or delete key to correct it just as you would when correcting text in a word processor. You can also delete an entire record by clicking on the first column to select an entire row (record) and then hitting the delete key. Because Access saves changes immediately, it will first remind you (via a small dialog box) that such a change will be permanent. If you indicate that this is your intent, Access will proceed to delete the record.

Ensuring Valid and Accurate Data Entry

The **data definition language (DDL)** of a DBMS enables users to define the record structure of any particular database table (i.e., the individual fields that each record will contain). Thus, DDL is the language that DBMSs use to create the data dictionaries that we described in Chapter 14. Well-conceived record structures also serve as controls over the accuracy of critical accounting data. For example, good data definitions could prevent errors such as typing "4)" instead of "40" for hours worked, "NU" instead of "NY" for the state code in a mailing address, or "UPC" instead of "UPS" for the shipper code. Although it is impossible to guard against every possible type of error, database designers can use the following tools found in typical DBMSs to catch many of them.

We will use the Parking Ticket database described in Chapter 14 to discuss methods for defining and extracting data from a database. Figure 15-8 illustrates the tables and relationships for this database. Note in this figure that there is a one-to-many relationship between "car registrations" and "tickets" (each car can have more than one ticket, but each ticket is for one car only) and also a one-to-many relationship between "parking violations" and "tickets" (each ticket is for one violation).

Most DBMSs enable users to make specific settings for the data fields in tables. In Access, you can make such settings using the field properties such as the one in Figure 15-4. In accounting applications, these settings include the following.

Proper Data Types for Fields. Using Microsoft Access, one input control is inherent in the data type that you assign to a particular data field. For example, if you create a

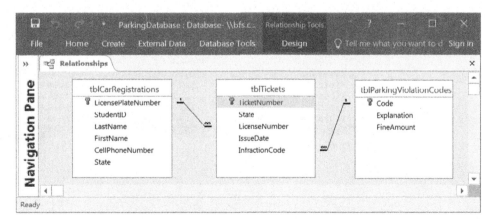

FIGURE 15-8 The tables and relationships for a parking database.

data field as a "number" data type, Access will reject all character inputs that are not numbers. Similarly, if you declare a data field as a "date" data type, Access will reject all input values (including alphabetic letters or punctuation marks) that cannot be part of a date. This is why it is often better to use data types other than "short text" for data fields.

Input Masks. **Input masks** limit user inputs to specific formats—for example, "123-45-6789" for a Social Security number, "(987) 456-7890" for a telephone number, or "7/9/18" for a date. Although system designers use special symbols for the mask, the DBMS interprets these symbols as input requirements and acts accordingly. At data-entry time, the user will see the formatted part of the mask. For example, this is the results of a mask designed for a Social Security number " ___-__ - ____". Input masks help users input data correctly by indicating a general input format, thereby reducing data-entry errors. Such masks also enable the system to reject incompatible data—for example, a letter input for a numeric field.

Default Values. A third control over the accuracy of data entry is to specify a **default value** for the data fields of new records. For example, a weekly payroll table might use the number "40" as the default value for the hours-worked data field. These default values help guard against input errors as well as speed data entry.

Drop-Down Lists. You have likely seen combo boxes on Web pages that contain drop-down lists of choices—for example, a list of shirt sizes of S, M, L, and XL. Databases like Access enable you to create similar lists for one or more of your table records. For example, the drop-down list in Figure 15-9 allows data-entry personnel to select a valid parking-infraction code. Drop-down lists are convenient alternatives to typing data manually. They also control input errors because (with specific settings) they can limit user entries to valid values. In Access, another advantage of using combo boxes is that you can store the choices for them separate tables, thereby enabling users to alter their values as needs require.

Validation Rules. One of the most versatile data entry controls is the ability to create custom validation tests using a **validation rule**. Using Microsoft Access, for example, you create such rules as a record-structure property of a data field. Figure 15-10

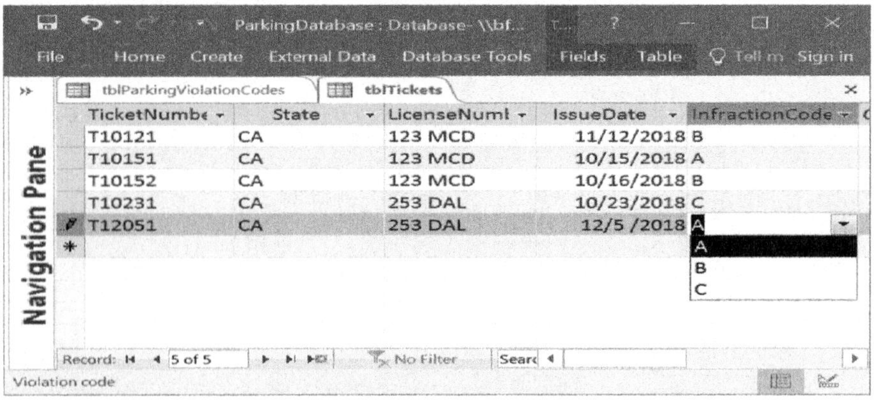

FIGURE 15-9 A drop-down list for the infraction code of the Tickets table.

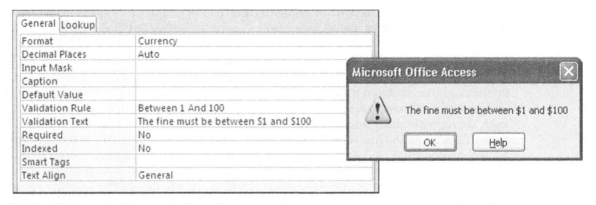

FIGURE 15-10   (Left) The properties window for the fine amount data field of the Ticket table. (Right) The error message that a user would see if he or she attempts to enter a value for this field that falls outside the specified range.

illustrates an example for the "Fine amount" data field of the Ticket table. This (numeric) data field shows the amount of money that a person must pay for a particular ticket. In Figure 15-10, the expression "Between 1 And 100" that appears in the Validation Rule specifies the acceptable range of values. The error message in the message box on the right displays the "Validation Text" that you specify in this field's properties window. This is what appears when a user attempts to enter a value (such as "200") that falls outside the allowable range.

Validation rules can be simple, such as the one in Figure 15-10, or more complex. For example, Access also enables you to use mathematical computations, predefined functions, and logical operators to create more complex validation rules. An example is "Between 1 And 100 AND Not 77," which means that the entry value must fall in the specified range and cannot be "77." Another example is "Between [StartDate] and [EndDate]," which means that the date entered must be between an employee's hire date and his or her termination date.

Case-in-Point 15.2   You have probably encountered validation rules many times when you signed up for online accounts that require passwords. Most systems require passwords to: have a minimum length, contain numbers and letters, and perhaps also include special characters or capital letters. Validation rules regulate the passwords that you can successfully create.

Referential Integrity.   A final data-entry control is to enforce **referential integrity** in relational databases. This feature controls for certain inconsistencies among the records in relational tables. Consider, for example, the possibility of *deleting* a parking violations code record from the third database table in Figure 15-8 (e.g., deleting the record for Code A—meter expired). We can't allow such a deletion because this would disrupt all of the *references* to that record in the Tickets table. For the same reason, we can't allow new records in the Tickets table to reference nonexistent codes in the parking violations code file—for example, a ticket with code "Z" (if such a code didn't exist). This would be a parking ticket for a nonexistent violation.

DBMSs make it easy to enforce referential integrity. In Access, for example, you simply check a box in the Edit Relationships dialog window at the time that you create the relationship—see Figure 15-6B. This enforcement performs two vital functions.

First, it does not allow record deletions in the "parent" table of a one-to-many relationship. Second, it does not allow a user to create a new record in the "many" table of a one-to-many relationship that references a nonexistent record on the "one" side. Case 15-20 illustrates these concepts in more detail.

In Figure 15-6B, note that the Edit Relationships window in Access provides two additional boxes that you might check: one that allows "cascade update related fields" and one that allows "cascade delete related records." These options enable you to override the referential integrity rules just described (although Access will warn you first). If you chose the first option, for example, you could delete a record in the Parking Violations Code File, and Access would also delete the reference to that record in the records of the Ticket File. (This would not be desirable here because it might leave you with tickets in the Tickets File with no violation code in them.) The second option allows you to delete a record from the one side of a one-to-many relationship, even if there are matching records on the many side. For example, if you delete a record in the Car Registration table, Access will then delete all the ticket records associated with that record (car) in the Ticket File table.

Tips for Creating Database Tables and Records

The preceding discussions described how to create tables and records in an Access database. There are many things that can go wrong when performing these tasks. Here are some guidelines to help you avoid them:

1. **Design first; create tables and records last.** Some people don't have time to do things right—only time to do things over. Don't be one of them. A careful definition of database entities and their relationships can prevent many problems later.

2. **Name tables systematically and use the conventional *tbl* prefix.** Even small databases can contain many tables, queries, forms, and reports. Using conventional prefixes such as "tbl" for tables and "qry" for queries enables database designers to distinguish among them. You may also find it useful to name related tables systematically—for example, use names like "tblCustomerMasterFile" or "tblCustomerReturns" for different types of customer files.

3. **Use mnemonic names for data fields.** Each data field within a record must have a name, and mnemonic names help you remember what each field means. For example, the name "State" is better than "Address Line 3" to represent the data field for the customer's state. Similarly, the names "StateAbbreviation" or "StateCode" may even be better if you allocate just two digits for this field. Finally, it is preferable to omit spaces when naming fields—for example, to define a field "StateCode" rather than "State Code."

4. **Assign correct and consistent data types to data fields.** If you plan to manipulate a data field mathematically, you must define this field as a number—not as a text field. You should use short-text data types for such fields as Social Security, credit card numbers, or phone numbers. These "numbers" are really codes that can be too long to store as numbers, but ones that Access can store easily as text values.

5. **Make certain that the data fields used to link tables together are the same data type.** If you use the data fields from separate tables to link two tables together, these fields *must* be the exact same data type. This is because you cannot link tables together if the foreign key in one table is, for example, a *text* field and the other is

a *date* field. As noted earlier, when using "number" data fields, the *type* of number must also match—for example, one data field cannot be an Integer data type and the other be a long integer data type. Violating this rule is one of the most common errors novices make when creating database tables and relationships in Access.

6. **Limit the size of data fields to reasonable lengths.** Access assigns a default size of "255" characters to text fields. If, for example, you designate a state code of only two digits, you should change the default size to two digits. This will limit users to entering no more than two digits. A similar guideline applies to Social Security numbers, telephone numbers, product numbers, and similar values of predetermined and fixed length.

7. **Use input masks.** As explained earlier, an input mask is a template that defines the required data format for a data field. An example of a phone number input mask is (999) 000-0000, which limits the values in a phone number field to 10 numeric digits. Input masks help ensure accurate data input and help reduce errors.

15.4 EXTRACTING DATA FROM DATABASES: DATA MANIPULATION LANGUAGES (DMLs)

The totality of the information in a database and the relationships between its tables are called the database **schema**. Thus, the schema is a map or plan of the entire database. Using the previous student-parking example, the schema would be all the information that a university might store about car registrations and parking tickets (see again Figure 15-8).

Any particular user or application program will normally be interested in (or might be limited to) only a subset of the information in the database. This limited access is a **subschema** or *view*. For example, one subschema for our parking database might be the information required by the university registrar—the student's name, number, and outstanding parking tickets. Subschemas are important design elements of a database because they dictate what data each user needs and also because they protect sensitive data from unauthorized access.

The terms *schema* and *subschema* describe a simple idea—the distinction between the *design* of a database on one hand and the *uses* of a database on the other. The goal is to design a database schema that is flexible enough to create all of the subschemas required by users. The following sections describe several ways to create subschemas.

Creating Select Queries

The purchasing agent of a manufacturing company needs to know what inventory balances are below their reorder points. A payroll manager wants to know which employees are eligible to receive year-end bonuses. A tax assessor is interested in those areas of the city that have experienced the most real estate appreciation.

What these individuals have in common is the need for specific information from one or more database tables. **Queries** allow database developers to create customized subschemas. For example, using the car registration database, you might want to (1) find out who owns a certain car parked on campus because the car's lights are on, (2) change the information in a specific record (e.g., update a student's phone number), (3) delete a record (e.g., because the person sells his or her car), or (4) list file information selectively (e.g., prepare a list of all students with California license plates). A **dynaset** is a dynamic subset of a database that you create with such queries, and the purpose of a **data manipulation language (DML)** is to help you create such dynasets.

> **Case-in-Point 15.3** Internal auditors must evaluate internal controls, an organization's operational efficiency, its business risks, and other critical success factors. The volume of data that internal auditors examine has expanded rapidly over the past decade, and internal auditors are developing new tools and testing procedures to detect risks and operational inefficiencies in complex environments. This is why knowing how to conduct database queries is now a valuable and important skill for internal auditors.

You can create several types of queries with Access 2016. One is a simple *select query* that references only one table. Another combines the information from several tables. A third type is an action query. We look at each of these queries in the following sections.

One-Table Select Queries. A **select query** creates a dynaset of database information based on two types of user-specified criteria: (1) criteria that determine which records to include and (2) criteria that determine which data fields to include *from* those records. Figure 15-11 illustrates a simple select query that displays particular information from a single table using Microsoft Access. This example asks the system to display the last name, first name, cell phone number, license plate state, and license plate number for all cars with California license plates.

Single Criterion. To create a simple select query, first click the Create tab on the main menu (refer back to Figure 15-2). In the Create menu, click "Query Design." Access will display a small dialog box that allows you to select the table(s) on which to base your query. To create the query in Figure 15-11, we only need the tblCarRegistrations table. Click on the tblCarRegistrations table and then click on the "Add" button.

The bottom portion of Figure 15-11 shows the layout in which to enter your data fields and the selection criteria for them. Your next task is to select the data fields in

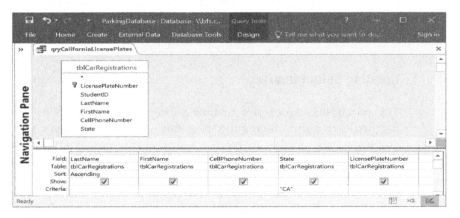

FIGURE 15-11 A simple query to select all car registrations with CA (California) license plates.

each record you wish to display. An easy way to do this is to double click on the field names in the table. Select the fields from this list as you continue to add field names to the query across the panel until you have selected all the fields you need.

Next, you must specify the selection criteria for the query. For example, to display only those records with California licenses, enter "CA" in the criteria box under "State." You will see that CA is now enclosed with quotation marks, which Access automatically adds for you. Basic comparison operators are also available for setting criteria—that is, = (equals), < (less than), > (greater than), >= (greater than or equal to), <= (less than or equal to), and <> (not equal to). For example, in a database of payroll records, the expression "<=60" for the HoursWorked field in a query would enable you to identify all employees who worked less than or equal to 60 hours.

You are now ready to run the query. To do this, click the exclamation point with the word "Run" on the left portion of the main menu. The results of your query will appear as shown in Figure 15-12. You can toggle back and forth between design and run modes by clicking on the View options in the Results section of the left side of the main menu.

After you have created a query, most DBMSs enable you to save it in a separate file for later use, thus eliminating the need to rewrite it. This allows end users to run premade queries that are created by designers and database experts. The letters "qry" are the standard naming prefix for queries. Thus, as you can see in Figure 15-12, we named our query "qryCaliforniaLicensePlates."

Multiple Criteria. It is also possible to specify multiple criteria in a query. For example, suppose that you wanted a list of all car registrants whose cars had California license plates *and* whose last names were "Curry." To create such a query in Access, simply type the name "Curry" in the "Last Name" column and in the *same* Criteria row as the "CA." Access interprets criteria appearing in the same row as an "and" operation. The results will be all those records with last name "Curry" *and* whose license plate state is "CA." Similarly, if you specify three criteria in the same row, then Access will find database records in the table satisfying all three requirements.

Sometimes, you might want to search for records that satisfy alternate requirements—for example, car registrants whose cars have either California license plates *or* Oregon license plates. To create such a query in Access, use multiple lines at the bottom of the Query dialog box in Figure 15-11. The result of this query

FIGURE 15-12 The results of the query in Figure 15-11. Note that the name of the query is qryCaliforniaLicensePlates.

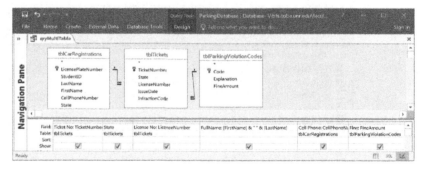

FIGURE 15-13 A multitable query—the results of the query in Figure 15-14.

will be all records that satisfy *either* requirement. The query output will also include records satisfying both requirements.

Multitable Select Queries. Many accounting applications require information from two or more database tables. For example, suppose that you wanted to create a listing of tickets similar to the one in Figure 15-13. Notice that this query draws information from all three of our tables—the ticket number (from the Tickets table), the owner's first and last names (from the CarRegistrations table), and the fine amount (from the ParkingViolationCodes table).

To construct this query, follow the steps outlined earlier for creating simple queries, but be sure to include all three tables in your query design before you begin to select data fields. Then select the fields shown in Figure 15-14. The results should be similar to those shown in Figure 15-13.

The tasks performed by a query like the one shown in Figure 15-14 are nontrivial. To appreciate this, imagine that you had to create the report described earlier manually. Assume that there were over 1,000 parking tickets and over 20,000 car registration records in the database. Sorting and organizing the records would take weeks. A computerized DBMS can accomplish this task and print the results almost immediately—an amazing accomplishment if you think about it!

Case-in-Point 15.4 The power of simple queries using Microsoft Access was what enabled internal auditors to discover the fraud at WorldCom.[1]

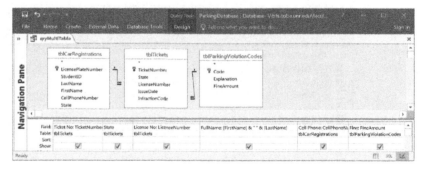

FIGURE 15-14 A multitable query.

---

[1] Loraas, T., and D. Searcy, 2010. Using queries to automate journal entry tests: Agile Machinery Group, Inc. *Issues in Accounting Education* 25(1): 155–174.

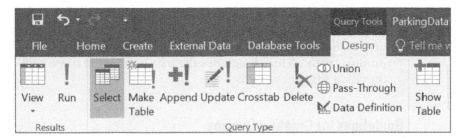

FIGURE 15-15   Some types of Action queries.

Creating Action Queries

The select queries described earlier extract information from database tables, but some accounting tasks require users to update or delete multiple records in a single operation. Microsoft Access supports the **action queries** listed as follows. You can create any of these queries by selecting the appropriate choice from the options that appear at the top of the screen after clicking on Create/Query design (see Figure 15-15).

1. ***Make-table queries*** enable you to create a new table from the records that you select in an existing table. For example, a university might want to create a separate table of all graduating seniors. Auditors might use a make-table query to create a separate table of all records that have been deleted in order to maintain an audit trail.

2. ***Append queries*** enable you to append records from one table to the end of another table. Accounting examples include the ability to add the payroll records for the current period to a year-to-date table or to consolidate the employees from two departments into a single table.

3. ***Update queries*** enable you to alter selected table records systematically. Accounting examples include the ability to raise the retail prices of particular products by 10%, raise the salaries of all those employees with high performance ratings by 5%, or delete a handling charge for all customers with purchases over a set limit.

4. ***Crosstab queries*** enable you to perform a statistical analysis of the data in a table and provide the cross-tabulation results in a row-and-column format similar to a pivot table in Excel. For example, a crosstab query might show the average invoice amount for each vendor in a vendor table or the average credit purchase amount for customers living in selected zip codes.

5. ***Delete queries*** enable you to delete table records selectively. Examples include the ability to delete employees who have left the organization, students who drop out of school or graduate from school, or inventory products no longer sold by the company.

Some other queries that are available through the Access Query Wizard are:

1. ***Find-duplicates queries*** enable you to find those records with duplicate entries. Many common auditing tasks require such queries—for example, finding duplicate customer orders, finding employees with the same Social Security or employee numbers, or finding different vendor records with the same address. Note that a simple select query might enable you to find *one example* of such duplicates. A find-duplicates query enables you to find *all duplicates* with a single query.

2. **Find-unmatched queries** enable you to find the records in one table with no matching record in another table. For example, such queries enable auditors to identify (1) those payroll records with no matching master employee records, (2) those products with no matching sales the past year, or (3) those vendor invoices with no matching supplier records.

Guidelines for Creating Queries

The preceding discussions described various kinds of select queries and action queries. Here are some guidelines to help you create error-free queries using Microsoft Access:

1. **Spell accurately and be sensitive to capitalization.** The criteria for Access select queries are case sensitive. For example, you will not get matches if you specify California licenses as "Cal" or "Ca" in a criteria line if the entries in the underlying database table are "CA."
2. **Specify AND and OR operations correctly.** If you want a query to satisfy two conditions simultaneously (i.e., to perform an AND operation), enter the criteria on the *same line* of your query. If you want a query to satisfy *either* of two conditions (i.e., perform an OR operation), place them on separate criteria lines.
3. **Join tables properly.** If you wish to construct a multitable query, the tables should first be joined properly in the Access Relationships window.
4. **Name queries systematically.** Query names should begin with the standard "qry" prefix. It also helps to assign mnemonic query names—for example, "qryCustomersInCalifornia" or "qryGraduatingSeniors."
5. **Choose data fields selectively.** Avoid including fields in your query that are not needed in the desired output. Extra fields tend to clutter reports and, accordingly, may do more harm than good.

Structured Query Language (SQL)

Another name for a DML is *data query language*. The American National Standards Institute (ANSI) has adopted standards for one such query language: **structured query language (SQL)**. This language is important because most relational databases support it, including Microsoft Access. Figure 15-16 shows how to request records with California license plates using SQL.

SQL is a useful tool for auditors because understanding SQL allows an auditor to retrieve data from many database systems, both small and large. In most contemporary business environments, an auditor can no longer retrieve data from paper reports. Instead, data must be acquired from the computerized accounting information

```
SELECT (LastName, FirstName, PhoneNumber, LicPlateState, LicPlateNo)
FROM ttblCarRegistrations
WHERE LicPlateState = CA;
```

FIGURE 15-16   An example of SQL instructions for the example of Figure 15-11. These instructions will list the last name, first name, phone number, license plate state, and license plate number of all cars with license plate state code "CA."

system (AIS). SQL allows a user to specify the table and fields that the user wants to retrieve, using commands such as FROM, SELECT, and WHERE. FROM identifies the table source, and SELECT chooses the data fields to include in the query. The WHERE command specifies the search criteria, such as selecting sales orders in excess of a specified dollar amount.

Sorting, Indexing, and Database Programming

In addition to accessing or listing records selectively, a DBMS also enables you to reorganize a table. One way to do this is by sorting records, which means physically rewriting records on a disk in the desired order. This is both time-consuming and usually unnecessary. It is faster and easier to **index** your records (by setting the Indexed property to "Yes" in Figure 15-10), which simply creates a table of record keys and disk addresses that accomplishes the same purpose as sorting. Thus, when users specify "sort" in queries, Access does not physically reorder records, but instead temporarily assembles the information in the specified order for display purposes. If you look carefully at the query specifications at the bottom of Figure 15-11, you will note the requirement to "sort" the records by last name.

Finally, even the best DBMS software cannot anticipate every user's processing needs. For this reason, advanced DBMSs include programming tools that enable users to develop their own processing applications. Users commonly develop customized data-entry screens, which enable them to include better data descriptions and more detailed instructions for data entry personnel on the input screens. Similarly, programming languages enable users to create custom processing routines—for example, to create their own data-validation routines. This end-user programming is important because it can enable users to perform their own data processing without the technical assistance of IT professionals.

AIS AT WORK
Finding Patterns in Financial Disclosures[2]

Typically, we think about looking for patterns in numbers when talking about data mining. For example, a firm might want to learn which products generate the most profits during different seasons, or it may seek to better understand its customers' purchasing patterns. Data mining, however, can also be applied to text, such as stories in the popular press, corporate e-mail, and even the financial statements themselves. Auditors, regulators, financial analysts, and investors may soon have a wide array of data mining tools available for predicting firms' future performance.

The SEC requires all publicly traded firms to file electronically, which has created a huge volume of corporate filings that users can mine to discover patterns in data. A new data mining technique involves analyses of the Management Discussion and Analysis (MD&A) section of the 10-K form, which the SEC requires. The MD&A is a narrative where management describes the prior year's results and discusses future

---

[2] Cecchini, M., H. Aytug, G. Koehler, and P. Pathak, 2010. Making words work: Using financial text as a predictor of financial events. *Decision Support Systems* 50(1): 164–175.

plans. The new data mining technique identifies firms that are likely to experience financial distress (such as bankruptcy) by studying the words in the MD&A section.

The main idea is to develop lists of keywords that are associated with firms that go bankrupt by examining the MD&A of all firms that go bankrupt during a period of time. Then, the system scans an individual firm's MD&A and determines whether there is a pattern of key words that is similar to those found for bankrupt firms. When the similarity is high, the likelihood of bankruptcy is also high. According to its developers, the system accurately distinguishes between firms that go bankrupt versus those that do not go bankrupt with 80% accuracy. Again, this prediction is based solely on the statements made by management in the MD&A, without any examination of the actual financial data. If analyzing only management statements can help predict bankruptcy, then advanced data mining systems that simultaneously analyze financial data, media coverage, MD&A, e-mails, and so on, may prove to have substantial predictive accuracy.

SUMMARY

✓ Database management systems (DBMSs) enable users to create their own databases using data definition languages (DDLs) and to manipulate file data using data manipulation languages (DMLs).

✓ Designers can integrate a variety of data-validation techniques to help ensure data integrity. Examples include choosing data types carefully for data fields, using input masks, using default values, creating a wide variety of validation rules, and enforcing referential integrity.

✓ Microsoft Access is a popular database management system that small businesses can use to create complete accounting systems. The final section illustrates the techniques you can use to create database tables and records with this software.

✓ An important use of databases is to extract selected information from it, and Access provides a number of tools for constructing select queries and action queries. These tools allow users to extract data from a single table or from multiple tables. Following the guidelines in this chapter can help you avoid errors when creating such queries.

✓ Structured query language (SQL) is a language for extracting information from databases that has been standardized by the American National Standards Institute (ANSI).

KEY TERMS YOU SHOULD KNOW

action queries	dynaset	record structure
data definition language (DDL)	field properties	referential integrity
data manipulation language (DML)	indexing	schema
data type	input masks	select query
database management system (DBMS)	navigation bar (Access)	structured query language (SQL)
default value	navigation pane (Access)	subschema
	primary key	validation rule
	queries	

TEST YOURSELF

Q15-1. What types of data can be stored in modern databases?

 a. Text and graphics only

 b. Text only

 c. Text, graphics, video files, audio files, and programming code

 d. None of the above can be stored in databases

Q15-2. The difference between (1) a database management system (DBMS) and (2) a database, is:

 a. nothing—these terms are synonyms

 b. the first is hardware, the second is software

 c. the first is program software, the second is proprietary data and related files

 d. the first refers to a complete accounting system, the second refers to a subset of that

Q15-3. An example of a *validation rule* is:

 a. an input value must be an integer

 b. an input value must also have a default value

 c. an input value must be between 0 and 40

 d. you cannot delete parent records that have child records associated with them

Q15-4. To construct a select query in Microsoft Access in which you want to satisfy two conditions simultaneously—that is, implement an *And* operation—you should:

 a. specify both criteria in *separate fields* of the Criteria line of the query

 b. specify both criteria in the *same field* of the Criteria line of the query

 c. specify each criteria in *separate fields and in separate Criteria lines* of the query

 d. give up; this is not possible in Microsoft Access.

Q15-5. To adjust the minimum wage of all payroll employees to the current federal level, you should use a(n):

 a. update query

 b. append query

 c. find minimums query

 d. tax expert

Q15-6. To identify all those employees receiving payroll checks but who have no matching record in a payroll master file, you should use a(n):

 a. auditor

 b. find unmatched records query

 c. crosstabs query

 d. update query

Q15-7. All of the following are examples of DBMSs *except*:

 a. Access

 b. Oracle

 c. DB2

 d. SQL

Q15-8. All of the following are examples of action queries *except:*

 a. update query

 b. append query

 c. delete query

 d. find missing data query

Q15-9. The difference between (1) using an update query and (2) updating a single record is:

 a. nothing—these are the same thing

 b. the first updates all selected records, the second only affects one record

 c. the first updates more than one table, the second updates only one record

 d. none of these is correct

Q15-10. SQL is an example of:

 a. a tool to perform online analytical processing

 b. a database management system

 c. a query language

 d. a multimedia database

DISCUSSION QUESTIONS

15-1. This chapter describes how to create tables and records in Microsoft Access. What other database management systems are available? Use the Internet to learn more about these systems.

15-2. Identify the different data types available for creating data fields in Microsoft Access. Similarly, identify the different types of numbers (e.g., Long integer) you can use if you define a field as a number. (Hint: Create a data field in a throwaway database table, assign it a "number" data type, and examine the possibilities for the "Field Size" property.)

15-3. What are database management systems? Are they the same as databases?

15-4. What are data definition languages (DDLs)? How are they related to DBMSs?

15-5. Why do database developers link tables together? How is this done using Access?

15-6. What is data validation? Why is it important? Give some examples of how to validate data inputs using Access.

15-7. A data-entry clerk at Watanabe and Associates recently questioned the need for validation rules in database tables. "After all," he stated, "if you make a mistake entering data, you can always go back and fix it later—if someone discovers your mistake." Do you agree with him?

15-8. What are data manipulation languages? How are these languages related to database management systems? How are these languages related to databases?

15-9. What is SQL? How is SQL like an Access query? How is it different?

PROBLEMS

15-10. Create a Salesperson table and a Customer Order table. The salesperson table should include the salesperson number, first name, last name, commission rate, and date of last sale. The customer order table includes the order number, customer number, salesperson number, order date, and total amount of the order. Create at least five records for each table. Finally, create a relationship for the two tables, using Figure 15-6 as a guide.

15-11. The Query Corporation employs the individuals listed in Figure 15-17. Use Access or another DBMS as required by your instructor to create a database of this information and then perform the following queries.

  a. List all employees in Department 5.

  b. List all employees with first name "Brenda."

  c. List all those employees with pay rates over $6.50.

  d. List all those employees eligible for overtime (T = yes; F = no).

15-12. Use the Web to find current examples of data warehousing software. Why do companies create data warehouses, and what are some accounting uses of such warehouses?

15-13. The information in Figure 15-18 is for the employees of the Marcia Felix Corporation.

  a. Use a DBMS software package to create a database for this figure.

  b. What is the average pay rate for these employees?

  c. What is the average pay rate for females? What is the average for males?

  d. What females scored over 70 on their examinations? What males scored over 50?

15-14. Consider the employee record in Figure 15-4, which illustrates the data structure of an employee table. Given the importance of this information, it is likely that the database developer would install validation tests to ensure its accuracy. Some possible restriction(s) are:

Data Field	Data type	Restriction
Department Code	Short Text	A or B or C or D
PayRate	Number	Must be between 9.25 and 15.50
DateHired	Date	Must be greater than January 1, 2018.

Record Number	Last Name	First Name	Social Security Number	Department	Pay Rate	Over-time
1	ADCOX	NORMAN	901795336	1	6.50	Yes
2	KOZAR	LINDA	412935350	1	6.50	Yes
3	MCLEAN	KAY	405751308	1	7.50	No
4	CUNNINGHAM	TOM	919782417	3	7.50	Yes
5	DANIELS	PATRICIA	517351609	3	5.50	Yes
6	MCGUIRE	ANNE	201891647	3	5.50	Yes
7	REEDER	BRENDA	619294493	3	5.50	Yes
8	BLOOM	BRENDA	513321592	4	6.25	Yes
9	DAVIS	DENISE	517351608	4	5.50	Yes
10	DUFFY	LESLIE	314532409	4	15.50	No
11	HARPER	LINDA	615824130	4	5.75	Yes
12	MORGAN	MEREDITH	704563903	4	6.25	Yes
13	WELSH	KAREN	216253428	4	15.25	No
14	CHAPIN	GEORGE	203767263	5	7.50	Yes
15	FINN	JOHN	715386721	5	6.25	Yes
16	HALPIN	MARSHA	913541871	5	6.50	Yes
17	LAURIN	PHILIP	514484631	5	6.50	Yes
18	MIAGLIO	PEGGY	414224972	5	6.25	Yes
19	TURNER	BRENDA	713589164	5	15.50	No
20	ZORICH	MILDRED	504455827	5	6.50	Yes

FIGURE 15-17 Employees of the Query Corporation.

Personnel File Date: October 10, 20xx	Employee Number	Score on Aptitude Test	Department ID	Current Pay Rate	Sex
BAKER, JEFFREY L.	1692	73	A	$7.50	M
BARRETT, RAYMOND G.	3444	53	B	7.45	M
BLISS, DONALD W.	6713	55	D	6.80	M
BOWERS, PAUL D.	2084	42	B	5.90	M
BUCHANAN, CINDY	3735	41	E	7.80	F
CHEUNG, WAI KONG	8183	55	C	7.80	F
CONRAD, MARK E.	8317	58	D	9.60	M
DAILY, REBECCA E.	2336	45	D	15.90	F
DRISCOLL, DAVID M.	5210	47	D	7.70	M
ERICKSON, KURT N.	2217	53	B	15.50	M
FRANTZ, HEIDI L.	6390	55	A	6.90	F
GARROW, SCOTT D.	8753	61	A	7.40	M
HARDENBROOK, LISA A.	7427	40	C	6.70	F
JACKSON, GREG W.	4091	67	D	15.90	M
LANGLEY, JERRY W.	3262	86	E	9.40	M
LUBINSKI, TRAVIS M.	3865	37	D	7.50	M
LYNCH, SHERENE D.	7857	66	D	15.90	F
MARKHAM, KYLE R.	6766	62	A	7.90	M
MCGUIRE, TANA B.	4052	55	A	9.20	F
MONACH, SHERI L.	8082	48	B	9.10	F
MOORE, MICHAEL S.	2431	67	E	15.50	M
NELSON, JOHN R.	5873	46	B	7.40	M
PAPEZ, PETER M.	7799	41	E	15.30	M
PETTINARI, DARIN M.	1222	56	B	15.40	M

FIGURE 15-18 Employee data for the Marcia Felix Corporation.

a. Using Access, create an employee table similar to the one shown in Figure 15-4. Create at least one record for this table.

b. Create validation rules for the listed restrictions and an accompanying validation text for each. Document your work by providing a table outlining exactly what rules you

created. (Hint: You can use the aforementioned expression for the department code as a validation rule.)

c. Test each validation rule by attempting to enter data that violate it. Screen capture the error messages for each of your three examples.

CASE ANALYSES

15-15. BSN Bicycles I (Creating a Database from Scratch with Microsoft Access)

Bill Barnes and Tom Freeman opened their BSN bicycle shop in 2010. Not counting Jake—a friend who helps out occasionally at the store—Bill and Tom are the only employees. The shop occupies a small commercial space that was once a restaurant. The former kitchen now stores spare parts and provides space for bicycles repairs while the former dining area in the front is now the retail sales area. The "corporate office" is just a desk and file cabinet in the back corner of the retail area.

Bill and Tom are more friends and bicycling enthusiasts than businessmen. They've pretty much sunk their life savings into the shop and are anxious that it succeed. In the first year of operations, they worked hard to convert the space into its present condition, which includes an old-timey sign above the door with their name "BSN Bicycles."

With all the other work that had to be done the first year, marketing efforts have been limited to chatting with friends, distributing flyers at bicycle races and similar sporting events, and placing a few ads on the Internet. Similarly, the owners haven't paid much attention to accounting tasks. Who has time with all the other things that must be done? But at least two things are now clear to the owners: (1) some of their loyal customers prefer to buy items on credit, and (2) all of their suppliers want to be paid on time.

Right now, BSN's "customer credit system" is a box of 3″ × 5″ cards. Each handwritten card contains customer information on the front and invoice information on the back (Figure 15-19). When a customer pays an invoice, one of the owners simply crosses off the invoice information on

<table>
<tr>
<td>

\#1234
Dan Donaldson
123 Maple Drive,   New City, Virginia 02345

home phone: (435) 765-6654   work: ?
cell: (232) 122-9843

Visa card #: 1234-4456-5432-0976   expires: 8/2019

</td>
<td>

Invoice #	Date	Amount
~~1023~~	~~5/15/2018~~	~~125.68~~
~~1028~~	~~5/18/2018~~	~~95.77~~
1056	8/12/2018	235.23

</td>
</tr>
<tr>
<td align="center">(A) The front of a 3×5 BSN customer card.</td>
<td align="center">(B) The back of a 3×5 BSN customer card.</td>
</tr>
</table>

FIGURE 15-19 A customer record for the BSN company.

the card. The "supplier accounts system" is similar, except that the vendor box of 3″ × 5″ cards is green, whereas the customer box is gray.

Jake is a student at the local university. He is taking an AIS course that includes a segment on Microsoft Access. He is still learning about database theory, but thinks that converting the shop's current "accounting systems" to a DBMS might be a good idea. He thinks, for example, that BSN needs a customer table and a vendor (supplier) table. He also thinks that BSN will need an inventory table to keep track of inventory, but that even more tables might be required. Can you help them?

Requirements

1. Identify the resources, events, and agents for BSN's accounting systems. Draw one or more E-R diagrams that illustrate the relationships between these items.
2. Identify the tables that you would need to create a working database for the company's receivables, payables, and inventory.
3. Using Access or another DBMS required by your instructor, create at least three records for each of the tables you identified in part 2. Hints: (1) Use the information on the front of the 3″ × 5″ card in Figure 15-19 for the customer record structure. (2) The data fields for the Vendors table should include the vendor ID, vendor name and address information, phone number, fax number, and contact person. (3) The data fields for the Inventory table should include item number, item description, units (e.g., dozen, each, etc.), unit cost, unit retail sales price, and quantity on hand.
4. Create relationships for your various tables.
5. Document your work by printing the relationships window.

15-16. BSN Bicycles II (Creating Queries in Access)

Business has been growing at BSN Bicycles, and the store owners have been using their Access database to store information about their customers. Now that the store is a little more established, the owners are thinking more about how best to attract more customers to their store. One idea is to see where their current customers live. The owners also want a complete list of their credit customers.

Requirements

1. If you have not already done so, create a database for BSN and the customer's table described in Case 15-17. Be sure to create at least 10 customer records for the company, including one with your name. Several of the customers should live in the states of Texas (TX) and Massachusetts (MA), and several customers should have zip code "12345." The customers in TX and MA and the customers with zip code 12345 do not have to be the same.
2. If you have not already done so, create several invoices for your customers.
3. Create a query that selects all customers living in TX or MA.
4. Create a query that selects all customers living in zip code 12345.
5. Create a query that selects all customers living in TX who also have zip code 12345.
6. Create a query that selects all credit customers. (Hint: Use the word "Yes" for the criteria in this query.)

15-17. Furry Friends Foundation I (Creating a New Database from Scratch)

The Furry Friends Foundation (FFF) is a nonprofit organization that finds homes for abandoned animals that are suitable for adoption. FFF began operations with a bequest from a wealthy gentleman who lived his life taking care of stray animals and wanted to make sure that such animals were looked after once he was gone. Although the amount the foundation started with was sufficient to set up an office and begin operations, it depends upon continuing donations to run daily operations.

FFF has not been keeping good records. Over the years, the foundation has had requests for year-end statements that document their donations to the Foundation for tax purposes. (Usually, donations are given with a particular type of animal in mind—for example, "for dogs.")

Now that the number of contributors exceeds 500, the president has decided to develop a database to handle the foundation's accounting and reporting needs. The following is a sample of some of the records at FFF.

Requirements

1. Using Access or a similar relational database, create the tables needed to set up a database for contributors, contributions, and whether the contributions are to be used for dogs, cats, or nonspecified.
2. What did you use for the primary record key of the FFF donation file table? Why did you use it?
3. Using *Access* or similar software as required by your instructor, add yourself as a contributor.
4. Create relationships for the tables.

FFF Contributor File

Contributor ID	Last Name	First Name	Street Address	City	State	Zip
13456	Aggies	Go	1845 Mays Ave	College Station	TX	77843
13480	Lawrence	Marie	9190 Bentley Road	Waltham	MA	02423
13484	Kitty	Robert	5815 AIS Lane	Tampa	FL	53887

FFF Donation File

Donation Date	Animal Code	Amount	Contributor ID
September 30, 2013	C	25	13456
September 20, 2013	D	125	13456
October 15, 2013	C	25	13456
October 15, 2013	D	10	13456
October 31, 2013	C	20	13456
October 31, 2013	D	20	13456
November 30, 2013	D	250	13456
November 15, 2013	C	25	13456
December 1, 2013	O	70	13456
December 10, 2013	C	100	13480
September 10, 2013	C	250	13480
October 10, 2013	C	500	13480
November 11, 2013	C	150	13480
December 14, 2013	D	100	13484
September 5, 2013	C	100	13484
October 10, 2013	O	100	13484
November 8, 2013	O	100	13484
December 15, 2013	D	50	13484

FFF Animal Code Table

Contribution for:	Code
Dogs	D
Cats	C
Hamster	H
Guinea Pig	G
Rabbit	R
Other	O

15-18. Furry Friends Foundation II (Creating Queries for Databases)

Recall from Case 15-17 that the Furry Friends Foundation is a nonprofit organization that finds homes for abandoned animals. The foundation has recently computerized some of its operations by storing its accounting data in a relational database. One reason for this was to enable it to more easily answer questions about donations. This portion of the case provides some examples of such questions and gives you practice creating database queries to answer them.

Requirements

1. If you have not already done so, create the tables and relationships described in Case 15-17.
2. Using *Access* or similar software as required by your instructor, create three donations for yourself. You should be donating to dogs in one contribution, cats in the second contribution, and unspecified in the third contribution.
3. Create a query that selects all customers donating to cats.
4. Create a query that selects all contributors who donated over $50.
5. Create a query that selects all contributors who donated over $100 to dogs.

15-19. Benjamin Department Store (Data Validation)

The payroll department at the Benjamin Department Store has defined the following record structure for employee records.

Date field	Data type	Example
Last Name	Text	Weiland
First Name	Text	Alice
Employee number	Text	E12345
Home phone number	Text	(987) 456-4321
Work phone extension	Number	123
Pay rate	Currency	$12.34
Number of tax exemptions	Number	3
Department	Text	A

All fields are required. The employee number serves as the primary key. Work phone extensions are always greater than "100" and less than "999." Hourly pay rates are always at least $12.50 and no more than $55.00. The maximum number of tax exemptions allowed is "6." Finally, there are only three departments: A, B, and C.

Requirements

1. Using a DBMS such as Access, create a record structure for the company.
2. Create data validation rules for as many data fields as you can. For each data validation rule, also create validation text that the system can use to display an appropriate error message.
3. Create employee records for yourself and employees with the last names Strawser, Smith, and Wolfe using data that you make up.
4. Attempt to create a record that violates a data validation rule.

15-20. North Beach College (Enforcing Referential Integrity)

North Beach College was founded as a small, liberal arts school just 3 years ago. Since that time, the institution has grown to the point where parking on campus is difficult and parking in illegal areas is common. Accordingly, the Board of Directors has reluctantly approved a policy requiring campus police to issue parking tickets.

Currently, the college requires students and faculty to register their cars with the parking office, which issues them parking decals that registrants must display inside the front windshield of their cars. At present, all recordkeeping at the parking office is done manually, severely limiting the ability of office personnel to create reports or perform meaningful statistical analyses about parking on campus. For example, it is currently not known how many students of each class (freshman, sophomore, etc.) register their cars or how many full-time faculty, part-time faculty, or clerical staff register their cars. The new policy of writing parking tickets will only add to this problem because it will require office staff to match parking tickets to student or faculty names. In addition, the Board of Directors would like an end-of-semester report indicating how many parking violations of each type (meter violation, invalid parking sticker, etc.) are issued by the campus police.

To help solve these problems, the College Board of Directors has hired you to create a computerized system for them. You realize that a database system might work for this, and accordingly, propose a database of tables with record structures similar to those in Figure 7-17. The Board of Directors approves your plan, but asks that you create a small system to demonstrate its features before creating a full-blown system.

Requirements

1. Use Microsoft Access (or an alternate DBMS designated by your instructor) to create the three tables illustrated in Figure 14-16.

2. Create at least three records in the car registration table. Be sure to use your own name as one of the registrants. Also, create at least three records for the Parking Violations Code File. Make up your own descriptions instead of using the ones shown in the figure.

3. For each record you create in the car registration table in the aforementioned step 2, create at least three parking tickets and input this information to the Tickets File. Thus, you should have at least nine records in this file. Be sure that at least one record in the Tickets File contains a reference to each of the records in the Parking Violations Code File (i.e., at least one person breaks every possible parking violation).

4. Attempt to create a record in the Ticket File that contains a nonexistent ticket code in the parking Violations Code File. Were you successful?

5. Link the tables together. Be sure to check "enforce referential integrity." When you get finished, your relationships window should resemble the one shown in Figure 15-15. What are the relationships among the records in the three tables?

6. Now again attempt to create a record in the ticket file that contains a nonexistent ticket code in the parking Violations Code File. Were you successful this time?

7. Finally, attempt to delete a record in the Parking Violations Code File. Why can't you do it?

READINGS AND OTHER RESOURCES

Alzubaidi, R. 2015. Query language application in accounting databases. *Proceedings for the Northeast Region Decision Sciences Institute* 1: 1–12.

Borthick, A. F., and G. P. Schneider. 2017. Analyzing data for decision making: integrating spreadsheet modeling and database querying. *Issues in Accounting Education* 32(1): 59–66.

Dow, K., M. Watson, and V. Shea. 2013. Understanding the links between audit risks and audit steps: The case of procurement cards. *Issues in Accounting Education* 28(4): 913–921.

Drum, D. M., and Pulvermacher, A. 2016. Accounting automation and insight at the speed of thought. *Journal of Emerging Technologies in Accounting* 13(1):181–186.

Go to www.wiley.com/go/simkin/videos to access videos on the following topics:

Create a Simple Query
Create a Table Using Microsoft Access

ANSWERS TO TEST YOURSELF

1. c **2.** c **3.** c **4.** a **5.** a **6.** b **7.** d **8.** d **9.** b **10.** c

Chapter 16

Database Forms and Reports

After reading this chapter, you will be able to:

1. *Create* simple forms in Access.

2. *Explain* the difference between a bound control and an unbound control on an Access form or report.

3. *Discuss* why calculated fields are not normally stored in databases.

4. *Create* advanced forms in Access with subforms.

5. *Create* a variety of reports in Access.

"Thanks to all the IT changes of the past few years, CPA firms need workers that can use the technological tools now at their disposal to help create new ways to analyze and present clients' financial data. Employers are looking for more than technical proficiency; they want candidates who can help make business decisions."

Baysden, C. 2013. Demand for accounting grads reaches all-time high.
Journal of Accountancy (June).

16.1 INTRODUCTION

The previous chapter illustrated how to design an Access database with several tables and also how to construct queries to select information from these tables. Two more important database objects are forms and reports. Database forms typically display complete information about *one* record on *one* screen, while database reports typically display selected information about many records using several pages or several screens.

The first section discusses how to create and use forms for input and output tasks. The second section discusses how to create reports. Both sections illustrate these tasks using Microsoft Access 2016, but many of the skills discussed here also apply to other database software.

16.2 FORMS

Figure 16-1 illustrates an example of a database **form**—a custom-designed screen for entering the data for a new record or for displaying the data for existing records. As you can see in Figure 16-1, a form has three major sections: (1) a **heading section**, which appears at the top of the form; (2) a **detail section**, which usually occupies the majority of the form and which displays the record information; and (3) a **footer section,** which

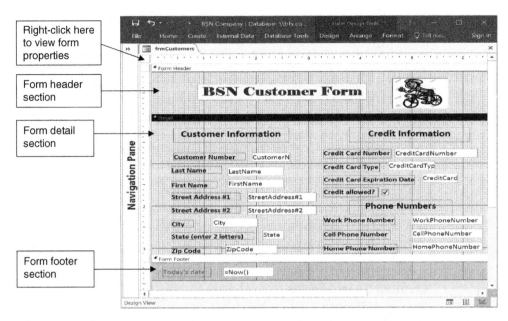

Right-click here to view form properties

Form header section

Form detail section

Form footer section

FIGURE 16-1   The three major sections of an Access form at design time.

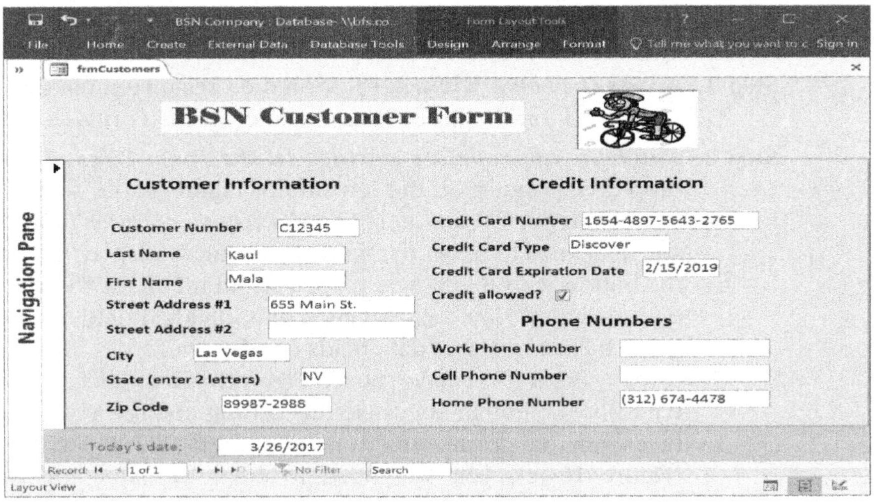

FIGURE 16-2   The form in Figure 16-1 in Form (or run) view.

appears at the bottom of the form (and which is often not used). Figure 16-1 shows the form in **design view**, while Figure 16-2 shows the same form in Form or run view.

Although there is no requirement to use a form for entering data into a database table, there are several reasons why using a form is better for this task than using a **datasheet screen** such as the one in Figure 15-3. One advantage is that a datasheet displays many records at once, making it possible to accidentally type over existing information instead of creating a new record. Another advantage is that developers can design a form to display all the data-entry textboxes for an entire record in one screen, whereas a datasheet typically requires users to keep scrolling to the right to enter data for off-screen items.

A third advantage of forms is that you can customize them. Figure 16-1 illustrates several examples of such customization, including: (1) custom header information (e.g., the label with the words "BSN Customer Form") at the top of a form, (2) text, logos, artwork, and (as shown) pictures for graphic interest, (3) more complete labels (instead of the default database names) to identify each field in the database table (e.g., "Customer Number" instead of "CustNo"), (4) the ability to group similar fields together in the form (e.g., the phone numbers in Figure 16-1), (5) the ability to add explanations or special instructions in the form to help users understand how to enter data (e.g., see the label for the State field), and (6) customized tab ordering that governs the order in which textboxes become active on the form.

Taken together, the various advantages of forms make them better for controlling data input than datasheet screens. In other words, forms help prevent data-entry errors, increase data reliability, can be an essential component of strong internal controls.

Creating Simple Forms

To create a custom form for a database table in Access, you can design a form from scratch by selecting *Blank Form* from the Create menu in Figure 16-3, but it is often easier to use the **Form Wizard** for this. Follow these steps to create a new form using the Form Wizard in Access.

Step 1. *Access the Form Wizard.* Click on the Create menu in the Access main menu. Then, click on the Form Wizard choice in the Forms section (Figure 16-3).

Step 2. *Enter the appropriate settings in the Form Wizard dialog boxes.* In the drop-down option on the left side of Figure 16-4a, select the table you want your form to reference (e.g., *tblBSN Customer Master Table*). In this screen, you will also need to select the fields you want to display *on* the form. Clicking on the button with the ≫ symbol selects all the fields from your source table—a typical choice. You can also click on individual field names and then click on the > button to select data fields one by one.

Use the second dialog box in Figure 16-4b to select a layout for your form—typically "Columnar" because this setting enables you to include all the data fields on one form. Finally, in the third dialog box of the Form Wizard (Figure 16-4c), you will need to create a name for your form. As with the database objects, you should use the conventional prefix for a form name—*frm*—and then create a name that helps you remember the form's

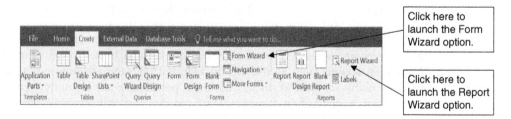

FIGURE 16-3 The options in the CREATE tab, showing the Form Wizard.

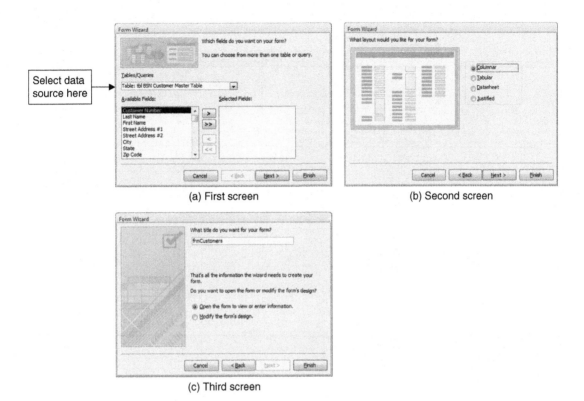

(a) First screen (b) Second screen

(c) Third screen

FIGURE 16-4   The three dialog boxes in the Form Wizard.

application.[1] In Figure 16-4c, for example, we have named the form *frmCustomers*. At this point, you can click on the Finish button in the last dialog box—you're done. The Form Wizard will then create the form with the settings you've indicated and list the completed form among those available for use in the main menu for forms.

Step 3: ***Customize the Form.*** If you open your form in design view, you will see something like the one in Figure 16-5. This figure helps make clear that a form has two modes—**run view**, which looks like that in Figure 16-1, and design view, which starts out looking like that in Figure 16-5. This screen contains form objects such as labels and textboxes that you can (1) delete (by first clicking on the object and then hitting the Del key on your keyboard), (2) reposition (by dragging them with your mouse), or (3) customize in other ways. As you can see, a lot of additional design work went into customizing the form in Figure 16-5 so that it looked like the one in Figure 16-2.

The objects such as textboxes and labels that appear on a form are examples of **form controls**. When customizing a form, it is important to distinguish between bound controls and unbound controls. **Bound controls** are textboxes, drop-down boxes, and similar form objects that depend upon the underlying data and therefore change from record to record. In contrast,

---

[1] We recommend prefixing all form names with the conventional prefixes of *tbl, qry, frm,* or *rpt.* Microsoft Access 2016 also includes icons on the left side of each file name that indicate the object type.

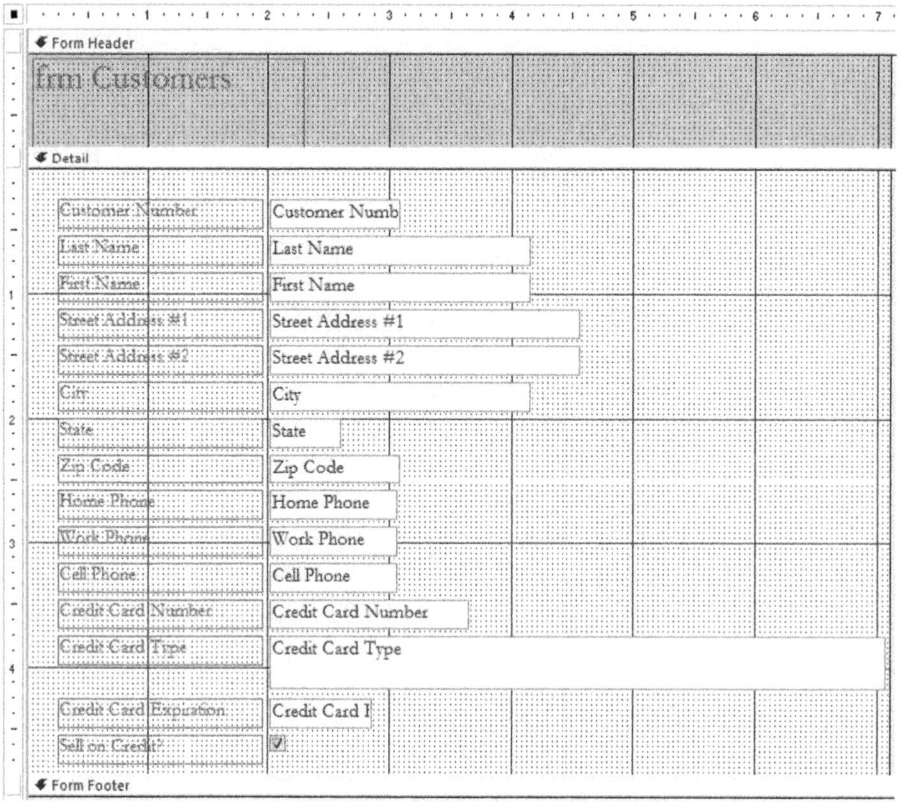

FIGURE 16-5 The starting format for the form in Figure 16-2.

unbound controls are labels, report headings, and similar items that are the same from record to record in a form and do not display underlying database information. On Access forms, labels and textboxes typically appear in pairs, but they are, in fact, separate objects. Thus, you can delete the label for a particular data field on a form, and the accompanying textbox will continue to display the database information to which it is bound.

You can add additional controls to your form by selecting them from the Form Design Tools (Figure 16-6a). Typical objects that you might add are labels and picture boxes in the form header. You can also add bound controls such as textboxes if you wish, but you can only do this when your form is in design mode.

To add a control to your form, left click on the control in the Toolbox, and then use your mouse to draw the selected object on your form. For example, in Figure 16-1, you can see additional labels (e.g., the heading "BSN Customers" in the header portion of the form or the label "Phone Numbers" in the detail portion of the form) and also a picture of a bicycle (which we created with an Image object from the Toolbox). The size of the object depends upon how large you drew it when you first created it, but you can resize any control on your form using the dots, or **sizing handles**, that appear on the border of your control when you click on it in the form.

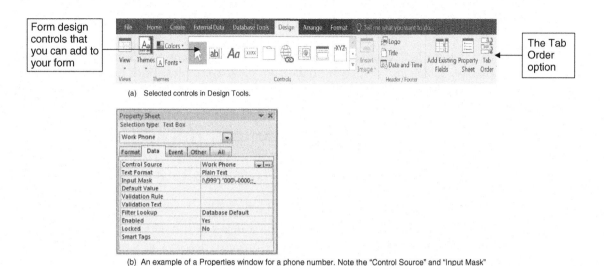

Form design controls that you can add to your form

The Tab Order option

(a) Selected controls in Design Tools.

(b) An example of a Properties window for a phone number. Note the "Control Source" and "Input Mask" settings for this particular control—a textbox that displays a work phone number.

FIGURE 16-6 An example of (a) the Form Controls window and (b) a Properties window.

Finally, to customize a control on a form, use that object's **Property Sheet window** (Figure 16-6b) to make individual settings for control objects. In effect, each form object has separate settings and its own Property Sheet window. To view the Property Sheet for a particular control, right click on an object in your form and select "Properties" from the drop-down list of choices that appears. This window allows you to change a wide range of settings—for example, the font size, font weight, or boldness of the text in labels. Of particular importance is the **Control Source property** of an object, which you will find among the settings in the Data tab portion of the Property Sheet window and which binds the control to an underlying data field. Bound controls have a Control Source setting, whereas unbound objects do not.

Step 3: *Refine your Design.* You can toggle back and forth between run mode and design mode by clicking on the *Form* and *Design* options. Form (i.e., Run) mode allows you to see how your form looks at run time and reveals what further work you need to perform to complete your form's design. In design mode, you can select multiple form objects at once (by depressing the Ctrl key and clicking on several objects successively) and then use the formatting options from the Format menu (on the main menu bar) to resize, align, and consistently space objects on your form.

Step 4: *Reset the Tab Order.* If you rearrange objects in your form in design mode, there is a good chance that you will also want to reset the **tab order** of your form controls—that is, the order in which each control becomes active in run mode. To do so, click on the Design tab in Figure 16-6a. One of the options you will see there is "Tab Order." If you click on this choice, Access will provide a small dialog window that enables you to reset this order. Here, you can create a custom order for the objects in your form or, more simply, click on the "Auto Order" button at the bottom of this window to have Access automatically reset the tab order. The new, auto-order sequence makes form controls become active sequentially from top to bottom and left to right.

Using Forms for Input and Output Tasks

As noted earlier, database forms provide a convenient tool for entering data into database tables and displaying data from database tables. Both tasks require the use of the **navigation bar** at the bottom of the form—that is, the portion of the screen that looks like this:

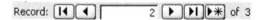

You can use this navigation bar for both the input and output tasks explained as follows.

Displaying or Changing Information.

The number in the middle of the navigation bar (e.g., "2" here) indicates which record currently displays in your form. Clicking on the ▐◀ symbol causes Access to display the first record in the underlying database table, while clicking on the ▶▐ symbol displays the last record in the table. Clicking on the ◀ symbol displays the record immediately before the current one, while clicking on the ▶ symbol displays the next record after the current one. You can also access the "previous record" or "next record" using the "Page up" and "Page Down" keys on your keyboard.

Forms also enable you to *change* the information already in a database record. For example, if a customer moves to a new address or changes his or her phone number, you would want to alter this information in the appropriate record of the Customer table. It is a simple matter to enter the new information for the appropriate record using a form for this task. Changing data in a form causes Access to automatically update the information in the underlying table.

Creating New Records.

If you wish to add a new record, you can use a form for this task as well. First, click on the ▶* button in the navigation bar. The system will then display the first available empty record (usually the one at the end of the underlying table) and allow you to enter the information for a new record—for example, the data for a new customer.

A useful feature in Access is that any data field that you include in a form automatically inherits all properties that you set for that field in the underlying table. This means that the same edit tests and data restrictions apply to the field for data entry, whether you enter the data in datasheet view for the table or in form view. For example, if you create an input mask for a phone number that looks like this: (999) 000-0000, Access will display the mask for this data field when you start entering data in your form at run time. Similarly, if you restrict a certain field to Integer data (e.g., a zip code), the system will not allow you to enter alphabetic text for that field. Finally, if you create a range test in your form (e.g., one that limits input values to between "0" and "40" hours), Access will not allow you to enter a value of "50" for that field. Thus, the properties that you set when you initially create the data fields of a table are powerful internal controls because they are also active when you update data or create new records.

Case-in-Point 16.1   Database forms are all around you. For example, when you make a purchase on a website like Amazon.com, you are interacting with a database form. The choices you select from menus and drop-down boxes enable you to enter data into the databases of the websites.

Printing Forms. You can print a form just as easily as you print any other Microsoft document—that is, by using the "Print" option from the File tab. You can also use Ctrl+P for this task. A word of caution: if you select All from the print dialog box, you will print a separate form for all the records the form can display—that is, potentially a lot of them!

Subforms: Showing Data from Multiple Tables

A **subform** is a form within a form. It displays data that are related to main form. Figure 16-7 is an example—the original customer form from Figure 16-1 with a new subform showing invoices for each customer. This explains why there are two navigation bars in the figure—the initial one at the bottom of Figure 16-1 and a new one in the subform of Figure 16-7. If you advance through the records of the customer table using the lower navigation bar, you will see the data for different customers in the main form. If you advance through the records of the subform, you will see the invoices for the same customer—if they exist.

Creating Subforms. Subforms display subordinate information related to the information in the main form. This reflects the one-to-many relationship of the underlying data. In Figure 16-7, for example, each customer might have several invoices, but each invoice is related to only one customer. To create a subform like the one in Figure 16-7 requires that "customers" and "invoices" have a one-to-many relationship. To create a form with a subform in Access, your first task is to make sure that the data in the two tables are related via the Relationships window and verify that the relationship is one-to-many.

In Access, there are two principle methods for creating a form with a subform. One approach is to identify the subform at the time you use the Form Wizard. First, you would use the dialog box in Figure 16-4a to select the data for the main form as explained earlier. But before continuing to the next form, you would also click on the drop-down menu in this dialog box and select a second table from the list. If a one-to-many relationship exists between the two tables, the Form Wizard will recognize your wish to create a subform within your main form and will create one for you.

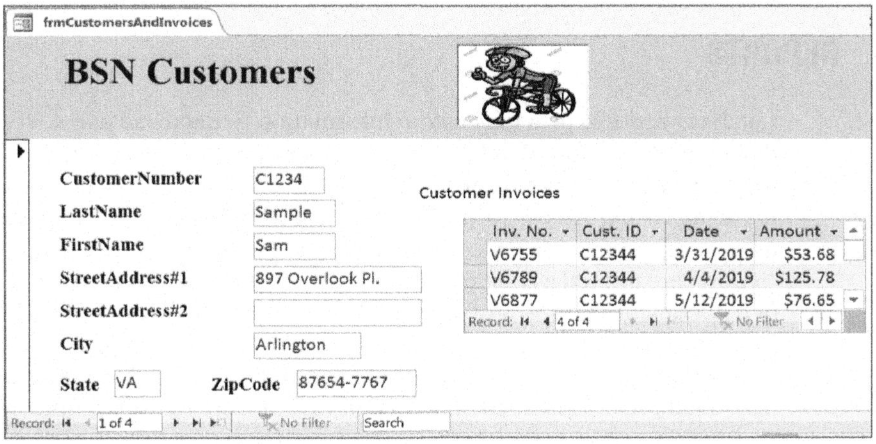

FIGURE 16-7 A form with a subform.

A second way to create a subform is to add one to an existing form *after* you've created the main form. To duplicate our form with a subform, open the form in Figure 16-1 in design view and use your mouse to extend the size of the details section of the form (to make room for the subform). Then, click on the Subform icon in the Design tab Toolbox and use your mouse to draw a rectangle in the detail section of your form. This procedure causes Access to launch the Subform Wizard, which will ask you for settings similar to those shown in Figure 16-5—for example, "Which table do you want to use for the subform?" or "How do you want the data to appear in the subform?"

In design mode, your resulting form and subform will not look exactly like the ones in Figure 16-7. For example, you will probably have to resize the outer dimensions of the subform to fit the data and perhaps reword the text in the label at the top of the subform. With a little bit of work, however, you should be able to design the forms to look like those in Figure 16-7. If you need to resize the column widths of your subform, however, you can do that at run time rather than at design time—a helpful advantage because you can see live data at run time.

Concluding Remarks about Forms

Database forms enable you to add records to a database table, modify the data in the existing records of a table, or simply view the data in a table. Although forms are not needed for such tasks, the ability to customize a form, provide explanations for data-entry fields within forms, and create convenient tab orderings is especially a useful feature for ensuring valid data entry. In commercial environments, the database developer is rarely the same person who enters data in database tables on a daily basis. Anything that the developer can do to make this job more convenient and straightforward for data-entry personnel helps avoid errors, streamlines the data-entry process, and saves time. Experts estimate that it costs about 10 times as much to *correct* an error in a database as it does to enter the data correctly.

Case-in-Point 16.2 Experian is a company that manages firm's credit risks, helps firms prevent fraud, and processes firms' payments. Experian recognizes the need for very strong validation controls within its database forms because its customers often enter data themselves. Even one letter or digit entered incorrectly can result in a failed payment.[2]

16.3 REPORTS

Database **reports** provide custom information to database users. Reports can be simple documents that only display the contents of a table or complex outputs that combine the information from several tables and show selected subsets of database information. If you are using Access to print something to paper, the chances are high that you are using a report for this task. This means that many items that you might not consider a "report" are treated as one by Access—for example, an invoice for a particular customer or a document that shows the name and address of a vendor. Access also treats mailing labels as reports.

Unlike forms, reports are strictly outputs and do not allow users to input data into databases. This section explains how to create (1) simple reports, (2) reports

---

[2] Experian, www.experian.com.

with calculated fields, (3) reports based on queries instead of tables, and (4) reports containing grouped data. In this section, we will use a slightly different version of the BSN database—that is, one that contains additional tables and modified records.

Creating Simple Reports

Figure 16-8 illustrates the print preview of a simple report—a listing of selected information about the customers in BSN's Customers table. The first step in creating such reports is *not* to use your database system at all, but rather to decide what information to include in the report and how best to display that information in a printed document. We stress again that spending a few minutes designing the general format of a report (even if on the back of an envelope) may save you hours of redesign work later.

A typical report has seven major components: (1) report heading, (2) page heading, (3) group heading, (4) detail or body, (5) group footer, (6) page footer, and (7) report footer. Figure 16-9 describes these items in greater detail. Perhaps the most important is the Detail section, which is similar to the detail section of a form. The detail section displays information from the records of database tables. After you have a general idea

BSN Customers

March 1, 2019

Customer Number	Last Name	First Name	Street Address	City	State	Zip Code	Sell on credit?
C12344	Sample	Sam	897 Overlook Pl.	Arlington	VA	87654-7767	☑
C12345	Kaul	Mala	655 Main St.	Las Vegas	NV	89987-2988	☑
C12346	Savage	Arline	78 Maple Ave	Burmingham	AL	34566-1234	☐
C12347	Salsberg	Ian	900 Oak St.	Forest Hills	NY	01233-3422	☑

Page 1 of 1

FIGURE 16-8 A simple report.

Component	Where It Appears	Typical Content
Report header	First page of the report	Company name and address, date prepared or relevant time period, company logo
Page header	Top of each page	Identification of each data field below it
Group header	Beginning of each group of records	Identification of a new group of data
Detail lines	Body of the report	The individual data fields of, and computed data fields from, underlying database tables
Group footer	End of each group	Control totals or other statistics such as maximums, minimums, or averages for the group
Page footer	Bottom of each page	Page number, report number
Report footer	Last page of the report	End-of-report identifier, grand totals

FIGURE 16-9 The major section of a database report.

of the format for your report, you can develop the report itself using these components. An easy way to do so is by using the Report Wizard in Access, following these steps:

Step 1: ***Launch the Report Wizard.*** To launch the **Report Wizard**, select the Create option from the main menu and then select "Report Wizard" (see again Figure 16-3). The first dialog box you will see is the one in Figure 16-10a.

Step 2: ***Select the Underlying Data Source and Desired Fields.*** You can base a report on a table, as we will do in this example, or a query (which can combine the data from several tables). To create the report in Figure 16-8, however, we will only need the Customers table. Thus, to replicate our work, select *tblBSN Customer Master Table* from the drop-down list in Figure 16-10a and then select the desired fields using the data field selector buttons (> and ≫) as needed.

Notice that not all the information in the Customers table appears in the Customer report of Figure 16-8. For example, the customer's home phone number and cell phone numbers are missing. This is typical of output reports—only selected information from underlying tables appears in them. The more information you include, the more complete the report, but also the more difficult it becomes to interpret. More data is not necessarily more information.

Step 3: ***Indicate Any Grouping Levels.*** When you click "Next" in Figure 16-10a, you will see the dialog box of Figure 16-10b. This is where you tell the Report Wizard how you would like to group your data. For example, you can group your customers by zip code. For the simple report in Figure 16-8, however, we do not need any such groupings, and you can simply click the Next button in this dialog box.

Step 4: ***Indicate Any Sort Fields and Select the Desired Report Format.*** The Report Wizard also allows you to sort up to four different fields. For example, Figure 16-10c indicates the settings to create a report of customers sorted by customers' last name within zip code. After selecting the sort fields, click Next in the dialog box. The fourth screen in the Report Wizard (Figure 16-10d) allows you to select a particular report layout. For line-by-line listings—the typical choice in simple reports—select "Tabular." You can also choose between "Portrait" and "Landscape" print options here.

Step 5: ***Name and Save the Report.*** After clicking Next in the dialog box shown in Figure 16-10d, you will see the dialog box in Figure 16-10e. Here, you have the opportunity to name your report. The standard prefix for a report is *rpt*, which is the reason we've named our report *rptCustomers_by_ZipCode*.

Step 6: ***Modify the Design of the Report as Desired.*** When you finish with the Report Wizard, you may need to modify the report design still further. If you open your new report in design view, you will see a screen similar to the one in Figure 16-11. This interactive screen enables you to modify the height or width of labels or textboxes (using their sizing handles), change the font size, italics, or boldness of headings (using the Properties Window for each element), or reposition items. You can also delete any element in the report by left clicking on it and pressing the Del key on your keyboard. In design view, the bar above any section of your report will darken to indicate which section of the report is active for design purposes.

There are many additional things you can do to modify your report's appearance. For example, you can cut and paste (or copy and paste) elements from one portion

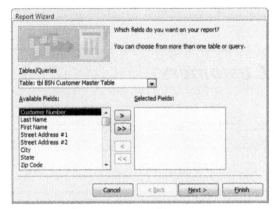

(a) The first screen in the Report Wizard.

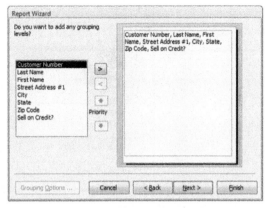

(b) The second screen in the Report Wizard.

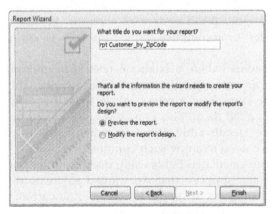

(c) The third screen in the Report Wizard.

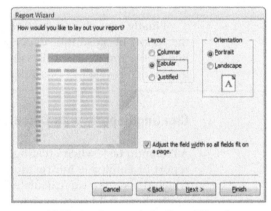

(d) The fourth screen in the Report Wizard.

(e) The fifth screen in the Report Wizard.

FIGURE 16-10 The dialog boxes of the Report Wizard.

of your report to another. Thus, we moved the date (with content "= Now()") from the footer section of the report to the header section using this cut-and-paste method. As with designing forms, you can also change background colors, or add charts, pictures, or logos to your report. To view these choices, click on the control's drop-down menu within the Design tab.

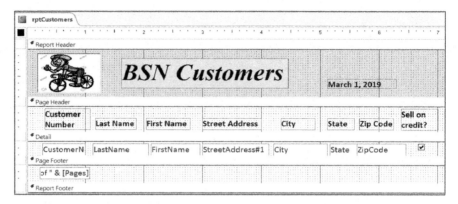

FIGURE 16-11 The Access report of Figure 16-8 in Design View.

Finally, you should be careful when moving anything into the "Detail" section of the report because the report will repeat any element in this section for each detail line of the report. For this same reason, you should try to make the detail section of the report as small as possible—it will save room on lengthy reports.

Creating Reports with Calculated Fields

A common task when creating reports is to include **calculated fields**. For example, a report of employee information might also include a field entitled "Years of Service," which the system can calculate from the employee's date of hire. Sometimes, you want a calculated field to appear in the detail section of a report while at other times, you want group or grand totals to appear in the group footer or the report footer sections of your report. In this section, we review the steps needed to accomplish the first task—creating a calculated field for the detail section of a report. In the following section, we review the steps needed to accomplish the second task—creating group summaries.

In accounting information systems (AISs), a common task is to multiply prices by quantities in order to compute an extension (line total) in an invoice. There is no reason to *store* such values in the records of a relational database because we can *compute* such values whenever we need them. This is why we only stored prices and quantities in the Customer_Invoice_Details table. However, when we print customer invoice information on a report, we need to show such computations.

It is usually the easiest to create calculated fields using queries rather than tables for the underlying data. To illustrate, suppose that we wanted to create the report shown in Figure 16-12—a report that shows invoice extensions for all current invoices for BSN. To create such a report, follow these steps:

Step 1: ***Create the Query with a Calculated Field.*** Figure 16-13 shows the query for our report. To create this query, we begin by selecting the tables needed to calculate invoice totals. One such table is the Customer_Invoice_Details table. The records in this table contain the item number and the quantity ordered, but not the name of the item purchased or its price. For this information, we need the BSN Inventory file.

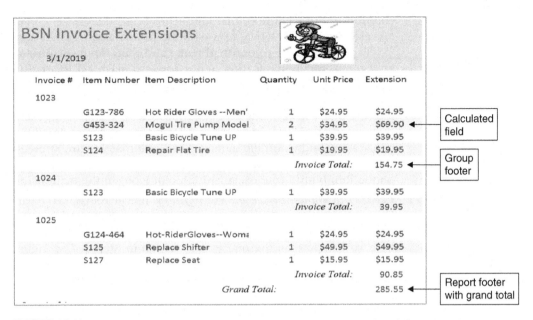

FIGURE 16-12 The print preview of a report that contains a calculated field (see last column of the report).

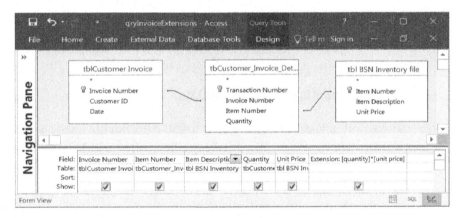

FIGURE 16-13 The query with a calculated field used to create the report in Figure 16-12.

Figure 16-13 is the design view for our query. We have selected the three tables we need for our task and also the desired fields—that is, the invoice number (on which we group the report), the item number and description of the good or service (both taken from the Customer_Invoice_Details table), and the Item description and unit price (both taken from the BSN Inventory table). For convenience, it is a good idea to select these items in the order in which you want them to appear in your final invoice, but this is not required.

To create the calculated field (called "Extension" here), select the first available column in the query design screen and type the *name* of your calculated field. We chose the name "Extension," but this choice is arbitrary. You can also choose a name with more than one word (e.g., "Extension Calculation"), but be careful *not* to choose a term with the same name as an existing data field.

Type a colon after your field name and then input the formula for it. Use an asterisk for multiplication and a forward slash (/) for division. Also, be careful to spell the field names in your formulas exactly as they appear in your underlying database tables. (If you misspell a field name, Access will not indicate that you've made an error, but instead will assume you're creating a parameter query and ask you for the data at run time.) Finally, place square brackets around your field names to indicate that you are referencing existing data fields. When you have completed your query, you can test it by clicking on the Run button (the exclamation point icon) in the main menu.

Step 2: *Create the Report Based on Your Query.* It now remains to create the report. Using the steps outlined earlier, use the Report Wizard to create the final report in Figure 16-12. To do so, launch the Report Wizard as before, but base your report on the query you created in Step 1. Use Figure 16-10 as a guide. In Figure 16-10a, make sure that you have selected your query as the basis of your report and then select all available fields. The second screen of the Report Wizard (Figure 16-10b) will ask you if you wish to group your data. Access will recognize that you have a one-to-many relationship between "invoice numbers" and "invoice details" and should show you this possibility by default. If it does not, however, select this option so that the report will group the detail lines for the same invoice together. Then continue with the remainder of the Report Wizard questions. Be sure to name your report something appropriate—for example, rptInvoiceExtensions. When you finish answering questions in the Report Wizard, you should then reformat your report as needed. The results should look similar to those in Figure 16-12.

Creating Reports with Grouped Data

The report in Figure 16-12 contains useful data, but obviously lacks some critical information. What is the name of the customer associated with each invoice? What is his or her address? A manager might want this information to appear in an invoice report. Finally, it might be useful to organize the report by customer's last name rather than by invoice number.

A **control break** is the technical term for the point at which a group changes from one type to the next in a report. Examples of control breaks include a change in zip code for the addresses in customer listings, or a change in the department number for a list of employees. Control breaks are often the points at which managers want to see subtotals, maximums, minimums, averages, or similar subgroup summaries.

To create control breaks for the report in Figure 16-12, we need to modify its design to include group totals for each invoice. Figure 16-14 illustrates the format for the final report, which includes new information and provides totals for each invoice. To create it, we will follow the steps outlined earlier for creating reports with calculated fields—that is, (1) create a query to generate the desired information, (2) use the Report Wizard to create an initial report based on this query, and (3) reformat the report as needed to achieve the desired end product. Here are the detailed steps:

Step 1: *Create the Underlying Query.* Your first task is to create the underlying query for this report. Figure 16-15 shows a portion of this query during its design.

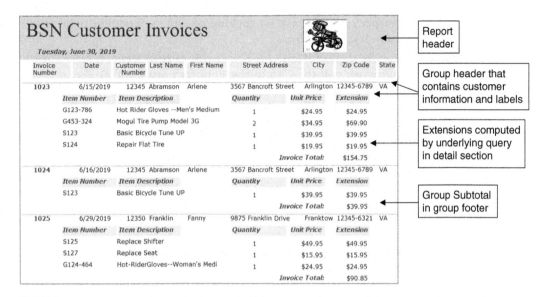

FIGURE 16-14 The invoice report of Figure 16-12, expanded to include customer information and invoice totals.

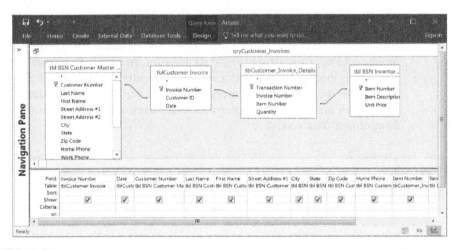

FIGURE 16-15 Part of the query used to create the report illustrated in Figure 16-14.

The upper portion of the query screen in Figure 16-15 identifies the four tables required to build the query. If you study the information contained in the report of Figure 16-14, you will realize *why* we needed four tables for this task. The *Customers* table provides the name and address information of each customer, while the *Invoice* table provides the invoice number. The *Customer Invoice Details* table provides the item number and the quantity ordered for each detail line of an invoice, and the *Products and Services* table provides the item description and sales price for each item purchased. Finally, we had to create a calculated field—the extension of quantity times price for each detail line—as described in the previous section.

When queries become as complex as this one, it is a good idea to run them and make sure that they work before using them in a report. Again, you can perform this task by clicking on the exclamation point (run icon) in the main Access menu.

Step 2: ***Use the Report Wizard to Create the Initial Report.*** After creating our initial query, we will then go to the Reports portion of Access and use the Report Wizard to create an initial report. You already know how to perform such a task, and we will not describe the process again here. The result is a report whose format will not look very much like the finished product in Figure 16-14, so we have additional work to do!

Step 3: ***Reformat the Report as Desired.*** It remains to reformat our report. Because we have also reviewed the activities for this step, we will not repeat them here. Again, it is useful to remember the following items: (1) you should expand the size of unbound labels so that their entire text shows, (2) you can delete any control you don't need, (3) you can move both bound and unbound controls from one part of a report to another, and (4) the Format menu enables you to resize, align, and reposition objects consistently on your report.

Concluding Remarks about Reports

This final section illustrates how to create reports in Access, including reports that contain calculated fields and reports that calculate subtotals for grouped data. Reports are the desired end product of complex database systems. That is, managers need to convert vast amounts of data into useful information for decision-making. This is the function of reports—they turn data into information. It is also important to remember at this point that reports cannot be created unless all of the needed data have been collected and appropriately organized. For this reason, database designers must speak with managers and other end users to determine what reports they need *before* designing a database.

AIS AT WORK
Mother Lode Bicycles

Although the BSN Bicycle Company is fictitious, Mother Lode Bicycles in Sparks, Nevada, is not. Founded in 1996 by two friends—Dave McDonald and Mark Kennedy—the 2,400-square-foot shop sells road and mountain bikes to local customers as well as out-of-towners visiting the area. Bike prices range from a few hundred dollars to several thousand dollars. Sales of bikes, clothing, and biking accessories make up the majority of the store's income, and repairs make up the rest.

In many ways, running a bike shop is similar to running any small business—it includes a division of labor. One partner manages the inventory, stocks the store shelves, and deals with the marketing and advertising parts of the business. The other partner deals with employees, supervises repairs, and interacts with customers. The owners need a system for storing and analyzing all of their transaction and on-transaction data.

For accounting tasks, the store's owners use off-the-shelf accounting software and the bookkeeping expertise of Mark's wife. With the exception of employees, the store does not sell items on credit, and there are no receivables. Mark personally supervises payables, taking advantage of cash discounts where possible and negotiating longer payment schedules with suppliers during the slower selling seasons of the year.

Most of the shop's inventory consists of items that sit on shelves and racks in the retail portion of the store, with just a few parts and unassembled bikes stored in the back room—a combination storeroom–warehouse–office–dining room. "Inventory control" is also a combination of elements, including "visual inspection," working with sales representatives to keep merchandise levels up, and the expertise of the owners for ordering or not ordering items for the slower or busier season to follow. The BSN database represents the type of database that a business like Mother Lode Bicycles can use to collect the data it needs to make critical business decisions.

 # SUMMARY

✓ Databases use forms to input data into, and to view data from, the records in tables.

✓ If you use forms to create new records, the data fields in the customized forms automatically inherit the same properties, attributes, and input restrictions that were created for them in the design of the table.

✓ The navigation bar at the bottom of a form enables you to view the first, last, next, and previous record in the underlying table.

✓ You can use subforms to display the "many" records related to the "one" record in the main form of a one-to-many relationship—for example, the outstanding invoices for a specific customer.

✓ You typically design and develop reports to create hard-copy outputs. In Access, reports are either based directly on tables or on queries that reference tables.

✓ A typical report has seven major components: (1) report heading, (2) page headings, (3) group headings, (4) detail or body, (5) group footer, (6) page footer, and (7) report footer.

✓ You should name forms and reports systematically. The standard prefix for a form is *frm*, and the standard prefix for a report is *rpt*.

✓ Most databases do not store calculated fields such as invoice line extensions (prices times quantities). Instead, we calculate these fields with queries.

✓ Many reports contain grouped data—for example, a set of lines for a given invoice or a set of invoices for a given customer. It is also possible to require a report to show control totals, averages, maximum, or minimum values for each group. In Access, you can create such figures using the Report Wizard and its grouping options.

KEY TERMS YOU SHOULD KNOW

bound control	footer section	Report Wizard
calculated fields	form	run view
control break	form control	sizing handles
Control Source property (form control)	Form Wizard	subform
	heading section (form or report)	tab order
datasheet screen	navigation bar	unbound control
design view	Property Sheet window	
detail section (form or report)	report	

TEST YOURSELF

Q16-1. In Access, you can use a *form* to perform all the following tasks *except*:

    a. create a new record in a specific table

    b. change the information in an existing record of a table

    c. view the information from many different records sequentially

    d. all of these are tasks that can be performed with an Access form

Q16-2. Each record in a database table of student records contains the name, address, total university credits, and total quality points for a specific student. The student's grade point average (GPA) is equal to total quality points divided by total university credits. Where would a database typically store a student's GPA information?

    a. In the same table as the student's other information

    b. In a new table of student details

    c. In a report stored in the Reports section of the database

    d. Nowhere; this is a calculated field that is typically created by a query at run time

Q16-3. A form control that does not change from record to record is probably:

    a. a design-time control

    b. a bound control

    c. an unbound control

    d. a mistake

Q16-4. The database of a veterinary clinic has records for the pets it treats in one table, records for pet owners in another table, and records for employees in a third table. Which of these is most likely to describe a database form and subform for this application?

    a. Employees in the main form and pets in the subform

    b. Pets in the main form and owners in the subform

    c. Owners in the main form and pets in the subform

    d. Owners in the main form and employees in the subform

Q16-5. If the form onscreen appears with grid lines and you can view the Toolbox, this form is mostly likely in:

    a. design mode

    b. run mode

    c. sleep mode

    d. wizard mode

Q16-6. What happens when you click on this symbol ▶❙ on a form's navigation bar?

    a. You will transition from run mode to design mode

    b. You will transition from design mode to run mode

    c. You will go to the first record in the table

    d. You will go to the last record in the table

Q16-7. Which of these best identifies the underlying data source for an Access report?

    a. Only tables

    b. Only queries

    c. Both tables and queries

    d. Tables, queries, and forms

Q16-8. The term "control break" is most closely associated with which of the following terms in Access?

    a. Groups of data

    b. Bathroom break

    c. Form control

    d. Report header

Q16-9. Which of these is *not* a typical part of a printed report using Access?

    a. Report header

    b. Report footer

    c. Navigation bar

    d. Detail line

DISCUSSION QUESTIONS

16-1. What are some of the advantages and disadvantages of database forms?

16-2. Would you rather use a form or a datasheet for entering data into a database table? Why?

16-3. To create a form, would you rather use the Form Wizard in Access or create the form from scratch? Why?

16-4. What is a subform? Why do forms have subforms? How do you create subforms in Access?

16-5. Why do database developers customize forms? Why isn't it sufficient to use the form as initially created by the Form Wizard?

16-6. What is the purpose of a database report? What information do such reports contain?

16-7. The chapter suggested that it is important to design the format of a report before creating the report itself. Do you agree or disagree?

16-8. Do you think that we will still use hard-copy reports in the future, or will they be replaced with soft-copy ones? Defend your answer.

16-9. Would you rather use the Report Wizard to create the format of a report or design one yourself from scratch? Why?

16-10. What is a calculated field in a report? Provide some examples. Why do reports contain calculated fields?

16-11. Access 2016 now enables users to store calculated fields as normal fields in database tables. Do you think they should?

16-12. Why are calculated fields created with database queries? Why not create them directly with reports?

16-13. An employee at Andrienne Hill Cosmetics believes that Access reports are a throwback to a former age when printed outputs were more common. Today, he said that they are no longer needed. Do you agree?

PROBLEMS

16-14. A form's navigation bar has five symbols on it. Identify each one and indicate its use.

16-15. A database report has seven major sections.

  a. Identify each one and provide a short explanation of each section.

  b. Identify a report that a database application might generate, and indicate what data might be found in each section of the report for your example.

16-16. Provide a short explanation of the difference between each of the following sets of terms:

  a. bound control versus unbound control

  b. design mode versus run mode

  c. ◀ symbol versus ▶ symbol on a form's navigation bar

  d. form versus subform

  e. normal data field versus calculated data field

  f. page header versus page footer

  g. report header versus report footer

  h. a report based on a table versus a report based on a query

16-17. Using the Customers table in the BSN database that accompanies this book, and following the directions in this chapter, create the form in Figure 16-1. Make sure that you reformat the default positions of the various textboxes as shown in the figure.

  a. Add a label in the heading portion of your form that contains the term "Prepared by:" and add your name. Print a single copy of your completed form.

  b. Use the navigation bar at the bottom of your form. What is the first record? What is the last record?

  c. Add a new record to this form with your name as the customer. Print a copy of this form.

  d. Close your form, go to the Tables portion of the database, and open the Customers table in datasheet view (see Figure 16-2). Verify that your new record is there. Now, add a second record with your name again. Are you surprised that you can do this?

16-18. If you have not done so already, use the Customers table in the BSN database that accompanies this book and the directions in this chapter to create the form in Figure 16-1. Make sure that you reformat the default positions of the various textboxes as shown in the figure. Now add a subform to your form so that it looks like that in Figure 16-7. To do this, open your initial form in design view, select the subform tool from the Toolbox Controls, and add a subform. Answer the questions for the Subform Wizard to select the Invoices table. When you have completed these tasks, also do the following:

a. Use the navigation bar of the main form to go to the last record in the Customers table. Print the form for this record.

b. Use the navigation bar of the main form to find a record with invoices. Then use the navigation bar of the subform to select a particular invoice. Which one did you select? Print this form.

16-19. Using the Customers table in the BSN database that accompanies this book, and following the directions in this chapter, create the report in Figure 16-8. Note that you will have to reformat and perhaps reposition several labels, and add both labels and a graphic in the header portion of the report.

a. Add a label in the heading portion of your report that contains the term "Prepared by:" and add your name. Print a single copy of your completed report.

b. Who is the first customer in your report? Who is the last customer in your report?

16-20. Use the Customers table in the BSN database that accompanies this book and the Report Wiz-ard to create the report in Figure 16-14. Note that you will have to reformat and perhaps reposition several labels, and add both labels and a graphic in the header portion of the report. Note that you will first have to create the underlying query for this report. Use Figures 16.12–16.19 as guides for this task. Print the final report.

16-21. Explain the use of each of the following options:

a. The navigation bar of a form

b. The Form Wizard in Access

c. The header section of a form

d. The tab order button for a form

e. A subform for a form

CASE ANALYSES

16-22. A Form for BSN Suppliers (Creating a Simple Form in Access)

The BSN Company requires a form with which to view its existing suppliers conveniently and also to create records for new suppliers. Figure 16-16 contains a suggested format for this form.

Requirements

1. Using the Vendors table in the BSN database that accompanies this book, create the initial form using the Form Wizard. Note that you will have to reposition some of the data fields in the form, add the term "Abbrev." to the label for the State field, and add the following items in the heading of the form: (1) a label with text "BSN Vendors," (2) a label with your name, and (3) a graphic (which can be different than the one shown in the figure).

2. Run your completed form to make sure that it works. What is the first record that shows in your form? What is the last record?

3. While in run mode, tab through the individual data fields of any particular record and note that you do *not* tab through the data fields column by column. Return to design view and adjust the tab order by selecting View/Tab Order from the main menu and make the necessary adjustments. What is the correct Tab Order, and how did you make these adjustments?

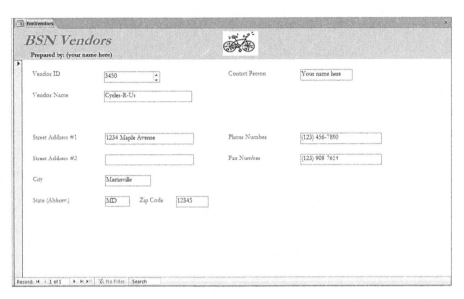

FIGURE 16-16   A form for entering and viewing vendor information in the BSN database.

4. Go back to run mode for your form and click on the ▶* symbol to add the information in Figure 16-16 to the Vendors table. Note that you should use your own name as the Contact Person for this vendor.

5. Print just this form to document your work, following the steps in the text for this task.

6. Now that you have used your new form, what additional improvements would you make to further streamline data-entry tasks?

16-23. A Form and Subform for BSN Suppliers (Creating Forms with Subforms in Access)

Create the form in Figure 16-16 and then add a subform to it that shows purchase orders for each vendor. Figure 16-17 provides a suggested format. To accomplish this task, follow these steps: (1) start with the Vendor form in design mode, (2) click on the subform control in the Toolbox, and (3) follow the steps in the Subform Wizard to complete your work.

Requirements

1. Run your new form to make sure that it works properly and then print a copy of your new form to document your work. Make sure that your name is in the header portion of the form.

2. Select a vendor for which there are outstanding purchase orders. Click on the ▶ symbol in the navigation bar of the main form. What happens?

3. Click on the ▶ symbol in the navigation bar of the subform. What happens?

4. Create a new purchase order for your current vendor using your new subform. Do you think it makes sense to be able to create a new purchase order that has no detail lines? Why or why not?

16-24. A Colorful, Read-Only Form for the BSN Company (Creating a Read-Only Form in Access)

Some employees only need to *retrieve* database information—not edit it or enter new data. Because forms are convenient for displaying the data for an entire record in a single screen, organizations

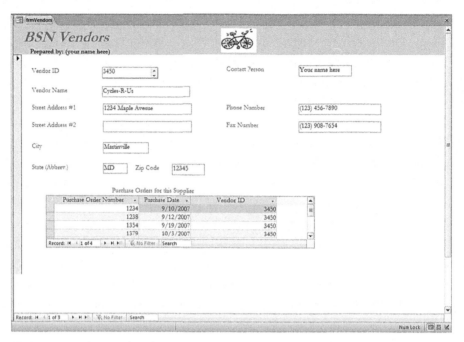

FIGURE 16-17 A suggested format for the form and subform described in Case 16-21.

also use forms for *outputs* rather than inputs. In these situations, the forms should be read-only—that is, should disallow user inputs. This protects the underlying data from changes that unauthorized personnel might introduce as well as from errors that might occur from random inputs or accidents. A similar comment applies to record deletions.

Create the Form

Here's how to create a read-only form that does not allow record insertions or deletions. To start, first create the Customer form shown in Figure 16-1. You can convert this form to a read-only one using the following steps, using Figure 16-18 to guide you.

1. After creating the form, open it in design view as shown in Figure 16-1.
2. Right click on the form (See Figure 16-1) and select "Form Properties" from the drop-down list that appears. Then, open the Data Tab of the Properties Sheet (Figure 16-18). If any object other than "Form" appears in the *Selection* object box at the top of this Properties Sheet, use the *Selection* drop-down menu to select "Form" from the set of options.
3. Set each of the following properties to "No:" (1) Data Entry, (2) Allow Additions, (3) Allow Deletions, and (4) Allow Edits.
4. Switch to Form view and test your new settings. Can you create a new record now? Can you delete an existing record? Can you edit an existing record? If not, your changes are working.

Select Colors for Your Form

The default colors for all three sections of an Access form are a dull gray. We can do better. To change the colors in the various sections of the form, perform the following steps.

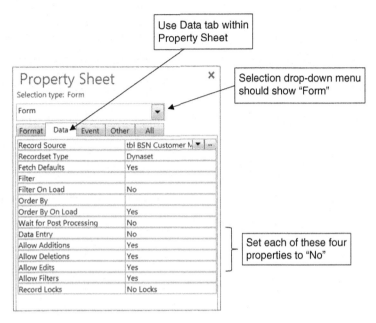

FIGURE 16-18 The settings for the Data tab of the Properties Sheet for a form.

1. Right click on any blank area of the Form header section, and then select Fill/Backcolor from the set of choices. Access will display a palette of colors from which to choose.
2. Select a color you like. The Form header section will change to the color you select.
3. Repeat steps 1 and 2 for the other two sections of the form.
4. You can also change the color in individual form objects—for example, textboxes. To do so, right click on the form object and then the Fill/Backcolor choice. The same color palette will appear, and you can select any color from it.

Requirements

1. Print the form in color. To do so, go to the File menu (see Figure 16-3) and select "Print" from the set of choices. In the print dialog box, make sure to select "Selected Record" so that you only print the record you want.
2. Write a report that documents what you did. What were your findings? Document them here.

16-25. A Listing of BSN Suppliers (Creating Simple Reports in Access)

The BSN Company would like a hard-copy report of all the current vendors in its database. Figure 16-19 provides a suggested format for the report. Note that your report header should include the company title, the current date, your name, and a graphic. Also note that the detail section contains multiple lines. Create a similar report for homework.

Requirements

1. Print the complete report.
2. Who is the first supplier, and who is the last supplier?

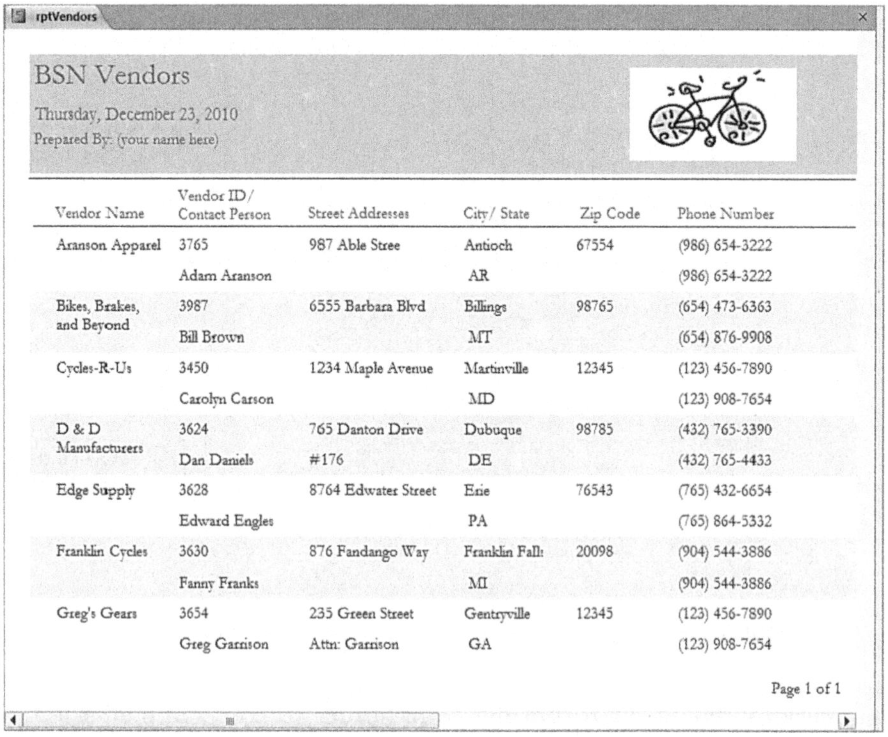

Vendor Name	Vendor ID/ Contact Person	Street Addresses	City/ State	Zip Code	Phone Number
Aranson Apparel	3765	987 Able Stree	Antioch	67554	(986) 654-3222
	Adam Aranson		AR		(986) 654-3222
Bikes, Brakes, and Beyond	3987	6555 Barbara Blvd	Billings	98765	(654) 473-6363
	Bill Brown		MT		(654) 876-9908
Cycles-R-Us	3450	1234 Maple Avenue	Martinville	12345	(123) 456-7890
	Carolyn Carson		MD		(123) 908-7654
D & D Manufacturers	3624	765 Danton Drive	Dubuque	98785	(432) 765-3390
	Dan Daniels	#176	DE		(432) 765-4433
Edge Supply	3628	8764 Edwater Street	Erie	76543	(765) 432-6654
	Edward Engles		PA		(765) 864-5332
Franklin Cycles	3630	876 Fandango Way	Franklin Falls	20098	(904) 544-3886
	Fanny Franks		MI		(904) 544-3886
Greg's Gears	3654	235 Green Street	Gentryville	12345	(123) 456-7890
	Greg Garrison	Attn: Garrison	GA		(123) 908-7654

FIGURE 16-19 A suggested format for the Report described in Case 16-25.

16-26. Furry Friends Foundation III (Creating Forms and Reports)

Recall from Cases 15-17 and 15-18 in Chapter 15 that the Furry Friends Foundation is a non-profit organization that finds homes for abandoned animals. The foundation has created a relational database to help it store data more easily and answer questions about donations. This portion of the case requires you to create database forms and reports.

Requirements

1. If you have not already done so, create the tables and relationships described in Case 15-17.
2. Create an intake form for the Contributor's Table. The form should be similar to that in Figure 16-1 and contain two columns for data entry. Make sure that the system tabs properly, so that form objects become active in a logical pattern from left to right and from top to bottom at run time. To document your work, provide a screen capture of your report at run time, which includes your name as the entered contributor.
3. Create an intake form for the Donation's Table. Again, the form should be similar to that in Figure 16-1 and contain two columns for data entry. Make sure that the system tabs properly, so that data entries proceed logically from left to right and from top to bottom. Provide a screen capture of your report at run time.
4. Create a report that contains a current list of contributors (including yourself as one of them). The report should include the following information in the header: Foundations Title, a graphic of a furry pet, your name as the developer, and the current date. The body of the report should

contain the name, address, and phone number of all contributors, listed alphabetically by contributor's last name. The information for each contributor should all be on one line. Print the complete report.

5. Expand the set of donors to include at least 10 contributors, and then change the entries in the donations file to include donations from all contributors. Create reports for both tables and then print complete lists. Finally, create a report that contains a complete list of all contributors who gave donations during the months of November and December 2017. (Hint: Base your report on a query instead of a table.) The report should include a header with the Foundations Title, a graphic of furry pets, your name as the developer, and the current date. The body of the report should list donations in order of the donor's last name and should include the donor's address and phone number. An example set of lines for this report is as follows:

Date	Contributor	Phone Number	Animal Code	Amount
November 11, 2017	Lawrence, Robert 9190 Teepee Road Doolittle, NV 54984	(775) 123-4567	C	150.00

READINGS AND OTHER RESOURCES

Alexander, M., and R. Kusleika. 2016. *Access 2016 Bible*. John Wiley and Sons, Publishers.

Conrad, J. 2013. *Microsoft Access 2013 Inside Out*. Microsoft Press.

Hernandez, P. 2017. Microsoft Access 2016 makes room for large numbers. *Eweek* (3/7): 2.

MacDonald, M. 2013. *Access 2013: The Missing Manual*. O'Reilly Media/Pogue Press.

Go to www.wiley.com/go/simkin/videos to access videos on the following topics:

Forms in Microsoft Access 2013
Reports in Microsoft Access 2013

ANSWERS TO TEST YOURSELF

1. d **2.** d **3.** c **4.** c **5.** a **6.** d **7.** c **8.** a **9.** c

Index

CPSIA information can be obtained
at www.ICGtesting.com
Printed in the USA
BVOW11s1645250118
506220BV00003B/33/P

VPT0000041309